FEDERAL TAXATION OF WEALTH TRANSFERS

FEDERAL TAXATION OF WEALTH TRANSFERS

Cases and Problems

Stephanie J. Willbanks

Professor of Law
Vermont Law School

PUBLISHERS

1185 Avenue of the Americas, New York, NY 10036
www.aspenpublishers.com

Permissions
Aspen Publishers
1185 Avenue of the Americas
New York, NY 10036

Printed in the United States of America.

1 2 3 4 5 6 7 8 9 0

ISBN 0-07355-4093-4

Library of Congress Cataloging-in-Publication Data

Willbanks, Stephanie J.
    Federal taxation of wealth transfers: cases and problems/
Stephanie J. Willbanks.—1st ed.
        p. cm.
Includes index.
ISBN 0-7355-4093-4 (hardcover)
    1.   Inheritance and transfer tax—Law and legislation—United States—Cases.
    2.   Gifts—Taxation—Law and legislation—United States—Cases. I. Title.

    KF6583.W55 2004
    343,7305'3—dc22   2003025529

About Aspen Publishers

Aspen Publishers, headquartered in New York City, is a leading information provider for attorneys, business professionals, and law students. Written by preeminent authorities, our products consist of analytical and practical information covering both U.S. and international topics. We publish in the full range of formats, including updated manuals, books, periodicals, CDs, and online products.

Our proprietary content is complemented by 2,500 legal databases, containing over 11 million documents, available through our Loislaw division. Aspen Publishers also offers a wide range of topical legal and business databases linked to Loislaw's primary material. Our mission is to provide accurate, timely, and authoritative content in easily accessible formats, supported by unmatched customer care.

To order any Aspen Publishers title, go to *www.aspenpublishers.com* or call 1-800-638-8437.

To reinstate your manual update service, call 1-800-638-8437.

For more information on Loislaw products, go to *www.loislaw.com* or call 1-800-364-2512.

For Customer Care issues, e-mail *CustomerCare@aspenpublishers.com;* call 1-800-234-1660; or fax 1-800-901-9075.

Aspen Publishers
A Wolters Kluwer Company

To my students

Summary of Contents

Contents

PART III
The Gross Estate   209

Preface

This textbook began more than 20 years ago as a set of problems to supplement a casebook. It reflects the input of the many students who have taken my course over the years; their analyses of the problems as well as their comments, questions, and suggestions have influenced the final product. I am most grateful for the contributions of my research assistants who have worked on this, and related projects. In particular, I want to recognize the work of Kristy Monteleone, who worked on Chapter 1, section A; and Catherine Richmond, who worked on Chapters 2, 4, 11, and 15. A special "thank you" goes to Sara Engelhardt, who helped me edit the manuscript. Without their valuable assistance, this project would still be in draft form.

This book is designed for problem-centered teaching. The problems focus primarily on the rules of law contained in the Code, the regulations, the cases, and the administrative interpretations. They also provide a base for discussing policy, *i.e.*, what the law should be, as well as planning, *i.e.*, how to achieve a client's wealth transfer objectives.

Despite the public rhetoric about the death of the "Death Tax," all three transfer taxes—the gift tax, the estate tax, and the generation-skipping transfer tax—are alive and well. In 2001, Congress enacted the Economic Growth and Tax Relief Reconciliation Act, which significantly increased the applicable exemption amount, modestly lowered rates, and repealed the estate and generation-skipping transfer taxes for the year 2010. Because of budget constraints, the repeal was made effective only for that one year. In 2011, the provisions of the gift, estate, and generation-skipping transfer taxes are scheduled to revert to their pre-2001 forms. As a result, both the pre-2001 provisions and the changes enacted in 2001 are discussed throughout this book.

Almost before the ink was dry on the 2001 Tax Act, voices were heard calling for acceleration of the amendments and for making them permanent. Proposals to do this have been introduced in Congress, but, so far, have failed to garner sufficient votes. Although the 2002 elections gave the Republicans control of the Senate, other issues have shifted the spotlight away from the transfer tax provisions. The Jobs and Growth Reconciliation Tax Act of 2003, which barely passed Congress and then only after long and bitter debate, amended the income tax but not the transfer taxes. Many people believe that further amendment of the transfer taxes is probable, but no one can predict what such amendments might be. Proposals to modify the existing transfer taxes but to increase the exemption amount have also failed. While Benjamin

Franklin once opined that the only two certainties in life were death and taxes, the federal death tax may no longer be one of the certainties. Only time will tell.

Stephanie J. Willbanks

March 2004

FEDERAL TAXATION OF
WEALTH TRANSFERS

PART I

Overview of Federal Taxation of the Transfer of Wealth

CHAPTER 1

Introduction to the Federal Transfer Tax System

A. HISTORY AND CONSTITUTIONALITY

Benjamin Franklin once wrote, "[I]n this world nothing can be said to be certain, except death and taxes."[1] The connection between death and taxes, however, arose much earlier. As early as 7 B.C. the Egyptians imposed a flat rate inheritance tax on real property.[2] The Greeks and Romans apparently borrowed this idea from the Egyptians. In 6 A.D., Emperor Augustus imposed an inheritance tax to create a pension fund for members of the Roman army.[3] Unlike the Egyptian tax, which allowed no exemptions, the Roman tax excluded property passing to specified relatives. As the tax rate increased and the allowable exemptions decreased, the Roman inheritance tax became more and more unpopular. The decline of Rome may have further weakened the tax, and it had disappeared by the time the Justinian Code was enacted in 533 A.D.[4]

During the Middle Ages death taxes were imposed by both the feudal lord and the church. Feudal tenure included two payments akin to an inheritance tax. The "relief" was paid to the lord by the heir of a deceased tenant.[5] The rationale for this payment was that the land, in essence, escheated to the lord, who then claimed payment for allowing the heir to retain possession. A second payment to the lord was the "heriot," which originated as a voluntary donation or legacy from the tenant to the lord, but over time became unavoidable.[6] The church also collected a payment at death, called the "mortuary," as compensation for tithes or other payments missed during life.[7] Anyone who died intestate leaving no wealth to the church was condemned to eternal damnation.

---

1. Benjamin Franklin, Letter to M. LeRoy, 1789, *quoted in* H.W. Brands, The First American — The Life and Times of Benjamin Franklin 706 (2000).

2. Randolph E. Paul, Federal Estate and Gift Taxation 3 (1942).

3. Max West, The Inheritance Tax 11-12 (1908).

4. *Id.* at 14; *see also,* Barbara R. Hauser, *Death Duties and Immortality: Why Civilization Needs Inheritances,* 34 Real Property, Probate and Trust Journal 363, 368 (1999).

5. West, *supra* note 3 at 15.

6. *Id.* at 17.

7. Hauser, *supra* note 4 at 370.; William J. Shultz, The Taxation of Inheritance 11 (1926).

The connection between these feudal payments and modern death taxes is speculative at best. In England, there does not appear to be any direct historical connection, but in some other European countries, particularly France, modern inheritance taxes may have grown out of the feudal relief. Other countries apparently modeled their death taxes on the Roman taxes.[8] The English first introduced a modern death tax as a stamp tax on the probate of wills and letters of administration in 1694.[9] The tax was simply the cost of stamps required to be affixed to legal documents.

Death taxes first appeared in the United States in the Stamp Act of July 6, 1797, which imposed an inheritance tax on the receipt of legacies and the probate of wills. This tax was enacted for a five-year period, but it was repealed in 1802 before the end of that term. With the War of 1812 creating the need for revenue, Congress debated, but did not enact, another inheritance tax.[10] During the Civil War, however, the need for revenue pushed Congress to impose a series of inheritance taxes on both personal and real property in 1862, 1864, and 1866. These inheritance taxes were graduated based on the degree of relationship between the heir or beneficiary and the decedent. In Scholey v. Rew, 90 U.S. 331 (1874), the Supreme Court upheld the constitutionality of this tax, concluding that the inheritance tax was an excise tax, permitted by Article I, section 8, of the Constitution, and not a direct tax under Article 1, section 9.[11] Despite this victory, Congress repealed the tax on personal property in 1870 and the tax on real property in 1872.

In response to the growing populist movement, Congress, in 1894, adopted the first national income tax and included inheritances as income.[12] This act quickly became the focus of another constitutional challenge, and the Supreme Court ruled the act unconstitutional because it was a direct tax and thus required apportionment among the several states. Pollock v. Farmer's Loan and Trust Co., 157 U.S. 429 (1895), *rehearing*, 158 U.S. 601 (1895).

In 1898, when war once more created the need for additional revenue, Congress reverted to the traditional inheritance tax. This tax was again challenged as unconstitutional, the taxpayer arguing that even if this tax was indirect, it was not uniform and therefore in violation of Article 1, section 9.

---

8. West, *supra* note 3 at 19-20.

9. Paul, *supra* note 2 at 4.

10. Paul, *supra* note 2 at 6.

11. Article 1, section 8, clause 1, provides:

> The Congress shall have the power to lay and collect taxes, duties, imposts, and excises, to pay the debts and provide for the common defense and general welfare of the United States; but all duties, imposts and excises shall be uniform throughout the United States.

Article I, section 9, clause 4, provides:

> No capitation, or other direct, tax shall be laid, unless in proportion to the census or enumeration herein before directed to be taken.

12. Paul, *supra* note 2 at 7.

The Supreme Court held that the tax was an excise tax, not a direct tax, and that the uniformity requirement of Article 1, section 9, only required geographic uniformity. Knowlton v. Moore, 178 U.S. 41 (1900). Despite this victory, Congress repealed this tax in 1902.

In 1916, Congress enacted an estate tax that became the foundation of the federal system of transfer taxation currently in place.[13] Although war was a primary motivating factor, the populist movement had succeeded in passing the Sixteenth Amendment, which paved the way for a national income tax. This set the stage for other attempts to tax large fortunes. Inheritance was viewed as a windfall increasing the ability to bear the burden of taxation.[14]

The estate tax, as enacted in 1916, encompassed not only transfers of property at death, but also transfers in contemplation of death and transfers that did not take effect in possession or enjoyment until death. It included an exemption of $50,000 and a progressive rate structure. Opponents once more challenged the constitutionality of the tax, but lost. New York Trust Co. v. Eisner, 256 U.S. 345 (1921). In upholding the tax, Justice Oliver Wendell Holmes noted that an estate tax has always been regarded as the antithesis of a direct tax and stated, "[u]pon this point, a page of history is worth a volume of logic." *Id.* at 349. Although the war ended and the immediate need for additional revenue abated, Congress did not repeal the estate tax.

Once it decided to retain the federal estate tax, Congress recognized the possibilities of tax avoidance through inter vivos gifts and adopted a gift tax in 1924. Although the initial gift tax was repealed in 1926, it was revived in 1932 and has continued in essentially the same format to present times. The gift tax, although designed to supplement the estate tax, was separate and distinct with its own exemption of $50,000 and a rate structure that was approximately 75 percent of the estate tax rates. Taxpayers challenged the 1924 gift tax as a direct tax, but lost. Bromley v. McCaughn, 280 U.S. 124 (1929). Growing tired of these challenges, the Supreme Court summarily rejected the claim, stating "The meaning of the phrase 'direct taxes' and the historical background of the constitutional requirements for their apportionment have been so often and exhaustively considered by this court, that no useful purpose would be served by renewing the discussion here." *Id.* at 136. The Court also rejected the argument that the graduated rates and exemptions violated the due process clause of the Fifth Amendment.

Congress and the courts continued to interpret and refine the estate and gift taxes. In 1948, Congress enacted a marital deduction for both the gift and the estate taxes that allowed a limited amount of property to pass tax-free between spouses. At the same time, Congress modified the income tax to allow married couples to file joint income tax returns.

---

13. During this time, the states also developed death taxes. Pennsylvania adopted the first inheritance tax in 1826. By the time Congress adopted the federal estate tax, 30 states had either an inheritance or an estate tax in place.

14. Paul, *supra* note 2 at 5-7.

The next significant amendment to the transfer tax system did not occur until 1976 when Congress integrated the gift and estate taxes, providing one rate structure and one unified credit. Shortly thereafter, in 1981, Congress amended the marital deduction to allow an unlimited amount of property to pass tax-free between spouses. In 1976, Congress also adopted a generation-skipping transfer tax designed to prevent tax avoidance through intergenerational transfers. This generation-skipping transfer tax was exceedingly complex, and Congress repealed it retroactively and substituted an entirely different generation-skipping tax in 1986.

Having survived, relatively unscathed, for most of the twentieth century, the federal system of transfer taxation came under attack in the late 1990s as unnecessary and an impediment to the economy. Congress finally succumbed to the political pressure and enacted the Economic Growth and Tax Relief Reconciliation Act of 2001. P.L. 107-16, 115 Stat. 38 (June 7, 2001). The Act gradually lowers the top marginal rate of tax and increases the exemption amount, but it does not fundamentally alter the transfer tax base or the rate structure. The Act also repeals the estate and the generation-skipping transfer taxes, but does so only for the year 2010. During that year the gift tax remains in full force and effect, and a new carryover basis regime becomes effective. The 2001 Tax Act, however, contains a sunset provision, so that in 2011 the transfer tax system reverts to its pre-2001 condition.[15]

The provisions of the 2001 Tax Act do not match the public discourse surrounding its enactment. It only repealed the "death tax" for one year, and further action will be required to make any of its provisions permanent. Both the economic and the political landscape changed significantly after adoption of the 2001 Act, and the future of the transfer taxes remains unsettled. Debate continues about whether to impose any tax at death and, if so, what form that tax should take. Section B describes the possible forms for taxing transfers of wealth at death, while section C reviews the primary arguments for and against imposing any tax at death.

B. FORMS OF WEALTH TAXATION

There are a number of different ways to tax property at death. Once the government decides that imposing a tax at death is appropriate, it must decide whether to focus on the decedent as owner of the property or on the recipient. The exact form of the tax will depend, at least in some measure, on the justification for the tax, on administrative feasibility, and, at least at the federal level, on constitutional considerations.

_____

15. For a commentary on the 2001 Act, _see_ Karen C. Burke & Grayson M.P. McCouch, _Estate Tax Repeal: Through the Looking Glass_, 22 Va. Tax Rev. 187 (2002).

There are three possible methods of taxing property at death. The first is simply to assess a tax based on the value of all property owned at death. This is not as simple as it might sound. First, one has to determine who owns the property at the moment of death. Sophisticated estate planning devices, including trusts and business entities, often make this task quite difficult. Second, one has to determine the value of the property. Most problematic, however, is that this form of taxation at the federal level would be unconstitutional as a direct tax. While this type of a wealth tax is employed by local and state governments during life, *e.g.*, a property tax, no jurisdiction has ever adopted this form of taxation at death.

The second possible death tax that focuses on the decedent is a transfer tax, *i.e.*, an excise tax on the privilege of transferring property at death. The focus of this tax is the decedent and his act of transferring property. While a transfer tax might exclude from the tax base transfers to certain favored people or organizations, the focus of the tax is not on the recipient. Another feature of this tax, in contrast to an inheritance tax, is that it will not matter how many beneficiaries a decedent designates. The tax base is the amount of property transferred by the decedent, not the amount received by individual beneficiaries. The federal estate tax adopts this structure.

The third possibility is an income tax based on the realization of gains at death. Under the current federal income tax system, unrealized gains are not taxed either during life or at death. As an alternative, the income tax could treat death as a realizing event and require the executor to include all unrealized gains in the decedent's final income tax return. While this theory has been proposed by some commentators, it has never been seriously considered as a viable form of death taxation in the United States.

Instead of imposing a death tax on the decedent, the government might choose to focus on the heirs and beneficiaries. In doing so, the government could enact a federal inheritance tax. Such a tax focuses on the receipt of property at death, and the beneficiary, not the estate of the decedent, would be liable for this tax. Rates can be graduated based on the amount of property received by each beneficiary and/or on the degree of kinship between the decedent and the recipient. Many states have adopted an inheritance tax.

An accessions tax, like an inheritance tax, would focus on the receipt of property by the taxpayer. It would not, however, be limited to receipt of property on death or from a specific decedent. Instead, it would accumulate all receipts of wealth from all sources in the tax base. In addition, it would impose an increasingly higher rate of tax with each addition to the tax base. No American jurisdiction has adopted, or even seriously considered, an accessions tax.

Another way of taxing beneficiaries is to treat all gifts and bequests as income. While federal and state income tax systems have excluded these items from the tax base, §102,[16] doing so is not constitutionally required. The advantage is that there is no need to construct or administer a separate tax system. The

---

16. All citations, unless otherwise indicated, are to the 1986 Internal Revenue Code as amended.

disadvantage is the perceived unfairness of taxing unusually large receipts at progressively higher tax rates. To counteract this perception, such a system would most likely need to include a special tax rate for gifts and bequests or some form of income averaging over a designated number of years.

Another way to tax beneficiaries is to require them to maintain the former owner's basis in the property.[17] Only when the beneficiary disposes of the property would he incur tax. At that point the tax would be based on the gain arising both during the donor's/decedent's ownership of the property and during the beneficiary's ownership of the property. This transferred basis system currently applies only to lifetime gifts. §1015. Transfers at death receive a stepped-up (or -down) basis equal to the fair market value of the property on the date of decedent's death. §1014. Congress did adopt a transferred basis system for transfers at death in 1976 when it unified the estate and gift taxes. This proved to be extremely unpopular, and Congress repealed it before it became effective. In the 2001 Tax Act, Congress, once again, enacted a transferred basis provision for transfers at death but delayed implementation until 2010, the year the estate tax is repealed. It remains to be seen whether this provision will survive longer than the 1976 version.

Once the tax base is determined, the next step is to decide on a rate of tax. While the ancient Egyptians imposed a flat rate of tax, most modern death taxes employ graduated rates. Graduated, or progressive, rates of tax are based on the theory that those with more wealth (or income) have a greater ability to pay and thus should assume the obligation of paying a greater share of the tax bill.

The federal transfer tax system adopts a graduated rate system, at least in part. Section 2001 contains graduated rates ranging from 18 percent to 50 percent.[18] The progressivity of the gift and estate taxes is, however, more apparent than real. With a $1,000,000 exemption amount, the lowest rate of tax actually imposed is 41 percent. Moreover, the benefit of the unified credit and graduated rates is phased out for estates greater than $10 million. §2001(c)(2).[19] The generation-skipping transfer tax imposes a flat rate of tax equal to the maximum federal estate tax rate. Under the amendments adopted in the 2001 Tax Act, both the gift and the estate taxes will have a flat rate of tax begining in 2006.

All states impose some form of death tax. A significant impetus was the state death tax credit, §2011, which allows an estate to exclude the amount of death tax paid to a state from the decedent's federal estate tax bill. Although limited in amount, this provision operates as a revenue sharing scheme. Twenty-seven jurisdictions have an estate tax equal to the §2011 credit, eight

---

17. Basis is simply the cost of property. §1012. Basis is the foundation for calculating gain or loss on the disposition of property for purposes of the income tax. §1001.

18. Prior to the 2001 Act, the top marginal rate was 55 percent. That act further reduces the top marginal rate to 49 percent for 2003, 48 percent for 2004, 47 percent for 2005, 46 percent for 2006, and 45 percent for 2007-2009. The estate tax is repealed for 2010, and the prior rates will become effective again in 2011.

19. Section 2001(c)(2) was repealed by the 2001 Tax Act.

states have an estate tax equal to the §2011 credit as it existed prior to the 2001 Tax Act, and four states have an estate tax based on a separate rate structure. Eleven jurisdictions have a combination of estate and inheritance taxes. A few states have recently repealed their inheritance taxes, but they have retained an estate tax equal to the §2011 credit. The 2001 Tax Act, however, repealed the §2011 credit and replaced it with a deduction for state death taxes. It is not clear what will happen in the states that base their tax on the §2011 credit without any adjustment for the 2001 amendment. At this time, state death systems are in a state of flux along with the federal transfer tax system.

C. POLICY CONSIDERATIONS

Evaluation of a particular tax depends on the overall structure of the tax system, the nature and rationale of the particular tax under consideration, and fundamental principles of tax policy. Most people agree that a tax system should include more than one tax base. Historically in the United States, the tax system has included income, property or wealth, and consumption. The choice of the tax base or combination of tax bases depends on the specific goals and principles that the government seeks to promote.

The fundamental goal of any tax system is to raise revenue. Other goals include promotion of economic or social policies, such as stimulation of the economy or redistribution of wealth. The goals of a tax system change from time to time as society and its needs change. The goals of a tax system may also be related to the tax base. The nature and characteristics of the tax base determine what goals it can accomplish. For example, an income tax system is much better at stimulating or depressing economic growth than a transfer tax system because the number of people paying the income tax is much greater and the flow of income is more certain.

No matter what the tax base or specific goals, there is general agreement on the fundamental principles that should be used to evaluate a tax system. One basic principle is equity, both horizontal and vertical. Stated most simply: Horizontal equity means that similarly situated individuals should be taxed similarly, while vertical equity means that individuals should be taxed according to their ability to pay. Of course, much of this debate depends on how one defines "similarly situated" or how one measures ability to pay.

A second principle involves the economic effects of the tax. While some argue that a tax system should not influence economic decisions, others recognize that taxation by its very nature influences such decisions. As a result, they would require only that the tax system have positive economic effects. Of course, there will be differences of opinion as to what is, or is not, a positive economic effect. This principle is, therefore, connected to the social or economic goals of the tax system.

A tax system should also be administratively feasible. It should not impose significant costs for enforcement, compliance, or planning. Other principles include: simplicity, stability, and directness, *i.e.*, how visible is the tax to those who pay it?

There has been significant commentary in the past 25 years arguing for and against repeal of the federal transfer tax system. Many commentators who favor retention also argue for significant reform of the system. The adoption of the 2001 Tax Act has not stifled this discussion. The following excerpts outline the arguments for and against repeal.[20]

Edward J. McCaffery, *Grave Robbers:*
The Moral Case Against the Death Tax
85 Tax Notes 1429, 1999 TNT 238-123 (Dec. 13, 1999)
Copyright © 1999 Tax Analysts. Used with permission.

. . . Only 1 to 2 percent of Americans who die each year leave enough wealth behind to generate any estate tax at all. One of the most surprising aspects of the death tax is that it contributes only about $24 billion a year, or just a little more than 1 percent of all federal revenues. At least since World War II, when both the income tax and the federal payroll tax system began to gather steam, the death tax has not been a significant revenue raiser; [since then] it has rarely accounted for more than 2 percent of total federal receipts. . . .

The low yield of the death tax does not, however, mean that the tax has no effects. The death tax features the highest rates of any major American tax, and families within its potential sting take great efforts to avoid it. A small percentage of taxable estates end up paying a large percentage of the total tax collected. When the estate tax was first imposed, it was targeted at the rich, with rates

---

20. These excerpts only summarize the basic arguments. For a complete analysis, read the articles themselves. Most footnotes have been omitted from these excerpts.

Other articles include: Mark L. Ascher, *Curtailing Inherited Wealth*, 89 Mich. L. Rev. 69 (1990); Joel C. Dobris, *A Brief for the Abolition of All Transfer Taxes*, 35 Syracuse L. Rev. 1215 (1984); Harold M. Dubroff, *The Teleological Case for Not Repealing the Estate Tax*, 84 Tax Notes 1433 (1999); Christopher E. Erblich, *To Bury the Federal Transfer Taxes Without Further Adieu*, 24 Seton Hall L. Rev. 1931 (1994); Michael J. Graetz, *To Praise the Estate Tax, Not to Bury It*, 93 Yale L. J. 259 (1983); Douglas Holtz-Eakin, *The Death Tax: Investments, Employment, and Entrepreneurs*, 84 Tax Notes 782 (1999); Edward J. McCaffery, *The Uneasy Case for Wealth Transfer Taxation*, 104 Yale L. J. 283 (1994); Eric Rakowski, *Can Wealth Taxes Be Justified?*, 53 Tax. L. Rev. 263 (2000); James R. Repetti, *Entrepreneurs and the Estate Tax*, 84 Tax Notes 1541 (1999); Richard Schmalbeck, *Does the Death Tax Deserve the Death Penalty? An Overview of the Major Arguments for Repeal of Federal Wealth Transfer Taxes*, 48 Clev. St. L. Rev. 749 (2000); John G. Steinkamp, *A Case for Federal Transfer Taxation*, 55 Ark. L. Rev. 1 (2002); Jay A. Soled & Charles Davenport, *Cremating Transfer Taxes: Is There Hope for a Resurrection?* 34 Wake Forest L. Rev. 229 (1999); Dennis J. Ventry, Jr., *Straight Talk about the "Death" Tax: Politics, Economics, and Morality*, 89 Tax Notes 1159 (2000); Mary R. Wampler, *Repealing the Federal Estate Tax: Death to the Death Tax or Will Reform Save the Day?*, 25 Seton Hall Legis. J. 525 (2001).

ranging from 1 to 10 percent. . . . [T]he maximum estate tax rate increased to 77 percent in 1941. After the Tax Reform Act of 1976, the estate and gift tax rates ranged from 18 percent to 70 percent. Today, the estate tax ranges from 37 to 55 percent. The U.S. estate tax is one of the highest in the world. . . .

In addition to numerous and complex special planning devices and opportunities, there are three major general exceptions and exclusions to the death tax that go a fair way toward explaining its limited yield. One, gifts or bequests left to a spouse are typically not taxable, under the so-called marital deduction. There are numerous complexities in this spousal deduction, nearly all of them unfortunate, but the bottom line is that most married couples do not pay an estate tax until both of them have died.

Two, each donor has a cumulative lifetime exemption level before any tax is due — this is the "zero bracket" of the estate tax. The unified credit amount, as it is called, became $600,000 in 1981; Congress agreed to raise it to $1 million over a number of years, beginning in 1997 and ending in 2006, but there has been some talk of accelerating the effective date of the higher amount. A husband and wife, with careful planning, can combine their lifetime exemption amounts so that they can leave $2 million to their heirs, tax-free.

Three, in addition to that $1 million benefit, there is an "annual exclusion amount" of $10,000. This can be given per donor, per donee, per year — all without counting against the $1 million lifetime exemption. Once again a husband and wife can combine their amounts. So a married couple can give $20,000 to each of their children each year, without incurring any tax or subtracting from their lifetime exemption amounts. . . .

Arguments for the Tax: A Summary

A survey of the academic and policy literature on the estate tax paints a picture of a tax in search of a coherent rationale. A variety of reasons for the tax has been offered over the years, with the dominant themes changing only in their relative emphasis.[16] The principal arguments are as follows:

- The tax is an important and growing source of revenue for the government.
- The tax adds a degree of progressivity to the tax system in a particularly nondistortionary way.
- The tax serves as a "backstop" to the income tax, which fails to completely tax savings, as it is theoretically committed to doing.
- The tax breaks up large concentrations of wealth across generations.
- Inheritances should be taxed away so that everyone begins the game of life on a level playing field, so as to ensure equality of opportunity.
- The tax is an important inducement to charitable giving at death.

---

16. For general arguments in favor of the estate tax, *see* Ascher, *Curtailing Inherited Wealth*, 89 Mich. L. Rev. 69 (1990); David G. Duff, *Taxing Inherited Wealth: A Philosophical Argument*, 6 Can. J. L. & Juris. 3 (1993); Michael J. Graetz, *To Praise the Estate Tax, Not to Bury It*, 93 Yale L. J. 259 (1983); D. W. Haslett, *Is Inheritance Justified?*, 15 Phil. & Pub. Aff. 122 (1986); McCaffery, *The Uneasy Case for Wealth Transfer Taxation*, 104 Yale L. J. 283 (1994).

Arguments Against the Tax: A Summary

First, it turns out that none of the arguments for the tax are compelling or even correct:[17]

- The death tax does not raise much revenue in gross, and it may actually lose money on net for the federal government when we account for administrative costs, revenue lost to other (e.g., income) taxes, and general economic distortions.
- Even if we accept "progressivity" as a legitimate aim of a fair tax system . . . the death tax gets its progressivity in the wrong place. It falls on savers, not spenders.
- Early and naive advocates of death taxes thought that such taxes would not distort behavior because they fell only on wealth that decedents left behind by accident. Now very strong evidence supports the common-sense idea that people are strongly motivated to leave wealth to their heirs. Death taxes distort the behavior and investment decisions of this important class of "intergenerational" savers.
- Not only does the income tax not need a "backstop," the income tax is actually a bad tax precisely because it falls on savings, in effect double taxing saving as opposed to immediate consumption. Death taxes compound the error by adding a third tax on savings. A fair tax system should consistently tax spending, not work or savings, and should use progressive rates to meet whatever liberal or redistributive objectives it has.
- Death taxes have not contributed to greater equality in America. In fact, the death tax has so many gaps, loopholes, and problems — and the motivation to pass on wealth to heirs is so strong — that the current death tax allows precisely the kind of wealth transmission it is designed to prevent or limit.
- The tax is an extremely costly, cumbersome, and indirect way to assist charities. Charitable giving can be helped or subsidized within the constraints of any tax system, so the unfair and inefficient death tax is not needed for that end.

Second, quite apart from rebutting the positive case for death taxation, there are many destructive elements to the death tax:

- The tax is economically inefficient. It distorts economic decisions, depresses the capital stock, and leads to less long-run growth.
- The tax is costly. It imposes very large private and public compliance costs and interferes with important long-run incentives.
- The tax is too porous to be effective in practice, yet a stronger tax would require invasive collection efforts. It is too hard to police and enforce gratuitous transfers, generally made within the family. The motive to pass on wealth

---

17. For general arguments against the estate tax, *see* Joel C. Dobris, *A Brief for the Abolition of All Transfer Taxes*, 35 Syracuse L. Rev. 1215 (1984); Charles O. Galvin, *To Bury the Estate Tax, Not to Praise It*, 52 Tax Notes 1413, Sept. 16, 1991; Edward J. McCaffery, *The Political Liberal Case Against the Estate Tax*, 23 Philosophy & Public Affairs 281 (1994); Edward J. McCaffery, *Being the Best We Can Be (A Reply to My Critics)*, 51 Tax Law Review 615 (1996); Edward J. McCaffery, *Rethinking the Estate Tax*, 67 Tax Notes 1678 (June 19, 1995).

runs too deep, and so tax avoidance and evasion haunt efforts to collect the tax. In the end, the death tax ends up encouraging just the kind of wealth transmissions its authors ostensibly deplored.

- The tax is unfair because it falls on the wrong people — savers, not spenders; intergenerational altruists, not selfish spendthrifts.
- An effective way to avoid death taxes is to spend all of one's wealth while alive and "die broke." But this is perverse. The death tax encourages behavior that supporters of the tax say they are trying to discourage: leisure, conspicuous consumption, luxurious spending, and the early and frequent transmission of wealth to subsequent generations.
- The death tax discourages the very behavior that a sound tax system ought to encourage: work, savings, thrift, and intergenerational altruism.
- The tax is unpopular with the American public, for perfectly legitimate reasons. . . .

It is time to forget complicated "carve-outs," complicated plans for taxing capital gains at death, or simple reform plans that leave the death tax in place. The optimal solution is to get rid of death taxation at its theoretically flawed root. We should consistently tax people as they spend, not as they work, save — or die. A consistent, backended consumption tax imposes a levy on our use of resources. If mom and dad work hard and save well and then pass on their left-over wealth to their children—not having needed to spend it themselves — we can and should tax the children when and as they spend the money. If we want some progressivity in our tax system, we can achieve it perfectly well under a variety of consumption tax models. We don't have to tax savings or savers two and three times, at the highest tax rates in America today.

We especially don't have to tax wealthy individuals who go to their graves leaving behind a store of capital unspent on their own personal whims. These are perfectly good and noble Americans, and it is little short of a sin that their distant Uncle Sam should be dancing on their graves. In short and in sum, for moral reasons above all, it is high time to kill the death tax.

John E. Donaldson, The Future of Transfer Taxation:
Repeal, Restructuring and Refinement, or Replacement
50 Wash. & Lee L. Rev. 539 (1993) Copyright © 1993
Washington & Lee Law Review. Used with permission.

. . . The adequacy of the [current transfer tax] system can be measured in terms of whether it accomplishes its objectives. Under this measure, the system, apart from raising comparatively insignificant revenue, is a failure. Its adequacy can also be measured in terms of the traditional tests of a good tax system, which employ standards of efficiency, fairness, and neutrality. Under this measure, the system also fails. Concededly, no tax system can be expected to be perfect. The extent to which imperfections can be reasonably tolerated and accepted is in part a function of the revenues produced by the system. . . . The current system is too costly. . . . The tax is imposed on the transferor and is measured by the type and value of wealth transferred, and the extent of imposition is determined by reference to the circumstances of the transferor and by exclusions and exemptions accorded the transferor. Such a system inherently invites manipulation and avoidance by the transferor and penalizes those who are unwary or who fail to pursue avoidance measures. The system's inherent invitation to manipulate and its penalties for failure to do so cause it to be unfair, inefficient, and nonneutral.

Whether accumulated wealth is a proper subject of taxation is a matter over which economists disagree and is essentially a political question. . . . [T]he question of how much revenue should be derived from such base is also a political question. However, the question of whether a particular system for taxing accumulated wealth is useful and worthwhile, . . . is essentially a practical and utilitarian matter. This essay suggests that as a practical and utilitarian matter, the present estate, gift, and generation-skipping tax system should be abandoned. . . .

Several goals have, from time to time, been ascribed to the transfer tax system. One that has been articulated from time to time, particularly during the 1930s, is the breaking up or reducing of concentrations of wealth. Another is that of producing revenue. More recently, the system has been "justified" for its role or potential in adding an element of progressivity to the overall federal tax system. An examination of the transfer tax system in relation to these perceived goals is in order.

However worthwhile the objective of breaking up or reducing concentrations of wealth may be, commentators generally agree that the transfer tax system has been ineffective in this regard. A study in 1978 concluded that transfer tax revenues were so small in relation to the wealth possessed by the top .5 percent of the population that the system could not have had a significant effect on wealth redistribution.[14] Another commentator writing in 1983 concluded that transfer taxes have done little to reduce concentrations of wealth. Notwithstanding occasional expressions to the contrary, Congress has shown little interest in the role of transfer taxes in breaking up concentrations of wealth. Its actions move in the opposite direction. In the Tax Reform Act of 1997 Congress, in enacting the reforms resulting in unification of the estate and gift tax systems and reduction in the number of persons affected, knowingly reduced revenues from transfer taxes. It did so again in the Economic Recovery Tax Act of 1981 when it expanded the unified credit thus exempting gratuitous transfers under $600,000 from tax, permitted an unlimited marital deduction and revised the rate structure to phase in a reduction of the maximum rate bracket from seventy percent to fifty percent. Congress did, however, restore a small element of progressivity to the system in 1988 by phasing out the benefit of the graduated structure for estates over $10,000,000. . . .

The transfer tax system simply has not made a significant contribution to a goal of breaking up wealth concentration. Although in 1992 transfer taxes

---

14. G. P. Verbit, *Do Estate and Gift Taxes Affect Wealth Distribution?*, 117 Tr. & Est. 598, 604 (1978) (constituting part one of a two-part article).

produced revenues of approximately $12 billion from the wealthiest one percent of the population, that amount is relatively minuscule in relation to the objective. Absent a significant change in the political climate, which appears unlikely in the foreseeable future, it is improbable that the system will be called upon to more effectively address perceived problems of wealth concentration.

The second, and perhaps the historically more important goal of the transfer tax system, is that of producing revenue. In the mid to late 1930s, the transfer tax system was a major component of the federal tax system, producing more than six percent of total revenues and in one year, 1936, ten percent. . . . Since World War II, however, transfer tax revenues have rarely exceeded two percent of total federal tax collections and as a result of recent changes, have diminished to approximately 1.1 percent. This decline reflects the greater importance of other taxes to the federal fisc. . . .

Although the $12 billion now produced annually by the transfer tax system is but a minuscule part of total federal revenues, it is a significant amount in the context of a federal fisc operating with inadequate revenues and large deficits. Assuming that these revenue dollars are too important to give up, and the class of wealthy on whom the burden falls should be largely unchanged, it is fair to ask whether the burden can be imposed more fairly and efficiently.

A third goal, or role, of transfer taxes advanced by some is that of contributing to the progressivity of the federal tax system. However, that role has a more historic than continuing significance and is a function both of the progressivity of other taxes, particularly the individual income tax, in relation to the amount of transfer tax revenues, and the number of persons burdened by the tax. In the mid to late 1930s, when estate tax revenues on occasion were as high as twenty-seven percent to fifty-six percent of individual income tax revenues, the transfer tax contributions to the goal of progressivity were substantial. Analysis of data for the early 1970s led one commentator to conclude that transfer taxes contributed a third as much to progressivity of the tax structure as did rates in excess of the average effective income tax rate.[39] However, the transfer tax contribution to progressivity had dropped to twelve percent by 1980 and would have been down to four percent for 1981 if the 1981 legislation had been fully effective in that year. When transfer taxes affect the top six or seven percent of the population, as they did in the mid-1970s, their contribution to progressivity may have meaningful significance. However, when the affected population drops to approximately one percent, today's level, the role of transfer taxes in contributing to progressivity of the tax system is minuscule. . . .

Adherence to generally accepted principles of sound tax policy requires that tax systems be fair, efficient, and neutral. The existing transfer tax system severely violates each of these principles.

First, the system is not fair, from considerations of both horizontal equity and vertical equity. Horizontal equity suggests that persons transferring equal

---

39. [Michael J. Graetz, *To Praise the Estate Tax, Not to Bury It,* 93 Yale L. J. 259, 272 (1983).]

wealth within the system be taxed in the same manner. Vertical equity (progressivity) suggests that persons of greater wealth be taxed more heavily on their transfers than persons of lesser wealth. Substantial horizontal inequity has been legislated into the system. For example, qualifying wealth represented by land used in farming and certain other business activities may be valued at "use" value rather than fair market value, permitting reductions in taxable estates of up to $750,000. Also, while some employment generated post-death payments are within the transfer tax base others are not. Further, life insurance proceeds, where the decedent has an incident of ownership, are included in the estate tax base. However, proceeds of life insurance, even when attributable to investment made by decedents, are excluded from the base where incidents of ownership are lacking or if once possessed, have been yielded more than three years prior to death.

More important to considerations of both horizontal and vertical equity is the simple fact that where transfer taxes that would otherwise have been imposed are avoided or postponed without penalty, equity is violated. A major industry, that pursued by estate planning professionals, has evolved to exploit opportunities for avoidance and penalty-free postponement of transfer taxes that would otherwise have been payable. A large number of attorneys, accountants, financial advisors, insurance specialists, and trust officers, having mastered the complexities and intricacies of the transfer tax system, devote all or substantial portions of their professional time in service of the cause of undermining horizontal and vertical equity within the transfer tax system.

A discussion of all of the tax avoidance and postponement devices available to avoid or delay imposition of transfer taxes is beyond the scope of this essay. The literature on estate planning directed to tax avoidance and minimization is extensive. To make the point, however, a mention of several techniques is sufficient. For example, persons having the greatest wealth, and thus benefitting most in circumventing vertical equity, are more readily able than those having less wealth to utilize the gift tax system, with its "tax exclusive" base to reduce the cost of donative transfers. . . . Another important device for avoiding imposition of transfer taxes is the utilization of the annual exclusion of $10,000 ($20,000 if husband and wife cooperate by using the split-gift election). . . . Trust arrangements where beneficiaries, including those with contingent interests, are given withdrawal powers are available to inflate the number of annual exclusions available. . . . Even more sophisticated techniques are available within the parameters of the generation-skipping trust provisions. . . .

A corollary to the foregoing observations regarding ease of tax avoidance and its effect on horizontal and vertical equity is the resulting consequence that to a significant extent transfer taxes are "voluntary taxes," paid largely by wealthy persons who are uninformed or ill-advised, or who simply die before putting their affairs in order — all too frequent occurrences. To the extent that the tax burdens those who bear it only because of the want of effective avoidance planning, it is especially unfair. . . . Similarly, lack of information or advice regarding opportunities to avoid or minimize taxes through lifetime giving arrangements causes imposition of otherwise avoidable taxes. A tax that is unduly borne by those who lack diligence and are uninformed or ill-advised, and is readily avoided by those who are diligent, well-informed and advised, is inherently an unfair tax.

Second, the transfer tax is inefficient. This is perhaps the system's most serious shortcoming. It requires an inordinate amount of attention at the highest levels of government, especially in relation to the relative insignificance of the revenues generated. . . . The creativity of estate planning professionals imposes a continuing drain on the attention of policy makers and legislators. The tax is comparatively expensive to administer. The system's complexity, coupled with the creative devices employed in estate planning, requires the Internal Revenue Service (IRS) to employ lawyers as estate tax examiners, who are compensated at a higher level than other IRS compliance personnel. While only a small fraction of individual income tax returns are examined, 12,000 of the 56,000 estate tax returns filed in 1989 were examined.

Efficiency is not properly measured by compliance costs to the government alone. The transfer tax system imposes enormous resource and opportunity costs in taxpayer compliance and avoidance endeavors and in the time and energy of lawyers, accountants, trust officers, and financial planners required to understand and apply the system. The magnitude of human resources involved is partially suggested by the American Bar Association's estimate that over 16,000 lawyers consider trust, probate, and estate law as their area of concentration. Lawyers, in drafting will and trust arrangements, understandably want their documents to stand the test of time. Because of the transfer tax system's focus on the circumstances of the decedent, wills for many are typically drafted not only in relation to existing circumstances and wealth patterns but in relation to possible changes. Lawyers may not cavalierly assume that clients of modest wealth when wills are executed will not have substantial wealth at death. Many clients who will, in fact, not have transfer tax exposure, receive legal services predicated on the possibility that they may face such exposure. Standard "sweetheart" wills leaving everything to a surviving spouse typically include disclaimer clauses with disclaimer amount trust provisions designed to offer the option of a formula-driven "by-pass" trust benefitting the spouse, if later needed to minimize transfer taxes. Standard wills typically include such boiler plate as tax apportionment clauses and tax election clauses, and durable powers of attorney instruments increasingly empower the attorney-in-fact to make gifts to enable "death bed" use of annual exclusions. Given the possibility, although nonlikelihood, that clients will face estate tax exposure, these provisions are prudent, even though in reality generally not necessary. Although the transfer tax system is intended to affect only a very small portion of the population, such protective drafting causes the system to affect a substantially larger segment, who prudently, but often unnecessarily, receive and pay for complex estate planning services. The system causes dispositive arrangements which could and should be simple to be exceedingly complex. Understandably, testators want to know the meaning of the language used in effecting their dispositive schemes. All too often the taxdriven complexity of language employed is incomprehensible to the testator.

The transfer tax system generates other resource and opportunity costs. Hundreds of law professors devote substantial portions of their careers in exposing thousands of students annually to the challenges and intricacies of transfer taxation and the related subject of estate planning, a major component of which is a study of techniques to avoid or minimize imposition of tax. Similar talent is devoted to the education of accountants, insurance agents, financial planners and others. Considerable resources are devoted to the presentation of continuing education courses for estate planning professionals and to the publication of articles, journals, and book devoted to their needs in understanding and applying the transfer tax system.

There are important consequential costs as well. Prudent fiduciaries are reluctant to distribute and settle decedents' estates before potential estate tax controversies have been settled. The transfer tax system prolongs the administration of estates. Prudent fiduciaries invest conservatively, and prolonged administration delays access to capital by beneficiaries, who may employ it more effectively within the economy. The system also promotes the "trustification" of assets that might otherwise have been transferred outright.

All of the foregoing energy, resources, and opportunity costs are sacrificed on the altar of a tax system that fails to achieve its supposed goals and yields only $12 billion in revenue. . . . The transfer tax system is manifestly inefficient. The resource and opportunity costs generated in relation to revenues obtained are alone sufficient to make the system unacceptable.

In addition to the standards of fairness and efficiency used to measure the desirability of tax systems is a third, that of neutrality. A good tax system should be neutral in that it ought to be nonintrusive — it should not alter choices and behavior that would have occurred in the absence of the system. The current tax system is decidedly nonneutral and intrusive. The system encourages lifetime gifts and penalizes the failure to make them. Further, the system virtually compels use of the marital deduction in most cases involving wealthy married couples. In those instances, it thus discourages substantial outright bequests to others. Also, the system discourages heavy use of joint and survivor arrangements that might otherwise be useful and desirable probate avoidance mechanisms. While the transfer tax system discourages substantial bequests to grandchildren and great grandchildren, it encourages limited bequests to, and certain trust arrangements of limited amounts for the benefit of, grandchildren. The system encourages certain trust arrangements for the benefit or charity and discourages all other trust arrangements for charity. Moreover, the system encourages the retention of farm and other land in some cases, and discourages the disposition of that land by surviving family members in those same cases. The system discourages certain employment related post-death benefit arrangements and encourages others. In varying circumstances the transfer tax system may encourage or discourage use of trust arrangements involving general or special powers of appointment. In inducing the making of gifts for minors and others considered unsuitable for the management of property, the system encourages the use of trusts. Given the tendency of most spouses to leave property to each other to the exclusion of children until the death of the surviving spouse, the system encourages the use of "by-pass" trusts. Because life insurance is a form of wealth that is fully realized at the death of the insured, and because life insurance arrangements can be structured to avoid imposition of transfer taxes, even when funded by the insured, the system encourages investment in life insurance products. The transfer tax system discourages the acquisition and retention of life insurance where the insured retains ownership incidents over the policy. Further, the system strongly encourages the obtaining of professional estate planning advice. The system discourages and renders difficult the prompt settlement of decedents' estates. On balance, the system contributes heavily to the "trustification" of wealth and thus channels the flow of substantial capital into arrangements where, given the prudence of fiduciaries, capital is conservatively invested. Thus to a substantial degree, the system operates to prevent people from making desired dispositions of their property and encourages undesired dispositions. The transfer tax system forces use of complex dispositive mechanisms when simple arrangements are desired. The system is severely intrusive in affecting human choices, investment decisions, and dispositive arrangements. In penalizing and rewarding different choices and decisions, it restricts investment decisions and donative and testamentary freedom and compromises personal liberty. Consequently, the transfer tax system is decidedly nonneutral.

James R. Repetti, *Democracy, Taxes, and Wealth*
76 N.Y.U. L. Rev. 825 (2001) Copyright © 2001 New York University
Law Review; James R. Repetti. Used with permission.

Proposals to repeal the estate tax reflect growing disfavor with the use of a tax system to redistribute wealth. This discontent is a reversal from prior years. Politicians had been concerned earlier about the adverse social effects of wealth concentration. . . . Wealth concentration in the United States decreased from 1929 to 1979. The share of our country's net worth held by the top one percent of wealthiest households declined from more than 44.2% in 1929 to 20.5% in 1979. During the same period, productivity grew rapidly. Beginning in the early 1980s, however, the share of net worth held by the top 1% increased markedly, and by 1989, it had grown to 35.7%. After 1989, the concentration of wealth held steady. The result was that at the end of the twentieth century, wealth was more concentrated in the United States than in the United Kingdom. This was a reversal from the early years of the twentieth century when the U.S. tradition of "economic democracy" had resulted in a much lower concentration than the "royalist legac[y]" of Britain.[9] . . .

---

9. Bruce Ackerman & Anne Alstott, The Stakeholder Society 95 (1999). . . .

Economic studies are remarkably unanimous in suggesting that high concentrations of wealth correlate with poor economic performance in the long run. A survey of the studies stated: "[S]everal studies have examined the impact of inequality upon economic growth. The picture they draw is impressively unambiguous, since they all suggest that greater inequality reduces the rate of growth."[39] Because data about wealth concentration are often difficult to obtain for extended periods in some countries, many studies use concentrations of income as a proxy for wealth. Economists believe that this does not alter the results, because concentrations of income follow the same patterns as concentrations of wealth in those countries for which both sets of data are available.

Published studies that have examined twenty-five-year periods have found that high income concentration at the beginning of the twenty-five-year period correlates with poor economic growth in the subsequent twenty-five years. . . . The long-term studies strongly challenge the conventional textbook maxim that "inequality is good for incentives and therefore good for growth. . . ." The conventional wisdom was that inequality should contribute to increased growth because: (1) the wealthy had a higher marginal propensity to save than the poor; (2) only the wealthy could make the large capital commitments necessary for industrial growth; and (3) the poor would be motivated to work harder than the wealthy.

However, the long-term studies suggest that other, more powerful forces may be involved. As a result, new explanations have been offered for why inequality corresponds with poor economic growth. . . . [T]he explanations with the most support — the presence of social unrest and the failure of countries with inequality to invest adequately in education — are also the explanations most likely to manifest themselves over a long period of time, not a short period. Thus, it is likely that the long-term studies better capture the relationship between inequality and poor economic growth than do the short-term studies. . . .

In addition to having an adverse economic effect in the long run, concentrations of wealth have a harmful impact on the effectiveness of democracies to the extent that an objective of democracy is to give all participants an equal voice. . . . While analysis of the influence of wealthy individuals on their employees and on the media has been anecdotal, analysis of the effect of wealth on the electoral process and conduct of public officials has been based upon statistical analysis. The analysis shows that nearly half of all contributors making large donations (at least $200) are individuals who have incomes over $250,000 per year, and that they wield significant influence. . . . A study of congressional campaign contributions made in 1997 found that 81% of the contributors of $200 or more to congressional candidates had annual family

---

39. Philippe Aghion et al., *Inequality and Economic Growth: The Perspective of the New Growth Theories*, 37 J. Econ. Lit. 1615, 1617 (1999).

incomes of over $100,000.[109] Forty-six percent of the donors had annual family incomes over $250,000 and 20% over $500,000.

The contributions clearly influence election results and, as a result, cause the wealthy to have a disproportionate voice. . . . Once a candidate is elected, do the contributors exert power over the candidate? The studies have been mixed in finding a direct relationship between contributions and how senators or members of the House actually vote in highly visible roll calls on the floor. However, the studies are much more consistent in finding evidence that the contributions do play a significant role in influencing the activities of legislators outside the limelight of roll call votes on the floor. . . .

A large portion of wealth in the United States is dynastic. Studies indicate that approximately fifty percent of wealth in the United States is inherited. In 1984, 241 of the wealthiest 400 individuals in the United States started with a significant inherited fortune. In 1999, 149 of the 400 wealthiest individuals in the United States started with a significant inherited fortune.

The harmful effects of wealth on the media and the political process are likely stronger in the case of dynastic wealth, as compared to wealth held by different families each generation. Where different families hold wealth each generation, it is likely that each new family will bring new perspectives, life experiences, and concerns to the political process and the media. Moreover, since the wealth will have been created by those that possess it, it is likely that such wealthholders also will have significant talents. In contrast, where wealth simply is transmitted from a generation that created it to subsequent generations in the same family, it is less certain that the subsequent generations will have new perspectives, life experiences, or great talent. . . .

Because of the concerns about dynastic wealth, society legitimately could decide to use the tax system to curb the transfer of wealth to those who did not create it. The tax system should do more, however, than merely help check wealth concentration. The macroeconomic literature . . . has emphasized the need for investment in human capital. This suggests that another objective of a tax system seeking to curb dynastic wealth should be to raise revenues to fund such investment. Also, it is important that the tax not create other problems that outweigh the foregoing benefits. . . .

An important goal of a tax to prevent wealth concentration should be to raise revenues to fund education and build an infrastructure (including communications and transportation) that will increase opportunities for all citizens. The increased investment in education could occur either by the government increasing its investment or by individuals increasing their investments with grants received from the government. Despite its many imperfections, our current wealth transfer tax appears to raise revenues that could be used for this purpose. Revenues from the estate and gift tax are projected to be $209 billion

---

109. John Green et al., *The Center for Responsive Politics, Individual Congressional Campaign Contributors: Wealthy, Conservative and Reform-Minded*, at http://www.opensecrets.org/pubs/donors/donors.htm (June 9, 1998).

for the years 2000 through 2005. These revenues are not insignificant. The 1999 revenue from the estate and gift tax of $27.8 billion is greater than the entire 1998 individual income tax liability of taxpayers with an adjusted gross income under $15,000 and forty-nine percent of the 1998 tax liability of taxpayers with an adjusted gross income between $15,000 and $30,000. . . .

[A] tax on wealth transfers raises significant revenue. However, even if it did not, the tax still would be justified if it helped curb wealth concentration, given the harms arising from wealth concentration. . . . Bequests and gifts account for approximately fifty percent of all wealth accumulations in the United States. Thus, it appears that a tax on wealth transfers should have an effect on concentrations of wealth.

The fact that the concentration of wealth in the United States has stayed relatively constant since 1989, after significant increases that occurred in the 1980s, does not mean that the estate tax has failed to affect wealth concentration and family dynasties. A recent study has sought to determine what the effect of the repeal of the estate and gift tax would be on wealth concentration.[185] The study determined that eliminating the estate and gift tax would increase the percentage of national wealth held by the top one percent from a conservative estimate of a ten percent increase to an aggressive estimate of a twofold increase.

Indirect evidence also suggests that the amount of wealth transferred from one generation to the next would have been larger without an estate tax. The amounts of estate tax paid by decedents with respect to taxable returns filed in 1997 represented twenty-four percent of the aggregate taxable estates reported in those returns. Moreover, the estate tax reduces wealth transferred within a family, not only because of the amount of taxes paid, but also because it encourages charitable contributions. Most studies have concluded that the estate tax encourages charitable contributions. . . . [T]he percentage of 1997 estate tax returns claiming charitable deductions and the average charitable bequest per 1997 return increased as the size of the gross estate increased. Approximately fifty percent of returns with gross estates exceeding $20 million claimed a charitable deduction, with an average contribution of $40,206,536 per return claiming the deduction. . . .

The combination of the estate tax liability and charitable contributions significantly reduces the amount of wealth transferred within a family. An important 1994 study that examined the tax returns for persons who died in 1982 found that the combination of charitable bequests, estate expenses, and taxes accounted on average for forty-one percent of the net worth (gross estate less debt) of decedents with gross estates over $10 million. The study's findings also suggest that taxing wealth transfers does not impose hardship on decedents' children. The study found that the average income of children of

---

185. John Laitner, *Simulating the Effects on Inequality and Wealth Accumulation of Eliminating the Federal Gift and Estate Tax* (Apr. 17, 2000) (unpublished manuscript, on file with New York University Law Review).

decedents with gross estates over $10 million at the time the decedents died was $271,254, measured in 1981 dollars. The children of decedents who died in 1982 with more modest estates, between $2.5 million and $10 million, had an average adjusted gross income of $123,452 the year before their parent's death, again measured in 1981 dollars. . . .

Another major criticism of the estate tax is that it imposes financial burdens on family businesses. Paying premiums for insurance to fund an estate tax liability reduces the cash available for investment in the business. Moreover, to the extent that insurance is inadequate to pay the estate tax, heirs may be forced to sell part of the business to fund the tax.

Most family business owners surveyed in the 1997 Family Business Survey stated that they rely on life insurance to pay the estate tax. A study has concluded, however, that businesses may not carry sufficient insurance to pay the entire estate tax. The study estimated the estate tax liability for owners of family businesses and compared the estimated tax liability to the amount of life insurance held on the owners' lives and other liquid assets held by the owner. It found that the mean gap between estimated estate tax liability on the one hand, and life insurance and liquid assets on the other hand, ranges from twelve to eighteen percent. The study also noted, however, that the gap might be attributable to the owners' expectations that various avoidance techniques, such as valuation discounts or favorable statutory provisions, will be used to reduce the estate tax liability.

The estate tax should have a minimal impact on most small businesses because of the numerous provisions . . . that currently provide relief to family businesses and farms. The difficulty is that current provisions are complex and require sophisticated advice before a taxpayer can benefit fully. . . . In addition to the substantial benefits conferred by statutory provisions, courts also have allowed significant discounts in valuing minority interests in businesses to reflect lack of control and lack of liquidity. Partial interests in real estate similarly are discounted to reflect the costs that an owner would incur in partitioning the land.

Although these provisions provide significant relief, they are complex. They create an equity problem because they provide the greatest benefit to those who seek sophisticated tax advice. To the extent that the estate tax does impose an unacceptable burden, policymakers need to identify the benefits provided by small businesses and family farms and to determine the best way to target tax relief to those companies providing the benefits. Family businesses normally have a low return on assets. However, the family business and farm may play an important humanizing role in a society where larger corporations are guided primarily by profit maximization. The family business or farm may contribute to the richness of community life through its willingness to help neighbors and the community in a way that does not maximize profits, but that nevertheless improves quality of life. As the business grows, however, these values may be lost as the use of the profit-maximizing formula becomes necessary to coordinate the activity of many participants. The task for policymakers is to identify the level at which this occurs so that tax relief is simple and does not require sophisticated planning. . . .

The final criticism of our current estate tax is that the costs of administration and compliance are high. The IRS incurs costs in administering the estate tax, and taxpayers incur costs in complying with it. Although the current estate and gift tax is full of loopholes and complex provisions, the costs to the IRS in administering the tax appear to be proportional to the amount of revenues generated.

The costs of taxpayer compliance are much more controversial. It is difficult to distinguish between the costs incurred by the taxpayers that are necessary to plan for an orderly succession of property under applicable state law and costs that are necessary to minimize the federal estate tax. The result is that the estimates of taxpayers' compliance have varied widely. . . .

[T]he current U.S. transfer tax does raise revenues and help curb wealth concentration without significantly influencing savings. The transfer tax need not harm farms or small businesses. All farms could be exempted with minimal revenue impact. Provisions to protect small businesses should be drafted clearly so that sophisticated advice is not required. Finally, valuation rules which allow taxpayers to decrease the value of assets subject to the tax should be eliminated.

Charles Davenport & Jay A. Soled,
Enlivening the Death-Tax Death-Talk
1999 TNT 142-93, 84 Tax Notes 591 (July 26, 1999)
Copyright © 1999 Tax Analysts. Used with permission.

. . . Our transfer taxes . . . are expected to raise about $27 billion in 1999. Over the next decade that amount is projected to grow to $44 billion. This is not a substantial portion of total taxes, and except for a year or two in the middle 1930s when they reached about 7 percent of the total, transfer taxes have never raised a substantial portion of our total taxes. . . . Transfer taxes amount to just 1.4 percent of total tax receipts. While not a large percentage of receipts, they are sufficiently great that elimination or reduction of them would force some fiscal offset: other taxes would have to be raised; other taxes could not be cut; borrowing would be greater; or spending would have to be cut. The loss of transfer taxes would further constrain fiscal action whether one is desirous of less government spending, the same, or more government spending. . . .

Complete elimination of transfer taxes would produce a 10-year revenue loss of $358 billion beginning in 2000. An across-the-board income tax cut equal to the estate tax receipts would reduce the income tax by about 3 percent for every current income tax payer. Alternatively, the same amount could fund changes to the AMT, provide funds for expiring provisions, reduce the marriage penalty, or allow other changes in existing provisions that are major irritants in the income tax. It could fund a substantial amount of personal savings accounts for phasing in retirement income privatization. The double tax on corporations could be substantially lightened. With these and other alternative tax cuts of more than $27 billion annually, we questioned what justified the [call for repeal of] the estate tax. . . .

[We] find that about 5 percent of decedents in any year is the greatest percentage that leave assets sufficient to require the filing of an estate return. . . . Estate tax returns show the wealth reported on the returns. In 1996, there were about 80,000 returns reporting about $137 billion. The average estate was about $1.7 million.

A study of wealth in 1992 found that the top 5 percent of the households (potential estate taxpayers) owned 58.3 percent (around $8.8 trillion) of all assets but 70.6 percent (about $8 trillion) of financial assets. The top 1 percent of wealth holders owned 35.9 percent of all assets, but 45.6 percent of financial assets. The top 1 percent held 63.5 percent of business assets and had an average household net worth of $7.6 million. Percentiles 2 through 5 held 22.4 percent of all assets in 1992 for total net worth of over $4.5 trillion and an average of about $1 million per household.[15]. . .

These facts tell us that most of the population is far out of the grasp of the estate tax. With the increase of the credit exemption to $1 million, even the three-quarters of the aspiring college students who expect to become millionaires have no concern about being swept into the clutches of the death tax. This dispersion of the estate tax would also argue that even the great multitudes who are reported to despise it have little reason to fear becoming subject to it. If the reported attitude is correct, it must either be based on a great misunderstanding or an unusual solicitude for financial betters. . . .

Potential estate taxpayers have ample resources. . . . They are a group able to pay taxes, and the opponents of the estate tax do not argue otherwise except in the context of assets claimed to be illiquid, businesses, and farms. If ability to pay were the only measure for tax policy, this group would seem to be a target for more taxation. There are, of course, other factors important in determining whether they should pay more tax.

Taxpayers subject to the estate tax have considerable property that has appreciated in their hands and never been subjected to tax. The estate tax is the last opportunity for society to tax these gains. They disappear at death due to the death-time step-up in basis of property to its fair market value. The amount of appreciation that passes free of the income tax is considerable. . . . Treasury estimates that the taxation of unrealized gains at death would increase revenues by $25.8 billion in 1999 and that would rise to $29.3 billion by 2004. . . . Put another way, about $18 billion of the 1999 revenue loss resulting from allowing unrealized gains to pass untaxed at death might reasonably be attributed to the top 5 percent of wealth holders. . . .

---

15. Wolff, Edward N., *Who Are the Rich? A Demographic Profile of High-Income and High-Wealth Americans,* Office of Tax Policy of the University of Michigan Business School, Working Paper Series No. 98-6 (1998).

The estate tax adds to the progressivity of the tax system, and that is believed by many to be a laudable aim. Sufficient defense of this position was eloquently made by Professor Michael Graetz.[30] He found that about one-third of the progressivity in our tax system is due to the estate tax.

The argument against progressivity is based on the notion that taxes should be proportional at best. Taxes that are not proportional are thought not to be fair. Proportionality, which apparently treats all persons as equals [at] least with respect to taxes as a percentage of income, seems based on a flawed premise. Not all persons have the same social and economic interests in a stable, conservative society. High-income and high-wealth members of society have a much greater stake in the stability of society. This stake does not rise merely linearly with income and wealth, but at least geometrically if not exponentially. A progressive burden places more societal costs on those who receive the most and benefit the most from our society. . . .

Early proponents of the estate tax argued that it would break up very large concentrations of wealth. . . . Its failure on this ground is frequently cited by opponents of the tax, a somewhat ironic dialectic since they seem so worried that their wealth will be unconcentrated by the tax. This criticism also admits of great concentrations of wealth. These great concentrations of wealth prove only that the tax has not been as effective as it might have been. We do not know whether they would have been greater, or lesser, if the estate tax had not existed. . . .

Not all power and wealth are concentrated at the national level. Much of it dispersed throughout large and small communities where the wealthy live. Many wealthy may have little influence on the national scene but have quite a bit of influence on smaller governmental units and economic life of their communities. At the lowest level, even small amounts of wealth may be sufficient to move either the legislature, the executive, or the bureaucracy in ways that citizens with lesser wealth cannot.

Wealth may also have a significant hold on the economic life of a community. Company towns still exist, and less melodramatic and less malevolent characters than Mr. Potter in "It's a Wonderful Life" abound. In these situations, power based on wealth lies on a spectrum from almost autocratic to barely significant. A reduction of family wealth will usually reduce the family power has over local authorities and the local economy. This is not an insignificant consideration. Local government likely has more influence on lives than the federal government does. The quality of schools, the need for safety, the need for building permits, local licensing ordinances, building and health codes, traffic tickets, road maintenance, zoning and rezoning, taxicab and cable TV monopolies, speed traps, discretionary and differential enforcement of laws and regulations, and many other irritations in daily life all spring from local government. Similarly, jobs may be dependent on a single employer and its satellites. . . .

---

30. Michael J. Graetz, *To Praise the Estate Tax, Not to Bury It*, 93 Yale L. J. 259 (1983).

Finally, if we believe practitioners and congressional testimony, constant concern about liquidity for estate taxes distracts businesses from tending to their own growth. Because of time spent in protecting transmission to the next generation and the sequestering of funds for that purpose, good business opportunities are forgone. Business managers are so distracted and assets so ill-used that businesses do not grow as rapidly as they otherwise would, and the tax has had, albeit probably unintended, an effect on the further concentration of wealth.

We conclude that the estate tax has had some unquantifiable effect on concentrations of wealth. A reduction or elimination of the tax will remove it as a factor in slowing what appears to be rapidly increasing concentration of wealth. . . .

One of the major charges against the death tax is inefficiency. The costs associated with it are claimed to be more, as great, or nearly as great as the tax collected. This claim is made irresponsibly and is frequently built on no foundation at all or on a foundation insufficient to support the extraordinary edifice built up on it. There are primarily three costs: (1) IRS costs of administration, (2) taxpayer planning costs, and (3) compliance costs. All have been greatly overstated. No prior estimate has been made with any analytic precision.

As a starting point, we ought to agree that the IRS administrative costs of the estate tax certainly cannot exceed the total budget of the IRS and likely is only a small percentage of that. . . .

A more refined estimate can be made. . . . [Between September 1996 and the same time in 1997] [t]he IRS examined 11,686, or 12.9 percent, of the estate tax returns and 2,085, or 0.9 percent, of the gift tax returns. Coverage for estates ran from about 7 percent for returns under $1 million to almost 48 percent for returns with a gross estate of more than $5 million.

At our request, the Internal Revenue Service supplied information on the cost of processing and examining gift and estate tax returns. The estimated cost . . . without giving any cost to buildings, electricity, or depreciation on furniture and the like was about $47 million. If we add 30 percent for this overhead, the total cost comes to $61 million. Appeals and litigation undoubtedly are less than the cost of examination, and we have assumed a cost for these activities of one-half that for examinations or $31 million. Some cost must also be assigned to the preparation of administrative guidance. . . . An overly generous figure assumes that the administrative cost is the same as the examining cost, or $61 million. All of these costs total $152 million annually. In light of the existing political and budget situation, there is little reason to think that this number will grow significantly over the next decade. This total is less than 2 percent of the IRS budget. The major cost of the tax systems, so we are told, is imposed not on the IRS but on the public, and we turn to it.

There are two distinct costs of the estate tax system to the public. First, the estate is planned. At death, an estate must be administered. We have estimated the first of these costs using the best information available from discussion with persons who plan estates. We have also estimated the costs of estate administration that we think are attributable to tax planning. There is admittedly more doubt about these costs, but we have been overly generous, we think, in allocating amounts due to the estate tax.

To estimate planning fees, we first consulted several professionals about their average charges for typical estate planning. . . . [Based on our assumptions and the analysis of the data collected] here are the fees attributable to decedents on 1996 estate tax returns:

Estate Size	Number	Fee per Estate	Gross Fee
$1.2 to $2 million	42,286	$2,500	$105.7
$2 to $5 million	28,441	3,500	99.5
$5 to $10 million	5,712	6,000	34.2
$10 to $20 million	1,871	10,000	18.7
$20 to $40 million	663	20,000	13.3
Over $40 million	372	50,000	18.6
Total gross fees stated in millions.			$290.0

This total was then halved because we assumed that the fee represented the planning of both married persons' estates. . . . [Based on our assumptions, we calculate] a fee of more than $5,000 for planning a couple's estate. This is very high in light of our conversations with estate planners, but we nevertheless will use it.

All of that fee is not attributable to the estate tax. Generally, instructions about health treatment are given. A power of attorney will be prepared. Dispositions of remains will be considered. Provisions and documents for the disposition of property must be drafted even if no estate tax existed. Discussions about the title to property will be necessary whether or not taxes are important. Executors and trustees must be selected, and guardians and conservators may even be discussed. Some people will want to protect minor or spendthrift children from inheriting vast sums of wealth that are freely available to them at a young age. . . .

All of this suggests that the drafting and the instruments would not be substantially different if there were no estate tax. We think the entire "estate planning" fee is not properly ascribed to the estate tax. . . . If an allocation were properly made between tax advice and general advice about the devolution of property, not all of the fee could be attributed to tax advice. In the lower-valued estates only about one-third of the fee is properly allocable to tax advice. This is rather a close question. If one drafts a QTIP trust that would be only slightly different if estate tax were no consideration, how much is attributable to estate taxes? Probably, not much. Yet, universally, our estate planning friends tell us that the entire fee is attributed to tax factors. When billing time comes around planners and clients simply forget about the worthless stepdaughters that would have harassed the son receiving the family business. The tax planning costs should be adjusted for this factor. Despite our thinking that tax considerations may not rise to more than one-third of the total work, we have estimated one-half of the total for tax planning, or $2,500 per couple.

That brings us to the number of people who will require tax estate planning. Decedents filing tax returns in 1996 were about 3.3 percent of the decedents that year, but decedents leaving estates large enough to require an estate tax return probably were not the only ones who took estate and gift taxes into account. . . .

A substantial part of the estate's attorney and executor fees has nothing to do with the estate tax. Even without an estate tax, assets must be marshalled, debts must be paid, heirs must be pacified, property must be valued, special orders may be sought, asset schedules must be prepared, claims and debts must be listed, income and expenses must be tracked, and many costs are incurred unrelated to the estate tax. If all assets were in a revocable trust, a smaller percentage of the costs might be attributed to routine estate administration, but despite the popularity of revocable trusts, we have not yet reached that Nirvana. . . .

Based on all of the assumptions and conclusions reached in the foregoing discussion about IRS cost, planning costs, and costs of administering the estate that might be attributed to the estate tax, the total cost, both public and private, of administering the estate tax, the estate tax estimated and projected receipts, and the [cost as a percentage of expected receipts for 1995-2007 ranges from a low of 6.17% in 2006 to a high of 9.04% in 2002.]. . .

The costs of administering the estate tax have been grossly overstated. We do not know why. In part, we think that few have tried very hard to analyze the costs, estimate them properly, and reach a number within the realm of reality. . . . Instead of high cost, we find the estate tax to be an efficient tax. . . .

Notwithstanding its flaws, the current U.S. transfer tax system works to some extent. The system raises and probably will continue to raise significant amounts of revenue that would be difficult to replace. Many people do not understand how transfer taxes work in practice. Such misunderstanding breeds concern and resentment. Minimal estate planning can alleviate the perceived burden transfer taxes considerably. Estate taxes operate unevenly among those people with portfolio and easily valued assets and those with hard-to-value small businesses and farms.

Planning is not terribly expensive for most estates and may have a beneficial effect for reasons unrelated to taxes. The tax cost associated with estate planning is only a marginally greater burden than is required for non-tax planning in an era of split families with multiple sets of children and others waiting to inherit property from people who have worked so hard to accumulate and save their fortunes.

Some of these concerns might be alleviated by taking a leaf from the 1986 income tax reform. Base broadening will permit a considerable restructuring of the system and a lowering of both the rates and the progression so that it would operate in a more even fashion and yet provide the same amount of revenue. One might also strengthen the tax by confining the gift tax annual per donee exclusion to its original purposes and cutting back on it. Valuation discounts should be eliminated because in most cases the discount is an illusion seen only by the courts.

If legislative reform is not undertaken to address these concerns, the potential and the fairness of the tax will continue to diminish. For that reason alone, these reforms should be made.

A primary role of any tax is to raise revenue. The initial impetus for the federal estate tax was the need to raise revenue for war efforts. While this particular rationale faded with time, the need for revenue did not disappear. In 2000, when the government predicted a $1.3 trillion budget surplus, the need for the revenue generated by the federal transfer tax system had diminished significantly. This budget surplus was a primary factor influencing the passage of the 2001 Act, particularly the repeal of the estate and the generation-skipping transfer taxes. The ink had barely dried on President George W. Bush's signature, however, when the economic and political landscapes changed dramatically, first with the slowing of the economy and then with the terrorist attacks of September 11, 2001, and then with the war in Iraq in 2003. The need to encourage economic growth in the latter half of 2001 has shifted attention away from the transfer tax provisions. Neither proponents nor opponents of the transfer tax system argue that these provisions provide an efficient and effective system for stimulating the economy. It remains to be seen whether Congress will make the repeal of the estate and generation-skipping transfer taxes permanent or whether Congress will be required to reverse even the temporary repeal.

Many commentators argue that some form of wealth taxation is necessary even if the current transfer tax system is abolished. Some would repeal §102 and include gifts and bequests in income.[21] The result would be a form of inheritance tax collected through the income tax structure. Others propose to tax unrealized appreciation at death, also a radical change to the income tax system.[22] An alternative to taxing unrealized gains at death is simply to repeal §1014 and tax the gain when the recipient ultimately sells the property.[23] Repeal of §1014 was enacted in 1976 but subsequently reversed before it became effective in 1980. Current proposals to eliminate the federal transfer tax system include repeal of §1014. Finally, one commentator has even

---

21. *See, e.g.,* Joseph M. Dodge, *Beyond Estate and Gift Tax Reform: Including Gifts and Bequests in Income,* 91 Harv. L. Rev. 1177 (1978); David M. Hudson, *Tax Policy and the Federal Taxation of the Transfer of Wealth,* 19 Willamette L. Rev. 1 (1983).

22. *See, e.g.,* Joseph M. Dodge, *Further Thoughts on Realizing Gains and Losses at Death,* 47 Vand. L. Rev. 1827 (1994); Lawrence Zelenak, *Taxing Gains at Death,* 46 Vand. L. Rev. 361 (1993); Charles O. Galvin, *Taxing Gains at Death: A Further Comment,* 46 Vand. L. Rev. 1525 (1993); Dan Subotnick, *On Constructively Realizing Constructive Realization: Building the Case for Death and Taxes,* 38 U. Kan. L. Rev. 1 (1989).

23. *See, e.g.,* Russell K. Osgood, *Carryover Basis Repeal and Reform of the Transfer Tax System,* 66 Cornell L. Rev. 297 (1981).

proposed an accessions tax[24] and others to include gifts and bequests in a consumption tax.[25]

PROBLEMS

1. You are a member of the United States House of Representatives and have been appointed to the House Ways and Means Committee, Subcommittee on Transfer Taxation. One of your colleagues has just introduced a bill to make the repeal of the estate and generation-skipping transfer taxes permanent. Be prepared to discuss and vote on this bill.
2. You are a member of the United States House of Representatives. The House Ways and Means Committee has introduced a bill to repeal §102 and tax all gifts and bequests as income. Be prepared to discuss and vote on this bill.
3. You are a member of the United States House of Representatives. The House Ways and Means Committee has introduced a bill requiring that all unrealized gains be taxed as income on the decedent's final income tax return. Be prepared to discuss and vote on this bill.
4. You are staff to a member of your State House of Representatives. Your state is debating whether to adopt an estate tax, an inheritance tax, or an accessions tax, *i.e.*, a cumulative tax on the receipt of gifts and inheritances. Compare and contrast these three alternatives for your boss, and make a recommendation.

D. THE ROLE OF STATE LAW

The federal transfer tax system is just that — a federal statute, regulations, interpretations, and judicial decisions. By its very nature, however, the system taxes property interests, and Congress has not supplemented the federal tax code with a federal system of property law. Instead, the tax system relies on state property law to define the nature and extent of property rights. This sounds simple and straightforward. Unfortunately, that is not the case. When there is little risk to the state property law system, state courts may be tempted to decide probate and other property law cases in a manner that maximizes the

---

24. Edward C. Halbach, Jr., *An Accessions Tax*, 23 Real Prop., Prob., & Trust J. 211 (1988). *See also* Joseph M. Dodge, *Comparing a Reformed Estate Tax with an Accessions Tax and an Income-Inclusion System, and Abandoning the Generation-Skipping Tax*, 56 SMU Law Rev. 551 (2003).

25. Karen C. Burke and Grayson M.P. McCouch, *A Consumption Tax on Gifts and Bequests?*, 17 Va. Tax Rev. 657 (1998); Joseph M. Dodge, *Taxing Gratuitous Transfers Under a Consumption Tax*, 51 Tax. L. Rev. 529 (1996).

federal transfer tax benefits or minimizes the tax. If the United States is not a party to these proceedings, there is no party to safeguard the interests of the tax system. How, then, should the federal courts construe state court decisions when deciding subsequent tax cases? The Supreme Court faced that issue in the following case.

Commissioner v. Estate of Bosch
387 U.S. 456 (1967)

Mr. Justice CLARK delivered the opinion of the Court.

These two federal estate tax cases present a common issue for our determination: Whether a federal court or agency in a federal estate tax controversy is conclusively bound by a state trial court adjudication of property rights or characterization of property interests when the United States is not made a party to such proceeding. [Both cases involved the marital deduction. In one case, the state court held a widow's alleged renunciation of a general power of appointment invalid. As a result, the trust established by the decedent qualified for the marital deduction. In the other case, the state court construed language in decedent's will to allocate claims, expenses, and taxes only to property not passing to the surviving spouse. This significantly increased the amount qualifying for the marital deduction.]. . .

We hold that where the federal estate tax liability turns upon the character of a property interest held and transferred by the decedent under state law, federal authorities are not bound by the determination made of such property interest by a state trial court. . . .

The problem of what effect must be given a state trial court decree where the matter decided there is determinative of federal estate tax consequences has long burdened the Bar and the courts. This Court has not addressed itself to the problem for nearly a third of a century. In Freuler v. Helvering, 291 U.S. 35 (1934), this Court, declining to find collusion between the parties on the record as presented there, held that a prior in personam judgment in the state court to which the United States was not made a party, "(o)bviously . . . had not the effect of res judicata, and could not furnish the basis for invocation of the full faith and credit clause. . . ." At 43. In *Freuler*'s wake, at least three positions have emerged among the circuits. The first of these holds that. . .

> if the question at issue is fairly presented to the state court for its independent decision and is so decided by the court the resulting judgment if binding upon the parties under the state law is conclusive as to their property rights in the federal tax case. . . .

Gallagher v. Smith, 223 F.2d 218, at 225. The opposite view is expressed in Faulkerson's Estate v. United States, 301 F.2d 231. This view seems to approach that of Erie R. Co. v. Tompkins, 304 U.S. 64 (1938), in that the federal court will consider itself bound by the state court decree only after independent examination of the state law as determined by the highest court of the State. The Government urges that an intermediate position be adopted; it suggests that a state trial court adjudication is binding in such cases only when the judgment is the result of an adversary proceeding in the state court. . . .

We look at the problem differently. First, the Commissioner was not made a party to either of the state proceedings here and neither had the effect of res judicata . . . nor did the principle of collateral estoppel apply. It can hardly be denied that both state proceedings were brought for the purpose of directly affecting federal estate tax liability. Next, it must be remembered that it was a federal taxing statute that the Congress enacted and upon which we are here passing. Therefore, in construing it, we must look to the legislative history surrounding it. We find that the report of the Senate Finance Committee recommending enactment of the marital deduction used very guarded language in referring to the very question involved here. It said that "proper regard," not finality, "should be given to interpretations of the will" by state courts and then only when entered by a court "in a bona fide adversary proceeding." S.Rep. No. 1013, Pt. 2, 80th Cong., 2d Sess., 4. We cannot say that the authors of this directive intended that the decrees of state trial courts were to be conclusive and binding on the computation of the federal estate tax as levied by the Congress. If the Congress had intended state trial court determinations to have that effect on the federal actions, it certainly would have said so — which it did not do. On the contrary, we believe it intended the marital deduction to be strictly construed and applied. Not only did it indicate that only "proper regard" was to be accorded state decrees but it placed specific limitations on the allowance of the deduction as set out in [IRC] §2056(b), (c), and (d). These restrictive limitations clearly indicate the great care that Congress exercised in the drawing of the Act and indicate also a definite concern with the elimination of loopholes and escape hatches that might jeopardize the federal revenue. This also is in keeping with the long-established policy of the Congress, as expressed in the Rules of Decision Act, 28 U.S.C. §1652. There it is provided that in the absence of federal requirements such as the Constitution or Acts of Congress, the "laws of the several states . . . shall be regarded as rules of deci-sion in civil actions in the courts of the United States, in cases where they apply." This Court has held that judicial decisions are "laws of the . . . state" within the section. Erie R. Co. v. Tompkins, *supra*; . . . Moreover, even in diversity cases this Court has further held that while the decrees of "lower state courts" should be "attributed some weight . . . the decision (is) not controlling . . ." where the highest court of the State has not spoken on the point. King v. Order of United Commercial Travelers, *supra*, at 160-161. And in West v. American Tel. & Tel. Co., 311 U.S. 223 (1940), this Court further held that "an intermediate appellate state court . . . is a datum for ascertaining state law which is not to be disregarded by a federal court *unless it is convinced by other persuasive data that the highest court of the state would decide otherwise*." At 237, 61 S.Ct. at 183 (Emphasis supplied). Thus, under some conditions, federal authority may not be bound even by an intermediate state appellate court ruling. It follows here then, that when the application of a federal statute is involved, the decision of a state trial court as to an underlying issue of state law should a fortiori not be controlling. This is but an application of the rule of Erie R. Co. v. Tompkins, *supra*, where state law as announced by the highest court of the State is to be followed. This is not a diversity case but the same principle may be applied for the same reasons, viz., the underlying substantive rule involved is based on state law and the State's highest court is the best authority on its own law. If there be no decision by that court then federal authorities must apply what they find to be the state law after giving "proper regard" to relevant rulings of other courts of the State. In this respect, it may be said to be, in effect, sitting as a state court. . . .

We believe that this would avoid much of the uncertainty that would result from the "non-adversary" approach and at the same time would be fair to the taxpayer and protect the federal revenue as well.

This cases raises two different issues. First: Is the question one of state property law, or is it one of interpreting the federal statute? Second: What court is making the decision, and what effect does its decision have in a subsequent proceeding? The situation becomes even more complicated when the federal law incorporates state law into its rules. These issues will be covered in greater depth in later chapters, particularly Chapters 8 and 14.

CHAPTER 2

Income Taxation of the Transfer of Wealth

A. GENERAL PRINCIPLES

The income tax differs in significant ways from the estate tax. It is imposed on an annual basis and focuses on the receipt, rather than the transfer, of money or property. The income tax is often used to encourage social or economic behavior, for example, to promote retirement savings or create new jobs. The gift tax and the estate tax are considered to be *in pari materia* (upon the same matter or subject) and therefore to be construed in the same manner, but no attempt has been made to coordinate the income tax with either the gift or the estate tax. Many transactions have income as well as gift and estate tax consequences. Because these tax systems developed independently of each other, a transaction may be treated one way for income tax purposes and another way for transfer tax purposes.

Although trusts are usually separate income-tax paying entities, §§671-679 dictate when the grantor or another will be treated as the owner of the trust and, thus, taxed on the income generated by the trust regardless of who actually receives distributions of trust income. The grantor trust rules differ from the rules governing the completion of gifts and the rules for including property in the gross estate in a number of instances. As a result, the grantor of a trust may be treated as the owner for income tax purposes even when the property is treated as owned by another for purposes of the gift and estate taxes and vice versa.

Example 2-1

Donald creates an irrevocable inter vivos trust to pay the income to Adam for Adam's life and then to distribute the trust property to Bob. Donald reserves the right to change trust beneficiaries at his death. That is, Donald cannot change the trust beneficiaries during his own lifetime, but he can do so in his will. This is not a completed transfer for gift tax purposes, Reg. §25.2511-2(b), and the property will be in Donald's gross estate for estate tax purposes, §2038. Donald, however, will not be treated as the owner of the trust property for income tax purposes, §674(b)(3). Instead, Adam will be taxed on the trust income that is distributed to him.

Likewise, some transactions will be treated as gifts for transfer tax purposes but not for income tax purposes. For gift tax purposes, a gift occurs whenever there is a transfer of property and the donor does not receive adequate and full consideration in money or money's worth. The donor's intent is irrelevant, except in business transactions. §2512(b). For income tax purposes, a gift is defined as a transfer that proceeds from "detached and disinterested generosity" or out of "affection, respect, admiration, charity, or like impulses." The primary consideration is the donor's intention. Commissioner v. Duberstein, 363 U.S. 278, 285 (1960). As a result, the same transaction may be classified as a gift for gift tax purposes but not for income tax purposes.

Example 2-2

Harvey proposes marriage to Wendy, and they sign a prenuptial agreement. In exchange for giving up all of her rights to his property upon death or divorce, Harvey will transfer $500,000 of stock to Wendy. This transaction will be treated as a sale for purposes of the income tax, and Harvey will be required to report any gain from this transaction on his income tax. *See* Farid-Es-Sultaneh v. Commissioner, 160 F.2d 812 (2d Cir. 1947). Because he received only Wendy's marital rights and did not receive money or money's worth in exchange for the stock, Harvey will owe gift tax on the transaction because it is treated as a gift for gift tax purposes. *See* Commissioner v.Wemyss, 324 U.S. 303 (1945); Merrill v. Fahs, 324 U.S. 308 (1945).[1]

Perfect symmetry may not be possible or even desirable. Developing one universal set of definitions and rules might impose a severe strain on both the income and the transfer taxes. Effective estate planning requires knowledge of both sets of rules, the connections between the systems, and the differences. This chapter does not purport to accomplish this goal; it is designed merely to introduce basic income tax concepts that are necessary for understanding the transfer tax system.

B. INCOME TAX CONSEQUENCES OF TRANSFERS OF PROPERTY
IRC §§61, 102, 165, 1001, 1012, 1014-1016, 1221-1223

Every transaction has at least two taxpayers, *e.g.*, a buyer and a seller or a donor and a recipient. In the income tax, there are potential tax consequences

---

1. Careful planning can avoid the adverse income and gift tax consequences in this example. As long as the parties make the agreement contingent upon the marriage and do not make the transfers until after the marriage, §1041 will prevent recognition of any realized gain to Harvey and §2523 will prevent the imposition of the gift tax. Wendy will receive Harvey's basis and recognize any gain when she sells the stock.

to both participants. In the transfer tax, the focus is on the donor or decedent's estate and the recipient, for the most part, is ignored. This section describes the basic income tax consequences to the buyer and seller or the donor and recipient from typical sales and gifts of property.

Section 61 imposes a tax on "gross income from whatever source derived." This includes not only compensation, interest, dividends, rents, and royalties, but also gains from the sale or exchange of property. Gain is defined as the difference between the amount the taxpayer receives and her adjusted basis. §1001. Basis is the taxpayer's cost, or investment, in the asset. §1012.

Example 2-3

Mary buys ten shares of stock for $1,000. Her basis in that stock is $1,000. Two years later she sells the stock to Sally for $5,000. Mary's gain is the difference between the amount she received ($5,000) and her basis ($1,000), *i.e.*, $4,000. §1001.

The taxpayer's basis in property will be increased for capital improvements to the property, and it will be decreased for depreciation deductions allowed with respect to the property. §1016.

Example 2-4

John buys rental real estate for $100,000. He builds an addition for $50,000. His adjusted basis in the property is now $150,000. Assume that John is allowed depreciation deductions of $10,000 each year. After four years, he sells the building for $180,000. His gain is the difference between the amount he realized ($180,000) and his adjusted basis in the property ($100,000 + $50,000 − $40,000 or $110,000), *i.e.*, $70,000. §1001.

Mere increases in value are not subject to the income tax. Increased value is only taxed when it is realized. Realization occurs when the taxpayer sells or exchanges the property. All gains from these transactions in property must be reported on the taxpayer's income tax return in the year the transaction occurs unless there is a specific section of the Internal Revenue Code that permits nonrecognition. For example, §1031 permits the nonrecognition of gain for like-kind exchanges of property used in business or held for the production of income. Likewise, §1041 permits nonrecognition of gain on exchanges between spouses or incident to divorce.

There are two types of gain: ordinary gain and capital gain. Capital gain results from the sale or exchange of a capital asset. The taxpayer's relationship with the property will determine whether or not it is a capital asset. Inventory and depreciable property held for use in business are not capital assets and will, therefore, produce ordinary income in a sale or exchange. §1221. To receive preferential income tax treatment, capital gains must be "long-term capital gain." That is, the taxpayer must own the assets for more than one year. §1222.

If the value of the taxpayer's property decreases, the taxpayer will be allowed to report a loss on her income tax return only if the loss occurred in a trade or business or in a transaction entered into for profit. §165. Losses are not allowed for property used for personal purposes, such as a home or an automobile, unless the loss results from theft, fire, or other casualty. §165(c)(3). The character of the loss, like the character of gain, depends on the taxpayer's relationship to the asset.

Example 2-5

Same facts as in Example 2-3, except that Mary's stock decreases in value to $500. When she sells it, she will have a loss of $500, the difference between her amount realized ($500) and her adjusted basis ($1,000). She can report this loss on her income tax return. Unless Mary is a stock trader, her loss will be a capital loss.

The same rule applies to John in Example 2-4. Assume that John sells the property for $90,000. He has a loss of $20,000, the difference between his amount realized ($90,000) and his adjusted basis ($110,000). John's loss will be considered an ordinary loss.

When a taxpayer sells property, she must report the gain or loss on her annual income tax return. The purchaser does not experience a gain or loss and, thus, does not have anything to report on his income tax return. The purchaser's basis in the property is whatever the purchaser paid for it. §1012. In Example 2-3, Sally's basis in the stock is $5,000. In Example 2-5, her basis would be $500.

When the taxpayer gives property away, the taxpayer is not required to report a gain, and she is not allowed to report a loss even though she has received nothing in return. The gift is not considered a sale or exchange for purposes of §1001. Although the recipient has an increase in wealth as a result of the gift, the recipient is not required to report that increase as income. Section 102 specifically excludes gifts, bequests, and inheritances from income for purposes of the income tax. When the donee receives appreciated property as a gift, however, the donee takes the donor's basis in the property. §1015. Any potential gain is thus transferred from the donor to the donee. If the donee receives a gift of income, however, such as a distribution of trust income, she must report that receipt as income. §102(b).

Example 2-6

Same facts as in Example 2-3, except that Mary makes a gift of the stock to Sally. Mary does not recognize any gain. Sally does not have to report any income, and her basis in the stock is now $1,000. Because Sally did not purchase the stock, she does not have an investment in it. Instead, Mary's basis transfers to Sally.

The transferred basis rule of §1015 is different in a loss situation. Section 1015 provides that if the donor's basis is greater than the fair market value on the date of the gift, then the donee's basis for determining loss will be that fair market value.

Example 2-7

Same facts as in Example 2-5, except that Mary makes a gift of the stock to Sally. Mary does not recognize a loss, Sally does not have to report any income, and Sally's basis will be $500. Assume that Sally sells the stock two years later for $400. She will then realize and recognize a loss of $100.

This rule only applies if Sally sells the stock at a loss. If the stock appreciates in value to $1,200, then Sally would realize a gain, not a loss. For purposes of computing the gain, her basis would be the same as Mary's, *i.e.*, $1,000. As a result, Sally would recognize a gain of $200, the difference between the amount realized and her adjusted basis.

In the unlikely event that Sally sold the stock for $800, she would recognize neither a gain nor a loss. Her basis for the purpose of determining loss is $500. If her basis is $500, she does not have a loss. Her basis for determining gain, however, is $1,000. If her basis is $1,000, she does not have a gain. In this situation, Sally would not have to recognize either a gain or a loss. Reg. §1.1015-1(a)(2).

This rule prevents the taxpayer, Mary in our example, from trafficking in losses. The difficulties of valuation and the potential for manipulation are simply too great. As a result, very few taxpayers will make a gift of loss property. Instead, they will sell the property, realize and recognize the loss for income tax purposes, and give the proceeds of the sale to the donee.

Section 1015 also allows the donee to increase her basis in gifted property by the amount of gift tax paid, but only to the extent that the gift tax results from appreciation in the value of the property while owned by the donor. §1015(d)(6). Given the many exclusions from the gift tax, such as the gift tax annual exclusion, the marital deduction, and the applicable exemption amount, few donors actually pay any gift tax. The rule of §1015(d)(6), thus, rarely applies.

Example 2-8

David buys stock for $20,000. The stock increases in value to $100,000, and David gives the stock to Robin. Assume that David is not married to Robin, that David has already given Robin gifts exceeding the gift tax annual exclusion, that David has already made gifts exceeding the applicable exemption amount in §2505, and that the gift tax on this particular gift is $40,000. Robin's basis in the stock is equal to David's basis plus the amount of the gift tax paid as a result of the appreciation in the value of the property. Section 1015(d)(6) limits the increase in Robin's basis to that portion of the gift tax paid ($40,000) attributable to the net appreciation in the value of the gift ($80,000/$100,000) or $32,000. Thus, Robin's basis is $52,000, *i.e.*, David's basis of $20,000 plus the $32,000 gift tax attributable to the appreciation.

Taxpayers, ever creative, sometimes combine sales and gifts into one transaction. Assume that David in Example 2-8 decides to "sell" the stock to Robin for $60,000. David has made a gift to Robin to the extent that the fair market value of the property ($100,000) exceeds the value of the consideration paid by Robin ($60,000). In this situation, there is a sale of the stock for $60,000 coupled with a gift of $40,000. David must report as income the gain on this transaction, that is, the difference between the amount realized ($60,000) and his adjusted basis ($20,000) or $40,000. He has also made a gift of $40,000. If David has already made gifts to Robin exceeding the annual exclusion and if David has already made gifts exceeding the applicable exemption amount, he will owe a gift tax on this transaction. Assume that the gift tax is $25,000. Robin has no income to report on this transaction. Her basis in the stock will be the greater of the amount she paid for the stock or the donor's basis increased by the gift tax paid. In this case, Robin's basis will be the amount she paid, the $60,000.

When the donor makes a gift, the length of time she has held the property, *i.e.*, her holding period, transfers to the recipient along with her basis. Section 1223(2) provides that if basis to the recipient is determined in whole or in part by reference to the basis of another person, the period of time for which that other person has held the property will be included in the taxpayer's holding period.

Example 2-9

David purchases stock for $20,000. Five years later the stock is worth $100,000, and David gives the stock to Robin. Assume that David does not pay any gift tax. Robin sells the stock six months later for $125,000. Robin has a gain on the sale of $105,000, the difference between the amount realized ($125,000) and her basis ($20,000). The gain will be long-term capital gain. Although Robin only owned the stock for six months, her holding period includes the five years that David owned the stock.

Section 1015 only applies to lifetime gifts. A different rule applies to bequests and inheritances. Section 1014 provides that if property is transferred at death, the recipient has a basis equal to the fair market value of the property on the date of the donor's death. This provides a "stepped-up" basis if the property has appreciated in value during the donor's life and a "stepped-down" basis if the donor's basis is greater than the property's fair market value at the date of death.

Example 2-10

Same facts as in Example 2-3, except that Mary dies and leaves the stock to Sally in her will. Mary's estate does not recognize any gain, and Sally's basis in the stock is now $5,000, the fair market value of the stock on the date of Mary's death.

If the stock, as in Example 2-5, has a fair market value of $500 on the date of Mary's death, Mary's estate will not recognize a loss, and Sally's basis will be $500.

As a result of §1014, any gain or loss realized during the decedent's life-time will not be included in anyone's income tax. Because the decedent did not sell the property before her death, she will not recognize any gain. Death is not treated as a realizing event for purposes of the income tax. The decedent's estate is a separate taxpaying entity. The estate, however, like the beneficiaries, receives a stepped-up basis in the property under §1014(b)(1). Thus, if the estate or any beneficiary disposes of the property before it appreciates in value, there will be no gain to recognize. The resulting loss of revenue is significant, and the estate tax does not entirely compensate for it because the estate tax only touches the estates of less than two percent of all decedents.

Property transferred at death not only receives a stepped-up basis, but also is treated as if it had been owned by the recipient for more than one year. §1223(11). As a result, most gains and losses recognized by an estate or bene-ficiaries will be long-term capital gains and long-term capital losses.

PROBLEMS

1. During the current year, Theresa earns a salary of $60,000, receives interest on her bank accounts and certificates of deposit of $2,000, and receives dividends of $3,000. In addition, Mary, her mother, sends Theresa a $10,000 check for her birthday. What is Theresa's gross income for the year?

2. Martha purchases stock for $100,000. Five years later, the stock has a value of $500,000, and she transfers it to Friendly National Bank as Trustee to pay the income to her son, Sam, for his life and, at his death, to distribute the corpus to his issue. The trust is irrevocable. The trust distributes $20,000 of income to Sam during the first year. What are the income tax consequences to Mary and Sam?

3. Angela purchases stock for $100,000. Five years later the fair market value of the stock is $300,000.
    a. Angela sells the stock to Barbara for $300,000. What are the income tax consequences to Angela? To Barbara?
    b. What are the income tax consequences if Barbara sells the stock six months later for $350,000?
    c. Instead, Angela gives the stock to Barbara. Angela does not pay any gift taxes. What are the income tax consequences to Angela? To Barbara?
    d. What are the income tax consequences to Barbara if she sells the stock six months later for $350,000?

4. Angela purchases stock for $100,000. Five years later the fair market value of the stock is $75,000.
    a. Angela sells the stock to Barbara for $75,000. What are the income tax consequences to Angela? To Barbara?

   b. What are the income tax consequences if Barbara sells the stock six months later for $50,000? What if she sells it for $125,000? What if she sells it for $80,000?
   c. Angela gives the stock to Barbara and does not pay any gift taxes. What are the income tax consequences to Angela? To Barbara?
   d. What are the income tax consequences if Barbara sells the stock six months later for $50,000? What if she sells it for $125,000? What if she sells it for $80,000?
5. Angela purchases stock for $50,000.
   a. Five years later, when the value of the stock is $200,000, Angela sells the stock to Barbara for $100,000. What are the income tax consequences to Angela? To Barbara?
   b. Six months later, Barbara sells the stock for $250,000. What are the income tax consequences?
6. Angela purchases stock for $50,000. Five years later, when the value of the stock is $200,000, Angela gives the stock to Barbara and pays a gift tax of $80,000. Barbara sells the stock six months later for $250,000. What are the income tax consequences to Angela? To Barbara?
7. Angela purchases stock for $50,000. Ten years later the value of the stock is $250,000.
   a. Angela dies. Her will leaves the stock to Barbara. What are the income tax consequences to Angela or her estate? To Barbara?
   b. Six months later, Barbara sells the stock for $300,000. What are the income tax consequences?

C. TRANSFERRED BASIS
IRC §§1014, 1015, 1022, 7701(a)(43)

The term "transferred basis" applies when the recipient of property acquires the transferor's basis in that property. §7701(a)(43). The donee of a gift receives a transferred basis pursuant to §1015. The recipient of property from a decedent's estate, however, receives a stepped-up basis pursuant to §1014. There is no justification for this difference. No gain or loss is recognized at death just as no gain or loss is recognized to the donor of a gift. As a result, the same transferred basis rules should apply in both situations.

Section 1014 has long been considered a loophole in the income tax resulting in significant revenue loss. Congress attempted to close this loophole in 1976 by repealing §1014 and replacing it with a transferred basis provision. The reaction, particularly by banks and other financial institutions serving as executors and trustees, was immediate and effective. The new transferred basis provision was, therefore, repealed before it ever became effective.

When Congress repealed the estate tax in 2001, it needed to offset the loss in revenue that would result. One of the revenue generators it adopted is new

§1022 that applies transferred basis rules to property acquired from a decedent. Section 1014 is repealed. The repeal of the estate tax and §1014 as well as the new transferred basis rules of §1022 applies only to decedents dying after December 31, 2009, and before January 1, 2011.

Like §1015, §1022 provides that the basis of property acquired from a decedent will be the lesser of (1) the fair market value of the property on the date of the decedent's death or (2) the decedent's basis in the property. Section 1022, however, does not allow an increase in basis as a result of the payment of the estate tax because the estate tax has been repealed for that same time period. Instead, §1022 provides for an increase in basis for property owned by the decedent on the date of death and acquired from the decedent by reason of death. There are two increases allowed by §1022. First, §1022(b) allows an increase in basis of $1,300,000. This applies to property transferred to any beneficiary. Second, §1022(c) allows an additional increase in basis of $3,000,000 for property acquired by a surviving spouse. The property passing to the surviving spouse must be either outright transfer property or qualified terminable interest property. Property passing to a surviving spouse may qualify for both the general basis increase as well as the spousal basis increase. The increase in basis under either subsection cannot exceed the fair market value of the property on the date of the decedent's death.

Section 1022(b) provides for a general basis increase of $1,300,000. This amount is increased by (1) the amount of capital loss carryovers under §1212(b) and net operating loss carryovers under §172 as well as (2) any losses that would have been allowable under §165 had the decedent sold the property immediately before death. If the decedent is a nonresident noncitizen of the United States, the basis increase is limited to $60,000. The executor must allocate the §1022(b) increase and report that allocation to the IRS.

Example 2-11

Debra dies on February 1, 2010. Her estate consists of stock in ABC, Inc. that she purchased for $50,000. On the date of her death, the stock had a fair market value of $2,000,000. Her will leaves the stock to her daughter, Ann. Under §1022, Ann will have a basis in the stock of $50,000 (Debra's basis) plus $1,300,000 (the §1022(b) basis increase) or $1,350,000.

Example 2-12

Instead, assume that Debra also owned stock in XYZ, Inc. Debra bought this stock for $100,000, and at the time of her death it had a fair market value of $80,000. Debra leaves her stock in both ABC, Inc. and XYZ, Inc. to her daughter, Ann. The basis increase of $1,300,000 is further increased by the $20,000 unrealized loss in the XYZ, Inc. stock. §1022(b)(2)(C)(ii). The basis of the XYZ, Inc. stock is limited to its fair market value on the date of decedent's death. §1022(d)(2). As a result, the entire increase in basis allowed by §1022(b), in this case $1,320,000, is allocated to the ABC,

Inc. stock. Ann will have a basis in that stock of $1,370,000; her basis in the XYZ, Inc. stock will be its fair market value of $80,000. §1022(a)(2)(B).

Section 1022(c) provides for an additional $3,000,000 increase in basis for property passing to a surviving spouse. The property passing to the surviving spouse must be either outright transfer property or qualified terminable interest property. §1022(c)(3). Outright transfer property does not include any property interest passing to a surviving spouse that terminates or fails on the lapse of time or the occurrence or failure of an event or contingency if an interest in that property also passes to someone else from the decedent. As a result, life estates, terms of years, and similar interests will not qualify for the basis increase. Bonds, notes, and similar contractual obligations, however, will qualify as outright transfer property. Qualified terminable interest property is property in which the surviving spouse has the right to receive all the income at least annually and no person has a power to appoint any part of the property to any person other than the surviving spouse. These limitations are analogous to the limitations on the marital deduction in §§2056 and 2523 discussed in Chapter 16.

Example 2-13

Debra dies on February 1, 2010. Her estate consists of stocks that she purchased for $100,000. On the date of her death, the stocks have a fair market value of $3,500,000. Her will leaves the stocks outright to her husband, Tom. Under §1022, Tom will have a basis in the stocks of $100,000 (Debra's basis) plus $3,000,000 (the §1022(c) basis increase) or $3,100,000.

Assume that the stocks had a fair market value of $5,000,000. The executor can allocate both the §1022(b) increase and the §1022(c) increase to this property. If the executor does so, Tom's basis would be $4,400,000.

The executor has discretion to allocate the basis increases of subsections (b) and (c) and must do so on the estate tax return. §1022(d)(2). There are some limitations on the exercise of the executor's discretion. First, the executor can only allocate the §1022(c) basis increase to property passing to the surviving spouse. Second, the executor cannot increase the basis of any asset above its fair market value on the date of the decedent's death. Beyond that, the only limitation on the executor is her fiduciary responsibility of impartiality and fair dealing.

Example 2-14

At the time of her death, Diane owns Blackacre, which has an adjusted basis of $1,000,000 and a fair market value of $4,000,000, and Greenacre, which has an adjusted basis of $1,000,000 and a fair market value of $2,000,000. Diane leaves Blackacre to her daughter, Anita, and Greenacre to her son, Ben. How should Ellen, her executor, allocate the $1,300,000 basis increase of §1022(b)?

Ellen's options include: (1) allocating the basis increase equally between the two parties, *i.e.*, $650,000 to each; (2) allocating the basis increase pro rata based on the adjusted basis of the properties, *i.e.*, ½ to Blackacre and ½ to Greenacre; (3) allocating the basis increase pro rata based on the fair market value of the properties, *i.e.*, ⅔ to Blackacre and ⅓ to Greenacre; and (4) allocating the basis increase pro rata based on the unrealized gain at the time of death, *i.e.*, ¾ to Blackacre and ¼ to Greenacre. Ellen might also need to consider the character of the gain and the income tax brackets of each beneficiary.

A similar dilemma occurs when the executor must allocate both the $1,300,000 basis increase and the $3,000,000 marital property basis increase.

Example 2-15

Assume that Diane is married to Sam and that they have one child, Carol. Diane leaves her stock, which has an adjusted basis of $500,000 and a fair market value of $5,000,000, to Sam, and she leaves Farmacre, which has an adjusted basis of $100,000 and a fair market value of $2,500,000, to Carol. Ellen must, of course, allocate the $3,000,000 basis increase to the stock left to Sam, but she has discretion to allocate the $1,300,000 basis increase to either the stock or Farmacre. The choice in this example is complicated by the fact that Sam is the surviving spouse.

The dilemma for executors may be far greater than these examples demonstrate. Decedents usually own a significant number of assets with varying amounts of long-term capital gain, ordinary gain, long-term capital loss, and even ordinary loss, and they leave these assets to a number of different beneficiaries. The decedent should provide guidance to the executor in allocating the basis increases. In the absence of such guidance, the executor should attempt to obtain the consent of the beneficiaries to the allocation of the basis increases.

The basis increases of §1022(b) and §1022(c) only apply to property that is owned by the decedent on the date of death. The decedent is not considered to be the owner of property over which she has a power of appointment. §1022(d)(1)(B)(iii). The decedent is, however, considered the owner of property transferred to a qualified revocable trust as defined in §645(b)(1). §1022(d)(1)(B)(ii). The decedent is also considered the owner of a portion of joint tenancy property. If the only other joint tenant is the surviving spouse, the decedent is considered to be the owner of 50 percent of that property. If the decedent acquired her joint tenancy interest by gift, bequest, devise, or inheritance, and if her interest is not otherwise determined by law, the decedent is considered to be the owner to the extent of a fractional interest in the property determined by the number of joint tenants. If neither of these rules applies, the decedent's ownership is determined by the consideration she furnished. §1022(d)(1)(B)(i). These rules mirror those in §2040 governing the inclusion of joint tenancy property in the gross estate.

The property must also be acquired from the decedent. Section 1022(e) defines this broadly to include (1) property acquired by bequest, devise, or inheritance or by the decedent's estate; (2) property transferred by the decedent during her lifetime to a qualified revocable trust or any other trust where the decedent reserved the right to alter, amend, or terminate the trust; or (3) any other property passing from the decedent by reason of death.

The basis increases of §1022(b) and §1022(c) do not apply to property acquired by the decedent by gift within three years of death. These increases also do not apply to stock or securities of a foreign personal holding company, stock of a DISC or former DISC, stock of a foreign investment company, and stock of a passive foreign investment company. Finally, the basis increases cannot exceed the fair market value of the property on the date of the decedent's death.

Section 1022 differs significantly from the transferred basis scheme adopted in 1976. First, §1022 allows basis increases of $1,300,000 and $3,000,000. These increases will allow a step-up in basis to fair market value for most estates. The estate tax currently only affects less than two percent of all decedents, and the transferred basis increases are higher than the current estate tax exemption amount. As a result, far fewer than two percent of all beneficiaries will receive a "transferred basis" and, thus, unrealized gain in assets acquired from a decedent. Section 1022, unlike the 1976 proposal, does not permit a "fresh start" basis as of the date of enactment or the effective date of the section. The fresh start provision of the 1976 act allowed preexisting gains and losses to be disregarded. Such a provision was not deemed necessary in the 2001 act because of the generous basis increases.

The future of §1022 is not clear. It was enacted as the *quid pro quo* for estate tax repeal. If the repeal of the estate tax is rescinded, §1022 may also disappear. Section 1022, like the estate tax repeal, has only a very short life, *i.e.*, the year 2010. Unless future legislation is enacted, the pre-2001 law will return on January 1, 2011. Moreover, the prior attempt to implement transferred basis at death failed, and it remains to be seen whether the same forces will undermine the current effort to impose transferred basis at death.

PROBLEMS

1. Debra dies in 2010 without a will. Her only heir is her sister, Ellen. At her death, Debra owned a house that she had purchased for $100,000 and that had a fair market value of $200,000, as well as stock that she had purchased for $200,000 and that had a fair market value of $500,000.

   a. What are the income tax consequences? What is Ellen's basis in the property?

   b. Same facts, except that Debra owned the house in joint tenancy with her sister, Ellen. Debra had paid the full $100,000 purchase price.

What are the income tax consequences? What is Ellen's basis in the property?

   c. Same as b, except that Debra and Ellen acquired the house in joint tenancy from their mother at her death. The fair market value of the house on the date of their mother's death was $100,000. What are the income tax consequences? What is Ellen's basis in the property?

2. David dies in 2010. At his death, David owned stock that he had purchased for $100,000. The stock had a fair market value on the date of David's death of $1,500,000. David's will left all his property to Frank.

   a. What are the income tax consequences? What is Frank's basis in the property?

   b. Assume that David had purchased the stock for $1,500,000 and that it had a fair market value at his death of $1,000,000. What are the income tax consequences? What is Frank's basis in the property?

   c. Assume that David had purchased the stock for $500,000 and that it had a fair market value at his death of $1,500,000. In addition, David owned Blackacre, which his father had given to him in 2008. David's adjusted basis in Blackacre was $200,000, and its fair market value on the date of his death was $500,000. What are the income tax consequences? What is Frank's basis in the property?

3. Donna is married to Harvey. They own a house in joint tenancy that has an adjusted basis of $200,000 and a fair market value of $600,000. In addition, Donna owns stock that she purchased for $500,000 and that has a fair market value of $2,000,000 on the date of her death.

   a. Donna dies in 2010. Her will leaves all of her property to Harvey. What are the income tax consequences? What is Harvey's basis in the property?

   b. Assume that the stock has a value of $4,500,000 and that Donna's will leaves all her property to the Friendly National Bank as Trustee to pay the income to Harvey for his life and at his death to distribute the trust corpus to Donna's children. What are the income tax consequences? What is the trust's basis in the property?

D. ESTATES AND TRUSTS AS TAXABLE ENTITIES: AN OVERVIEW OF SUBCHAPTER J
IRC §§ 641-643, 651-652, 661-662, 665, 671-678

Estates and trusts are considered as separate entities and, as such, are subject to income tax. Subchapter J of the Internal Revenue Code, §§641-692, governs the taxation of these entities. The complexities of subchapter J, and there are many, are beyond the scope of this chapter and this book. The tax practitioner and the estate planner, however, must learn these rules in detail, because the income tax treatment of trusts and estates is frequently as important as the transfer tax issues.

To some extent, estates and trusts are treated as distinct taxpaying entities. They must file annual income tax returns (Form 1041), and they are subject to the same basic rules as individuals and corporations when they earn ordinary income and capital gains. In calculating taxable income, they are also allowed a personal exemption deduction. §642(b). Section 1(e) contains the tax rate structure applicable to these entities. Estates and trusts, however, are also treated as mere conduits to the extent that they distribute current income to their beneficiaries. In this situation, the estate or trust receives a deduction for the income distributed, and the beneficiary must report the amount of the distribution as income.

The income taxation of trusts depends on whether the trust is a simple trust, a complex trust, or a grantor or Mallinckrodt trust. Simple trusts are those that distribute all current income each year, that make no distributions other than current income, *i.e.*, they do not distribute trust principal or accumulated income, and that make no charitable contributions. §651. Simple trusts receive a deduction equal to the amount of income distributed to the beneficiary and, therefore, the trust will pay no tax. Instead, the beneficiary must report the income, which retains its character as ordinary income, long-term capital gain, or tax-free income. §652.

Complex trusts are those that accumulate income, distribute accumulated income, or distribute principal. §661. Estates are treated like complex trusts. Complex trusts and estates also receive a deduction for current income that is distributed, §661, and the beneficiaries must report that income on their individual income tax returns. §662.

When the trust does not distribute all of its current income, the trust will have taxable income that is subject to the rates in §1(e). §641. These rates are designed to discourage the accumulation of income in a trust. In 2003, the 27 percent rate applied to taxable income beginning at $1,900 and the 38.6 percent rate (the highest rate) applied to taxable income beginning at $9,350. Given these rates, there is very little tax advantage to creating trusts simply to shelter or split income. The clever taxpayer who creates multiple trusts with substantially the same beneficiaries to avoid these rates will be foiled by §643(f), which treats those trusts as one trust if the principal purpose was the avoidance of income tax.

When a complex trust distributes all of its current net income and only current net income, it is treated as a simple trust. When it distributes accumulated income or principal, a tier system applies to the beneficiaries. §662(a). The tier system requires the beneficiary to report as gross income amounts that are required to be distributed. The amount of gross income is limited to the trust's distributable net income, which is defined in §643. Distributable net income is taxable income with certain adjustments. The beneficiary must also report as gross income amounts distributed from accumulated income or principal but only to the extent that distributable net income exceeds required distributions. §662(a)(2). As a result, most distributions of accumulated income and principal are not taxed as gross income to the beneficiary. To do otherwise would be to tax the income twice, once when it was earned and taxed to the trust and a second time when it was in fact distributed to the beneficiary.

Not all trusts are subject to these two rules. Instead, the income earned by a trust may be taxed to the grantor or someone else under §§671-679. These rules treat the grantor as if she still owned the trust property, received the income from it, paid the resulting income tax, and then made a gift of that income to the beneficiary. In these cases, the beneficiary is not taxed on the income. The grantor trust rules developed in response to taxpayers' attempts to shift income to family members in lower tax brackets or to retain significant control over trust property.

In Helvering v. Clifford, 309 U.S. 331 (1940), the taxpayer established a trust for the benefit of his wife that was to last for five years and, at termination, the trust principal (marketable securities) would return to the taxpayer while all accumulated income would be distributed to his wife. The taxpayer was the sole trustee and had absolute discretion to distribute or accumulate income; the right to vote, sell, or pledge the securities; and the power to invest in any property even if the investment was highly speculative. At the time George Clifford created this trust, each individual, regardless of marital status, filed his or her own tax return. The ability to file a joint tax return as a married couple did not occur until 1948. The Clifford trust, in funneling income to the wife, significantly decreased George's income tax without depriving him of the benefit of that income. The Commissioner, however, claimed that George, not his wife, should be taxed on the trust's income, and the Supreme Court agreed, saying, ". . . the short duration of the trust, the fact that the wife was the beneficiary, and the retention of control over the corpus by respondent all lead irresistibly to the conclusion that respondent continued to be the owner [of the trust property] for purposes of [§61]." *Id.* at 335. The Court found that Clifford's control over the trust property remained essentially the same after creating the trust and that the trust was "at best a temporary reallocation of income within an intimate family group." Because the taxpayer did not suffer "any substantial change in his economic position," the Court held that he must report the trust income as his own. *Id.*

After the Clifford decision, taxpayers wondered how long they had to forgo income to prevent taxation. The Treasury's answer was: more than ten years, and this was eventually codified in §673. Clifford trusts, lasting for ten years plus one day, became popular devices to shift income to lower bracket taxpayers. Congress eventually amended §673 in 1986 to eliminate these trusts.

An individual other than the grantor can also be treated as the owner of a trust for purposes of the income tax. This principle was established in Mallinckrodt v. Nunan, where the taxpayer's father created a trust for the benefit of the taxpayer and his family. 146 F.2d 1 (8th Cir. 1945), *cert. denied* 324 U.S. 871 (1945). The trustees were to pay the taxpayer's wife $10,000 out of the net income annually and then to pay the residue of the net income to the taxpayer at his request. Any income not distributed was added to principal. Even though the taxpayer did not request distribution of income, the Commissioner determined that he should report the income, other than the $10,000 distributed to his wife, as his own. The Court of Appeals agreed, noting that the general principles of income tax law "justify, if they do not compel, the conclusion that the undistributed net income of the trust in suit, during the years in question, was taxable to [taxpayer] under section [61]. This, because the power of [taxpayer] to receive this trust income each year, upon request, can be regarded as the equivalent of ownership of the income for purposes of taxation." *Id.* at 5. The result in *Mallinckrodt* has been codified at §678.

The grantor trust provisions in §§671-679 extend far beyond the *Clifford* and *Mallinckrodt* cases. Definitions and basic rules that apply to all grantor and *Mallinckrodt* trusts are found in §672. The definitions of adverse and nonadverse parties are particularly important as sharing power with an adverse party will usually prevent the grantor from being taxed as the owner of the trust. An adverse party is one who has a beneficial interest in the trust, whose beneficial interest is substantial, and who will be adversely affected by the exercise of the power. §672(a). A trustee is not an adverse party simply because she is a trustee; however, if a trustee has a beneficial interest in the trust, she may be an adverse party depending on the nature of her interest and the grantor's retained power. Reg. §1.672(a)-1(a). The holder of a general power of appointment is considered to have a beneficial interest in the trust and, like other beneficiaries, may or may not be an adverse party. *Id.*

Example 2-16

George creates an irrevocable inter vivos trust by transferring property to Friendly National Bank as Trustee to pay the income to Ann for life and the remainder to Ben. George retains the right to add income beneficiaries but only with the consent of Ann. Ann is an adverse party because she has a beneficial interest in the trust that is substantial and that would be adversely affected by the addition of other income beneficiaries. As a result, George is not treated as the owner of the trust under §674.

Assume the same facts, except that George must obtain the consent of Ben instead of Ann to add income beneficiaries. Although Ben has a substantial beneficial interest in the trust, it is not adversely affected by the addition of other income beneficiaries. As a result, George will be treated as the owner of the trust under §674. If George retained the right to add remaindermen but only with the consent of Ben, then Ben would be an adverse party and George would not be considered the owner under §674.

Section 672(b) prevents the grantor from adding conditions to a power in an attempt to avoid the consequences of the grantor trust rules. This subsection provides that a person is deemed to have a power even though it is subject to conditions precedent, such as giving notice, or arises only after a specified period of time or on the happening of an event. Section 672(c) attributes powers held by a grantor's spouse to the grantor.

A reversionary interest will cause the grantor to be treated as the owner if that interest exceeds five percent of the value of the trust at the time the trust is created. §673. The primary issue is the valuation of the reversionary interest. If the grantor retains a reversionary interest for a specific term of years or upon the death of a beneficiary, valuation is determined under the general principles of §7520 and depends on the applicable interest rate and the length of the beneficiary's interest. If the reversion occurs on the happening of an event that cannot be valued actuarially, for example, the birth of a child or the death of a beneficiary without a child, valuation becomes problematic. In valuing the grantor's reversionary interest, §673(c) assumes the maximum exercise of discretion in favor of the grantor. The grantor will not be treated as the owner of a trust if the reversionary interest occurs because of the death of a lineal descendant who dies before age 21 as long as that individual holds all of the present interests in the trust. §673(b).

Example 2-17

Greg creates an irrevocable inter vivos trust to pay the income to his nephew, Alex, for life and, at Alex's death, the trust property is to revert to Greg or his estate. If the value of Greg's reversionary interest is greater than five percent of the value of the trust, Greg will be treated as the owner of the trust under §673(a).

Example 2-18

Greg creates an irrevocable inter vivos trust for the benefit of Beth, his daughter. The Trustee, Friendly National Bank, has discretion to use the income and principal for the benefit of Beth until she is 21. At age 21, the trust property will be distributed to Beth. Greg will not be treated as the owner of this trust because Beth is his lineal descendant and holds all of the present interests in the trust even though the property will revert to Greg, as Beth's parent, should she die before age 21. §673(b).

The remoteness concept of §673 is incorporated into §§674, 676, and 677. These sections provide that if the grantor has a prohibited power, the power will not be sufficient to classify the trust as a grantor trust if the power only arises after the occurrence of an event or contingency that, had it been a reversionary interest, would have escaped the reach of §673 because it was of little value. This means that if the event or occurrence is so remote that the power, were it a reversionary interest, would be less than five percent of the value of the trust corpus, the grantor will not be treated as the owner. Of course, if the event happens, the grantor's power will no longer be remote and she will be treated as the grantor unless she relinquishes the power. §§674(b)(2), 676(b), 677(a).

Section 674 treats the grantor as the owner of a trust over which the grantor, a nonadverse person, or both have the power to control the beneficial enjoyment of trust property, for example, by adding or deleting beneficiaries. This broad, general rule is overshadowed by many exceptions. Section 674(b) excludes the following powers regardless of who holds them: (1) the power to apply income for the support of a dependent; (2) the power affecting beneficiary enjoyment of income for a period that commences after an event that is so remote that the grantor would not be treated as the owner under §673 if the power were a reversionary interest; (3) the power exercisable only by will, other than a power to appoint accumulated income; (4) the power to allocate among charitable beneficiaries; (5) the power to distribute corpus that is limited by a reasonably definite external standard specified in the trust; (6) the power to distribute corpus to a current income beneficiary that is chargeable against that beneficiary's separate portion of the trust; (7) the power to withhold income temporarily or during the disability of a beneficiary; and (8) the power to allocate receipts and disbursements between corpus and income. Section 674(c) allows independent trustees to distribute or accumulate income or distribute corpus. This does not, however, include the power to add beneficiaries other than after-born or after-adopted children. Independent trustees cannot include the grantor, and no more than half can be related or subordinate parties as defined in §672(c). Section 674(d) allows the trustee to allocate income pursuant to a reasonably definite external standard as long as the trustee is not the grantor or the grantor's spouse.

Section 675 treats the grantor as the owner of the trust if the grantor has any of the following administrative powers: (1) the power to deal with trust property for less than adequate and full consideration; (2) the power to borrow trust property without adequate interest or security; (3) the power to borrow trust funds unless the loan is made by a trustee who is the grantor, the grantor's spouse, or a related or subordinate trustee who is subservient to the grantor; or (4) a power of administration exercisable in a nonfiduciary capacity.

Section 676 treats the grantor as the owner if the grantor can revest trust property in himself. As a result, all revocable trusts are grantor trusts.

Section 677(a) treats the grantor as the owner of a trust where the income is, or may be, used for the benefit of the grantor or the grantor's spouse without the consent of an adverse party. This includes the ability to distribute income to the grantor or the grantor's spouse, the ability to accumulate income for future distribution to the grantor or the grantor's spouse, and the ability to apply income to the payment of life insurance premiums on the life of the grantor or the grantor's spouse. In addition, if income is actually used to discharge the grantor's or the grantor's spouse's legal obligation of support, the grantor will also be considered the owner of the trust. §677(b). The difference between subsections (a) and (b) is that the mere existence of the power to use income for the benefit of the grantor or his spouse is sufficient to render the grantor the owner, while the power to use income to discharge the legal obligation of support must actually be exercised before the grantor is treated as the owner.

Section 678 treats a person other than the grantor as the owner if that person has the power to vest corpus or income in himself or that person has released such a power but retains a power described in §§671-677. This section does not apply, however, to a power over income if the grantor herself is treated as the owner of the trust for income tax purposes under §§671-679. Moreover, §678(c) does not treat a third person as the owner if that person is the trustee and, as such, can distribute income to someone that the trustee has the legal obligation to support.

Example 2-19

Gloria creates an irrevocable, inter vivos trust by transferring property to Friendly National Bank as Trustee. The Trustee has absolute discretion to distribute or accumulate income. Owen has the ability to demand payment of the income for his own benefit. Because of this, Owen will be treated as the owner of the trust pursuant to §678.

Example 2-20

Gloria creates an irrevocable, inter vivos trust by transferring property to Paula as Trustee. The Trustee has the discretion to distribute income to, or for the benefit of, Arthur and Barbara. Paula is the mother of Arthur and Barbara, who are minor children. Paula's ability to distribute income for their benefit will not make her the owner of the trust for income tax purposes. If she does in fact distribute income for their support or maintenance, however, she will be treated as the owner to the extent of that distribution. §678(c).

PROBLEMS

Who will be taxed on the trust income in each of the following situations where Gillian creates an irrevocable, inter vivos trust by transferring $2,500,000 to the Trustee? The trust is known as The Smith Family Trust.

1. The Trustee, Friendly National Bank, is required to distribute all income, at least quarterly, in equal shares to Ann and Bert. After the death of Ann and Bert, the Trustee is to distribute the trust property to their lineal descendants by right of representation. Friendly National Bank distributes all the income each year to Ann and Bert.
2. The Trustee, Friendly National Bank, has discretion to distribute income among Carol, David, and Ellen or to accumulate it. The Trustee also has the discretion to distribute trust corpus to Carol, David, or Ellen for their support and maintenance. After the death of Carol, David, and Ellen the Trustee is to distribute the trust property to their lineal descendants by right of representation. The trust earns $100,000 of net income each year.
    a. In year 1, Friendly National Bank distributes $100,000 in equal shares to Carol, David, and Ellen.
    b. In year 2, Friendly National Bank distributes $100,000 to Ellen.

    c. In year 3, Friendly National Bank makes no distributions.

    d. In year 4, Friendly National Bank distributes $25,000 to Carol and $25,000 to David.

    e. In year 5, Friendly National Bank distributes $50,000 to Carol, $50,000 to David, and $50,000 to Ellen.

    f. In year 6, Friendly National Bank distributes $100,000 to Carol, $100,000 to David, and $100,000 to Ellen.

3. The Trustee, Friendly National Bank, is required to distribute income to Frank annually. At Frank's death, the Trustee is to distribute the trust property to Harriet.

    a. Gillian retains the right to terminate the trust; on termination, the trust property will return to her.

    b. Gillian retains the right to terminate the trust if Frank dies before age 50 without children.

4. The Trustee, Friendly National Bank, is required to distribute all income to Gillian's mother, Isabel, for her life. At Isabel's death, the trust property will return to Gillian if living, otherwise to her lineal descendants by right of representation.

5. The Trustee, Friendly National Bank, has absolute discretion to distribute income to, or for the benefit of, Gillian's grandson, John. When John reaches age 21, the Trustee is to distribute all accumulated income and principal to John. If John dies before age 21, the accumulated income and principal is to be distributed to his estate.

6. The Trustee, Tom (Gillian's brother), is to distribute income to Karen and Linda for their lives and, at their deaths, to distribute the trust property to their lineal descendants by right of representation.

    a. Gillian, who is not a Trustee, retains the right to add beneficiaries to the trust.

    b. Gillian, who is not a Trustee, retains the right to add beneficiaries to the trust but only in her will.

    c. The Trustee, Tom, has the power to accumulate or distribute income to Karen and Linda.

    d. The Trustee, Tom, has the power to distribute income to Karen and Linda for their health, education, or support.

7. The Trustee, Gillian, is to distribute income to Mark and Nancy for their lives and, at their deaths, to distribute the trust property to their lineal descendants by right of representation.

    a. The Trustee has the power to distribute corpus to Mark or Nancy for their medical needs or for tuition.

    b. The Trustee has absolute discretion to allocate receipts between income and corpus.

    c. Gillian has the right to borrow money or other property from the trust.

8. The Trustee, Friendly National Bank, has the power to distribute income or corpus to, or for the benefit of, Sam, Gillian's husband.

9. The Trustee, Friendly National Bank, has the power to distribute income or corpus to, or for the benefit of, Peter, Gillian's son.
10. The Trustee, Friendly National Bank, has discretion to distribute income to Sam, Gillian's husband, or to Peter, her adult son. Sam has the power to withdraw any amount of trust principal for his own benefit. At Sam's death, the trust property is to be distributed to Gillian's and Sam's children.

CHAPTER 3

Valuation

A. GENERAL PRINCIPLES
IRC §§2031, 2033, 2512

Valuation is one of the most frequently litigated issues in federal transfer taxation. Despite its importance, the Internal Revenue Code does not define value; that task is left to the regulations. Regulation §20.2031-1(b) provides:

> The value of every item of property includible in a decedent's gross estate . . .
> is its fair market value at the time of the decedent's death. . . . The fair market
> value is the price at which the property would change hands between a willing
> buyer and a willing seller, neither being under any compulsion to buy or to sell
> and both having reasonable knowledge of relevant facts. The fair market value
> of a particular item of property . . . is not to be determined by a forced sale price.
> Nor is the fair market value of an item of property to be determined by the sale
> price of the item in a market other than that in which such item is most
> commonly sold to the public.

The same definition applies to gifts, Reg. §25.2512-1, and, by implication, to generation-skipping transfers.

The gift, estate, and generation-skipping taxes focus on the transfer of property by a donor or decedent. The transmission of property, not its receipt, is taxed. As a result, changes in value that result from splitting property into shares for multiple recipients or imposing restrictions on it during the transfer are generally ignored.

Valuation of property in the decedent's estate determines not only the amount of the estate tax, but also the basis of that property in the hands of heirs and beneficiaries. Section 1014 provides that the basis of property acquired from a decedent is its fair market value on the date of death.[1] Basis will determine gain or loss if, or when, the heirs and beneficiaries sell the property.

Fair market value is just that — market value. It is the amount of money that a willing buyer would pay a willing seller. It is not the value of an item to a particular individual. An individual may place a higher value on a particular

---

1. The 2001 Tax Act repealed §1014 and substituted a transferred-basis provision, §1022.

piece of property for sentimental reasons, for example, because it was the house in which she was raised. This is highly subjective and incapable of measurement. Value for transfer tax purposes is also not the intrinsic or inherent value hidden in an object. As the court in American National Bank & Trust Company v. United States observed:

> Two conceptions of value are possible. First it is apparent that an asset always has some theoretical, underlying value which is revealed or made apparent by subsequent events. For example, an unsigned painting by Botticelli languishing in a second hand art shop with a minimal price tag always had the same inherent value which it acquires when the creator of the painting is later discovered. In a second sense, however, value is a practical process, always changing in accord with the price that it will yield on the market at a given time. In this sense, the undiscovered Botticelli has a value far less than its "inherent" value. The Code and the Regulations clearly enshrine this second sense of value.

594 F.2d 1141, 1144 at note 2 (7th Cir. 1979).

Value is determined in the market where the item is commonly bought and sold. If the property is typically sold to the general public, that retail market determines the value. If there is a specialized market, for example, for certain types of art, that market establishes the value.

Different methods are used to determine value, depending on the nature of the asset. The three basic methods of valuation are the market approach, capitalization of income, and the cost approach. For a more detailed explanation of each approach, *see* The IRS Valuation Guide for Income, Estate and Gift Taxes, Federal Estate and Gift Tax Reports, CCH Number 239, January 28, 1994; L. Paul Hood, Jr., *Valuation: General and Real Estate*, 830-2d BNA Tax Mgt. Portfolio A-13 – A-25 (1995).

The market approach uses both actual sales of the particular piece of property and sales of comparable properties. Actual sales data are only used if the date of the sale is reasonably close to the date of death or the date of the gift and the sale is an arm's-length transaction. Intrafamily sales are closely scrutinized and rarely establish fair market value. Sales after the valuation date may be considered but are of limited value if they are influenced by events that were not known on the valuation date. Subsequent events are generally ignored when valuing either property or claims against the estate. When comparable sales are used to establish value, there must be a sufficient number to ensure accuracy, they must be within a reasonable time of the valuation date, and they must be of similar property. The market approach is most often used to value assets such as stocks, bonds, and real estate.

Assets held for investment or for use in a trade or business or the business itself may be valued using the capitalization of income method. The first step is to determine the income the property will produce over time. Once the income is established, it is then capitalized. Capitalization is simply the application of the anticipated rate of return to the projected income. This method is often used to value commercial real estate and closely held business interests for which there is no readily ascertainable market.

The cost approach estimates how much it would take to replace or reproduce the asset. It takes into consideration both historical cost and depreciation. It is used in valuing certain business interests and has been used in valuing a life insurance policy for gift tax purposes. Guggenheim v. Rasquin, 312 U.S. 254 (1941); United States v. Ryerson, 312 U.S. 260 (1941).

The valuation of a particular piece of property is a question of fact, although the principles that govern that valuation are questions of law. Because the issue is factual, each case depends on its unique facts and circumstances. Moreover, some property interests are easy to value because they are regularly bought and sold in public markets. Others are difficult to value because the property interest is unique, complex, or rarely sold. In determining the gift tax consequences of alternate contingent remainders, the Supreme Court noted, "[w]e cannot accept any suggestion that the complexity of a property interest created by a trust can serve to defeat a tax. . . . Even though these concepts of property and value may be slippery and elusive they can not escape taxation so long as they are used in the world of business." Smith v. Shaughnessy, 318 U.S. 176, 180 (1943).

In the companion case of Robinette v. Helvering, the donor retained a reversionary interest if her daughter died without issue who reached the age of 21, which caused the Court to hold:

> The petitioner does not refer us to any recognized method by which it would be possible to determine the value of such a contingent reversionary remainder. It may be true, as the petitioners argue that trust instruments such as these before us frequently create "a complex aggregate of rights, privileges, powers and immunities and that in certain instances all these rights, privileges, powers and immunities are not transferred or released simultaneously." But before one who gives this property away by this method is entitled to [a] deduction from his gift tax on the basis that he had retained some of these complex strands it is necessary that he at least establish the possibility of approximating what value he holds. Factors to be considered in fixing the value of this contingent reservation as of the date of the gift would have included consideration of whether or not the daughter would marry; whether she would have children; whether they would reach the age of 21; etc. Actuarial science may have made great strides in appraising the value of that which seems to be unappraisable, but we have no reason to believe from this record that even the actuarial art could do more than guess at the value here in question.

318 U.S. 184, 188-189 (1943). As a result, the Court valued the retained interest at zero, thereby increasing the value of the transferred property and the gift tax on it.

The donor or the estate has the burden of proving valuation. If the donor or estate produces sufficient evidence, the burden then shifts to the IRS. Frequently the issue of valuation becomes grounds for the battle of experts. The court is not bound to accept the opinion of any expert and must make its own determination of value. As noted by the court in Estate of Crossmore v. Commissioner,

Although a determination of value frequently involves "a conjecture, a guess, a prediction, a prophecy," . . . we refrain from picking values at random simply because we disagree with the valuations of both petitioner and respondent. . . . We endeavor to reach a conclusion on valuation which is capable of logical explanation. . . . But, as observed in the past, the inherent inexactitude of the valuation process sometimes requires us to make "Solomon-like" pronouncements. . . . That consequence cannot be avoided here where we are working within the parameters set by the opinion of petitioner's expert which we rejected and the actual results of the will contest settlement relied upon by respondent. The best we can do is set forth the underpinnings of our ultimate decision providing, in the event of an appeal, a "trail for the appellate court to follow.". . . This we now proceed to do.

56 T.C.M. (CCH) 483, 487 (1988).

The following case demonstrates the complexities of valuation as well as its intensely factual nature.

Estate of Andrews v. United States
850 F. Supp. 1279 (E.D. Va. 1994)

PAYNE, District Judge.

The Estate of Virginia C. Andrews (the "Estate") instituted this action to secure the refund of federal estate tax and interest in the amount of $947,483.87 which the Internal Revenue Service ("IRS") assessed on the value of the name of Virginia C. Andrews ("Andrews") who, at the time of her death on December 19, 1986, was an internationally known, best-selling author. . . . The Estate did not list Andrews' name as among its assets and consequently none of the estate taxes it paid were based on the value of Andrews' name. On November 16, 1990, the IRS issued a notice of deficiency, asserting that the Andrews' name was an asset of the Estate having a value of $1,244,910.84 on the date of her death, and thereupon assessed deficient taxes in the amount of $649,201.77. . . .

Statement of Facts

The value of an author's name at date of death is an issue of first impression the resolution of which depends in substantial part on the facts known and reasonably knowable at the date of death. . . . When V.C. Andrews died on December 19, 1986, she had achieved international recognition as an author of paperback fiction novels. Her literary career began with the publication of short stories and, as is usually the case, many of her early works met with rejection by publishers. However, in 1978, Andrews' career began its remarkable ascent upon the publication of "Flowers in the Attic" which achieved substantial commercial success and introduced a genre of literature which came to be known as "children in jeopardy" of which Andrews soon became the undisputed master. . . .

Pocket Books [Andrews' publisher] understandably was interested in further capitalizing on the commercial success of the "children in jeopardy" books. To this end, Pocket Books had initiated, earlier in 1986 before the publication of "Dark Angel," negotiations for another contract calling for Andrews to produce a sequel to "Dark Angel" in October 1987 and a prequel to "Flowers in the Attic" in October 1988. Diamant [Andrews' agent] handled these negotiations for Andrews' company, Vanda Productions, Ltd. ("Vanda"). During the negotiations, which took place in October 1986, Diamant was unaware that Andrews was terminally ill. She only learned of Andrews' impending death after mailing the proposed contract to Andrews in early November. Diamant and Andrews never discussed the proposed contract.

The proposed contract was much like its predecessors in form and content. For instance, it too permitted the publisher to use Andrews' "name and likeness and biographical material about the writer for purposes of advertising and trade in connection with" Andrews' works. The proposed contract required Andrews to produce two manuscripts and provided for $3 million in advances against royalties, and, like its predecessors, the proposed contract keyed payment of the greater part of the advances to the acceptance and publication of the manuscripts. The $3 million advance was the largest advance ever offered to Andrews. . . . Like the 1984 contract, the proposed contract contained an option clause under which the publisher was entitled to the first right of refusal on subsequent works of fiction submitted by Andrews. . . .

Although Romanos [President of Simon & Schuster's Consumer Group, which included Pocket Books (Andrews' publisher)] knew that Andrews was too ill to complete the editorial process on "Dark Angel," neither he nor Diamant ever discussed the possibility of Andrews' death or the subject of using a ghostwriter to continue the "children in jeopardy" books. Nonetheless, on December 19, 1986, immediately after learning of Andrews' death from Ann Patty [Andrews' editor at Pocket Books], Romanos expressed the view that it would be possible to continue publication of books in that genre under Andrews' name if another author could mimic Andrews' style.

Considering that ghostwritten novels were not unusual and that, at the time, "Dark Angel" occupied a high place on the national best-seller lists, the reaction of Romanos was not unexpected. In fact, Romanos was then of a mind to publish ghostwritten books under the terms of the contract which Andrews had executed before she died. . . . Shortly thereafter, Payne [Andrews' executor] and Romanos revised the proposed 1986 contract, which Andrews had executed before her death, to reflect that the project would proceed with a ghostwriter. Romanos executed it on behalf of Pocket Books late in March 1987. This contract will be referred to as the "First Publishing Contract."

At about the same time, Payne was negotiating a contract with Niederman [an author of horror stories also represented by Diamant, Andrews' agent] ("Writer's Contract 1") which was executed on March 20, 1987. . . . All participants in the effort to continue the "children in jeopardy" genre recognized that ghostwriting was a difficult, and not always successful, venture. . . . As it happened, all of these apprehensions were ill-founded. Within a week after it was released in October 1987, Niederman's first work, "Garden of Shadows," was pronounced a commercial success by Romanos. Indeed, there is evidence that, even before publication, the Estate and Pocket Books considered that Niederman's efforts would be successful because they undertook negotiations for a second contract (the "Second Publishing Contract"). This contract, which was executed on January 19, 1988, called for the Estate to provide three additional manuscripts for publication under Andrews' name. . . .

While the central focus of the ghostwriting project was to mimic Andrews' style, plot construction and character development, there also were concerted efforts to maintain the illusion that Niederman's works were those of Andrews. Accordingly, the project proceeded on the fundamental premise that the works would bear only Andrews' name. Neither Payne, the executor, nor Romanos thought it advisable to have Niederman's name appear on the ghostwritten books. In fact, Writer's Contract 2 obligated Niederman not to disclose that he had written, or was writing, books "under the name of" Andrews. The succeeding writer's contracts contained the same restriction.

Moreover, although the fact of Andrews' death was the subject of newspaper obituaries, it was not until publication of the fifth ghostwritten book in 1990 that her death was confirmed to her audience in the preliminary pages of "Dawn." Even then, the text of that notice led the reader to believe that the stories had been largely completed by Andrews before she died. . . . The record, however, is clear that the predominant reason for concealing Niederman's identity was that Andrews was the preeminent author in this unique genre and that books written by a well-known author have an enhanced chance of commercial success. . . .

The IRS valuation was the work of Janna Levinstein, an IRS Estate Tax Examiner with fourteen years of experience in valuing decedents' estates for tax purposes. . . . The starting point of the IRS valuation was the First Publishing Contract which Levinstein considered to be a ratification by the Estate of the contract signed on behalf of Vanda by Andrews in November 1986 approximately a month before her death. . . . Levinstein then interviewed Romanos and Diamant in September 1990, almost four years after Andrews' death. At that time, the two books called for by the First Publishing Contract had been published successfully. So too had three other post-death books authored by Niederman under the subsequent publishing contracts. Romanos informed Levinstein that he then thought the scope of the project would constitute those five books and three more yet to be published. . . . Levinstein then established a base value of $12 million for all post-death novels, published and to be published. . . . Levinstein then projected a value for all eight ghostwritten novels ". . . which would be enhanced by the V.C. Andrews name, reputation, and mystique . . ." at the amount of $1.5 million each. This, according to Levinstein, would produce a "gross amount of $12 million."

The gross amount then was discounted by: (i) deducting 10% for the agent's commission; (ii) establishing a present value for the remaining balance by applying a 15% discount factor principally on the basis that it was the factor used by the Estate's appraiser to value the copyrights on novels written by Andrews; (iii) applying a uniform factor of 40% of net present value to account for the value of the work itself, marketing, promotions and advertising; and (iv) applying a discount for the contingency of the failure of the ghostwriter to produce a manuscript acceptable to the publisher, applying a higher discount factor to later novels on the theory that "success becomes less predictable the [further] in the future it occurs."

Applying this approach to each "set" of books (i.e., to the required output of each publishing contract entered into by the Estate), Levinstein valued the name and likeness of Andrews as: $621,218.07 for the first two post-death books; $391,702.30 for the next three post-death books; and $231,990.54 for the last three post-death books. This method yielded a total claimed date of death value for Andrews' name and likeness of $1,244,910.84. . . .

The IRS also offered the testimony of Peter Jaszi, an expert in intellectual property law, to support the testimony of Levinstein and the IRS valuation. . . . Recognizing that the value of Andrews' name must be determined at date of death, Jaszi concluded that the best evidence of the Estate's rights was "the final contract which Pocket Books had offered to Andrews, for two books which would complete the Dollanganger series, and continue the Casteel series, respectively." The advance figures of $1.5 million for each novel, in Jaszi's view, "offered the best available basis for estimating the value of additional novels in the 'V.C. Andrews' line.'"

The expert evidence about valuation presented by the Estate was offered by Philip W. Moore, President of Seligman Valuations. Moore had extensive experience in valuing closely-held corporations and securities as well as various investments and other tangible and intangible assets. Like Levinstein, Moore had no previous experience in valuing an author's name, but he had been involved in valuing the name of a deceased famous designer of men's clothes. Moore applied what he described as generally accepted valuation techniques in conducting a study of the publishing industry, the market for Andrews' books, the general economic conditions extant in late 1986 and early 1987, and the investment market generally in the same timeframe. Using this general information as background, Moore then expressed an opinion about the facts which would be considered by the buyer and seller in the hypothetical transaction required by the IRS regulations and the decisional law. Having done that and mindful of the evidence offered at trial respecting facts reasonably knowable on the date of death, Moore opined that on the date of Andrews' death a willing buyer and seller, neither acting under compulsion and both being informed as to the reasonably knowable facts, would have arrived at a price of $140,000 in a hypothetical sale and purchase of Andrews' name.

Mr. Moore posited that the investment opportunity for the buyer was an unattractive one because: (1) it was fraught with uncertainties; (2) it presented a risk that there would be no return on the investment; and (3) there were other more attractive alternatives. Accordingly, it was Moore's opinion that the buyer would discount by 85% the price that otherwise would be required to purchase the name. . . .

Discussion

The basic principles of law which govern valuation of property in a decedent's estate are well-settled. First, the controlling statute, 26 U.S.C. §2031(a), provides that:

> The value of the gross estate of the decedent shall be determined by including . . . the value at the time of his death of all property, real or personal, tangible or intangible, wherever situated.

The regulations which implement this statute, and hence have the force of law, specify that the value of every item to be taxed is its "fair market value at the time of decedent's death." The regulations further provide that: "[t]he fair market value is the price at which the property would change hands between a willing buyer and a willing seller, neither being under any compulsion to buy or sell and both having reasonable knowledge of the relevant facts." 26 C.F.R. §20.2031-1(b).

The decisional law has defined the "relevant facts" for purposes of setting value on the date of death to be those that the hypothetical willing buyer and seller "could reasonably have been expected to know at that time." First Nat. Bank of Kenosha v. United States, 763 F.2d 891, 893-94 (7th Cir.1985). This has spawned the related rule that ". . . subsequent events are not considered in fixing fair market value, except to the extent that they were reasonably foreseeable at the date of valuation — in estate tax cases, the date of death." *Id.* at 894 (citations omitted). That rule is, in turn, modified by the principle that "[s]ubsequent events may serve to establish both that the expectations were entertained and also that such expectations were reasonable and intelligent." Estate of Jephson v. Commissioner of Internal Revenue, 81 T.C. 999, 1983 WL 14908 (1983). To that extent then, events which occur after the date of death may be taken into account in making the valuation decision. When considered together, these principles governing consideration of events occurring subsequent to death have become a rule of relevance which precludes, as irrelevant, information that the hypothetical willing buyer could not have known and permits, as relevant, evidence of the actual price received after the date of death "so long as the sale occurred within a reasonable time after death and no intervening events drastically changed the value of the property." First Nat. Bank of Kenosha, *supra.*

The applicable regulations also teach that the relevant market to be considered in determining the fair market value of an asset is the market in which that asset is usually and commonly the subject of commerce. 26 C.F.R. §20.2031-1(b). In that regard: "[a]ll relevant facts and elements of value as of the applicable valuation date shall be considered in every case." This requires that each case be judged on its own facts, taking into account the nature of the asset and the market in which its monetary value ordinarily would be set, "subject to such uncertainty as ordinarily attaches to such an inquiry." *See, e.g.*, Estate of Vardell v. Commissioner of Internal Revenue, 307 F.2d 688, 693 (5th Cir.1962).

Finally, as a procedural point of departure, it is settled that, in an action for refund, the determination of the IRS enjoys a presumption of correctness, which the taxpayer must overcome by showing that no tax at all is owed or that the amount of tax owed is in a lesser amount than that determined by the IRS. Compton v. United States, 334 F.2d 212, 216 (4th Cir. 1964). This presumption exists because a suit for refund is in the nature of an action of assumpsit for money had and received, Lewis v. Reynolds, 284 U.S. 281, 283(1932), in which it is the taxpayer's burden to establish by a preponderance of the evidence that the taxes sought to be refunded were in fact overpaid. *Id.*

The starting point for the analysis required by these legal principles is to determine the facts reasonably knowable on December 19, 1986 to the parties to the hypothetical sale transaction. The record shows that those parties would have had access to much information of significance.

For instance, the parties to the transaction would have known that Andrews was a best-selling author whose name was internationally recognized as the preeminent author of "children in jeopardy" books; and that Andrews' books, although not written to a formula, contained similar themes and similar kinds of characters and in many other ways bore the distinctive imprint of Andrews' unique style. Informed buyers and sellers also would have known that no other author had approximated Andrews' success in this rather unique genre of literature. And, it would be known to both buyer and seller that Andrews' most recent book was still high on the national best-seller lists.

The relevant market would have been in the publishing industry. The parties to the hypothetical sale transaction would therefore be expected to know the role of a famous author's name in commerce within the publishing industry. In that regard, they would understand, as Diamant and Romanos made clear, that the author's name is instrumental in promoting the sales of books particularly where, as here, there exists a well-defined readership audience as the consequence of seven previous best-selling novels.

Knowledge of the relevant market also would have made the hypothetical parties aware that the content of a book is another key element in its commercial success. They also would know, however, that Andrews' books were published in the paperback segment of the market and therefore they would understand that publication of Andrews' books would not be preceded by, or attended with, critical reviews of the work because that practice is confined generally to that segment of the market for publication of hardcover books. Considering this factor, the parties would perceive that the commercial success of a new book in the "children in jeopardy genre" would be heavily dependent upon association with the name of an author whose similar works were well-accepted by an extensive and faithful audience.

On the other hand, the hypothetical buyer and seller would fully appreciate that a poorly received book bearing Andrews' name could have an adverse impact on the sales of the books she wrote before her death. Both parties would recognize that the economic consequences to the Estate would be a diminished stream of royalty income from the pre-death books.

Because the parties would be familiar with the publishing industry, they would know that the continuation of related books or of books in series, by use of ghostwriters following an author's death is not an uncommon practice. . . . The parties to the hypothetical sale could reasonably have been expected to make themselves aware of previous contractual arrangements between Andrews and her publisher. Therefore, they would have known that previous contracts permitted the publisher to use Andrews' name and likeness to promote books written pursuant to the previous contracts, and that all previous rights to the use of Andrews' name had been in association with the production or promotion of a literary work. For these reasons and because of the other provisions of the previous contracts, the parties to the hypothetical transaction would expect that use of the name likely would be linked with acceptance of a manuscript which, of course, would have to be ghostwritten.

Any party to a transaction involving the right to use Andrews' name in conjunction with a ghostwritten manuscript would have appreciated, as did the executor, the publisher and the agent, that there was no assurance that a ghost-writer would be able to produce a manuscript acceptable to the publisher. Hence, the parties would know that purchase of the right to use Andrews' name in conjunction with a ghostwritten book would entail the risk that the purchase transaction might be for naught. On the other hand, both parties would appreciate that there was the prospect of substantial commercial success if a ghost-writer could mimic Andrews' unique style. . . .

Taken as a whole, the record shows that the principal obstacle to, and risk associated with the purchase of Andrews' name was presented by the significant uncertainty attendant upon the production of a ghostwritten manuscript acceptable to a publisher. That, as the record establishes, was a significant risk which, in turn, would motivate the buyer to discount the purchase price substantially. In fact, both the IRS and the Estate acknowledge that a buyer would significantly discount the purchase price for the risk of failure to produce an acceptable manuscript. . . .

Having ascertained the relevant facts reasonably knowable to the hypothetical seller and buyer of Andrews' name on the date of her death, it is necessary now to consider how those facts would have been applied to the negotiation of the price at which the seller would have parted with, and a buyer would have acquired, the rights to the use of Andrews' name. . . .

Both the IRS and the Estate have used the First Publishing Contract, albeit in different ways, as the principal point of departure in valuing Andrews' name. The First Publishing Contract may appropriately be considered in determining the value of Andrews' name because its existence and the possibilities it presented were reasonably knowable on the date of death to the buyer and seller in the hypothetical transaction which forms the framework for valuing Andrews' name. . . . Accordingly, it is peculiarly instructive to a buyer and seller respecting the economic parameters sought to be established in the hypothetical negotiation required by the IRS regulations. This is in keeping with the now accepted principle that contracts for the sale of assets made after, but reasonably near, the date of death are persuasive evidence of fair market value except where a material change in circumstances between the date of sale and the date of death operates to render the sale unforeseeable on the date of death. . . .

The IRS also used the Second and Third Publishing Contracts, each of which called for three books, in arriving at its valuation because the IRS determined that the First, Second and Third Publishing Contracts, requiring the production of eight books, all were foreseeable on the date of death. . . . The record does not support reliance on the Second and Third Publishing Contracts in any way. To the contrary, the record establishes that, although Romanos, Diamant and the Estate, were hopeful that the ghostwriting venture would succeed, all considered the venture to be risky and speculative. Romanos and Diamant unequivocally stated that, if the first ghostwritten book failed, there would be no more published. Romanos also explained that, if the first book failed, it would be pulled from the shelves to avoid damage to market for pre-death books. . . . In fact, the IRS valuation considers the risk of failure associated with subsequent books to be materially greater than the risk associated with the first book. Thus, the record establishes that the project was sufficiently risky that an informed buyer and seller would have been negotiating on the basis that neither of them could expect numerous subsequent books which would produce income of such magnitude as to warrant increasing the price at which the hypothetical sale of Andrews' name would be made in December 1986.

The determination that the First Publishing Contract may be used in determining the value of Andrews' name on this date of her death does not, however, itself result in establishing the value of Andrews' name because the right to use the name is only part of a bundle of rights made subject to commerce and the contract does not allocate specific value to the name or to the other subjects of the contract. . . .

As explained previously, the First Publishing Contract does not allocate any segment of the consideration to the right to use the name which is clearly among the consideration flowing to the publisher under the contract. Of the total advance of $3 million, $1,550,000 is attributable to the first book ($500,000 upon execution of the contract; $200,000 on acceptance of the first half of the manuscript; $350,000 on acceptance of the second half of the manuscript; $500,000 sixty days after publication).

Moore, Jaszi and Levinstein all use $1,500,000 as either the starting point or a principal focal point of their approach to valuing Andrews' name at the date of death. In fact, it is the common denominator in the otherwise substantially different approaches taken by the experts in valuing Andrews' name. And, that amount is a focal point of their respective opinions. The soundness of using the amount advanced for the first book under the First Publishing Contract as a benchmark for valuing Andrews' name is confirmed by other evidence in the record, such as the correlation between the success of past books and the size of advances in ensuing contracts and the fact that the author has no personal obligation to repay advances after each payment benchmark is reached. It receives further confirmation from the fact that no expert sought to determine value by predicting the amount of royalty revenue from the first ghostwritten books and, of course, this is the only other reasonably available source of revenue from the use of the name. For the foregoing reasons, the court concludes that the hypothetical buyer and seller would start their respective determinations of the price component at $1.55 million, the advance for the first book under the First Publishing Contract.

Moore testified, and common sense confirms, that the parties to the transaction would realize that the expense of producing the literary product would have to be taken into account in setting the value. Neither Levinstein nor Jaszi disagreed with this logical proposition. Nor does the post-trial brief of the IRS dispute it. The only specific evidence on this subject comes from Moore who testified that expenses would be approximately $500,000. On this record, Moore's estimate of expenses is a reasonable one.

Both Moore and Levinstein agreed that it was necessary to apply a discount to allow for the risky nature of the project. Moore used a risk factor of 85%. Levinstein used a "contingency factor" of 33% for the risk associated with the venture in producing the first book.

Levinstein concluded that there was a greater prospect for success of the first ghostwritten books than for later ones. For this reason, she applied a lower risk factor discount of 33% for the first such book. Although subsequent developments proved that Levinstein was in error as to the later books, that evidence cannot be considered. However, Levinstein's conclusion respecting the prospects for the first ghostwritten book is borne out by the fact that Andrews' name was associated with a unique genre of literature for which there was an existing, highly loyal and expanding readership as is evidenced by the rapid growth in sales of books actually written by Andrews. It is underscored by the fact that Andrews' last pre-death book was high on the national best-seller lists at the time she died. It is confirmed by the immediate judgment of Romanos to undertake ghostwritten sequels to the same books for which the original 1986 was proposed upon essentially the same contract terms.

Taken as a whole, the record does not support Moore's use of an 85% discount factor. . . . The 85% discount factor does not properly allow for the strong market for Andrews' works on the date of her death, as evidenced by the prominent place on the best-seller lists held in December 1986 by "Dawn." Nor does it properly recognize the extremely unique nature of Andrews' past success and the scope of her renown in this highly unusual genre of literature which enjoyed a ready-made market in which, as Romanos acknowledged to his staff a few days after Andrews' death, significant sales were generated simply by virtue of the fact that Andrews was the author.

To be sure, the quality of the literary work was a key element in the volume of sales, but it does too little credit to the undisputed evidence of Andrews' popularity and achievement to say that the prospect of finding a ghostwriter who could satisfy the publisher with a manuscript was so risky as to warrant an 85% discount factor. Moreover, the use of the 85% risk factor does not properly reflect the extent to which ghostwriters had succeeded in generating manuscripts acceptable to publishers.

Considering the success of other ghostwriting ventures and the immense popularity of Andrews' name and the substantial size of her very loyal established audience, the court finds that a 33% discount factor would have been appropriate to use in arriving at the price for the hypothetical transaction here at issue. Applying the mathematical method used by both Moore and Levinstein to these findings, the valuation of Andrews' name at date of death would be $703,500.

B. VALUATION DATE
IRC §§2001, 2031, 2032, 2504, 2511, 2512

Gifts are valued on the date the gift is complete, that is, on the date that the donor has given up all power to change the beneficial ownership of the property. Reg. §25.2511-2. Property in the decedent's estate is valued as of the day of death, unless the executor elects the alternative valuation date. Reg. §20.2031-1(b). The value of property subject to the generation-skipping transfer tax is determined on the date of the transfer, that is, on the date of the direct skip, the taxable distribution, or the taxable termination.

The decedent's death itself can affect the valuation of property. For example, in Goodman v. Granger, the decedent's employment contracts provided for additional payments when he terminated his employment, but the payments would be forfeited if the decedent competed with his employer. 243 F.2d 264 (3d Cir. 1957), *cert. denied* 355 U.S. 835 (1957). Decedent died during his employment and his employer made the payments required by the contracts. The district court accepted the estate's argument that the contracts had no value because of the forfeiture provision. The Third Circuit reversed, holding that the payments were to be valued "as of the time of [decedent's] death when the limiting factor of the contingencies would no longer be considered. Death ripened the interest in the deferred payments into an absolute one, and death permitted the imposition of the tax measured by the value of that absolute interest in property." *Id.* at 269.

This same principle was applied in United States v. Land to the valuation of decedent's partnership interest that was subject to a buy-sell agreement restricting the value of that interest to two-thirds of its calculated value. 303 F.2d 170 (5th Cir. 1962), *cert. denied* 371 U.S. 862 (1962). The court ignored the provisions of the buy-sell agreement because "[t]he possibility that [decedent] would withdraw from the partnership and surrender his interest at the two-thirds valuation was foreclosed. There was then no contract or option outstanding except in the partners to purchase at full value. Death sealed the fact that their interests would be purchased or redeemed at full value. The fair market value, therefore, of the partnership interest at the time of the death of the partner was its full value." *Id*. at 175.

Not every restriction will be ignored. In Estate of McClatchy v. Commissioner, 147 F.3d 1089 (9th Cir. 1998), the decedent owned stock that was subject to federal securities law restrictions, which limited its marketability, because of his status as an affiliate. As a result of decedent's death, the stock passed to his estate, which was not an affiliate. The court held that the value of stock was determined by the interest of the decedent at the time of his death as restricted by the federal securities law. It distinguished Goodman v. Granger and United States v. Land, saying, "[i]n these cases, death clearly is the precipitating event and is the only event required to fix the value of the property. Similarly, the death of a key partner can instantly decrease the value of a business. . . . But in the instant case, death alone did not effect the transformation of the stock's value. The value of the stock was transformed only because the estate was a non-affiliate. . . . If the estate had been an affiliate, the securities law restrictions still would have applied." *Id*. at 1092-1093.

Events occurring after the date of death are generally not considered in assessing valuation.

Estate of Curry v. Commissioner
74 T.C. 540 (1980), *acq.* **1981-2 C.B. 1**

WILBUR, Judge:
. . . In 1966, the decedent executed an agreement with another attorney which provided that the decedent would receive a stated percentage of any attorney's fees which might be awarded in a list of docketed cases pending before the Indian Claims Commission. Any award of attorney's fees in the cases was contingent upon an ultimate recovery on behalf of the plaintiff tribal members and would be measured by the extent of the recovery. When Mr. Curry died in 1972, 13 of the cases were still in various unresolved stages of litigation before the Commission. The issue for our decision is whether the contractual right to share in contingent attorney's fees with regard to these 13 pending cases is property which must be valued and included in the decedent's gross estate. Petitioners argue that because the decedent's right to share in the attorney's fees was not compensable as of the date of death, i.e., that because by their very nature, contingent fees do not accrue until a final judgment is rendered, the decedent's interest in the fees had no market value when he died. Respondent contends that the contractual right to share in future attorney's fees is an interest in property includable in the decedent's gross estate, and that notwithstanding the contingent nature of the fees, the decedent's interest had substantial value on the date of death. We agree with respondent that the

contractual right is includable in the gross estate, although we disagree some-what with his methodology in valuing the interest.

First, we deal with the contention that as a matter of law, contingent legal fees are not includable in the gross estate because there is no compensable interest as of the date of death. We find nothing in the statute to sustain such a proposition. Section 2031 provides that the value of the gross estate shall be determined by including the value of all property, real or personal, tangible or intangible. Section 2033 provides that the value of the gross estate shall include the value of all property to the extent of the interest therein of the dece-dent. As used in the statute, the term "property" encompasses all choses in action, including claims for services performed. . . . A right of a deceased partner to share in future profits of the partnership is an interest in property, includable in the gross estate. . . . The date-of-death values of existing claims of the decedent which pass to his estate are includable in the gross estate. . . .

The fact that the legal fees we are concerned with were contingent upon future recovery by the Indian tribes is a critical consideration in trying to deter-mine what the contract right was worth as of the date of death. However, the contingent nature of the contract right must bear on the factual question of valuation. It cannot, as a matter of law, preclude the inclusion of the interest in the decedent's gross estate or command that the value be fixed at zero. Although uncertainty as to the value of a contract right may postpone the inclu-sion of the income until it is actually realized for *income* tax purposes, for *estate* tax purposes, the value of an asset must be determined in order to close the estate. . . . We therefore hold that, under the circumstances before us, the contractual right herein to share in future attorney's fees which are contingent in nature, is property to be included in the decedent's gross estate under section 2033.

We must next address the factual issue of the value at the date of death of the contractual right to share in contingent attorney's fees for the 13 cases then pending before the Indian Claims Commission. . . . First of all, we must reject petitioner's contention that because the claims here involved had not been reduced to judgment, they were too remote and speculative to be valued. Valuation for estate tax purposes frequently involves difficult and somewhat imprecise calculations. *See* Estate of Smith v. Commissioner, 57 T.C. 650 (1972), *affd.* 510 F.2d 479 (2d Cir. 1975). However, uncertainties and difficul-ties encountered in determining value have never been considered justifica-tions for obviating this necessary task. *See* Ithaca Trust Co. v. United States, 279 U.S. 151 (1929), and Estate of Smith v. Commissioner, *supra*. Approximately half of the cases listed in the agreement executed between Mr. Weissbrodt and Mr. Curry in 1966 were reduced to judgment by 1972, the year in which Mr. Curry died. These cases resulted in substantial awards of attorney's fees. Although there are distinctions between the cases decided prior to 1972 and some of the cases still pending as of the date of death, it is clear that the contractual right to share in any future award of attorney's fees for this kind of litigation had substantial value when the decedent died.

Respondent asserts that the value of the contract right as of the date of death is $260,444. He arrives at this figure by adding two distinct sums. First, he valued the right to fees in two of the docketed cases (22-D and 22-J) as the amount of income, $100,544, which actually was paid to the estate for these two cases 4 months after the date of death. In order to value the 11 other cases, he took the compromise agreement executed between the two residuary beneficiaries in which Ms. Bullard [a friend of Mr. Curry] assigned her right to one-half of any future recoveries in the 11 cases to Ms. Curry-Cloonan [Mr. Curry's daughter] in exchange for Ms. Curry-Cloonan's agreement to arrange to have certain joint ownership bonds and bank accounts brought into the estate. Respondent reasons that since the result of this arrangement was to benefit Ms. Bullard in the amount of $79,950, one can double that figure to arrive at the value of an undivided right to share in the 11 pending cases. By adding the income for the 2 cases which were completed shortly after Mr. Curry's death with the computation of the value of the 11 other cases, respondent concludes that the date-of-death value of the entire contract right is $260,444.

Although appealing because of the simplicity, we must reject respondent's methodology in valuing the contract right of the decedent. With regard to the first two docketed cases (22-D and 22-J), respondent has erred in failing to distinguish between a contractual right to receive future income and the actual receipt of the income subsequent to the date of death. . . . In addition, we do not share respondent's view that the "sale" of Ms. Bullard's right to receive half of any future attorney's fees in the remaining 11 cases fits neatly into the "willing seller, willing buyer" criteria of the regulations. It seems clear from the record that the agreement was drawn up by Mr. Dowdey [the attorney representing Mr. Curry's estate in probate] and accepted by the residuary beneficiaries primarily for reasons apart from economic considerations. Mr. Dowdey realized he had made a serious mistake in advising the residuary beneficiaries that the joint ownership bonds and accounts were to be part of Mr. Curry's estate and in his initial attempt to collect the bonds from the surviving owners. In addition, it is clear that he was guided by a strong desire on the part of one of the beneficiaries, Ms. Curry-Cloonan, to avoid being locked into a continuing relationship with Ms. Bullard at any cost, and by many other personal considerations of both women. The agreement appears to us to be a carefully orchestrated solution to most of the problems confronting those involved with the estate — not a disinterested sale between a willing buyer and a willing seller, both having knowledge of the relevant facts. Therefore, we do not consider the compromise agreement as indicative of the economic value of the contract right as of the date of death, and we disregard it in valuing the right.

Clearly, there is no way to value with exactness a contractual right to share in attorney's fees for 13 Indian claims cases, all of which were in various stages of litigation when Mr. Curry died. However, respondent produced an expert witness (Mr. Webb) who elucidated the procedures of the Indian Claims Commission and gave helpful testimony as to the three broad characteristics of cases covered by the agreement (land, accounting, and damages) and the general potential for recovery in each classification. In addition, the parties submitted voluminous exhibits relating to each of the separate claims, which we have examined with great care.

It must be remembered, however, that we are not estimating the potential amount of recovery of the underlying claims in general, but rather the contractual right to share in a percentage (18 percent to 24 percent) of a percentage (usually 10 percent) of any recovery on behalf of specific clients. The two most critical factors in valuing the contract right are the classifications of the cases still pending and the stage to which each had progressed. For instance, Mr. Webb testified that the land cases had by far the best potential for recovery on behalf of the tribes. Of the 13 cases, 4 were land cases. However, Mr. Webb also testified that accounting and damage cases, of which the other nine cases were comprised, were much more problematic. It was not at all clear how the Indian Claims Commission would react to these claims, and Mr. Webb was hesitant to try to set any value on them because of the uncertainty and the substantial delay in their resolution.

Among the land cases, the stage to which each had proceeded is important in setting a value as of August 23, 1972, the date of death. For example, the two cases for which the estate recovered $100,544.40 4 months after the date of death were substantially complete, at least as far as the real issues were concerned. Title had been determined, liability had been set, and a compromise settlement had been approved by the parties. The remaining steps — approval by the Commission of the settlement, and application to and approval by the Commission of attorney's fees — are basically pro forma steps.

However, the other land cases were in some aspects less promising, at least in terms of the estate's receiving a share of the attorney's fees. While we recognize that the estate ultimately received substantial attorney's fees in one land case ($150,000), the potential for recovery in even this case was clouded by several factors at the date of death. For, while it was clear that some tribe or a group of tribes was going to make a substantial recovery in this case, it was not clear which tribes these were going to be in 1972. Many tribes had intervened in the suit, and title to and the boundaries of the land were not determined until 1975. Therefore, although the potential for some recovery was good, it was not at all clear how much of the recovery might eventually accrue to Mr. Curry's estate.

Additionally, as noted earlier, recovery of attorney's fees in the damage and accounting cases was subject to several contingencies at the date of death, the date critical to our inquiry. And even though the estate ultimately recovered substantial legal fees in one of the damage cases, we note that seven of the damage and accounting cases were still pending at the date of trial, and all of these cases must be viewed in the light of the circumstances existing on August 23, 1972, the date of death.

Additional relevant considerations in valuing, on August 23, 1972, the contractual right to share in a percentage of future attorney's fees are: Mr. Weissbrodt's past successes as a prosecuting attorney for the tribes; the delays involved in this kind of litigation; and the fact that there were claims by other attorneys on Mr. Curry's share of the fees except for the first two awards, which were made shortly after his death.

After a careful consideration of the entire record before us, we find that the date-of-death value of the contractual right to share in the attorney's fees for the two land cases (22-D and 22-J) which were substantially completed and not subject to competing claims was $95,000.

The date-of-death value of the right to share in the attorney's fees for the remaining 11 cases presents a more difficult problem. We have carefully evaluated the nature and the type of cases involved in the light of the expert testimony received, the stage of the litigation at the date of death, Mr. Weissbrodt's experience and past successes in this relatively esoteric area, the impact of delay so characteristic of Indian Claims litigation, and the possibility of competing claims for some of the fees. We recognize that, while there were ultimately substantial awards in some instances, in estimating the date-of-death value of these claims, we must be satisfied with some imprecision. But inexactitude is often a byproduct in estimating claims or assets without an established market and provides no excuse for failing to value the claims before us in the light of the vicissitudes attending their recovery. In the light of all the factors we have enumerated as of the date of death, August 23, 1972, and considering that critical issues were still unresolved, we conclude that the date-of-death value of the remaining 11 cases was $70,000. Therefore, the amount includable in the decedent's estate under section 2033 is $165,000.

Not all events occurring after death are ignored. While the court in Estate of Andrews v. Commissioner, *supra*, refused to consider the second and third publishing contracts or the success of the novels, it relied on the first publishing contract. In both *Estate of Andrews* and *Estate of Curry*, the parties relied on expert appraisals to establish valuation. Both courts took that evidence into consideration, but made their own determinations of value.

Some events subsequent to death will be considered if the executor elects the alternate valuation date in §2032. This provision is designed to protect beneficiaries from decreases in value occurring after death. Assessing the estate tax on the higher values could result in the tax substantially diminishing, or even eliminating, the amount of property available for distribution to the beneficiaries. The alternate valuation date also establishes the value for purposes of §1014. If an estate did not have sufficient assets to incur a tax and the executor elected the alternate valuation date, the beneficiaries would receive a higher basis for income tax purposes if the value of the assets increased after the decedent's death. Recognizing the potential for abuse, Congress in 1984 added subsection (c), which allows the executor to elect the alternate valuation date only if both the value of the gross estate and the amount of the estate tax will decrease as a result of the election.

The election is made on the estate tax return and is irrevocable. As a result of the election:

(1) assets sold, distributed, or otherwise disposed of within six months of decedent's death are valued on the date of the sale, distribution, or disposition;
(2) other assets are valued as of the date six months after the decedent's death; and
(3) interests that are affected only by the mere lapse of time are valued without consideration of that lapse of time.

Example 3-1

Doris died on February 1, owning Blackacre, stock in X, Inc., stock in Y, Inc., stock in Z, Inc., and a remainder interest in a trust established by her grandfather. On February 1 the value of these assets was:

Blackacre	$ 350,000
stock in X, Inc.	$ 500,000
stock in Y, Inc.	$ 1,000,000
stock in Z, Inc.	$ 350,000
remainder	$ 265,000

On May 5, the executor sold the stock in Z, Inc. for $330,000. On June 15, when the value of the stock in Y, Inc. was $600,000, the executor distributed it to Beneficiary. On August 1, the property remaining in the estate had the following values:

Blackacre	$ 375,000
stock in X, Inc.	$ 400,000
stock in Y, Inc.	$ 700,000
remainder	$ 263,000

Doris's executor may elect the alternate valuation date because the value of the assets and any estate tax liability would decrease between February 1 and August 1. If the executor elects the alternate valuation date, the assets will be valued on the estate tax return as follows:

Blackacre	$ 375,000
stock in X, Inc.	$ 400,000
stock in Y, Inc.	$ 600,000
stock in Z, Inc.	$ 330,000
remainder	$ 265,000

The gift and the estate taxes are part of a unified transfer tax system. Despite this, some gifts are brought back into the gross estate (*see, e.g.*, §§2036, 2037, 2038, and 2040(a)). While these transfers were valued on the date the gift was completed for gift tax purposes, the property will be revalued as of the date of death, because it is included in the decedent's gross estate. Gifts that are not brought back into the gross estate are "adjusted taxable gifts" and are included in the calculation of the estate tax under §2001. Taxable gifts made in one year are also included in the calculation of the gift tax for gifts made in subsequent years under §2502. Because of this, the IRS could assert a higher gift tax on a subsequent gift or a higher estate tax if it revalued prior gifts even when the statute of limitations on the prior gifts had expired.

Prior to 1997, §2504(c) protected against the revaluation of prior gifts if the period of limitations had passed and the gift tax had been assessed and paid. This section, however, applied only to the calculation of the gift tax on subsequent gifts, and the IRS succeeded in establishing higher values for adjusted taxable gifts for purposes of calculating the estate tax in cases such as Estate of Smith v. Commissioner, 94 T.C. 872 (1990), *acq.* 1990-2 C.B. 1, Stalcup v. United States, 792 F. Supp. 714 (W.D. Okla. 1991), and Evanson v. United States, 30 F.3d 960 (8th Cir. 1994). In 1997, Congress overruled these cases by enacting §2001(f), which precludes the revaluation of gifts in the calculation of the estate tax if the statute of limitations for assessing the gift tax has expired but only if the value of the gift was disclosed on the gift tax return "in a manner adequate to apprise the Secretary of the nature of [the gift]." While this amendment overrules cases such as *Estate of Smith*, *Stalcup*, and *Evanson*, the door is still open for the IRS to claim that the nature of the gift transaction was not adequately disclosed on the gift tax return.

PROBLEMS

1. Peter purchased Whiteacre, commercial real estate, 20 years ago for $30,000. Three years ago, when the local property tax appraisal on it was $225,000, Peter gave Whiteacre to his daughter, Deanna. Deanna died this year. Two months before her death, Bert offered to purchase Whiteacre for $350,000, but Deanna refused to sell. Five months after Deanna's death, chemical waste from a manufacturing business that predated Peter's purchase was discovered on the property. Two years after Deanna's death, Whiteacre was distributed to her sister, Sally, who sold it for $50,000. What is the value of Whiteacre for gift and estate tax purposes? How would you establish that value in an IRS audit or at trial?

2. Duncan died on September 1. He was the sole beneficiary of Ellen, his neighbor and lifelong friend. Ellen owned property valued at $750,000, and she was survived by a sister, Faith, and eight nieces and nephews. Although earlier wills had divided her property among her nieces and nephews, the more recent versions gave larger and larger shares of her estate to Duncan. Ellen informed the attorney who drafted her wills that she and her husband had been friends with Duncan and his wife for over 50 years, that after her husband's death Duncan helped her take care of her property and manage her financial affairs, and that she had little contact with her nieces and nephews particularly in the five years before her death. Ellen died in the February preceding Duncan, and three of her

nephews challenged her will on grounds of lack of mental capacity and undue influence. One year after Duncan's death, the will contest settled when the nephews agreed to accept $100,000. Duncan's estate eventually received property valued at $600,000 from Ellen's estate. You are the executor of Duncan's will. What do you report on his estate tax return? How would you establish value in an IRS audit or at trial?

3. Daniel died on March 15. He owned the following assets, which were valued on that date and on September 15 as follows:

Asset	March 15 Value	September 15 Value
stock in A, Inc.	$100,000	$ 60,000
stock in B, Inc.	$250,000	$150,000
stock in C, Inc.	$325,000	$200,000
Farmacre	$450,000	$500,000
Greenacre	$600,000	$500,000

Daniel also owned a life insurance policy that paid $1,000,000 to his estate.

a. What is the value of Daniel's estate for estate tax purposes?
b. What if the estate had sold Farmacre on June 10 to Daniel's nephew, Ned, for $350,000 as they had agreed prior to Daniel's death?
c. Same as 3.a., except that the estate had distributed Greenacre to Ann on May 10 when it had a value of $580,000.
d. Same as 3.a., except that Daniel did not own any insurance, Greenacre had a September 15 value of $750,000, and Farmacre had a September 15 value of $600,000.

C. VALUATION OF SPECIFIC ASSETS
IRC §§2031, 2512, 7520

Valuation depends on all the facts and circumstances, including the nature of the asset. The regulations provide detailed rules for valuing stocks and bonds. If stocks and bonds are sold in an established market, such as a stock exchange, the fair market value is the mean between the highest and the lowest quoted selling price on the valuation date. If there are no sales on the valuation date, then a weighted average is used. If there are sales on more than one exchange, the sales prices from the exchange where the stocks and bonds are principally sold are used. If there are no sales within a reasonable time, then the value is the mean between the bona fide bid and asked prices. If there are no selling or bid and asked prices available, stock will be valued by considering the corporation's net worth, earning power, and dividend-paying capacity, while bonds will be valued considering the soundness of the security, the interest yield, and the date of maturity. In both cases, other relevant factors are listed in the regulations. Reg. §§20.2031-2, 25.2512-2.

Real estate is valued at its highest and best use, unless it qualifies for special use valuation. §2032A. The use of the real estate — residential, commercial, or vacant — will determine the method of valuation. In all cases, qualified appraisers are relied on to give an opinion as to value.

Household and personal effects must also be valued. Items worth less than $100 may be grouped together. Individual items worth more than $3,000 and collections that have an aggregate value exceeding $10,000 must be appraised. If the executor does not list each item separately, the executor can furnish a written statement of the aggregate value based on an appraisal. Reg. §20.2031-6; Form 706, Schedule F.

The value of a promissory note is presumed to be the unpaid principal plus the amount of interest accrued to the date of death. The interest rate, the date of maturity, or issues of collectibility might diminish the value of the note. Reg. §§20.2031-4, 25.2512-4. The value of cash deposits is the amount in the account on the date of death. If the bank honors checks after the decedent's death, the diminished value of the account can be reported as long as the amounts paid after death are not claimed as deductions. Reg. §20.2031-5. Checks issued as gifts that are cashed after death do not diminish the value of the account.

Life insurance is valued differently for purposes of the gift tax and the estate tax. For gift tax purposes, the value of a life insurance policy is the replacement cost. Reg. §25.2512-6(a). If the policy has been in force for some time, its value is the interpolated terminal reserve plus the proportionate amount of the last premium. *Id.* The interpolated terminal reserve is equivalent to the cash surrender value of the policy, that is, the amount that the insurance company would pay if the insured cashed in the policy. The easiest way to value an insurance policy is to request that information from the insurance company.

If the decedent owned life insurance on her own life, §2042 requires that the amount included in the gross estate is the amount received by the estate or the beneficiary. This is the value that is transferred from the decedent as a result of her death. The reason for this rule is obvious.

Example 3-2

David purchases a life insurance policy with a face amount of $1,000,000, names his wife, Wendy, as the beneficiary, and pays the first year's premium of $1,000. He dies in a car accident the following day. The value of the policy is essentially the amount of the premium, $1,000, but the amount received because of David's death is $1,000,000. The amount received, *i.e.*, $1,000,000, not the "value" of the life insurance policy, will be included in David's gross estate under §2042(2).

If the decedent owns life insurance on the life of another, that policy would be included in the decedent's gross estate under §2033 and valued the same as for gift tax purposes. Reg. §20.2031-8(a).

The value of life estates, remainders, and similar interests depends on the value of the property as well as such factors as the life expectancy of the life tenant or the probability of the occurrence of events that trigger the reversion or remainder, for example, marriage, birth of issue, or death without issue. The present value of the interest must then be calculated using a discount factor. The value of a specific interest depends on the unique facts and circumstances of each case. Individualized valuation of these interests would be extraordinarily time consuming and subject to challenge and negotiation. Instead, the regulations prescribe actuarial factors for valuing life estates, terms of years, annuities, reversions, and remainders. Reg. §§20.2031-7, 25.2512-5. Initially, the regulations included tables based on an established interest rate. When interest rates change rapidly, taxpayers are able to manipulate valuation to avoid taxation. As a result, Congress enacted §7520, which directs the Secretary of the Treasury to issue tables and requires that the appropriate interest rate be designated on a monthly basis. The valuation tables now contain actuarial factors for a series of interest rates and are revised every ten years to reflect changes in mortality rates. §7520(c). The most recent valuation tables were issued in 1999 as IRS Publication 1457: Actuarial Values — Book Aleph and IRS Publication 1457: Actuarial Values — Book Beth. Table B, containing the term certain remainder factors, Table K, containing the annuity adjustment factors, and Table S, containing the life remainder factors, are reproduced in regulation §20.2031-7(d)(6) and (7).

The value of a remainder interest based on one person's life is simply the value of the property multiplied by the appropriate actuarial factor. Reg. §§2031-7(d)(2)(ii), 25.2512-5(d)(2)(ii). The value of the life estate based on one life is the difference between the value of the property and the value of the remainder. Reg. §§20.2031-7(d)(2)(iii), 25.2512-5(d)(2)(iii).

Example 3-3

Gary establishes an irrevocable trust to pay the income to John for life and the remainder to John's children. Gary transfers $100,000, to the trust. On the date of the transfer John is 45 years old and the interest rate designated by the Secretary for that month is five percent. The value of the remainder interest is the value of the property ($100,000) multiplied by the factor for age 45 at five percent (.23772) or $23,772. The value of the life estate is $100,000 less $23,772 or $76,228.

The value of a term certain and a reversion is calculated in the same manner. Reg. §§20.2031-7(d)(2)(ii) and (iii), 25.2512-5(d)(2)(ii) and (iii).

Example 3-4

Grace establishes an irrevocable trust to pay the income to her mother, Mary, for 15 years. At the end of the 15 years, the trust property will be distributed to Grace. Grace transfers $500,000 to the trust. The applicable interest rate for the month is six percent. The value of Grace's reversion is $500,000 multiplied by .417265 or $208,632.50. The value of Mary's term certain is $500,000 less $208,632.50 or $291,367.50.

If the interest depends on more than one life, marriage, or other contingencies, the tables in the regulations will not provide the appropriate actuarial factor. Publication 1457 provides guidance in some cases, but beyond that a ruling must be requested from the IRS. Reg. §§20.2031-7(d)(4), 25.2512-5(d)(4).

An annuity is the right to receive a periodic payment for a specified number of years, for one life, or for more than one life. The value of an annuity paid annually is the amount of the payment multiplied by an actuarial factor provided in Publication 1457. If the annuity is payable more frequently, the payment is also multiplied by the applicable adjustment factor in Table K. Reg. §§20.2031-7(d)(2)(iv), 25.2512-5(d)(2)(iv).

Lottery payments are often paid over a term of years and, as the following case demonstrates, usually may not be transferred without a court order.

Cook v. Commissioner
349 F.3d 850 (5th Cir. 2003)

DUHE, Circuit Judge:

Appellants ask this Court to reverse the Tax Court's conclusion that a nontransferrable lottery prize payable in seventeen annual installments is a private annuity that must be valued, for estate tax purposes, in accordance with 26 U.S.C. § 7520. Because we conclude that the prize is properly characterized [as] a private annuity, and that nonmarketability does not render the valuation of the prize under § 7520 and the regulations unreasonable, we affirm.

Gladys Cook and her sister-in-law Myrtle Newby had a longstanding informal agreement under which they jointly purchased Texas lottery tickets and shared the winnings. On July 8, 1995, Cook bought a winning ticket valued at $17 million, payable in 20 annual installments. The initial payment of $858,648 was made July 10, 1995, and the remaining payments of $853,000 each would be made on July 15th of the next 19 years. Texas law prohibited the assignment, other by court order, of the right to receive the lottery payments; neither could the prize be collected in a lump sum.

On July 12, 1995, Cook and Newby converted their informal partnership to a formal limited partnership . . . and each assigned her interest in the lottery winnings to the partnership. In exchange, each received a 48% limited partnership interest and a 2% general partnership interest.

Cook died November 6, 1995. The partnership's assets on that date, the valuation date for estate Tax purposes, were $391,717 in cash and the right to receive 19 annual lottery payments of $853,000 each. The parties stipulated that, because of the prohibition on transfer of the lottery prize, no market for the right to lottery payments existed in Texas at the time of Cook's death. . . . [T]he parties stipulated that the only remaining disputed issue was whether the lottery prize must be valued according to the annuity tables for purposes of valuing the partnership interest. The parties stipulated to alternate values for the partnership interest, agreeing that if the prize must be valued under the annuity tables, the value of the partnership interest was $2,908,605; if not, it was $2,237,140.

The Tax Court held that it was bound under a previous Tax Court case, Gribauskas v. Commissioner, 116 T.C. 142 (2001), to value the lottery payments using the annuity tables. *Gribauskas,* which has since been reversed by the Second Circuit, held that a lottery prize is a private annuity that must be valued under the annuity tables. The Estate appeals, asserting that the Tax Court erred in valuing the lottery prize rather than the partnership, and alternatively, in determining that the annuity tables do not assign an unreasonable value to the lottery prize. . . .

Treasury Regulations § 20.2031-1(b) governs valuation generally, providing that "the value of every item of property includible in a decedent's gross estate under sections 2031 through 2044 is its fair market value at the time of decedent's death." Fair market value is defined as "the price at which the property would change hands between a willing buyer and a willing seller, neither being under any compulsion to buy or sell and both having reasonable knowledge of relevant facts. . . ." *Id.*

In the case of a private annuity, fair market value is determined not under the general willing-buyer-willing-seller test, but under the method prescribed by 26 U.S.C. § 7520 and the accompanying regulations. In general, the value of a private annuity is determined by a factor composed of an interest rate component and a mortality component. When the annuity is for a term of years rather than an interest for life, the mortality component is equal to the term of years. The interest rate component is determined using a rounded interest rate equal to 120 percent of the Federal midterm rate in effect for the month in which the valuation date falls. 26 U.S.C. § 7520; Treas. Reg. § 20.7520-1(b).

Thus, for the property interests subject to § 7520 and the accompanying regulations, the sometimes wide variation produced by experts' fair market valuation methods gives way to certainty provided by the valuation tables. In enacting § 7520(a)(I) and requiring valuation by the tables, Congress displayed a preference for convenience and certainty over accuracy in the individual case. . . . The applicability of the annuity tables is not, however, unassailable. They must be used to value annuities "unless it is shown that the result is so unrealistic and unreasonable that either some modification in the prescribed method should be made, or complete departure from the method should be taken, and a more reasonable and realistic means of determining value is available." O'Reilly v. Commissioner, 973 F.2d 1403, 1407 (8th Cir. 1992) (quoting Weller v. Commissioner, 38 T.C. 790, 803, 1962 WL 1155 (1962)). The party challenging applicability of the tables has the substantial burden of demonstrating that the tables produce an unreasonable result. *Id.* at 1409.

Recently, the Ninth and Second Circuits have, surprisingly enough, dealt with cases in which facts very similar to those before us have arisen. *Gribauskas,* 342 F.3d 85; Shackleford v. United States, 262 F.3d 1028 (9th Cir. 2001). In previous cases, courts departed from valuation tables only when individual cases involved facts substantially at variance with factual assumptions underlying the tables. . . . Now, however, the Second and Ninth Circuits have recognized limits to the policy of standardization and a concurrent breadth in the exception to applicability of actuarial tables. *Gribauskas* at *1, *3;

Shackleford at 1033. Both circuits held that marketability must be considered in valuing the enforceable right to receive a series of cash payments.

The Estate argues that the lottery prize is not a private annuity, and therefore it is not susceptible to valuation under the tables. The Tax Court relied on its previous decision in Gribauskas v. Commissioner, 116 T.C. 142 (2001), *rev'd on other grounds,* Gribauskas v. Commissioner, 342 F.3d 85 (2d Cir. 2003), which addressed at length the same arguments presented by the Estate in this case, in holding that the lottery prize is a private annuity. Section 7520 does not define "annuity," but we find the reasoning of the Tax Court in *Gribauskas* on this issue persuasive: a lottery prize is within the customary meaning of the term annuity, which is " 'An obligation to pay a stated sum, usually monthly or annually, to a stated recipient.' " *Id.* (quoting Black's Law Dictionary). *Gribauskas* considered the characteristics of a nontransferrable lottery prize payable in yearly installments against those of notes receivable, leaseholds, patents, and royalty payments, none of which are valued under actuarial tables and all of which share some characteristics with the lottery prize. The court distinguished the nonannuity assets, however, as having value dependent on market forces that affect the value of the underlying asset or the likelihood of continued payments. In contrast, a private annuity may be defined broadly, as the right to a series of fixed payments independent of market forces. The lottery prize, an unsecured right to a series of fixed payments for a certain term with virtually no risk of default, falls within the definition of a private annuity, valuable under the § 7520 tables.

The Estate holds out the three results from valuation experts against the result from the tables as speaking for themselves on the question of reasonableness. The annuity-table valuation of the lottery prize exceeds the lowest expert valuation by $3,982,850, and the highest by $2,504,661. The difference in the numbers is attributable to nonmarketability discounts applied by the experts to the lottery prize but not taken into account by the valuation tables. The Tax Court observed that the wide discrepancies between the three expert valuations made "a compelling argument justifying use of the valuation tables," given Congress's policy of standardizing valuation.

The result produced by the valuation tables is not unreasonable because the factor accounting for the disparity between the expert and the table valuation, *i.e.,* a marketability discount, is not properly applied to the lottery prize. The nonmarketability of a private annuity is an assumption underlying the annuity tables. For example, the value of survivor annuities payable under qualified plans (transfer of which is prohibited by ERISA); charitable remainder annuity trusts; and grantor retained annuity trusts (GRATS); which are not marketable, are determined by use of the tables. *See*, Treas. Reg. § 1.664-2(c); 20.2039-2(c)(1)(viii) and (c)(2). . . . [T]he cases in which courts have seen fit to depart from the valuation tables have involved facts that disproved assumptions underlying the tables. The holdings in *Shackleford* and *Gribauskas* depart from that longstanding trend based on the premise that the right to alienate is fundamental to the valuation of *any* property. *Gribauskas* at *2; *Shackleford*, 262 F.3d at 1032 ("The right to transfer is 'one of the most essential sticks in the bundle of rights that are commonly characterized as property.' ") (quoting Youpee v. Babbitt, 67 F.3d 194, 197 (9th Cir. 1995), *aff'd,* Babbitt v. Youpee, 519 U.S. 234, 117 S.Ct. 727, 136 L.Ed. 2d 696 (1997)). We agree that the right to alienate is necessary to value a capital asset; however, we think it unreasonable to apply a nonmarketability discount when the asset to be valued is the right, independent of market forces, to receive a certain amount of money annually for a certain term. *Youpee* involved restrictions on the right to devise land, a capital asset. The remaining cases relied upon by the Ninth Circuit also involved capital assets, such as corporate stock, for which value is not readily ascertainable absent a transfer from buyer to seller. . . .

The Second Circuit recognized that previous cases departing from the tables involved not simply a disparity in numbers but factual assumptions in the tables that were inconsistent with the facts of an individual case. *Gribauskas* at *3. The court reasoned that the exception recognized by previous cases is broader than the Commissioner suggests, as evidenced by the standard of an "unreasonable and unrealistic result." *Id.* While an extraordinary case whose facts are not duplicative of previous cases might justify departure, the exception is not so broad as to include a case involving a factor not necessary to determine the asset's value. We note that the Second Circuit relied in *Gribauskas* on the parties' stipulations that the nonmarketability of the lottery prize reduced its value. *Id.* at *1 ("Notably, the parties stipulated that a market for the Lotto winnings *did exist* at the time the return was filed [and] that the prize's market value was diminished considerably due to transfer restrictions. . . ."). In the case at bar, the parties stipulated that *no market existed* for the lottery prize.

Marketability is important to the valuation of an asset when capital appreciation is an element of value or when the value would otherwise be difficult to ascertain. Other kinds of private annuities are valued under the tables despite being nonmarketable. As the Tax Court stated, nonmarketability does not "alter or jeopardize the essential entitlement to a stream of fixed payments." The value of the lottery prize is readily ascertainable by simple aggregation of the payments to be received. The value of the prize must be discounted because it is payable over time, rather than in a lump sum; the tables account for that feature by discounting the payments to present value. We disagree with the Second and Ninth Circuits that a reasonable valuation of the lottery prize requires a discount for nonmarketability. The Tax Court was correct in holding that departure from the annuity tables is not warranted for valuation of the lottery prize.

We find no error in the Tax Court's construction of the stipulations. The stipulations provided alternate values for the value of the partnership, thus leaving only the question of the lottery prize's valuation. We conclude that the lottery prize is a private annuity, and the value produced under the valuation tables is not so unreasonable or unrealistic as to warrant resort to a different valuation method. We affirm the judgment of the Tax Court holding that the prize must be valued under the tables.

In other situations, departure from the actuarial tables is allowed as specified in regulations §§20.7520-3 and 25.7520-3. For example, the actuarial tables may not be used to value interests measured by the life of an individual who is terminally ill on the valuation date. Regulations §§20.7520-3(b)(3) and 25.7520-3(b)(3) provide:

> For purposes of this paragraph (b)(3), an individual who is known to have an incurable illness or other deteriorating physical condition is considered terminally ill if

there is at least a 50 percent probability that the individual will die within 1 year. However, if the individual survives for eighteen months or longer after the date of the decedent's death, that individual is presumed to have not been terminally ill at the [valuation date] unless the contrary is established by clear and convincing evidence.

Terminal illness is not considered in valuing a decedent's reversionary interest under §2037 or §2042(2). If it were, those sections would rarely, if ever, be applicable. Reg. §§20.7520-3(b)(3)(ii) and 25.7520-3(b)(3)(ii).

PROBLEMS

1. At the time of his death, Dwight owned the following assets. How will they be valued for estate tax purposes?
       Stock in AT&T
       Municipal bonds
       A ten percent interest in a family business
       Money market fund
       Checking account
       Savings account
       House
       Car
       Sailboat
       Life insurance policy
       Promissory note
       Paintings
       Household furnishings
       Golden retriever

2. Glen established an irrevocable inter vivos trust by transferring $200,000 to Friendly National Bank as Trustee to pay the income to Ann for her life and then to distribute the trust property to Beth.
    a. What are the values of the life estate and the remainder for gift tax purposes? Assume that Ann is 60 years old and that the applicable interest rate is 4.6 percent.
    b. What are the values if the income is to be paid to Ann for 15 years?
    c. If Ann dies two months after the trust is created, will that affect the valuation?

3. Donna and her sister, Jenny, won the State Lottery and elected to receive the $40 million prize in equal annual installments over 20 years. Donna died after receiving two payments. Although the winner of State Lottery has the option to receive either a lump sum (approximately half the face value of the prize), once a winner has chosen annual installments, the winner cannot transfer or assign the right to receive those payments.
    a. Ellen, Donna's executor, asks for your advice on how to value this asset on Donna's estate tax return. What do you tell her?

b. Would valuation be different if Donna and Jenny had formed a limited partnership, transferred the winning ticket to the limited partnership, and the limited partnership had elected the annual installments?

D. BUSINESS INTERESTS
IRC §§2031, 2032A, 2057

The valuation of closely held business interests is particularly difficult because there is relatively little market data and there are often restrictions on the sale of such interests.

Revenue Ruling 59-60
1959-1 C.B. 237

In valuing the stock of closely held corporations, or the stock of corporations where market quotations are not available, all other available financial data, as well as all relevant factors affecting the fair market value must be considered for estate tax and gift tax purposes. No general formula may be given that is applicable to the many different valuation situations arising in the valuation of such stock. However, the general approach, methods, and factors which must be considered in valuing such securities are outlined. . . .

Closely held corporations are those corporations the shares of which are owned by a relatively limited number of stockholders. Often the entire stock issue is held by one family. The result of this situation is that little, if any, trading in the shares takes place. There is, therefore, no established market for the stock and such sales as occur at irregular intervals seldom reflect all of the elements of a representative transaction as defined by the term "fair market value.". . .

It is advisable to emphasize that in the valuation of the stock of closely held corporations or the stock of corporations where market quotations are either lacking or too scarce to be recognized, all available financial data, as well as all relevant factors affecting the fair market value, should be considered. The following factors, although not all-inclusive are fundamental and require careful analysis in each case:

(a) The nature of the business and the history of the enterprise from its inception.
(b) The economic outlook in general and the condition and outlook of the specific industry in particular.
(c) The book value of the stock and the financial condition of the business.

(d) The earning capacity of the company.

(e) The dividend-paying capacity.

(f) Whether or not the enterprise has goodwill or other intangible value.

(g) Sales of the stock and the size of the block of stock to be valued.

(h) The market price of stocks of corporations engaged in the same or a similar line of business having their stocks actively traded in a free and open market, either on an exchange or over-the-counter.

The following is a brief discussion of each of the foregoing factors:

(a) The history of a corporate enterprise will show its past stability or instability, its growth or lack of growth, the diversity or lack of diversity of its operations, and other facts needed to form an opinion of the degree of risk involved in the business. . . . The detail to be considered should increase with approach to the required date of appraisal, since recent events are of greatest help in predicting the future; but a study of gross and net income, and of dividends covering a long prior period, is highly desirable. The history to be studied should include, but need not be limited to, the nature of the business, its products or services, its operating and investment assets, capital structure, plant facilities, sales records and management, all of which should be considered as of the date of the appraisal, with due regard for recent significant changes. Events of the past that are unlikely to recur in the future should be discounted, since value has a close relation to future expectancy.

(b) A sound appraisal of a closely held stock must consider current and prospective economic conditions as of the date of appraisal, both in the national economy and in the industry or industries with which the corporation is allied. It is important to know that the company is more or less successful than its competitors in the same industry, or that it is maintaining a stable position with respect to competitors. . . . The public's appraisal of the future prospects of competitive industries or of competitors within an industry may be indicated by price trends in the markets for commodities and for securities. The loss of the manager of a so-called "one-man" business may have a depressing effect upon the value of the stock of such business, particularly if there is a lack of trained personnel capable of succeeding to the management of the enterprise. In valuing the stock of this type of business, therefore, the effect of the loss of the manager on the future expectancy of the business, and the absence of management-succession potentialities are pertinent factors to be taken into consideration. On the other hand, there may be factors which offset, in whole or in part, the loss of the manager's services. For instance, the nature of the business and of its assets may be such that they will not be impaired by the loss of the manager. Furthermore, the loss may be adequately covered by life insurance, or competent management might be employed on the basis of the consideration paid for the former manager's services. These, or other offsetting factors, if found to exist, should be carefully weighed against the loss of the manager's services in valuing the stock of the enterprise.

(c) Balance sheets should be obtained, preferably in the form of comparative annual statements for two or more years immediately preceding the date of appraisal, together with a balance sheet at the end of the month preceding that date, if corporate accounting will permit. . . . These statements usually will disclose to the appraiser (1) liquid position (ratio of current assets to current liabilities); (2) gross and net book value of principal classes of fixed assets; (3) working capital; (4) long-term indebtedness; (5) capital structure; and (6) net worth. Consideration also should be given to any assets not essential to the operation of the business, such as investments in securities, real estate, etc. . . . If the corporation has more than one class of stock outstanding, the charter or certificate of incorporation should be examined to ascertain the explicit rights and privileges of the various stock issues including: (1) voting powers, (2) preference as to dividends, and (3) preference as to assets in the event of liquidation.

(d) Detailed profit-and-loss statements should be obtained and considered for a representative period immediately prior to the required date of appraisal, preferably five or more years. Such statements should show (1) gross income by principal items; (2) principal deductions from gross income including major prior items of operating expenses, interest and other expense on each item of long-term debt, depreciation and depletion if such deductions are made, officers' salaries, in total if they appear to be reasonable or in detail if they seem to be excessive, contributions (whether or not deductible for tax purposes) that the nature of its business and its community position require the corporation to make, and taxes by principal items, including income and excess profits taxes; (3) net income available for dividends; (4) rates and amounts of dividends paid on each class of stock; (5) remaining amount carried to surplus; and (6) adjustments to, and reconciliation with, surplus as stated on the balance sheet. . . . Potential future income is a major factor in many valuations of closely-held stocks, and all information concerning past income which will be helpful in predicting the future should be secured. Prior earnings records usually are the most reliable guide as to the future expectancy, but resort to arbitrary five-or-ten-year averages without regard to current trends or future prospects will not produce a realistic valuation. . . .

(e) Primary consideration should be given to the dividend-paying capacity of the company rather than to dividends actually paid in the past. Recognition must be given to the necessity of retaining a reasonable portion of profits in a company to meet competition. Dividend-paying capacity is a factor that must be considered in an appraisal, but dividends actually paid in the past may not have any relation to dividend-paying capacity. Specifically, the dividends paid by a closely held family company may be measured by the income needs of the stockholders or by their desire to avoid taxes on dividend receipts, instead of by the ability of the company to pay dividends. Where an actual or effective controlling interest in a corporation is to be valued, the dividend factor is not a material element, since the payment of such dividends is discretionary with the controlling stockholders. The individual or group in control can substitute salaries and bonuses for dividends, thus reducing net income and understating the dividend-paying capacity of the company. It follows, therefore, that dividends are less reliable criteria of fair market value than other applicable factors.

(f) In the final analysis, goodwill is based upon earning capacity. The presence of goodwill and its value, therefore, rests upon the excess of net earnings over and above a fair return on the net tangible assets. While the element of goodwill may be based primarily on earnings, such factors as the prestige and renown of the business, the ownership of a trade or brand name, and a record of successful operation over a prolonged period in a particular locality, also may furnish support for the inclusion of intangible value. In some instances it may not be possible to make a separate appraisal of the tangible and intangible assets of the business. The enterprise has a value as an entity. Whatever intangible value there is, which is supportable by the facts, may be measured by the amount by which the appraised value of the tangible assets exceeds the net book value of such assets.

(g) Sales of stock of a closely held corporation should be carefully investigated to determine whether they represent transactions at arm's length. Forced or distress sales do not ordinarily reflect fair market value nor do isolated sales in small amounts necessarily control as the measure of value. This is especially true in the valuation of a controlling interest in a corporation. Since, in the case of closely held stocks, no prevailing market prices are available, there is no basis for making an adjustment for blockage. It follows, therefore, that such stocks should be valued upon a consideration of all the evidence affecting the fair market value. The size of the block of stock itself is a relevant factor to be considered. Although it is true that a minority interest in an unlisted corporation's stock is more difficult to sell than a similar block of listed stock, it is equally true that control of a corporation, either actual or in effect, representing as it does an added element of value, may justify a higher value for a specific block of stock. . . .

Because valuations cannot be made on the basis of a prescribed formula, there is no means whereby the various applicable factors in a particular case can be assigned mathematical weights in deriving the fair market value. For this reason, no useful purpose is served by taking an average of several factors (for example, book value, capitalized earnings and capitalized dividends) and basing the valuation on the result. Such a process excludes active consideration of other pertinent factors, and the end result cannot be supported by a realistic application of the significant facts in the case except by mere chance.

Closely held business interests receive special consideration in the estate tax. One provision is §2032A, which allows the executor to elect "special-use," rather than fair market, valuation for real property used in farming or another trade or business. Without §2032A, such real property would be valued at its highest and best use, which could force heirs and beneficiaries to sell the family business to pay the resulting estate tax. While §2032A does not necessarily prevent such sales, it does diminish their likelihood.

The requirements of §2032A are many and complex:

1. The decedent must have been a citizen or resident of the United States, and the real property must be located in the United States.
2. The decedent or a member of his family must have been using the property for farming or business on the date of death. Members of the family include (a) ancestors, (b) a spouse, and (c) lineal descendants and their spouses.
3. The decedent must transfer the property to a qualified heir, *i.e.*, a member of his family.
4. The qualified heir must continue to use the property in farming or business for the next ten years.
5. At least 50 percent of the gross estate must consist of real and personal property used in farming or business.
6. At least 25 percent of the gross estate must consist of the real property used in farming or business.
7. During five of the eight years immediately preceding death, the decedent or a member of his family must have used the real property for farming or business and materially participated in the operation of the farm or business.

If these requirements are met, the executor can elect to value the property at its use in farming or other business rather than at its fair market value. The estate, however, can only reduce the value of the real property by $750,000 (as adjusted for inflation). If the heir disposes of the property within ten years, other than to another qualified member of the family, the tax benefit will be recaptured.

Deeming these provisions inadequate to protect family-owned businesses, Congress enacted §2033A in 1997. This section excluded from the gross estate the value of a qualified family-owned business. This exclusion could not exceed $1,300,000 less the applicable exclusion amount, *i.e.*, the amount of property shielded by the unified credit. As a result, the exclusion decreased from a maximum of $675,000 in 1998 when the applicable exclusion amount was $625,000 to a maximum of $300,000 in 2006 when the applicable exclusion amount was scheduled to be $1,000,000. The eligibility requirements were patterned after §2032A, although they were not identical, and were complex and confusing.

Because of confusion surrounding this new section, Congress repealed §2033A before it went into effect and replaced it with a deduction, §2057, for the value of family-owned businesses. The requirements are similar, but not identical, to §2032A:

1. The decedent must be a citizen or resident of the United States, and the principal place of the business must be in the United States.

2. The value of the business interest in the decedent's gross estate, plus any gifts of that business to a member of the family, must exceed 50 percent of the value of the adjusted gross estate, as defined in §2057(c).
3. During five of the eight years immediately preceding death, the decedent or a member of his family must have owned the business interest and materially participated in the operation of the business.
4. The business interest must be left to a "qualified heir," *i.e.*, a member of the decedent's family or an active employee who has worked in the business for at least ten years before the decedent's death.
5. The qualified heir must materially participate in the business for ten years after the decedent's death.
6. The decedent must either operate the business as a proprietor or the decedent and members of his family must own 50 percent of the business entity. The business interest also qualifies if decedent and members of his family own 30 percent of the business entity and (a) 70 percent is owned by members of two families or (b) 90 percent is owned by members of three families.

If all these requirements are met, then the estate is allowed to deduct the value of the decedent's business interest up to $675,000. If the estate elects to deduct the $675,000, the decedent's applicable exclusion amount under §2010 is limited to $625,000 regardless of the year of death. The result is a maximum exclusion of $1,300,000.

Section 2057 applies in addition to §2032A. The executor should first elect special use valuation under §2032A and value the real property used in the business accordingly. That value is then used to determine the value of the business for purposes of §2057. The interplay of these two sections is complicated, and great care must be taken in their application because their requirements and restrictions are not identical.

The 2001 Tax Act increased the unified credit exemption amount to $1,500,000 for decedents dying after December 31, 2003. Section 2057, therefore, provides no additional benefit and Congress repealed it, except for the recapture provisions. The provisions of the 2001 Tax Act are themselves repealed effective January 1, 2011, so §2057 will become effective again at that time. Because the exemption amount will then be $1,000,000, the benefit of §2057 will be limited to $300,000.

E. DISCOUNTS AND PREMIUMS

Factors such as the amount of stock owned by the decedent or the lack of a ready market for the property can affect valuation. Regulation §20.2031-2(e) states:

In certain exceptional cases, the size of the bock of stock to be valued in relation to the number of shares changing hands in sales may be relevant in determining whether selling prices reflect the fair market value of the bock of stock to be valued. If the executor can show that the block of stock to be valued is so large in relation to the actual sales on the existing market that it could not be liquidated in a reasonable time without depressing the market, the price at which the clock could be sold as such outside the usual market, as through an underwriter, may be a more accurate indiction of value than market quotations.

Blockage discounts have been recognized in valuing art as well as stock.

Estate of O'Keeffe v. Commissioner
63 T.C.M. (CCH) 2699 (1992)

COHEN, Judge:

Findings of Fact

. . . [Georgia T.] O'Keeffe died on March 6, 1986, at the age of 98. At the time of her death, there remained in her estate approximately 400 works or groups of works of art that she had created. The total of the individual fair market values of each of O'Keeffe's works in the estate as of the date of death exceeded $72,759,000. If, however, all or a substantial portion of those works had been simultaneously offered for sale on the date of death, the availability of such a large block of O'Keeffe's works would have depressed the price to be paid for each of the individual works.

The fair market value of the aggregate of the works in the estate, therefore, as of the date of death, was substantially less than the total of the fair market values of each individual work. The amount of the discount (the blockage discount) to be anticipated with respect to each work of art in the collection, however, would depend on the market for that work or works of the type represented by that work. In order to determine the appropriate discount for particular segments of the aggregate, therefore, it is necessary to examine the history of the market for O'Keeffe's works, the prospects for the market for O'Keeffe's works as of the date of death, the types of works to be valued, and the art market in the United States.

O'Keeffe began painting in 1914. . . . O'Keeffe became one of the best known American artists of the period between the two World Wars. Although she lived well past the post-War period and became a celebrity, the bulk of her work, as well as her reputation among art dealers and critics, was based on her connection with early Modernist painting in America. . . . Sales of O'Keeffe's works in the late 1970s and early 1980s increased, partly as a result of a generalized boom in the art market and partly because of a more aggressive personal sales approach taken by O'Keeffe. In 1979, the average price of a work sold by O'Keeffe jumped from tens of thousands of dollars to $121,000. The average price of paintings O'Keeffe sold personally rose to a high of $631,250 in 1983. . . .

At the date of her death, O'Keeffe had produced between 1,100 and 1,200 substantial works. The market for her works was essentially limited to the United States. . . . O'Keeffe was able to transcend her traditional market, collectors of American Modernism, and appeal to a far broader range of buyers. The buyers to whom her works appealed included art collectors and persons who enjoyed the beauty of her pictures, the fascination of her myth, and the subject of her pictures. O'Keeffe's diverse range of subject matters, such as flowers, trees and leaves, landscapes (New Mexico and New York), and abstractions (early and late), and her various "periods" appealed to different segments of the public. The market for O'Keeffe's works included small and large museums that bought the works or sought donors for the works, private collectors, and the general public. Her works appealed to those who collected American "modern" art as well as those who simply liked what she painted.

The works of significant value in the estate at the date of O'Keeffe's death ranged from early works on paper through works on canvas done in the 1970s. . . . The paintings that are part of a particular series show the differences in O'Keeffe's technique in the treatment of medium, light, form, and perspective of one theme and show O'Keeffe's progression as an artist. The paintings that are part of a series are an essential part of her lifetime output and will often have a value greater than the value each would have if it were not part of a series. . . .

From 1979 to 1986, with the exception of the 1982 recession, the art market in the United States experienced a boom period, with the values of individual works of art rising dramatically over those years. Increased market activity and competition drove up the prices of works of art. . . . In 1986, the art market in the United States was strong. . . . By 1986, it had become apparent to knowledgeable dealers and collectors that the art market, particularly the highly inflated market for American art, had grown so fast that it was becoming unstable and unreliable. A dealer could still make a profit on the quick turnover of individual works, particularly on outstanding examples of an individual artist's work. Knowledgeable dealers and collectors, however, would have approached with caution the purchase of a large block of works of mixed quality identified with early American Modernism, such as those in the estate. . . .

The estate employed Eugene Victor Thaw (Thaw) to appraise O'Keeffe's works in the estate for the Federal estate tax return and for trial of this case. Thaw had been involved in all aspects of the art market since 1950. He was well qualified to appraise the works of O'Keeffe. Thaw had testified as a witness on the blockage discount appropriate in the Tax Court case of Estate of Smith v. Commissioner, 57 T.C. 650 (1972), *affd.* 510 F.2d 479 (2d Cir. 1975). The *Smith* case was the first litigated case to apply a blockage discount to works of art. In Thaw's opinion, however, there was no similarity between the content of the Smith estate and the content of the O'Keeffe estate except that the two cases were tried in the Tax Court. The individual values of all of O'Keeffe's works in the estate were determined by agreement between Thaw, on behalf of petitioner, and the Internal Revenue Service (IRS).

It was Thaw's opinion that the appropriate blockage discount that should be allowed for O'Keeffe's works in the estate on the date of death is 75 percent. Thaw's opinion was based on the understanding and assumption that all of the works in the estate would be sold to a single buyer as a bulk purchase, which would require a syndicate of investors. The hypothetical buyer would have to hold the works for many years and, in determining the price to be paid, would take into account interest, selling costs, promotion, maintenance costs, and carrying charges. Thaw also based his opinion on the assumption that a buyer would consider "fluctuations from the very high market plateau for O'Keeffes in 1986," although he would have advised a potential buyer that prices of works by O'Keeffe, on average, were unlikely to go down.

Thaw would not, however, have advised a hypothetical seller of the works in the estate to sell the total of those works at a 75-percent discount. Thaw was under the impression that determination of blockage discount required him to assume a hypothetical buyer on the date of death who would have been required to purchase all of the works of the estate in bulk on that date. Although Thaw's written report categorized the works in the estate by medium and price, he did not differentiate among the works in determining the discount to be applied.

Barbara Rose (Rose), an art historian who had assisted O'Keeffe in relation to the publication of the 1976 book, also prepared a written report on behalf of petitioner. Rose identified traditional factors establishing value in the art market as rarity, quality, size, subject matter, medium, and condition. With reference to O'Keeffe's works, she identified lack of scholarly reviews or a catalogue raisonne, the "mystical and religious content of her art," and prejudices of sex, age, and provincialism as negative factors. Rose concluded that a bulk sale of O'Keeffe's works on the date of death would have resulted in a two-thirds to three-fourths loss in value. Rose, however, would not have advised a seller to sell O'Keeffe's works in bulk on the date of death at the discounted value. Rose's opinion was based in part on her view that many of O'Keeffe's works in the estate were in poor condition.

Warren Adelson (Adelson), a dealer in American art, prepared a written report on behalf of respondent. Adelson divided the art into two categories, "Bequested Art" and "Remaining Art." Adelson assumed and understood that:

> Blockage discounts have been applied to recognize the impact of a huge number of works of art coming on the market at the same time, thereby disrupting the normal economics of supply and demand. Clearly blockage is applicable to works of art that are for sale, works that impact the marketplace. It is not applicable to works which are unavailable for sale, in this case, bequested works.

The total value of the 80 pieces of "Bequested Art" for which Adelson did not determine a blockage discount was $32,228,000. With respect to the "Remaining Art," Adelson noted that the 72 most valuable items totaled $30,975,000. He opined that these pieces could be sold "within a few years"; he determined "only a nominal discount" of 10 percent for those 72 items. In his opinion, a blockage discount of 37 percent would be "fair and reasonable" for the other 177 pieces that would "take years, perhaps a decade, to dispose of."

Opinion

. . . The parties in this case agree that the total of the individual fair market values of each of O'Keeffe's works in the estate exceeded $72,759,000 on March 6, 1986. They disagree, however, as to the appropriate blockage discount to be applied to the total. In our view, the disagreement is in large part the result of erroneous instructions to the experts with respect to the concept of blockage. . . .

In this case, the opinions of petitioner's experts that O'Keeffe's works in the estate, individually valued in excess of $72 million, could have been sold on the date of her death for $18 million, defies common sense. Our conclusion is based in substantial part on the particular content of the works. The individual values of 44 pieces totaled almost one-half of the agreed value of the whole group!

Respondent's expert's opinion is erroneous as a matter of law. There is no justification for his exclusion of the bequeathed art from the total subject to discount. Determination of fair market value assumes that works are in the market and precludes consideration that works are "unavailable for sale." He was not entitled to consider the actual disposition of the works of art of the estate any more than fair market value may be determined by assuming that particular purchasers will purchase works of art from the estate. . . .

Although each of the experts was qualified to express an opinion on the subject matter on which he or she was called to testify, each of them suffered from the same tendency to ignore relevant facts inconsistent with the position of the party employing the expert and to exaggerate facts consistent with the view espoused. Thus, each conclusion as to the appropriate blockage discount suffers from substantial defects and is patently unreliable. Thaw, for example, in effect assumed a forced sale in bulk of all of the works of the estate to a single buyer. Petitioner tries to justify that assumption by arguing that ascertainment of fair market value requires that property "must change hands" on the date of death. That argument is unsupported by authority or reason and ignores the concepts of willing buyers and willing sellers acting without compulsion — the defining actors in a fair market value transaction. . . . Expert testimony based on a flawed legal basis or presumption is irrelevant. . . . The Court also rejects proposed transactions that are contrary to the interests of a hypothetical seller.

Rose's opinion relied on her concern with the condition of certain of the works of art in the estate, although the individual condition of each work presumably would have been taken into account by Thaw in reaching the individual appraisals of the work. Thaw never indicated otherwise. Both Thaw and Rose conceded that they would not have recommended to a seller that the works in the estate be sold for the $18 million that they opined was the blocked value of the estate on the date of death. . . .

While the parties each purportedly rely on Estate of Smith v. Commissioner, 57 T.C. 650 (1972), *affd.* 510 F.2d 479 (2d Cir. 1975), each takes parts of the opinion in that case out of context. In that case, the Court was required to determine the fair market value of 425 pieces of nonrepresentational metal sculptures created by David Smith. Respondent claimed that no discount should be applied to the total and that the fair market value of each item should simply be determined by the price at which the item could be sold separately in the retail art market on a "one-at-a-time" basis. The estate applied a 75-percent discount to the total. The Court stated:

> We find it unnecessary, in this unusual case, to make any hard-and-fast choice between the two approaches urged by the parties. On the one hand, we think that the initial 75-percent discount, which petitioner has applied to the "one-at-a-time" value in order to determine the price which a purchaser would pay for all the sculptures, is too high. On the other hand, we think that respondent should have given considerable weight to the fact that each item of sculpture would not be offered in isolation. We think that, at the very least, each willing buyer in the retail art market would take into account, in determining the price he would be willing to pay for any given item, the fact that 424 other items were being offered for sale at the same time. The impact of such simultaneous availability of an extremely large number of items of the same general category is a significant circumstance which should be taken into account. In this connection, the so-called blockage rule utilized in connection with the sale of a large number of securities furnishes a useful analogy. . . . We think that a museum or individual collector of art objects would not completely ignore the resale value of a given item, although it obviously has far less significance than in the case of a dealer. Moreover, the "retail market" claimed by respondent may well encompass the use of an auction method of disposal (to be distinguished from the usual forced-sale concept) for at least a part of the art objects; in such a situation the presence of a large number of pieces on the market at one time would be a most material factor. Under the foregoing circumstances, we think that, in this case, the amount which an en bloc purchaser for resale would pay and the aggregate of the separate "one-at-a-time" values to be obtained by a variety of dispositions in the "retail market" would be the same. [57 T.C. at 657-658; fn. refs. omitted.]

The Court took into account other elements involved in the valuation process as they existed at the time of death and rejected the estate's claim that future commissions on sales of the work should be considered. The Court concluded that the fair market value of the 425 sculptures at the moment of Smith's death was $2,700,000. Because the total of the individual values of the sculptures was $4,284,000, the parties in this case translate the Court's conclusion to a 37-percent discount. Nothing in the opinion, however, explains the conclusion of value by application of a particular percentage to the total. . . .

Petitioner's experts acknowledge that there is a vast difference in quality among the pieces in the estate, although Thaw disagreed with Adelson's assumption that it would be appropriate to dispose of the most valuable pieces first. Although they mentioned, and purportedly relied on, their experience with estates of other artists, Thaw and Rose provided insufficient information for us to make a judgment on the comparability of those situations. The attempted comparisons to the estate of David Smith showed lack of meaningful "comparability." Unlike the situation in Estate of Smith v. Commissioner, 57 T.C. 650 (1972), *affd*. 510 F.2d 479 (2d Cir. 1975), the evidence in this case shows that the amount that would be paid for individual purchases of O'Keeffe's works and the amount that would be paid by a hypothetical en bloc purchaser would not be the same. There is too much variation among the different O'Keeffe works by type, quality, period, price, and other factors affecting the probable market for each work. Overall, petitioner's experts' testimony was limited to the perceptions of dealers and art critics and ignored less sophisticated elements of the art market.

From the evidence, it is apparent to us that different works in the estate would be of interest to different segments of the art market. The parties have not reasonably quantified assumptions about the specific markets in which segments of the works in the estate would be salable. Petitioner has erroneously assumed that all of the art would initially be sold to a bulk purchaser, who would purchase for resale. Petitioner thus ignores the market of collectors who, while taking into account resale value, are not primarily interested in the rate of return on the investment.

Petitioner strenuously objects to evidence that, in fact, a substantial number of the most valuable works in the estate have been or will be distributed to museums. We are not persuaded that the market for O'Keeffe's works did not include museums, and petitioner's assertions on this point are disingenuous. Petitioner's experts stated, without supporting data, that museums were not in the market for O'Keeffe's works. This testimony, however, does not consider whether museums were not in the market for O'Keeffe's works only because they anticipated distributions of 42 major works from the estate to 8 major art museums. The evidence of actual distributions and subsequent sales to museums refutes petitioner's experts' opinions about the interest of museums in O'Keeffe and thus cannot be ignored.

Petitioner and its experts also argue that the market for O'Keeffe's works depended on her personality and personal sales efforts, but the objective evidence of sales of her works after her death belies that contention. Those sales may be considered for that purpose. It is equally plausible and more consistent with the objective evidence to infer that the methods of sale and the postsale constraints that O'Keeffe imposed limited the market for her works, so that the market opened up after her death.

We conclude that the respective experts in this case each failed to consider the relevant market for particular works of O'Keeffe or groups of works in the estate. *See* sec. 20.2031-1(a), Estate Tax Regs. . . . We cannot rely on the burden of proof in this case. There is evidence from which we can determine a value, although we are frustrated and imposed upon by the lack of reliable expert opinion supporting the discounts claimed by the opposing parties. We are persuaded that O'Keeffe's works in the estate on the date of her death should be segmented, not necessarily by value but by quality, uniqueness, and salability. There should be at least two categories, i.e., works that are salable within a relatively short period of time at approximately their individual values and works that can only be marketed over a long period of years with substantial effort. We believe that petitioner's experts' opinion is valid only as applied to the second category of works. Respondent's argument is meritorious with regard to the first category. For want of a more reliable breakdown, we conclude that one-half of the value of O'Keeffe's works in the estate would be appropriately subjected to petitioner's experts' analysis and should be discounted 75 percent. Using our best judgment on the entire record, we conclude that the other half of the total value of O'Keeffe's works should be discounted 25 percent. After considering the entire record, we conclude that the fair market value of O'Keeffe's works in the estate at the date of death was $36,400,000.

An adjustment for blockage reflects a discount for the difficulty of selling the property. Courts have also recognized discounts for problems of marketability particularly with respect to stock in closely held business interests. As the court in Mandelbaum v. Commissioner noted:

> When determining the value of unlisted stock by reference to listed stock, a discount from the listed price is typically warranted in order to reflect the unlisted stock's lack of marketability. Such a discount, commonly known as a "lack of marketability discount" (or, more succinctly, a "marketability discount"), reflects the absence of a recognized market for closely held stock and accounts for the fact that closely held stock is generally not readily transferable. A marketability discount also reflects the fact that a buyer may have to incur a subsequent expense to register the unlisted stock for public sale. . . .
>
> The parties have stipulated the "freely traded" values of Big M's class B common stock on the pertinent valuations dates. These stipulated values take into account any applicable minority discount. The stipulated values must be discounted to reflect the fact that Big M's stock is unlisted and is not easily marketable. Ascertaining the appropriate discount for limited marketability is a factual determination. Critical to this determination is an appreciation of the fundamental elements of value that are used by an investor in making his or her investment decision. A nonexclusive list of these factors includes: (1) The value of the subject corporation's privately traded securities vis-a-vis its publicly traded securities (or, if the subject corporation does not have stock that is traded both publicly and privately, the cost of a similar corporation's public and private stock); (2) an analysis of the subject corporation's financial statements; (3) the corporation's dividend-paying capacity, its history of paying dividends, and the amount of its prior dividends; (4) the nature of the corporation, its history, its position in the industry, and its economic outlook; (5) the corporation's management; (6) the degree of control transferred with the block of stock to be valued; (7) any restriction on the transferability of the corporation's stock; (8) the period of time for which an investor must hold the subject stock to realize a sufficient

profit; (9) the corporation's redemption policy; and (10) the cost of effectuating a public offering of the stock to be valued, e.g., legal, accounting, and underwriting fees.

69 T.C.M. (CCH) 2852, 2863-2864 (1995), *aff'd* 91 F.3d 124 (3d Cir. 1996).

A marketability discount may be combined with a premium for holding a controlling interest or a discount for holding a minority interest. The marketability discount is separate from these other adjustments.

If a donor or decedent transfers a controlling interest in a business, an additional value may be assigned to the element of control. Revenue Ruling 59-60, 1959-1 C.B. 237. In recognizing that valuation of decedent's stock should include a premium because it represented a 51.8 percent voting control element, the court in Estate of Salsbury v. Commissioner stated:

> Before describing and analyzing the theories of the expert witnesses, the powers of a 51.8 percent owner should first be summarized. A 51.8 percent owner could elect the entire board of directors. A director could be removed at any time by such owner. The owner of 51.8 percent voting control, through his power to elect the entire board of directors, could control the business and affairs of Salsbury Laboratories, elect and remove all of the corporate officers, fix their salaries, and control the declaration of dividends, subject to the provisions of the Articles of Incorporation. In addition, a 51.8 percent owner, through the board, could issue the 210,000 shares of unissued class A stock to himself, upon payment of not less than $1 per share, and thus could obtain 62.7 percent voting control.

34 T.C.M. (CCH) 1441, 1451 (1975).

In Estate of Chenoweth v. Commissioner, 88 T.C. 1577 (1987), the court held that the estate was entitled to a control premium for purposes of the marital deduction. In that case the decedent owned all of the stock in the company and bequeathed 51 percent to his surviving spouse and 49 percent to his daughter by a prior marriage. Although the only issue before the court was whether a control premium could be applied to the marital deduction bequest, the court noted:

> While we would tend to agree that the sum of the parts cannot equal more than the whole — that is, the majority block together with the control premium, when added to the minority block of the company's stock with an appropriate discount for minority interest, should not equal more than the total 100 percent interest of the decedent, as reported for purposes of section 2031 — it might well turn out that the sum of the parts can equal less than the whole — that is, that the control premium which is added to the majority block passing to decedent's surviving spouse might be less than the proper minority discount to be attributed to the shares passing to decedent's daughter Kelli.

Id. at 1589-1590.

Discounts for minority interests are well recognized. The amount of the appropriate discount, like valuation itself, is a factual question and one on which experts frequently differ. Minority discounts reflect the lack of control that the owner of such an interest has over business decisions. A minority interest, however, may have such control if it represents the "swing vote," that is, if that interest can be combined with another owner to exert control. In these cases, the minority discount may be greatly diminished or a control premium may be added.

Example 3-5

Debra owned 100 percent of the stock of Family, Inc. She gave 30 percent of the stock to each of her four children and retained 10 percent of the stock. For gift tax purposes, each of the gifts will be valued separately, and the swing vote attributes of each block will be taken into account in determining the value of each gift. TAM 9436005.

For estate tax purposes, the decedent's interest must be valued because that is the interest that will be transferred as a result of death. For gift tax purposes, each gift is valued separately. After losing a number of cases, the IRS finally conceded that it will not attribute ownership by other family members in determining control premiums and minority discounts. Revenue Ruling 93-12, 1993-1 C.B. 202.

The availability of discounts for minority ownership coupled with the recognition that family interests will not be aggregated has promoted the growth of the family limited partnership, or limited liability company, as an estate planning device. In the typical family limited partnership an individual or a couple creates a partnership and transfers their assets to it, taking back both general and limited partnership interests. At the time of creation and subsequently, they transfer interests in the partnership to their children. The gifts to the children will be minority interests in the partnership, and their value will be decreased by discounts that reflect that minority status. The goal of the individual, or couple, who created the partnership is to own only a minority interest in the partnership at death. If they succeed in doing this, the value of that interest will also enjoy a minority discount. The individual, or couple, will be able to transfer assets to their children or others at significantly reduced transfer tax cost if this device is successful.

When an individual forms a family limited partnership with his children, he will be deemed to have made gifts to the children only if the partnership interests received by the individual and his children are not proportionate to the property contributed to the partnership. Shepherd v. Commissioner, 115 T.C. 376 (2000) *aff'd* 283 F.3d 1258 (11th Cir. 2002). In *Shepherd*, a father and his two sons created a partnership with the father as a 50 percent owner and each son as a 25 percent owner. The father then contributed land and stock to the partnership. Because the sons did not make proportionate contributions, the court held that the father had made gifts to the sons.

If all the partners make proportionate contributions, there will be no gifts on formation even if the value of the partnership interest is less than the value of the property transferred to the partnership. Any difference in value in this situation would be attributable to the minority and marketability discounts. Estate of Jones II v. Commissioner, 116 T.C. 121 (2001); Estate of Strangi v. Commissioner, 115 T.C. 478 (2000) *aff'd in part, rev'd in part,* 293 F.3d 279 (5th Cir. 2002).[2]

Gifts of family partnership interests, whether general partnership interests or limited partnership interests, will be valued under traditional valuation principles and may include marketability and minority discounts. Similar discounts may be applied to the estate tax valuation of family partnership interests at death. In addition, family partnership interests may be subject to restrictions. Whether or not such restrictions will affect valuation depends on the application of §§2703 and 2704, which are discussed in the next section. Although the IRS has been thwarted on many fronts in its attack on family limited partnerships, it has succeeded in including the value of such interests in the decedent's gross estate under §2036 under some circumstances.

PROBLEMS

1. Henry owns 100 percent of the stock in Family Business, Inc.
   a. Henry gives 40 percent of the stock outright to his spouse, Wanda. Henry also creates a trust for Wanda's benefit that qualifies for the marital deduction as Qualified Terminable Interest Property, and he transfers 40 percent of the stock to it. Henry also gives 5 percent of the stock to each of his four children. How will the gifts be valued?
   b. Instead, Henry dies owning all the stock. He bequeaths the property as designated in problem 1.a. How will the stock be valued for purposes of his estate?
   c. Same as 1.b., then Wanda dies. How will the stock be valued in her estate? Would it make any difference if Henry had left the stock to a trust that qualified for the marital deduction by giving Wanda a testamentary general power of appointment?
   d. Same as 1.b., except that Henry gave 60 percent of the stock to Wanda outright and gave each of his children 10 percent. How will the stock be valued for purposes of Henry's estate? How should it be valued for purposes of the marital deduction?

---

2. The Fifth Circuit reversed the Tax Court's refusal to allow the IRS leave to amend in order to argue that the decedent's partnership interest should have been included in his gross estate under §2036. The Fifth Circuit did affirm the Tax Court's decision that the partnership agreement would not be disregarded for federal income tax purposes. Estate of Strangi v. Commissioner, 293 F.3d 279 (5th Cir. 2002). On remand, the Tax Court held that the value of property transferred to the family limited partnership was included in the decedent's gross estate under §2036. Estate of Strangi v. Commissioner, 85 T.C.M. (CCH) 1331 (2003). *See* page 292.

2. Henry (from problem 1) comes to you for estate planning advice. Family Business, Inc. has a value of $5,000,000. Henry also owns investment real estate valued at $2,000,000 and a portfolio of stocks valued at $3,000,000. He and Wanda own a house, cars, and household effects. Henry wants to retire from operating Family Business, Inc.; he wants to ensure a stream of income to himself and Wanda; and he wants to pass his assets to his four children at minimal transfer tax cost.

    a. Should Henry establish a Family Limited Partnership? Why?
    b. If so, what assets should he transfer to it?
    c. What arguments might the IRS raise on incorporation? On Henry's death?
    d. What advice do you give Henry to minimize the likelihood that the IRS will succeed?
    e. Assume that Henry dies owning a 2 percent general partnership interest and a 30 percent limited partnership interest. How will those interests be valued for estate tax purposes?

3. Duane is an unmarried, U.S. citizen who has operated a sheep farm for the past 25 years. Duane owns the farmland and other farming property (equipment, sheep, etc.) in fee simple, and he operates the farm as a sole proprietor. His son, Sam, has worked for Duane for the past ten years. Duane dies, leaving all of his property to his son, Sam. Sam intends to continue to run the sheep farm as long as possible. Sam, as executor of Duane's estate, will make all the necessary elections and agreements. On the date of death, Duane's property was valued as follows:

Residence (not part of the sheep farm)	$ 150,000
Life insurance, payable to Sam	$ 250,000
Investments (stocks and bonds)	$ 100,000
Farm real property	
Highest and best use	$ 2,000,000
Use as sheep farm	$ 1,000,000
Farm personal property	$ 500,000

    Assume there are no mortgages, debts, claims, taxes, or expenses.

    a. Does Duane's estate qualify under §2032A? Explain why. If so, what is the effect?
    b. Same as a., except that Duane's investments have a value of $500,000, the farm real property has a highest and best use value of $500,000, the farm real property has a value of $200,000 for use as a sheep farm, and the farm personal property has a value of $100,000. Does the estate qualify under §2032A?
    c. What advice might you give Duane if the estate does not qualify under §2032A?
    d. Same facts as in a. What is the value of Duane's gross estate? (Consider the application of §2057.)

4. Assume that the provisions of the 2001 Tax Act have been repealed and
    that Congress has raised the exemption amount to $2,000,000. Congress
    is debating whether to revive §2057 and, if so, what the amount of the
    deduction will be. What arguments would you make in favor of retain-
    ing the section? In favor of repealing it? How would you vote? Why?

F. CHAPTER 14
IRC §§2701-2704

Taxpayers attempt to minimize their taxes through devices to freeze or
diminish the value of assets in their estates. One estate freezing device for
owners of closely held business interests involves the recapitalization of the
corporation with the older generation retaining preferred stock and giving
common stock to their descendants. If the preferred stock included sufficient
dividend, liquidation, and conversion rights, most if not all, of the value in the
company was assigned to the preferred stock. The common stock could then be
transferred at little, or no, transfer tax cost to the descendants, taking with it all
future appreciation in the value of the business. If the preferred shareholders
did not exercise their rights, additional value would shift to the common shareholders often without any transfer tax consequences. The IRS challenged this
and similar schemes on a variety of fronts but was not particularly successful.
In 1990, Congress finally enacted Chapter 14, §§2701-2704, creating special
valuation rules for transfers of certain interests in corporations, partnerships, or
trusts as well as rules governing the valuation of business interests that included
certain rights and restrictions. Sections 2701-2704 are primarily valuation rules.

Section 2701 applies to the transfer of certain business interests to members
of the transferor's family, but only if the transferor or specified family
members retain an interest in the business. The section does not apply to transfers at death, if the retained interest has market quotations readily available on
an established securities market, if the retained interest and the transferred
interest are of the same class, or if the retained interest and the transferred
interest are proportionally the same. When §2701 applies, it determines the
value of the transferred interest for gift tax purposes.

For §2701 to apply, there must be a transfer to a member of the transferor's
family. Members of the transferor's family are: the transferor's spouse, lineal
descendants of the transferor or the transferor's spouse, and spouses of such
lineal descendants. §2701(e)(1). In addition, the transferor or an applicable
family member must retain an applicable interest. Applicable family members
are the transferor's spouse, ancestors of the transferor or the transferor's spouse,
and spouses of such ancestors. §2701(e)(2). An applicable interest is a liquidation, put, call, conversion, or distribution right. Distribution rights are only
considered applicable retained interests if immediately before the transfer, the

transferor and applicable family members control the business. Control is defined as 50 percent of the stock of a corporation, determined by value or voting rights, or as 50 percent of the capital or profits interest in a partnership. §2701(b)(2). To determine control, interests of a corporation, partnership, trust, or other entity are attributed to the transferor and applicable family members. §2701(e)(3).

Section 2701 requires that any junior equity interest, *e.g.*, common stock in a corporation, have a minimum value of ten percent. §2701(a)(4). Any applicable retained interest has a value of zero unless it is a qualified payment. §2701(a)(3). A qualified payment is a dividend payable on a periodic basis at a fixed rate on cumulative preferred stock. §2701(c)(3). If there is a qualified payment, then other rights are valued as if they will be exercised to produce the lowest possible value. §2701(a)(3)(B).

Example 3-6

Father owns all the common stock in Family, Inc., which has a value of $1,000,000. He recapitalizes the corporation with common and preferred stock. He transfers the common stock to Daughter and retains the preferred stock. Section 2701 will apply to this transfer and will value the common stock at $1,000,000 unless the preferred stock is cumulative and will pay dividends at a fixed rate on a periodic basis.

If the preferred stock is cumulative and will pay dividends at a fixed rate on a periodic basis, any liquidation, put, call, or conversion rights will be valued at their lowest possible value. The common stock will have a minimum value of $100,000.

By requiring that retained distribution rights be cumulative, paid periodically, and paid at a fixed rate, §2701 attempts to prevent transferors from not enforcing their rights and thereby allowing value to shift to the other shareholders. If dividends are not paid, §2701 requires that the value of those unpaid dividends accrue to the retained preferred stock. As a result, the value of that stock will be increased if it is later given away or at the transferor's death. §2701(d). Recognizing that there may be good and sufficient business reasons for not paying dividends, even on cumulative preferred stock, §2701(d)(2)(C) provides a four-year grace period for the payment of dividends.

Section 2702 is similar in structure and purpose to §2701. It applies to transfers to members of the transferor's family where the transferor, or an applicable family member, retains an interest such as a life estate, a term of years, or a remainder. Section 2702 does not apply if the gift is incomplete, if the only property transferred is a personal residence, or if the regulations exempt the transfer because it is not inconsistent with the purposes of the section. §2702(a)(3).

For §2702 to apply, the transferor must transfer an interest to a family member, which includes the transferor's spouse, any ancestor or lineal descendant of the transferor or the transferor's spouse, a sibling of the transferor, or a spouse of any ancestor, lineal descendant, or sibling. §2702(e). This is a broader definition of family than that contained in §2701. In addition, the transferor or an applicable family member must retain an interest. Applicable family members are the transferor's spouse, an ancestor of the transferor or the transferor's spouse, or the spouse of an ancestor. §2702(a)(1). Section 2702 will apply if the transferor, or an applicable family member, retains a life estate, a term of years, a remainder, a reversion, or a power to alter, amend, or revoke. Reg. §25.2702-2(a)(4).

A retained interest will be valued at zero unless it is a qualified interest. §2702(a)(2). There are three types of qualified interests — a qualified annuity interest, a qualified unitrust interest, and a qualified remainder interest. A qualified annuity interest is an irrevocable right to a fixed amount payable at least annually. The fixed amount may be a dollar amount or a fraction or percentage of the initial fair market value of the property transferred to the trust. §2702(b)(1), Reg. §25.2702-3(b)(1). A qualified unitrust interest is an irrevocable right to receive a fixed percentage of the net fair market value of the trust assets determined annually. Like a qualified annuity interest, a qualified unitrust interest must be paid at least annually. Unlike a qualified annuity interest, the trust assets are valued each year and the stated percentage is applied to this value. §2702(b)(2), Reg. §25.2702-3(c). An annuity interest will remain the same from year to year even if the value of the trust assets fluctuate. A unitrust interest, on the other hand, will change each year as the value of the trust assets change. A qualified remainder interest must be noncontingent, and all other interests in the trust must be either qualified annuity interests or qualified unitrust interests. A qualified remainder interest may be the right to receive all or only a fractional share of the trust property. A reversion may be a qualified remainder interest if all other requirements are met. §2702(b)(3), Reg. §25.2702-3(f).

Section 2703 provides that any option, agreement, or right to acquire or use property at a price less than fair market value and any restriction on the right to sell or use property will be ignored in valuing that property. While §§2701 and 2702 only affect valuation for gift tax purposes, §2703 applies to valuation for purposes of the gift, estate, and generation-skipping transfer taxes. This section applies to any arrangement that affects the use or sale of property and is not limited to transfers between family members.

Section 2703 does not apply if all three of the following three requirements are met:

(1) The agreement restricting sale or use is a bona fide business arrangement.
(2) It is not a device to transfer property to family members for less than full and adequate consideration.
(3) Its terms are comparable to similar arrangements negotiated in an arm's-length transaction.

The regulations create a safe harbor for restrictions on interests of minority owners. If more than 50 percent of the value of the property is owned by individuals who are not members of the transferor's family and if the interests owned by these other individuals are subject to the same restriction, then the restriction on the transferor's property interest is deemed to satisfy the three-prong statutory test. Reg. §25.2703-1(b)(3). The attribution rules of regulation §25.2701-6 apply to determine the extent of the transferor's interest in the property.

Outside the regulatory safe harbor, it is difficult to qualify for the §2703(b) exception. While most restrictive agreements will be bona fide, many are designed to retain control of the business within the family. Determining what is full and adequate consideration is difficult because of the closely held nature of the business. Moreover, it is difficult to obtain information about comparable arrangements, few of which are negotiated at arm's length. Thus, while buy-sell agreements and similar restrictions will affect the owner's ability to transfer her interest, such restrictions will rarely affect the value of the property for transfer tax purposes.

Section 2704 provides that the lapse of certain rights and restrictions will be treated as a transfer and may, as a result, be subject to gift or estate tax. This section only applies to the lapse of a voting or liquidation right in a corporation or partnership and then only if the individual holding the right and her family control the entity. Section 2704 adopts the §2701 definition of control, *i.e.,* 50 percent. The amount of the transfer is the difference between the value of all interests held by the individual immediately before the lapse and the value of all interests immediately after the lapse. As a result, individuals are no longer able to transfer value in a business to the other owners by creating rights that are not meant to be exercised or that lapse on the occurrence of events, such as the individual's death.

PROBLEMS

1. Does §2701 apply in each of the following situations?
   a. Dinah owns 1,000 shares of common stock in A, Inc. There are no other shares outstanding. She recapitalizes A, Inc., receiving 1,000 shares of preferred, nonvoting stock and 1,000 shares of common voting stock.
      (1) Dinah sells the common stock to her son, Simon.
      (2) Dinah gives each of her three children 200 shares of common stock and 200 shares of preferred stock.
      (3) Dinah gives 200 shares of common stock to each of her four nieces.
   b. Ed, Frank, and Greg are brothers, and each owns 1,000 shares of common, voting stock and 2,000 shares of preferred nonvoting stock in B, Inc.
      (1) Ed transfers 500 shares of preferred stock to each of his two children.
      (2) Frank transfers his common stock to his spouse, Sally.
      (3) Greg transfers his common stock to his grandchildren.
      (4) Greg dies owning only preferred stock.
   c. What if Ed, Frank, and Greg are friends, not brothers?

2. How should the preferred stock in problem 1 be structured to minimize the transfer taxes?

3. Does §2702 apply in each of the following situations?

   a. Joan establishes an irrevocable inter vivos trust with Friendly National Bank to pay the income to herself for her life and, at her death, to distribute the trust property to her children in equal shares.

   b. Joan establishes an irrevocable inter vivos trust with Friendly National Bank to pay the income to her husband for his life and, at his death, to distribute the trust property to their children in equal shares.

   c. Joan establishes an irrevocable inter vivos trust with Friendly National Bank to pay the income to herself for ten years and, at her death, to distribute the trust property to her niece.

   d. Joan and her husband transfer their home to a trust, retaining the right to live in the house for 15 years. At the end of the 15 years, the house will belong to their daughter.

   e. Joan purchases Blackacre, undeveloped real property, by paying the entire purchase price and creating a life estate in herself and a remainder interest in her son.

   f. Joan purchases Blackacre, undeveloped real property, by paying the entire purchase price and taking title as joint tenants with the right of survivorship with her son.

   g. How would you structure the life interest in problem 3.a. to make it a qualified interest?

CHAPTER 4

Calculation of the Gift and Estate Taxes

A. GENERAL PRINCIPLES

Prior to 1976, the gift tax and the estate tax were separate and distinct taxes, and there was no generation-skipping transfer tax. 1976, Congress unified these two taxes by enacting one rate schedule that applies to both the gift and the estate taxes and one unified credit.[1] The same year, Congress also enacted a generation-skipping transfer tax, but only ten years later repealed this tax and enacted a substantially different generation-skipping transfer tax. Calculation of the generation-skipping transfer tax is described in Chapter 18. In 2001, Congress repealed the estate and generation-skipping transfer taxes, but retained the gift tax. Congress, however, delayed the effective date of the repeal to January 1, 2010. During the transition period, the rate structure for the estate and gift tax will remain unified, with the maximum rate decreasing gradually to 45 percent in 2007. The applicable credit amounts will, however, no longer be unified. Beginning in 2002, the gift tax exemption amount will be $1,000,000 while the estate tax exemption amount will increase from $1,000,000 for decedents dying in 2002 to $3,500,000 for decedents dying in 2009. In 2010, the estate tax is repealed, and the maximum tax rate for inter vivos gifts will be 35 percent. The amendments made by the 2001 Tax Act do not extend beyond 2010. As a result, the rate structure is scheduled to revert to a 55 percent maximum rate, and the estate tax applicable exemption amount will diminish to $1,000,000 in 2011.

This chapter describes the calculation of the estate and gift taxes under three different scenarios. Section B describes calculation of the tax under a unified system, where the rates and the applicable exemption amounts are identical for the gift and estate taxes. This structure applies to years 1976 through 2003 and again beginning in 2011, assuming there are no further amendments to the gift and estate taxes. Section C describes the transition period of 2004 through

---

1. Sections 2010 and 2505 now refer to "the applicable credit amount" rather than "the unified credit."

2009, when the exemption amounts diverge. Section D describes the year 2010, when the gift tax has a maximum rate of 35 percent and the estate tax is repealed.

The following overview of the gift and estate taxes is necessary to understand the sample calculations in this chapter. The gift tax is imposed only on transactions where the donor has given up dominion and control over the property and received nothing in return. Transfers to political and charitable organizations, transfers to spouses, and transfers for medical expenses or education are excluded from the gift tax. §§2501(a)(5), 2503(e), 2522, 2523. In addition, each donor can transfer $11,000 each year to as many recipients as he desires before using up the exemption amount.[2] Finally, the donor will not actually pay any gift tax until his taxable transfers exceed the $1,000,000 applicable exemption amount. §2505.

The federal estate tax begins with a calculation of the gross estate, which includes:

Property owned at death	§2033
Certain gifts made within three years of death	§2035(a)
Gift tax paid on gifts within three years of death	§2035(b)
Property over which the decedent retained an income interest or the right to designate beneficiaries	§2036
Revocable transfers	§2038
Joint tenancy property	§2040
Property over which the decedent had a general power of appointment	§2041
Life insurance owned by the decedent	§2042
Qualified Terminable Interest Property	§2044

To compute the taxable estate, deductions are allowed for:

Expenses, claims against the estate, and certain taxes	§2053
Charitable transfers	§2055
Transfers to a surviving spouse	§2056

The estate tax is computed on the taxable estate, increased by the amount of adjusted taxable gifts. Adjusted taxable gifts are all the taxable gifts made during life that are not otherwise included in the gross estate. §2001. The amount of any gift tax paid is then subtracted, §2001(b)(2). Credits against the estate tax include:

Unified credit	§2010
Credit for state death taxes	§2011
Credit for certain "prior transfers"	§2013

---

2. Section 2503(b) provides for a gift tax annual exclusion of $10,000 to be adjusted periodically for inflation. The first inflation adjustment, to $11,000, became effective for 2002. Rev. Proc. 2001-59, 2001-2 C.B. 623 (2001).

B. SAMPLE CALCULATIONS: A UNIFIED TRANSFER TAX SYSTEM
IRC §§2001, 2010, 2502, 2503(b), 2505

Since 1976, the gift and estate taxes have been a truly unified transfer tax system. Most transfers are subject to only one tax.[3] The same rate schedule in §2001 applies to taxable gifts and the taxable estate. §§2001, 2502. And there is one applicable credit amount. §§2010, 2505. The applicable credit is just that — a credit against the tax. As such, it reduces the amount of tax owed rather than the amount of taxable gifts or the taxable estate. It operates as a zero bracket amount, that is, the amount that may be transferred without paying any tax. Most people, however, do not refer to the applicable credit amount, but to the amount of property sheltered by this credit, *i.e.*, the applicable exemption amount.

All taxable transfers are cumulative. That is, once the taxpayer begins making taxable gifts, the first gift is taxed, at least in part, at the lowest rates in §2001.[4] The next gift is taxed at a higher rate, and so on. Section 2502 ensures this by requiring the taxpayer to calculate a tentative tax on the aggregate sum of taxable gifts made during the current and all prior years. The taxpayer then subtracts the tentative tax on the aggregate sum of taxable gifts made in prior tax years. The result is the gift tax due on the taxable gifts in the current year.

Example 4-1

Assume that Dan has not made any taxable gifts before the current year, that he has already made gifts equal to the gift tax annual exclusion amount in the current year,[5] and that he then makes a taxable gift of $1,250,000 in the current year. Assume further that the applicable exemption amount is $1,000,000 and the maximum rate of tax in §2001(c) is 50 percent.

The gift tax is calculated under §2502 on the $1,250,000, using the rates in §2001(c). Then the applicable credit amount is subtracted. §2505. The applicable credit amount is $345,800, *i.e.*, the amount of tax on $1,000,000. The tax due is:

Taxable gift	$1,250,000	
Tentative tax on taxable gift		$448,300
Applicable credit amount		$345,800
Tax due		$102,500

---

3. There are a few exceptions to this. For example, if the decedent purchases property with someone other than his surviving spouse as joint tenants with the right of survivorship and the decedent pays the entire purchase price, the value of the joint tenancy given to the other person will be taxed as a completed gift, and the entire value of the property will be in the decedent's gross estate pursuant to §2040(a).

4. Actually, no gifts are taxed until the taxpayer has exceeded the applicable exemption amount. *See* §§2502, 2505. Once the taxpayer has exceeded this amount, gifts are taxed beginning at the 41 percent rate.

5. *See* Chapter 7 for a discussion of the gift tax annual exclusion.

Dan then makes another taxable gift in the following year of $1,250,000. Section 2502 ensures that this second gift will incur a higher tax by requiring that all prior taxable gifts be added to the current taxable gifts. A tentative tax is then calculated on the aggregate taxable gifts. To determine the tax on the second gift, the tax on the prior gift is then subtracted. Using this process, the gift tax on Dan's second gift of $1,250,000 is $577,500, calculated as follows:

Prior taxable gifts	$1,250,000	
Current taxable gifts	$1,250,000	
Aggregate taxable gifts	$2,500,000	
Tentative tax on aggregate taxable gifts		$1,025,800
Tentative tax on prior taxable gifts		$ 448,300
Tax on current taxable gifts		$ 577,500

Dan is not allowed any applicable credit amount for this second gift, because the full amount of the credit had been used on the prior taxable gift.

Notice that the gift tax, even before application of the credit, is higher in the second year than in the first year even though the gifts were equal in value. Section 2502 requires the taxpayer to use increasingly higher rates of tax once he begins making taxable gifts, *i.e.*, those over the $11,000 annual exclusion amount.

This same concept applies to the estate tax.

Example 4-2

Now assume Dan dies with a taxable estate of $2,500,000. Section 2001 ensures that the taxpayer will pay a higher rate of tax because of the prior $2,500,000 taxable gifts than a decedent who had not made taxable gifts and dies with a taxable estate of $2,500,000. This result occurs because §2001 requires the inclusion of adjusted taxable gifts in the calculation of the tax.

Taxable estate	$2,500,000	
Adjusted taxable gifts	$2,500,000	
Total	$5,000,000	
Tax on $5,000,000		$2,275,800
Less gift tax paid		$ 680,000
Less applicable credit amount		$ 345,800
Estate tax due		$1,250,000

Notice that the estate tax paid, $1,250,000, is more than the gift tax paid on the same amount of taxable gifts even without subtracting the applicable credit amount, *i.e.*, the tentative tax on the $2,500,000 aggregate of taxable gifts was $1,025,800. This difference occurs because there is one progressive rate schedule that is applied to the cumulative amount of taxable transfers, whether occurring during life or at death.

Example 4-3

Now compare Dan with Debra, who made no taxable gifts and also had a taxable estate of $2,500,000. Debra's estate tax is calculated as follows:

Taxable estate	$2,500,000
Adjusted taxable gifts	$ 0
Total	$2,500,000
Tax on $2,500,000	$1,025,800
Less applicable credit amount	$ 345,800
Estate tax due	$ 680,000

There are two things to notice. First, Dan paid significantly more estate tax than Debra because of his prior taxable gifts. Second, Debra's estate tax ($680,000) is exactly the same as Dan's total gift tax paid, *i.e.*, $102,500 plus $577,500.

Notice that Dan's estate is allowed to subtract the amount of gift tax actually paid. This is necessary because the tentative tax of $2,275,800 is calculated on an amount that includes his taxable gifts. For the same reason, §2010 allows the estate to subtract the applicable credit amount even if it has been used to shelter lifetime gifts. If §2010 did not allow this, the decedent's estate would pay a tax on those gifts at the time of death.

Example 4-4

To demonstrate this, compare Dan's estate tax with the estate tax of David, who had a taxable estate of $5,000,000 but who did not make any taxable gifts during his lifetime. David will pay a tax calculated as follows:

Taxable estate	$5,000,000
Adjusted taxable gifts	$ 0
Total	$5,000,000
Tax on $5,000,000	$2,275,800
Less applicable credit amount	$345,800
Estate tax due	$1,930,000

Notice that the total amount of tax paid is the same for Dan and David. David paid $1,930,000 as an estate tax, while Dan paid an estate tax of $1,250,000 plus a gift tax of $102,500 on the first taxable gift and $577,500 on the second taxable gift, for a grand total of $1,930,000. Had Dan not been allowed to deduct the applicable credit amount and the amount of gift tax paid from the tentative estate tax, he would have ended up paying a total tax of $3,301,600 ($2,275,800 plus $680,000 plus $345,800), far more than David.

Remember:

(1) the gift tax and the estate tax are one unified system so that it does not matter whether the taxpayer transfers property during life or at death;

(2) there is only one applicable credit amount that will shelter $1 million from the transfer tax whether the transfers occur during life or at death; and

(3) once the taxpayer begins making taxable transfers, the taxpayer is taxed at an increasingly higher rate.

Congress did not attempt to unify the generation-skipping transfer tax with either the gift or the estate tax. The tax rate on generation-skipping transfers is the maximum estate tax rate, and there is a separate $1 million exemption amount for this tax. The calculation of the generation-skipping transfer tax and its relationship to the gift tax and the estate tax are described in Chapter 18.

PROBLEMS

Prior to 2002, the amount of the gift tax annual exclusion was $10,000. For purposes of these problems, assume that all the gifts were made prior to 2002 and thus the annual exclusion amount was $10,000. Assume that each person died in 2002, when the maximum estate tax rate was still 50 percent and the applicable exemption amount was $1,000,000. The estate tax on $1,000,000 is $345,800.

1. Debra makes annual gifts of $10,000 to each of her two children for many years. Debra dies in 2002 owning property valued at $1,600,000. Her estate claims expenses and deductions of $100,000. Calculate the federal estate tax due.

2. David makes annual gifts of $10,000 to each of his two children for many years. In 2001, David made gifts of $250,000 to each of his children in addition to his annual $10,000 gifts. David died in 2002 owning property valued at $1,100,000. His estate claims expenses and deductions of $100,000. Calculate the gift and estate taxes due.

3. In 1999, Doris gave her daughter, Ann, $260,000 cash. In 2000, Doris gave her son, Bob, $510,000 cash. In 2001, Doris gave her daughter, Ann, $510,000 cash and her son, Bob, $260,000 cash. In 2002, Doris died. At the time of her death she owned property valued at $990,000. Her estate claims expenses and deductions of $200,000. Calculate the gift and estate taxes due. Note that §2035(b) includes in the gross estate the amount of gift taxes paid on gifts made within three years of death.

4. In 1998, Donald established an irrevocable trust to pay the income to himself for his life and the remainder to Ellen (who is unrelated). (Assume that the value of the remainder interest is $500,000 at the time of the gift.) In 1999, Donald purchased Blackacre by paying the full purchase price of $520,000 in cash and taking title as joint tenants with the right of survivorship with Fred. (Assume that the value of Fred's interest is 50 percent of the total value.) In 2000, Donald gave Ellen $510,000 cash. In 2001, Donald gave Fred $760,000 cash. Donald dies in 2002. At that time the joint tenancy property has a fair market value of $600,000. The trust corpus has a value of $1,300,000. Donald also

owns other property valued at $1,665,000. His estate claims expenses and deductions of $250,000. Calculate the gift and estate taxes due.

C. SAMPLE CALCULATIONS: 2004-2009
IRC §§2001, 2010, 2502, 2503(b), 2505

During the years 2004-2009, the calculation of the gift tax and the estate tax remains the same as in prior years but with two differences. First, the gift tax and estate tax applicable exemption amounts will differ. The gift tax exemption amount will remain at $1,000,000. (This is equivalent to a credit amount of $345,800.) The estate tax exemption amount in §2010 will increase as follows:

Year	Applicable Exemption Amount
2004 and 2005	$1,500,000
2006, 2007, and 2008	$2,000,000
2009	$3,500,000

Second, the maximum tax rate in §2001 will decrease as follows:

Year	Maximum Tax Rate
2002	50 percent
2003	49 percent
2004	48 percent
2005	47 percent
2006	46 percent
2007, 2008, and 2009	45 percent

The Secretary of the Treasury is to publish tax rate tables incorporating these new maximum rates. In the absence of these tables, assume that beginning in 2003 the maximum rate will apply to taxable estates of $2,000,000 and greater until the year 2007. Beginning in 2007, assume that the maximum rate will apply to taxable estates of $1,500,000 and greater.

The examples that follow are the same as in section B.

Example 4-5

Dan makes a taxable gift of $1,250,000 in 2006. The gift tax continues to be calculated under §§2001 and 2502 as follows:

Taxable gift	$1,250,000
Tax on taxable gift	$448,300
Applicable credit amount	$345,800
Tax due	$102,500

Dan makes another taxable gift in 2007 of $1,250,000. The tax on this gift is $557,500, calculated as follows:

Prior taxable gifts	$1,250,000
Current taxable gifts	$1,250,000
Aggregate taxable gifts	$2,500,000
Tentative tax on aggregate taxable gifts	$ 555,800
	+ $1,000,000
	× .45
	$ 450,000
	$1,005,800
Less tentative tax on prior taxable gifts	$ 448,300
Tax on current taxable gifts	$ 557,500

There is no applicable credit amount available for the second gift because the full amount of the credit had been used on the prior taxable gift. Dan is now paying $20,000 less in gift taxes because of the decrease in the maximum marginal rate.

Example 4-6

Now assume Dan dies in 2008 with a taxable estate of $2,500,000. His taxable estate includes the $660,000 of gift tax paid because of §2035(b).[6] Remember that §2001 requires that the donor's taxable gifts be added to the amount of the taxable estate prior to calculation of the tax.

Taxable estate	$2,500,000
Adjusted taxable gifts	$2,500,000
Total	$5,000,000
Tax on $5,000,000	$ 555,800
	+ $3,500,000
	× .45
	$1,575,000
	$2,130,800
Less gift tax paid	$ 660,000
Less applicable credit amount	$ 780,800
Estate tax due	$ 690,000

Example 4-7

Debra, on the other hand, had a taxable estate of $5,000,000 but did not make any taxable gifts during her lifetime. Debra's estate tax is calculated as follows:

Taxable estate	$5,000,000
Adjusted taxable gifts	$ 0

---

6. *See* Chapter 10, section F for a discussion of §2035(b).

Total	$5,000,000	
Tax on $5,000,000		$2,130,800
Less applicable credit amount		$ 780,800
Estate tax due		$1,350,000

Notice that the total amount of tax paid is the same for both Dan and Debra. While Debra paid $1,350,000 as an estate tax, Dan paid an estate tax of $690,000 plus a gift tax of $102,500 on the first taxable gift and $557,500 on the second taxable gift, for a total of $1,350,000.

Dan and Debra are now paying less total transfer taxes because of the decrease in the maximum rate of tax.

PROBLEMS

1. Debra dies in 2008 with a taxable estate of $6,000,000. Calculate the estate tax due.
2. David makes taxable gifts in 2006 of $2,000,000. He makes taxable gifts in 2007 of $2,000,000. He dies in 2008 with a taxable estate of $2,000,000. (Assume that the taxable estate includes the gift taxes paid.) Calculate the estate and gift taxes due.

D. SAMPLE CALCULATIONS: 2010
IRC §§2001, 2010, 2502, 2503(b), 2505

The estate tax is repealed for the year 2010. The gift tax will remain in place, and the maximum rate of tax will be 35 percent. For the year 2010, §2502 provides a gift tax rate table with graduated rates of 18 percent to 35 percent. The 35 percent rate, however, is effective for taxable gifts of $500,000. This means that there will be a flat rate of tax on the amount of taxable gifts that exceed the applicable exemption amount, which is $1,000,000. The gift tax attributable to this amount is $330,800.

Example 4-8

Del makes a taxable gift of $500,000 in the year 2010. Assume that Del has not made any prior taxable gifts. The gift tax is:

Taxable gift	$500,000
Tentative tax	$155,800
Less applicable credit amount	$330,800
Gift tax due	$ 0

If Del made a taxable gift of $1,000,000 in 2010, no tax would be due because the gift tax exemption amount is $1,000,000. Del will owe a gift tax only when his taxable gifts exceed this amount.

The estate tax is repealed for decedents dying in the year 2010. It makes no sense for a donor who might die in that year to make taxable gifts. Doing so means paying gift tax unnecessarily. If, however, the rates in effect before the 2001 Tax Act was passed return for tax years beginning after 2010, there will be a strong incentive to make taxable gifts in 2010. These rates that are scheduled to return in 2011 are much higher than the gift tax rates that will be effective in 2010.

Example 4-9

Assume that Doris has made no prior taxable gifts and then makes taxable gifts of $5,000,000 in 2010. Her gift tax will be:

Taxable gift	$5,000,000
Tentative tax	$ 155,800
	+ $5,000,000
	− 500,000
	$4,500,000
	× .35
	$1,575,000
	$1,730,800
Less applicable credit amount	$ 330,800
Gift tax due	$1,400,000

Now assume that the rate schedule that existed before the 2001 Tax Act was passed is reinstated and that Doris waits and makes taxable gifts of $5,000,000 in 2011. The gift tax would be:

Taxable gift	$5,000,000
Tentative tax	$1,290,800
	+ $5,000,000
	− 3,000,000
	$2,000,000
	× .55
	$1,100,000
	$2,390,800
Less applicable credit amount	$ 345,800
Gift tax due	$2,045,000

The effective tax rate on the gift in 2010 is only 28 percent, while it is 41 percent on the same gift in 2011.

There is no estate tax in 2010. For decedents dying in that year, however, the transferred basis rules of §1022 will apply. These rules were explained in section C of Chapter 2.

PROBLEMS

1. Doris makes taxable gifts in 2010 of $2,000,000. Calculate the gift tax due.

2. Donald dies in 2010. He had make no taxable gifts during his lifetime. At the time of his death he owns stocks that had an adjusted basis of $500,000 and a fair market value of $2,000,000. His will leaves all his property to his son, Sam. What are the tax consequences?

PART II

Taxation of Gifts

CHAPTER 5

The Definition of a Gift

A. GENERAL PRINCIPLES
IRC §§102, 2501, 2511, 2512

Everyone knows what a gift is. It is something you receive from family or friends on your birthday, a holiday, or a special occasion. For purposes of a gift tax, this definition is inadequate. It is too narrow because it excludes some transactions that should be taxed as gifts, and, at the same time, it is too broad because it includes some transactions that should not be taxed as gifts. The law requires a precise definition before imposing a tax. Without an explicit definition taxpayers can neither plan transactions nor report them appropriately. Definition is also necessary so the government can assess and collect the tax effectively and efficiently.

The common law test of "donative intent" is not sufficient. This test is highly subjective and would allow similar transactions to be taxed differently, depending on the taxpayer's proof of motive at the time of the transaction as well as the identity of the fact finder. It would also require significant administrative and judicial resources to make case by case determinations, and it would provide little guidance to taxpayers in planning and reporting their transactions.

Given the importance of a definition, one would expect the Internal Revenue Code to provide one. Unfortunately, it does not. While §2501 imposes a tax on "the transfer of property by gift," it does not even purport to define the term "gift." It does limit the imposition of the tax to "transfers" of "property," both of which are important limitations on the reach of the gift tax. These terms do not, however, supply the required definition. That job is left to §2512, which is entitled "Valuation of Gifts" and which provides: "[w]here property is transferred for less than an adequate and full consideration in money or money's worth, then the amount by which the value of the property exceeded the value of the consideration shall be deemed a gift."

This definition differs from that used for income tax purposes. In Commissioner v. Duberstein, 363 U.S. 278, 285 (1960), the Court defined a gift for purposes of §102 as a transfer that arises from "detached and disinterested generosity" or from "affection, respect, admiration, charity, or like impulses." This income tax definition focuses on the donor's intent, a factor that is of secondary importance in the gift tax. For purposes of the gift tax, the primary consideration is a comparison values — what the donor gave up versus what the donor received.

The gift tax is also imposed on the transfer of property by the donor rather than on receipt of the property by the donee. It is measured by the value of what the donor has given away, and the donee need not even be identified at the time of the transfer. Reg. §25.2511-2(a).

B. BUSINESS TRANSACTIONS
IRC §§2511, 2512

A gift occurs when the transferor receives less than adequate and full consideration in money or money's worth. Determining whether the transferor has received adequate consideration depends on the value of the property transferred as well as the value of the consideration received. Valuation depends on all the facts and circumstances and can be difficult to establish for assets that are not bought and sold regularly in an established market. The regulations provide a safe harbor for business transactions, defined as "a transaction that is bona fide, at arm's length, and free from donative intent." Reg. §25.2512-8.

Estate of Anderson v. Commissioner
8 T.C. 706 (1947)

[Taxpayers, senior executives, transferred common stock in a corporation to certain junior executives in accordance with a plan to change stockholdings among the management group as responsibilities shifted. The Commissioner determined gift tax deficiencies of approximately $870,000.]

ARUNDELL, Judge:

At the threshold we are met with the question of whether the sales of stock by Anderson and Clayton to the six individuals actively engaged in the Anderson-Clayton business enterprise are in any event subject to gift tax. Respondent concedes that these sales were bona fide and at arm's length; but he contends that they were not made in the ordinary course of business, that the value of the stock was greater than the value of the consideration received, and that the excess is therefore taxable as a gift under §2512(b). . . .

The first issue therefore reduces itself to the question of whether the sales of common stock of corporation were "made in the ordinary course of business." Petitioners contend that the sales were so made. They argue that, while donative intent may not be material in determining whether a gift has been made, the presence or absence of donative intent is an important circumstance in determining whether a sale or other disposition of property is made in the ordinary course of a business as "a transaction which is bona fide, at arm's length, and free from any donative intent."

For the purposes of deciding the first issue thus raised, we shall assume that the stock had a value in excess of the consideration.

All the sales of stock were made pursuant to what was essentially a profit-sharing plan. Profit participation by the active management was a common practice in the cotton merchandising business generally. The evidence makes clear that cotton merchandising is primarily a management business and one of the most difficult and complex merchandising operations in the world, and that the success of the business is dependent, by and large, upon efficient and well trained management having long experience in all phases of cotton merchandising.

Prior to the organization of [the] corporation, Clayton, Fleming and Whittington held profit sharing or commission contracts with [the] association which yielded them large annual returns and removed considerable cash from the business. When [the] corporation was organized, its common stock was substituted for the profit sharing contracts, and that had the two-fold effect of keeping cash in the business as invested capital and compelling the executives to acquire a proprietary interest in the business. From the beginning, the common stock of [the] corporation was designed to be held only by persons actively engaged in the Anderson-Clayton business enterprise. Clayton and Anderson were the holders of the largest equities in the business, and the real value of their large investments in preferred stock could be maintained and preserved only by a continued efficient management. In order to build up a responsible management which could continue the business in the event of the retirement or death of Anderson or Clayton, they believed it essential that the junior executives acquire proprietary interests in the business and that such proprietary interests should grow in proportion to the shifting of responsibilities from the seniors to the juniors.

And so the plan was put into operation upon the organization of [the] corporation. All the common stockholders understood that the relative proportions of their holdings would change from time to time as responsibilities were shifted from the older to the younger executives. At the beginning of each cotton season it was customary to reexamine the management situation and the relative contributions to management on the part of the several executives and to determine what readjustments, if any, in the relative ownership of common stock should be made. All the sales of common stock here in issue, as well as other sales not in issue, were made pursuant to the agreement between [the] corporation and all the common stockholders, all of whom were actively engaged in the business. Under that agreement a method was provided for determining annually . . . a price at which transfers of the common stock should be made. . . . It was contemplated not only that Clayton and Anderson would sell some of their common stock from time to time to their juniors, but also that as the latter should pass the peak of responsibility, they in turn would sell part of their holdings to their juniors who were taking on more responsibility. In other words, the common stock was designed not to be marketable, but to be held in direct proportion to the active participation of each stockholder in the business enterprise.

It is obvious from all these circumstances that the sales of common stock were motivated by the peculiar importance of expert and continuous management to the cotton merchandising business. They were intended to preserve or augment the value of the estates of Clayton and Anderson, as well as to relieve them of obligations to corporation. . . . There was no intent on the part of Anderson and Clayton in selling the stock to confer, nor intent on the part of their vendees to receive, gratuitous benefits. Clearly, then, these transactions were not gifts in any ordinary sense of the word.

In contending that the sales of stock were not "made in the ordinary course of business," respondent's position appears to be that it was neither ordinary for Anderson and Clayton nor ordinary for business men in general to enter into transactions of the type here involved. We do not agree. On the contrary, it is apparent from the numerous occasions on which Clayton and Anderson sold common stock to their junior executives, both those in issue and others not in issue, that it was a quite customary and ordinary thing for them to do. The record also proves that profit sharing or participation among the active management was quite the ordinary and customary practice in the cotton merchandising business generally. Furthermore, from facts within the range of judicial knowledge, we know that nothing is more ordinary, as business is conducted in this country, than profit-sharing arrangements and plans for the acquisition of proprietary interests by junior executives or junior partners, often for inadequate consideration, if consideration is to be measured solely in terms of money or something reducible to a money value. . . .

The pertinent inquiry for gift tax purposes is whether the transaction is a genuine business transaction, as distinguished, for example from the marital or family type of transaction involved in *Wemyss* and its companion case, Merrill v. Fahs, 324 U.S. 308. Surely it will not be said that there may not be a genuine business transaction not directly connected with the taxpayer's trade or business or even though the taxpayer be not engaged in "carrying on any trade or business," within the scope of that term as limited by Higgins v. Commissioner, 312 U.S. 212. Bad bargains, sales for less than market, sales for less than adequate consideration in money or money's worth are made every day in the business world, for one reason or another; but no one would think for a moment that any gift is involved, even in the broadest possible sense of the term "gift.". . .

We have found that the sales of stock in issue were bona fide and made at arm's length, in the ordinary course of business. Therefore, assuming, without deciding, that the value of the stock was greater than the value of the consideration, we hold that the transfers are not subject to gift tax.

PROBLEMS

1. Ann transfers ten shares of stock in XYZ, Inc. to Brad. Ann purchased the ten shares of stock for $1,000 (the adjusted basis); at the time of the transfer the stock has a fair market value of $25,000.
   a. Has Ann made a gift? If so, what is the amount of the gift?
   b. What if Ann sells the stock to Brad for $10,000?
2. Car Dealer sells Customer a car listed at $35,000 for $23,000.
   a. Has Car Dealer made a gift? If so, what is the amount of the gift?
   b. What are the gift tax consequences if Car Dealer is Customer's parent?
3. Allison, Bert, Carol, and Dan are the sole shareholders of Widgett Manufacturing, Inc. Each owns 1,000 shares of common stock and 1,000 shares of preferred stock.
   a. Allison transfers Blackacre, which has a fair market value of $100,000, to Widgett Manufacturing, Inc. Has Allison made a gift? If so, what is the amount of the gift?
   b. Allison retires from the business and sells all of her shares to the corporation pursuant to a preexisting agreement for $350,000. Has she made a gift?
   c. What if the IRS establishes that the fair market value of the stock was $500,000?
   d. Instead, Allison, Bert, Carol, and Dan each sell 100 shares of common stock to Ellen and 100 shares of common stock to Frank pursuant to a preexisting agreement. Each sale of 100 shares is for $20,000. Have they made gifts?
   e. What if the IRS claims that the fair market value of each block of 100 shares of stock is $35,000?
   f. Does it matter who Ellen and Frank are? Does it matter what the reason for the sale is?
4. Why is there a separate definition of a gift in regulation §25.2512-8?

C. ADEQUATE AND FULL CONSIDERATION
IRC §2512

Section 2512(b) defines a gift as a transfer of property for less than an adequate and full consideration in money or money's worth. It is relatively easy to determine if any monetary consideration received by the transferor is equal to the value of the transferred property once that value has been determined. A problem, however, arises when the transferor receives something other than money.

Commissioner v. Wemyss
324 U.S. 303 (1945)

Mr. Justice FRANKFURTER delivered the opinion of the Court.

In 1939 taxpayer proposed marriage to Mrs. More, a widow with one child. Her deceased husband had set up two trusts . . . with provision that, in the event of Mrs. More's remarriage, her part of the income ceased and went to the child. . . . On Mrs. More's unwillingness to suffer loss of her trust income through remarriage the parties on May 24, 1939, entered upon an agreement whereby taxpayer transferred to Mrs. More a block of shares of stock. Within a month they married. The Commissioner ruled that the transfer of this stock, the value of which, $149,456.13, taxpayer does not controvert, was subject to the Federal Gift Tax. . . . Accordingly, he assessed a deficiency which the Tax Court upheld, 2 T.C. 876, but the Circuit Court of Appeals reversed the Tax Court, 144 F.2d 78. We granted certiorari. . . .

In view of the major role which the Tax Court plays in federal tax litigation, it becomes important to consider how that court dealt with this problem. Fusing, as it were, [§§2501(a) and 2512(b)], the Tax Court read them as not being limited by any common law technical notions about "consideration." And so, while recognizing that marriage was of course a valuable consideration to support a contract, the Tax Court did not deem marriage to satisfy the requirement of [§2512(b)] in that it was not a consideration reducible to money value. Accordingly, the Court found the whole value of the stock transferred to Mrs. More taxable under the statute and the relevant Treas. Reg. [§25.2512-8]: "A consideration not reducible to a money value, as love and affection, promise of marriage, etc., is to be wholly disregarded, and the entire value of the property transferred constitutes the amount of the gift." In the alternative, the Tax Court was of the view that if Mrs. More's loss of her trust income rather than the marriage was consideration for the taxpayer's transfer of his stock to her, he is not relieved from the tax because he did not receive any money's worth from Mrs. More's relinquishment of her trust income, and, in any event, the actual value of her interest in the trust, subject to fluctuations of its stock earnings, was not proved. . . . The Circuit Court of Appeals rejected this line of reasoning. It found in the marriage agreement an arm's length bargain and an absence of "donative intent" which it deemed essential: "A donative intent followed by a donative act is essential to constitute a gift; and no strained and artificial construction of a supplementary statute should be indulged to tax as a gift a transfer actually lacking donative intent."

Sections [2501(a) and 2512(b)] are not disparate provisions. Congress directed them to the same purpose, and they should not be separated in application. Had Congress taxed "gifts" simpliciter, it would be appropriate to assume that the term was used in its colloquial sense, and a search for "donative intent" would be indicated. But Congress intended to use the term "gifts" in its broadest and most comprehensive sense. Congress chose not to require an ascertainment of what too often is an elusive state of mind. For purposes of the gift tax it not only dispensed with the test of "donative intent." It formulated a much more workable external test, that where "property is transferred for less than an adequate and full consideration in money or money's worth," the excess in such money value "shall, for the purpose of the tax imposed by this title, be deemed a gift. . . ." And Treasury Regulations have emphasized that common law considerations were not embodied in the gift tax.

To reinforce the evident desire of Congress to hit all the protean arrangements which the wit of man can devise that are not business transactions within the meaning of ordinary speech, the Treasury Regulations make clear that no genuine business transaction comes within the purport of the gift tax by excluding "a sale, exchange, or other transfer of property made in the ordinary course of business (a transaction which is bona fide, at arm's length, and free from any donative intent)." Treas. Reg. [§25.2512-8]. Thus on finding that a transfer in the circumstances of a particular case is not made in the ordinary course of business, the transfer becomes subject to the gift tax to the extent that it is not made "for an adequate and full consideration in money or money's worth." . . .

The Tax Court in effect found the transfer of the stock to Mrs. More was not made at arm's length in the ordinary course of business. It noted that the inducement was marriage, took account of the discrepancy between what she got and what she gave up, and also of the benefit that her marriage settlement brought to her son. These were considerations the Tax Court could justifiably heed, and heeding, decide as it did.

If we are to isolate as an independently reviewable question of law the view of the Tax Court that money consideration must benefit the donor to relieve a transfer by him from being a gift, we think the Tax court was correct. . . . The section taxing as gifts transfers that are not made for "adequate and full (money) consideration" aims to reach those transfers which are withdrawn from the donor's estate. To allow detriment to the donee to satisfy the requirement of "adequate and full consideration" would violate the purpose of the statute and open wide the door for evasion of the gift tax. . . . Reversed.

Merrill v. Fahs
324 U.S. 308 (1945)

Mr. Justice FRANKFURTER delivered the opinion of the Court.

On March 7, 1939, taxpayer, the petitioner, made an antenuptial agreement with Kinta Desmare. Taxpayer, a resident of Florida, had been twice married and had three children and two grandchildren. He was a man of large resources, with cash and securities worth more than $5,000,000, and Florida real estate valued at $135,000. Miss Desmare's assets were negligible. By the arrangement entered into the day before their marriage, taxpayer agreed to set up within ninety days after marriage an irrevocable trust for $300,000, the provisions of which were to conform to Miss Desmare's wishes. The taxpayer was also to provide in his will for two additional trusts, one, likewise in the amount of $300,000, to contain the same limitations as the inter vivos trust, and the other, also in the amount of $300,000, for the benefit of their surviving children. In return Miss Desmare released all rights that she might acquire as wife or widow in taxpayer's property, both real and personal, excepting the right to maintenance and support. The inducements for this agreement were stated to be the contemplated marriage, desire to make fair requital for the release of marital rights, freedom for the taxpayer to make appropriate provisions for his children and other dependents, the uncertainty surrounding his financial future and marital tranquillity. That such an antenuptial agreement is enforceable in Florida is not disputed . . . nor that Florida gives a wife an inchoate interest in all the husband's property, contingent during his life but absolute upon death. . . . The parties married, and the agreement was fully carried out.

On their gift tax return for 1939, both reported the creation of the trust but claimed that no tax was due. The Commissioner, however, determined a deficiency of $99,000 in taxpayer's return in relation to the transfer of the $300,000. . . . The District Court sustained the taxpayer, . . . but was reversed by the Circuit Court of Appeals for the Fifth Circuit. . . . We granted certiorari in connection with Commissioner v. Wemyss, *supra*, and heard the two cases together. . . .

Taxpayer claims that Miss Desmare's relinquishment of her marital rights constituted "adequate and full consideration in money or money's worth." The Collector, relying on the construction of a like phrase in the estate tax, contends that release of marital rights does not furnish such "adequate and full consideration.". . . The guiding light is what was said in Estate of Sanford v. Commissioner, 308 U.S. 39, 44: "The gift tax was supplementary to the estate tax. The two are in pari materia and must be construed together." The phrase on the meaning of which decision must largely turn — that is, transfers for other than "an adequate and full consideration in money or money's worth" — came into the gift tax by way of estate tax provisions. It first appeared in the Revenue Act of 1926. Section 303(a)(1) of that Act . . . allowed deductions from the value of the gross estate of claims against the estate to the extent that they were bona fide and incurred "for an adequate and full consideration in money or money's worth." It is important to note that the language of previous Acts which made the test "fair consideration" was thus changed after courts had given "fair consideration" an expansive construction.

The first modern estate tax law had included in the gross estate transfers in contemplation of, or intended to take effect in possession or enjoyment at, death, except "a bona fide sale for a fair consideration in money or money's worth." Dower rights and other marital property rights were intended to be included in the gross estate since they were considered merely an expectation, and in 1918 Congress specifically included them. This provision was for the purpose of clarifying the existing law. In 1924 Congress limited deductible claims against an estate to those supported by "a fair consideration in money or money's worth," employing the same standard applied to transfers in contemplation of death. Similar language was used in the gift tax, first imposed by the 1924 Act, by providing, "Where property is sold or exchanged for less than a fair consideration in money or money's worth" the excess shall be deemed a gift.

The two types of tax thus followed a similar course, like problems and purposes being expressed in like language. In this situation, courts held that "fair consideration" included relinquishment of dower rights. Ferguson v. Dickson, 3 Cir., 300 F. 961; and *see* McCaughn v. Carver, 3 Cir., 19 F.2d 126; Stubblefield v. United States, 6 F. Supp. 440, 79 Ct.Cl. 268. Congress was thus led as we have indicated to substitute in the 1926 Revenue Act the words "adequate and full consideration" in order to narrow the scope of tax exemptions. *See* Taft v. Commissioner, 304 U.S. 351. When the gift tax was re-enacted in the 1932 Revenue Act, the restrictive phrase "adequate and full consideration" as found in the estate tax was taken over by the draftsman.

To be sure, in the 1932 Act Congress specifically provided that relinquishment of marital rights for purposes of the estate tax shall not constitute "consideration in money or money's worth." The Committees of Congress reported that if the value of relinquished marital interests "may, in whole or in part, constitute a consideration for an otherwise taxable transfer (as has been held so), or an otherwise unallowable deduction from the gross estate, the effect produced amounts to a subversion of the legislative intent. . . ." Plainly, the explicitness was one of cautious redundancy to prevent "subversion of the legislative intent." Without this specific provision, Congress undoubtedly intended the requirement of "adequate and full consideration" to exclude relinquishment of dower and other marital rights with respect to the estate tax. . . .

We believe that there is every reason for giving the same words in the gift tax the same reading. Correlation of the gift tax and the estate tax still requires legislative intervention. . . . But to interpret the same phrases in the two taxes concerning the same subject matter in different ways where obvious reasons do not compel divergent treatment is to introduce another and needless complexity into this already irksome situation. Here strong reasons urge identical construction. To hold otherwise would encourage tax avoidance. . . . And it would not fulfill the purpose of the gift tax in discouraging family settlements so as to avoid high income surtaxes. . . . There is thus every reason in this case to construe the provisions of both taxes harmoniously. . . .

Affirmed.

A gift is not taxed until the transaction has been completed, *i.e.*, until the donor has given up dominion and control over the property.[1] Reg. §25.2511-2(b). In Revenue Ruling 69-347, 1969-1 C.B. 227, the IRS ruled that a gift made

---

1. The completion requirement is explained in Chapter 6.

pursuant to a legally enforceable antenuptial agreement is effective on the date of the marriage. The rationale was that a promise to make a gift becomes taxable in the year in which the obligation becomes binding and not when the discharging payments are made. In Revenue Ruling 69-347, the antenuptial agreement became binding only upon the parties' marriage.

At the time Commissioner v. Wemyss and Merrill v. Fahs were decided, there was no deduction in the gift or estate tax for transfers to spouses. Sections 2056 and 2523 now govern the tax consequences of antenuptial agreements that are conditioned upon marriage. Likewise, the income tax consequences are dictated by §1041, which provides that transfers between spouses are to be treated as gifts with the recipient spouse acquiring a transferred basis, rather than a stepped-up basis, in the property. As a result of these sections, a carefully drafted antenuptial agreement should create neither gift nor income tax consequences.

Another problem occurs when the transferor requires the recipient to pay the gift tax due on the transaction. Because the payment of the gift tax is the donor's "primary and personal liability," Reg. §25.2511-2(a), payment of that debt by the recipient is consideration flowing to the donor. Assume that Uncle transfers stock valued at $200,000 to his Niece on condition that she pay the resulting gift tax of $82,000.[2] Is this two transactions, *i.e.*, a transfer of $200,000 from Uncle to Niece and a separate transfer of $82,000 by Niece to the government on behalf of Uncle? Or is this only one transaction, *i.e.*, a "net gift" to Niece of $118,000? The tax consequences depend on how this transaction is characterized.

In Diedrich v. Commissioner, 457 U.S. 191 (1982), the Court held that a "net gift" was a part sale/part gift for income tax purposes. As a result, the donor realized income equal to the difference between the gift tax paid by the recipient (the amount realized) and the donor's adjusted basis in the property. This decision requires analogous treatment for gift tax purposes. If the transaction is actually a sale, at least in part, then the consideration paid by the recipient diminishes the amount of the gift.

While this result is dictated by the nature of the transaction, after all the donor's transfer was conditioned on the recipient's agreement to pay the resulting gift tax, it creates a further problem for computing the gift tax due. The gift tax of $82,000 in our example is based on the stock value of $200,000. Under the net gift theory, however, the value of the gift is not $200,000 but only $118,000, *i.e.*, the difference between the value of the property transferred and the value of the consideration received. If the gift is only $118,000, the gift tax is only $48,380. This would mean that the amount of the gift is $151,620 rather than $118,000. How, then, does one determine the true value of the "net gift"? The answer lies in a simple algebraic formula. Revenue Ruling 75-72, 1975-1

---

2. For the sake of simplicity, the calculations in this example assume that the donor has already used the §2505 applicable credit amount and that the tax rate on the resulting gift is 41 percent.

C.B. 310, provides that the gift tax due is equal to the tentative tax (computed on the full fair market value of the property transferred) divided by one plus the rate of tax. In our example, the gift tax due would be $82,000 divided by 1.41 or $58,156.

Many transactions, whether "net gifts" or antenuptial agreements, have income tax as well as gift tax consequences. Because the definition of a gift for income tax purposes is not the same as for gift tax purposes, a transaction could be considered a gift for one tax but not the other. Antenuptial agreements present just such a situation. In Farid-Es-Sultaneh v. Commissioner, 160 F.2d 812 (2d Cir. 1947), the taxpayer sold stock she had received from her former husband pursuant to an antenuptial agreement. The Court held that her release of marital rights was sufficient consideration to support the contract and, thus, removed the transaction from the income tax definition of a gift. The taxpayer was treated as having purchased the stock from her former husband and, therefore, her basis was the fair market value of the stock. As a result, her income tax liability on the subsequent transaction was greatly diminished. The Court refused to adopt the gift tax definition of a gift, holding that there was no reason to coordinate the definitions because the purposes of the taxes were different.

The difference in definitions caused the court in Commissioner v. Beck's Estate, 129 F.2d 243, 246 (2d Cir. 1942), to suggest using the term "gift" for gift tax purposes, the term "gaft" for income tax purposes, and the term "geft" for estate tax purposes. This suggestion, although cited by other courts and even the IRS, has never been taken seriously.

PROBLEMS

1. Amy transfers stock with a fair market value of $150,000 to Bruce on condition that Bruce pay the $55,500 gift tax due. Amy's adjusted basis in the stock is $20,000. What are the gift and income tax consequences?

2. Aaron promises to establish a trust for the benefit of his son, Brian, if Brian will quit working as a lobbyist for the tobacco industry. Aaron does not restrict Brian's employment in any other way. Brian quits his job as a lobbyist and takes a position with the consumer protection division of the attorney general's office. Aaron then transfers $500,000 to Friendly National Bank as Trustee, to pay the income to Brian during his life and, at his death, to distribute the property to Brian's issue. What are the gift tax consequences, if any, to Aaron?

3. Amanda is in her 70s, is in good health, and lives in a large house in a rural area. Amanda asks Bridget, the granddaughter of a close friend, to live in the house with her. Amanda does not need nursing care, but wants someone for companionship and to help with housework and repairs. Amanda promises to transfer the house to Bridget if she will live with her for five years. Bridget does so and continues to work full-time in a

nearby town. Amanda transfers title in the house to Bridget. What are the gift tax consequences?

4. Adrian is divorced, has two children, and owns substantial assets. Adrian and Beatrice are planning to marry and are considering an antenuptial agreement. Adrian would transfer stock (fair market value $500,000, adjusted basis $100,000) to Beatrice.

    a. Beatrice will lose substantial trust income established by her former husband upon her remarriage. What are the gift tax consequences if Beatrice signs the antenuptial agreement? Assume that she does not release any support or property rights. Her only promise in the antenuptial agreement is to marry Adrian.

    b. Instead, assume that Beatrice releases her rights to share in Adrian's property upon death or divorce. She does not release any support rights. What are the gift tax consequences of this arrangement?

    c. Instead, assume that Beatrice releases both her property and her support rights. What are the gift tax consequences of this arrangement? *See* Revenue Ruling 68-379, 1968-2 C.B. 414, *infra*, section D.

D. DISCHARGE OF SUPPORT OBLIGATIONS
IRC §§2503, 2512, 2516

If love and affection are insufficient consideration to remove a transaction from the reach of the gift tax, are all intrafamily transfers taxable gifts? What happens when Parent takes Teenager shopping for clothes and Parent buys Teenager the latest fashions? If Teenager expresses appropriate thanks, this is not sufficient consideration because it is not money or money's worth. Even if Teenager promises to make her bed and keep her room picked up, and in fact does so, Parent has not received sufficient consideration.

This transaction, however, is not a gift for purposes of the gift tax because Parent has a legal obligation to support Teenager. In Converse v. Commissioner, 5 T.C. 1014 (1945), *aff'd* 163 F.2d 131 (2d Cir. 1947), the Commissioner conceded that support of a child was not a gift. The rationale for this decision appears to be that transfers pursuant to a legal obligation of support are more akin to consumption than to a gratuitous transfer; that is, they are for the taxpayer's own benefit. In Revenue Ruling 68-379, the IRS agreed, providing:

> Generally, a husband has a duty to support his wife during their joint lives or until she remarries. The satisfaction of this legal obligation does not have the effect of diminishing the husband's estate any more than the satisfaction of any other legal obligation. A transfer to a wife in settlement of inheritance rights is, on the other hand, a present transfer of what would otherwise be a major portion

of the husband's estate on death. Section 25.2512-8 of the regulations specifically states that the release of dower or curtesy or a statutory substitute for dower or curtesy (inheritance rights) is not a consideration in money or money's worth which would prevent taxation of the transfer. The regulations make no reference to support rights. Consequently, since support rights are distinguishable from inheritance rights, a surrender of support rights is not a surrender of "other marital rights," as that phrase is used in the regulations. A release of support rights by a wife constitutes a consideration in money or money's worth.

1968-2 C.B. 414.

While the gift tax does not explicitly exclude transfers that qualify as support, the estate tax provides that claims founded only on a promise or agreement must be supported by adequate and full consideration in money or money's worth. §2053(c)(1)(A). As a result, obligations imposed by law may be deducted without regard to consideration. The Supreme Court incorporated this principle into the gift tax in Harris v. Commissioner, 340 U.S. 106 (1950). In that case the husband received property of greater value than the wife in a divorce, and the Commissioner assessed a gift tax. The Supreme Court disagreed:

> If the parties had without more gone ahead and voluntarily unravelled their business interests on the basis of this compromise, there would be no question that the gift tax would be payable. For there would have been a "promise or agreement" that effected a relinquishment of marital rights in property. It therefore would fall under the ban of the provision of the estate tax which by judicial construction has been incorporated into the gift tax statute.
>
> But the parties did not simply undertake a voluntary contractual division of their property interests. They were faced with the fact that Nevada law not only authorized but instructed the divorce court to decree a just and equitable disposition of both the community and the separate property of the parties. The agreement recited that it was executed in order to effect a settlement of the respective property rights of the parties "in the event a divorce should be decreed"; and it provided that the agreement should be submitted to the divorce court "for its approval." It went on to say, "It is of the essence of this agreement that the settlement herein provided for shall not become operative in any manner nor shall any of the recitals or covenants herein become binding upon either party unless a decree of absolute divorce between the parties shall be entered in the pending Nevada action."
>
> If the agreement had stopped there and were in fact submitted to the court, it is clear that the gift tax would not be applicable. That arrangement would not be a "promise or agreement" in the statutory sense. It would be wholly conditional upon the entry of the decree; the divorce court might or might not accept the provisions of the arrangement as the measure of the respective obligations; it might indeed add to or subtract from them. The decree, not the arrangement submitted to the court, would fix the rights and obligations of the parties. . . .
>
> But the present case is distinguished by reason of a further provision in the undertaking and in the decree. The former provided that "the covenants in this

agreement shall survive any decree of divorce which may be entered." And the decree stated "It is ordered that said agreement and said trust agreements forming a part thereof shall survive this decree.". . . If "the transfer" of marital rights in property is effected by the parties, it is pursuant to a "promise or agreement" in the meaning of the statute. If "the transfer" is effected by court decree, no "promise or agreement" of the parties is the operative fact. In no realistic sense is a court decree a "promise or agreement" between the parties to a litigation. If finer, more legalistic lines are to be drawn, Congress must do it.

If, as we hold, the case is free from any "promise or agreement" concerning marital rights in property, it presents no remaining problems of difficulty. The Treasury Regulations §25.2512-8 recognize as tax free "a sale, exchange, or other transfer of property made in the ordinary course of business (a transaction which is bona fide, at arm's length, and free from any donative intent)." This transaction is not "in the ordinary course of business" in any conventional sense. Few transactions between husband and wife ever would be; and those under the aegis of a divorce court are not. But if two partners on dissolution of the firm entered into a transaction of this character or if chancery did it for them, there would seem to be no doubt that the unscrambling of the business interests would satisfy the spirit of the Regulations.

Id. at 109-112.

Subsequently, Congress enacted §2516, which excludes from the gift tax transfers made (1) in settlement of marital or property rights and (2) to provide a reasonable allowance for child support. To qualify under §2516, there must be a written agreement between the parties and divorce must occur within the year before the agreement is signed or two years afterwards. Section 2516 does not resolve all the gift tax issues arising in a divorce context. If a couple separates but does not receive a final divorce decree or if they fail to meet the timing requirements of §2516, their transfers will be governed by the principles enunciated in Harris v. Commissioner, Merrill v. Fahs, and Revenue Ruling 68-379.

If a couple uses the divorce settlement as a means of transferring property in addition to that required to settle their marital or property rights or to provide a reasonable allowance for support for a minor child, the gift tax may still apply.

Spruance v. Commissioner
60 T.C. 141 (1973)
aff'd without published opinion, 505 F.2d 731 (3d Cir. 1974)

DAWSON, Judge:
. . . The facts, as we have found them, can be summarized as follows: Preston Lea Spruance (Lea) and his wife Margaret, entered into a written separation agreement in July 1955 settling their marital (including support) and property rights and their minor children's support rights. . . . Pursuant to the agreement . . . Lea transferred duPont and Christiana Securities stock having a

fair market value of $1,058,575.13 in trust for the benefit of Margaret and their four children. On the date of the transfer one child was an adult and the others were age 20, 17, and 10. The income interest in the stock . . . transferred in part to Margaret for her support and maintenance and in part to his children for their support and maintenance while minors. Upon the death of Lea and Margaret the remainder interest in the stock will pass to the children. . . . Respondent determined that there was a gift for gift tax purposes to the extent that the total value of the separately held stock at the time of transfer exceeded the value of the income interest in the stock transferred to Margaret and the value of the income interest in the stock transferred to the minor children. Petitioner contends that the entire transfer was for full and adequate consideration.

We hold that there was a taxable gift in the amount determined by the respondent. . . . We interpret [§§2512(b) and 2516] to mean, in the context of this case, that petitioner must prove that the transfer of stock in trust was either to settle his wife's marital or property rights or to provide a reasonable allowance for the support of the minor children. Having failed to prove this with respect to a portion of the property transferred, that portion must be taxed as a gift. Incident to the problem of proof, we observe that respondent has not determined that the value of the income interest going to the minor children was excessive, i.e., that the transfer provided for more than a reasonable support allowance. Respondent has simply calculated the value of Margaret's income interest and the children's minority income interests — all according to the tables appearing in section 20.2031-7(f), Estate Tax Regs. — and subtracted the sum of these values from the total value of the stock transferred. The end result is that the value of the taxable gift is $448,158.37. Petitioner does not challenge respondent's calculations or his use of the estate tax tables.

Petitioner argues that no gift was intended and that, in fact, no gift occurred. . . . But it is well settled that donative intent on the part of the transferor is not an essential element in the application of the gift tax to a given transfer. . . . [A] taxpayer-transferor who transfers property (a) in return for his or her spouse's marital rights or property rights, (b) to provide a reasonable allowance for the support of their minor children, and (c) to put the property in the hands of adult children, has made a taxable gift to the extent of (c). "To construe the statute as suggested by petitioner would open a means for a divorcing parent to transfer property to his adult child free of both gift tax and estate tax." Estate of Hubert Keller, 44 T.C. 851, 860 (1965).

Finally, with regard to this issue, petitioner stresses that the portion of the transfer determined to be taxable by the respondent is not a gift because Margaret bargained her own rights in return for the transfer to the children. We cannot assume, however, that this was the case. The lone statement of the petitioner, in response to his attorney's question, that the wife did so insist is not sufficient evidence on this vital point, especially where other sources of the desired information were not explored and where the petitioner's memory admittedly was not very good with respect to what transpired approximately 17 years ago.

The legal obligation of support is governed by state law both in terms of how much child support is required in the divorce context and in terms of the extent of that obligation outside of divorce. The extent of the legal obligation of support may also be determined, at least in part, by economic circumstances. Is a $25,000 diamond necklace a gift for the poor taxpayer who has saved for 20 years to give this to his spouse on their wedding anniversary but not for the wealthy taxpayer?

This issue is rarely encountered for many reasons. First, gifts to spouses are excluded from the gift tax by the unlimited marital deduction. §2523. Second, most gifts that exceed the legal obligation of support fall within the gift tax annual exclusion. §2503(b). Third, Congress has enacted §2503(e) that excludes payments of educational and medical expenses from the gift tax. To some extent, §2503(e) is far broader than any support obligation because it applies to any individual, not just family members. On the other hand, §2503(e) is quite limited. It extends only to specific payments made directly to educational organizations and medical care providers; it does not cover room and board paid for a student, nor does it cover payments made directly to individuals to reimburse them for expenses they have paid. It does not extend to support provided to family and friends when there is no legal obligation of support.

PROBLEMS

1. Alice buys her 14-year-old child the latest in designer tennis shoes, and the 14-year-old is eternally grateful. What are the gift tax consequences?
2. What are the gift tax consequences to Alice if she buys her 18-year-old child a car? What if the car is a Mercedes? What if the child is 19? 24? What do you advise the client who plans to buy a car for her child?
3. What are the gift tax consequences in the following circumstances?
   a. Alice pays $15,000 tuition, $5,000 room and board, and $1,000 for books to send her 14-year-old child to private boarding high school.
   b. Alice pays $18,000 tuition, $6,000 room and board, and $1,500 for books to send her 19-year-old to college. She also sends the child $100 per month as an allowance.
   c. Alice pays $20,500 tuition, $2,000 for books, and $12,000 for living expenses for her 24-year-old child-who is a law student.
   d. Same as c, only the person is Alice's niece, not her child.
   e. Alice pays the medical bills of:
      (1) the 14-year-old child;
      (2) the 19-year-old child;

>   (3)   the 24-year-old child;
>   (4)   her niece who is 24;
>   (5)   her 63-year-old mother, who does *not* live with her;
>   (6)   her best friend, who also does *not* live with Alice.
>   f.   Alice pays the rent, utilities, and food bills of the following individuals who do not live with her:
>   (1)   her 24-year-old child;
>   (2)   her mother;
>   (3)   her best friend.

4.   Alan and Betsy have been married for 15 years and have two minor children. When they separate, they sign an agreement that requires Alan to pay Betsy $1,000 per month in maintenance and $600 per child per month in child support. The agreement also requires Alan to transfer his interest in the family home to Betsy as well as 100 shares of stock in XYZ, Inc. (Alan and Betsy had owned the home in joint tenancy with the right of survivorship. Their adjusted basis was $50,000, and the fair market value was $200,000. Alan owned 500 shares of XYZ, Inc. He had a basis of $10 in each share. At the time of the agreement, each share had a fair market value of $25.) The agreement requires Betsy to release all her rights to support and to share in Alan's property and to waive all of her rights in his pension fund. Eighteen months after Alan and Betsy sign the separation agreement, the court issues a final divorce decree.
   a.   What are the gift tax consequences if the court decree incorporates the agreement by reference?
   b.   What are the gift tax consequences if the court decree contains identical terms as the separation agreement but does not mention the agreement?
   c.   What are the gift tax consequences if the court decree does not provide for maintenance, child support, or a property settlement and does not mention the separation agreement?
   d.   What are the gift tax consequences if the court decree incorporates the agreement, but the decree is not issued until 30 months after the agreement is signed?
   e.   What are the gift tax consequences if the court decree does not mention the separation agreement and is not issued until 30 months after the agreement is signed?

5.   Agnes and Boris obtain a divorce. Agnes establishes an irrevocable trust for the support of their minor children Chloe and Duncan, as provided in the divorce agreement, which provides:

   The Trustee is to pay Boris a reasonable allowance for the support of Chloe and Duncan on a quarterly basis out of trust income. The Trustee is instructed to distribute at least $2,000 per child per quarter, but has the discretion to distribute more. Distributions may be made directly to Chloe and Duncan after the age of 18. Distributions for support (other than distributions for education) cease when the child reaches age 21.

The Trustee is also directed to use trust income for the education of Chloe and Duncan including private boarding school, college, and graduate school. The Trustee may invade corpus to pay for education but may not distribute to either child (or for their benefit) more than that child's proportionate share of trust corpus.

Any income not distributed will be accumulated and added to corpus. Undistributed income and corpus will be distributed in equal shares when the youngest child is 30.

What are the gift tax consequences?

E. TAXABLE TRANSFERS
IRC §§2501, 2511, 2512, 7278

Lack of consideration, alone, does not make a gift. There must still be a transfer of property. §2501. The terms "transfer" and "property" have been interpreted expansively in §2511 and regulation §25.2511-1.

Example 5-1

Sam creates a joint bank account with Tom and transfers $50,000 into it. Sam makes a gift to Tom whenever Tom withdraws funds from the account. Reg. §25.2511-1(h)(4).

Example 5-2

Jane establishes an irrevocable trust with Friendly National Bank as Trustee to pay the income to Ann for her life and, at Ann's death, to distribute the property to Carol. Jane has made a gift of the life income to Ann and a gift of the remainder interest to Carol. Reg. §25.2511-1(h)(7).

Example 5-3

Bob owns a house, and he has a mortgage of $125,000 on it with Marble State Bank. Anna pays Marble State Bank $125,000 to satisfy the mortgage. She has made a gift to Bob equal to the amount she paid.

Example 5-4

Max transfers Blackacre, which has a fair market value of $100,000, to ABC, Inc. and receives nothing in exchange. Max has made a gift to the shareholders of ABC, Inc. Reg. §25.2511-1(h)(1).

The scope of the gift tax was established early in its history by a series of cases where taxpayers challenged the imposition of the gift tax to a variety of arrangements. In Burnet v. Guggenheim, 288 U.S. 280 (1933), the taxpayer established a revocable trust prior to the enactment of the gift tax statute in

1924. Subsequently, the taxpayer released the power to revoke, and the Commissioner assessed a gift tax on the release. The Supreme Court upheld the imposition of the gift tax, stating that the gift occurred when the taxpayer released his command over the property rather than when he had transferred title to it to the trust. The Court noted that the gift tax was enacted to supplement the estate tax, that courts had continued to construe the concept of transfer for purposes of the estate tax in an ever-broadening manner, and that Congress expected this expansive definition of transfer to apply in the gift tax context as well.

Next, the Supreme Court imposed the gift tax on the relinquishment of the power to designate new beneficiaries in Sanford's Estate v. Commissioner, 308 U.S. 39 (1939) and in Rasquin v. Humphreys, 308 U.S. 54 (1939). Although the Court again noted that the primary purpose of the gift tax was to prevent avoidance of the estate tax, it held that the two taxes were not always mutually exclusive and that, as a result, some transfers might be subject to both taxes. The fact that these trusts might be included in the grantor's gross estate did not, therefore, prevent imposition of the gift tax.

Not long after, the Supreme Court applied the gift tax to the creation of trusts where the remaindermen could not be identified and might not have been in existence at that time. Smith v. Shaughnessy, 318 U.S. 176 (1943); Robinette v. Helvering, 318 U.S. 184 (1943). The Court refused to allow the taxpayers' complex arrangements to defeat the gift tax, stating: "Even though these concepts of property and value may be slippery and elusive they cannot escape taxation so long as they are used in the world of business. The language of the gift tax statute . . . is broad enough to include property, however conceptual or contingent." Smith v. Shaughnessy, 318 U.S. at 180.

The next challenges to the gift tax came in the companion cases of Commissioner v. Wemyss, 324 U.S. 303 (1945), and Merrill v. Fahs, 324 U.S. 308 (1945). In *Wemyss*, the Court held that the gift tax applied to a transfer of stock in exchange for a promise to marry where no consideration passed to the donor although the donee suffered a detriment by losing income from a trust established by her former husband. In Merrill v. Fahs, the Court held that the gift tax encompassed the transfer of stock in exchange for a release of marital rights, holding that those rights were not consideration in money or money's worth. These cases established the essence of the gift tax: a transfer of property that diminished the donor's estate.

These efforts did not end taxpayers' attempts to avoid the gift tax while transferring benefits to their family and friends. As interest rates rose in the 1960s and 1970s, the interest-free loan became a popular device for shifting economic benefits to lower-bracket taxpayers. In the typical situation, the taxpayer loaned money to a family member, either for a specified term or requiring that the money be repaid "upon demand" and charged little, or no, interest. The Commissioner attempted to impose a gift tax on these arrangements but had little success until the following case reached the Supreme Court.

Dickman v. Commissioner
465 U.S. 330 (1984)

Chief Justice BURGER delivered the opinion of the Court.

. . . Paul and Esther Dickman were husband and wife; Lyle Dickman was their son. Paul, Esther, Lyle, and Lyle's wife and children were the owners of Artesian Farm, Inc. (Artesian). . . . Between 1971 and 1976 . . . the outstanding balances for the loans from Paul to Lyle varied from $144,715 to $342,915; with regard to Paul's loans to Artesian, the outstanding balances ranged from $207,875 to $669,733. During the same period, Esther loaned $226,130 to Lyle and $68,651 to Artesian. With two exceptions, all the loans were evidenced by demand notes bearing no interest.

Paul Dickman died in 1976, leaving a gross estate for federal estate tax purposes of $3,464,011. The Commissioner of Internal Revenue audited Paul Dickman's estate and determined that the loans to Lyle and Artesian resulted in taxable gifts to the extent of the value of the use of the loaned funds. . . . Reaffirming its earlier decision in Crown v. Commissioner, 67 T.C. 1060 (1977), *aff'd*, 585 F.2d 234 (CA7 1978), the Tax Court concluded that intrafamily, interest-free demand loans do not result in taxable gifts. . . . Because the Tax Court determined that all the loans to Lyle and Artesian were made payable on demand, it held that the loans were not subject to the federal gift tax. . . . The United States Court of Appeals for the Eleventh Circuit reversed. . . .

The statutory language of the federal gift tax provisions purports to reach any gratuitous transfer of any interest in property. . . . The language of [§§2501 and 2511] is clear and admits of but one reasonable interpretation: transfers of property by gift, by whatever means effected, are subject to the federal gift tax.

The Committee Reports accompanying the Revenue Act of 1932, ch. 209, 47 Stat. 169, which established the present scheme of federal gift taxation, make plain that Congress intended the gift tax statute to reach all gratuitous transfers of any valuable interest in property. Among other things, these Reports state:

> The terms "property," "transfer," "gift," and "indirectly" are used in the broadest and most comprehensive sense; the term "property" reaching every species of right or interest protected by law and having an exchangeable value. The words "transfer . . . by gift" and "whether . . . direct or indirect" are designed to cover and comprehend all transactions . . . whereby, and to the extent . . . that, property or a property right is donatively passed to or conferred upon another, regardless of the means or the device employed in its accomplishment. H.R.Rep. No. 708, 72d Cong., 1st Sess., 27-28 (1932); S.Rep. No. 665, 72d Cong., 1st Sess., 39 (1932).

The plain language of the statute reflects this legislative history; the gift tax was designed to encompass all transfers of property and property rights having significant value.

On several prior occasions, this Court has acknowledged the expansive sweep of the gift tax provisions. . . .

In asserting that interest-free demand loans give rise to taxable gifts, the Commissioner does not seek to impose the gift tax upon the principal amount of the loan, but only upon the reasonable value of the use of the money lent. The taxable gift that assertedly results from an interest-free demand loan is the value of receiving and using the money without incurring a corresponding obligation to pay interest along with the loan's repayment.[5] Is such a gratuitous transfer of the right to use money a "transfer of property" within the intendment of §2501(a)(1)?

We have little difficulty accepting the theory that the use of valuable property — in this case money — is itself a legally protectible property interest. Of the aggregate rights associated with any property interest, the right of use of property is perhaps of the highest order. One court put it succinctly:

> "Property" is more than just the physical thing — the land, the bricks, the mortar — it is also the sum of all the rights and powers incident to ownership of the physical thing. It is the tangible and the intangible. Property is composed of constituent elements and of these elements the right to *use* the physical thing to the exclusion of others is the most essential and beneficial. Without this right all other elements would be of little value. . . .

Passailaigue v. United States, 224 F. Supp. 682, 686 (M.D. Ga.1963) (emphasis in original).

What was transferred here was the use of a substantial amount of cash for an indefinite period of time. An analogous interest in real property, the use under a tenancy at will, has long been recognized as a property right. *E.g.*, Restatement (Second) of Property §1.6 (1977); 3 G. Thompson, Commentaries on the Modern Law of Real Property §1020 (J. Grimes ed. 1980). For example, a parent who grants to a child the rent-free, indefinite use of commercial property having a reasonable rental value of $8,000 a month has clearly transferred a valuable property right. The transfer of $100,000 in cash, interest-free and repayable on demand, is similarly a grant of the use of valuable property. Its uncertain tenure may reduce its value, but it does not undermine its status as property. In either instance, when the property owner transfers to another the right to use the object, an identifiable property interest has clearly changed hands.

The right to the use of $100,000 without charge is a valuable interest in the money lent, as much so as the rent-free use of property consisting of land and buildings. In either case, there is a measurable economic value associated with

---

5. The Commissioner's tax treatment of interest-free demand loans may perhaps be best understood as a two-step approach to such transactions. Under this theory, such a loan has two basic economic components: an arm's-length loan from the lender to the borrower, on which the borrower pays the lender a fair rate of interest, followed by a gift from the lender to the borrower in the amount of that interest. *See* Crown v. Commissioner, 585 F.2d 234, 240 (CA7 1978).

the use of the property transferred. The value of the use of money is found in what it can produce; the measure of that value is interest — "rent" for the use of the funds. We can assume that an interest-free loan for a fixed period, especially for a prolonged period, may have greater value than such a loan made payable on demand, but it would defy common human experience to say that an intrafamily loan payable on demand is not subject to accommodation; its value may be reduced by virtue of its demand status, but that value is surely not eliminated. . . .

Against this background, the gift tax statutes clearly encompass within their broad sweep the gratuitous transfer of the use of money. Just as a tenancy at will in real property is an estate or interest in land, so also is the right to use money a cognizable interest in personal property. The right to use money is plainly a valuable right, readily measurable by reference to current interest rates; the vast banking industry is positive evidence of this reality. Accordingly, we conclude that the interest-free loan of funds is a "transfer of property by gift" within the contemplation of the federal gift tax statutes.

In order to make a taxable gift, a transferor must relinquish dominion and control over the transferred property. Treas. Reg. §25.2511-2(b), 26 CFR §25.2511-2(b) (1983). At the moment an interest-free demand loan is made, the transferor has not given up all dominion and control; he could terminate the transferee's use of the funds by calling the loan. As time passes without a demand for repayment, however, the transferor allows the use of the principal to pass to the transferee, and the gift becomes complete. *See ibid.;* Rev. Rul. 69-347, 1969-1 C.B. 227; Rev. Rul. 69-346, 1969-1 Cum. Bull. 227. As the Court of Appeals realized, 690 F.2d, at 819, the fact that the transferor's dominion and control over the use of the principal are relinquished over time will become especially relevant in connection with the valuation of the gifts that result from such loans; it does not, however, alter the fact that the lender has made a gratuitous transfer of property subject to the federal gift tax.

Our holding that an interest-free demand loan results in a taxable gift of the use of the transferred funds is fully consistent with one of the major purposes of the federal gift tax statute: protection of the estate tax and the income tax. The legislative history of the gift tax provisions reflects that Congress enacted a tax on gifts to supplement existing estate and income tax laws. Failure to impose the gift tax on interest-free loans would seriously undermine this estate and income tax protection goal.

A substantial no-interest loan from parent to child creates significant tax benefits for the lender quite apart from the economic advantages to the borrower. This is especially so when an individual in a high income tax bracket transfers income-producing property to an individual in a lower income tax bracket, thereby reducing the taxable income of the high-bracket taxpayer at the expense, ultimately, of all other taxpayers and the Government. Subjecting interest-free loans to gift taxation minimizes the potential loss to the federal fisc generated by the use of such loans as an income tax avoidance mechanism for the transferor. Gift taxation of interest-free loans also effectuates Congress' desire to supplement the estate tax provisions. A gratuitous transfer of income-producing property may enable the transferor to avoid the future estate tax liability that would result if the earnings generated by the property — rent, interest, or dividends — became a part of the transferor's estate. Imposing the gift tax upon interest-free loans bolsters the estate tax by preventing the diminution of the transferor's estate in this fashion.

Petitioners contend that administrative and equitable considerations require a holding that no gift tax consequences result from the making of interest-free demand loans. . . . Petitioners first advance an argument accepted by the Tax Court in Crown v. Commissioner: "[O]ur income tax system does not recognize unrealized earnings or accumulations of wealth and no taxpayer is under any obligation to continuously invest his money for a profit. The opportunity cost of either letting one's money remain idle or suffering a loss from an unwise investment is not taxable merely because a profit could have been made from a wise investment." 67 T.C., at 1063-1064. Thus, petitioners argue, an interest-free loan should not be made subject to the gift tax simply because of the possibility that the money lent might have enhanced the transferor's taxable income or gross estate had the loan never been made.

This contention misses the mark. It is certainly true that no law requires an individual to invest his property in an income-producing fashion, just as no law demands that a transferor charge interest or rent for the use of money or other property. An individual may, without incurring the gift tax, squander money, conceal it under a mattress, or otherwise waste its use value by failing to invest it. Such acts of consumption have nothing to do with lending money at no interest. The gift tax is an excise tax on transfers of property; allowing dollars to lie idle involves no transfer. If the taxpayer chooses not to waste the use value of money, however, but instead transfers the use to someone else, a taxable event has occurred. That the transferor himself could have consumed or wasted the use value of the money without incurring the gift tax does not change this result. Contrary to petitioners' assertion, a holding in favor of the taxability of interest-free loans does not impose upon the transferor a duty profitably to invest; rather, it merely recognizes that certain tax consequences inevitably flow from a decision to make a "transfer of property by gift." 26 U.S.C. §2501(a)(1).

Petitioners next attack the breadth of the Commissioner's view that interest-free demand loans give rise to taxable gifts. Carried to its logical extreme, petitioners argue, the Commissioner's rationale would elevate to the status of taxable gifts such commonplace transactions as a loan of the proverbial cup of sugar to a neighbor or a loan of lunch money to a colleague. Petitioners urge that such a result is an untenable intrusion by the Government into cherished zones of privacy, particularly where intrafamily transactions are involved.

Our laws require parents to provide their minor offspring with the necessities and conveniences of life; questions under the tax law often arise, however, when parents provide more than the necessities, and in quantities significant enough to attract the attention of the taxing authorities. Generally, the legal obligation of support terminates when the offspring reach majority. Nonetheless, it is not uncommon for parents to provide their adult children with such things as the use of cars or vacation cottages, simply on the basis of the family relationship. We assume that the focus of the Internal Revenue Service is not on such traditional familial matters. When the Government levies a gift tax on routine neighborly or familial gifts, there will be time enough to deal with such a case.

Moreover, the tax law provides liberally for gifts to both family members and others; within the limits of the prescribed statutory exemptions, even substantial gifts may be entirely tax free. First, under §2503(e) of the Code, 26 U.S.C. §2503(e) (1982 ed.), amounts paid on behalf of an individual for tuition at a qualified educational institution or for medical care are not considered "transfer[s] of property by gift" for purposes of the gift tax statutes. More significantly, §2503(b) of the Code provides an annual exclusion from the computation of taxable gifts of $10,000 per year, per donee; this provision allows a taxpayer to give up to $10,000 annually to each of any number of persons, without incurring any gift tax liability. The "split gift" provision of Code §2513(a), which effectively enables a husband and wife to give each object of their bounty $20,000 per year without liability for gift tax, further enhances the ability to transfer significant amounts of money and property free of gift tax consequences. Finally, should a taxpayer make gifts during one year that exceed the §2503(b) annual gift tax exclusion, no gift tax liability will result until the unified credit of Code §2505 has been exhausted. These generous exclusions, exceptions, and credits clearly absorb the sorts of de minimis gifts petitioners envision and render illusory the administrative problems that petitioners perceive in their "parade of horribles."

Finally, petitioners urge that the Commissioner should not be allowed to assert the gift taxability of interest-free demand loans because such a position represents a departure from prior Internal Revenue Service practice. This contention rests on the fact that, prior to 1966, the Commissioner had not construed the gift tax statutes and regulations to authorize the levying of a gift tax on the value of the use of money or property. *See* Crown v. Commissioner, 585 F.2d, at 241; Johnson v. United States, 254 F. Supp. 73 (N.D. Tex.1966). From this they argue that it is manifestly unfair to permit the Commissioner to impose the gift tax on the transactions challenged here.

Even accepting the notion that the Commissioner's present position represents a departure from prior administrative practice, which is by no means certain, it is well established that the Commissioner may change an earlier interpretation of the law, even if such a change is made retroactive in effect. . . . This rule applies even though a taxpayer may have relied to his detriment upon the Commissioner's prior position. . . . The Commissioner is under no duty to assert a particular position as soon as the statute authorizes such an interpretation. . . . Accordingly, petitioners' "taxpayer reliance" argument is unavailing.

As we have noted . . . Congress has provided generous exclusions and credits designed to reduce the gift tax liability of the great majority of taxpayers. Congress clearly has the power to provide a similar exclusion for the gifts that result from interest-free demand loans. Any change in the gift tax consequences of such loans, however, is a legislative responsibility, not a judicial one. Until such a change occurs, we are bound to effectuate Congress' intent to protect the estate and income tax systems with a broad and comprehensive tax upon all "transfer[s] of property by gift.". . .

We hold, therefore, that the interest-free demand loans shown by this record resulted in taxable gifts of the reasonable value of the use of the money lent. Accordingly, the judgment of the United States Court of Appeals for the Eleventh Circuit is

Affirmed.

Section 7872 now governs both the income tax and the gift tax consequences of interest-free and below-market loans. This section encompasses not only gift loans but also compensation-related and corporation-shareholder loans. Section 7872 creates two imputed transfers for gift loans and for loans payable on demand: a transfer from the lender to the borrower equal to the amount of forgone interest and a second transfer from the borrower to the lender of the same amount. These deemed transfers occur on the last day of the calendar year in which the loan is outstanding. For term loans, §7872(b) imputes a transfer on the day of the loan from the lender to the borrower equal to the amount loaned less the present value of all required payments, *i.e.*, the present value of the amount of forgone interest. The tax consequences of these deemed transfers depend on the taxpayers' relationship to each other and whether the loan is payable on demand or is for a specified term.

Example 5-5

Parent loans Child $500,000, interest-free. Child signs a promissory note agreeing to repay the loan 30 days after Parent makes a written request. Assume that the applicable federal rate of interest is five percent. On the last day of the calendar year, Parent is deemed to have made a transfer to Child equal to the amount of forgone interest, *i.e.*, $25,300. This transfer will be considered a gift. While Child does not have to report it as income because of §102, Parent will have made a taxable gift of $25,300, assuming that Parent has already made gifts to Child that year equal to the amount of the gift tax annual exclusion. On the same day, Child is deemed to have made a transfer to Parent equal to the $25,300 forgone interest. This deemed transfer is not gratuitous, and, as a result, Parent will have interest income of $25,300.

The fear that *Dickman* would be extended to the loan of the proverbial cup of sugar between neighbors has not been realized. The Internal Revenue Service has not attempted to apply the rationale of *Dickman* to loans of personal, or even real, property. The enactment of §7872, the difficulty of discovering such transactions, and the valuation problems inherent in such transactions have undoubtedly restrained the IRS. Moreover, §7872 itself excludes gift loans between individuals that do not exceed $10,000. Finally, the gift tax annual exclusion shelters most rent-free or interest-free transactions from the gift tax.

Where it has perceived abuse, however, the IRS has invoked *Dickman*, for example, by claiming that the failure to require distribution of preferred dividends, the failure to redeem preferred stock, or the failure to convert preferred to common stock resulted in a gift. TAM 9420001, TAM 8726005, PLR 8723007. Courts, however, have resisted these efforts. In Snyder v. Commissioner, 93 T.C. 529 (1980), the Court refused to hold that a shareholder's failure to exercise her right of redemption was a gift. The Court did, however, hold that the shareholder's failure to convert preferred stock with a noncumulative dividend to preferred stock with a cumulative dividend resulted in a significant shift of economic benefit and thus a gift to the common shareholders. In Hutchens Non-Marital Trusts v. Commissioner, 66 T.C.M. (C.C.H.) 1599 (1993), and Daniels v. Commissioner, 68 T.C.M. (C.C.H.) 1310 (1994), the Tax Court refused to extend this principle further. In these cases the boards of directors had retained corporate earnings rather than declare dividends. Relying on the fiduciary responsibilities of directors and majority shareholders and the existence of sufficient business reasons for retention of the earnings, the Tax Court held that these arrangements did not constitute gifts.

The enactment of §§2701 and 2702 in 1990 has apparently stifled any attempts by the IRS to extend *Dickman* beyond loans of money. *See* Chapter 3, section F for a discussion of these provisions. These sections require that retained interests in the business context or irrevocable trusts pay a fixed rate of return on a periodic basis. If not, the interest is valued at zero, and the donor is deemed to have made a gift of the full value of the property to the remainder beneficiaries. This is a far more draconian result than that in *Dickman* and prevents the shifting of untaxed economic benefits from grantors to beneficiaries.

These sections, however, do not prevent the shifting of all economic benefits from clever donors to the natural objects of their bounty. To escape the gift tax, these donors need only perform services free-of-charge, as the following case demonstrates.

Commissioner v. Hogle
165 F.2d 352 (10th Cir. 1947)

PHILLIPS, Circuit Judge.

. . . The question presented is whether or not annual earnings of two trusts, one known as the Copley Trust, and one known as the Three Trust, during the years in question, from trading in securities and commodities carried on by the trusts under Hogle's direction, amounted to gifts by Hogle to the trusts. These trusts were before this court in Hogle v. Commissioner, 10 Cir., 132 F.2d 66, and the facts with respect to such trusts are there fully set out.

The Copley Trust was created in 1922 by Hogle and his wife for the benefit of their three children. It consisted of a securities trading account to be managed and operated under Hogle's direction, the property accruing to the trust to be divided among the children on April 15, 1945. The trust was irrevocable and Hogle retained no right to alter or amend the trust instrument, or to change the beneficial interests. None of the principal or income could revest in Hogle. It provided that any losses resulting from trading in excess of the "profits and various income returns thereof" should be made good by Hogle, and that any such losses should not become an indebtedness of the trustee or the beneficiaries, but that any such losses made good by Hogle should be returned to him out of the first profits that accrued from further transactions.

On October 7, 1922, a margin account was opened for the trust with J. A. Hogle & Company, a brokerage partnership, consisting of Hogle and his wife, and in which the three children subsequently became partners. The trading resulted in profits in every year, except 1928 and 1929. In those years, certain securities were given to the trust by Hogle and his wife. The profits and benefits in the trust were divided on April 15, 1945, among the three children, and the trust was terminated.

In 1932, Hogle opened a trading account with the partnership in the name of the Three Trust account and a few days thereafter, Hogle and his wife created the Three Trust, consisting of a securities trading account for the benefit of the three children. The trust was irrevocable and was in all respects like the Copley Trust, with the exception it was to terminate on April 15, 1950, and income could be distributed in the meantime in the discretion of Hogle and any two of the three trustees. Although the trading was conducted in the name of the trust, receipts and disbursements were credited and debited to the individual beneficiaries according to the specified share of each during the term of the trust. Gains and profits were realized in every year, including the taxable years.

The net worth of each trust in each of the years for which the gift taxes were assessed was more than sufficient to provide the margins required to cover the trading carried on for it.

In Hogle v. Commissioner, *supra*, we held, under the doctrine of Helvering v. Clifford, 309 U.S. 331, 60 S.Ct. 554, 84 L.Ed. 788, that the net income resulting from trading on margin was taxable to Hogle. We do not think it follows, however, that the net income in each of the taxable years derived from trading constituted a gift thereof by Hogle to the trusts. . . .

The net income derived from trading carried on in behalf of the trusts accrued immediately and directly to the trusts, and did not consist of income accruing to Hogle which he transferred by anticipatory gift to the trusts. Hogle never owned or held an economic interest in such income. Likewise, since the funds in the trusts were sufficient to provide the margins required to cover the trading carried on in the taxable years, any losses resulting from trading would have been suffered immediately and directly by the trusts. What, in fact and in realty, Hogle gave to the trusts in the taxable years was his expert services in carrying on the trading, personal services in the management of the trusts.

Hogle could give or withhold his personal services in carrying on trading on margin for the trusts. He could not withhold from the trusts any of the income accruing from trading on margin. How could he give what he could not withhold? There was no transfer directly or indirectly from Hogle to the trusts of title to, or other economic interest in, the income from trading or margin, having the quality of a gift. In short, there was no transfer directly or indirectly by Hogle to the trusts of property or property rights.

The Commissioner places strong reliance upon Hogle v. Commissioner, *supra*, to sustain the contention that the income arising from the trading on margin represented personal earnings of Hogle; and that Hogle in substance gave to the trusts the profits derived from part of his individual efforts. Certain excerpts from the opinion are emphasized in support of the argument that the net income arising from the trading on margin for the benefit of the trusts represented earnings of Hogle, and that, upon the accrual of such income to the trusts, a transfer having the quality of a gift was effectuated within the meaning of §2501(a). But, we think a critical reading of the opinion in that case in its entirety will indicate that it does not support the Commissioner's contention. While the court drew a distinction between the income tax liability of Hogle on profits accruing to the trusts from trading on margin and gains accruing to the trusts from other sources, and held that he was liable for the tax on net income derived from such trading but not on gains accruing from other sources, his liability for tax on the net income derived from trading on margin was predicated upon his power to control indirectly the extent of the profit derived from such trading by determining the extent and amount of such trading. Despite certain statements contained in the opinion on which the Commissioner relies, the basis of the holding that Hogle was liable for income tax on the net income resulting from trading on margin was his power to control the extent of such trading and therefore the extent of the income therefrom. It was predicated on his power to dominate the amount of income that would accrue from trading, That was the essence of our holding. We did not hold that such income accrued first to Hogle and was by him transferred by anticipatory gift to the trusts.

Our holding in Hogle v. Commissioner, *supra*, was an extreme application of the doctrine of the *Clifford* case, *supra*. To hold that the profits accruing from trading in margins constitute gifts from Hogle to the trusts, we think, would be an unjustified extension of the doctrine of the *Clifford* case.

Affirmed.

PROBLEMS

1. Anthony loans his daughter Belinda $250,000. Belinda signs a promissory note agreeing to repay the $250,000 within ten days of a written demand by Anthony. The note does not require the payment of interest.
   a. What are the gift tax consequences? Does it matter how Belinda uses the $250,000?

      b.   What if Anthony charges her interest at two percent above what he could earn on a certificate of deposit?

2. If you were a judge on the United States Tax Court, how would you decide each of the following cases? The IRS claims that each of these transactions creates gift tax liability.

      a.   Althea allows Basil to use her summer cabin for one month without paying any rent.

      b.   Althea allows Basil to use her house for one year without paying any rent.

      c.   Anita allows her son, Ben, who is 22 and just graduated from college, to live with her for one year. Ben contributes nothing to the household expenses.

      d.   Amelia owns a successful cosmetics company. Bess and Charles, her children, have been employed by the cosmetics company for over ten years. When Amelia decides to produce a new line of cosmetics, Amelia has her children, Bess and Charles, form a new company to develop Amelia's idea. Amelia consults with the new company for no fee, but she does not work for the company on a regular basis. Bess and Charles resign their positions with Amelia's company to work full time for their own company.

      e.   Angela practices law as a sole practitioner. She hires Brad, a new law school graduate, to work for her. Three years later she retires, and Brad takes over the practice.

3. Grace creates an irrevocable trust to pay the income to Sam (her spouse) for life, and at his death to distribute the trust property to their children, Ellen and Frank. Ellen and Frank are Co-Trustees. Sam, Ellen, and Frank agree that Ellen and Frank will each be paid $50,000 a year to serve as Trustee and that this amount will be paid from the trust's income. What are the tax consequences, if any, of this arrangement?

4. Greg creates an irrevocable trust with Friendly National Bank as Trustee. The Trustee has discretion to distribute income to Sally (Greg's spouse) for her health, education, or support. At Sally's death, the trust property is to be distributed to their children, Joan and Karl. Sally has substantial property in her own name. She and the children petition the court to terminate the trust and distribute the trust property to Joan and Karl. What are the tax consequences if the court grants the petition?

F. DISCLAIMERS
IRC §2518

A disclaimer occurs when the recipient of property refuses to accept it or relinquishes her right to it. State law provides that the disclaimed property will pass as if the recipient had predeceased the donor. Who, then, will be treated as the transferor of the property for transfer tax purposes?

Example 5-6

Chris dies, leaving Greenacre to Adam. Adam disclaims his interest, and the, property passes to Adam's son, Ben. Has Adam made a gift to Ben? It would appear that he has. Adam had a right to Greenacre. He could have accepted the property and then immediately transferred it to Ben. His disclaimer creates exactly the same result. Because he has diminished his estate through disclaiming his interest, it would seem that Adam has made a gift to Ben.

Section 2518 provides otherwise, as long as specific requirements are followed. First, the disclaimer must be irrevocable and unqualified. Second, it must be written. Third, the writing must be received by the transferor, the transferor's legal representative, or the holder of legal title to the property no later than nine months after the creation of the interest or the date on which the disclaimant turns 21. Fourth, the person disclaiming cannot have accepted the property interest or any of its benefits. Finally, the disclaimed property interest must pass without any direction by the person disclaiming either to the decedent's spouse or to a person other than the one disclaiming.

It would appear that the disclaimer must also satisfy state law requirements; otherwise, the person disclaiming will be considered the owner of the property. Imposing this additional requirement, however, conflicts with the revisions to §2518 made in 1976. In that year, Congress eliminated satisfaction of state law as a requirement for a qualified disclaimer to provide uniformity. Recognizing the dilemma, Congress provided in §2518(c)(3) that a written transfer of one's entire interest in property that otherwise meets the requirements of §2518 will be treated as a qualified disclaimer if the transfer is to a person who would have received the property had the transferor made a qualified disclaimer.

One can disclaim an entire interest in property. One can also disclaim an undivided portion of property. One can disclaim a partial interest in property if that is all that one receives. One can even disclaim the survivorship interest passing at the death of a joint tenant.

Example 5-7

Joan died, leaving her household property and art collection to Mary, the family home to Paul, and $1,000,000 to Peter. Mary disclaimed her interest in Joan's furniture and two paintings but not her interest in the rest of the art collection. Peter disclaimed his interest in $400,000 of the $1,000,000 bequest. Assuming that the other requirements of §2518 have been met and that Mary and Peter will not acquire an interest in the disclaimed property pursuant to state law, the disclaimers will be valid. Reg. §25.2518-3(d)(Ex.1).

Example 5-8

Jean creates an irrevocable trust to pay the income to Martha until Martha is 40 years old. When Martha is 40, the trust property will be distributed to her or, if she has died, to her issue. Martha disclaims her interest in the remainder of the trust but retains her right to the trust income. Assuming Martha's disclaimer satisfies the other requirements of §2518, the disclaimer of the remainder interest is qualified. Reg. §25.2518-3(d)(Ex. 8).

Instead, Martha disclaimers her interest in the trust income but retains her interest in the remainder. Assume that the income is then paid to her issue. Again, assuming that her disclaimer satisfies the other requirements of §2518, the disclaimer of the income interest is qualified. *Id.*

Example 5-9

John and Mike purchased Blackacre in 1980 as joint tenants for $50,000. Mike dies when the fair market value is $200,000. Within nine months of Mike's death, John files a disclaimer of the interest in Blackacre that he would receive as a result of Mike's death. Assuming that the other requirements of §2518 have been met, John will have made a qualified disclaimer of the one-half interest in Blackacre that would pass to him as a result of Mike's death. John is still considered the owner of the interest he acquired in 1980. Reg. §25.2518-2(c)(5)(Ex. 7). The result is the same whether or not the joint tenancy is unilaterally severable under state law. Reg. §25.2518-2(c)(4)(i).

Section 2518 allows taxpayers to avoid transfer tax consequences from successive transfers of property. In Example 5-6, Adam disclaims the property because he knows that it will pass to his son. Because Adam did not need or want the property, he avoided the tax consequences of transferring the property himself to his son. Disclaimers also allow a surviving spouse to adjust the amount of the marital deduction or take advantage of an unused applicable credit amount in the estate of the first spouse to die. If state law allows a personal representative to disclaim property on behalf of a decedent, the personal representative may be able to avoid estate tax for the decedent who never possessed or enjoyed the property.

PROBLEMS

1. David dies with a will that provides:
   I leave Blackacre to my son, Abel.
   I leave $500,000 to my daughter, Brenda.
   I leave my IBM stock to my daughter, Carol.
   I leave the residue of my estate to my children in equal shares.
   Assume that David makes no provision in his will for the distribution of property in the event of a disclaimer or if any of the beneficiaries prede-

cease him. Assume further that under state law disclaimed property passes to the disclaimant's heirs.

   a. May Abel disclaim a one-half interest in Blackacre?

   b. What are the tax consequences if Brenda disclaims an interest in $200,000?

   c. What are the tax consequences if Carol disclaims 40 percent of the IBM stock?

2. Debra died, leaving her stock portfolio to her neighbor, Ellen, her real estate to her friend, Frank, and the residuary of her estate to Ellen and Frank in equal shares. Debra makes no provision in her will for the distribution of property in the event of a disclaimer or if a beneficiary predeceases her. Assume that under state law disclaimed property become part of the residuary estate. What are the tax consequences if Ellen disclaims her interest in the stock portfolio?

3. On September 5, 1998, Grace established an irrevocable trust by transferring property to Friendly National Bank as Trustee to pay the income to John for his life, and at his death to distribute the trust property to Karen and Laura in equal shares. John dies on March 10, 2004, and Karen sends the Trustee written notice on June 26, 2004, disclaiming her interest in the trust property. Assume that Karen's interest would pass to her heirs under state law. What are the tax consequences?

CHAPTER 6

Completion

A. GENERAL PRINCIPLES
Regulation §25.2511-2

A transfer of property without adequate and full consideration in money or money's worth will not be subject to the gift tax until the transfer is complete. A gift is complete when the donor has "so parted with dominion and control as to leave in him no power to change its disposition, whether for his own benefit or the benefit of another." Reg. §25.2511-2(b). This regulation essentially codifies the common law requirement of delivery. Prior to delivery, the donor has the ability to retract the gift. It is, after all, a transfer made without consideration. If the donor merely promises to transfer property and never follows through on her promise, there is no gift and no transaction on which to impose the tax.

Example 6-1

Aunt tells Nephew, "I will send you $500 next week." This is simply a promise; it is not yet a gift. If Aunt never sends the $500, Nephew has no recourse because he has paid nothing for the promise. If Aunt never sends the $500, she has not made a transfer — a fundamental requirement of the gift tax.

Now assume that Aunt hands Nephew $500 cash. By doing so, Aunt has given up her right to the money; she cannot change her mind. At that point the gift is complete.

Notice that the rule focuses on the donor and her loss of control over the property. This arises from the fact that the gift tax, like the estate tax, is imposed on the transfer of property away from the donor — on the diminution of her estate — rather than on any benefit flowing to the recipient. The regulations state: "[T]he [gift] tax is a primary and personal liability of the donor, is an excise upon his act of making the transfer, is measured by the value of the property passing from the donor, and attaches regardless of the fact that the identity of the donee may not then be known or ascertainable." Reg. §25.2511-2(a).

This rule is necessary to fulfill the fundamental purpose of the gift tax, *i.e.*, to backstop the estate tax. The gift tax must reach those transfers of wealth that are not caught by the estate tax. Any transfer of property that is not included in the gross estate by §§2035-2044 must be subjected to the gift tax. There is not, of course, perfect symmetry. There are some completed gifts that are brought back into the gross estate. These situations result from the application of the estate tax rules, not the gift tax definition of a completed gift.

The question of when a gift is complete arises in a variety of contexts. When a donor sends the recipient a check, or promises to pay a sum of money when the recipient graduates from college, or enters into an antenuptial contract, the issue of timing determines when the gift tax will be imposed. When a donor establishes a trust, each interest must be examined to determine whether the donor has the ability to change the beneficial ownership of that interest. This issue is important because the gift tax, like the income tax, is imposed on an annual basis. The gift tax return for all transfers made within a given year is due on April 15 of the following year. §6075(b)(1). To properly complete the gift tax return, the taxpayer must know which transfers in that year will be subject to the tax. The timing of a gift also determines which gifts qualify for the annual exclusion, which is analyzed in Chapter 7.

PROBLEMS

1. Ellen establishes a joint bank account with Ned, her nephew, by depositing $100,000 in the Friendly National Bank on November 17, 2003. Ned makes no deposits into the account, but he withdraws $25,000 on March 15, 2004. Has Ellen made a gift to Ned? If so, when is the gift complete?

2. Fred purchases Blackacre, taking title with Mary, his daughter, as joint tenants with the right of survivorship. Has Fred made a gift? If so, when is it complete?

3. Henry signs a deed transferring title to Greenacre to Linda, his daughter, on September 1, 1999. Linda records the deed on October 15, 2004. Is this a gift? When is it complete?

4. Isabel is an expert in the cosmetics field. In 1999, she creates a corporation with the intent of establishing Joan, her niece, who has no experience in the field, in the cosmetics field. Isabel, in consultation with her legal advisor, creates a corporation, retaining 51 shares of common stock and transferring 49 shares to Joan. Following the incorporation, Isabel sent Joan a letter stating that she (Isabel) has no ownership interest in the corporation, that she has established the corporation to allow Joan to take advantage of her expertise in the area, and that she will execute any and all documents necessary to transfer title to Joan at any time that Joan requests. Isabel is the president and chief executive officer of the company. In 2004, Isabel transferred title to the 51 shares of stock to Joan. What are the gift tax consequences of this arrangement?

B. PROMISES, CHECKS, AND NOTES
IRC §§2053(c), 2503(b)
Regulation §25.2511-2

A contract, by definition, involves consideration. When the consideration is not sufficient or it is not money or money's worth, there is a gift. In this situation, the gift is complete when the contract becomes legally enforceable.

Example 6-2

In 1999, Parent promises to pay Child $25,000 if Child graduates from college. Child graduates in June 2003, and Parent sends Child $25,000 in January 2004. Parent has not made a gift in 1999 because Parent has merely promised to make a gift at some time in the future. Parent is obligated to pay Child in June 2003 because Child has fulfilled the terms of the agreement. There is now a contract that is legally binding on Parent. At this point, Parent has made a completed gift to Child because Parent can no longer refuse to pay Child. Revenue Ruling 79-384, 1979-2 C.B. 344.

Aunt gives Nephew $500. If Aunt hands Nephew $500 cash, the gift is complete at that moment because Aunt has given up her ability to take the money back. If the gift is made by check, it is not complete until the check is paid or is negotiated for value to a third person because the payor can stop payment on the check at any time before the payee has received payment. Revenue Ruling 67-396, 1967-2 C.B. 351. As a result, the gift is not complete until this right has terminated.

In the majority of cases, no question is ever raised about the date of completion of a gift made by check. The issue becomes important only when checks are given at the end of the tax year and not cashed until the following year or when the donor dies before the checks are cashed. These problems arise because the gift tax contains an exclusion for the first $11,000 of gifts made by the donor in each year to a recipient. §2503(b). This exclusion is an annual per donee exclusion. Thus, the donor may give as many people as she wishes $11,000 and exclude those gifts from the gift tax. The donor may also give the same person $11,000 each year and still exclude those gifts from the gift tax. For example, assume the donor makes gifts of $11,000 to each of his three children each year. He sends the gifts as checks in December 2002 and then in March 2003. If a recipient does not cash the December 2002 check until January 2003, the donor would have made two gifts in 2003, only one of which will qualify for the gift tax annual exclusion.

Another problem arises because the gross estate includes all property owned by the decedent at the moment of death. Only claims that are founded on adequate and full consideration may be deducted pursuant to §2053(c)(1)(A). Thus, gratuitous promises are not valid claims against the estate. When a donor has made gifts immediately before death, the effective date of completion can determine whether the property is included in the gross estate or escapes taxation under the gift tax annual exclusion.

<hr>

Metzger v. Commissioner
38 F.3d 118 (4th Cir. 1994)

<hr>

WILLIAMS, Circuit Judge:

This is an appeal by the Commissioner of Internal Revenue from a decision of the United States Tax Court in favor of the taxpayer, the estate of Albert F. Metzger. The issue presented is whether noncharitable gifts in the form of checks are complete for federal gift tax purposes at the time of the unconditional delivery and deposit of the checks, or when the checks were actually honored by the drawee bank. The Tax Court concluded that, in the limited circumstances of this case, the bank's acceptance of the checks should "relate back" to the year in which they were delivered and deposited. We agree and affirm.

On August 26, 1985, Albert F. Metzger signed a power of attorney authorizing his son, John Metzger, to make gifts of property to Albert Metzger's heirs, legatees, and their spouses. Pursuant to this power of attorney, on December 14, 1985, John wrote four checks on his father's bank account, each in the amount of $10,000, payable to himself, his wife, his brother, and his brother's wife. John and his wife deposited their checks into their joint bank account on December 31, 1985, but the checks did not clear Albert Metzger's account until January 2, 1986, after the New Year's holiday. Albert Metzger made additional gifts of $10,000 each to John and his wife in 1986, which cleared Albert Metzger's account in 1986.

Albert Metzger died on May 29, 1987, his estate was probated, and an estate tax return was filed with the IRS. . . . In the course of the audit of Albert Metzger's estate tax return, the IRS determined that the checks delivered to John and his wife in December 1985 were gifts made in 1986 for gift tax purposes, because the drawee bank did not honor the checks until 1986. Consequently, the IRS concluded that in 1986 Albert Metzger had made gifts to John and his wife of $20,000 each, $40,000 total, of which $20,000 were taxable gifts that should have been reported on Albert Metzger's federal estate tax return. . . .

The Tax Court agreed with the Commissioner that, under the applicable Maryland law, gifts in the form of checks are not completed until they are actually honored by the drawee bank. Nevertheless, the Tax Court granted summary judgment to the taxpayer under the "relation-back" doctrine. Applying the relation-back doctrine, the Tax Court held that, once the checks were honored by the bank, the completed gifts related back to the date they were deposited for federal gift tax purposes. The Commissioner appeals. . . .

The question we must decide in this case is whether the $10,000 gifts that Albert Metzger made to his son and daughter-in-law were completed in 1985 or in 1986 for gift tax purposes. If the gifts were completed in 1985, they qualify for the annual exclusion under §2503(b); if the gifts were not completed until 1986, they must be combined with the other $10,000 gifts made to the son and daughter-in-law in that year. Therefore, Albert Metzger would have exceeded the annual exclusion for 1986, resulting in $20,000 of taxable gifts.

According to the gift tax regulations, a gift is complete when "the donor has so parted with dominion and control as to leave in him no power to change its disposition, whether for his own benefit or for the benefit of another." 26 C.F.R. §25.2511-2(b) (1993). The regulations further provide that "relinquishment or termination of a power to change the beneficiaries of transferred property . . . is regarded as the event that completes the gift and causes the tax to apply," 26 C.F.R. §25.2511-2(f) (1993), and "[a] gift is incomplete in every instance in which a donor reserves the power to revest the beneficial titles to the property in himself," 26 C.F.R. §25.2511-2(c) (1993).

We refer to state law to determine whether a donor has relinquished dominion and control over a gift in the form of a check, Estate of Dillingham v. Commissioner, 903 F.2d 760, 763 (10th Cir.1990), and the parties agree that Maryland law is controlling. The Tax Court held, and we agree, that under Maryland law the delivery of a personal check is only conditional payment, and the gift remains incomplete until the donee presents the check for payment and the check is accepted by the drawee bank. *See* Malloy v. Smith, 265 Md. 460, 290 A.2d 486, 487-88 (1972). . . . Thus, applying Maryland law, Albert Metzger did not completely relinquish dominion and control of the funds given to his son and daughter-in-law until January 2, 1986, when the check was accepted by his bank and his account was debited. Therefore, under §25.2511-2(b) the gift was not completed until 1986. This brings us to the Tax Court's application of the relation-back doctrine, which the IRS contends is contrary to the regulations.

The Tax Court first applied the relation-back doctrine in the context of income tax deductions for charitable contributions. Estate of Spiegel v. Commissioner, 12 T.C. 524, 1949 WL 182 (1949). In *Spiegel*, the IRS disallowed tax deductions for charitable contributions in the year checks were delivered because they were not deposited until the following year. The Tax Court found that because the checks had been unconditionally delivered, promptly presented for payment, and duly paid upon presentment, the payment of the checks related back to the date of delivery, and thus the charitable deductions should have been allowed for the year of delivery. *Id.* at 533.

The Tax Court subsequently applied the relation-back rule from Spiegel in the context of estate taxes and charitable donations in Estate of Belcher v. Commissioner, 83 T.C. 227 (1984). In *Belcher*, checks were mailed to charitable donees prior to the donor's death but not paid until after his death. The Tax Court held that the funds were not part of the gross estate because the conditional payment that occurred when the checks were delivered became absolute upon presentment and payment by the drawee bank, and related back to the date of delivery. It is significant to note that the very same gift tax regulations applicable in *Belcher* are relevant in this case. The IRS contends that a strict interpretation of the gift tax regulations does not support invocation of the relation-back doctrine in the estate tax context. Even if this assertion is true, *Belcher* was equally inconsistent with the regulations, and the Commissioner did not challenge that application of the relation-back doctrine. Rather, the Commissioner merely asserted that for policy reasons noncharitable gifts should be treated differently. Because the Tax Court has incorporated the doctrine into the estate tax area in cases such as *Belcher* where circumstances warranted, we also look beyond the regulation to consider whether its incorporation is warranted here.

Despite its extension of the relation-back doctrine to charitable donations and estate taxes in *Belcher*, the Tax Court, following the reasoning of the Seventh Circuit in McCarthy v. United States, 806 F.2d 129 (7th Cir.1986), declined to extend the doctrine to noncharitable gifts in the estate tax context in the specific circumstances presented in Estate of Dillingham v. Commissioner, 88 T.C. 1569 (1987), *aff'd*, 903 F.2d 760 (10th Cir.1990), and Estate of Gagliardi v. Commissioner, 89 T.C. 1207 (1987). The IRS argues that these precedents cannot be adequately distinguished from the present case and thus require our rejection of the relation-back doctrine. We disagree.

In *McCarthy*, 806 F.2d at 130, the donor wrote and either mailed or delivered nine checks of $3,000 each during the period between May 15 and 22, 1980. The checks were intended as gifts to various relatives. *Id.* The donor died on May 24, 1980, and none of the checks were cashed before that time. *Id.* The Seventh Circuit first concluded that under the applicable state law the donor had not relinquished dominion and control over the checks, "thus preventing completion of the intended gifts" and requiring that the funds be included in the gross estate. *Id.* at 131. The Seventh Circuit then declined to extend the relation-back doctrine because there was no offsetting deduction as there was in the *Belcher* case, and also because application of the relation-back doctrine might foster estate tax avoidance if donors issued checks with the understanding that they not be cashed until after the donor's death. *Id.* at 132.

Similar facts were present in *Gagliardi*. The donor delivered checks to his children on February 4 and 18, and died on February 22. 89 T.C. at 1209. Some of the checks were cashed before the donor's death and some were cashed after his death. *Id.* The Tax Court held, for the same reasons discussed in *McCarthy*, that the relation-back doctrine should not be extended in the estate tax context to the checks that were not cashed before the donor's death. *Id.* at 1212-13. We do not dispute the wisdom of declining to extend the relation-back doctrine in the circumstances presented in *McCarthy* and *Gagliardi*, when the donor died while the checks were still outstanding. Clearly there is a very real danger of fostering estate tax avoidance in cases in which checks are not cashed until after the donor dies. However, that is not the situation in this case.

More analogous to this case are the facts presented in *Estate of Dillingham*. In *Dillingham*, the donor delivered six checks in the amount of $3,000 each to six different individuals on December 24, 1980. 88 T.C. at 1570. The donees did not present the checks for payment at the drawee bank until January 28, 1981, over thirty days after the checks were delivered and on the same day that six additional checks for $3,000 each were delivered to these individuals. *Id.* The donor died June 7, 1981. *Id.* The question presented in *Dillingham* was the same as it is in this case, namely, whether the oncharitable gifts made by check were complete for gift and estate tax purj)ses in the year the checks were delivered to the donee. *Id.* Although the Ta\ Court declined to apply the relation-back doctrine and hold that the gifts were complete in 1980, it stated:

> [b]ecause the checks in the present cases were cashed before the decedent's death, the concern of this Court in *Belcher* and the Circuit Court in *McCarthy* that the donees might have a secret agreement with the donor that the checks would not be cashed until after the donor's death is not present.

Id. at 1574. Rather, the Tax Court based its decision not to extend the relation-back doctrine on its concern about the delay between the time of delivery of the checks and the time the checks were cashed. *Id.* Specifically, the Tax Court held that this delay cast doubt as to whether the checks were unconditionally delivered, and the taxpayer's reliance on the delivery of the checks alone, without proof of unconditional delivery, did not warrant extension of the relation-back doctrine. *Id.* at 1574-75.

In affirming the Tax Court's decision in *Dillingham*, the Eleventh Circuit referred to the Seventh Circuit's reasoning in *McCarthy* and declined to extend the relation-back doctrine to the circumstances in *Dillingham*. 903 F.2d at 764-65. In doing so, however, the Eleventh Circuit explicitly stated that it "express[ed] no opinion as to circumstances where the late December gifts are cashed immediately after the New Year holidays, when financial institutions are closed. Sufficient to say that those are not the circumstances of this case." *Id.* at 765 n. 7.

They are the circumstances with regard to the Estate of Albert Metzger and, in these limited circumstances, application of the relation-back doctrine is appropriate. Here the checks were delivered and deposited in December 1985, more than a year before Albert Metzger died. The checks did not clear Albert Metzger's account until 1986 due to applicable bank procedures, the New Year's holiday, and the fact that Albert Metzger's account was with a different bank than his son and daughter-in-law's account. In contrast to *McCarthy* and *Gagliardi*, the facts in this case do not implicate the concern with averting estate tax avoidance because there was no intervening death between the time the checks were delivered and the day they were deposited. Moreover, unlike *Dillingham*, the son and daughter-in-law in this case timely deposited the checks, leaving no legitimate dispute regarding Albert Metzger's intent to make a gift and his unconditional delivery of the checks.

Thus, we are presented with a very limited situation in which there is no uncertainty as to the donor's intent and unconditional delivery of the gifts, and no danger of a scheme to avoid estate taxes. In such a limited circumstance, where noncharitable gifts are deposited at the end of December and presented for payment shortly after their delivery but are not honored by the drawee bank until after the New Year's holiday, we agree with the Tax Court that the gifts should relate back to the date of deposit. As the Tax Court held:

> We see no reason for refusing to apply the relation-back doctrine to noncharitable gifts where the taxpayer is able to establish: (1) The donor's intent to make a gift, (2) unconditional delivery of the check, and (3) presentment of the check within the year for which favorable tax treatment is sought and within a reasonable time of issuance. Assuming these elements are present, the practical realities of everyday commerce recognized in Estate of Spiegel v. Commissioner, 12 T.C. 524, 529 (1949), require a limited extension of the relation-back rule.

We agree with this limited extension, and are not persuaded that it is inconsistent with the regulations as they have been applied or inconsistent with other precedent. Accordingly, we affirm.

The IRS has agreed to follow *Metzger*. Revenue Ruling 96-56 provides:

> the delivery of a check to a noncharitable donee will be deemed to be a completed gift for federal gift and estate tax purposes on the earlier of (i) the date on which the donor has so parted with dominion and control under local law as to leave in the donor no power to change its disposition, or (ii) the date on which the donee deposits the check (or cashes the check against available funds of the donee) or presents the check for payment, if it is established that: (1) the check was paid by the drawee bank when first presented to the drawee bank for payment; (2) the donor was alive when the check was paid by the drawee bank; (3) the donor intended to make a gift; (4) delivery of the check by the donor was unconditional; and (5) the check was deposited, cashed, or presented in the calendar year for which completed gift treatment is sought and within a reasonable time of issuance.

1996-2 C.B. 161.

A promissory note, like a check, is a negotiable instrument. Usually, promissory notes are given in exchange for a loan of money. They may also be given in exchange for the transfer of property. In such situations, promissory notes are given for adequate and full consideration in money or money's worth and are not gifts. A promissory note, like a check, may also be given as a gift. If the promissory note is a mere promise to pay, it is not a completed gift until the note is paid or transferred for value. Revenue Ruling 67-396, *supra*. If, however, the promissory note creates a legally enforceable agreement that has a determinable value, the note is a completed gift on the date it is signed. Revenue Ruling 84-25, 1984-1 C.B. 191.

Bradford v. Commissioner
34 T.C. 1059 (1960), *acq.* 1961-2C.B. 3

DRENNEN, Judge:

. . . Eleanor A. Bradford, hereafter referred to as petitioner, and her husband, J. C. Bradford, hereafter referred to as J. C., were married in 1926 and reside in Nashville, Tennessee. . . . J. C. was a member of J. C. Bradford & Co., a partnership engaged in the investment banking and securities business in Nashville. The partnership was a member of the New York Stock Exchange. In addition, J. C. was a partner in an insurance agency located in Nashville.

Prior to and during 1938, J. C. was indebted in a substantial amount to the American National Bank, Nashville, hereafter referred to as the bank. During this time, J. C. had been a good customer of the bank and the officers of the bank were willing to cooperate with him concerning the retirement of his obligations to the bank. On October 26, 1938, the New York Stock Exchange adopted a rule which required each general partner in a member firm to submit a detailed account of his indebtedness. At this time J.C.'s indebtedness to the bank totaled $305,000, evidenced by his promissory notes. He feared that this large bank indebtedness would cause J. C. Bradford & Co. to lose its seat on the exchange. This would seriously curtail his earning power.

Thereupon, J. C. requested the bank to substitute a promissory note signed by his wife, the petitioner, for $205,000 in lieu of his own notes for that amount. The bank agreed. On November 25, 1938, petitioner signed an interest-bearing, negotiable demand note payable to the bank, which was dated November 1, 1938, in the amount of $205,000. This note was delivered to the bank by J. C., along with his own notes of $53,000 and $47,000, which were endorsed by petitioner, whereupon the bank returned to J. C. his own notes totaling $305,000, which were marked paid. The collateral which had been on J. C.'s prior notes of $305,000 was placed on the $205,000 note signed by petitioner. Petitioner did not receive any monetary consideration for the execution of her note in the amount of $205,000. . . .

When J. C. requested petitioner to execute the note for $205,000, he explained to her that he was in a "predicament" because of the New York Stock Exchange requirements. He advised her that the bank would accept a note signed by her and, further, that the bank would then release his notes in an equal amount.

At the time petitioner executed the note for $205,000 her net worth was approximately $15,780, which consisted of an equity of approximately $12,000 in the family residence, the sum of $1,280 in a margin account in the J. C. Bradford & Co. brokerage office, and personal effect[s] having an estimated value of $2,500. The bank was aware of petitioner's net worth at the time. Petitioner was not employed and had no independent source of income, nor the prospects of any inheritance except from her husband. . . .

The issue here is whether petitioner's substitution of her note in the amount of $205,000 for notes of her husband of equal amount held by a bank in 1938 constituted a taxable gift in the amount of $205,000 by petitioner to her husband in 1938.

Petitioner contends that the transaction did not constitute a transfer of property by gift within [§2501(a)] because the note executed by petitioner and delivered to the bank was not "property" in her hands, and, further, that even if she did transfer property to her husband by gift in 1938, the value of the property transferred was substantially less than the exemption and exclusion . . . allowable . . . so there is no gift tax liability.

Respondent's position is that the subject of the gift was the entire transaction whereby petitioner's husband was relieved of his indebtedness by the execution and delivery of petitioner's note to the bank, thereby resulting in a transfer of economic benefits which would qualify as a "gift" in the broad and comprehensive sense of that word as used in the statute. . . .

We are of the opinion that the transactions . . . did not constitute a taxable gift from petitioner to her husband in the year 1938 within the purview of the statute. We have found no gift tax cases involving facts similar to those here present, but most gift tax cases must be decided on their own facts anyway. Various general principles have developed through case law and the regulations, and our conclusion is based on the application of some of these principles which seem founded on common sense to the facts in this case.

The gift tax is an excise tax on the transfer of property without adequate and full consideration. Gift tax liability is dependent on the transfer of property by the donor, not the receipt of property by the donee, and the measure of the tax is the value of the property passing from the donor at the time the transfer is completed. . . . While the presence of donative intent on the part of the donor is said no longer to be a necessary element to make a transfer subject to gift tax, as it had always been considered to be in the common law connotation of gifts, the transfer must be donative in character, and we think donative intent may still be a material factor in determining whether a taxable gift has been made. . . . It is true that application of the tax is determined more from the objective facts and circumstances of the transfer and what was accomplished, rather than the subjective motives of the donor, Commissioner v. Wemyss, 324 U.S. 303, but the objective standards used in the tax concept of a gift in effect supply the necessary donative intent of which the donor may not have been conscious. But in any event it seems clear that to constitute a gift for tax purposes there must be a transfer of property owned by the donor with a clear and unequivocal intent on the part of the donor to divest himself presently of the property transferred, and dominion and control thereof. . . .

The facts and circumstances surrounding the transaction here involved do not convince us that petitioner intended to divest herself of any property or interest therein owned by her in 1938, or that any of the parties involved anticipated that any of her property would ever be used to satisfy the obligation to the bank. In the first place she did not own property in 1938 that would have come anywhere near satisfying the obligation to the bank, and she had no prospects of acquiring any except through her husband. Secondly, the entire transaction was arranged by J. C., his collateral was retained as security for petitioner's note, and he testified that it was understood that the bank would look first to his collateral for liquidation of the obligation, and he hoped and expected that the collateral would increase sufficiently in value to cover the entire obligation. J. C. paid the interest on the loan and it is reasonable to assume that all parties involved looked to J. C.'s assets and his earning power to liquidate the loan.

This does not mean that petitioner was not obligated on the indebtedness evidenced by her note. We assume the bank could have taken judgment against her on the note had it not been paid, and levied on her property to help satisfy the judgment, and that it probably would have done so had that course of action become necessary. But unless and until such action was taken we do not believe petitioner parted with, or intended to part with, dominion and control of any property owned by her which would give rise to a gift tax.

Granted that section [2501(a)] is comprehensive enough to "include property, however conceptual or contingent," Smith v. Shaughnessy, 318 U.S. 176, and to reach any passage of control over the economic benefits of property, Estate of Sanford v. Commissioner, 308 U.S. 39; nevertheless, no matter how intangible, the donor must own a property right or interest which is capable of being, and is, transferred. Commissioner v. Mills, 183 F.2d 32 (C.A. 9, 1950), affirming 12 T.C. 468. Petitioner transferred no property or interest in property in 1938 but only made a promise to pay in the future if called upon to do so. John D. Archbold, 42 B.T.A. 453. The fact that J. C. may have derived some economic benefit in 1938 as a result of this promise is not controlling. . . .

We hold that petitioner did not make a transfer of property by gift in 1938. . . . We might add . . . that taxation is a practical matter and it seems incredible that a person having a net worth of only $15,780 could make a gift of $205,000.

The issue of completion also arises in the context of employee death benefits. Most such benefits qualify for special income and estate tax treatment under specific statutory provisions. In some cases, however, an employer will establish an unqualified benefit plan. If properly structured, the death benefit may avoid estate taxation. Having lost a series of estate tax cases, the IRS proposed to tax such benefits as gifts. In Revenue Ruling 81-31, 1981-1 C.B. 475, the IRS held that there was an inter vivos gratuitous transfer where the employer agreed to pay a death benefit in exchange for past and future services. Because the value could not be ascertained until the employee's death, the IRS held that the gift was not completed until the taxpayer died. This ruling was challenged in the following case.

Estate of DiMarco v. Commissioner
87 T.C. 653 (1986), *acq.* 1990 - 2 C.B. 1

STERRETT, Chief Judge:

. . . [T]he only issue presented in this case is whether the present value of a survivors income benefit payable with respect to the decedent by decedent's employer is an adjusted taxable gift within the meaning of section 2001. . . .

Anthony F. DiMarco (hereinafter referred to as the decedent) was born on August 31, 1925. He died on November 16, 1979, survived by his wife, Joan M. DiMarco, and five children. He had been employed continuously by the International Business Machines Corporation (IBM) as an active, regular, full-time, permanent employee from January 9, 1950, until his death. On May 2, 1953, decedent and Joan M. DiMarco were married; he had not been previously married. Decedent's parents were not dependent upon him for their support at any time between the date when his employment with IBM began and the date of his marriage to Joan M. DiMarco. At the time of his death, decedent was employed as an electrical engineer at a salary of $5,250 per month. . . .

On November 16, 1979, and at all other times relevant to this proceeding, IBM maintained a non-contributory Group Life Insurance and Survivors Income Benefit Plan (hereinafter referred to as the Plan) for the benefit of its regular employees. IBM established the Plan in September of 1934, and while the Plan has been amended on many occasions since that time, it has, since January of 1935, provided two basic benefits: (i) group term life insurance, and (ii) an uninsured and unfunded survivors income benefit. . . .

The Plan also provided a survivors income benefit on an uninsured and unfunded basis; that is, all survivors income benefits were paid out of IBM's general assets. With the exception of fewer than 30 top executives, all regular IBM employees, including decedent, were covered automatically by the survivors income benefit portion of the Plan. At the time of decedent's death, the amount of the survivors income benefit was equal to three times the employee's regular annual compensation. Under the terms of the Plan, the benefit was payable only to an employee's surviving spouse, certain minor and dependent children, and dependent parents. Payment was made semi-monthly, at the monthly rate of one-quarter of the employee's regular monthly compensation, and continued until the total benefit was paid. However, payments continued only so long as there remained at least one eligible survivor, and if the employee left no eligible survivor at death, no benefit was payable.

Decedent never had any power to alter, amend, revoke, or terminate the Plan in whole or in part. He had no power to select or change the beneficiaries of the survivors income benefit; no power to change the amount, form, or timing of the survivors income benefit payments; no power to substitute other benefits for the survivors income benefit; and, other than by resigning his employment with IBM, no power to terminate his coverage under the Plan. However, IBM expressly reserved the right, in its discretion, to modify the Plan if it determined that it was advisable to do so.

Joan M. DiMarco, as decedent's surviving spouse, was entitled under the Plan to receive a survivors income benefit, payable semi-monthly, in the amount of $656.25. Decedent did not report the survivors income benefit as a gift on a gift tax return, and petitioner did not report it either as part of the gross estate or as an adjusted taxable gift on decedent's Federal estate tax return. . . .

In his notice of deficiency, respondent "determined that an adjusted taxable gift of the present value of the IBM Survivor Annuity was made by the decedent on the date of death as it was not susceptible of valuation until the date of death." Respondent then determined that the present value of the survivors income benefit was $135,885.00, and he added this amount, as an adjusted taxable gift, to the taxable estate of decedent in computing the amount of the deficiency.

The only issue for decision in this case is whether the present value of the survivors income benefit that is payable by IBM to Joan M. DiMarco is an adjusted taxable gift within the meaning of section 2001. The term "adjusted taxable gifts" is defined by section 2001(b) as "the total amount of the taxable gifts (within the meaning of section 2503) made by the decedent after December 31, 1976, other than gifts which are includible in the gross estate of the decedent." Section 2503(a) in turn defines "taxable gifts" as the "total amount of gifts" made during the applicable period less certain statutory deductions. Thus, the survivors income benefit that is payable by IBM to Joan M. DiMarco is an adjusted taxable gift within the meaning of section 2001 only if it is also a taxable gift within the meaning of section 2503 that was made by decedent after December 31, 1976. . . .

After reviewing carefully respondent's briefs, the statutory notice of deficiency, and the stipulation of facts, it appears to us that respondent is making two arguments in this case. First, it appears that respondent argues that decedent made a completed transfer of a property interest in the survivors income benefit for gift tax purposes on January 9, 1950, but that because the interest could not be valued at that time, it was necessary to treat the transfer as an open transaction and to value the transferred property and impose the gift tax on the date of decedent's death, when the property interest finally became subject to valuation. In the alternative, respondent appears to argue that decedent made an incomplete transfer of a property interest in the survivors income benefit for gift tax purposes on January 9, 1950, because the property interest could not be valued at that time, but that the transfer became complete on November 16, 1979, when decedent died, because the transferred property could then and for the first time be valued.

Petitioner argues, for a variety of reasons, that decedent never made a taxable gift of the survivors income benefit. Petitioner argues that decedent never owned a property interest in the survivors income benefit that he was capable of transferring. Petitioner further contends that, even if decedent owned such an interest, he never transferred it, and if he did transfer it, he never did so voluntarily. Petitioner also asserts that transfers of property cannot become complete for gift tax purposes upon the death of the donor, and that decedent never made a completed transfer of any property interest he may have owned in the survivors income benefit before his death because he always had the power to revoke the transfer, if any was made, simply by resigning his employment with IBM. Petitioner finally argues that, if the decedent made a taxable gift of the survivors income benefit, he did so before December 31, 1976, and that such a gift does not qualify as an adjusted taxable gift within the meaning of section 2001. For the reasons set forth below, we find for petitioner. . . .

[A] transfer of property qualifies as a taxable gift only if the transfer is complete, and a transfer is complete for gift tax purposes only when the transferor relinquishes dominion and control over the transferred property. Sec. 25.2511-2(b), Gift Tax Regs.; Estate of Sanford v. Commissioner, 308 U.S. 39, 42-43 (1939). At the time the transfer is complete, the transferred property must be valued. Sec. 2512(a). This value is then used in determining the gift tax that is due. Sec. 2502.

Respondent argues that decedent transferred a property interest in the survivors income benefit for gift tax purposes on January 9, 1950. This transfer was either complete or incomplete for gift tax purposes. If the transfer was complete, we have little difficulty in disposing of this case because a completed transfer would have been a taxable gift that was made by decedent before December 31, 1976, and section 2001 expressly defines an adjusted taxable gift as a taxable gift that was made after December 31, 1976. On the other hand, if the transfer was incomplete for gift tax purposes, we do not believe that it became complete or that we can deem that it became complete at the time of decedent's death. Section 25.2511-2(f), Gift Tax Regs., provides that —

> the relinquishment or termination of a power to change the beneficiaries of transferred property, *occurring otherwise than by the death of the donor (the statute being confined to transfers by living donors)*, is regarded as the event that completes the gift and causes the tax to apply. . . . (Emphasis added.)

We believe that this regulation precludes our finding in this case that the alleged transfer of property by decedent on January 9, 1950, became complete for gift tax purposes by reason of decedent's death.

We recognize, of course, that respondent does not assert in this case that the alleged transfer on January 9, 1950, became complete and subject to the gift tax because decedent's death terminated a power to change the beneficiaries of the transferred property. Even so, in view of the fact that a transfer of property that becomes complete because the donor's death terminates a power to change the beneficiaries of the transferred property is not subject to the gift tax, we decline to hold that a transfer of property that becomes complete because the donor's death makes it possible for the first time to value the transferred property is subject to the gift tax. We perceive nothing in the gift tax statute or the regulations that would justify such a result.

In addition, we believe that respondent has confused the issues of completion and valuation in this case. Respondent appears to argue that, because the value of the survivors income benefit could not be determined on January 9, 1950, when the alleged transfer occurred, the transfer should be treated as incomplete for gift tax purposes until the survivors income benefit became susceptible of valuation, when decedent died, at which time the transfer became complete and subject to the gift tax. For the reasons stated above, we have already held that transfers of property do not become complete for gift tax purposes by reason of the death of the donor. We also question, however, whether the fact that the value of transferred property cannot be readily determined at the time of transfer is relevant in determining whether the transfer is complete for gift tax purposes. We have noted above that transfers of property are complete and subject to the gift tax at the time the donor relinquishes dominion and control over the transferred property. Nothing in the statute or the regulations suggests that, even if a donor relinquishes dominion and control over transferred property, the transfer is or can be considered to be incomplete for gift tax purposes if the value of the property is uncertain. . . .

Respondent also argues that completed transfers of property for gift tax purposes can and should be treated as open transactions in those cases where the transferred property is difficult to value, and that valuation of the transferred property and the imposition of the gift tax should be postponed until the value of the property can be readily determined. We reject this contention. The clear language of the statute and the regulations requires that transferred property be valued for gift tax purposes at the time the transfer becomes complete. . . . As a result, property must be valued and the gift tax imposed at the time a completed transfer of the property occurs.

We also agree with petitioner that decedent never made a taxable gift of any property interest in the survivors income benefit because we find no act by decedent that qualifies as an act of "transfer" of an interest in property. His participation in the Plan was involuntary, he had no power to select or change the beneficiaries of the survivors income benefit, no power to alter the amount or timing of the payment of the benefit, and no power to substitute other benefits for those prescribed by the Plan. These facts are substantially similar to the facts of Estate of Miller v. Commissioner, 14 T.C. 657 (1950), an estate tax case wherein we also concluded that the decedent had performed no qualifying act of transfer. In *Estate of Miller*, respondent argued, relying on cases where the decedent had purchased for a lump sum joint and survivor annuity contracts and at the time of purchase irrevocably designated the surviving annuitants, that the decedent had, for purposes of section 811(c) of the 1939 Code, transferred property during his life that was intended to take effect at his death. We rejected this contention and concluded that the decedent could not have transferred any property interest for any purpose because he had not performed any act that possibly could be construed as an act of transfer. . . .

Respondent argues, however, that decedent's simple act of going to work for IBM on January 9, 1950, constituted an act of transfer by decedent for gift tax purposes. We disagree. None of the cases cited by respondent hold that, without more, the simple act of going to work for an employer that has an automatic, non-elective, company-wide survivors income benefit plan similar to the one at issue in this case constitutes a "transfer" of an interest in the benefit for either estate or gift tax purposes. Moreover, we doubt that it can be maintained seriously that decedent began his employment with IBM on January 9, 1950 (when he was 24, unmarried, and without dependents), for the purpose or with any intention of transferring property rights in the survivors income benefit. While we agree with respondent that a taxable event may occur without a volitional act by the donor, as in a case where an incomplete transfer of property becomes complete because of the occurrence of an event outside the donor's control, we do not believe that a taxable event can occur for gift tax purposes unless there is first and in fact an act of transfer by the donor; and there can be no act of transfer unless the act is voluntary and the transferor has some awareness that he is in fact making a transfer of property, that is, he must intend to do so. . . . It is apparent to us that decedent never intended and never voluntarily acted to transfer any interest that he may have owned in the survivors income benefit. There being no act of transfer by decedent, there can be no transfer of property by gift.

Moreover, we question whether decedent ever owned a property interest in the survivors income benefit that he was capable of transferring during his lifetime. He had no voice in selecting the beneficiaries of the survivors income benefit and no ability to affect or determine the benefits payable to them. The categories of beneficiaries, the determination whether a claimant is an eligible beneficiary, and the amounts payable to the beneficiaries all were controlled directly by the provisions of the Plan and indirectly by IBM, and payments were made directly to the beneficiaries by IBM. Furthermore, the benefits were payable out of the general assets of IBM, not out of any fund in which decedent had a vested interest, and the benefits did not accrue until decedent's death. Most importantly, IBM had the power and the right to modify the Plan and the survivors income benefit at any time and in its sole discretion. Under these circumstances, we have little difficulty in concluding that decedent never acquired fixed and enforceable property rights in the survivors income benefit that he was capable of transferring during his lifetime. . . .

In our opinion, decedent never made a taxable gift of any interest in the survivors income benefit to his wife. It follows that the present value of the survivors income benefit is not an adjusted taxable gift within the meaning of section 2001.

Not all courts agree with the Tax Court's analysis of the transfer issue. In Estate of Tully v. Commissioner, 528 F.2d 1401 (Ct. Cl. 1976), the court held that the decedent had made a transfer by entering into an employment agreement. In *Tully*, however, the decedent was married at the time he began his employment. The *Tully* case is at page 340.

PROBLEMS

1. On August 1, 2003, Agnes promises to send Ned, her nephew, $50,000. Agnes sends the check on March 1, 2004. What are the gift tax consequences?

2. On April 15, 2001, Arthur promises to pay Nancy, his niece, $50,000 if Nancy refrains from smoking for two years. Nancy agrees to do so, and she keeps her promise. Arthur sends Nancy the check for $50,000 on May 1, 2003.
   a. What are the gift tax consequences?
   b. Instead, what are the gift tax consequences if Arthur does not send the check until March 5, 2004?

3. On December 15, 2003, Amanda sends Peter, her son, a check for $11,000.
   a. Peter deposits the check in his bank on December 29, 2003. The check clears Amanda's bank on January 3, 2004. What are the gift tax consequences?
   b. Instead, Peter deposits the check in his bank on January 2, 2004. The check clears Amanda's bank on January 5, 2004. What are the gift tax consequences?
   c. Amanda dies on December 29, 2003. Peter cashes the check on January 3, 2004. What are the gift tax consequences?

4. Alex decides to give Blackacre to Paul, his son, as a wedding gift. Alex sends Paul a letter on October 15, 2002, promising to transfer Blackacre as a wedding present. Alex transfers title to Paul on February 25, 2003, the day after Paul is married.
   a. What are the gift tax consequences?
   b. What if Alex does not transfer title until March 5, 2004?

5. Did Eleanor Bradford make a gift to her husband at the time she signed the demand note payable to the bank? What facts support your conclusion? What would be the gift tax consequences if Eleanor Bradford paid $100,000 to the bank?

6. Was the court in *DiMarco* correct?
   a. Why is the decedent's marital status at the time he begins his employment relevant?
   b. If an employee benefit, such as IBM's survivors' income benefit, is not taxed by the estate tax because the decedent has no power or control over it, how should it be taxed?

C. REVOCABLE TRUSTS AND RETAINED INTERESTS
Regulation §25.2511-2

A gift is complete when the donor has "so parted with dominion and control as to leave in him no power to change its disposition, whether for his own benefit or for the benefit of another." Reg. §25.2511-2(b). Where the donor reserves power over the disposition of property, the transfer may be wholly incomplete or only partially incomplete. *Id.* Where the donor creates multiple interests, for example in trusts, each interest must be analyzed separately to determine whether or not it is complete.

Obviously, where the donor retains the power to revoke the gift, it is not complete. What happens when a grantor creates a trust in one year, retaining the power to revoke it, and then releases the power to revoke in a subsequent year? The trust property will not be in the grantor's gross estate because she has not retained a power over the trust property for her lifetime nor does she have a power over it at the time of her death. §§2036(a)(2), 2038(a)(1). These estate tax provisions strongly suggest that there must be a completed gift at some point in time, either when the trust was originally created or when the power to revoke was released.

In Burnet v. Guggenheim, 288 U.S. 280 (1933), the grantor released the power to revoke the trust after the gift tax was enacted and the Court held that the gift tax applied at the time the grantor released the power.

> "Taxation is not so much concerned with the refinements of title as it is with actual command over the property taxed — the actual benefit for which the tax is paid." Corliss v. Bowers, 281 U.S. 376, 378. . . . While the powers of revocation stood uncanceled in the deeds, the gifts, from the point of view of substance, were inchoate and imperfect. By concession there would have been no gift in any aspect if the donor had attempted to attain the same result by the mere delivery of the securities into the hands of the donees. A power of revocation accompanying delivery would have made the gift a nullity. Basket v. Hassell, 107 U.S. 602. By the execution of deeds and the creation of trusts, the settlor did indeed succeed in divesting himself of title and transferring it to others, . . . but the substance of his dominion was the same as if these forms had been omitted. . . . He was free at any moment, with reason or without, to revest title in himself, except as to any income then collected or accrued. As to the principal of the trusts and as to income to accrue thereafter, the gifts were formal and unreal. They acquired substance and reality for the first time in July, 1925, when the deeds became absolute through the cancellation of the power. . . .
>
> Congress did not mean that the tax should be paid twice, or partly at one time and partly at another. If a revocable deed of trust is a present transfer by gift, there is not another transfer when the power is extinguished. If there is not a present transfer upon the delivery of the revocable deed, then there is such a transfer upon the extinguishment of the power. There must be a choice, and a consistent choice, between the one date and the other. To arrive at a decision, we have therefore to put to ourselves the question: Which choice is it the more likely

that Congress would have made? Let us suppose a revocable transfer made on June 3, 1924, the day after the adoption of the Revenue Act of that year. Let us suppose a power of revocation still uncanceled, or extinguished years afterwards, say in 1931. Did Congress have in view the present payment of a tax upon the full value of the subject-matter of this imperfect and inchoate gift? The statute provides that, upon a transfer by gift, the tax upon the value shall be paid by the donor . . . and shall constitute a lien upon the property transferred. . . . By the act now in force, the personal liability for payment extends to the donee. . . . A statute will be construed in such a way as to avoid unnecessary hardship when its meaning is uncertain. . . . Hardship there plainly is in exacting the immediate payment of a tax upon the value of the principal when nothing has been done to give assurance that any part of the principal will ever go to the donee. The statute is not aimed at every transfer of the legal title without consideration. Such a transfer there would be if the trustees were to hold for the use of the grantor. It is aimed at transfers of the title that have the quality of a gift, and a gift is not consummate until put beyond recall. . . .

The tax upon gifts is closely related both in structure and in purpose to the tax upon those transfers that take effect at death. What is paid upon the one is in certain circumstances a credit to be applied in reduction of what will be due upon the other. . . . The two statutes are plainly *in pari materia*. There has been a steady widening of the concept of a transfer for the purpose of taxation under the provisions of [the estate tax]. . . . There is little likelihood that the lawmakers meant to narrow the concept, and to revert to a construction that would exalt the form above the substance, in fixing the scope of a transfer for the purposes of [the gift tax]. We do not ignore differences in precision of definition between the one part and the other. They cannot obscure identities more fundamental and important. The tax upon estates, as it stood in 1924, was the outcome of a long process of evolution; it had been refined and perfected by decisions and amendments almost without number. The tax on gifts was something new. Even so, the concept of a transfer, so painfully developed in respect of taxes on estates, was not flung aside and scouted in laying this new burden upon transfers during life. Congress was aware that what was of the essence of a transfer had come to be identified more nearly with a change of economic benefits than with technicalities of title. The word had gained a new color, the result, no doubt in part, of repeated changes of the statutes, but a new color none the less.

Id. at 283-287.

Six years later the Supreme Court faced a similar issue in the companion cases of Estate of Sanford v. Commissioner, 308 U.S. 39 (1939), and Rasquin v. Humphreys, 308 U.S. 54 (1939), where the donors retained the power to designate new beneficiaries but subsequently released that power. The IRS took inconsistent positions in these two cases because it was uncertain which construction of the gift tax would produce greater revenue. Relying on Burnet v. Guggenheim, the Court held that the tax would be imposed at the time the grantor relinquished the power to designate new or different beneficiaries, stating:

> In ascertaining the correct construction of the statutes taxing gifts, it is necessary to read them in the light of the closely related provisions of the revenue laws

taxing transfers at death, as they have been interpreted by our decisions. . . . When the gift tax was enacted Congress was aware that the essence of a transfer is the passage of control over the economic benefits of property rather than any technical changes in its title. . . . The rule was thus established, and has ever since been consistently followed by the Court, that a transfer of property upon trust, with power reserved to the donor either to revoke it and recapture the trust property or to modify its terms so as to designate new beneficiaries other than himself is incomplete, and becomes complete so as to subject the transfer to death taxes only on relinquishment of the power at death.

There is nothing in the language of the statute, and our attention has not been directed to anything in its legislative history to suggest that Congress had any purpose to tax gifts before the donor had fully parted with his interest in the property given, or that the test of the completeness of the taxed gift was to be any different from that to be applied in determining whether the donor has retained an interest such that it becomes subject to the estate tax upon its extinguishment at death. The gift tax was supplementary to the estate tax. The two are in pari materia and must be construed together. Burnet v. Guggenheim, *supra*, 288 U.S. page 286. An important, if not the main purpose of the gift tax was to prevent or compensate for avoidance of death taxes by taxing the gifts of property inter vivos which, but for the gifts, would be subject in its original or converted form to the tax laid upon transfers at death. . . .

It is plain that the contention of the taxpayer in this case that the gift becomes complete and taxable upon the relinquishment of the donor's power to revoke the trust cannot be sustained unless we are to hold, contrary to the policy of the statute and the reasoning in the *Guggenheim* case, that a second tax will be incurred upon the donor's relinquishment at death of his power to select new beneficiaries, or unless as an alternative we are to abandon our ruling in the *Porter* case. The Government does not suggest, even in its argument in the *Humphreys* case, that we should depart from our earlier rulings, and we think it clear that we should not do so both because we are satisfied with the reasoning upon which they rest and because departure from either would produce inconsistencies in the law as serious and confusing as the inconsistencies in administrative practice from which the Government now seeks relief.

There are other persuasive reasons why the taxpayer's contention cannot be sustained. By [§6324(b)], the donee of any gift is made personally liable for the tax to the extent of the value of the gift if the tax is not paid by the donor. It can hardly be supposed that Congress intended to impose personal liability upon the donee of a gift of property, so incomplete that he might be deprived of it by the donor the day after he had paid the tax. Further, [§2522] exempts from the tax, gifts to religious, charitable, and educational corporations and the like. A gift would seem not to be complete, for purposes of the tax, where the donor has reserved the power to determine whether the donees ultimately entitled to receive and enjoy the property are of such a class as to exempt the gift from taxation. Apart from other considerations we should hesitate to accept as correct a construction under which it could plausibly be maintained that a gift in trust for the benefit of charitable corporations is then complete so that the taxing statute becomes operative and the gift escapes the tax even though the donor should later change the beneficiaries to the non-exempt class through exercise of a power of modify the trust in any way not beneficial to himself.

Estate of Sanford v. Commissioner, 308 U.S. 39, 42-47.

A grantor is deemed to have a power over the trust property even if she can only exercise the power in conjunction with another person. If the other person has an interest in the trust that is both substantial and adverse, then the grantor will not be considered as having retained a power. Reg. §25.2511-2(e).

Example 6-3

Gretchen establishes an irrevocable trust, appointing herself and her brother, Ben, as Trustees. The Trustees have discretion to distribute income to, or for the benefit of, Gretchen's nieces and nephews or to accumulate the income and add it to the principal. The Trustees also have discretion to distribute corpus to any income beneficiary if the Trustees determine that the distribution is necessary for their comfort and happiness. At the death of the last of Gretchen's nieces and nephews, the trust property is to be distributed to Gretchen's surviving heirs. Both Trustees must agree on distributions of income or corpus.

The gifts to Gretchen's nieces and nephews as well as to her surviving heirs are incomplete. Gretchen has retained the power to change the beneficial enjoyment of the trust property. This is sufficient to make the gifts incomplete, even though Gretchen cannot receive trust property herself. Reg. §25.2511-2(c). It is irrelevant that Ben must consent. His interest as Trustee is not adverse to the exercise of discretion, either over income or over corpus. Reg. §25.2511-2(e). Gretchen will also be taxed on the income from the trust pursuant to §674 because Ben does not have an interest adverse to the exercise of this power.

Example 6-4

Gretchen establishes an irrevocable trust, appointing herself as Trustee. As Trustee, Gretchen has discretion to distribute trust income to, or for the benefit of, her brother, Ben, his wife, Wendy, or their children, Nancy and Peter. Any trust income not distributed is added to the principal. At the death of the last surviving income beneficiary, the trust property is to be distributed to Ben's surviving descendants. The gift of income is incomplete because Gretchen can change the beneficial enjoyment of the trust income through distribution or accumulation of the income. Reg. §25.2511-2(c). The gift of the remainder interest is complete, because Gretchen cannot alter the beneficiaries even though she can increase the amount of the gift through accumulation of the income. Gretchen's power over the income is sufficient to make her the owner for purposes of the income tax. §674.

Assume that Ben must consent to any distribution or accumulation of trust income. Ben's interest as a possible recipient of trust income is adverse to the distribution of trust income to anyone else or to the accumulation of trust income. As a result, the gift of the income interest is now complete. Reg. §25.2511-2(e). Since Ben has an adverse interest, Gretchen is no longer taxable on the income. §674(a).

The grantor may retain control over trust property as long as that control is a fiduciary power and is limited by a fixed or ascertainable standard. Reg. §25.2511-2(g). An ascertainable standard is an objective, external standard that a beneficiary can force the trustee to exercise. It is one that is related to health, education, support, or maintenance or one designed to maintain the beneficiary's accustomed standard of living. *See* Reg. §25.2511-1(g)(2). In Example 6-3, Gretchen can distribute corpus for the comfort and happiness of her nieces and nephews. This is not an ascertainable standard. If, however, her discretion was limited to distributing corpus for their health, education, or support, the standard would be ascertainable and the gift of the remainder would be a completed gift. If the grantor's power is over corpus and is limited by an ascertainable standard, then the grantor is no longer taxed as the owner. §674(b)(5)(A).

On the other hand, the existence of an ascertainable standard makes a gift in trust incomplete where the grantor is the trust beneficiary.

Example 6-5

Greg establishes an irrevocable trust with Friendly National Bank as Trustee. The Trustee has discretion to pay the income to Greg or his children during Greg's life. At his death, the trust property will be distributed to Greg's surviving issue. The gifts of income and principal are complete because Greg has not retained the power to change the beneficial enjoyment of the trust property. Reg. §25.2511-2(b).

Assume instead that the Trustee has discretion to distribute either income or corpus for the health and maintenance of Greg. This is an ascertainable standard. Greg can force the Trustee to distribute trust property to him for these needs. As a result, the transfer to the trust is not a completed gift. Reg. §25.2511-2(b).

Although the Supreme Court in *Estate of Sanford* and Rasquin v. Humphreys suggested that a transfer should be taxed either as a gift during life or as a testamentary transfer at death, the rules governing when a gift is complete and the rules governing what interests are included in the gross estate for estate tax purposes are not entirely consistent. There are many situations where a completed gift will be included in the decedent's gross estate. For example, Daniel purchases Blackacre, taking title as joint tenants with the right of survivorship with his daughter, Betsy, and paying the entire purchase price himself. The creation of the joint tenancy is a completed gift. At Daniel's death, however, the full value of Blackacre will be in his gross estate. §2040(a).

Another example is when Ellen creates an irrevocable trust with Friendly National Bank as Trustee to pay the income to her during her life and then to distribute the trust property to her surviving issue at her death. The gift of the remainder interest is complete because Ellen has given up all dominion and control over the trust property. The full value of the trust, however, will be in her gross estate pursuant to §2036(a)(1). The same result occurs if Fred creates an irrevocable trust with Friendly National Bank as Trustee to pay the income to Ann for her life, and at her death to distribute the trust property to Bob, and Fred retains the right to terminate the trust and distribute the trust property to Bob. The gift of the income interest is incomplete because Fred has retained the ability to change the recipient of the trust income by terminating the trust; the gift of the remainder is complete because Fred can only alter the time and manner of enjoyment. Reg. §25.2511-2(d). The full value of the trust will be in Fred's gross estate under §2038 if he dies without exercising the power because of his right to terminate the trust.

The gift completion rules and the gross estate provisions are also not completely consistent with the grantor trust rules described in Chapter 2. It is possible for the grantor of a trust to make a completed gift and still be taxed as the owner of the trust.

In the 2001 Tax Act, Congress repealed the estate tax but retained the gift tax.[1] The retention of the gift tax is designed to prevent shifting income to lower bracket taxpayers. To reinforce this policy, Congress also amended §2511 by adding subsection (c), which provides:

> Treatment of certain transfers in trust, — Notwithstanding any other provision of this section and except as provided in regulations a transfer in trust shall be treated as a transfer of property by gift, unless the trust is treated as wholly owned by the donor or the donor's spouse under subpart E of part I of subchapter J of chapter 1.

In other words, if the grantor or the grantor's spouse is treated as the owner of a trust for income tax purposes, the transfer to that trust will be treated as an incomplete transfer. Distribution of income from that trust to someone other than the grantor or his spouse will be a completed gift, and the relinquishment of the power that made the trust a grantor trust will also be a completed gift. This rule only becomes effective in 2010 when the estate tax is repealed. Until then, the regulations, case law, and administrative rulings delineating when a gift is, or is not, complete will continue to prevail.

PROBLEMS

1. Gail establishes a trust to pay the income to Eric for ten years, with the remainder to Faith.
   a. What are the gift tax consequences if the trust is irrevocable?
   b. What are the gift tax consequences if the trust is revocable?
   c. What are the gift tax consequences if the trust is irrevocable but the corpus reverts to Gail after ten years rather than going to Faith?

---

1. Because of the sunset provision of this Act, the repeal of the estate tax is only effective for the year 2010.

2. Gail establishes an irrevocable trust with Friendly National Bank as Trustee to pay the income to Eric for life with the remainder to Faith. What are the gift tax consequences in each of the following situations?

    a. Gail retains the power to add or delete beneficiaries.
    b. Gail retains the power to alter only the remaindermen.
    c. Same as a, only Gail must obtain the consent of Calvin (her spouse) to alter the beneficiaries.
    d. Same as c, only the remainder is to be paid to Calvin.
    e. What if instead Gail *as Trustee* retains the power to distribute the corpus for the education of Faith?
    f. What if Gail *as Trustee* retains the power to distribute corpus to Faith in an emergency?
    g. What if Gail *as Trustee* retains the power to distribute corpus to Faith for her comfort and happiness?

D. INSTALLMENT SALES AND LOANS
IRC §2503(b)

Installment sales and similar transactions have potential income, gift, and estate tax advantages. Because most installment sales occur within the family context, the first issue is whether the consideration paid is adequate and full and in money or money's worth. Because the fair market value of the property is often difficult to establish, intrafamily transactions are subject to close scrutiny. Even if the consideration stated in the contract is full and adequate, a further issue arises if the seller/parent forgives the annual payments as they come due. Is this a series of gifts? Or is it one gift at the time the contract was signed? The answer will determine whether the parent will receive only one annual exclusion in the year the contract is signed or a series of annual exclusions as the payments are forgiven. Sellers/parents, of course, try to achieve the latter result.

Estate of Kelley v. Commissioner
63 T.C. 321 (1974)

FEATHERSTON, Judge:

. . . On August 5, 1954, J. W. Kelley, since deceased, and his wife, Margaret I. Kelley (hereinafter referred to as petitioners), executed five warranty deeds transferring to their three children, N. Ray Kelley, M. E. Kelley, and Beulah Danforth, and to their two grandchildren, Jerry E. Devenport and Sybil Devenport Angeley, specific tracts of land in Lamb, Castro, and Palmer Counties, Tex., subject to stated reservations. In each conveyance, petitioners reserved to themselves the full possession, benefits, and use of the properties, as well as the rents, issues, and profits thereof during both of their natural lives.

Each of the deeds recites that it was given in consideration of a stated cash payment and vendor's lien notes. Each grantee executed four non-interest-bearing vendor's lien notes in favor of petitioners, the first of which matured January 1, 1955. The second note matured January 1, 1956; the third one on January 1, 1957; and the last one on January 1, 1958. The face amount of each vendor's lien note executed by N. Ray Kelley, M. E. Kelley, and Beulah Danforth was $6,000; the face amount of each vendor's lien note executed by Jerry E. Devenport and Sybil Devenport Angeley was $3,000. The downpayments made by the grantees in connection with the conveyances were gifts to the grantees by petitioners.

Each deed of conveyance described each of the notes given therefor and recited that a vendor's lien was retained against the property conveyed to secure the payment of such notes. A valid lien was thereby created under Texas law against each such tract to secure the payment of the notes given therefor. The deeds were filed in the office of the county clerk of each county in which the deeded land is located.

None of the aforementioned vendor's lien notes was actually paid by the grantees; instead the notes were forgiven by petitioners at or about the time they became due. . . . Gift tax returns for 1954 were filed for Margaret I. Kelley, individually, and for J. W. Kelley's estate. In each such gift tax return, there was deducted from the reported value of the donor's conveyance an amount equal to such donor's community portion of the vendor's lien notes.

In his statutory notice of deficiency, respondent increased the taxable gifts of each petitioner for 1954 by such petitioner's community one-half of the above-described vendor's lien notes, being $48,000 for each petitioner. Petitioners here contend that, in August 1954, they sold remainder interests in their land to their children and grandchildren in consideration of the cash and vendor's lien notes reserving an estate for both of their lives, and that they did not make gifts of such interests.

We hold for petitioners. The notes received by petitioners, secured by valid vendor's liens, constituted valuable consideration in return for the transfer of the property. Petitioners have reported as taxable gifts the value of the transferred interests in excess of the face amount of the notes. The notes were extinguished without payment as they became due, but the vendor's liens continued in effect as long as a balance was due on the notes. At any time prior to the forgiveness of the final note relating to a particular transfer, petitioners could have demanded payment of the amounts falling due and, in case of default, could have foreclosed the vendor's lien on the property to satisfy the obligations. In addition, the notes, to the extent of the unpaid balances, were subject to sale or assignment by petitioners at any time, and a purchaser or assignee could have enforced the liens.

This Court has held that when property is transferred in exchange for a valid, enforceable, and secured legal obligation, there is no gift for Federal tax

purposes. In Selsor R. Haygood, 42 T.C. 936 (1964), a mother deeded properties to each of her two sons and in return took a vendor's lien note from each
son for the full value of the property, payable $3,000 per year. In accordance
with her intention when she transferred the properties, the mother canceled the
$3,000 payments as they became due. Holding that the mother did not make
gifts of the properties at the time of the transfer and receipt of the notes, the
Court said (Selsor R. Haygood, *supra* at 946):

> If the notes of petitioner's sons were as a matter of law unenforceable, there
> might be validity to respondent's argument that there was no debt secured by the
> vendor's liens and deeds of trust which would be collectible. However, under the
> facts in this case where the very deeds conveying the properties recited that
> vendor's lien notes were being given in consideration therefor, the evidence
> certainly supports the fact that the notes did create enforceable indebtedness
> even though petitioner had no intention of collecting the debts but did intend to
> forgive each payment as it became due. . . .

See also Geoffrey C. Davies, 40 T.C. 525, 531 (1963); Nelson Story III, 38
T.C. 936, 941 (1962).

Respondent maintains that the vendor's lien notes received by petitioners
lacked economic substance and were a mere "facade for the principal purpose
of tax avoidance." However, there are two answers to this contention. First, the
notes and vendor's liens, without evidence showing they were a "facade," are
prima facie what they purport to be. There is nothing in the trial record to
support a finding that the notes and vendor's liens, both in proper legal form
and regular on their face, were not valid and enforceable. Nor is there any
evidence of any agreement between petitioners and the donees qualifying the
rights of petitioners under either the liens or the notes. There is no solid
evidence indicating that petitioners did not purposely and consciously reserve
all rights given to them under the liens and notes until they actually forgave the
notes. Nothing in the record suggests the notes were not collectible. Indeed,
since the gift tax returns, accepted as a basis for the computations in the notices
of deficiency, reflect that the transferred remainder interests had substantial
value in excess of the amounts of the notes, Thus, there is no real evidence to
support respondent's argument that the notes and liens were a mere facade.

Second, since the notes and liens were enforceable, petitioners' gifts in 1954
were limited to the value of the transferred interests in excess of the face amount
of the notes. Petitioners retained the rights over the remainder interests
conferred by the vendor's liens and notes, including the rights of assignment
and foreclosure in case of default. Any sale or other transfer of such interests by
the donees would have been subject to the liens. Thus, a gift was not made of
the remainder interests; only the excess of the value of the remainder interests
over and above the agreed consideration for the sale was the subject of a gift.

We are not unmindful of the elementary proposition of tax law that family
transactions are subject to rigid scrutiny. *See* Estate of Carr v. Van Anda, 12
T.C. 1158, 1162 (1949). In the instant case, however, there is no substantial

evidence to negate the legal effect of the secured obligations other than the suspicions which may arise from any transaction between family members. The subsequent forgiveness of the notes as they came due is not sufficient to support an inference that the notes and liens were without substance in 1954, when the initial transaction occurred. In the absence of additional evidence, we feel constrained to adhere to our prior holdings in similar cases.

Revenue Ruling 77-299
1977-2 C.B. 343

. . . G had given A and B, G's grandchildren, $3,000 per year at Christmas since each grandchild was 10 years old. When A and B were, respectively, 21 and 22 years old and enrolled in graduate school, G proposed to give Blackacre, with a fair market value of $27,000, to A and Whiteacre, with a fair market value of $24,000, to B. Both Blackacre and Whiteacre were unimproved tracts of nonincome-producing real property. A and B had spent the money previously given them by G, did not have any other funds, and did not have an independent source of income. When informed of G's intent, G's attorney, in order to minimize G's Federal gift tax on the transfer, suggested a sale of the property to each grandchild in return for installment notes that would be payable in yearly amounts equal to the annual gift tax exclusion.

The plan was implemented in July 1972, at which time A and B each received a package of instruments in the mail from G's attorney. A's package contained a check from G for $50, a deed to Blackacre, a mortgage on the property, one note with a face amount of $2,950 and eight notes each in the amount of $3,000. B's package contained a check from G for $50, a deed to Whiteacre, a mortgage on the property, one note with a face amount of $2,950 and seven notes each in the amount of $3,000. A letter also accompanied each package explaining the transaction to A and B and indicating that G did not intend to collect on the notes, but intended to forgive each payment as it became due. A and B did not have prior knowledge of the transaction. There were no negotiations concerning the transaction, and G's attorney represented all of the parties to the transaction.

The notes were noninterest-bearing and nonnegotiable. The notes provided that A owed $26,950 on Blackacre and B owed $23,950 on Whiteacre. The first note of each grandchild in the amount of $2,950 matured on January 1, 1973, and each additional note in the amount of $3,000 matured on January 1 of each succeeding year. Each of the deeds recited that it was given in consideration of a cash payment of $50 and the notes. Additionally, each deed described the notes and recited that the mortgages on the property were taken to secure the payment of the notes. The deeds, mortgage, and notes were executed on July 15, 1973, and at the same time A and B each transferred $50 to G. Thereafter, the deeds (but not the mortgages) were recorded with the proper county authorities.

On December 25, 1972, G forgave the $2,950 due from A and B on January 1, 1973. On December 25 of 1973 and 1974, G forgave the $3,000 due from A and B on January 1 of the following years.

The specific question presented is whether the transfer of the property in return for the notes secured by a purchase money mortgage was a bona fide sale between the parties or whether the transaction was in substance a gift of the transferor's entire interest in the property structured to avoid the Federal gift tax.

Section 2501 . . . imposes a tax on the transfer of property by gift. . . . [T]he gift tax applies to all transactions whereby property or property rights or interests are gratuitously passed or conferred upon another, regardless of the means or device employed. *See* section 25.2511-1(c) of the regulations.

In the case of present interests, section 2503 of the Code excludes $3,000 of gifts per calendar year for each donee from gifts subject to the gift tax. [The IRS then quotes §2512 and regulation §25.2512-8.]

In Minnie E. Deal, 29 T.C. 730 (1958), the taxpayer transferred in trust a remainder interest in unimproved, nonincome-producing property to the taxpayer's children in return for noninterest-bearing, unsecured demand notes. The taxpayer cancelled $3,000 of each child's indebtedness each year until the balance due was completely cancelled. The Tax Court held the notes executed by the children were not intended as consideration for the transfer and, rather than a bona fide sale, the taxpayer made a gift of the remainder interest to the children. A similar result was reached in Estate of Pearl Gibbons Reynolds, 55 T.C. 172, 202 (1970), and a similar rationale was applied in Marie-Anne De Goldschmidt-Rothschild, 9 T.C. 325 (1947), *aff'd* 168 F.2d 975 (2d Cir. 1948).

Thus, in the instant case, whether the transfer of property was a sale or a gift depends upon whether, as part of a prearranged plan, G intended to forgive the notes that were received when G transferred the property.

It should be noted that the intent to forgive notes is to be distinguished from donative intent, which, as indicated by section 25.2511-1(g)(1) of the regulations, is not relevant. A finding of an intent to forgive the note relates to whether valuable consideration was received and, thus, to whether the transaction was in reality a bona fide sale or a disguised gift. Therefore, such an inquiry is necessary in situations such as the one described here. . . . Donative intent, on the other hand, rather than relating to whether a transaction was actually a sale or a gift, relates to whether the donor intended the transaction to be a sale or a gift. Although the same facts would be used in determining either type of intent, they relate to two entirely different inquiries.

In the instant case, the facts clearly indicate that G, as part of a prearranged plan, intended to forgive the notes that were received in return for the transfer of G's land. Therefore, the transaction was merely a disguised gift rather than a bona fide sale.

The Service will not follow the decisions in Selsor R. Haywood, 42 T.C. 936 (1964), acq. in result, 1965-1 C.B. 4, nonacq., 1977-2 C.B. 2, and J. W. Kelley, 63 T.C. 321 (1974), nonacq., 1977-2 C.B. 2, that held that forgiveness of notes constituted a gift of a present interest, under circumstances similar to the present ruling.

Accordingly, for Federal gift tax purposes, G made a transfer by gift to A in 1972 in the amount of $27,000. In addition, G made a transfer by gift to B in 1972 in the amount of $24,000.

Although the courts are more sympathetic to taxpayers than the IRS, not all taxpayers prevail. *See, e.g.*, Estate of Maxwell v. Commissioner, 3 F.3d 591 (2d Cir. 1993), at page 247. Taxpayers have also tried to extend the benefits of annual debt forgiveness to outright loans.

Estate of Berkman v. Commissioner
38 T.C.M. (CCH) 183 (1979)

FAY, Judge:

. . . The first issue for our decision is whether the decedent's transfer of $275,000 to his daughter, son-in-law, and their wholly owned corporation in exchange for five promissory notes resulted in taxable gifts, and if so, to what extent. . . .

It is well established that [the exception in regulation §25.2512-8] is not limited to strictly business transactions but includes all bona fide transfers at arm's length in which no donative intent is present. Harris v. Commissioner, 340 U.S. 106, 112 (1950); Stern v. United States, 436 F.2d 1327, 1330 (5th Cir. 1971); Anderson v. Commissioner, 8 T.C. 706, 720 (1947). Moreover, even a family transaction may, for gift tax purposes, be treated as one "in the ordinary course of business" if each one of the parenthetical criteria in section 25.2512-8, Gift Tax Regs., is fully met. Stern v. United States, *supra*; Rosenthal v. Commissioner, 205 F.2d 505, 509 (2d Cir. 1953).

With these principles in mind, to resolve the issue of whether the transfers made by the decedent were taxable gifts, we must determine to what extent the notes he received in exchange represented consideration for these transfers.

The respondent first contends there was no intention on the part of the decedent to collect the $275,000 and, thus, the promissory notes were not valid obligations and did not represent any consideration for the transfers made by the decedent. Consequently, all five transactions resulted in taxable gifts to the full extent of the amounts transferred. In the alternative, the respondent argues that even if the promissory notes were valid obligations, the transfers the decedent made were not at arm's length, therefore, the difference between the amount of each transfer and the fair market value of each note given in exchange constitutes a taxable gift.

Petitioner maintains that the decedent entered into an arm's-length loan arrangement with each transferee and the promissory notes he received were valid, enforceable obligations which constituted full and sufficient consideration for each transfer. Therefore, none of the transfers resulted in taxable gifts.

With respect to the respondent's first contention, while we recognize that intrafamily transfers are subject to special scrutiny to determine if they are in reality what they appear to be on their face, we believe the promissory notes were valid, enforceable obligations. Examination of the notes reveals that they were executed in proper legal form and signed by the obligors. Moreover, the transferees carried out their obligations under the notes; they paid the interest due every month without exception. Finally, there is no evidence to support the respondent's contention that at the time of the transfers the decedent did not intend to collect the notes.

Although we have rejected the respondent's primary contention, with respect to the first four transfers made by the decedent, we agree with his alternative argument that these transfers were not at arm's length, and therefore, the difference between the amount of each transfer and the fair market value of each promissory note given in exchange constitutes a taxable gift.

While the petitioner contends that the transfers were arm's-length transactions, the evidence in the record simply does not support its position. Even though the decedent may have had a profit motive in making these transfers because the interest rate on the notes was higher than he was earning on his money otherwise, this factor alone does not mean that the transfers were made at arm's length. There are other factors here which must be considered. To begin with, the decedent was over 75 years old when he began making these transfers in exchange for notes due in 20 years. In addition, the decedent took no security on these notes. Moreover, the notes did not require any principal payments until maturity. Finally, the transferees, the decedent's daughter and son-in-law, were the natural objects of his bounty. In his will, the decedent directed that all his property be divided equally between his two daughters. As a result, Barbara Given was bequeathed one half of the notes on which she was a debtor. Taking all of these factors into account, we conclude that the petitioner has failed to meet its burden of proof that the transfers were at arm's length and free of donative intent. . . .

Since these transfers were not at arm's length or free of donative intent, the parenthetical criteria of section 25.2512-8, Gift Tax Regs., have not been met. Consequently, the promissory notes cannot be considered adequate and full consideration under this section of the regulations. However, because the notes were valid, enforceable obligations that paid interest we believe they did constitute consideration to the extent of their fair market values. We, therefore, hold that the difference between the amount of each of the first four transfers and the fair market value of each promissory note given in exchange constitutes a taxable gift. *See* Estate of Reynolds v. Commissioner, 55 T.C. 172, 201 (1970); Blackburn v. Commissioner, 20 T.C. 204, 207 (1953).

With respect to the transfer of $55,000 on March 2, 1972, since the interest payable on the note the decedent received was 6 percent and the prime rate at that time was only 4.75 percent, we hold that this transfer was made for adequate and full consideration and, therefore, the decedent made no taxable gift on this exchange.

Where a gift of property is made its fair market value on the date of the gift, less the fair market value on such date of any consideration received by the donor, shall constitute the amount of the gift. Section 2512(a) and (b). Thus, to calculate the amount of the gifts made by the decedent, we must determine the fair market value of each promissory note on the date of execution.

The question of valuation is a subjective one and requires the Court to exercise its best judgment in light of all the facts of the case. While the record leaves much to be desired, having considered the rate of interest, date of maturity, lack of security and the solvency of the debtors, we have determined the fair market value of each note on the date of execution and the resulting amount of gifts to be as follows:

Date of Execution	Face Amount	Fair Market Value	Amount of Gift
11/15/68	$100,000	$85,000	$15,000
04/24/69	50,000	37,500	12,500
11/19/70	30,000	24,000	6,000
11/19/70	40,000	32,000	8,000

Evidencing a purported loan with a promissory note, however, is not sufficient to escape the gift tax. In Estate of Flandreau v. Commissioner, 63 T.C.M. (CCH) 2512 (1992), *aff'd* 994 F.2d 91 (2d Cir. 1993) and Muserlian v. Commissioner, 58 T.C.M. (CCH) 100 (1989), *aff'd* 932 F.2d 109 (2d Cir. 1991), the taxpayers transferred large sums of money to their children and immediately borrowed the money back. The children then forgave each debt payment as it came due. In these cases the courts found the loan transactions to be shams and imposed gift tax consequences on the original transaction. In Miller v. Commissioner, the taxpayer transferred money to her two sons, who signed promissory notes. 71 T.C.M. (CCH) 1674 (1996), *aff'd* 113 F.3d 1241 (9th Cir. 1997). In treating the initial transfers as gifts, the Tax Court found that there was no real expectation that the sons would repay the loans and that the taxpayer did not intend to enforce the terms of the promissory notes. The Tax Court also noted that neither son gave security for the loan, there was no discussion of the terms of the promissory notes, including the repayment dates, and there was no demand for repayment by the taxpayer. Other factors that the court will review in determining whether a sale or a loan is actually a gift include whether interest is charged, whether there is a fixed maturity date for the note, whether there is a demand for repayment, whether there are actual payments on the note, whether the purchaser or borrower has the ability to pay or repay, the seller's/lender's health, the records kept by the seller/lender, and how the seller/lender reported the transaction for income and gift tax purposes.

PROBLEMS

1. Angela owns Greenacre (fair market value $100,000; adjusted basis $20,000). What are the gift tax consequences of the following arrangements?
    a. Angela gives Greenacre to Nina, her niece.
    b. Angela sells Greenacre to Nina for $50,000.
    c. Angela sells Greenacre to Nina for $100,000. Nina signs a promissory note for $100,000 plus interest at the applicable federal rate. Nina also gives Angela a mortgage on the property. The mortgage is recorded. Angela forgives each payment of principal and interest ($11,000) as it comes due.
2. Angela loans Nina, her niece, $500,000 to start a business. Nina signs a promissory note. What are the gift tax consequences of the following arrangements?
    a. Angela charges Nina no interest. She secures the promissory note with liens against the business property. Nina pays each installment of principal as it comes due.
    b. Angela charges Nina five percent interest.
    c. Angela charges Nina interest at the applicable federal rate. She forgives each payment as it comes due.

CHAPTER 7

The Annual Exclusion

A. GENERAL PRINCIPLES
IRC §2503(b)

Not every completed gift is subject to tax. If it were, the IRS would be flooded with tax returns and taxpayers would rise up in revolt. Every day taxpayers give millions of birthday, wedding, holiday, and other presents to family, friends, and colleagues. They also buy lunch, loan books or the proverbial cups of sugar, and make countless other transfers of property without receiving any consideration in return. The burden of keeping track of these transactions is incomprehensible, and ordinary citizens would resent the intrusion into their private lives that such an accounting would require.

The answer to this dilemma is the gift tax annual exclusion, codified in §2503(b). Originally the amount was set at $5,000. This was lowered to $4,000 in 1938, then lowered to $3,000 in 1942, then raised to $10,000 in 1981. In 1997, Congress indexed the gift tax annual exclusion for inflation, but only in increments of $1,000. In was not until 2002 that indexing made a difference in the amount of the exclusion, which was then raised to $11,000. Rev. Pro. 2001-59, 2001-2 C.B. 623.

Because the annual exclusion applies to each recipient, the ability to diminish gift tax liability is significant.

Example 7-1

Taxpayer has two children, each of whom is married and has two children. Taxpayer can give $11,000 each year to each child, to each child-in-law, and to each grandchild for a total of $88,000 per year. If the taxpayer maintains this level of giving for only ten years, the taxpayer can exclude $880,000 from her estate without paying any transfer tax and without ever filing a gift tax return. This amount is in addition to the applicable exemption amount in §2505.

The gift tax, like the income tax, is payable on an annual basis. The taxpayer, however, need not report gifts that qualify for the annual exclusion.

§6019(a). This avoids the problems of record keeping and governmental intrusion that this exclusion is designed to prevent.

B. GIFT SPLITTING
   IRC §2513

A taxpayer who is married can double the benefit of the annual exclusion. Section 2513 allows the taxpayer to treat gifts as if made one-half by her husband, as long as he consents. The taxpayer in Example 7-1 could then transfer $22,000 to each person for a total of $176,000 each year. In this situation, if her husband later makes separate gifts of $11,000 to each recipient, those gifts will not qualify for the annual exclusion because he has used his annual exclusion by agreeing to split the taxpayer's gifts. Section 2513, therefore, does not double the amount of the annual exclusion, but it does allow taxpayers to fully utilize the exclusion when only one spouse is making gifts.

Congress adopted §2513 in 1948 in conjunction with other provisions designed to equalize the income, estate, and gift tax treatment of couples in community property and common law property jurisdictions. Because gifts of community property were already considered as made one-half by each spouse, §2513 merely gave the same benefit to couples in common law property states. When Congress adopted the unlimited marital deduction in 1981, the need for §2513 all but disappeared. Since 1981, the married couple can achieve the same result as §2513 by having the wealthy spouse transfer property to the poorer spouse. Each then gives the children and grandchildren $11,000 of his or her own money. Although this technique is more cumbersome than gift splitting, it does avoid the need for the couple to file a gift tax return, which is required for electing §2513 treatment, no matter how small the gift.

Despite the unlimited marital deduction, §2513 will not disappear. The transaction costs of double transfers may be too high for some gifts, and there will be some situations where the spouse would not transfer property to the recipient on his own but would be willing to split the donor's gift.

There are a number of requirements in §2513. Both spouses must be citizens or residents of the United States; the donor must not give the spouse a general power of appointment over the property; the donor must be married to the spouse at the time of the gift and not remarry during the calendar year; and both spouses must consent to split all gifts made during the calendar year. Gift splitting must be elected by filing a gift tax return signed by both spouses, and, once that return is filed, both spouses become jointly and severally liable for the tax. Finally, the amount of a split gift will not be included in the spouse's gross estate, but it will be considered in determining his gift and estate tax liability. If, for example, a donor makes a gift of $100,000 and her spouse consents to gift splitting, the spouse has made a $50,000 gift and therefore used up $39,000 of his §2505 applicable exemption amount.

PROBLEMS

1. Adam gives Beth $5,000. What are the gift tax consequences?
    a. What if he gives her $11,000?
    b. What if he gives her $50,000?
    c. Does it matter what Adam's relationship to Beth is?
    d. What are the gift tax consequences in 1.b if Adam is married to Carol?
2. Abby sends Mark, her son, a painting (fair market value $1,000) for his birthday in March. She sends him a set of china (fair market value $2,000) for his wedding in June. In December, she sends him a check for $10,000. What are the gift tax consequences of these transactions?
3. Teresa gives her daughter, Sally, stock valued at $11,000. On the same day, Teresa gives her ten nieces and nephews stock in the same company; each gift of stock is valued at $11,000. One week later all ten nieces and nephews transfer the stock to Sally. What are the gift tax consequences?
4. Art and Ben are brothers. Art is married to Carol; they have three children — Ed, Faith, and Gail. Ben is married to Diane; they have three children — Henry, Isaac, and Joan. On December 1, Art sends $11,000 each to Ed, Faith, Gail, Henry, Isaac, and Joan. On December 5, Ben sends $11,000 each to Ed, Faith, Gail, Henry, Isaac, and Joan. What are the gift tax consequences?
5. Debra owns Blackacre (fair market value $176,000; adjusted basis $25,000). She deeds Blackacre to her two sons, her two daughters, her two sons-in-law, her two daughters-in-law, and her eight grandchildren as tenants in common.
    a. What are the gift tax consequences?
    b. Instead, Debra sells Blackacre to her two sons, Larry and John, as tenants in common. Larry and John each make a down payment of $5,000 and sign a promissory note agreeing to pay the principal plus interest on an annual basis. Each payment is $11,000, and Debra forgives each payment as it comes due. What are the gift tax consequences?
6. What is the proper amount of the gift tax annual exclusion: $1,000? $5,000? $10,000? $25,000?
7. Instead of a flat amount per year, should there be a de minimis exclusion applied to each gift? For example, the first $100 or $1,000 of each gift is excluded? Or should only gifts of a certain amount be excluded?

C. PRESENT INTEREST REQUIREMENT
IRC §2503(b)

The annual exclusion is only available for gifts of present interests — those that give the recipient the "unrestricted right to the immediate use, possession, or enjoyment of property or the income from property." Reg. §25.2503-3(b). The requirement that the gift be one of a present interest avoids the administrative problem of determining the number of ultimate donees and the value of their rights. This might be impossible in some cases because all donees might not be identified, or even in existence, at the time the gift is completed.

A gift of cash or a fee interest in Blackacre is a present interest and qualifies for the annual exclusion. A gift of a remainder interest in Blackacre, even a vested remainder, is not a present interest because the recipient does not have an unrestricted right to the immediate use, possession, or enjoyment of the property until sometime in the future when the life tenant dies. It does not matter that the remainderman could immediately sell her interest and obtain cash or other property for it. On the other hand, some gifts that do not bestow benefits until the future will qualify as present interests. For example, if the donor buys a life insurance policy on her own life and gives it to her nephew, that gift qualifies as a present interest. Revenue Ruling 55-408, 1955-1 C.B. 113. A promissory note where payments will begin in the future is a present interest. Reg. §25.2503-3(a). These gifts qualify for the annual exclusion because the nature of the assets themselves produce the deferral of any economic benefit, rather than the donor's actions in carving out certain rights or interests.

A gift of corporate stock is also a gift of a present interest. The recipient has the right to the full and immediate enjoyment of that property, even if the corporation is a small, family-held corporation that never pays dividends. TAM 9346003. If there are substantial restrictions on the stock, however, such as a buy-sell agreement, the stock may be considered a future interest. Revenue Ruling 76-360, 1976-2 C.B. 298. A gift of a partnership interest, even a limited partnership interest, is generally considered a present interest despite the fact that the interest may not pay income on a regular basis or, in the case of a limited partnership, the general partner controls the flow of income. *See, e.g.,* Wooley v. United States, 736 F. Supp. 1506 (S.D. Ind. 1990); TAM 9131006; TAM 8611004. In Hackl v. Commissioner, 118 T.C. 279 (2002), the court held that units in a limited liability company were not present interests because the recipients did not receive a substantial present economic benefit. The court examined all the facts and circumstances, including the operating agreement. These facts indicated that the recipients could not compel distributions, could not withdraw their capital accounts without managerial consent, and could not freely transfer their interests. As a result, they did not receive any substantial economic benefit and the donor did not receive the benefit of the gift tax annual exclusion. Likewise, in TAM 9751003 the IRS held that the gift of a limited partnership interest did not qualify as a present interest because the general partner, an S corporation controlled by the donor, had complete discretion over income distributions, retention of funds, and could retain funds for any reason whatsoever.

When a transferor creates a trust, each interest must be analyzed to determine if it is a present or a future interest. The first issue is whether the donor is making a transfer to the trustee or to the beneficiaries. If the transfer were to the trustee, the donor would be entitled to only one annual exclusion. If the gift is to the beneficiaries, the donor would be entitled to an annual exclusion for each beneficiary who receives a present interest. Originally the lower courts held that the gift was to the trustee, which allowed the donor to create multiple trusts for the benefit of a single recipient. *See, e.g.,* United States v. Ryerson, 114 F.2d 150 (7th Cir. 1940), *rev'd* 312 U.S. 260, 312 U.S. 405 (1941); Cox v. Commissioner, 38 B.T.A. 865 (1938); Rheinstrom v. Commissioner, 37 B.T.A. 308 (1938), *rev'd* 105 F.2d 642 (8th Cir. 1939); Knox v. Commissioner, 36 B.T.A. 630 (1938). In 1938, Congress denied the annual exclusion for all gifts in trust to prevent tax avoidance. Revenue Act of 1938, §505, 52 Stat. 447. After the Supreme Court decided that the beneficiary and not the trustee was the recipient of a gift in trust, Helvering v. Hutchings, 312 U.S. 393 (1941), Congress restored the annual exclusion for gifts in trust.

Example 7-2

David creates an irrevocable trust to pay the income to Ann for life, then the income to Beth for life, with the remainder to Carol. Carol's interest is a vested remainder and a future interest. Ann and Beth each have a life estate. Beth's life estate is a future interest because it will not begin until Ann's death. Whether or not Ann's life estate is a future interest will depend on the terms of the trust.

In United States v. Pelzer, 312 U.S. 399, 404 (1941), the taxpayer created a trust and directed the trustee to accumulate the income for ten years before distributing income to his grandchildren. The Supreme Court held that the gifts to the grandchildren were future interests because the beneficiaries had no right to the present enjoyment of the corpus or the income unless they survived the ten-year period. In Fondren v. Commission, 324 U.S. 18 (1945), the Supreme Court held that gifts in trust where the trustee had discretion to distribute income for a grandchild's "comfort, support, maintenance, and welfare" were gifts of future interests, stating:

> [I]t is not enough to bring the exclusion into force that the donee has vested rights. In addition he must have the right presently to use, possess or enjoy the property. These terms are not words of art, like "fee" in the law of seizin . . . but connote the right to substantial present economic benefit. The question is of time, not when title vests, but when enjoyment begins. Whatever puts the barrier of a substantial period between the will of the beneficiary or donee now to enjoy what has been given him and that enjoyment makes the gift one of a future interest. . . .
>
> The trusts' stated purpose was "to provide for the personal comfort, support, maintenance, and welfare" of the grandchildren. But from the explicit recitals of the instruments, as well as the evidence, including a stipulation, it is clear that the parents of each child were so situated that, when the gifts were made, they were fully able to provide for and educate him. And, from the same recitals, it is clear there was little reason to believe that any parent would not continue so until

the child's majority. Accordingly, in each instance, the trust was to continue until the child should attain the age of thirty-five. . . .

[The beneficiaries'] right was not absolute and immediate, but was conditioned, during minority and afterward until the times specified for distribution, upon a contingency which might never arise. That contingency by the explicit terms of the trust, was the existence of need which was then nonexistent and, in the stated contemplation of the donors, was not likely to occur in the future, at any rate during the child's minority. The circumstances surrounding the donors and the donees confirm these recitals. The case is one therefore in which the gift, if presently vested, made enjoyment contingent upon the occurrence of future events, not only uncertain, but by the recitals of the instrument itself improbable of occurrence. The gifts consequently were of "future interests in property" within the meaning of Section [2503(b)].

Id. at 20, 22, 24.

PROBLEMS

1. Alice transfers shares of stock in XYZ, Inc. (fair market value $11,000) to her nephew, Michael.
    a. What are the gift tax consequences?
    b. What if XYZ, Inc. is a closely held family business that has never paid dividends?
    c. What if Alice transfers a limited partnership interest to Michael rather than shares of stock?
2. Andrew transfers a term life insurance policy on his life to his niece, Nancy.
    a. What are the gift tax consequences, assuming Andrew has a life expectancy of 15 years?
    b. What are the gift tax consequences if Andrew transfers the policy to Friendly National Bank as Trustee for the benefit of Nancy?
3. Agnes transfers Blackacre (fair market value $200,000) to RST, Inc., whose shareholders are her five nieces and nephews. What are the gift tax consequences?
4. Gwen establishes an irrevocable trust and transfers $1,000,000 to Friendly National Bank as Trustee. What are the gift tax consequences of the following alternatives?
    a. Income to Alex for life, remainder to Evan.
    b. Income to Alex for life, remainder to Evan. The Trustee has complete discretion whether to distribute income to Alex or to accumulate it. Accumulated income will be paid to Alex's issue.
    c. Income to Alex and Betsy in equal shares, remainder to Evan.
    d. The Trustee has complete discretion to distribute income in whatever proportion to Alex, Betsy, Claude, and Dinah. The remainder goes to Evan at the death of the last income beneficiary.

e.   Income to Alex for life, remainder to Evan. Alex is 25 years old when the trust is established. The Trustee has discretion to accumulate income or distribute it to Alex for health, education, or an emergency.

D.   GIFTS TO MINORS
IRC §2503(b), (c)

Parents often make gifts to their minor children. Outright gifts, such as a bicycle or a new computer, qualify as present interests. No parent, however, wants to give a child control over a substantial amount of money, and state law prevents minors from owning certain property interests. A parent could, of course, have a legal guardian appointed for the child and transfer the money or other property to the guardian for the benefit of the child. A guardian is usually restricted in her ability to deal with property for the benefit of the minor and must obtain court approval for most transactions. As a result, parents avoid this option.

Every state has adopted either the Uniform Gifts to Minors Act or the Uniform Transfers to Minors Act. Both statutes give the custodian broad power to deal with property without court supervision. Transfers pursuant to these statutes are simple. Parents can establish bank accounts or purchase investments for the minor child simply by having title read "to X as custodian for child." Because the statutes require the custodian to use the property for the benefit of the child, these gifts are completed gifts of present interests. Revenue Ruling 59-357, 1959-2 C.B. 212; Revenue Ruling 73-287, 1973-2 C.B. 321.

There are income and estate tax disadvantages to making gifts pursuant to the Uniform Gifts to Minors Act or the Uniform Transfers to Minors Act. If the custodian actually uses the property for the support of the minor, the parent (even if not the donor or the custodian) will be taxed on the income from the property. Section 677 treats the parent as the owner because of the parent's legal obligation of support. Moreover, if the donor is the custodian and dies while the child is a minor, the property will be in the donor's gross estate under §2038 because of the broad powers of the custodian. If the parent is the custodian and not the donor, the property will still be in the parent's gross estate under §2041 because of the parent's legal obligation of support and the ability of the custodian to use the transferred property for the support of the minor child.

Given these disadvantages, many parents prefer to establish trusts for the benefit of their minor children. Requiring the trustee to make mandatory payments of income to the minor child, however, presents the same problems as outright gifts. Parents, and other donors, simply do not want to give minor children access to substantial wealth. Congress provided an alternative in

§2503(c), which provides that no part of a gift to a minor will be considered a future interest if (1) the property and its income may be expended by or for the benefit of the donee before age 21, and (2) to the extent not expended, the property and any accumulated income must (a) be distributed to the child at age 21 or (b) should the donee die before age 21 be payable to the donee's estate or as the donee may appoint under a general power of appointment. Section 2503(c) provides that the entire value of the property, not just the value of the income interest, will qualify for the annual exclusion. Although the requirements of this section appear reasonable and clear, there has been significant litigation to determine its exact boundaries.

Ross v. United States
348 F.2d 577 (5th Cir. 1965)

WISDOM, Circuit Judge:

The question this gift tax exclusion case presents is whether a gift in trust to a minor, under a trust agreement authorizing the trustee to exercise all the powers of a guardian, must be "considered" a gift of a future interest for purposes of section 2503(c) of the Internal Revenue Code of 1954. The district court granted a summary judgment in favor of the United States, dismissing the taxpayers' claim for a gift tax refund. 226 F. Supp. 333. We reverse.

The facts are stipulated. On November 15, 1956, the taxpayers, Nell K. Ross and her husband James H. Ross, now dead, set up three trusts, one for each of their minor grandchildren. The trusts are identical, except for the names of the beneficiaries. Article III of each trust gives the trustees complete discretion to use all or part of the trust income for the "support, maintenance, and education" of the beneficiary. It also authorizes the trustees to hold and dispose of the income:

> To the same extent as if (the trustees) were the guardian of the beneficiary's person and estate and as if payments and distribution for his use and benefit were being made by him in that capacity as well as Trustee.

Article IV directs the trustees to pay the trust principal to the beneficiary on his attaining the age of twenty-one, or to his estate if he dies before he is twenty-one. Article V sets forth the administrative powers of the trustees. Paragraph two of that article empowers the trustees:

> To exercise all powers which guardians of the persons or estates of minors may, [by] order of [the] Court or otherwise, be authorized to exercise from time to time under the laws of the domicile of the beneficiary of this Trust.

. . . The trust instruments, in spirit and in letter, give the trustees, at the very least, all the powers of a guardian under Texas law. (In a sense, paragraph two of article V gives the trustees even greater power than a guardian would have, because the trustees may do without a court order whatever a guardian may do only with a court order.) As to this power, the district court reached the same conclusion as this Court, but held that Texas law so restricts the powers of a guardian over the corpus of his ward's estate that the gifts failed to meet the requirements of section 2503(c). We disagree.

It is true that under Texas law, a guardian may spend the corpus of his ward's estate (1) only for the maintenance and education of the ward, (2) only where the parents of the ward cannot provide adequate support, and, (3) except in cases of emergency, only after obtaining a court order. But these restrictions, in themselves, do not require that a gift through a Texas guardian be treated as a future interest for purposes of section 2503. An outright gift by a donor to the guardian of a minor is considered a gift of a present and not a future interest under section 2503(b); and limitations imposed by state law on the guardian's use of the property do not make the gift one of a future interest. Beatrice B. Briggs, 1960, 34 T.C. 1132. A gift in trust for a minor "as if the trustee herein were holding the property as guardian" for the donee has been held to be a gift of a present interest under section 2503(b) of the Code and is, therefore, entitled to the $3,000 exclusion from taxable gifts permitted by that section. That state laws pertaining to guardianships might pose barriers to the immediate enjoyment of a gift in trust will not cause the gift to be denied present interest status. United States v. Baker, 4 Cir. 1956, 236 F.2d 317. . . . [W]e read the words *"may be expended"* in section 2503(c) to mean *"may be expended within the limitations imposed on guardians by state law."*

Legislative history supports this reading of section 2503(c). This section, enacted in 1954, had no antecedent. It was enacted as a result of the courts' having given unexpectedly broad scope to the future interest exception to the annual exclusion. The future interest exception, adopted in 1932, was a legislative response to the specific administrative difficulty, in some cases, "of determining the number of eventual donees and the values of their respective gifts." H.Rep.No.708, 72d Cong., 1st Sess. 29 (1932); S.Rep.No.665, 72d Cong., 1st Sess. 41 (1932). The courts, perhaps because the language of the statute was so broad, extended the future interest concept beyond the limits to which Congress, later, was willing to go. Before the enactment of 2503(c) a gift in trust was held to create a future interest, for purposes of the annual exclusion, whenever the trustee had discretion to accumulate income or restrict distribution of corpus. . . .

The status of gifts made through guardians was uncertain, though there were strong suggestions that such gifts might be considered present interest[s]. Section 2503(c) "partially relaxe(d) the 'future interest' restriction contained in subsection (b), in the case of gifts to minors, by providing a specific type of gift for which the exclusion (would) be allowed." H.Rep.No.1337, 83rd Cong. 2d Sess. (3 U.S.C.Cong. & Adm.News (1954) pp. 4017, 4465). . . .

Section 2503(c) does not demand that the trust instrument require the expenditure of corpus. Thus, the Senate Committee Report states:

> Subsection (c), a new provision adopted in the House bill, describes a certain type of gift to a minor which will not be treated as a gift of a future interest. Your

committee has amended the provisions of the House bill to provide that it is not necessary that the property or income therefrom be actually expended by or for the benefit of a minor during minority so long as all such amounts not so expended will pass to the donee upon attaining majority and, in the event of his prior death, will be payable to his estate or as he may appoint under a general power of appointment. S.Rep.No.1622, 83rd Cong., 2d Sess. 478 (1954), 3 U.S.C.Cong. & Adm.News (1954), p. 5123. Nor does section 2503(c) require that the trust instrument state in so many words that the trustees have the power to expend corpus for the benefit of the minor beneficiaries.

The language of this report, read in the context of the entire legislative history of section 2503(c), describes the legislator's objective: to liberalize the law by removing from the future interest restriction of subsection (b) gifts for the benefit of a minor made through the garden variety guardianship. . . . If we read the statute as the Government suggests, interpreting it to mean that a gift through a guardian can qualify for the exclusion only if the guardian has unlimited power to invade corpus for the benefit of the donee, whether or not for his maintenance or education, we would disqualify from exclusion virtually all gifts made through the ordinary type of guardianship. . . .

We find that the existence of reasonable, prudent, and ordinary restrictions imposed by state law on the powers of a guardian do not, in themselves, disqualify a gift to a minor represented by a guardian. Here the trustees had all the powers of a guardian, and more. We hold, therefore, that the taxpayers were entitled to the annual exclusion for the gifts in question.

Estate of Levine v. Commissioner
526 F.2d 717 (2d Cir. 1975)

IRVING R. KAUFMAN, Chief Judge:

One suspects that because the Internal Revenue Code of 1954 piles exceptions upon exclusions, it invites efforts to outwit the tax collector. The case before us is an example of adroit taxpayers seizing upon words in the Code which, if interpreted as they urge, would distort congressional intent and violate well-established rules of statutory construction. We therefore reverse the decision of the Tax Court favoring the taxpayers, 63 T.C. 136 (1974).

The facts in this case have been stipulated. On December 30, 1968, David H. Levine, a Connecticut resident, established identical irrevocable trusts for five grandchildren whose ages then ranged from 2 to 15 years. . . . Unless a designated "Independent Trustee" saw fit in his discretion to direct otherwise, the trustees were to retain all income generated until the grandchild-beneficiary reached age 21. At that time, the accumulated income would be distributed in toto. Thereafter, the beneficiary would receive payments at least annually of all income earned by the trust. If the grandchild died before his or her twenty-first birthday, all accumulated income would go to the estate of the grandchild.

During the lifetime of the beneficiary, control over the trust corpus was vested exclusively in the "absolute and uncontrolled discretion" of the Independent Trustee. He could permit the principal to stand untouched or he could pay out any portion directly to, or for the benefit of, the beneficiary. In addition, the trustee could terminate the trust at any time by distributing the entire corpus. The trust also provided the beneficiary with a limited power of appointment in the event that any of the principal remained in the trust upon his or her death. The corpus, or any part of it, could be designated to pass to some or all of David H. Levine's lineal descendants. The original beneficiary could not elect to leave corpus to his or her own estate, his or her creditors, or the creditors of the original beneficiary's estate. . . .

At first blush, it might seem that the Levine trusts clearly fail to satisfy the requirements of §2503(c)(2). The "property" — if defined as the corpus — would not pass to the donee when the beneficiary turned 21. Nor would it be payable to the donee's estate if death occurred before the age of 21 years. The power of appointment established by each trust over the corpus also fails the tests set forth in §2514(c).

The problem, however, is somewhat more complex. The Supreme Court in *Disston* and *Fondren, supra*, recognized that a gift may be divided into component parts for tax purposes. One or more of those elements may qualify as present interests even if others do not. The Tax Court applied these principles in a 1961 decision involving a trust similar to Levine's. Herr v. C.I.R., 35 T.C. 732 (1961). Treating the income to be accumulated to age 21 (the "pre-21 income interest") as a separate element of "property," *id.* at 737, the Tax Court held that this segment satisfied the requirements of §2503(c) and the taxpayer could therefore benefit from the §2503(b) exclusion. The Third Circuit affirmed the Tax Court, 303 F.2d 780 (3d Cir. 1962). The Commissioner has acquiesced in the *Herr* decision, 1968-2 C.B. 2, and accordingly concedes in the present case that the pre-21 income interest is eligible for the gift tax exclusion.

The pre-21 income interests in the Levine trusts do not, however, exhaust the $3,000 per donee annual exclusion. Knowing that the remainder interests cannot qualify as present interests under either §2503(b) or §2503(c), the Levines have concentrated their attention on the post-21 income interests. Although the taxpayer in *Herr* did not suggest that the post-21 segment could properly be considered a present interest, the Tax Court explicitly spoke to the issue: "(I)ncome (after) 21 . . . (is a) future interest." 35 T.C. at 736. And the Court of Appeals commented similarly: "(T)he right(s) to income and principal after minority are future interests." 303 F.2d at 782. The taxpayers ask us to disregard these views and to extend the holding of *Herr* so that the post-21 income interests will be treated as present interests. We decline to do so.

If the post-21 income interests are looked upon as separate gifts, they cannot be considered present interests under §2503(b). As in the case of the remainder interests, initial enjoyment is delayed until a time in the future. Moreover, the requirements of §2503(c)(2) are not satisfied.

The taxpayers urge that we are required to treat the post-21 income interests as one with the pre-21 income interests, but that the remainder interests should be considered a separate gift. The taxpayers recognize that the combined pre- and post-21 income interests do not qualify as a present interest when viewed solely in the light of §2503(b). This is so because the accumulation of income before age 21 works as a postponement of immediate enjoyment. In addition, the combined income interests fail to meet the criteria of §2503(c)(2).

The Levines seek to overcome these obstacles by means of an ingenious argument. The combination of pre-21 and post-21 income interests resembles a unitary life estate, they argue. The only reason it cannot qualify as a §2503(b) present interest, they urge, is the accumulation provision that permits enjoyment to be delayed until age 21. But, they say, §2503(c) as interpreted by *Herr* permits the future interest characteristic of the pre-21 income interests to be disregarded for the purpose of receiving the §2503(b) exclusion. In other words, they assert that *Herr* and §2503(c) in effect transform the pre-21 income interests into present interests. Then, by a giant leap, the taxpayers conclude that a single, lifetime present interest is produced by linking the pre-21 constructive present interests with the post-21 income interests.

A study of the statutory language, however, convinces us that Congress did not contemplate such an "off-again, on-again" elusive treatment of the pre-21 segment of the transfers in trust. Moreover, we cannot be unmindful of the rule of construction that Congress permits exclusions only as a matter of grace, and the exclusions sections are to be strictly construed against the taxpayer. . . . Nor does the legislative history prove more helpful to the taxpayers. The House Report, H.R.Rep. No. 1337, 83d Cong., 2d Sess. A322, 3 U.S.Code Cong. & Admin.News, p. 4465 (1954), explained that §2503(c):

> *partially* relaxes the "future interest" restriction contained in (§2503(b)), in the case of gifts to minors, by providing a *specific type of gift* for which the exclusion will be allowed. If *the gift* may be expended by, or for the benefit of, the minor donee prior to his attaining the age of 21 years, and, to the extent not so expended, will pass to the donee at that time, but if the donee dies prior to that time, will pass to the donee's estate or as he may appoint by will under a general power of appointment, the gift will not be treated as a future interest. (Emphasis added).

See also 3 U.S.Code Cong. & Admin.News at p. 5123 (Senate Report, refers to a "*certain type* of gift to a minor which will not be treated as a gift of a future interest" (emphasis added)). The special treatment of pre-21 income interests in *Herr* could be justified as not *penalizing* the taxpayer for linking pre-21 income interests with other interests. But, the Levines would have us *reward* such a combination, since the post-21 income interest clearly could not, by itself, qualify for the annual exclusion.

There is one additional factor that we cannot ignore. The *Herr* opinions rejecting the contention that a post-21 income interest can be a §2503 present interest were rendered more than a decade ago. Extensive attention has been paid by the treatises, commentators, and tax services to the *Herr* decisions, and "no other field of legislation receives as much continuous, sustained and detailed attention" from Congress as does tax law. 3 Sutherland on Statutory Construction §66.02 at 184 (4th ed. 1974). Congress has had ample opportunity to amend the Code if it disagreed with the interpretation of §§2503(b) and (c) set forth in *Herr. See* Georgia v. United States, 411 U.S. 526, 533 (1973).

Accordingly, we reverse the decision of the Tax Court and remand.

E.   CRUMMEY TRUSTS
IRC §§2503(b), 2514

Not all parents are satisfied with a §2503(c) trust. Many want to delay distribution far beyond age 21 and yet take full advantage of the annual exclusion. Others do not want the trustee to distribute income to the minor children for any purpose. In these cases, parents have created present interests in their children by giving the children general powers of appointment. A general power of appointment is the right to withdraw, demand, or appoint property for the benefit of oneself, one's creditors, one's estate, or the creditors of one's estate. §2514(c). Because of the substantial control that a general power of appointment gives to the holder, the Code treats the exercise or release of a general power as a transfer of property by the power holder. §2514(b). In other words, the power holder is the virtual owner of the property. The question whether the creation of a general power of appointment in a minor child creates a present interest in that child is answered in the following case.

Crummey v. Commissioner
397 F.2d 82 (9th Cir. 1968)

BYRNE, District Judge:

. . . On February 12, 1962, the petitioners executed, as grantors, an irrevocable living trust for the benefit of their four children. . . . Originally the sum of $50 was contributed to the trust. Thereafter, additional contributions were made by each of the petitioners. . . .

The Commissioner of Internal Revenue determined that each of the petitioners was entitled to only one $3,000 exclusion for each year. This determination was based upon the Commissioner's belief that the portion of the gifts in trust for the children under the age of 21 were "future interests" which are disallowed under §2503(b). . . .

The key provision of the trust agreement is the "demand" provision which states:

THREE. Additions. The Trustee may receive any other real or personal property from the Trustors (or either of them) or from any other person or persons, by lifetime gift, under a Will or Trust or from any other source. . . . With respect to such additions, each child of the Trustors may demand at any time (up to and including December 31 of the year in which a transfer to his or her Trust has been made) the sum of Four Thousand Dollars ($4,000.00) or the amount of the transfer from each donor, whichever is less, payable in cash immediately upon receipt by the Trustee of the demand in writing and in any event, not later than December 31 in the year in which such transfer was made. Such payment shall be made from the gift of that donor for that year. If a child is a minor at the time of such gift of that donor for that year, or fails in legal capacity for any reason, the child's guardian may make such demand on behalf of the child. The property received pursuant to the demand shall be held by the guardian for the benefit and use of the child.

The whole question on this appeal is whether or not a present interest was given by the petitioners to their minor children so as to qualify as an exclusion under §2503(b). The petitioners on appeal contend that each minor beneficiary has the right under California law to demand partial distribution from the Trustee. In the alternative they urge that a parent as natural guardian of the person of his minor children could make such a demand. As a third alternative, they assert that under California law a minor over the age of 14 has the right to have a legal guardian appointed who can make the necessary demand. . . .

It was stipulated before the Tax Court in regard to the trust and the parties thereto that at all times relevant all the minor children lived with the petitioners and no legal guardian had been appointed for them. In addition, it was agreed that all the children were supported by petitioners and none of them had made a demand against the trust funds or received any distribution from them.

The tax regulations define a "future interest" for the purposes of §2503(b) as follows:

> "Future interests" is a legal term, and includes reversions, remainder, and other interests or estates, whether vested or contingent, and whether or not supported by a particular interest or estate, which are limited to commence in use, possession or enjoyment at some future date or time. Treasury Regulations of Gift Tax, §25.2503-3.

This definition has been adopted by the Supreme Court. Fondren v. Commissioner, 324 U.S. 18, 65 S.Ct. 499, 89 L.Ed. 668 (1945); Commissioner v. Disston, 325 U.S. 442, 65 S.Ct. 1328, 89 L.Ed. 1720 (1945). In *Fondren* the court stated that the important question is when enjoyment begins. There the court held that gifts to an irrevocable trust for the grantor's minor grandchildren were "future interests" where income was to be accumulated and the corpus and the accumulations were not to be paid until designated times commencing with each grandchild's 25th birthday. The trustee was authorized to spend the income or invade the corpus during the minority of the beneficiaries only if need were shown. The facts demonstrated that need had not occurred and was not likely to occur.

Neither of the parties nor the Tax Court has any disagreement with the above summarization of the basic tests. The dispute comes in attempting to narrow the definition of a future interest down to a more specific and useful form.

The Commissioner and the Tax Court both placed primary reliance on the case of Stifel v. Commissioner, 197 F.2d 107 (2d Cir. 1952). In that case an irrevocable trust was involved which provided that the beneficiary, a minor, could demand any part of the funds not expended by the Trustee and, subject to such demand, the Trustee was to accumulate. The trust also provided that it could be terminated by the beneficiary or by her guardian during minority. The court held that gifts to this trust were gifts of "future interests." They relied upon *Fondren* for the proposition that they could look at circumstances as well as the trust agreement and under such circumstances it was clear that the minor could not make the demand and that no guardian had ever been appointed who could make such a demand.

The leading case relied upon by the petitioners is Kieckhefer v. Commissioner, 189 F.2d 118 (7th Cir. 1951). In that case the donor set up a trust with his newly born grandson as the beneficiary. The trustee was to hold the funds unless the beneficiary or his legally appointed guardian demanded that the trust be terminated. The Commissioner urged that the grandson could not effectively make such a demand and that no guardian had been appointed. The court disregarded these factors and held that where any restrictions on use were caused by disabilities of a minor rather than by the terms of the trust, the gift was a "present interest." The court further stated that the important thing was the right to enjoy rather than the actual enjoyment of the property. . . .

Although there are certainly factual distinctions between the *Stifel* and *Kieckhefer* cases, it seems clear that the two courts took opposing positions on the way the problem of defining "future interests" should be resolved. As we read the *Stifel* case, it says that the court should look at the trust instrument, the law as to minors, and the financial and other circumstances of the parties. From this examination it is up to the court to determine whether it is likely that the minor beneficiary is to receive any present enjoyment of the property. If it is not likely, then the gift is a "future interest." At the other extreme is the holding in *Kieckhefer* which says that a gift to a minor is not a "future interest" if the only reason for a delay in enjoyment is the minority status of the donee and his consequent disabilities. The *Kieckhefer* court noted that under the terms there present, a gift to an adult would have qualified for the exclusion and they refused to discriminate against a minor. The court equated a present interest with a present right to possess, use or enjoy. The facts of the case and the court's reasoning, however, indicate that it was really equating a present interest with a present right to possess, use or enjoy except for the fact that the beneficiary was a minor. In between these two positions there is a third possibility. That possibility is that the court should determine whether the donee is legally and technically capable of immediately enjoying the property. Basically this is the test relied on by the petitioners. Under this theory, the question would be whether the donee could possibly gain immediate enjoyment and the emphasis would be on the trust instrument and the laws of the jurisdiction as to minors. It was primarily on this basis that the Tax Court decided the present case, although some examination of surrounding circumstances was apparently made. . . .

Under the provisions of this trust the income is to be accumulated and added to the corpus until each minor reaches the age of 21, unless the trustee feels in his discretion that distributions should be made to a needy beneficiary. From 21 to 35 all income is distributed to the beneficiary. After 35 the trustee again has discretion as to both income and corpus, and may distribute whatever is necessary up to the whole thereof. Aside from the actions of the trustee, the only way any beneficiary may get at the property is through the "demand" provision, quoted above.

One question raised in these proceedings is whether or not the trust prohibits a minor child from making a demand on the yearly additions to the trust. The key language from paragraph three is as follows:

> If a child is a minor at the time of such gift of that donor for that year, or fails in legal capacity for any reason, the child's guardian may make such demand on behalf of the child.

The Tax Court interpreted this provision in favor of the taxpayers by saying that "may" is permissive and thus that the minor child can make the demand if allowed by law, or, if not permitted by law, the guardian may do it. Although, as the Commissioner suggests, this strains the language somewhat, it does seem consistent with the obvious intent in drafting this provision. Surely, this provision was intended to give the minor beneficiary the broadest demand power available so that the gift tax exclusion would be applicable.

There is very little dispute between the parties as to the rights and disabilities of a minor accorded by the California statutes and cases. The problem comes in attempting to ascertain from these rights and disabilities the answer to the question of whether a minor may make a demand upon the trustee for a portion of the trust as provided in the trust instrument.

It is agreed that a minor in California may own property. . . . He may receive a gift. . . . A minor may demand his own funds from a bank . . ., a savings institution . . ., or a corporation. . . . A minor of the age of 14 or over has the right to secure the appointment of a guardian and one will be appointed if the court finds it "necessary or convenient". . . . It is further agreed that a minor cannot sue in his own name . . . and cannot appoint an agent. . . . With certain exceptions a minor can disaffirm contracts made by him during his minority. . . . A minor under the age of 18 cannot make contracts relating to real property or personal property not in his possession or control. . . . The parent of a child may be its natural guardian, but such a guardianship is of the person of the child and not of his estate. . . .

After examining the same rights and disabilities, the petitioners, the Commissioner, and the Tax Court each arrived at a different solution to our problem. The Tax Court concentrated on the disabilities and concluded that David and Mark could not make an effective demand because they could not sue in their own name, nor appoint an agent and could disaffirm contracts. The court, however, concluded that Janet could make an effective demand because Cal.Civ.Code, §33 indirectly states that she could make contracts with regard to real and personal property.

The Commissioner concentrated on the inability to sue or appoint an agent and concluded that none of the minors had anything more than paper rights because he or she lacked the capacity to enforce the demand.

The petitioners urge that the right to acquire and hold property is the key. In the alternative they argue that the parent as a natural guardian could make the demand although it would be necessary to appoint a legal guardian to receive the property. Finally, they urge that all the minors over 14 could make a demand since they could request the appointment of a legal guardian.

The position taken by the Tax Court seems clearly untenable. The distinction drawn between David and Mark on the one hand, and Janet on the other, makes no sense. The mere fact that Janet can make certain additional contracts does not have any relevance to the question of whether she is capable of making an effective demand upon the trustee. We cannot agree with the position of the Commissioner because we do not feel that a lawsuit or the appointment of an agent is a necessary prelude to the making of a demand upon the trustee. As we visualize the hypothetical situation, the child would inform the trustee that he demanded his share of the additions up to $4,000. The trustee would petition the court for the appointment of a legal guardian and then turn the funds over to the guardian. It would also seem possible for the parent to make the demand as natural guardian. This would involve the acquisition of property for the child rather than the management of the property. It would then be necessary for a legal guardian to be appointed to take charge of the funds. The only time when the disability to sue would come into play, would be if the trustee disregarded the demand and committed a breach of trust. That would not, however, vitiate the demand.

All this is admittedly speculative since it is highly unlikely that a demand will ever be made or that if one is made, it would be made in this fashion. However, as a technical matter, we think a minor could make the demand.

Given the trust, the California law, and the circumstances in our case, it can be seen that very different results may well be achieved, depending upon the test used. Under a strict interpretation of the *Stifel* test of examining everything and determining whether there is any likelihood of present enjoyment, the gifts to minors in our case would seem to be "future interests." Although under our interpretation neither the trust nor the law technically forbid a demand by the minor, the practical difficulties of a child going through the procedures seem substantial. In addition, the surrounding facts indicate the children were well cared for and the obvious intention of the trustors was to create a long term trust. No guardian had been appointed and, except for the tax difficulties, probably never would be appointed. As a practical matter, it is likely that some, if not all, of the beneficiaries did not even know that they had any right to demand funds from the trust. They probably did not know when contributions were made to the trust or in what amounts. Even had they known, the substantial contributions were made toward the end of the year so that the time to make a demand was severely limited. Nobody had made a demand under the provision, and no distributions had been made. We think it unlikely that any demand ever would have been made. . . .

Under the general language of *Kieckhefer* which talked of the "right to enjoy," all exclusions in our case would seem to be allowable. The broader *Kieckhefer* rule which we have discussed is inapplicable on the facts of this case. That rule, as we interpret it, is that postponed enjoyment is not equivalent to a "future interest" if the postponement is solely caused by the minority of the beneficiary. In *Kieckhefer*, the income was accumulated and added to the corpus until the beneficiary reached the age of 21. At that time everything was to be turned over to him. This is all that happened unless a demand was made. In our case, on the contrary, if no demand is made in any particular year, the additions are forever removed from the uncontrolled reach of the beneficiary since, with the exception of the yearly demand provision, the only way the corpus can ever be tapped by a beneficiary, is through a distribution at the discretion of the trustee.

We decline to follow a strict reading of the *Stifel* case in our situation because we feel that the solution suggested by that case is inconsistent and unfair. It becomes arbitrary for the IRS to step in and decide who is likely to make an effective demand. Under the circumstances suggested in our case, it is doubtful that any demands will be made against the trust — yet the Commissioner always allowed the exclusion as to adult beneficiaries. There is nothing to indicate that it is any more likely that John will demand funds than that any other beneficiary will do so. The only distinction is that it might be easier for him to make such a demand. Since we conclude that the demand can be made by the others, it follows that the exclusion should also apply to them. In another case we might follow the broader *Kieckhefer* rule, since it seems least arbitrary and establishes a clear standard. However, if the minors have no way of making the demand in our case, then there is more than just a postponement involved, since John could demand his share of yearly additions while the others would never have the opportunity at their shares of those additions but would be limited to taking part of any additions added subseuent to their 21st birthdays. . . .

The decision of the Tax Court denying the taxpayers' exclusions on the gifts to David and Mark Crummey is reversed. The decision of the Tax Court allowing the taxpayers' exclusions on the 1962 gift to Janet Crummey is affirmed.

Since the victory in *Crummey*, taxpayers have used *Crummey* powers to create present interests in trust beneficiaries, both adults and children. The IRS has recognized that such powers create present interests if there is no agreement that the beneficiaries will not exercise their powers and if the beneficiaries receive notice of contributions to the trust and have a realistic opportunity to exercise their powers. The IRS, however, has held that *Crummey* powers in beneficiaries that have only a contingent interest in the trust do not create valid present interests because there is an implicit agreement that such beneficiaries will not exercise their powers.

Estate of Cristofani v. Commissioner
97 T.C. 74 (1991)

RUWE, Judge:

. . . The issue for decision is whether transfers of property to a trust, where the beneficiaries possessed the right to withdraw an amount not in excess of the section 2503(b) exclusion within 15 days of such transfers, constitute gifts of a present interest in property within the meaning of section 2503(b).

Petitioner is the Estate of Maria Cristofani, deceased, Frank Cristofani, executor. . . . Decedent has two children, Frank Cristofani and Lillian Dawson. . . . Decedent has five grandchildren. . . . On June 12, 1984, decedent executed an irrevocable trust entitled the Maria Cristofani Children's Trust I (Children's Trust). Frank Cristofani and Lillian Dawson were named the trustees of the Children's Trust.

In general, Frank Cristofani and Lillian Dawson possessed the following rights and interests in the Children's Trust corpus and income. Under Article Twelfth, following a contribution to the Children's Trust, Frank Cristofani and Lillian Dawson could each withdraw an amount not to exceed the amount specified for the gift tax exclusion under section 2503(b). Such withdrawal period would begin on the date of the contribution and end on the 15th day following such contribution. Under Article Third, Frank Cristofani and Lillian Dawson were to receive equally the entire net income of the trust quarter-annually, or at more frequent intervals. After decedent's death, under Article Third, the Trust Estate was to be divided into as many equal shares as there were children of decedent then living or children of decedent then deceased but leaving issue. Both Frank Cristofani and Lillian Dawson survived decedent, and thus the Children's Trust was divided into two equal trusts. . . .

In general, decedent's five grandchildren possessed the following rights and interests in the Children's Trust. Under Article Twelfth, during a 15-day period following a contribution to the Children's Trust, each of the grandchildren possessed the same right of withdrawal as described above regarding the withdrawal rights of Frank Cristofani and Lillian Dawson. Under Article Twelfth, the trustee of the Children's Trust was required to notify the beneficiaries of the trust each time a contribution was received. Under Article Third, had either Frank Cristofani or Lillian Dawson predeceased decedent or failed to survive decedent by 120 days, his or her equal portion of decedent's Children's Trust would have passed in trust to his or her children (decedent's grandchildren).

Under Article Third, the trustees, in their discretion, could apply as much of the principal of the Children's Trust as necessary for the proper support, health, maintenance and education of decedent's children. In exercising their discretion, the trustees were to take into account several factors, including "The Settlor's desire to consider the Settlor's children as primary beneficiaries and the other beneficiaries of secondary importance."

Decedent intended to fund the corpus of the Children's Trust with 100 percent ownership of improved real property. . . . Decedent intended that a one-third undivided interest in the Spring Street property be transferred to the Children's Trust during each of the 3 taxable years 1984, 1985, and 1986. . . .

Consistent with her intent, decedent transferred, on December 17, 1984, an undivided 33-percent interest in the Spring Street property to the Children's Trust by a quitclaim deed. Similarly, in 1985, decedent transferred a second undivided 33-percent interest in the Spring Street property to the Children's Trust by a quitclaim deed which was recorded on November 27, 1985. Decedent intended to transfer her remaining undivided interest in the Spring Street property to the Children's Trust in 1986. However, decedent died prior to making the transfer, and her remaining interest in the Spring Street property remained in her estate.

The value of the 33-percent undivided interest in the Spring Street property that decedent transferred in 1984 was $70,000. The value of the 33-percent undivided interest in the Spring Street property that decedent transferred in 1985 also was $70,000.

Decedent did not report the two $70,000 transfers on Federal gift tax returns. Rather, decedent claimed seven annual exclusions of $10,000 each under section 2503(b) for each year 1984 and 1985. These annual exclusions were claimed with respect to decedent's two children and decedent's five grandchildren.

There was no agreement or understanding between decedent, the trustees, and the beneficiaries that decedent's grandchildren would not exercise their withdrawal rights following a contribution to the Children's Trust. None of decedent's five grandchildren exercised their rights to withdraw under Article Twelfth of the Children's Trust during either 1984 or 1985. None of decedent's five grandchildren received a distribution from the Children's Trust during either 1984 or 1985.

Respondent allowed petitioner to claim the annual exclusions with respect to decedent's two children. However, respondent disallowed the $10,000 annual exclusions claimed with respect to each of decedent's grandchildren claimed for the years 1984 and 1985. . . .

In the instant case, petitioner argues that the right of decedent's grandchildren to withdraw an amount equal to the annual exclusion within 15 days after decedent's contribution of property to the Children's Trust constitutes a gift of a present interest in property, thus qualifying for a $10,000 annual exclusion for each grandchild for the years 1984 and 1985. Petitioner relies upon Crummey v. Commissioner, 397 F.2d 82 (9th Cir. 1968). . . .

Subsequent to the opinion in *Crummey*, respondent's revenue rulings have recognized that when a trust instrument gives a beneficiary the legal power to demand immediate possession of corpus, that power qualifies as a present interest in property. *See* Rev. Rul. 85-24, 1985-1 C.B. 329, 330 . . . ; Rev. Rul. 81-7, 1981-1 C.B. 474. . . . While we recognize that revenue rulings do not constitute authority for deciding a case in this Court, . . . we mention them to show respondent's recognition that a trust beneficiary's legal right to demand immediate possession and enjoyment of trust corpus or income constitutes a present interest in property for purposes of the annual exclusion under section 2503(b). . . . We also note that respondent allowed the annual exclusions with respect to decedent's two children who possessed the same right of withdrawal as decedent's grandchildren.

In the instant case, respondent has not argued that decedent's grandchildren did not possess a legal right to withdraw corpus from the Children's Trust within 15 days following any contribution, or that such demand could have been legally resisted by the trustees. In fact, the parties have stipulated that "following a contribution to the Children's Trust, each of the grandchildren possessed the SAME RIGHT OF WITHDRAWAL as . . . the withdrawal rights of Frank Cristofani and Lillian Dawson." (Emphasis added.) The legal right of decedent's grandchildren to withdraw specified amounts from the trust corpus within 15 days following any contribution of property constitutes a gift of a present interest. Crummey v. Commissioner, *supra*.

On brief, respondent attempts to distinguish *Crummey* from the instant case. Respondent argues that in *Crummey* the trust beneficiaries not only possessed an immediate right of withdrawal, but also possessed "substantial, future economic benefits" in the trust corpus and income. Respondent emphasizes that the Children's Trust identified decedent's children as "primary beneficiaries," and that decedent's grandchildren were to be considered as "beneficiaries of secondary importance."

Generally, the beneficiaries of the trust in *Crummey* were entitled to distributions of income. Trust corpus was to be distributed to the issue of each beneficiary sometime following the beneficiary's death. *See* Crummey v. Commissioner. . . . Aside from the discretionary actions of the trustee, the only way any beneficiary in *Crummey* could receive trust corpus was through the demand provision which allowed each beneficiary to demand up to $4,000 in the year in which a transfer to the trust was made. . . .

In the instant case, the primary beneficiaries of the Children's Trust were decedent's children. Decedent's grandchildren held contingent remainder interests in the Children's Trust. Decedent's grandchildren's interests vested only in the event that their respective parent (decedent's child) predeceased decedent or failed to survive decedent by more than 120 days. We do not believe, however, that *Crummey* requires that the beneficiaries of a trust must have a vested present interest or vested remainder interest in the trust corpus or income, in order to qualify for the section 2503(b) exclusion.

As discussed in *Crummey*, the likelihood that the beneficiary will actually receive present enjoyment of the property is not the test for determining whether a present interest was received. Rather, we must examine the ability of the beneficiaries, in a legal sense, to exercise their right to withdraw trust corpus, and the trustee's right to legally resist a beneficiary's demand for payment. Crummey v. Commissioner, 397 F.2d at 88. Based upon the language of the trust instrument and stipulations of the parties, we believe that each grandchild possessed the legal right to withdraw trust corpus and that the trustees would be unable to legally resist a grandchild's withdrawal demand. We note that there was no agreement or understanding between decedent, the trustees, and the beneficiaries that the grandchildren would not exercise their withdrawal rights following a contribution to the Children's Trust.

Respondent also argues that since the grandchildren possessed only a contingent remainder interest in the Children's Trust, decedent never intended to benefit her grandchildren. Respondent contends that the only reason decedent gave her grandchildren the right to withdraw trust corpus was to obtain the benefit of the annual exclusion.

We disagree. Based upon the provisions of the Children's Trust, we believe that decedent intended to benefit her grandchildren. Their benefits, as remaindermen, were contingent upon a child of decedent's dying before decedent or failing to survive decedent by more than 120 days. We recognize that at the time decedent executed the Children's Trust, decedent's children were in good health, but this does not remove the possibility that decedent's children could have predeceased decedent.

In addition, decedent's grandchildren possessed the power to withdraw up to an amount equal to the amount allowable for the 2503(b) exclusion. Although decedent's grandchildren never exercised their respective withdrawal rights, this does not vitiate the fact that they had the legal right to do so, within 15 days following a contribution to the Children's Trust. Events might have occurred to prompt decedent's children and grandchildren (through their guardians) to exercise their withdrawal rights. For example, either or both of decedent's children and their respective families might have suddenly and unexpectedly been faced with economic hardship; or, in the event of the insolvency of one of decedent's children, the rights of the grandchildren might have been exercised to safeguard their interest in the trust assets from their parents' creditors. In light of the provisions in decedent's trust, we fail to see how respondent can argue that decedent did not intend to benefit her grandchildren.

Finally, the fact that the trust provisions were intended to obtain the benefit of the annual gift tax exclusion does not change the result. As we stated in Perkins v. Commissioner, *supra,*

> regardless of the petitioners' motives, or why they did what they in fact did, the legal rights in question were created by the trust instruments and could at any

time thereafter be exercised. Petitioners having done what they purported to do, their tax-saving motive is irrelevant. [Perkins v. Commissioner, 27 T.C. at 606.]

Based upon the foregoing, we find that the grandchildren's right to withdraw an amount not to exceed the section 2503(b) exclusion, represents a present interest for purposes of section 2503(b). Accordingly, petitioner is entitled to claim annual exclusions with respect to decedent's grandchildren as a result of decedent's transfers of property to the Children's Trust in 1984 and 1985.

The IRS acquiesced in the result, but not the rationale, of *Crisofani*. 1992-C.B. 1, 1996-2 C.B. 1. The IRS, however, has continued to challenge *Crummey* powers given to individuals who are not the primary beneficiaries of the trust, but has been unsuccessful. *See* Estate of Kohlsaat v. Commissioner, 73 T.C.M. (C.C.H.) 2732 (1997), and Estate of Holland v. Commissioner, 73 T.C.M. (C.C.H.) 3236 (1997).

PROBLEMS

1. Gladys has substantial wealth and wants to transfer money to, or for the benefit of, her ten grandchildren. She also wants to minimize transfer tax consequences. She has four children, all of whom are living at the time.
    a.   What options does Gladys have?
    b.   What are the advantages and disadvantages of each option?
    c.   If Gladys wants to transfer money in trust, should Gladys establish one trust for all ten grandchildren or separate trusts for each grandchild? Why?
    d.   If Gladys wants to delay distribution of corpus to the grandchildren for as long as possible, what form of trust would you recommend? Why?
2. Gil establishes an irrevocable trust for the benefit of his minor child, Alan. The Trustee is required to distribute all income annually to, or for the benefit of, Alan. When Alan is 50, the Trustee is to distribute the principal to Alan. If Alan dies before age 50, the principal is to be distributed to whomever Alan designates in his will. Gil transfers $11,000 to the trust each year for five years.
    a.   What are the gift tax consequences?
    b.   What if the Trustee has discretion whether to distribute income to Alan or to accumulate it?
    c.   Same as b, only Gil also gives Alan the right to withdraw the lesser of (1) the amount contributed to the trust or (2) $11,000.

3. Gil establishes an irrevocable trust for the benefit of his minor child, Alan. The Trustee has the discretion to use the income and the principal for the benefit of Alan until Alan is 21. At that time the principal is to be distributed to Alan. Gil transfers $11,000 to the trust.

   a. What are the gift tax consequences to Gil if the principal is to be paid to Alan's brother, Brad, if Alan dies before age 21?

   b. What if the principal is to be paid to Alan's heirs at law?

   c. What if, in the event of Alan's death before age 21, the principal is to be paid to whomever Alan designates and in default of appointment to Brad?

   d. Assume that the principal goes to Alan's estate if Alan dies during the term of the trust. The Trustee is not to distribute principal to Alan until age 35. What are the gift tax consequences?

   e. Assume that the principal goes to Alan's estate if Alan dies during the term of the trust. The Trustee is instructed to use the income and principal only for Alan's health, education, support, and maintenance. What are the gift tax consequences? What if the Trustee is to use the income and principal only for Alan's comfort and happiness?

4. Graham establishes an irrevocable trust with Friendly National Bank as Trustee. The Trustee is to pay the income to Aaron and Barbara (Graham's children) in whatever amount the Trustee decides. Any income not distributed is to be added to the principal. After the death of Aaron and Barbara, the principal is to be distributed to Aaron's and Barbara's children (Cindy, Dexter, Emery, and Florence). Graham gives Aaron and Barbara each the power to withdraw the lesser of (1) $11,000 or (2) the amount contributed to the trust. If Aaron and Barbara do not exercise this power, it lapses at the end of the year.

   a. What are the gift tax consequences to Graham if Graham transfers $22,000 to the trust?

   b. What are the gift tax consequences to Graham if instead he transfers $50,000 to the trust?

   c. What are the gift tax consequences if Graham transfers $66,000 to the trust and gives withdrawal powers to Cindy, Dexter, Emery, and Florence as well as Aaron and Barbara?

   d. What are the gift tax consequences if Graham transfers $110,000 to the trust and gives withdrawal powers to Jane, Keith, Larry, and Martha as well as Aaron, Barbara, Cindy, Dexter, Emery, and Florence? Is there any limit to the number of withdrawal powers Graham can create? Should there be?

5. Should Congress eliminate the annual exclusion for gifts in trust?

PART III

The Gross Estate

CHAPTER 8

Property Owned at Death

A. GENERAL PRINCIPLES
IRC §2033

The estate tax is an excise tax on the transfer of property at death. It is neither a wealth tax, imposed on the value of property owned by decedent at the moment of her death, nor an inheritance tax, imposed on the value of property received by the heirs or beneficiaries. The tax is imposed on the value of the "gross estate" less certain deductions. The gross estate includes those property interests transferred by the decedent to another at, or as a result of, the decedent's death.

The first estate tax defined the gross estate to include all property "[t]o the extent of the interest therein of the decedent at the time of his death which after his death is subject to the payment of the charges against his estate and the expenses of its administration and is subject to distribution as part of his estate." Revenue Act of 1916 §202(a). This language influenced the Supreme Court to restrict the scope of this section. In United States v. Field, 255 U.S. 257 (1921), the Court held that the gross estate did not include property transferred pursuant to the exercise of a general power of appointment because that trust property was not in the decedent's probate estate and thus not subject to claims against the estate.

Congress then amended this provision so that the gross estate included all property "[t]o the extent of the interest therein of the decedent at the time of his death." Revenue Act of 1926 §302(a). Despite this less restrictive language, the Supreme Court refused to extend it to property subject to an unexercised general power of appointment. Helvering v. Safe Deposit & Trust Co., 316 U.S. 56 (1942). The Court emphasized that Congress had enacted a separate provision to include property subject to an *exercised* general power of appointment in the gross estate. Because Congress had not addressed the issue of an unexercised general power in revising the language of §302(a), the Court reasoned that Congress did not intend to tax unexercised general powers at the power holder's death.

As a result of these cases, Congress has had to enact specific provisions to bring powers of appointment, retained interests, and other such property interests into the gross estate. *See* §§2035-2044. Despite these provisions, there is still a need for a general "catch-all" provision to bring fee simple and similar property interests into the decedent's gross estate, and §2033 serves that function.

Section 2033 includes in the gross estate "the value of all property to the extent of the interest therein of the decedent at the time of his death." This includes property that will be subject to probate in state court, that is, those property interests that are subject to the payment of the claims and expenses and that are subject to distribution as part of the decedent's estate. Section 2033 reaches beyond the probate estate to any property interest that the decedent has an interest in at the moment before death and that passes from the decedent to another as a result of the decedent's death, such as a vested remainder in trust property that is transmissible at death. There is a broad range of property interests that fall within this section. For example, the name of a well-known author was included as an asset of the estate in Estate of Andrews v. United States, 850 F. Supp. 1279 (E.D. Va. 1994). State law in that case recognized a right of publicity that could be transferred to the decedent's beneficiaries, and the only issue was valuation. The *Andrews* case is discussed at page 60.

Not all property passing to decedent's heirs or his estate will be in his gross estate. Wrongful death benefits paid directly to the decedent's heirs or next of kin are excluded because the decedent did not have an interest in that benefit before his death. Revenue Ruling 54-19, 1954-1 C.B. 179; Revenue Ruling 68-88, 1968-1 C.B. 397. In Connecticut Bank and Trust Co. v. United States, 465 F.2d 760 (2d Cir. 1972), the court extended this rationale to wrongful death benefits received by the decedent's estate, not just his heirs. Any recovery for pain and suffering or expenses incurred before death are included in the gross estate, however, because the decedent would have recovered those amounts had he survived. Revenue Ruling 69-8, 1969-1 C.B. 219; Revenue Ruling 75-127, 1975-1 C.B. 297.

TAM 9152005

The Decedent stole a number of art objects while serving in the United States Army in France and Germany. . . . In 1957, the Decedent returned to his home town and . . . leased an apartment (in a nearby city) that he lavishly furnished and maintained until his death. . . . In 1977, the Decedent reported a taxable income of approximately $15,150. In 1978, the Decedent reported a taxable income of approximately $16,350 and, in 1979, he reported that he had no taxable income. . . . The Decedent's brother . . . has indicated in depositions that, over the 35-year period from the end of the Second World War until the Decedent's death, the brother had known of the art objects and had seen the art objects in the Decedent's possession on countless occasions. The Decedent's sister . . . her spouse, and her children apparently visited the Decedent's home town residence regularly. . . .

The Decedent died in February 1980, a resident of Texas. No federal estate tax return has been filed for the Decedent's estate. In his will, executed in

January 1979, the Decedent bequeathed all of his silver, china and crystal to two nieces and a nephew. The Decedent bequeathed and devised all the rest of his property to his sister and brother. . . .

Under Texas law, an individual's possession of personal property gives rise to the inference that the individual has a right to such possession. That is, an individual's possession of personal property is prima facie evidence of ownership. Therefore, the individual has a superior claim to converted property as against everyone except the person from whom it was converted. *See* Hickey v. Couchman, 797 S.W.2d 103 (1990); Worth Tool & Die Co. v. Atlantis Electronics, 398 S.W.2d 656 (1966); Cook v. Kern, 277 S.W.2d 946 (1955). For this reason, if an individual is in possession of converted (stolen) property and the property is, in turn, stolen or otherwise taken from the individual by another person (who was not the original owner), the individual may legally reclaim the property from the latter person. However, an individual in possession of converted (stolen) property is unable to convey clear title to a bona fide purchaser when the property is sold within the boundaries of Texas. Olin Corporation v. Cargo Carriers, 673 S.W.2d 211 (1984).

Section 2033 of the Code provides that the value of the gross estate shall include the value of all property to the extent of the interest therein of the decedent at the time of death. Section 20.2033-1 of the Estate Tax Regulations provides that the gross estate includes under section 2033 the value of all property beneficially owned by the decedent at the time of death. . . . In determining the nature of ownership that is required for inclusion of property in a decedent's gross estate under section 2033, we note that the estate tax inclusionary statutes, including section 2033, are based upon a decedent's possession of the economic equivalent of ownership rather than upon the decedent's possession of a technical legal title. . . . Consequently, even if a decedent lacked technical legal title to property at the time of death, if the decedent possessed the use and economic benefits of the property that were equivalent to ownership and if, by reason of that possession, the decedent does, in fact, successfully transfer the same use and economic benefits to the objects of his bounty at death, to be enjoyed by those persons for an indefinite period after the decedent's death, then the value of property is includible in the decedent's gross estate under section 2033 of the Code.

In the present case, on the date of the Decedent's death, he possessed art objects that he had stolen. During the entire 35-year period ending with his death, the Decedent had the exclusive possession, enjoyment, and *actual* command (including the unfettered ability of sale when he chose) of the art objects that was tantamount to ownership. [Emphasis in original.] From the income information provided by the Decedent to the Internal Revenue Service over the years, it does not appear that the Decedent had any job or profession that would enable him to acquire a vast orchid collection, travel so extensively, or live so lavishly. It is a compelling inference that the Decedent successfully sold a substantial quantity of stolen art objects to finance his lifestyle. Thus, not only did the Decedent have the full use, possession, and enjoyment of the stolen art property, but also he had the apparent ability to easily sell that property if, as, and when he felt he needed money. As such, he was the substantive owner of the beneficial interest in that property at his death.

On his death, the Decedent successfully transferred to his designated heirs (his sister and brother), the same use and economic benefits that he had enjoyed during his lifetime. In this way, the sister and brother (and, with their permission, their children) assumed the exclusive possession, actual command of the art objects, and the ability to dispose of them in the discreet markets for their own profit. . . . In the present case, it is evident from the circumstances that, over the 35-year period ending at the Decedent's death, the various family members, including the sister and brother, were well aware of the Decedent's possession of the stolen art objects and that the art objects had significant value. . . . Thus, by reason of surviving the Decedent and inheriting control over his assets, the Decedent's heirs became the substantive owners of the art objects, acquiring the same exclusive possession, command, and economic benefit of the property that the Decedent had enjoyed. Therefore, the property is includible in the Decedent's gross estate under section 2033 of the Internal Revenue Code. . . .

The question whether property that was stolen by a taxpayer can be regarded as owned by the taxpayer, when the taxpayer did not have legal title to the property, was resolved for income tax purposes in James v. United States, 366 U.S. 213 (1961). . . . Similarly, for federal estate tax purposes, no distinction should be drawn between a decedent's property that has been obtained by theft and decedents' property that has been lawfully obtained. If the decedent, at death, possessed the use and economic benefits of the stolen property that are equivalent to ownership, the decedent's lack of title to the stolen property does not affect its inclusion in the decedent's gross estate under section 2033 when the decedent can successfully transfer the property to his heirs. . . .

Section 2031(a) of the Code provides that the value of the gross estate of the decedent shall be determined by including to the extent provided the value at the time of death of all property wherever situated. Section 20.2031-1(b) of the regulations provides that the value of every item of property includible in a decedent's gross estate is its fair market value at the time of the decedent's death. The fair market value is the price at which the property would change hands between a willing buyer and a willing seller, neither being under any compulsion to buy or to sell and both having reasonable knowledge of the relevant facts. Thus, in the case of an item of property which is generally obtained by the public in the retail market, the fair market value of such an item of property is the price at which the item or a comparable item would be sold at retail. . . .

In this case, because the art objects that are includible in the Decedent's gross estate were stolen and, thus, would, under most circumstances, have been transferrable only in an illicit market, the appropriate market for establishing the fair market value, on the date of the Decedent's death, includes the discreet retail markets of the international network of traffickers in stolen art as well as the legitimate retail art markets consisting of international auction firms, advertised displays in antiques publications, and legitimate art and antiques dealers. . . . At the Decedent's death, these discreet retail markets consisted of the middlemen and dealers who sold stolen art objects to the many thousands of individual collectors (including crime barons) eager to purchase otherwise unobtainable art and antiques. . . .

Because 1) all of the art objects held by the Decedent were of great histori-cal, artistic, cultural, and religious significance and 2) the clients in the discreet retail market were eager to purchase such otherwise unobtainable objects at premium prices, we conclude that, for purposes of section 2031 of the Code, the price that would have been paid, on the Decedent's date of death, by a willing buyer of each of the art objects is the highest price that would have been paid at that time whether in the discreet retail market or in the legitimate art market.

PROBLEMS

1. Edna has been appointed executor of Denise's estate and consults you about the estate tax consequences of Denise's death. Denise purchased a house in Montpelier, Vermont, 15 years ago for $100,000. Her mortgage was $80,000. Two weeks before her death she received an offer for $250,000 for the house. Denise and Connie purchased a condominium in Acapulco for $100,000 ten years ago. They owned it as tenants in common. Denise purchased an apartment building in Boston 12 years ago for $450,000. She had claimed $75,000 in depreciation deductions on her income tax returns. The apartment building generates $120,000 net income a year. Four years ago, Denise purchased a car for $18,000. Eight years ago, Denise purchased a sailboat for $50,000.

    At the time of her death, Denise owned 500 shares of IBM, Inc., stock, 2,000 shares of Microsoft, Inc., 700 shares of 3M, Inc., and 100 shares of XYZ, Inc., a family business (her shares represent a 20 percent interest). Denise also owned municipal bonds with face amounts total-ing $100,000. They produce $8,000 of income per year, which is exempt from federal income tax pursuant to §103. Denise had a checking account (balance of $1,200), savings account (balance of $5,000), and a money market account (balance of $50,000). Denise owned a cemetery plot for her own burial. Denise also owned furniture purchased for $45,000, clothes, and household furnishings. In addition, she owned an art collection, which was insured for $250,000, and a ruby ring, which was insured for $1,500. Denise also owned a golden retriever and a Siamese cat.

    Denise died on July 2. After her death, Edna received (1) a check for $5,000 representing Denise's earned, but unpaid, salary; (2) a check for $2,000 from her employer designated "bonus"; and (3) checks totaling

$20,000 each month representing rent from the apartment complex owned by Denise.

Denise died as a result of an automobile accident. Edna sued the other driver and received $500,000 in settlement. Before her death, Denise had sued Geoffrey for patent infringement on a device that Denise had patented. Discovery did not begin until after Denise's death, and the case is scheduled to come to trial one year from the date of Denise's death.

What is included in Denise's gross estate? At what value? Why?

2. Donna was a personal injury attorney. Most of her work was performed on a contingent fee basis.

   a. At the time of her death, she had just settled the Arlington case. The defendant in that case paid the plaintiff three months after Donna's death, and the plaintiff sent Ed, Donna's executor, a check for $50,000 for her fee.

   b. Shortly before her death, Donna had completed the trial in the Bennington case, including argument on post-trial motions. Two weeks after her death the trial judge denied the motions, and no appeal was taken. Plaintiff received payment 15 months after Donna's death and sent Ed, her executor, a check for $100,000.

   c. A week before her death, Donna had filed a complaint in the Caldwell case. After her death, the case was referred to Attorney Jones, who tried the case three years after Donna's death. Defendant appealed, lost, and finally paid Jones five years after Donna's death. Jones sent Ed, her executor, a check for $25,000.

      Are any of these amounts in Donna's gross estate? Explain. *See* Estate of Curry v. Commissioner at page 70.

3. Six months before her death, Debra sent checks for $11,000 to Adrian, Bruce, and Claire. None of the checks had been presented for payment before Debra's death. *See* Metzger v. Commissioner at page 156.

   a. Are the checks included in Debra's gross estate?

   b. What if Adrian, Bruce, and Claire had deposited the checks in their respective bank accounts two days before Debra's death but the checks had not cleared Debra's bank before her death?

   c. What if Debra had sent the checks three days before her death?

4. Diane loaned $150,000 to her son, Tom, five years before her death. Tom signed a promissory note, agreeing to repay the money "upon demand by Diane." The note did not require interest, and it was not secured by any collateral.

   a. Is the promissory note included in Diane's gross estate? If so, at what value?

   b. What if the note required interest at eight percent per year, payable on December 15 each year? Assume that Tom has paid interest each year but has not repaid any principal. Diane dies on December 14. What is in her gross estate?

    c. What if Diane's will directs that all debts owed to her be canceled?

    d. What if there was only an oral agreement and no promissory note?

5. At the time of his death, David was the beneficiary of three trusts. Are any of these trusts in his gross estate?

    a. A trust was established by David's maternal grandmother that provided income to David for his life and distribution of the trust property to David's children at his death. The trust property had a value of $500,000 at the time of David's death. What if David also had the power to appoint the trust property in his will to anyone, including his own estate? Does it matter whether David exercised this power in his will or not?

    b. A trust was established by David's uncle to pay the income to his spouse for her life with the remainder to David or his estate. The trust was irrevocable. At the time of David's death, the trust property had a value of $1,000,000, and both David's uncle and aunt were still living.

    c. A trust was established by David's aunt to pay the income to Mary for life with the corpus to Nancy if she was living at Mary's death, otherwise to David or his estate. At the time of David's death, the value of the trust property was $800,000, and Mary and Nancy were still alive. David's aunt was dead.

6. The police suspected for many years that Dominic was a drug dealer, and he was under surveillance at the time of his death. Dominic had never been arrested or convicted of any crimes. Dominic was murdered in his home, and the investigation revealed a large quantity of illegal drugs hidden in the house. The value of the drugs, had they been sold on the street, was $2,500,000. The police seized the drugs and destroyed them. The state also instituted a forfeiture procedure to seize Dominic's house (fair market value $350,000) and his car (fair market value $35,000).

    a. What should Dominic's executor include in the gross estate?

    b. How should the executor determine the value of the property in the gross estate?

B. MARITAL INTERESTS IN PROPERTY
IRC §2034

In community property jurisdictions, the surviving spouse may have an interest in the decedent's community property. The community property share of the surviving spouse is owned by that spouse and is, therefore, excluded from the decedent's gross estate. Similar benefits are provided by elective share statutes in common law property jurisdictions.[1] The existence of these

---

1. Georgia is the only state that does not provide this benefit to surviving spouses.

rights, however, does not diminish the value of the decedent's gross estate, and §2034 specifically provides that the value of the gross estate includes the value of these rights. Of course, property passing to a surviving spouse pursuant to an elective share statute will qualify for the marital deduction in §2056 unless the property interest passing to the surviving spouse is a non-deductible terminable interest, such as a life estate.

PROBLEMS

Willa is married to Harold, and they have four adult children. At the time of her death, Willa owns the following property in her own name: a house (fair market value, $300,000); clothes, jewelry, car, and similar items (fair market value, $50,000); stock (fair market value, $600,000); a bank account (balance, $50,000). Willa does not own any other property.

1. What is the value of Willa's gross estate if she leaves all of her property to Harold, her spouse?
2. What is the value of Willa's gross estate if she leaves half of her property to Harold and the remainder in equal shares to her children?
3. What is the value of Willa's gross estate if she leaves all of her property in equal shares to her children, and Harold elects against the will. Under state law, Harold receives an undivided one-half interest in each asset.

CHAPTER 9

Joint Ownership

A. GENERAL PRINCIPLES
IRC §§2033, 2040

There are three basic forms of concurrent property ownership: (1) tenancy in common, (2) joint tenancy with the right of survivorship,[1] and (3) community property. In a tenancy in common each owner has the current right to use and possess the property. Tenants in common may have unequal interests in the property; that is, if A and B own Blackacre as tenants in common, A could own a one-third interest, and B could own the other two-thirds interest. There is no right of survivorship in a tenancy in common. As a result, each tenant in common's interest may be passed by will or intestacy to another. The estate tax consequences are, therefore, governed by §2033.

Joint tenancy is distinguished by survivorship rights. The surviving joint tenant acquires the entire interest in the property as a matter of law at the death of the other joint tenant. For example, C and D own Greenacre as joint tenants. At C's death, D becomes the absolute owner of Greenacre despite any provision in C's will to the contrary. Each joint tenant is an equal owner in the entire property. Under the common law, joint tenancy ownership was characterized by the four unities of time, title, interest, and possession. That is, all joint tenants had to acquire their interests at the same time, by the same instrument, in the same share, and with the same rights to use and possession. This has changed in many jurisdictions, particularly with respect to the acquisition of the joint tenancy interest. If C and D are joint tenants, they each own an undivided half interest in Greenacre. If there are more than two joint tenants, each owns the same percentage interest.

The common law also presumed that property deeded or willed to two or more persons was given to them as joint tenants with the right of survivorship.

---

1. Tenancy by the entirety is a form of joint tenancy with the right of survivorship available only to a married couple; it is not recognized in every jurisdiction. Because it cannot be unilaterally severed, valuation will depend on the relative ages of the husband and wife. The discussion in this chapter of joint tenancy, particularly the discussion of §2040(b), also applies to tenancy by the entirety.

This presumption has been abolished in most American jurisdictions. As a result, if property is deeded or willed to A and B, they are considered tenants in common. On the other hand, a deed or will giving property to C and D "jointly" or as "joint tenants" or "joint owners" will usually be interpreted as creating a joint tenancy with the right of survivorship. State law dictates what language is necessary to create a joint tenancy.

Example 9-1

Mary and Joan are sisters and own Blackacre as equal tenants in common. Joan dies without a will. Under the applicable intestacy statute Joan's interest passes to her two children, Dana and Leslie, in equal shares. Dana and Leslie become tenants in common with Mary; Mary owns a one-half interest, and Dana and Leslie each own a one-quarter interest.

Example 9-2

John and Luke are brothers and own Greenacre as joint tenants with the right of survivorship. Luke dies. His will leaves his interest in Greenacre to his daughter, Nancy. After Luke's death, John owns Greenacre in fee simple. Luke's will does not affect the ownership of Greenacre because his interest terminated at the moment of his death, and he had nothing to devise to Nancy.

Joint tenancy with the right of survivorship is a popular estate planning device. At death, the property passes immediately to the survivor by operation of law without the delay or expense of a probate proceeding. If one joint tenant has incurred debts in his own name, that creditor cannot reach the property after the debtor's death unless the creditor has filed a lien against the property prior to the debtor's death. Usually, joint tenancy property is not subject to a spouse's election against the will. Joint tenancy property *is* included in the augmented estate and, thus, subject to the elective share in jurisdictions that have adopted the Uniform Probate Code. U.P.C. §§2-205 to 2-207. Joint tenancy can, however, have negative consequences, particularly for a married couple. Because §2040(b) includes only one-half the value of joint tenancy property of a married couple in the gross estate of the first to die, only that half qualifies for the stepped-up basis provided by §1014. Moreover, if the couple own substantially all of their property as joint tenants, they may lose the benefit of the applicable credit amount provided by §2010 in the estate of the first to die. As a result, the couple may pay more estate tax than necessary.[2]

Joint bank accounts may be treated as true joint tenancy accounts, as trust accounts, or as nominal or convenience accounts. State law defines the characteristics of such accounts. The transfer tax consequences will depend on these state law characteristics.

---

2. This issue is discussed in Chapter 16, section F.2.

Community property considers all property acquired during marriage as belonging to both the husband and the wife. Property gifted or devised to only one spouse individually may be held as separate property. Husband and Wife each own an undivided one-half interest in the community property regardless of title. If Husband and Wife own property as joint tenants with the right of survivorship, however, such property is not considered community property. Husband and Wife share income produced by community property equally, and each has the right to dispose of half of the community property at death. Because there are no survivorship rights in community property, §2033 brings the decedent's share of community property into his gross estate. The full value of the community property is not included even if the decedent alone paid all of the consideration and held the property in his sole name during the marriage. Both spouses must consent to gifts of community property, and such gifts are treated as made equally by each spouse.

B.   CREATION AND TERMINATION OF JOINT INTERESTS DURING LIFE
IRC §§2511, 2512, 2523(a)

The creation of a joint tenancy is a gift to the extent that the joint tenants do not provide any consideration for their interests. §2512(b). Donor, D, can create a joint tenancy in others by deeding the property to A and B as joint tenants. D can also create a joint tenancy with herself by deeding property to A, B, and D as joint tenants.

The gift is complete at the time of the property transfer because D has given up the power to retract the gift. Reg. §25.2511-2(b). Joint bank accounts, even true joint tenancy bank accounts, are an exception to this rule in many jurisdictions. When D deposits money into a joint bank account with A, D has not made a completed gift if D has the power to withdraw the entire amount of the deposit without the consent of A. D's deposit is a revocable transfer and will not be a completed gift until A withdraws the money. In jurisdictions where the donor does not have this right of revocation, the gift is complete at the time of deposit because the other joint tenant's right becomes vested at that moment. When Donor purchases a United States Savings Bond payable to "Donor or A," she can reclaim all of the funds; thus, the gift is incomplete until maturity, when the joint owner receives his share. Reg. §25.2511-1(h)(4).

The value of the gift depends on whether the joint tenancy can be severed unilaterally, which is a question of state law. If any joint tenant can sever the joint tenancy without the consent of the other joint tenants, then the value of each joint tenant's interest is the same. If a joint tenant must obtain the consent of the other joint tenants to sever the joint tenancy, the value of each tenant's interest will depend on his or her age in relation to the age of the other joint tenants. The difference in value results from the probability that the youngest joint tenant will survive and, thus, will most likely become the sole owner of the property.

In most circumstances, the joint tenancy interest created by a gift is considered a present interest for purposes of the gift tax annual exclusion. The creation of a joint tenancy by one spouse with another will also qualify for the unlimited marital deduction of §2523.

The termination of a joint tenancy during the life of all joint tenants does not create any further gift tax consequences as long as each joint tenant receives his or her proportionate share of the property or proceeds. If the property or proceeds from it are distributed in any manner that is not proportional, the difference will be a gift to the extent that the donor does not receive adequate and full consideration in money or money's worth. This can happen when joint tenants transfer their ownership interests into a new form of ownership, such as a partnership or a trust, where there are nonproportional interests.

C. TERMINATION OF JOINT INTERESTS BY DEATH
IRC §§2033, 2040, 2056(a)

Section 2033 includes in the gross estate all property owned at death that passes from the decedent to another as a result of death. Because the decedent may transfer an interest in property held as a tenant in common by will or intestacy, §2033 brings those interests into the gross estate. Section 2033 also includes the decedent's share of community property in the gross estate because each spouse has the right to devise or bequeath his share of such property.

On the other hand, property owned as joint tenants with the right of survivorship or as tenants by the entirety passes to the survivor at death by operation of law, not from the decedent. As a result, such interests are not governed by §2033. Instead, §2040(a) includes in the gross estate the full value of property owned as joint tenants with the right of survivorship subject to the exceptions discussed below.

1. The Tracing Rule of §2040(a)

Section 2040(a) provides that "[t]he value of the gross estate shall include the value of all property to the extent of the interest therein held as joint tenants with right of survivorship by the decedent and any other person . . . except such part thereof as may be shown to have originally belonged to such other person and never to have been received or acquired by the latter from decedent for less than an adequate and full consideration in money or money's worth." This language creates a rebuttable presumption that the first joint tenant to die provided all of the consideration for the acquisition of the property. The surviving joint tenant has the burden of proving his contribution. This presumption does not apply if all the joint tenants received their interests in the property by gift, bequest, or inheritance from a third party. In this situation, only the decedent's fractional interest is brought into her gross estate by §2040(a).

If the executor establishes that the surviving joint tenant furnished some, or all, of the consideration to acquire the property, that portion of the property attributable to the survivor's contribution is excluded. That is, the amount excluded equals the date of death value of the property times the consideration provided by the survivor divided by the total consideration paid to acquire the property. The formula is:

$$\text{amount excluded} = \text{value of property} \times \frac{\text{survivor's consideration}}{\text{total consideration paid}}$$

Example 9-3

Decedent and Survivor acquired Greenacre as joint tenants with the right of survivorship. Decedent paid $80,000 and Survivor $20,000. At the time of Decedent's death Greenacre has a fair market value of $200,000. The amount excluded from Decedent's gross estate is:

$$\$200,000 \times \frac{\$20,000}{\$100,000}$$

Thus, $40,000 will be excluded from, and $160,000 will be included in, Decedent's gross estate by §2040(a).

The §2040(a) presumption creates a significant problem for the executor, because he must be able to prove the surviving joint tenant's contribution to the purchase price. The executor must have the records necessary to establish these contributions. This is not an easy burden to satisfy, as frequently the joint tenants make differing contributions over time to the acquisition of property or sell the original property and reinvest the proceeds in new joint tenancy property, as the following case demonstrates.

Estate of Fratini v. Commissioner
76 T.C.M. (CCH) 342 (1998)

RUWE, Judge:

. . . Albert Fratini (decedent) . . . was not married when he died. For 18 years preceding his death, decedent continuously lived with Marion Friedeberg. Ms. Friedeberg is the estate's personal representative and the sole beneficiary under decedent's holographic will. . . . At the time decedent and Ms. Friedeberg began their relationship in 1974, decedent owned, among other things, several pieces of real property [(known as Laidley, Valencia, and South Fitch). He also owned a 10 percent undivided interest in Acadia. On December 10 and 11, 1987, decedent transferred to Ms. Friedeberg an undivided one-half joint tenancy interest in each of these properties.]. . .

Decedent and Ms. Friedeberg jointly obtained interests in several other properties after they began living together. [On February 10, 1983, they purchased Chenery with money from their joint bank account. On September 12, 1984, they purchased Dolores with a downpayment provided by both and a promissory note signed by both. On March 27, 1985, they purchased Onondaga. The downpayment was one check from Ms. Friedeberg and two checks drawn on their joint bank account. Both signed the promissory note for the remaining cost of Onondaga.] . . . In addition to land and buildings, decedent and Ms. Friedeberg maintained joint bank accounts and purchased a number of certificates of deposit with funds drawn from those accounts. . . . On or about December 15, 1987, a fire occurred at the Dolores property. Decedent and Ms. Friedeberg received a total of $50,471.61 [which was] . . . deposited on March 18, 1988, into a joint savings account held at Continental Bank in decedent's and Ms. Friedeberg's names. . . .

In 1988 and 1989, decedent reported on his individual Federal income tax return rental income and loss from the Valencia, Chenery, Dolores, Onondaga, and South Fitch properties. Ms. Friedeberg did not report rental income or loss on her Federal income tax returns for 1988 and 1989. For the years 1990 through 1992, decedent and Ms. Friedeberg both reported income and loss from the rental properties. For the years 1981 through 1992, Ms. Friedeberg reported taxable interest income of $133,051. With respect to the $133,051 of interest income reported, approximately $3,440 was earned from accounts titled in Ms. Friedeberg's name alone. . . .

We must first decide whether the estate is entitled to contribution credits pursuant to section 2040 regarding the value of the real properties, bank accounts, and certificates of deposit that were held in the joint names of decedent and Ms. Friedeberg on the date of decedent's death. . . . Section 2040 governs the value of jointly owned property to be included in a decedent's estate. . . . Section 2040 establishes a "contribution test," whereby the estate of the deceased joint tenant must generally include the value of the entire property less the portion of the property attributable to the consideration furnished by the surviving joint tenant. Hahn v. Commissioner, 110 T.C. 140, 144, (1998). If part of the consideration is found to have been contributed in money or money's worth by the surviving joint tenant, then the part of the value of the property that is proportionate to such consideration is not included in decedent's gross estate. . . .

Section 2040 creates a rebuttable presumption that the value of the entire property is includable in the deceased joint tenant's estate, and the burden of showing original ownership or contribution to the purchase price by the surviving joint tenant falls upon the estate. Hahn v. Commissioner, *supra* at 144. . . . Where evidence indicates that the surviving joint tenant did contribute money or money's worth under section 2040, courts have held that the executor's burden has been met notwithstanding that the exact amount of the contribution could not be proven by the taxpayer. . . . In those circumstances, we have applied the rule enunciated in Cohan v. Commissioner, 39 F.2d 540 (2d Cir.1930), and allowed taxpayers to approximate where amounts were not definitely determinable. . . .

With respect to amounts that Ms. Friedeberg received after June 1974, the point at which Ms. Friedeberg and decedent began living together, Ms. Friedeberg claims that she received total monthly restitution payments of $57,220.15 from the German Government. Ms. Friedeberg also received $15,000 in August 1976 as a result of her divorce. Ms. Friedeberg received a distribution from the estate of Lucian Lubinski of $29,177.53 on December 8, 1981. On November 5, 1983, and May 13, 1985, Ms. Friedeberg received $7,500 and $6,185.46, respectively, from the estate of Hirtha Gray.

From the above-listed amounts, Ms. Friedeberg contributed $4,000 to the purchase of a jointly owned CD in July of 1979. In or around October of 1980, Ms. Friedeberg purchased a CD in the amount of $10,000 in her name with the money she received as restitution payments from the German Government. Upon maturity of the $10,000 CD, Ms. Friedeberg testified that the proceeds were ultimately contributed to the purchase of a CD in the joint names of decedent and Ms. Friedeberg. Ms. Friedeberg testified that during 1981 she contributed the $29,177 she received from the estate of Lucian Lubinski toward the purchase of a CD in the amount of $30,000 in the joint names of herself and decedent.

As evidence, Ms. Friedeberg offered a number of items in support of her testimony. Ms. Friedeberg offered summary schedules showing that she received from the German Government a total of $57,220.15 from June 1974 to June 2, 1992, the date of decedent's death. Ms. Friedeberg also offered bank statements dated in early 1981, which indicate that she owned a CD in the amount of $10,000. Ms. Friedeberg offered numerous bank statements that indicated that CD's were later purchased in the joint names of decedent and herself in amounts corresponding to the amounts Ms. Friedeberg testified that she and decedent purchased. Ms. Friedeberg offered probate documents from the Superior Court of San Francisco County, California, dated March 2, 1981, indicating that she received a distribution of $29,177.53 from the estate of Lucian Lubinski. With respect to the jointly acquired real properties, Ms. Friedeberg testified that the downpayments for Chenery, Dolores, and Onondaga were all paid with funds from bank accounts held in the joint names of decedent and Ms. Friedeberg. . . . From 1974 to 1985, Ms. Friedeberg has shown that she received at least $71,862. One-half of the total downpayments for the properties would require a contribution of $69,586.82. We find Ms. Friedeberg to be a credible witness, and we accept the veracity of her testimony. Thus, notwithstanding the fact that Ms. Friedeberg was unable to provide every receipt for each bank deposit, purchase of a CD, and receipts for each reinvestment into another CD, it is reasonable to conclude that she contributed one-half toward the total purchase prices of the Chenery, Dolores, and Onondaga properties. Cohan v. Commissioner, supra.

Petitioner also argues that Ms. Friedeberg provided services in the form of management of the rental properties from 1974 until 1992. Petitioner argues that these services constitute adequate consideration contributed in "money's worth" to the values of the Laidley, Valencia, South Fitch, and Acadia properties, such that petitioner is entitled to exclude one-half of the total value of these properties from decedent's estate under section 2040(a). Respondent asserts that the services Ms. Friedeberg performed were minimal and that petitioner has not established a value for Ms. Friedeberg's services.

Our determination of whether Ms. Friedeberg provided full and adequate consideration is necessarily one of fact. . . . In determining the consideration furnished by the surviving joint tenant, amounts furnished by decedent to the surviving joint tenant for less than full and adequate consideration are to be ignored. . . . If part of the consideration is found to have been contributed by the surviving joint tenant, then the part of the value of the property as is proportionate to such consideration is not included in decedent's gross estate. Sec. 20.2040-1(a)(2), Estate Tax Regs.

In the instant case, Ms. Friedeberg testified that for a number of years she managed the rental properties. In support of Ms. Friedeberg's testimony, petitioner offered a number of check registers indicating that Ms. Friedeberg regularly kept the financial records regarding income and expenses related to the rental properties. Ms. Friedeberg submitted a substantial number of documents regarding the rental properties from sellers, insurance companies, mortgage banks, tenants, and title companies addressed to both decedent and Ms. Friedeberg. Ms. Friedeberg submitted many letters from tenants of the rental properties addressed to her alone. She had signature authority over the joint accounts and regularly wrote checks and paid expenses related to the rental properties. Ms. Friedeberg maintained the buildings on the rental properties by providing janitorial services and maintaining the landscape. We find that Ms. Friedeberg did provide various services including management of the properties, maintenance, and janitorial services.

Petitioner introduced Mr. Paul Chahin as an expert witness, and offered his expert report for the purpose of proving the fair market value of the real estate management and other services provided by Ms. Friedeberg. In his report, Mr. Chahin indicated that his valuation was based on an understanding that Ms. Friedeberg managed the Valencia property and the properties which decedent and Ms. Friedeberg jointly acquired. Mr. Chahin indicated in his report that, based on his experience as a property manager, the property management, leasing, janitorial and maintenance services performed by Ms. Friedeberg had an average fair market value of $24,000 per year.

Mr. Chahin's report did not distinguish between the amount of services provided for each of the different properties based on the number of rental units in each building or otherwise. Mr. Chahin's report did not distinguish a difference in value over the course of 18 years, notwithstanding the fact that more units were acquired over time. The report simply states that the fees charged in general have remained "relatively constant in California since the early 1980's." Also, it is unclear from Mr. Chahin's report which properties the valuation is based on. Mr. Chahin's report does not appear to address the Laidley, South Fitch, or Acadia properties. Because the value assigned by Mr. Chahin is arrived at in a conclusory fashion, without taking into account the changes in the amount of services or the value of the services over time, Mr. Chahin's report does not persuade us that the value of Ms. Friedeberg's services was $24,000 per year, and we are not bound by it. Parker v. Commissioner, 86 T.C. 547, 561 (1986). . . . Using our best judgment under these circumstances, we hold that petitioner is entitled to section 2040 contribution credits for Valencia and South Fitch of 21.13 percent and 21.61 percent, respectively. Cohan v. Commissioner, *supra*.

However, petitioner has not offered any evidence which would persuade us that Ms. Friedeberg performed substantial services in connection with the Laidley or Acadia properties. Petitioner reported no contribution credits on Form 706 for the Laidley and Acadia properties. Although Ms. Friedeberg testified that she regularly cleaned Laidley, she also resided in Laidley with decedent for all the years in which she and decedent lived together. Laidley was never used as a rental property. Also, decedent did not receive any rental income from Acadia subsequent to his divorce from Ms. Fratini. . . . [W]e find that petitioner has failed to carry the burden of proving that adequate consideration in money's worth was contributed by Ms. Friedeberg to the joint interests in the Laidley or Acadia properties. . . .

With respect to the remaining assets, petitioner argues that the estate is entitled to deduct one-half of the date-of-death value of two checking accounts containing $29,724, a savings account containing $5,214, and a CD valued at $100,000.

Generally, income produced by property belongs to the person who owns the property at the time the property produces such income and does not originate with a donor who has made a completed gift of that property prior to the production of such income. Harvey v. United States, 185 F.2d 463, 467 (7th Cir.1950); *see also* Estate of Howard v. Commissioner, 9 T.C. 1192, 1202-1203 (1947); sec. 20.2040-1(c)(5), Estate Tax Regs. Where a surviving joint tenant receives property gratuitously from a decedent, the property thereafter produces income, and the income is used as consideration for the acquisition of the jointly held property, the income from the time of receipt of the gift has been held to be the surviving joint tenant's income. Estate of Goldsborough v. Commissioner, 70 T.C. 1077, 1083 (1978), *affd. without published opinion* 673 F.2d 1310 (4th Cir.1982). . . .

Ms. Friedeberg testified that amounts received through rental of the properties were equally shared and deposited in the jointly owned bank accounts and were used regularly to purchase CD's. For the time period after December 10, 1987, decedent and Ms. Friedeberg, as joint owners of the properties, equally shared the net rentals. Again, we accept the veracity of Ms. Friedeberg's testimony and find that the rental income received and deposited into joint accounts constitutes sufficient consideration such that Ms. Friedeberg acquired a 50-percent ownership interest in the bank accounts and CD deposits as of the date of decedent's death. Therefore, we hold that petitioner is due a contribution credit pursuant to section 2040 equal to 50 percent of the joint bank account holdings in the savings, checking, and CD accounts.

In determining the amount included in decedent's estate pursuant to section 2040, petitioner reduced the value of decedent's interest in several of the jointly held real properties by fractional interest discounts. Petitioner argues that the reported discounted fair market values of the joint tenancy interests in Laidley, Valencia, South Fitch, Chenery, Dolores, and Onondaga are valid. In the notice of deficiency, respondent disallowed the claimed fractional discounts.

In our recent opinion in Estate of Young v. Commissioner, 110 T.C. 297, (1998), we addressed the issue of whether, and to what extent, a fractional interest discount or lack of marketability discount should be applied to a decedent's property held in joint tenancy with right of survivorship. In Estate of Young v. Commissioner, *supra* at 315-316, we stated:

> Under the scheme of section 2040(a), the amount includable in a decedent's gross estate does not depend on a valuation of property rights actually transferred at death, or on a valuation of the actual interest held by the decedent (legal title); instead, decedent's gross estate includes the entire value of property held in a joint tenancy by him and any other person, except to the extent the consideration for the property was furnished by such other person. . . . Section 2040(a) provides an artificial inclusion of the joint tenancy property: the entire value of the property less any contribution by the surviving joint tenant. Except for the statutory exclusions in section 2040(a), there is no further allowance to account for the fact that less than the entire interest is being included. [Citation and fn. ref. omitted.]

Applying the same reasoning to the instant case, we conclude that petitioner is not entitled to fractional interest discounts on any of the properties based on joint ownership with Ms. Friedeberg.

Improvements paid for by one of the joint tenants are considered a contribution toward the acquisition of the property. Estate of Peters v. Commissioner, 386 F.2d 404 (4th Cir. 1967). Mortgage payments as well as joint liability for a mortgage are also deemed equal contributions by the joint tenants. Revenue Ruling 79-302, 1979-2 C.B. 328.

Not all contributions by the surviving joint tenant qualify for exclusion. Any money or other property received from the decedent as a gift will not be considered a contribution by the surviving joint tenant. Reg. §20.2040-1(c)(4).

Example 9-4

Decedent purchases Whiteacre as joint tenants with her Son. If she pays the entire purchase price of $100,000, the full date of death value will be in her gross estate. Instead, she gives her Son $50,000, and they purchase Whiteacre, both paying $50,000 cash. Section 2040(a) prevents this obvious attempt at tax evasion by including the full value of Whiteacre in Decedent's gross estate.

Example 9-5

Assume that Decedent and Son exchange Whiteacre from Example 9-4 for new property held as joint tenants, Grayacre. This is considered a mere change in form, and the Son is deemed to have contributed nothing toward the purchase of Grayacre. If Decedent and her Son sell Whiteacre and use the proceeds to purchase Grayacre, the same rule applies. In all of the situations, Decedent paid the entire consideration for the property, and the full date of death value is in her gross estate. *See, e.g.*, Endicott Trust Co. v. United States, 305 F. Supp. 943 (N.D.N.Y. 1969).

A different rule applies if the Son uses his own resources as a contribution to the purchase of property held jointly with the Decedent. Income earned on property, even property originally given to the Son by Decedent, qualifies as the Son's contribution.

Example 9-6

Decedent gives her Son stock in XYZ, Inc. Son uses the dividends he has received on the stock to purchase Greenacre as joint tenants with Decedent. When Decedent dies, the amount that Son paid is considered his contribution. Reg. §20.2040-1(c)(5); Harvey v. United States, 185 F.2d 463 (7th Cir. 1950).

A similar rule applies to appreciation in value realized by Son.

Example 9-7

Assume that the XYZ, Inc., stock in Example 9-6 was worth $10,000 when Decedent gave it to Son. When the stock had appreciated in value to $15,000, Son sold it. He used the $5,000 appreciation to purchase stock in ABC, Inc., with Decedent as joint tenants. The $5,000 will be considered Son's contribution. Revenue Ruling 79-372, 1979-2 C.B. 330; Estate of Goldsborough v. Commissioner, 70 T.C. 1077, 1083, (1978), *aff'd without published opinion*, 673 F.2d 1310 (4th Cir.1982).

If Son had contributed the entire sales proceeds of $15,000 to the purchase of the ABC, Inc., stock as joint tenants with Decedent, only $5,000 would qualify as his contribution. Estate of Goldsborough v. Commissioner, *supra*.

The surviving joint tenant may contribute services that will count as consideration toward the acquisition of the jointly owned property. Services provided in a business context between unrelated parties generally will qualify as adequate consideration. Even services provided by related parties (including spouses in the days before §2040(b)) will qualify as consideration if the services are performed in a business context and the survivor provides more than minimal services. *See, e.g.,* United States v. Neel, 235 F.2d 395 (10th Cir. 1956); Singer v. Shaughnessy, 198 F.2d 178 (2d Cir. 1952); Berkowitz v. Commissioner, 108 F.2d 319 (3d Cir. 1939). *But see* Estate of Awrey v. Commissioner, 5 T.C. 222 (1945); Bushman v. United States, 8 F. Supp. 694, 80 Ct. Cl. 175 (1934), *cert. denied* 295 U.S. 756 (1935). If the joint tenants are related, the issue will be whether the services are gratuitous. *See* Estate of Kjorvestad v. United States, 81-1 U.S.T.C. ¶13,401 at 87,471 (D.N.D., 1981). Where the joint tenants are spouses, any services rendered within the context of the marriage will be excluded. Estate of Loveland v. Commissioner, 13 T.C. 5 (1949); Bushman v. United States, *supra.* Services by a spouse are no longer an issue because of §2040(b), discussed below.

No valuation discount is allowed for joint tenancy property based on partial ownership. Courts have emphasized that the statutory language of "full value" in §2040(a) precludes such a discount. Estate of Fratini v. Commissioner, *supra*; Estate of Young v. Commissioner, 110 T.C. 297 (1998).

2. Spousal Joint Interests: §2040(b)

Section 2040(b) provides that only half the value of a "qualified joint tenancy," *i.e.*, joint tenancy property owned only by a husband and wife or property owned as tenants by the entirety, will be included in the decedent's gross estate. The rule of §2040(b) is simple. Only half of the date of death value of the jointly owned property will be in the gross estate of the first to die. It does not matter who provided what portion of the consideration or where the consideration originated. The decedent's estate will also receive a marital deduction for the value of the property included in the gross estate.

The enactment of §2040(b) eliminated any need for spouses to keep track of who provided what consideration for jointly owned property. It also eliminated all disputes over agreements to provide services whether in a business context or the family context. It did, however, limit the value of the jointly held property that would receive a step-up in basis under §1014 to the one-half that is included in the decedent's gross estate.

Example 9-8

Husband and Wife bought Blackacre for $100,000 and held title as joint tenants with the right of survivorship. Wife dies when Blackacre has a fair market value of $400,000. Only $200,000 is in her gross estate under §2040(b). Wife's estate will not pay any estate tax because of the unlimited marital deduction. Husband's basis in Blackacre after Wife's death is $250,000, *i.e.*, $50,000 for his half from the purchase and $200,000 for the half he acquired as a result of Wife's death.

Instead, Wife purchased Blackacre for $100,000 and took title in fee simple. Wife dies when Blackacre has a fair market value of $400,000. The full $400,000 is in her gross estate under §2033 because she owned the property in her name alone. If Wife willed Blackacre to Husband, her estate will not pay any estate tax because of the unlimited marital deduction. Husband's basis in Blackacre after Wife's death is $400,000 because of §1014.

The limit in the stepped-up basis resulting from the 1981 legislation led to litigation over the applicability of §2040(b) to joint tenancy interests acquired prior to 1976. To understand the issue, one must know something of the history of §2040. In 1954, Congress enacted §2515, which provided that the creation of a joint tenancy in real property between spouses was not a gift unless the spouses affirmatively elected to treat the transaction as a gift. This provision codified what most people believed the law to be. The only reason to elect gift treatment on the creation of the joint tenancy was to avoid gift tax consequences when the joint tenancy was terminated. In 1976, when Congress unified the gift and estate tax provisions, it also enacted §2040(b), which included only one-half of the value of spousal joint tenancy property in the gross estate of the first to die regardless of the contributions of the decedent and the survivor as long as the creation of the joint tenancy had been treated as a gift pursuant to §2515.

In 1981, when Congress removed all limits from the marital deduction, the need for §2515 disappeared, and Congress repealed the section. It also amended §2040(b) to apply to all spousal joint tenancies and tenancies by the entirety for decedents dying after 1981. In Gallenstein v. United States, 975 F.2d 286 (6th Cir. 1992), however, the court held that the effective date provisions of the 1981 act did not repeal the effective date provisions of the 1976 act and, therefore, property acquired before 1977 was subject to the rules of §§2515 and 2040(a). Consequently, if spouses had not elected to treat the acquisition of jointly owned property as a gift, the full value of the jointly held property was in the estate of the first to die if he provided the consideration. As a result, the survivor received a stepped-up basis in the full value of the jointly held property. Other courts have agreed with the Sixth Circuit, opening the door to substantial estate planning opportunities for spouses who acquired jointly owned property prior to 1977. *See* Anderson v. United States, 96-2 U.S.T.C. ¶60,235 at 86,544 (D. Md. 1996); Hahn v. Commissioner, 110 T.C. 140 (1998); Patten v. United States, 116 F.3d 1029 (4th Cir. 1997). The IRS has acquiesced in *Hahn*, AOD 2001-06, and will no longer litigate this issue.

A married couple that owns all of their property as joint tenants or tenants by the entirety also loses the benefits of the applicable credit amount in §2010 in the estate of the first to die. Failure to consider this issue can have disastrous consequences.

Example 9-9

Husband and Wife own $10 million of property as joint tenants, and Husband dies. Husband's gross estate includes only $5 million because of §2040(b), and his estate will receive a $5 million marital deduction under §2056, resulting in a taxable estate of zero. Because Husband's taxable estate is zero, it does not receive the benefit of the applicable credit amount in §2010. When Wife dies, her estate will pay an increased estate tax. By severing the joint tenancies and setting up credit shelter trusts, this couple could have decreased the estate tax due when Wife died. Failure to create such an estate plan will be considered malpractice by the attorney. *See* discussion in Chapter 16, section F.2.

The qualified joint tenancy provision of §2040(b) does not apply if the surviving spouse is not a citizen of the United States. *See* §2056(d)(1)(B).

PROBLEMS

1. David owns Blackacre, fair market value $120,000, and deeds it to his two children, Adam and Beth.
    a. What are the gift tax consequences?
    b. What are the estate tax consequences in this situation when Adam dies?
    c. What are the gift tax consequences if David deeds Blackacre to Adam and Beth as joint tenants?
    d. What are the estate tax consequences in this situation when Adam dies?
    e. What are the gift tax consequences if David deeds Blackacre to himself, Adam, and Beth as joint tenants?
    f. Some years later, they sell Blackacre for $150,000, and each receives $50,000. Are there any gift tax consequences?
    g. What if David received nothing on the sale and Adam and Beth each received $75,000?
2. Diane buys Greenacre for $100,000 (cash, no mortgage) and takes title in joint tenancy with Carl. Carl provides nothing toward the purchase of Greenacre. Assume that Diane and Carl are unrelated and that either can defeat the survivorship rights of the other unilaterally.
    a. What are the gift tax consequences?
    b. What are the estate tax consequences if Diane dies before Carl when Greenacre has a value of $200,000?
    c. What are the estate tax consequences if Carl dies first?
    d. What are the gift tax consequences if Diane paid $75,000, and Carl paid $25,000 of the purchase price of Greenacre?
    e. What are the estate tax consequences if Diane dies before Carl when Greenacre has a value of $200,000?

    f.   What are the estate tax consequences if Carl dies first?

    g. What are the gift and estate tax consequences in problems 2.a. and 2.b. if Diane and Carl were married?

3. Doris establishes a joint savings account with Ellen. Doris deposits $50,000 in the savings account.

    a. What are the gift tax consequences?

    b. What are the gift tax consequences when Doris withdraws $5,000?

    c. What are the gift tax consequences when Ellen withdraws $15,000?

    d. What are the estate tax consequences when Doris dies and there is $35,000 in the account?

4. Donald is 70 years old and owns a house valued at $200,000. Although Donald is in good health, he is concerned about living alone and keeping the property repaired. Donald moves into Megan's house, and he resides there until his death. Donald has his own room, but he eats all of his meals with Megan and her family. He pays no rent and makes no monetary contribution to the cost of the house or food. Donald does, however, transfer title in his own home to himself and Megan as joint tenants with the right of survivorship. What are the estate tax consequences when Donald dies?

5. Debra and Sam purchase Farmacre in 1982 as joint tenants with the right of survivorship. The down payment of $10,000 is made from Debra's prior earnings. Debra and Sam both work on the farm. Proceeds from farming are used to pay off the mortgage on the farm. There is no formal business agreement between Debra and Sam. Debra dies when Farmacre has a fair market value of $500,000. How much is included in Debra's gross estate?

6. Doug purchases Whiteacre, investment real estate, with his daughter, Sally, taking title as joint tenants. Doug pays the entire $100,000 purchase price of Whiteacre.

    a. Five years later when Whiteacre is worth $150,000, Doug and Sally exchange Whiteacre for Greyacre in a §1031 like-kind exchange. (In a like-kind exchange, the taxpayers do not recognize, *i.e.*, report, any income for purposes of the income tax.) Doug dies six years after the exchange when Grayacre is worth $180,000. What is included in his gross estate? Why?

    b. Instead, when Whiteacre is worth $150,000, Doug and Sally sell it and use the full amount of the proceeds to purchase stock in ABC, Inc. as joint tenants. Doug dies when the stock is worth $180,000. What is included in his gross estate? Why?

7. In a unified transfer tax system where the creation of a joint tenancy is treated as a gift, is §2040(a) necessary? Why?

CHAPTER 10

Retained Interests

A. HISTORICAL PERSPECTIVE

Sections 2035 through 2038 include in the gross estate property that the decedent transferred during his life if he retained an interest in, or power over, that property. These four provisions began as a single sentence in the Revenue Act of 1916, which included in the gross estate all property "[t]o the extent of any interest therein of which the decedent has at any time made a transfer, or with respect to which he has created a trust, in contemplation of or intended to take effect in possession or enjoyment at or after his death." §202(b). Because there was no gift tax at this time, §202(b) was necessary to prevent evasion of the estate tax through lifetime transfers. The current structure and interpretation of §§2035-2038 owe much to the initial judicial interpretation of this provision, and "[u]pon this point a page of history is worth a volume of logic." O.W. Holmes, Jr. J., in New York Trust Co. v. Eisner, 256 U.S. 345, 349 (1921).

1. Gifts in Contemplation of Death: §2035

Immediately after enactment of the Revenue Act of 1916 there was substantial litigation interpreting the "contemplation of death" language even though the act included a rebuttable presumption that any transfer of a material part of the decedent's property within the two years prior to his death was made in contemplation of death. Courts examined all the evidence to determine the decedent's motive for such transfers. Unless the decedent had been terminally ill or obsessed with thoughts of death, courts excluded even obvious testamentary transfers from the gross estate. Frustrated with the continuous litigation, Congress created an irrebuttable presumption in the Revenue Act of 1926. §302(c). The Supreme Court, however, held the irrebuttable presumption unconstitutional on due process grounds in Heiner v. Donnan, 285 U.S. 312 (1932). Congress then returned to the rebuttable presumption and also enacted a gift tax. Revenue Act of 1932, §§501-532. Enactment of the gift tax did not resolve the problem because the gift tax rates were substantially lower than the estate tax rates and there were separate exemption amounts for each tax.

Litigation continued, and in 1950 Congress tried again, extending the rebuttable presumption from two to three years, eliminating the requirement that the transfer be a material part of the decedent's estate, and excluding all transfers that occurred more than three years before the decedent's death. Revenue Act of 1950, §501(a). This provided some, but not total, relief. In 1976, Congress unified the gift and the estate taxes, creating a single rate schedule and a unified credit. At that time Congress substituted a flat three-year rule for the rebuttable presumption, requiring that all gifts made within three years of death be included in the gross estate regardless of the donor's motive. Tax Reform Act of 1976, §2001(a)(5).

Unification of the two transfer taxes did not completely eliminate the differences between lifetime and testamentary transfers because the gift tax is tax exclusive and the estate tax is tax inclusive. In other words, the donor pays the gift tax with funds in addition to the gift. The decedent's estate pays the estate tax on the total value of property in the gross estate (less certain deductions) but from funds included in the gross estate. The decedent's beneficiaries receive less property because the amount of tax is subtracted before they receive their distribution. To remedy this, Congress enacted what is now §2035(b), which includes in the gross estate the amount of gift tax paid on transfers within three years of death.

Recognizing that the unification of the transfer taxes and the addition of §2035(b) eliminated the need for the inclusion of deathbed transfers, Congress repealed the three year rule for most gifts in 1981. It retained the rule only for (1) gifts of life insurance made within three years of death and (2) transfers where the value of property would have been in the decedent's gross estate under §§2036-2038 but the decedent relinquished the retained interest or power within three years of death. §2035(a).

2. *Retained Life Estates: §2036*

While there was less litigation involving the phrase "intended to take effect in possession or enjoyment at or after death," this provision proved equally troubling to the courts. One of the most valuable rights in property is the ability to possess that property or to obtain income from it. One would, therefore, assume that if the decedent owned property and made a lifetime transfer reserving to himself the right to use, possess, or enjoy that property or to receive the income from it, that such a transfer would be one "intended to take effect in possession or enjoyment at or after death." After all, the remainderman will not be able to possess or enjoy the property or its income until after the decedent's death. State courts had, in fact, interpreted similar language to include such transfers. *See, e.g.*, In re Keeney's Estate, 194 N.Y. 281, 87 N.E. 428 (1909), *aff'd*, 222 U.S. 525 (1912). The Supreme Court, however, rejected this interpretation of the postponed possession and enjoyment clause in May v. Heiner, 281 U.S. 238 (1930). The hope that May v. Heiner would be restricted to the reservation of a secondary life estate disappeared when the Supreme Court applied the same rule to the reservation of any life estate in Burnet v. Northern Trust Co., 283 U.S. 782 (1931), Morsman v. Burnet, 283 U.S. 783 (1931), and McCormick v. Burnet, 283 U.S. 784 (1931). This prompted the Treasury to appeal to Congress the day after these opinions were issued, and Congress responded with a joint resolution that became §2036(a).

The result in May v. Heiner, while surprising, was presaged by earlier opinions of the Court. In Shukert v. Allen, 273 U.S. 545 (1927), the decedent at age 56 established a trust to accumulate income for 30 years and then distribute it and the trust corpus to his three children. Despite the testamentary nature of this transfer, the Commissioner did not argue that it was made in contemplation of death. Instead, the only question was whether the trust was intended to take effect in possession or enjoyment at or after the decedent's death. The Court rejected the Commissioner's claim, stating, "The transfer was immediate and out and out, leaving no interest remaining in the testator. The trust in its terms has no reference to his death but is the same and unaffected whether he lives or dies." *Id*. at 547.

Shortly thereafter, the Court decided Reinecke v. Northern Trust Co., 278 U.S. 339 (1929), where the decedent established trusts to terminate five years after the death of the settlor or the life income beneficiary, whichever occurred first. Again, the Court refused to include these trusts in the decedent's gross estate, stating:

> In its plan and scope the tax is one imposed on transfers at death or made in contemplation of death and is measured by the value at death of the interest which is transferred. . . . One may freely give his property to another by absolute gift without subjecting himself or his estate to a tax, but we are asked to say that this statute means that he may not make a gift inter vivos, equally absolute and complete, without subjecting it to a tax if the gift takes the form of a life estate in one with remainder over to another at or after the donor's death. It would require plain and compelling language to justify so incongruous a result and we think it is wanting in the present statute.

Id. at 348. In doing so, the Court ignored the language of the statute that included in the gross estate transfers "intended to take effect in possession or enjoyment at or after death."

Given the Supreme Court's extremely narrow reading of the postponed possession and enjoyment clause, it was not surprising that it dealt with the issue of a retained life estate in May v. Heiner summarily:

> The transfer . . . was not made in contemplation of death within the legal significance of those words. It was not testamentary in character and was beyond recall by the decedent. At the death of Mrs. May no interest in the property held under the trust deed passed from her to the living; title thereto had been definitely fixed by the trust deed. The interest therein which she possessed immediately prior to her death was obliterated by that event.

Id. at 243. It was not until 1949 that the Supreme Court finally repudiated May v. Heiner. Commissioner v. Church's Estate, 335 U.S. 632 (1949). By that time, Congress had enacted the predecessor of §2036(a).

3. Retained Reversions: §2037

The Supreme Court also struggled with the application of the postponed possession and enjoyment clause to reversionary interests. In Klein v. United States, 283 U.S. 231 (1931), decedent had conveyed land to his wife for her life, retaining a reversion if she died before he did. The Court rejected arguments based on the niceties of property law and included the property in the gross estate saying, "It is perfectly plain that the death of the grantor was the indispensable and intended event which brought the larger estate into being for the grantee and effected its transmission from the dead to the living, thus satisfying the terms of the taxing act and justifying the tax imposed." *Id*. at 234. Ignoring both the rationale and the result in *Klein*, the Court relied on just those niceties of property law a mere four years later to hold the postponed possession and enjoyment clause inapplicable to reversions retained in trusts. Helvering v. St. Louis Union Trust Co., 296 U.S. 39 (1935); Becker v. St. Louis Union Trust Co., 296 U.S. 48 (1935). The Court finally resolved the conflict in Helvering v. Hallock, 309 U.S. 106 (1940), reversing its position in the *St. Louis Union Trust Co*. cases. Having decided to include the extinguishment of decedent's reversionary interest in the gross estate, the Court then applied that rule to a reversion worth approximately $70 in a trust valued at $1.1 million. Estate of Spiegel v. Commissioner, 335 U.S. 701 (1949). Congress, recognizing the absurdity of this result, enacted the predecessor of §2037 in 1949.

4. Powers to Alter, Terminate, or Revoke: §2038

The Supreme Court had far less trouble applying the postponed possession and enjoyment clause to transfers where the decedent retained the power to revoke, alter, or terminate a trust. In upholding the constitutionality of the estate tax as applied to life insurance, the Court had said, "Such an outstanding power residing exclusively in a donor to recall a gift after it is made is a limitation on the gift which makes it incomplete as to the donor as well as to the donee, and we think that the termination of such a power at death may also be the appropriate subject of a tax upon transfers." Chase National Bank v. United States, 278 U.S. 327, 336-337 (1929). Having determined the estate tax constitutional, the Court, without further analysis, upheld its application to two trusts where the decedent retained the power of revocation. Reinecke v. Northern Trust Co., 278 U.S. 339 (1929).

In §302(d) of the Revenue Act of 1924 Congress added explicit language including transfers where the decedent "created a trust" and where the decedent retained "alone or in conjunction with any person [the power] to alter, amend, or revoke." The Supreme Court had no difficulty applying this language to a trust where the decedent retained the power to appoint the trust property to anyone other than himself or his estate. Porter v. Commissioner, 288 U.S. 436 (1933). In Commissioner v. Chase National Bank, the court followed *Porter*, holding that a trust where the decedent retained the power to appoint the property in her will among her lawful descendants was included in her gross estate. 82 F.2d 157 (2d Cir. 1936), *cert. denied* 299 U.S. 552 (1936).

The only issue of any significance was whether the phrase "alter, amend, or revoke" included the power to terminate a trust and distribute the property to the beneficiaries other than the decedent-grantor. The Supreme Court was able to avoid this question in White v. Poor, 296 U.S. 98 (1935), and Congress immediately revised the estate tax to include the power to terminate. That did not, however, resolve the issue, because Congress retained the original language for transfers made on or before June 22, 1936. In Commissioner v. Holme's Estate, the Supreme Court finally faced the issue squarely and decided that the power to terminate a trust was a power to "alter, amend, or revoke" because the power affected not only the time of enjoyment but also the persons who would actually enjoy the property. 326 U.S. 480 (1946). Finally, in Lober v. United States, 346 U.S. 335 (1953), the Supreme Court applied the statute to a power to terminate that only affected the time of enjoyment, stressing the concepts of "present economic benefit" and "full enjoyment of the property" and saying: "A donor who keeps so strong a hold over the actual and immediate enjoyment of what he puts beyond his own power to retake has not divested himself of that degree of control which [the statute] requires in order to avoid the tax." *Id.* at 337.

The postponed possession and enjoyment clause only applied to transfers where the decedent had retained an interest or power. The Supreme Court, therefore, refused to apply that clause to a decedent who had retained the power to terminate as one of three trustees, then resigned as trustee, and was later reappointed to the position. White v. Poor, 296 U.S. 98 (1935). The Court found that the power arose from her appointment as trustee by others and not by an express reservation. The Supreme Court applied the same reasoning to a power to revoke or modify the trust when the decedent could only exercise the power in conjunction with all the beneficiaries and the trustee. Helvering v. Helmholz, 296 U.S. 93 (1935). The Court was not troubled by the need for others to agree with the decedent, having upheld the inclusion of a joint power in Helvering v. City Bank and Farmers Trust Co., 296 U.S. 85 (1935), decided the same day. What prevented the Court from including the trust in *Helmholz* was that the decedent's power to terminate the trust if all the beneficiaries consented was also a power granted by state law. The inclusion of such language in the trust added nothing to the decedent's powers. In other words, the decedent in *Helmholz* did not really "retain" the power at issue. Congress again responded, adding the language "without regard to when or from what source the decedent acquired such power." Revenue Act of 1936, §805.

5. *Relationship to the Gift Tax and the Income Tax*

After Congress enacted a gift tax in 1932, questions arose about the interplay of the two taxes. Even before unification in 1976, most completed gifts were excluded from the estate tax. Courts reasoned that the two taxes were "in pari materia," *i.e.*, "upon the same subject matter," and to be construed together. Courts did not apply this rule slavishly so that some completed transfers were also subjected to the estate tax.

Example 10-1

Dexter establishes an irrevocable trust with Friendly National Bank to pay the income to himself for life and, at his death, to distribute the trust property to his three nieces. Assuming that Dexter has not retained any powers to alter, amend, revoke, or terminate the trust, the creation of the trust is a completed gift of the remainder interest. The value of the remainder will depend on Dexter's age, but it will be a taxable gift. When Dexter dies, the entire value of the trust property will be in his gross estate under §2036(a)(1) because he has the right to the income from the entire trust property.

Depending on the decedent's powers, the decedent may be treated as the owner of the trust for purposes of the income tax. Although courts have often referred to the grantor trust rules in analyzing decedent's powers under §§2036(a)(2) and 2038, they have recognized the differing language and purpose of the income tax. For example, the decedent will not be treated as the owner of a trust if the power can only be exercised in conjunction with someone who has a substantial adverse interest in the trust. Sections 2036(a)(2) and 2038(a) apply to powers exercisable "in conjunction with any person" even if that person has a substantial adverse interest in the trust. The rules governing when a gift is considered complete are more closely aligned with the income tax rules. Joint powers are excluded if the donor shares the power with a person having a substantial adverse interest. *See* Reg. §25.2511-2(e). Congress has codified the connection between the income tax and the gift tax for gifts occurring after December 31, 2009. §2511(c). Whether this connection will remain if the repeal of the estate tax is itself repealed is unclear. The grantor trust rules are discussed in Chapter 2, section D.

The complexities of the retained interest provisions and inconsistencies between these provisions, the gift tax completion rules, and the grantor trust rules have lead many commentators to propose wholesale revision. *See, e.g.*, Task Force on Transfer Tax Restructuring, Report on Transfer Tax Restructuring, American Bar Association Section of Taxation, reprinted in 41 Tax Law. 395 (1988); Joseph M. Dodge, *Redoing the Estate and Gift Taxes Along Easy-to-Value Lines*, 43 Tax L. Rev. 241 (1988); Harry L. Gutman, *A Comment on the ABA Section Task Force Report on Transfer Tax*

Restructuring, 41 Tax Law. 653 (1988); Joseph Isenbergh, *Simplifying Retained Life Interests, Revocable Transfers, and the Marital Deduction,* 51 U. Chi. L. Rev. 1 (1984); W. Leslie Peat and Stephanie J. Willbanks, *A Page of Logic Is Worth a Volume of History: The Treatment of Retained Interests Under the Federal Estate and Gift Tax Statutes,* 8 Va. Tax Rev. 639 (1989). These proposals have largely been ignored by Congress.

B.   THE RIGHT TO INCOME
IRC §§2036(a)(1), 2702

1.   General Principles

If a decedent transfers property during his life and retains the right to the possession or enjoyment of it or the right to the income from it, §2036(a)(1) will bring that property into the decedent's gross estate. In these situations, the decedent is only transferring a remainder interest in the property and that interest is a future interest, *i.e.,* one that will not take effect in possession or enjoyment until at or after the decedent's death. The decedent, of course, will continue to enjoy the economic benefits from the property until his death even though he cannot alter the identity of the ultimate beneficiaries, the remaindermen. This type of transfer serves as a substitute for a will and is considered testamentary in nature.

Section 2036(a)(1) applies whether the decedent retains possession or enjoyment or the right to income for life, for a period which does not in fact end before his death, or for a period that is not ascertainable without reference to his death.

Example 10-2

Debra establishes an irrevocable trust with Friendly National Bank as Trustee to pay the income to her for 15 years. At the end of 15 years, the Trustee is to distribute the trust property to Debra's issue. Debra dies in year 12. The value of the trust property is in her gross estate because she retained the right to the income for a period that did not in fact end before her death.

If Debra lived for 16 years, nothing would be in her gross estate because she did not retain the right to income for any of the periods specified in §2036(a)(1).

Example 10-3

David establishes an irrevocable trust with Friendly National Bank as Trustee to pay the income to him each quarter. The right to income terminates with the quarterly payment immediately preceding his death. Any income generated between the last payment and the termination of the trust will be distributed, along with the trust property, to David's surviving issue. Section 2036(a)(1) forecloses this tax avoidance scheme by including in the gross estate transfers where decedent retained the right to income for a "period not ascertainable without reference to his death." Reg. §20.2036-1(b)(1)(i).

Section 2036(a)(1) also applies to the reservation of a secondary life estate, as in May v. Heiner, even if the primary life tenant is still alive at the decedent's death. Reg. §20.2036-1(b)(1)(ii).

Example 10-4

Doris creates an irrevocable trust with Friendly National Bank as Trustee to pay the income to Adam for life. After Adam's death, the Trustee is to pay the income to Doris for her life. After the death of both Adam and Doris, the Trustee is to distribute the trust property to Ben. Doris dies before Adam. The value of the trust property, less the value of Adam's life estate, is in Doris's gross estate under §2036(a)(1). Reg. §20.2036-1(b)(1)(ii).

When the decedent makes a transfer and reserves a life estate, either in trust or otherwise, the decedent makes a taxable gift of the remainder interest. The value of the remainder depends on the decedent's age and the applicable interest rate. §7520. Section 2702 will preempt this basic rule of valuation if (1) the remainder interest is transferred to a member of the decedent's family and (2) the decedent or any applicable member of his family retains an interest in the trust. "Member of the family" is defined in §2704(c)(2) to include the transferor's spouse, any ancestor or lineal descendant of the transferor or the transferor's spouse, and the transferor's siblings as well as the spouses of any ancestor, lineal descendant, or sibling. "Applicable family member" is defined in §2701(e)(2) as the transferor's spouse, an ancestor of the transferor or his spouse, and the spouse of any such ancestor. Section 2702 thus reaches beyond §2036(a)(1) transfers to any transfer where interests are not only retained by the transferor, but given to the transferor's spouse or their ancestors.

Section 2702 applies to transfers to the decedent's spouse, siblings, and lineal descendants. It thus applies to gifts to the decedent's children, grandchildren, and great-grandchildren, but not to gifts to nieces, nephews, cousins, or unrelated individuals. When §2702 applies, it values any retained interest at zero unless the retained interest is a "qualified interest." Qualified interests are (1) the right to receive fixed amounts payable not less frequently than annually (an annuity interest) §2702(b)(1), Reg. §25.2702-3(b)(1); (2) the right to receive a fixed percentage of the fair market value of the property in the trust determined annually and payable not less frequently than annually (an unitrust interest) §2702(b)(2), Reg. §25.2702-3(c)(1); and (3) any noncontingent remainder interest if all the other interests are either annuity interests or unitrust interests. Section 2702 also excludes transfers to a qualified personal residence trust (QRPT), *i.e.*, a trust that consists only of a personal residence for the beneficiary who has a term interest in the trust. §2702(a)(3).

Example 10-5

Daniel creates an irrevocable trust with Friendly National Bank as Trustee to pay the income to himself for life. At his death, the Trustee is to distribute the trust property to Daniel's daughter, Sally, and if she predeceases him, to her surviving issue. Because Daniel has retained an interest in the trust and transferred the remainder to a family member, §2702 applies. If Daniel's income interest is not a qualified annuity interest or unitrust interest, it will be valued at zero. As a result, the full value of the trust property will be treated as a completed gift. Because the gift is a future interest, it will not qualify for the gift tax annual exclusion. When Daniel dies, the full value of the trust property will be in his gross estate under §2036(a)(1) because he has retained the right to the income for his life. It is irrelevant that the full value of the trust was taxed as a completed gift.

On the other hand, if Daniel's income interest is a qualified annuity interest or unitrust interest, that interest is valued using standard valuation techniques. The value of the remainder will be the difference between the value of the trust property and the value of Daniel's retained interest. Reg. §25.2702-1(b). This difference will be the value of the taxable gift. When Daniel dies, the trust property will still be in his gross estate under §2036(a)(1) because he has retained the right to the income for his life, but it will be limited to the amount of trust property needed to produce the income distributed to Daniel. If Daniel's interest is a grantor retained *annuity* interest, however, the full value of the trust property will be in his gross estate under §2039(a), which is discussed in Chapter 11.

There are a number of exceptions to §2036(a)(1). It does not apply to bona fide sales for adequate and full consideration in money or money's worth. What qualifies as sufficient consideration is discussed in the following subsection as well as in section F of this chapter. The principles are the same whether the case involves §§2035, 2036, 2037, or 2038. Moreover, §2036(a)(1) does not apply to private annuities. Whether a particular transfer involves a retained interest or an annuity depends on all the facts and circumstances and is discussed in section B of Chapter 11. Finally, §2036(a)(1) does not apply where decedent establishes a trust giving the trustee absolute discretion to accumulate income or to distribute it to the decedent. In this situation, the decedent does not have a *right* to the income; he has given the trustee the right to determine what happens to the income.

This last rule is obviously ripe for abuse and, thus, it does not apply if there is an understanding between the decedent and the trustee, either express or implied, that the trustee will distribute income to the decedent whenever the decedent requests or if the decedent herself is the trustee. In these situations the decedent in fact continues to control the flow of income and is considered to have a *right* to it. If state law provides that the decedent's creditors can reach the trust income even though the trustee has discretion whether or not to distribute it to the decedent, the trust property will, once again, be in the decedent's gross estate under §2036(a)(1). In this situation, the decedent can force distributions by not paying his creditors and requiring them to seek reimbursement from the trust. Likewise, if the trustee's discretion to distribute income is limited by an ascertainable standard relating to the decedent's health, education, support, or maintenance, the trust property will be in the decedent's gross estate under §2036(a)(1). If the trustee's discretion is limited by an ascertainable standard, the trustee must make distributions to the decedent for the specified purposes. If the trustee does not, a court will enforce the decedent's right to such distributions. In all these situations, the decedent has in fact retained a right to the income, and the trust property will be included in his gross estate under §2036(a)(1). The ascertainable standard exception is discussed in section C.2. of this chapter and in Chapter 12 in reference to powers of appointment.

2. *Retained Possession or Enjoyment*

Section 2036(a)(1) applies if the decedent retains the possession or enjoyment of property even if it does not produce any income. Frequently, decedent will transfer her residence to her children. The residence will be in the decedent's gross estate if there is an agreement, even an implicit one, allowing decedent to remain there. Continued occupancy by the decedent until death is a primary factor in determining the existence of such an agreement.

Estate of Rapelje v. Commissioner
73 T.C. 82 (1979)

DAWSON, Judge:
. . . On August 11, 1969, the decedent transferred his personal residence (hereinafter residence) in Saratoga Springs, N.Y., to his two daughters. The decedent received no consideration for the transfer and reported the transfer as a taxable gift. The decedent continued living at the residence until November 1969 when he went to Florida for a vacation. During his stay in Florida, he considered purchasing a house in Fort Lauderdale but decided against it and returned to the residence in Saratoga Springs in May 1970. In July 1970, the decedent suffered a stroke which left him paralyzed on his right side and unable to speak. His health deteriorated thereafter and he died on November 18, 1973. From the time of the stroke until his death, the decedent lived at the residence.

Sometime in September 1969, Mrs. Mulligan's niece moved into the residence with her husband and they lived there until January 1970. In September

1971, Mrs. Mulligan's daughter moved in and stayed for several months. Thereafter, the decedent was the only occupant of the residence.

Neither Mrs. Mulligan nor Mrs. Wright ever moved into the residence during the decedent's life. The decedent continued to pay the real estate taxes on the property after the transfer, although Mrs. Wright did pay some utility bills. The decedent paid no rent for the use of the home. Neither daughter made any attempt to sell or rent the residence prior to decedent's death. They also made no attempt to sell their own homes. Although no express agreement existed between the decedent and his daughters regarding his continued use of the home after the gift, the parties nevertheless intended that the decedent would be allowed to live there until he purchased another home. . . .

The issue presented here is whether the value of decedent's residence must be included in his gross estate pursuant to section 2036. . . . This section requires property to be included in the decedent's estate if he retained the actual possession or enjoyment thereof, even though he may have had no enforceable right to do so. Estate of Honigman v. Commissioner, 66 T.C. 1080, 1082 (1976); Estate of Linderme v. Commissioner, 52 T.C. 305, 308 (1969). Possession or enjoyment of gifted property is retained when there is an express or implied understanding to that effect among the parties at the time of transfer. Guynn v. United States, 437 F.2d 1148, 1150 (4th Cir. 1971); Estate of Honigman v. Commissioner, *supra* at 1082; Estate of Hendry v. Commissioner, 62 T.C. 861, 872 (1974); Estate of Barlow v. Commissioner, 55 T.C. 666, 670 (1971). The burden is on the petitioner to disprove the existence of any implied agreement or understanding, and that burden is particularly onerous when intrafamily arrangements are involved. . . .

In the present case, there was no express agreement allowing decedent to retain possession and enjoyment of the home. Respondent, however, contends that the facts support an inference of an implied understanding between the decedent and his daughters whereby decedent was allowed to live in the house until he was able to locate a new home. Petitioners maintain that although such an understanding may have arisen after decedent suffered his stroke, there was no such agreement in existence at the time of the gift. Based on our review of the record before us, we conclude that petitioners have failed to meet their burden of proving that a tacit agreement did not arise contemporaneously with the transfer.

In determining whether there was an implied understanding between the parties, all facts and circumstances surrounding the transfer and subsequent use of the property must be considered. The continued exclusive possession by the donor and the withholding of possession from the donee are particularly significant factors. Guynn v. United States, *supra* at 1150; *compare* Estate of Linderme v. Commissioner, *supra* at 309, *with* Estate of Gutchess v. Commissioner, 46 T.C. 554, 557 (1966). In the present case, the donor maintained almost exclusive occupancy of the residence until his death in 1973. The transfer took place in August 1969. Decedent continued to live there alone until September 1969. Sometime in September, Mrs. Mulligan's niece moved in with her husband and they stayed until January 1970. In November 1969, the decedent went to Florida and did not return until May 1970. From May 1970 until September 1971, the decedent lived alone at the residence. In September 1971, Mrs. Mulligan's daughter moved in and stayed for several months. Thereafter, the decedent was the sole occupant of the residence.

A plausible argument could be made that the donees were making indirect use of the property by allowing their relatives to stay there, particularly if they did so over the decedent's objection. There is nothing in the record, however, to support that proposition. Decedent may have been wholly indifferent to their use of the property, or he may even have invited them himself. Even if he had violently opposed the presence of the guests, that would only tend to show an intent by the donees to exercise dominion and control over the property, which is only one factor to be considered in deciding whether decedent retained possession pursuant to an implied agreement.

In spite of the donees' continued residence in their original houses after the gift, petitioners argue that the conduct of the parties subsequent to the transfer negates the existence of any implied agreement. For example, they contend that the primary purpose of decedent's 6-month sojourn in Florida soon after the transfer was to purchase a new house. We disagree. Although decedent did look at one house for sale in Fort Lauderdale, the record does not reveal any extensive house hunting activity. Moreover, the decedent had made identical winter trips to Florida every year for the past 10 years. Thus, we are not convinced that the decedent felt any compelling need to locate a new home on this particular visit.

Petitioners also maintain that Mrs. Mulligan intended to move into the residence in 1971 when her husband was due to retire. In anticipation of this event, the couple visited the home frequently on weekends and vacations and made some repairs. Mrs. Mulligan also notified her employer in Buffalo that she would be leaving in 1971. This planned move was abandoned, of course, when the decedent suffered his stroke. We think that Mrs. Mulligan did intend to move into the residence eventually, but the facts suggest to us that the move was implicitly conditioned on the successful conclusion of the decedent's search for a new home.

There are other facts which support an inference of an implied understanding between the parties. The decedent paid no rent to his daughters for the continued use of the property. Although Mrs. Wright did pay some utility bills relating to the property, the decedent continued to pay the real estate taxes. Neither daughter made any attempt to sell her own house. Nor did they ever attempt to sell or rent the residence prior to the decedent's death. The plain fact of the matter is that with the exception of the change in record title, the gift of the property did not effect any substantial changes in the relationship of the parties to the residence. Thus, we find that there was an implied understanding between the parties arising contemporaneously with the transfer whereby the decedent was allowed to retain possession or enjoyment of the residence for a period which did not in fact end before his death.

Accordingly, we hold that under section 2036 the value of the residence must be included in decedent's gross estate.

The decedent's continued occupancy must be adverse to that of the new owners. For example, if Husband transfers the family home to Wife and both continue to occupy it, the property will not be in his gross estate at death. Estate of Gutchess v. Commissioner, 46 T.C. 554 (1966). In this case the court refused to imply an agreement because "[t]he transferor husband's use of the property by occupancy after the transfer is a natural use which does not diminish transferee wife's enjoyment and possession and which grows out of a congenial and happy family relationship. Such post-transfer use is insufficient to indicate any prior agreement or prearrangement for retention of use by the transferor." *Id.* at 557. The same rationale has been applied to cases where decedents transfer partial interests to their children as tenants in common. *See, e.g.,* Estate of Wineman v. Commissioner, 79 T.C.M. (CCH) 2189 (2000); Estate of Powell v. Commissioner, 63 T.C.M. (CCH) 3192 (1992). In *Powell,* the decedent was not in fact living in the house at the time of her death nor were the other tenants in common residing there either. In *Wineman,* decedent continued to occupy and use only part of the property while one child occupied a portion of the property and a family corporation leased another portion of it.

Decedent can avoid §2036(a)(1) if she transfers the property for full and adequate consideration in money or money's worth. Intrafamily transfers, however, are closely scrutinized to determine if the sale is a bona fide arm's-length transaction.

Estate of Maxwell v. Commissioner
3 F.3d 591 (2d Cir. 1993)

LASKER, Senior District Judge:

. . . On March 14, 1984, Lydia G. Maxwell (the "decedent") conveyed her personal residence, which she had lived in since 1957, to her son Winslow Maxwell, her only heir, and his wife Margaret Jane Maxwell (the "Maxwells"). Following the transfer, the decedent continued to reside in the house until her death on July 30, 1986. At the time of the transfer, she was eighty-two years old and was suffering from cancer.

The transaction was structured as follows:

1) The residence was sold by the decedent to the Maxwells for $270,000;
2) Simultaneously with the sale, the decedent forgave $20,000 of the purchase price (which was equal in amount to the annual gift tax exclusion to which she was entitled);

3) The Maxwells executed a $250,000 mortgage note in favor of decedent;
4) The Maxwells leased the premises to her for five years at the monthly rental of $1800; and
5) The Maxwells were obligated to pay and did pay certain expenses associated with the property following the transfer, including property taxes, insurance costs, and unspecified "other expenses."

While the decedent paid the Maxwells rent totaling $16,200 in 1984, $22,183 in 1985 and $12,600 in 1986, the Maxwells paid the decedent interest on the mortgage totaling $16,875 in 1984, $21,150 in 1985, and $11,475 in 1986. As can be observed, the rent paid by the decedent to the Maxwells came remarkably close to matching the mortgage interest which they paid to her. . . .

Not only did the rent functionally cancel out the interest payments made by the Maxwells, but the Maxwells were at no time called upon to pay any of the principal on the $250,000 mortgage debt; it was forgiven in its entirety. As petitioner's counsel admitted at oral argument, although the Maxwells had executed the mortgage note, "there was an intention by and large that it not be paid." Pursuant to this intention, in each of the following years preceding her death, the decedent forgave $20,000 of the mortgage principal, and, by a provision of her will executed on March 16, 1984 (that is, just two days after the transfer), she forgave the remaining indebtedness.

The decedent reported the sale of her residence on her 1984 federal income tax return but did not pay any tax on the sale because she elected to use the once-in-a-lifetime exclusion on the sale or exchange of a principal residence provided for by 26 U.S.C. §121.

She continued to occupy the house by herself until her death. At no time during her occupancy did the Maxwells attempt to sell the house to anyone else, but, on September 22, 1986, shortly after the decedent's death, they did sell the house for $550,000. . . .

On the decedent's estate tax return, the Estate reported only the $210,000 remaining on the mortgage debt (following the decedent's forgiveness of $20,000 in the two preceding years). The Commissioner found that the 1984 transaction constituted a transfer with retained life estate—rejecting the petitioners' arguments that the decedent did not retain "possession or enjoyment" of the property, and that the transaction was exempt from section 2036(a) because it was a bona fide sale for full and adequate consideration—, and assessed a deficiency against the Estate to adjust for the difference between the fair market value of the property at the time of decedent's death ($550,000) and the reported $210,000.

The Estate appealed to the tax court, which, after a trial on stipulated facts, affirmed the Commissioner's ruling, holding:

On this record, bearing in mind petitioner's burden of proof, we hold that, notwithstanding its form, the substance of the transaction calls for the conclusion that decedent made a transfer to her son and daughter-in-law with the understanding, at least implied, that she would continue to reside in her home until her death, that the transfer was not a bona fide sale for an adequate and full consideration in money or money's worth, and that the lease represented nothing more than an attempt to add color to the characterization of the transaction as a bona fide sale.

There are two questions before us: Did the decedent retain possession or enjoyment of the property following the transfer. And if she did, was the transfer a bona fide sale for an adequate and full consideration in money or money's worth. . . .

In numerous cases, the tax court has held, where an aged family member transferred her home to a relative and continued to reside there until her death, that the decedent-transferor had retained "possession or enjoyment" of the property within the meaning of §2036. . . . [C]ourts have held that §2036(a) requires that the fair market value of such property be included in the decedent's estate if he retained the actual possession or enjoyment thereof, even though he may have had no enforceable right to do so. Estate of Honigman v. Commissioner, 66 T.C. 1080, 1082; Estate of Linderme v. Commissioner, 52 T.C. 305, 308 (1969). *Id.* In such cases, the burden is on the decedent's estate to disprove the existence of any adverse implied agreement or understanding and that burden is particularly onerous when intrafamily arrangements are involved. Skinner's Estate v. United States, 316 F.2d 517, 520 (3d Cir. 1963); Estate of Hendry v. Commissioner, *supra* at 872; Estate of Kerdolff v. Commissioner, 57 T.C. 643, 648 (1972). *Id.*

As indicated above, the tax court found as a fact that the decedent had transferred her home to the Maxwells "with the understanding, at least implied, that she would continue to reside in her home until her death." This finding was based upon the decedent's advanced age, her medical condition, and the overall result of the sale and lease. The lease was, in the tax court's words, "merely window dressing"—it had no substance.

The tax court's findings of fact are reversible only if clearly erroneous. . . . We agree with the tax court's finding that the decedent transferred her home to the Maxwells "with the understanding, at least implied, that she would continue to reside in her home until her death," and certainly do not find it to be clearly erroneous. The decedent did, in fact, live at her residence until she died, and she had sole possession of the residence during the period between the day she sold her home to the Maxwells and the day she died. There is no evidence that the Maxwells ever intended to occupy the house themselves, or to sell or lease it to anyone else during the decedent's lifetime. Moreover, the Maxwells' failure to demand payment by the estate, as they were entitled to do under the lease, of the rent due for the months following decedent's death and preceding their sale of the property, also supports the tax court's finding. . . .

[P]etitioner . . . argues that the decedent's payment of rent sanctifies the transaction and renders it legitimate. [This] argument ignore[s] the realities of the rent being offset by mortgage interest, the forgiveness of the entire mortgage debt either by gift or testamentary disposition, and the fact that the decedent was eighty-two at the time of the transfer and actually continued to live in the residence until her death which, at the time of the transfer, she had reason to believe would occur soon in view of her poor health.

The Estate relies primarily on Barlow v. Commissioner, 55 T.C. 666 (1971). In that case, the father transferred a farm to his children and simultaneously leased the right to continue to farm the property. The tax court held that the father did not retain "possession or enjoyment," stating that "one of the most valuable incidents of income-producing real estate is the rent which it yields. He who receives the rent in fact enjoys the property." *Barlow*, 55 T.C. at 671. . . . However, *Barlow* is clearly distinguishable on its facts: In that case, there was evidence that the rent paid was fair and customary and, equally importantly, the rent paid was not offset by the decedent's receipt of interest from the family lessor.

Nor is there any merit to petitioner's contention that the "decedent's status as a tenant" exempts her from §2036(a) "as a matter of law." *Barlow* itself recognized that where a transferor "by agreement" "reserves the right of occupancy as an incident to the transfer," §2036(a) applies. *Barlow*, 55 T.C. at 670. The court there simply reached a different conclusion on its facts: [The] substance-versus-form argument, *while theoretically plausible*, depends upon the facts, and we do not think the record as a whole contains the facts required to give it life. . . . *Id.* at 670 (emphasis added).

For the reasons stated above, we conclude that the decedent did retain possession or enjoyment of the property for life and turn to the question of whether the transfer constituted "a bona fide sale for adequate and full consideration in money or money's worth."

Section 2036(a) provides that even if possession or enjoyment of transferred property is retained by the decedent until her death, if the transfer was a bona fide sale for adequate and full consideration in money or money's worth, the property is not includible in the estate. Petitioner contends that the Maxwells paid an "adequate and full consideration" for the decedent's residence, $270,000 total, consisting of the $250,000 mortgage note given by the Maxwells to the decedent, and the $20,000 the decedent forgave simultaneously with the conveyance.[3]

The tax court held that neither the Maxwells' mortgage note nor the decedent's $20,000 forgiveness constituted consideration within the meaning of the statute. . . .

There is no question that the mortgage note here is a fully secured, legally enforceable obligation on its face. The question is whether it is actually what it

---

3. As noted above, the parties have stipulated that the fair market value of the property on the date of the purported sale was $280,000. The Estate contends that $270,000 was full and adequate consideration for the sale, with a broker, for a house appraised at $280,000. We assume this fact to be true for purposes of determining whether the transaction was one for "an adequate and full consideration in money or money's worth."

purports to be—a bona fide instrument of indebtedness—or whether it is a facade. . . . We agree with the tax court that where, as here, there is an implied agreement between the parties that the grantee would never be called upon to make any payment to the grantor, as, in fact, actually occurred, the note given by the grantee had "no value at all." . . . As the Supreme Court has remarked, the family relationship often makes it possible for one to shift tax incidence by surface changes of ownership without disturbing in the least his dominion and control over the subject of the gift or the purposes for which the income from the property is used. Commissioner v. Culbertson, 337 U.S. 733, 746 (1949). There can be no doubt that intent is a relevant inquiry in determining whether a transaction is "bona fide." As another panel of this Court held recently . . . in a case involving an intrafamily transfer: "when the bona fides of promissory notes is at issue, the taxpayer must demonstrate affirmatively that 'there existed at the time of the transaction a real expectation of repayment and an intent to enforce the collection of the indebtedness.'" [citing] Estate of Van Anda v. Commissioner, 12 T.C. 1158, 1162 (1949), aff'd per curiam, 192 F.2d 391 (2d Cir.1951). . . . Flandreau v. Commissioner, 994 F.2d 91, 93 (2d Cir. 1993) (case involving IRC §2053(c)(1)). In language strikingly apposite to the situation here, the court stated: "it is appropriate to look beyond the form of the transactions and to determine, as the tax court did here, that the gifts and loans back to decedent were 'component parts of single transactions.'" Id. (citation omitted).

The tax court concluded that the evidence "viewed as a whole" left the "unmistakable impression" that regardless of how long decedent lived following the transfer of her house, the entire principal balance of the mortgage note would be forgiven, and the Maxwells would not be required to pay any of such principal. Id.

The petitioner's reliance on Haygood v. Commissioner, 42 T.C. 936 (1964), not followed by Rev. Rul. 77-299, 1977-2 C.B. 343 (1977), Kelley v. Commissioner, 63 T.C. 321 (1974), not followed by Rev. Rul. 77-299, 1977-2 C.B. 343 (1977), and Wilson v. Commissioner, 64 T.C.M. (CCH) 583 (1992), is misplaced. Those cases held only that intent to forgive notes in the future does not per se disqualify such notes from constituting valid consideration. In contrast, in the case at hand, the decedent did far more than merely "indicate[ ] an intent to forgive the indebtedness in the future." Wilson, 64 T.C.M. (CCH) 583, 584 (1992).

In Haygood, Kelley, and Wilson, the question was whether transfers of property by petitioners to their children or grandchildren in exchange for notes were completed gifts within the meaning of the Internal Revenue Code. None of the notes was actually paid by the grantees; instead the notes were either forgiven by petitioners at or about the time they became due (Haygood and Kelley) or the petitioner died prior to the date when the note was due (Wilson). In those circumstances, the tax court held that the notes received by petitioners, secured by valid vendor's liens or by deeds of trust on the property, constituted valuable consideration for the transfer of the property.

The *Kelley* court made no finding as to intent to forgive the notes. In *Haygood*, although the court did find that the "petitioner had no intention of collecting the debts but did intend to forgive each payment as it became due," it also found that the transfer of the property to the children had been a mistake.[5] And, the *Wilson* court found that:

> The uncontradicted testimony in this case establishes that petitioner and her children intended that the children would sell the property and pay the note with the proceeds. *Wilson*, 64 T.C.M. (CCH) at 584.

By contrast, in the case at hand, the tax court found that, at the time the note was executed, there was "an understanding" between the Maxwells and the decedent that the note would be forgiven. In our judgment, the conduct of decedent and the Maxwells with respect to the principal balance of the note, when viewed in connection with the initial "forgiveness" of $20,000 of the purported purchase price, strongly suggests the existence of an understanding between decedent and the Maxwells that decedent would forgive $20,000 each year thereafter until her death, when the balance would be forgiven by decedent's will. . . . To conclude, we hold that the conveyance was not a bona fide sale for an adequate and full consideration in money or money's worth. . . .

The decision of the tax court is affirmed.

WALKER, Circuit Judge, dissenting:

Nearly 60 years ago, in words as true today as they were then, Judge Learned Hand wrote that "[a]ny one may so arrange his affairs that his taxes shall be as low as possible; he is not bound to choose that pattern which will best pay the Treasury; there is not even a patriotic duty to increase one's taxes." *Helvering v. Gregory*, 69 F.2d 809, 810 (2d Cir.1934), *aff'd*, 293 U.S. 465, 55 S.Ct. 266, 79 L.Ed. 596 (1935). . . . There is no doubt that the decedent and the Maxwells structured the transaction at issue here to maximize tax benefits. However, it is far from clear that the transaction was a sham, and thus could be ignored for tax purposes by the IRS. . . .

I. The Decedent's "Possession" of the Property

The majority correctly states that, under §2036(a)(1), an individual may retain possession or enjoyment of a property, following a legal transfer of ownership, pursuant to an express agreement or an implied understanding to that effect among the parties at the time of transfer. *See* Estate of Honigman v. Commissioner, 66 T.C. 1080, 1082 (1976). However, physical occupation of a property is not necessarily equivalent to possession or enjoyment of it. Rather, the statute looks to whether an individual gratuitously resides on a property

---

5. The court stated that it was "eminently clear from the testimony that it was petitioner's intent to give only a $3,000 interest [in the property] to each of her sons" that year but her lawyer accidentally structured the transaction to give the entire property to the petitioner's sons. Haygood v. Commissioner, 42 T.C. 936, 942 (1964).

following a sale until her death, thereby effectively retaining an ownership interest in the land. *See* Estate of Barlow v. Commissioner, 55 T.C. 666, 670 (1971); *see also* Estate of Kerdolff v. Commissioner, 57 T.C. 643 (1972); Estate of Nicol v. Commissioner, 56 T.C. 179, 182 (1971). . . . I believe the crucial question under §2036(a)(1) is not whether the Maxwells intended the decedent to remain on the property, or indeed whether she physically occupied the house until her death. Rather, it is whether she retained incidents of ownership of the land until her death.

In this case, the stipulated facts establish that the decedent remained on the land not as an owner, but as a tenant who fulfilled her duties under a lease by paying a rent of $1,800 per month. After the sale, the Maxwells assumed the burdens and costs of ownership, including insurance and property tax payments that were not off-set by the decedent's rents.

Tax Court case law makes clear that a rent-paying tenant does not retain possession or ownership of property. In *Estate of Barlow*, the decedent parents gave farmland to their children who leased the property back. Focusing on the terms of the lease, the court held that the children were in possession of the property because of their right to receive rental payments. . . . In this case, there is no evidence of an agreement qualifying the Maxwells' right to receive rents under the lease. Indeed, the decedent made rental payments until her death. The majority seeks to distinguish *Estate of Barlow* on [the] ground that the decedent's rental payments approximated the Maxwells' mortgage payments. However, the fact that the payments approximated each other does not obviate the economic significance of the lease, transforming it into a mere "facade." It is reasonable to expect that a market rent would approximate, if not exceed, the carrying costs of the property.

The proper result here might be different if the Tax Court found that the decedent paid an inflated, above-market rent for the use of the property as a means of subsidizing the Maxwells' mortgage payments. Estate of DuPont v. Commissioner, 63 T.C. 746, 766 n. 3 (1975). However, the Tax Court did not consider the market-rental value of the property—let alone make findings on the issue. The majority's reliance on the Maxwells' decision not to demand rent from the estate after the decedent's death is misplaced. In *Estate of Barlow*, a delay in the payment of rents for four years did not obviate the economic significance of the lease. *See* 55 T.C. at 668. . . .

II. The "Sham" Purchase

The majority holds that the Maxwells proffered no consideration in connection with their purchase of the property from the decedent and, thus, that there was not a bona fide sale within the meaning of §2036(a). However, in examining the economic results of the transaction, the majority misconstrues both Tax Court case law and the stipulated facts in the record. . . . In a line of cases beginning nearly 30 years ago, the Tax Court has stated that where "property is transferred in exchange for a valid, enforceable, and secured legal obligation to pay full value, there is no gift for Federal tax purposes." Wilson v.

Commissioner, 64 Tax Ct.Mem.Dec. (CCH) 583, 584 (1992); *see* Laughinhouse v. Commissioner, 80 T.C. 425, 431 n. 8 (1983); Estate of Kelley v. Commissioner, 63 T.C. 321, 323-24 (1974); Haygood v. Commissioner, 42 T.C. 936, 946 (1964). "This is true even if the parties are related and the seller/obligee *indicates an intent to forgive the indebtedness in the future*." *Wilson*, Tax Ct.Mem.Dec. (CCH) at 584 (emphasis added); *see* Laughinhouse v. Commissioner, 80 T.C. at 431 n. 8; Estate of Kelley, 63 T.C. at 323-24; *Haygood*, 42 T.C. at 946; *see also* Story v. Commissioner, 38 T.C. 936, 942 (1962) (the question is "not whether [the payee] intended to collect the debt, but whether [the payee] intended to make a gift of the amount when it was advanced or to create an obligation portions of which could be forgiven from time to time as gifts in the future"). While the Commissioner has consistently expressed disagreement with the reasoning of and refused to acquiesce in the Tax Court's reasoning in these cases, *see, e.g.*, Rev. Rul. 77-299, 1977-2 C.B. 343 (1977), the Commissioner's disagreement does not impair their precedential value. Neither does the Commissioner's nonacquiescence affect the reasonableness of taxpayer reliance upon the Tax Court precedents.

The majority suggests that *Haygood, Estate of Kelley* and *Wilson* only stand for the proposition that an "intent to forgive notes in the future does not per se disqualify such notes from constituting valid indebtedness." Majority Opinion at 597. However, I read these cases to state that the inquiry ends in the taxpayer's favor upon a finding that the payee received a legally enforceable note or other instrument of indebtedness in return for a property.

The purposes of the transactions at issue in *Haygood* and *Estate of Kelley* and the transaction in this case were the same: to remove properties from estates without paying taxes by selling them to close relatives in exchange for secured notes. And the notes at issue here were legally valid, like the notes at issue in the earlier Tax Court cases. Yet, in *Haygood* and *Estate of Kelley*, the Tax Court found such sales bona fide, while, in this case, the Tax Court found that the mortgage notes were without substance.

In attempting to distinguish *Haygood* and *Estate of Kelley*, the majority distorts them. For example, the majority suggests that the Tax Court's finding that the decedent and the Maxwells had an "understanding" that the mortgage would eventually be forgiven at the time the property was transferred makes this case unique. However, the payee in *Haygood* also intended to forgive the notes executed in her favor from the time she received them. *See* 42 T.C. at 946. And, while the majority correctly states that the *Estate of Kelley* court never explicitly found that the payee had formulated the intent to forgive the notes on the day she received them, the majority fails to note that the *Estate of Kelley* opinion focused upon the enforceability of the notes—the fact that they could be enforced—quoted approvingly language in *Haygood* stating that an intent to forgive would not defeat the economic substance of a transaction. *See* 63 T.C. at 324-25. . . .

The economic substance of the mortgages is established not only by the lack of evidence contradicting their validity and enforceability, but also by the actions of the parties. The majority states that the Maxwells were never called upon to make payments upon the notes. *See* Majority Opinion at 595-96. It is unclear whether the majority means that the Maxwells made no interest or no principal payments. In fact, they made both.

First, as I've discussed, the Maxwells made monthly interest payments on the notes until the decedent's death. The unremarkable fact that the mortgage payments approximated the decedent's rent, which the majority relies upon in considering whether the decedent retained possession of the property, does not in itself vitiate the economic substance of the rents.

Second, the decedent forgave annually $20,000 of the principal amounts the Maxwells owed on the mortgages, starting with an initial forgiveness at the time of the conveyance of the property to the Maxwells. The amounts forgiven corresponded to the decedent's $10,000 per donee exclusion from the gift tax. *See* 26 U.S.C. §2503. Thus, each time the decedent forgave a portion of the amounts owed on the mortgages, she effectively made a gift to the Maxwells by reducing their mortgage obligations. The substance of these transactions would have been exactly the same had the decedent made annual cash gifts totaling $20,000 to the Maxwells and the Maxwells then independently chose to use those or other monies to make principal payments on the mortgages. The fact that the decedent chose to benefit the Maxwells by reducing their obligations directly rather than by sending them a check and receiving another check in return does not make the Maxwells' satisfaction of portions of the principal amounts any less genuine. . . .

I respectfully dissent.

It is possible to avoid §2036(a)(1) by creating a qualified personal residence trust for a specified term of years. If the decedent survives the term, nothing will be in her gross estate because she did not in fact possess the property at the time of her death. The problem with this approach is that the decedent is then without a place to live. In Private Letter Ruling 9829002, the decedent continued to occupy the residence after the termination of the personal residence trust. The IRS ruled that the payment of fair market rent by the decedent would prevent inclusion of the residence in the decedent's gross estate. *See also* Estate of Barlow v. Commissioner, 55 T.C. 666 (1971), cited in Estate of Maxwell v. Commissioner, *supra*, where the payment of rent precluded the application of §2036(a)(1).

3. *Legal Obligation of Support*

The decedent is deemed to have retained possession or enjoyment or the right to income from property if the property, or its income, is to be used to discharge his legal obligations or for his pecuniary benefit. This includes the legal obligation to support a dependent during the decedent's lifetime. Reg. §20.2036-1(b)(2).

Estate of Gokey v. Commissioner
72 T.C. 721 (1979)

WILES, Judge:

. . . On October 1, 1961, decedent, then 57, executed a trust agreement creating, in part, separate irrevocable trusts for the benefit of Bridget, Gretchen and Patrick. . . . Mrs. Gokey was the sole trustee of both trusts through decedent's date of death. The relevant portion of that trust agreement provides:

> Section 2: Until each beneficiary becomes twenty-one (21) years of age, the Trustee shall use such part or all of the net income of his or her trust for the support, care, welfare, and education of the beneficiary thereof, payments from such net income to be made to such beneficiary or in such other manner as the Trustee deems to be in the best interest of the beneficiary, and any unused income shall be accumulated and added to the principal of such beneficiary's trust. After each beneficiary becomes twenty-one (21) years of age, the Trustee shall pay to him or her, in convenient installments, the entire net income of his or her trust. In the Trustee's discretion, said income payments may be supplemented at any time with payments of principal from a beneficiary's share whenever the Trustee deems any such payments necessary for the support, care, welfare, or education of the beneficiary thereof.

[Decedent died in 1969 when Gretchen was 15 and Patrick as 13. Bridget was 18, the statutory age of majority, and no issue was raised concerning her share of the trust.]

The first issue is whether decedent retained the possession or enjoyment of, or the right to the income from, property transferred by him to irrevocable trusts for the benefit of Gretchen and Patrick. If so, the value of the property in those trusts is properly includable in decedent's gross estate under section 2036. The resolution of this issue depends upon whether, within the meaning of section 20.2036-1(b)(2), Estate Tax Regs., the income or property of the trusts was to be applied toward the discharge of the decedent's legal obligation to support Gretchen and Patrick during his lifetime.

Respondent contends that under Illinois law, decedent was under a legal duty to support his minor children, Gretchen and Patrick; that the terms of the children's trusts clearly require the trustees to use the trust's income and property for their support; and that, therefore, the value of the trust property is includable in decedent's gross estate.

Petitioners do not dispute decedent's obligation to support Gretchen and Patrick under Illinois law; however, they contend that the use of the property or income therefrom for the children's support was within the unrestricted discretion of the trustees; that even if trusts did not give the trustees any discretion in this matter, the decedent nevertheless intended to grant them this discretion; that the use of the term "welfare" in the trusts creates an unascertainable standard which, even if ascertainable, is much broader than the standard for support; and that, therefore, the value of the trust property is not includable in decedent's gross estate. We agree with respondent on this issue.

Respondent relies upon section 20.2036-1(b)(2), Estate Tax Regs., which states that the use, possession, right to the income, or other enjoyment of the transferred property is considered as having been retained by or reserved to the decedent within the meaning of section 2036(a)(1) to the extent that the use, possession, right to the income, or other enjoyment is to be applied toward the discharge of a legal obligation of decedent which includes an obligation to support a dependent. "Is to be applied" is not to be read as "may be applied," which exists where an independent trustee is vested with discretion over distributions. . . . This creates a factual question as to whether the income from the trust property must be restricted or confined to fulfilling the settlor's obligation to support his dependents. . . .

We believe the language of the children's trusts found in section 2 of the 1961 trust agreement which relates "shall use such part or all of the net income . . . for the support, care, welfare, and education of the beneficiary" clearly manifests decedent's intent to require the trustees to apply the income for the stated purpose. In our view, it is impossible to construe the instrument as one which gives the trustees discretion as to whether or not income shall be used for "support, care, welfare, and education." That standard completely controls the application of the trust's funds. If those needs exceed the trusts' income, principal may be utilized. If those needs do not absorb all the trusts' income, the remaining income is accumulated and added to principal. Moreover, the section 2 phrase "payments from such net income to be made to such beneficiary or in such other manner as the Trustee deems to be in the best interest of the beneficiary" does not alter our interpretation. Clearly, this phrase only grants the trustee discretion in the method of payment adopted. Since we find decedent's intent clearly expressed in the trust instrument, we need not look beyond the four corners of the instrument to determine intent.

Petitioners next argue that the use of the word "welfare" within the phrase "the Trustee shall use such part or all of the net income of his or her trust for the support, care, welfare, and education of the beneficiary thereof" in section 2 of the 1961 trust instrument, gives the trustee authority to make nonsupport expenditures which, in turn, violates the "is to be applied" language of section 20.2036-1(b)(2), Estate Tax Regs. They support this theory by arguing that the standard "support, care, welfare, and education" is not ascertainable under, among others, sections 2036(a)(2) and 2041; and even if ascertainable, "welfare" is broader than "support" under Illinois law.

In determining whether "support, care, welfare, and education" is subject to an ascertainable external standard, we must rely upon Illinois law. . . . In Estate of Wood v. Commissioner, 39 T.C. 919, 923-924 (1963), we held that the phrase "support, maintenance, welfare, and comfort" was subject to an ascertainable standard:

> We think that these four somewhat overlapping nouns were intended in the aggregate to describe the life beneficiary's standard of living in all its aspects. . . .
>
> Admittedly, the words "support," and "maintenance" are regarded as referable to a standard of living, and the addition of the naked words "comfort" and "welfare" in the context of the instrument before us merely rounds out the standard of living concept.

In Estate of Bell v. Commissioner, 66 T.C. 729, 734-735 (1976), we found that the phrase "well being and maintenance in health and comfort" was subject to an ascertainable standard in Illinois:

> Although providing a modicum of discretion to the trustees, this language created a standard enforceable in a court of equity. Under Illinois law, a court of equity would look to the beneficiary's accustomed living standard in compelling compliance by the trustees, either to require income distributions for the stated purposes or to restrain distributions for unauthorized purposes. In Re Whitman, 22 Ill. 511 (1859) ("support, education, and maintenance"); French v. Northern Trust Co., 197 Ill. 30, 64 N.E. 105, 106 (1902) ("properly maintained and comfortably provided for out of such property"); Burke v. Burke, 259 Ill. 262, 102 N.E. 293, 294 (1913) ("the comforts and necessities of life").

We similarly believe that under Illinois law, a court of equity would look to Gretchen's and Patrick's accustomed living standard in compelling compliance by the trustee to require income distributions for the stated purposes. As a result, we find that the terms "support, care, welfare, and education," when viewed in the aggregate, were intended to describe the children's standard of living and are, therefore, subject to an external ascertainable standard. . . . Having found that the phrase in the aggregate created an ascertainable standard requiring the trustee to make expenditures for the children's accustomed living standard, we must reject petitioners' argument that the term "welfare" in the phrase allows the trustee to make nonsupport payments because "welfare" is broader than "support" under Illinois law.

Thus, it only remains for us to decide whether, under Illinois law, support is synonymous, for this purpose, with accustomed standard of living. In Rock Island Bank & Trust Co. v. Rhoads, 353 Ill. 131, 187 N.E. 139, 144 (1933), the Illinois Supreme Court stated: "The word 'comfort' must be construed as relating to her *support* and ease. . . . Had this clause provided only for her comfort, it cannot be doubted that such would be a limitation . . . to maintain her *in the station in life to which she was accustomed*." (Emphasis added.) We view this language as indicative that, under Illinois law, support is equivalent to accustomed standard of living. We are satisfied that the instrument before us provides an ascertainable standard under Illinois law. Accordingly, we find that decedent's gross estate includes the value of Gretchen's and Patrick's trusts since we find them to be support trusts within the meaning of section 2036(a)(1) and section 20.2036-1(b)(2), Estate Tax Regs.

Section 2036(a)(1) also applies to the decedent's obligation to support his spouse. In Estate of Sullivan v. Commissioner, 66 T.C.M. (CCH) 1329 (1993), the court recognized that a spouse may make a gift to the other spouse without affecting the duty of support, but included the trust in the decedent's gross estate because the decedent, as trustee, had discretion to invade corpus for his spouse's "proper care, support, maintenance, and health." This language restricted the decedent-trustee to distributions for her support. The court then determined what her support needs were, examining tax returns and records of the couple's living expenses, and included in decedent's gross estate that portion of the trust principal necessary to fund the obligation of support.

PROBLEMS

1. What are the gift and estate tax consequences if Donald establishes the following irrevocable trusts?
   a. Income to Donald for life, remainder to Ann.
   b. Income to Donald for ten years, remainder to Ann. Donald dies in year 12. What if Donald dies in year 8?
   c. Income to Ann for life, then income to Donald for life, remainder to Bob. Donald predeceases Ann.
2. Donald establishes an irrevocable trust with Friendly National Bank as Trustee to pay the income to Ann and Bob until the youngest is 21. The Trustee has the discretion to either accumulate the income or use it for the support, care, welfare, health, and education of Ann and Bob. After an income beneficiary becomes 21, the Trustee must distribute the beneficiary's share of trust income to the beneficiary. When the oldest beneficiary turns 21, the trust is to be divided into two shares. Each beneficiary will receive half of his or her share of the corpus at age 30 and the other half at age 40.
   a. What are the estate tax consequences if Donald dies when Ann and Bob, his children, are eight and ten?
   b. What if Donald dies when his children are 18 and 20 and they are both attending college?
3. In 1995, Doris transferred her house (fair market value $150,000, adjusted basis $50,000) to Ethan, her son. Doris continued to live in the house until her death in September 2002.
   a. Assume that Doris filed a gift tax return reporting the transfer as a gift, but she paid no gift tax because of §2505. Assume further that Doris paid no rent. What are the estate tax consequences?

    b. Same as 3.a., except that Doris moves to a nursing home in August 2000 and remains there until her death. Ethan does not occupy the house or rent it during this time.

    c. Same as 3.a., except Doris paid Ethan $1,500 per month as rent.

    d. Instead, Doris sold the house to Ethan for $150,000 on the installment basis. Each annual payment of principal and interest was $10,000. Doris forgave each payment as it became due. What are the estate tax consequences? What if Doris's will forgave this debt?

    e. Instead, Doris transferred the house to Ethan in exchange for Ethan's promise to pay Doris $20,000 per year until death. Doris remained living in the house until her death. What are the estate tax consequences? What if Doris did not remain in the house but Ethan lived there? What if neither Doris nor Ethan lived there and Ethan rented the house to others for $1,500 per month?

    f. Instead, Doris transferred her house to Tom as Trustee, retaining the right to live in the house for ten years. What are the estate tax consequences if Doris dies during the ten-year term? What if she dies in year 12? What if Doris dies in year 12 when she is renting the house from the trust for $1,500 per month?

4. Diane transferred property to Friendly National Bank as Trustee. The Trustee has absolute discretion to distribute income to, or for the benefit of, Diane during her life. At her death, the Trustee is to distribute the trust property to Diane's surviving issue.

    a. What are the estate tax consequences?

    b. What if the trustee distributed trust income to Diane on a quarterly basis?

5. In a unified transfer tax system where the transfer of a remainder interest is a completed gift, is §2036(a)(1) necessary? Why?

C. THE RIGHT TO DETERMINE ENJOYMENT OF PROPERTY
IRC §§2036(a)(2), 2038(a)(1)

1. General Principles

If the decedent transfers property and retains the right to designate who shall possess or enjoy the property or its income, §2036(a)(2) will include that property in the decedent's gross estate. If the decedent transfers property and the enjoyment of that property is subject to the decedent's power to alter, amend, revoke, or terminate the trust at the moment of the decedent's death, §2038(a)(1) will include that property in the decedent's gross estate. These two sections encompass almost every conceivable power to affect the beneficial enjoyment of property, and they are not limited to situations where the decedent can obtain beneficial enjoyment of the property for herself. Often both sections will apply to a particular property interest; however, the sections are not identical.

United States v. O'Malley
383 U.S. 627 (1966)

Mr. Justice WHITE delivered the opinion of the Court.

. . . Edward H. Fabrice, who died in 1949, created five irrevocable trusts in 1936 and 1937, two for each of two daughters and one for his wife. He was one of three trustees of the trusts, each of which provided that the trustees, in their sole discretion, could pay trust income to the beneficiary or accumulate the income, in which event it became part of the principal of the trust. Basing his action on [§2036(a)(2)] and [§2038(a)(1)], the Commissioner included in Fabrice's gross estate both the original principal of the trusts and the accumulated income added thereto. . . . The District Court found the original corpus of the trusts includable in the estate, a holding not challenged in the Court of Appeals or here. It felt obliged, however, . . . to exclude from the taxable estate the portion of the trust principal representing accumulated income and to order an appropriate refund. D.C., 220 F. Supp. 30. The Court of Appeals affirmed, 340 F.2d 930. . . . We now reverse the decision below.

The applicability of [§2036(a)(2)], upon which the United States now stands, depends upon the answer to two inquiries relevant to the facts of this case: first, whether Fabrice retained a power "to designate the persons who shall possess or enjoy the property or the income therefrom"; and second, whether the property sought to be included, namely, the portions of trust principal representing accumulated income, was the subject of a previous transfer by Fabrice.

Section [2036(a)(2)] . . . requires the property to be included not only when the grantor himself has the right to its income but also when he has the right to designate those who may possess and enjoy it. Here Fabrice was empowered, with the other trustees, to distribute the trust income to the income beneficiaries or to accumulate it and add it to the principal, thereby denying to the beneficiaries the privilege of immediate enjoyment and conditioning their eventual enjoyment upon surviving the termination of the trust. This is a significant power . . . and of sufficient substance to be deemed the power to "designate" within the meaning of [§2036(a)(2)]. . . . [T]he first condition to taxing accumulated income added to the principal is satisfied, for the income from these increments to principal was subject to the identical power in Fabrice to distribute or accumulate until the very moment of his death.

The dispute in this case relates to the second condition to the applicability of [§2036(a)(2)]—whether Fabrice had ever "transferred" the income additions to the trust principal. Contrary to the judgment of the Court of Appeals, we are sure that he had. At the time Fabrice established these trusts, he owned all of the rights to the property transferred, a major aspect of which was his right to the present and future income produced by that property. . . . With the creation of the trusts, he relinquished all of his rights to income except the power to distribute that income to the income beneficiaries or to accumulate it and hold it for the remaindermen of the trusts. He no longer had, for example, the right to income for his own benefit or to have it distributed to any other than the trust beneficiaries. Moreover, with respect to the very additions to principal now at issue, he exercised his retained power to distribute or accumulate income, choosing to do the latter and thereby adding to the principal of the trusts. All income increments to trust principal are therefore traceable to Fabrice himself, by virtue of the original transfer and the exercise of the power to accumulate. Before the creation of the trusts, Fabrice owned all rights to the property and to its income. By the time of his death he had divested himself of all power and control over accumulated income which had been added to the principal, except the power to deal with the income from such additions. With respect to each addition to trust principal from accumulated income, Fabrice had clearly made a "transfer" as required by [§2036(a)(2)]. Under that section, the power over income retained by Fabrice is sufficient to require the inclusion of the original corpus of the trust in his gross estate. The accumulated income added to principal is subject to the same power and is likewise includable. . . .

Respondents rely upon two cases in which the Tax Court and two circuit courts of appeals have concluded that where an irrevocable inter vivos transfer in trust, not incomplete in any respect, is subjected to tax as a gift in contemplation of death under [§2035(a)], the income of the trust accumulated prior to the grantor's death is not includable in the gross estate. Commissioner of Internal Revenue v. Gidwitz' Estate, 7 Cir., 196 F.2d 813, *affirming* 14 T.C. 1263; Burns v. Commissioner of Internal Revenue, 5 Cir., 177 F.2d 739, *affirming* 9 T.C. 979. The courts in those cases considered the taxable event to be a completed inter vivos transfer, not a transfer at death, and the property includable to be only the property subject to that transfer. The value of that property, whatever the valuation date, was apparently deemed an adequate reflection of any income rights included in the transfer since the grantor retained no interest in the property and no power over income which might justify the addition of subsequently accumulated income to his own gross estate. . . .

This reasoning, however, does not solve those cases arising under [§§2036 to 2038]. The courts in both *Burns*, 9 T.C. 979, 988-989 and *Gidwitz*, 196 F.2d 813, 817-818, expressly distinguished those situations where the grantor retains an interest in a property or its income, or a power over either, and his death is a significant step in effecting a transfer which began inter vivos but which becomes final and complete only with his demise. *McDermott's Estate* failed to note this distinction and represents an erroneous extension of *Gidwitz*. In both McDermott and the case before us now, the grantor reserved the power to accumulate or distribute income. This power he exercised by accumulating and adding income to principal and this same power he held until the moment of his death with respect to both the original principal and the accumulated income. In these circumstances, [§2036(a)(2)] requires inclusion in Fabrice's gross estate of all of the trust principal, including those portions representing accumulated income.

Reversed.

Both §2036(a)(2) and §2038(a)(1) apply whether the decedent can exercise the power alone or "in conjunction with any other person." It does not matter whether the additional person has an interest that is adverse to the exercise of the power. Although the "substantial adverse interest" standard applies in the income tax, to determine if the grantor will be treated as the owner of the trust, as well as in the gift tax, to determine if the donor has made a completed gift, this standard is irrelevant for estate tax purposes.

Example 10-6

Decedent creates an irrevocable trust to pay the income to her children for their lives. After the death of all Decedent's children, the trust property is to be distributed to her descendants. There are three Trustees, one of whom is decedent. Decedent has the discretion to add or delete income or remainder beneficiaries as long as all Trustees agree. The trust will be in Decedent's gross estate under §§2036(a)(2) and 2038(a)(1) because Decedent has retained for her life the right to determine who will enjoy the trust property and has, at the moment of her death, the power to alter or amend the trust. It is not relevant under either §2036(a)(2) or §2038(a)(1) that Decedent can only act in conjunction with the two other Trustees.

Example 10-7

Decedent creates an irrevocable trust, transferring property to himself as Trustee to pay the income to his son, Adam, for his life. At Adam's death, the trust property is to be distributed to Adam's surviving issue. Decedent retains the right to revoke the trust, but only with Adam's consent. Upon revocation, the trust property reverts to Decedent. The trust property will be in Decedent's gross estate under §2036(a)(2) and §2038(a)(1). It is irrelevant that Adam must consent to the exercise of the power and that Adam has a substantial adverse interest to the exercise of that power.

While there is substantial similarity between §2036(a)(2) and §2038(a)(1), there are also differences. Section 2036(a)(2) applies to the right to designate enjoyment if the decedent retains that right for his life, for a period that is not ascertainable without reference to his death, or for a period that does not in fact end before his death. Section 2038(a)(1), on the other hand, applies to a power that exists on the date of decedent's death. The decedent need not have specifically retained the power; he may obtain the power other than through an express reservation. Section 2038(a)(1) will not apply to a power that can be exercised only if a specified contingency happens and that contingency does not in fact occur before decedent's death. Section 2036(a)(2) is not so limited.

2. Ascertainable Standards

An ascertainable standard is an objective, external standard that will be enforced by a court. If Donor transfers property and retains the power to distribute income or corpus, the gift is incomplete. If Donor's power to make such distributions is restricted by an ascertainable standard, however, the gift is complete. Reg. §25.2511-2(g). The same rule applies to powers of appointment; if the power is limited by an ascertainable standard relating to health, education, support, or maintenance, it is not a general power of appointment. §§2041(b)(1)(A), 2514(c)(1); *see* Regs. §§20.2041-1(c)(2), 25.2514-1(c)(2). Neither §§2036 and 2038 nor the regulations interpreting these sections make any reference to ascertainable standards. Nonetheless, courts have interpreted these sections to include this exception.

Old Colony Trust Company v. United States
423 F.2d 601 (1st Cir. 1970)

ALDRICH, Chief Judge.

The sole question in this case is whether the estate of a settlor of an inter vivos trust, who was a trustee until the date of his death, is to be charged with the value of the principal he contributed by virtue of reserved powers in the trust. . . . The court ruled for the government, 300 F. Supp. 1032, and the executor appeals.

The initial life beneficiary of the trust was the settlor's adult son. Eighty per cent of the income was normally to be payable to him, and the balance added to principal. Subsequent beneficiaries were the son's widow and his issue. The powers upon which the government relies to cause the corpus to be includible in the settlor-trustee's estate are contained in two articles. . . .

Article 4 permitted the trustees to increase the percentage of income payable to the son beyond the eighty per cent,

> in their absolute discretion . . . when in their opinion such increase is needed in case of sickness, or desirable in view of changed circumstances.

In addition, under Article 4 the trustees were given the discretion to cease paying income to the son, and add it all to principal, "During such period as the Trustees may decide that the stoppage of such payments is for his best interests."

Article 7 gave broad administrative or management powers to the trustees, with discretion to acquire investments not normally held by trustees, and the right to determine, what was to be charged or credited to income or principal, including stock dividends or deductions for amortization. It further provided that all divisions and decisions made by the trustees in good faith should be conclusive on all parties, and in summary, stated that the trustees were empowered, "generally to do all things in relation to the Trust Fund which the Donor could do if living and this Trust had not been executed."

The government claims that each of these two articles meant that the settlor trustee had "the right . . . to designate the persons who shall possess or enjoy the (trust) property or the income therefrom" within the meaning of section 2036(a)(2) . . . and that the settlor-trustee at the date of his death possessed a power "to alter, amend, revoke, or terminate" within the meaning of section 2038(a)(1). . . .

If State Street Trust Co. v. United States, 1 Cir., 1959, 263 F.2d 635, was correctly decided in this aspect, the government must prevail because of the Article 7 powers. There this court, Chief Judge Magruder dissenting, held against the taxpayer because broad powers similar to those in Article 7 meant "as long as he lived, in substance and shift the economic benefits of the trusts between the life tenants and the remaindermen," so that the settlor "as long as he lived, in substance and effect and in a very real sense . . . retained for his life . . . the right . . . to designate the persons who shall possess or enjoy the property or the income therefrom. . . ." 263 F.2d at 639-640, quoting 26 U.S.C. 2036(a)(2). We accept the taxpayer's invitation to reconsider this ruling.

It is common ground that a settlor will not find the corpus of the trust included in his estate merely because he named himself a trustee. Jennings v. Smith, 2 Cir., 1947, 161 F.2d 74. He must have reserved a power to himself that is inconsistent with the full termination of ownership. The government's brief defines this as "sufficient dominion and control until his death." Trustee powers given for the administration or management of the trust must be equitably exercised, however, for the benefit of the trust as a whole. . . . The court in *State Street* conceded that the powers at issue were all such powers, but reached the conclusion that, cumulatively, they gave the settlor dominion sufficiently unfettered to be in the nature of ownership. With all respect to the majority of the then court, we find it difficult to see how a power can be subject to control by the probate court, and exercisable only in what the trustee fairly concludes is in the interests of the trust and its beneficiaries as a whole, and at the same time be an ownership power.

The government's position, to be sound, must be that the trustee's powers are beyond the court's control. Under Massachusetts law, however, no amount of administrative discretion prevents judicial supervision of the trustee. Thus in Appeal of Davis, 1903, 183 Mass. 499, 67 N.E. 604, a trustee was given "full power to make purchases, investments and exchanges . . . in such manner as to them shall seem expedient; it being my intention to give my trustees . . .

the same dominion and control over said trust property as I now have." In spite of this language, and in spite of their good faith, the court charged the trustees for failing sufficiently to diversify their investment portfolio.

The Massachusetts court has never varied from this broad rule of accountability. . . .

We do not believe that trustee powers are to be more broadly construed for tax purposes than the probate court would construe them for administrative purposes. More basically, we agree with Judge Magruder's observation that nothing is "gained by lumping them together." State Street Trust Co. v. United States, *supra*, 263 F.2d at 642. We hold that no aggregation of purely administrative powers can meet the government's amorphous test of "sufficient dominion and control" so as to be equated with ownership.

This does not resolve taxpayer's difficulties under Article 4. Quite different considerations apply to distribution powers. Under them the trustee can, expressly, prefer one beneficiary over another. Furthermore, his freedom of choice may vary greatly, depending upon the terms of the individual trust. If there is an ascertainable standard, the trustee can be compelled to follow it. If there is not, even though he is a fiduciary, it is not unreasonable to say that his retention of an unmeasurable freedom of choice is equivalent to retaining some of the incidents of ownership. Hence, under the cases, if there is an ascertainable standard the settlor-trustee's estate is not taxed. . . .

The trust provision which is uniformly held to provide an ascertainable standard is one which, though variously expressed, authorizes such distributions as may be needed to continue the beneficiary's accustomed way of life. . . . On the other hand, if the trustee may go further, and has power to provide for the beneficiary's "happiness," . . . or "pleasure," . . . or "use and benefit," . . . or "reasonable requirement(s)," . . . the standard is so loose that the trustee is in effect uncontrolled.

In the case at bar the trustees could increase the life tenant's income "in case of sickness, or (if) desirable in view of changed circumstances." Alternatively, they could reduce it "for his best interests." "Sickness" presents no problem. Conceivably, providing for "changed circumstances" is roughly equivalent to maintaining the son's present standard of living. . . . The unavoidable stumbling block is the trustees' right to accumulate income and add it to capital (which the son would never receive) when it is to the "best interests" of the son to do so. Additional payments to a beneficiary whenever in his "best interests" might seem to be too broad a standard in any event. . . .

Power, however, to decrease or cut off a beneficiary's income when in his "best interests," is even more troublesome. When the beneficiary is the son, and the trustee the father, a particular purpose comes to mind, parental control through holding the purse strings. The father decides what conduct is to the "best interests" of the son, and if the son does not agree, he loses his allowance. Such a power has the plain indicia of ownership control. The alternative, that the son, because of other means, might not need this income, and would prefer to have it accumulate for his widow and children after his death, is no better. If the trustee has power to confer "happiness" on the son by generosity to someone else, this seems clearly an unascertainable standard. . . .

The case of Hays' Estate v. Commr. of Internal Revenue, 5 Cir., 1950, 181 F.2d 169, is contrary to our decision. The opinion is unsupported by either reasoning or authority, and we will not follow it. With the present settlor-trustee free to determine the standard himself, a finding of ownership control was warranted. To put it another way, the cost of holding onto the strings may prove to be a rope burn. State Street Bank & Trust Co. v. United States, *supra*.

Affirmed.

Leopold v. United States
510 F.2d 617 (9th Cir. 1975)

ALFRED T. GOODWIN, Circuit Judge:

. . . The first issue is the includibility in the decedent's gross estate of the entire corpus and accumulated income of two inter vivos trusts, one for the primary benefit of his daughter Catherine, and the other for the primary benefit of his daughter Celeste. . . .

The government contends that the powers of decedent and his co-trustee to distribute principal to decedent's daughters whenever they deemed such payments to be "necessary and proper" and to accumulate trust income or to pay it out in their "uncontrolled discretion" for the girls' "support, education, maintenance and general welfare" constituted a power "to alter, amend, revoke, or terminate" within the meaning of section 2038. The government also contends that these powers gave the decedent the ability to shift income from his daughters to their heirs and, thus, to designate the persons who would receive the enjoyment of the property within the meaning of section 2036(a)(2).

The district court concluded, and the taxpayers do not dispute, that since the decedent had the power to pay out principal as he deemed "necessary and proper," he retained sufficient control over the remainder interest of each trust to justify its inclusion in his gross estate. However, the court also held that the decedent had retained no power to affect the beneficial enjoyment of the income of either trust, except to the extent that such power was limited by an ascertainable, external, objective standard. Although the question is a close one, we agree with the district court that the standard was ascertainable. The Court of Appeals for the First Circuit has said:

> The trust provision which is uniformly held to provide an ascertainable standard is one which, though variously expressed, authorizes such distributions as may be needed to continue the beneficiary's accustomed way of life. . . . Old Colony Trust Co. v. United States, 423 F.2d 601, 604 (1st Cir. 1970).

The provision at issue here, authorizing payments of income for the "support, education, maintenance and general welfare" of decedent's daughters, requires the trustees to maintain the daughters in their accustomed way of life and, hence, provides a sufficiently objective standard. . . . From this conclusion it follows that the present value of a portion of the income interests was properly excluded from the decedent's gross estate. At the time of decedent's death, the daughters had an enforceable right to enjoy that portion of the trust income necessary to maintain them in their accustomed way of life. The government has elsewhere conceded the propriety of excluding from the gross estate the present value of a fixed, indefeasible income right even though the decedent retained the power to pay corpus prematurely to the income beneficiary. *See* Walter v. United States, 295 F.2d 720 (6th Cir. 1961). *See also* Revenue Ruling 70-513, 1970-72 C.B. 194, which holds that under section 2038 only the value of the remainder interest, and not the entire corpus, of a trust is includible in the decedent's gross estate where the enjoyment of a life estate is vested in the beneficiary and is not subject to reduction through exercise of the decedent's reserved power to terminate the trust and to pay over the corpus to the life beneficiary.

But the daughters here had an enforceable right to enjoy currently only a portion of the full income stream prior to reaching twenty-one years of age— i.e., that amount necessary to maintain them in their accustomed way of life. With respect to the remaining income, the decedent had two options: he could either allow that income to accumulate until the girls reached 21, or he could provide for present enjoyment of the income by paying over the corpus with its full income-generating capacity. Thus, the decedent possessed a degree of control over the enjoyment of that segment of the future income he was not required to distribute currently which precludes exclusion of its actuarial value from his gross estate. *See* United States v. O'Malley, 383 U.S. 627, 631 (1966); Lober v. United States, 346 U.S. 335, 337 (1953).

The government argues that under Estate of Varian v. Commissioner, 396 F.2d 753 (9th Cir. 1968), *aff'g* 47 T.C. 34 (1966), the entire corpus of the trusts must be included in the gross estate. Varian does not compel such a result. In *Varian*, the trust instrument provided:

> 3. Distribution of Income and Principal
> (a) The Trustees shall pay to or apply for the benefit of the child such sums as may in the Trustees' discretion be necessary for the child's support, maintenance and education.
> (b) In the discretion of Trustees, the principal and income or any portion thereof, may be payable to the child at any time before attaining the age of 21 years. . . .
> 47 T.C. at 38.

The Tax Court held that the second clause conferred a completely unrestricted power over the distribution of income and principal which destroyed whatever objective standard may have been contained in the first clause. 47 T.C. at 43–44. We are presented with trust provisions which are substantially similar to those in *Varian* in all significant respects but one: Here, the unrestricted power extends only to the payment of principal. We recognize, of course, that in terms of economic effect the addition of an unrestricted power over a future income stream adds very little to the discretion possessed by a trustee with an unrestricted power over the principal.

But in determining whether an unrestricted power in one provision of a trust destroys an ascertainable income standard in another trust provision, we refuse to extend the logic of *Varian* to the situation where the unfettered power applies only to payment of principal. To do so would create conflict with the concededly proper principle that the present value of a fixed income right is excludible where the decedent retains a discretionary power to pay the corpus prematurely to the income beneficiary.

The amount of previously accumulated income was properly excluded. Once the decision had been made to accumulate part of the income, this accumulation was placed beyond the reach of the trustees. The accumulated income would be paid to the children when they reached 21. Although the trustees could pay out the principal early, they could not prematurely distribute the accumulated income. Unlike the accumulated income held taxable in United States v. O'Malley, the accumulated income here did not become part of the trust principal and was not subject to the powers decedent reserved over the principal.

We hold, then, that under sections 2036(a)(2) and 2038(a)(1) the decedent's reserved power to distribute the principal of the trusts at any time requires the inclusion of the corpus of each trust, reduced by the actuarial value of that segment of the future income stream which the decedent would be obligated to distribute currently to his daughters. We further hold that the exclusion of previously accumulated income was proper. The case must be remanded to the district court for a factual determination of the amount of the includible sum.

3.   *Power to Appoint Trustees*

When the trustee has discretion to retain or distribute income or the power to designate beneficiaries, the trust property will not be in the decedent's gross estate if the decedent is not the trustee. But what if the decedent has the power to appoint successor trustees? Will the trustee's powers then be imputed to the decedent?

Estate of Farrel v. United States
553 F.2d 637 (Cl. Ct. 1977)

DAVIS, Judge.

The stipulated facts in this tax refund suit thrust upon us a narrow but knotty issue of estate tax law under Section 2036(a)(2) of the Internal Revenue Code of 1954. In 1961 Marian B. Arrel established an irrevocable trust with a corpus of various securities and her grandchildren as beneficiaries. Two individuals were named as trustees. They were given discretionary power to pay or apply all or part of the net income or principal to or for the benefit of any one or more of the beneficiaries (and their issue). The instrument also provided for a "time of division" when the corpus was to be divided into various portions, each of which (according to specified circumstances) was either to be paid over immediately to a specified beneficiary, or held in a new trust with the trustee having discretionary power to make payments to or for the benefit of specified beneficiaries until a later time when required payments were to be made. No provision was made in the trust for any distribution to Mrs. Farrel in any circumstances.

The trust called for two trustees at all times, and provided for Mrs. Farrel to appoint a successor trustee if a vacancy occurred in that position through death, resignation or removal by a proper court for cause. However, neither the instrument nor Connecticut law (which governed the trust) permitted Mrs. Farrel to remove a trustee and thereby create a vacancy. The trust was silent as to whether Mrs. Farrel could appoint herself as a successor trustee in the event of a vacancy, but neither the trust instrument nor Connecticut law would have prevented her from doing so.

Two vacancies occurred in the office of trustee during Mrs. Farrel's life. In 1964 a named trustee died and Mrs. Farrel appointed a third person as successor trustee. In 1965 that successor trustee resigned and Mrs. Farrel, as settlor, appointed another individual to succeed him. . . .

Both parties agree that (a) the trustees had "the right, either alone or in conjunction with any person, to designate the persons who shall possess or enjoy the property or the income therefrom" within the meaning of Section 2036(a)(2); (b) Mrs. Farrel, the decedent-settlor, could lawfully designate herself (under the trust and Connecticut law) as successor trustee if a vacancy occurred during her life; (c) the occurrence of a vacancy in the office of trustee was a condition which Mrs. Farrel could not create and which was beyond her control; and (d) Mrs. Farrel had the opportunity, before her 1969 death, to appoint a successor trustee only during the two periods in 1964 and 1965 mentioned above. The legal conflict is whether the right of the trustees (as to who should enjoy or possess the property or income) should in these circumstances be attributed to the decedent under §2036(a) for any of the three periods designated in that statutory provision—her life; any period not ascertainable without reference to her death; any period which does not in fact end before her death. The Government's answer is yes and the plaintiff of course says no.

Only Section 2036(a) is now before us but, since taxpayer's presentation emphasizes a comparison of that provision with Section 2038 (a cognate but separate part of the estate tax), it is important to set out, at the beginning, the relevant aspects of the latter, as we do in the margin. Plaintiff's primary point is that (i) it is now and has long been settled that Section 2038 does not cover a power or right subject to a conditional event which has not occurred prior to and does not exist at the decedent's death, such as a discretionary power to distribute income or principal under specified conditions which have not occurred before the death, and (ii) the same rule has been and is applicable to Section 2036(a).

There is no question that taxpayer is correct as to the construction of Section 2038. That slant was given by the courts to the provision's predecessor under the 1939 Code (*see* Jennings v. Smith, 161 F.2d 74, 77-78 (2d Cir. 1947); Estate of Want v. Commissioner, 29 T.C. 1223 (1958), *rev'd on other grounds*, 280 F.2d 777 (2d Cir. 1960); Estate of Kasch v. Commissioner, 30 T.C. 102 (1958)), and the Treasury has itself adopted the same interpretation for the 1954 Code as well. Treasury Regulations on Estate Tax (1954 Code), Section 20.2038-1(a) and (b); *see also* Rev. Bul. 55-393, 1955-1 Cum. Bull. 448.

The initial and fundamental question we have to face is whether this settled understanding of Section 2038 necessarily governs Section 2036(a), as it now stands. We think not for two reasons which we shall consider in turn: first, that the critical points-of-view of the two provisions differ, and, second, that the regulations governing the two sections take diametrically opposed positions on the narrow issue of contingent rights and powers of the kind involved here.

The two separate provisions appear to diverge sharply in their perspective—the point from which the pertinent powers and rights are to be seen. Section 2038(a) looks at the problem from decedent's death—what he can and cannot do at that specific moment. Excluded are contingent rights and powers (beyond the decedent's control) which are not exercisable at that moment because the designated contingency does not exist at that time. Section 2036(a), on the other hand, looks forward from the time the decedent made the transfer to see whether he has retained any of the specified rights "for his life or for any period not ascertainable without reference to his death or for any period which does not in fact end before his death." This language makes the transferor's death one pole of the specified time-span but the whole of the time-span is also significant. Because of the statute's reference to the time-span, differences of interpretation are quite conceivable. It is possible for instance, to hold the words to mean that the retained right has to exist at all times throughout one of the periods, but it is also possible to see the language as covering contingencies which could realistically occur at some separate point or points during the designated periods—always including the moment [of] decedent's death. We take it (from the argument's insistence on the parallel to 2038) that the taxpayer would not stand on the former ("at all times") interpretation if a vacancy in the trusteeship's existed and had not been filed at Mrs. Farrel's death. But under the language of 2036(a) there is no compelling reason why the moment of death has to be exclusively important. Unlike Section 2038, this provision seems to look forward from the time of transfer to the date of the transferor's death, and can be said to concentrate on the significant rights with respect to the transferred property the transfer or retains, not at every moment during that period, but whenever the specified contingency happens to arise during that period (so long as the contingency can still occur at the end of the period).

There is nothing unreasonable about this latter construction, which accords with Congress' over-all purpose to gather into the estate tax all transfers which remain significantly incomplete—on which the transferor still holds a string—during his lifetime. It is hard to believe, for instance that, whatever may be true of 2038, 2036(a) would have to be seen as failing to cover a trust where the trustee, with discretionary powers, could be removed by the settlor, and the settlor substituted as trustee, whenever economic conditions fell below a stated level (*e.g.*, a designated level on a certain stock exchange index or a level of earnings of the trust) even though fortuitously that condition did not happen to exist at the time of death. In a case like that, the lifetime link between the decedent and the trust property (and income) would be so strong as plainly to measure up to both the letter and the spirit of 2036(a) if the Treasury chose to see it that way. This case, though perhaps less clear, falls into the same class of a continuing substantial tie.

The other element that leads us to reject plaintiff's attempt to equate 2036(a) with 2038, for this case, is that the Treasury has affirmatively chosen to separate the two sections—there is a Treasury regulation under the former §20.2036-1, which, to our mind, clearly covers this decedent's situation (in contrast to the regulation under 2038, which excludes it). [Reg. §20.2036-1(b)(3)]. Taxpayer urges us to read the regulation otherwise, and if we cannot to hold it invalid.

The regulation says flatly . . . that it is immaterial "(iii) whether the exercise of the power was subject to a contingency beyond the decedent's control which did not occur before his death (*e.g.*, the death of another person during the decedent's lifetime)." This would seem on its surface to blanket this decedent's position under her trust, but plaintiff would read it very literally and narrowly to apply only where the contingency relates to the "exercise" of an already existing power, and conversely, to be inapplicable where the power only springs into existence when a trustee vacancy occurs. Similarly, taxpayer sees in the broad sweep of the last sentence of §20.2036-1(b)(3) the implied negative pregnant that a restricted power in the decedent to appoint herself a substitute trustee only in the event of a vacancy lies outside 2036(a). We cannot accept these strained (if not casuistic) analyses of the regulation because they go directly counter to its apparent purpose to cover just such contingencies as we have here. If proof of that objective is needed it is fully supplied by the companion regulation under 2038 (Treasury Regulation on Estate Tax (1954 Code), §20.2038-1(b)) which declares in coordinate terms that "section 2038 is not applicable to a power the exercise of which was subject to a contingency beyond the decedent's control which did not occur before his death (*e.g.*, the death of another person during the decedent's life). *See, however, Section 2036(a)(2) for the inclusion of property in the decedent's gross estate on account of such a power.*" (Emphasis added).

We are required, then, to consider whether §20.2036-1(b)(3) should be overturned as invalid. Recognizing the deference due Treasury Regulations . . . we cannot take that step. We have pointed out that 2036 is not the same as 2038 in its wording or in the viewpoint from which it appraises the decedent's link to the transferred property. We have also said that it is not unreasonable to regard 2036(a), in the way the Treasury does, as a blanket overall sweeping-in of property over which the decedent still has at death some significant, though contingent, power to choose those who shall have possession or enjoyment. . . .

We end by noting that the contingent right of Mrs. Farrel to make herself a trustee in the event of a vacancy—unlike the *de facto* "powers" involved in United States v. Byrum, 4089 U.S. 125 (1972) and in Estate of Tully v. United States, 528 F.2d 1401, 208 Ct.Cl. 596 (1976)—was a legally enforceable right, in effect imbedded in the trust instrument, which bore directly on the designation of the persons to possess or enjoy the trust property or income. That the exercise of this right was foreseeable when the trust was created—that it was a real right, neither insignificant nor illusory—is shown by the fact that Mrs. Farrel had two opportunities to exercise it in eight years and, if she had lived, may well have had more.

Estate of Wall v. Commissioner
101 T.C. 300 (1993)

NIMS, Judge:

. . . Mrs. Wall, the grantor, retained the right in each trust indenture to remove the corporate sole trustee and replace it with another corporate trustee which had to be "independent" from the grantor. In each case the trustee was given the authority to distribute principal and income to a beneficiary essentially unrestrained by an ascertainable standard. Did the right to replace the corporate trustee in turn encompass the right to exercise the powers of the trustee? For the following reasons, we think not.

The underlying assumption of Rev. Rul. 79-353 and respondent's argument is that even a corporate trustee will be compelled to follow the bidding of a settlor who has the power to remove the trustee; otherwise the settlor will be able to find another corporate trustee which will act as the settlor wishes. In other words, says respondent, under these circumstances the settlor has the de facto power to exercise the powers vested in the trustee. But the Supreme Court has said in *Byrum* that the section 2036(a)(2) right connotes an ascertainable and legally enforceable power, as exemplified by the facts in United States v. O'Malley, 383 U.S. 627 (1966). As the Supreme Court states in *Byrum*, "*O'Malley* was covered precisely by the statute [section 2036(a)(2)] for two reasons: (1) there the settlor had reserved a legal right, set forth in the trust instrument; and (2) this right expressly authorized the settlor, 'in conjunction' with others, to accumulate income and thereby 'to designate' the persons to enjoy it." United States v. Byrum, 408 U.S. at 136.

In the case before us respondent simply speculates that Mrs. Wall, by merely threatening First Wisconsin to replace it, could indirectly have exercised powers of the trustee similar to, though broader than, those in *O'Malley*. In

Estate of Beckwith v. Commissioner, 55 T.C. 242 (1970), the trust indenture explicitly provided for the periodic distribution of trust income to a named beneficiary. Under the terms of the trust indenture the settlor retained no power or right to control the amounts or the timing of the distributions. The Commissioner, however, relied upon certain "practical considerations" which, he contended, enabled the decedent to control the flow of the income. The so-called practical considerations included the authority for the trust to retain stock in the settlor's closely held corporation; the power given the trustee to vote the stock; the settlor's retained right to remove a trustee and appoint a successor other than himself; and the close business relationships between the settlor and the individual trustees. We held that none of the so-called practical considerations nor all of them combined provided a basis for an inference that the settlor, by prearrangement or informal understanding or otherwise, reserved the right to cause the trustees to retain the closely held stock or to give the settlor proxies with respect thereto. Estate of Beckwith v. Commissioner, 55 T.C. at 248-249.

While it is true that First Wisconsin's power to distribute income and principal is not restricted to the extent existing in *Estate of Beckwith*, it is also true that, under established principles of the law governing trusts, a trustee would violate its fiduciary duty if it acquiesced in the wishes of the settlor by taking action that the trustee would not otherwise take regarding the beneficial enjoyment of any interest in the trust, or agreed with the settlor, prior to appointment, as to how fiduciary powers should be exercised over the distribution of income and principal. The trustee has a duty to administer the trust in the sole interest of the beneficiary, to act impartially if there are multiple beneficiaries, and to exercise powers exclusively for the benefit of the beneficiaries. *See, e.g.*, Bogert, The Law of Trusts and Trustees, section 543, at 217 (2d ed. 1993) ("Perhaps the most fundamental duty of a trustee is that he must display throughout the administration of the trust complete loyalty to the interests of the beneficiary and must exclude all selfish interest and all consideration of the interests of third persons."). While the parties and amicus have not briefed the Wisconsin law on this virtually universal rule, it would seem highly unlikely that there is a variance between Wisconsin and other jurisdictions.

In irrevocable trusts such as those under scrutiny, the trustee is accountable only to the beneficiaries, not to the settlor, and any right of action for breach of fiduciary duty lies in the beneficiaries, not in the settlor. Bogert, *supra*, sec. 42, at 431-433. It also seems incontrovertible that the trustee's duty of sole fidelity to the beneficiary remains the same regardless of whether or not distributions are discretionary and whether or not limited by a standard such as one related to health, education, support in reasonable comfort, and the like.

In the absence of some compelling reason to do so, which respondent has not shown, we are not inclined to infer any kind of fraudulent side agreement between Mrs. Wall and First Wisconsin as to how the administration of these trusts would be manipulated by Mrs. Wall. Instead, since the language of the trust indentures provides maximum flexibility as to distributions of income and principal, the trustee would be expected to look to the circumstances of the beneficiaries to whom sole allegiance is owed, and not to Mrs. Wall, in order to determine the timing and amount of discretionary distributions.

It seems also likely that Mrs. Wall might have conceived that a beneficiary might move to a distant location, making the beneficiary's personal contact with the trust department impractical, or that First Wisconsin might merge with an out-of-state bank in a way that would change the character of its trust department. These motives, if they indeed existed, are not the equivalent of a retained right contemplated by section 2036(a)(2). Nor do they imply arrangements, not previously contemplated, made after a transfer has been completed to permit the transferor to enjoy the benefits of the property. *See* Estate of Barlow v. Commissioner, 55 T.C. 666, 670 (1971). We therefore apply the Supreme Court's definition of a section 2036(a)(2) retained right; namely, that it must be an ascertainable and legally enforceable power. United States v. Byrum, 408 U.S. at 136. We hold that Mrs. Wall did not retain such an ascertainable and enforceable power to affect the beneficial enjoyment of the trust property.

On brief respondent points out that sections 2036(a)(2) and 2038(a)(1) frequently overlap and urges that in this case both are equally applicable. We agree that these sections frequently overlap, but for reasons stated above we hold that neither is applicable. We have focused essentially on section 2036(a)(2), but for the reasons given, Mrs. Wall's retained power to substitute another independent corporate trustee for First Wisconsin is not the type of power which would affect the "enjoyment" of the trust property contemplated by section 2036(a)(2) or section 2038(a)(1).

Revenue Ruling 95-58
1995-2 C.B. 191

The Internal Revenue Service has reconsidered whether a grantor's reservation of an unqualified power to remove a trustee and appoint a new trustee (other than the grantor) is tantamount to a reservation by the grantor of the trustee's discretionary powers of distribution. . . . For purposes of §§2036 and 2038, it is immaterial in what capacity the power was exercisable by the decedent. Thus, if a decedent transferred property in trust while retaining, as trustee, the discretionary power to distribute the principal and income, the trust property will be includible in the decedent's gross estate under §§2036 and 2038. The regulations under §§2036 and 2038 explain that a decedent is regarded as having possessed the powers of a trustee if the decedent possessed an unrestricted power to remove the trustee and appoint anyone (including the decedent) as trustee. Sections 20.2036-1(b)(3) and 20.2038-1(a) of the Estate Tax Regulations. . . . Rev. Rul. 77-182 is modified to hold that even if the decedent had possessed the power to remove the trustee and appoint an individual or corporate successor trustee that was not related or subordinate to the decedent (within the meaning of §672(c)), the decedent would not have retained a trustee's discretionary control over trust income.

4. *Reciprocal Trusts*

Courts developed the reciprocal trust doctrine in response to schemes developed to avoid the rules of §2036 and §2038. It is but one example of a more pervasive issue that appears throughout both the income and the transfer taxes: when does the substance of a transaction dictate its tax consequences, and when will the form of the transaction chosen by the taxpayer be respected? The general rule, of course, is that the form of a transaction will govern. Taxpayers have the right to structure their affairs to minimize the impact of taxes. When taxpayers, however, ignore the formalities or subvert the form, courts will exalt substance over form to prevent tax evasion.

United States v. Estate of Grace
395 U.S. 316 (1969)

Mr. Justice MARSHALL delivered the opinion of the Court.

This case involves the application of [§2036] of the Internal Revenue Code of 1939 to a so-called "reciprocal trust" situation. After Joseph P. Grace's death in 1950, the Commissioner of Internal Revenue determined that the value of a trust created by his wife was includible in his gross estate. A deficiency was assessed and paid, and, after denial of a claim for a refund, this refund suit was brought. The Court of Claims, with two judges dissenting, ruled that the value of the trust was not includible in decedent's estate under §2036 and entered judgment for respondent. . . . We reverse.

Decedent was a very wealthy man at the time of his marriage to the late Janet Grace in 1908. Janet Grace had no wealth or property of her own, but, between 1908 and 1931, decedent transferred to her a large amount of personal and real property, including the family's Long Island estate. Decedent retained effective control over the family's business affairs, including the property transferred to his wife. She took no interest and no part in business affairs and relied upon her husband's judgment. Whenever some formal action was required regarding property in her name, decedent would have the appropriate instrument prepared and she would execute it.

On December 15, 1931, decedent executed a trust instrument, hereinafter called the Joseph Grace trust. Named as trustees were decedent, his nephew, and a third party. The trustees were directed to pay the income of the trust to Janet Grace during her lifetime, and to pay to her any part of the principal which a majority of the trustees might deem advisable. Janet was given the power to designate, by will or deed, the manner in which the trust estate remaining at her death was to be distributed among decedent and their children. The trust properties included securities and real estate interests.

On December 30, 1931, Janet Grace executed a trust instrument, hereinafter called the Janet Grace trust, which was virtually identical to the Joseph Grace trust. The trust properties included the family estate and corporate securities, all of which had been transferred to her by decedent in preceding years.

The trust instruments were prepared by one of decedent's employees in accordance with a plan devised by decedent to create additional trusts before the advent of a new gift tax expected to be enacted the next year. Decedent selected the properties to be included in each trust. Janet Grace, acting in accordance with this plan, executed her trust instrument at decedent's request.

Janet Grace died in 1937. The Joseph Grace trust terminated at her death. Her estate's federal estate tax return disclosed the Janet Grace trust and reported it as a nontaxable transfer by Janet Grace. The Commissioner asserted that the Janet and Joseph Grace trusts were "reciprocal" and asserted a deficiency to the extent of mutual value. Compromises on unrelated issues resulted in 55% of the smaller of the two trusts, the Janet Grace trust, being included in her gross estate.

Joseph Grace died in 1950. The federal estate tax return disclosed both trusts. The Joseph Grace trust was reported as a nontaxable transfer and the Janet Grace trust was reported as a trust under which decedent held a limited power of appointment. Neither trust was included in decedent's gross estate.

The Commissioner determined that the Joseph and Janet Grace trusts were "reciprocal" and included the amount of the Janet Grace trust in decedent's gross estate. A deficiency in the amount of $363,500.97, plus interest, was assessed and paid. . . .

The doctrine of reciprocal trusts was formulated in response to attempts to draft instruments which seemingly avoid the literal terms of [§2036], while still leaving the decedent the lifetime enjoyment of his property. The doctrine dates from Lehman v. Commissioner of Internal Revenue, 109 F.2d 99 (C.A.2d Cir.), *cert. denied*, 310 U.S. 637 (1940). In *Lehman*, decedent and his brother owned equal shares in certain stocks and bonds. Each brother placed his interest in trust for the other's benefit for life, with remainder to the life tenant's issue. Each brother also gave the other the right to withdraw $150,000 of the principal. If the brothers had each reserved the right to withdraw $150,000 from the trust that each had created, the trusts would have been includible in their gross estates as interests of which each had made a transfer with a power to revoke. When one of the brothers died, his estate argued that neither trust was includible because the decedent did not have a power over a trust which he had created.

The Second Circuit disagreed. That court ruled that the effect of the transfers was the same as if the decedent had transferred his stock in trust for himself, remainder to his issue, and had reserved the right to withdraw $150,000. The court reasoned: "The fact that the trusts were reciprocated or 'crossed' is a trifle, quite lacking in practical or legal significance. . . . The law searches out the reality and is not concerned with the form." 109 F.2d, at 100. The court ruled that the decisive point was that each brother caused the other to make a transfer by establishing his own trust.

The doctrine of reciprocal trusts has been applied numerous times since the *Lehman* decision. It received congressional approval in §6 of the Technical Changes Act of 1949, 63 Stat. 893. The present case is, however, this Court's first examination of the doctrine.

The Court of Claims was divided over the requirements for application of the doctrine to the situation of this case. Relying on some language in *Lehman* and certain other courts of appeals' decisions, the majority held that the crucial factor was whether the decedent had established his trust as consideration for the establishment of the trust of which he was a beneficiary. The court ruled that decedent had not established his trust as a quid pro quo for the Janet Grace trust, and that Janet Grace had not established her trust in exchange for the Joseph Grace trust. Rather, the trusts were found to be part of an established pattern of family giving, with neither party desiring to obtain property from the other. Indeed, the court found that Janet Grace had created her trust because decedent requested that she do so. It therefore found the reciprocal trust doctrine inapplicable.

The court recognized that certain cases had established a slightly different test for reciprocity. Those cases inferred consideration from the establishment of two similar trusts at about the same time. The court held that any inference of consideration was rebutted by the evidence in the case, particularly the lack of any evidence of an estate tax avoidance motive on the part of the Graces. In contrast, the dissent felt that the majority's approach placed entirely too much weight on subjective intent. Once it was established that the trusts were interrelated, the dissent felt that the subjective intent of the parties in establishing the trust should become irrelevant. The relevant factor was whether the trusts created by the settlors placed each other in approximately the same objective economic position as they would have been in if each had created his own trust with himself, rather than the other, as life beneficiary.

We agree with the dissent that the approach of the Court of Claims majority places too much emphasis on the subjective intent of the parties in creating the trusts and for that reason hinders proper application of the federal estate tax laws. It is true that there is language in *Lehman* and other cases that would seem to support the majority's approach. It is also true that the results in some of those cases arguably support the decision below. Nevertheless, we think that these cases are not in accord with this Court's prior decisions interpreting related provisions of the federal estate tax laws.

Emphasis on the subjective intent of the parties in creating the trusts, particularly when those parties are members of the same family unit, creates substantial obstacles to the proper application of the federal estate tax laws. As this Court said in Estate of Spiegel v. Commissioner of Internal Revenue, 335 U.S. 701, 705-706 (1949):

> Any requirement . . . (of) a post-death attempt to probe the settlor's thoughts in
> regard to the transfer, would partially impair the effectiveness of . . . ([§2036]) as
> an instrument to frustrate estate tax evasions.

We agree that "the taxability of a trust corpus . . . does not hinge on a settlor's motives, but depends on the nature and operative effect of the trust transfer." *Id.*, at 705. . . .

We think these observations have particular weight when applied to the reciprocal trust situation. First, inquiries into subjective intent, especially in intrafamily transfers, are particularly perilous. The present case illustrates that it is, practically speaking, impossible to determine after the death of the parties what they had in mind in creating trusts over 30 years earlier. Second, there is a high probability that such a trust arrangement was indeed created for tax-avoidance purposes. And, even if there was no estate-tax-avoidance motive, the settlor in a very real and objective sense did retain an economic interest while purporting to give away his property.[8] Finally, it is unrealistic to assume that the settlors of the trusts, usually members of one family unit, will have created their trusts as a bargained-for exchange for the other trust. "Consideration," in the traditional legal sense, simply does not normally enter into such intrafamily transfers.[9]

For these reasons, we hold that application of the reciprocal trust doctrine is not dependent upon a finding that each trust was created as a quid pro quo for the other. Such a "consideration" requirement necessarily involves a difficult inquiry into the subjective intent of the settlors. Nor do we think it necessary to prove the existence of a tax-avoidance motive. As we have said above, standards of this sort, which rely on subjective factors, are rarely workable under the federal estate tax laws. Rather, we hold that application of the reciprocal trust doctrine requires only that the trusts be interrelated, and that the arrangement, to the extent of mutual value, leaves the settlors in approximately the same economic position as they would have been in had they created trusts naming themselves as life beneficiaries.[10]

---

8. For example, in the present case decedent ostensibly devised the trust plan to avoid an imminent federal gift tax. Instead of establishing trusts for the present benefit of his children, he chose an arrangement under which he and his wife retained present enjoyment of the property and under which the property would pass to their children without imposition of either estate or gift tax.

9. The present case is probably typical in this regard. Janet Grace created her trust because decedent requested that she do so; it was in no real sense a bargained-for quid pro quo for his trust. . . .

10. We do not mean to say that the existence of "consideration," in the traditional legal sense of a bargained-for exchange, can never be relevant. In certain cases, inquiries into the settlor's reasons for creating the trusts may be helpful in establishing the requisite link between the two trusts. We only hold that a finding of a bargained-for consideration is not necessary to establish reciprocity.

Applying this test to the present case, we think it clear that the value of the Janet Grace trust fund must be included in decedent's estate for federal estate tax purposes. It is undisputed that the two trusts are interrelated. They are substantially identical in terms and were created at approximately the same time. Indeed, they were part of a single transaction designed and carried out by decedent. It is also clear that the transfers in trust left each party, to the extent of mutual value, in the same objective economic position as before. Indeed, it appears, as would be expected in transfers between husband and wife, that the effective position of each party vis-a-vis the property did not change at all. It is no answer that the transferred properties were different in character. For purposes of the estate tax, we think that economic value is the only workable criterion. Joseph Grace's estate remained undiminished to the extent of the value of his wife's trust and the value of his estate must accordingly be increased by the value of that trust.

The judgment of the Court of Claims is reversed and the case is remanded for further proceedings consistent with this opinion.

PROBLEMS

1. Derrick transfers $500,000 to Friendly National Bank to pay the income to Anita for life with the remainder to Ben. What are the gift and estate tax consequences in the following situations?
   a. Derrick retains the right to revoke the trust.
   b. The trust is irrevocable, but Derrick retains the right to add or delete beneficiaries.
   c. The trust is irrevocable, but Derrick retains the right to alter the amount of income or corpus allocated to any beneficiary, including to add beneficiaries.
   d. The trust is irrevocable, but Derrick retains the right to add income or remainder beneficiaries to the trust in his will.
   e. The trust is irrevocable, but Derrick retains the right to terminate the trust. Upon termination, the corpus goes to Ben.
   f. The trust is irrevocable, but Derrick *as Trustee* retains the right to invest funds, to sell trust property, and to borrow money.
2. Same as 1.a. except that Derrick may revoke only with the consent of Emma, his spouse. What if Derrick can only revoke with the consent of Ben?
3. Derrick establishes an irrevocable trust to pay the income to Anita for life with the remainder to Ben. Derrick is the sole Trustee. What are the gift and estate tax consequences of the following arrangements?
   a. Derrick retains the power to accumulate income or distribute it to Anita. Accumulated income is added to the corpus.
   b. Derrick retains the power to distribute corpus to Anita to maintain Anita in the station in life to which Anita is accustomed.

    c. Derrick retains the power to distribute corpus to Anita for health, education, welfare, and support.

    d. Derrick retains the power to distribute corpus to Anita in an emergency.

    e. Derrick retains the power to distribute corpus to Anita if Derrick decides that it is in Anita's best interests.

    f. Derrick retains the power to distribute corpus to Anita for her welfare and happiness.

    g. Derrick retains the power to distribute corpus to Anita as is necessary and proper.

4. Same as 3.a. except that Derrick is not the Trustee. What are the estate tax consequences of the following?

    a. Derrick has the power to appoint a Successor Trustee if a vacancy occurs. Derrick cannot appoint himself as Trustee. No vacancy occurs before Derrick dies.

       What if a vacancy had occurred and Derrick had filled it?

    b. Derrick has the power to remove a Trustee for cause and appoint another Trustee other than himself. Derrick dies without having exercised the power.

    c. Derrick has the power to remove a Trustee for any reason or for no reason and to appoint another Trustee other than himself. Derrick dies without having exercised the power.

    d. How would your answers change if Derrick could appoint himself as Trustee?

5. Derrick established an irrevocable trust with Friendly National Bank as Trustee to pay the income to Anita for life and the remainder to Anita's issue. Derrick retains the right to designate new beneficiaries if Anita dies before her oldest child reaches age 35. What are the estate tax consequences if Derrick dies survived by Anita?

6. Diane established an irrevocable trust and appointed herself as one of three Trustees. The Trustees have discretion to accumulate income or distribute it to Diane's three children. Accumulated income is added to the trust property. The Trustees must agree on any accumulation or distribution of income. At the death of all Diane's children, the trust property is to be distributed to their issue. There is a provision for appointment of Successor Trustees if any Trustee should die or resign.

    a. What are the estate tax consequences if Diane is serving as Trustee at the time of her death?

    b. What if Diane had not appointed herself as Trustee but was appointed by the other Trustees as a Successor Trustee and was serving as Trustee at the time of her death?

7. Is anything in Debra's gross estate in the following situations? If so, what?

    a. Debra creates an irrevocable trust by transferring $1 million to Friendly National Bank as Trustee, to pay the income to her spouse,

Sam, for his life. At Sam's death, the trust property is to be distributed to their surviving issue. On the same day, Sam creates an irrevocable trust by transferring $1 million to Friendly National Bank as Trustee to pay the income to Debra for life. At Debra's death, the trust property is to be distributed to their surviving issue. What if Debra transferred $3 million to the trust she created and Sam only transferred $1 million to the trust he created? What if they transferred the same amounts, but Sam created his trust three months later? Six months later? Two years later?

b. Debra creates an irrevocable trust by transferring $1 million to Friendly National Bank as Trustee, to pay the income to her mother, Mary, for her life, and then to pay the income to her spouse, Sam, for his life. At Sam's death, the trust property is to be distributed to their surviving issue. On the same day, Sam creates an irrevocable trust by transferring $1 million to Friendly National Bank as Trustee to pay the income to Mary for her life, and then the income to Debra for life. At Debra's death, the trust property is to be distributed to their surviving issue.

What if Sam did not create a life estate in Mary, but only in Debra?

c. Debra and Sam are married and have four children. Neither has any other children. Debra creates an irrevocable trust by transferring $1 million to Friendly National Bank as Trustee, to pay the income to her children, for their lives. When the last surviving child dies, the trust property is to be distributed to their surviving issue. Debra gives Sam the right to modify the trust or to terminate it. On termination, the trust property will be distributed to the beneficiaries in proportion to their actuarial values in the trust. On the same day, Sam creates an irrevocable trust by transferring $1 million to Friendly National Bank as Trustee to pay the income to his children, for life. When the last surviving child dies, the trust property is to be distributed to their surviving issue. Sam gives Debra the right to modify the trust or to terminate it. On termination, the trust property will be distributed to the beneficiaries in proportion to their actuarial values in the trust.

d. Would the results in 7.a., b., and c. be the same if Sam were Debra's brother and they created the trusts for the benefit of each other's children?

8. Donald and Ronald are twin brothers. Each is married and has three children. What are the gift or estate tax consequences in the following situations?

a. Donald gives each of his children and each of his nieces and nephews $11,000 each year. Ronald does the same.

b. Donald creates an irrevocable trust with Friendly National Bank as Trustee. He gives each of his children and each of his nieces and nephews the right to withdraw the lesser of $11,000 or their proportionate amount contributed to the trust in that tax year. Donald contributes $66,000 to the trust each year. Ronald creates an irrevocable trust with Friendly National Bank as Trustee. He gives each of his children and each of his nieces and nephews the right to withdraw the lesser of $11,000 or their proportionate amount contributed to the trust in that tax year. Ronald contributes $66,000 to the trust each year.

c.   Donald creates irrevocable trusts for each of his children under §2503(c) and appoints Ronald as Trustee. Ronald creates irrevocable trusts for each of his children under §2503(c) and appoints Donald as Trustee. Donald dies when all of the children are less than 20 years old.

9.   For the most part, the gift completion rules in reg. §25.2511-2 coordinate with §§2036(a)(2) and 2038(a)(1). These rules reflect a "hard to complete" transfer tax regime, *i.e.*, one where the transfers are taxed at death rather than at the time of the initial gift. The alternative, *i.e.*, an "easy to complete" transfer tax regime, would tax transfers at the time of the initial transfer. *See* articles cited at pages 240-241. Which regime is better? Why?

D.   RETENTION OF BUSINESS INTERESTS
IRC §§2036, 2701

1.   *Retention of Voting Rights*

United States v. Byrum
408 U.S. 125 (1972)

Mr. Justice POWELL delivered the opinion of the Court.

Decedent, Milliken C. Byrum, created in 1958 an irrevocable trust to which he transferred shares of stock in three closely held corporations. Prior to transfer, he owned at least 71% of the outstanding stock of each corporation. The beneficiaries were his children or, in the event of their death before the termination of the trust, their surviving children. The trust instrument specified that there be a corporate trustee. Byrum designated as sole trustee an independent corporation, Huntington National Bank. The trust agreement vested in the trustee broad and detailed powers with respect to the control and management of the trust property. These powers were exercisable in the trustee's sole discretion, subject to rights reserved by Byrum: (i) to vote the shares of unlisted stock held in the trust estate; (ii) to disapprove the sale or transfer of any trust assets, including the shares transferred to the trust; (iii) to approve investments and reinvestments; and (iv) to remove the trustee and "designate another corporate Trustee to serve as successor." . . .

When he died in 1964, Byrum owned less than 50% of the common stock in two of the corporations and 59% in the third. The trust had retained the shares transferred to it, with the result that Byrum had continued to have the right to vote not less than 71% of the common stock in each of the three corporations. There was minority stockholders, unrelated to Byrum, in each corporation.

Following Byrum's death, the Commissioner of Internal Revenue determined that the transferred stock was properly included within Byrum's gross estate under §2036(a). . . . The Commissioner determined that the stock transferred into the trust should be included in Byrum's gross estate because of the rights reserved by him in the trust agreement. It was asserted that his right to vote the transferred shares and to veto any sale thereof by the trustee, together with the ownership of other shares, enabled Byrum to retain the "enjoyment of . . . the property," and also allowed him to determine the flow of income to the trust and thereby "designate the persons who shall . . . enjoy . . . the income. . . ."

I

The Government relies primarily on its claim, made under §2036(a)(2), that Byrum retained the right to designate the persons who shall enjoy the income from the transferred property. The argument is a complicated one. By retaining voting control over the corporations whose stock was transferred, Byrum was in a position to select the corporate directors. He could retain this position by not selling the shares he owned and by vetoing any sale by the trustee of the transferred shares. These rights, it is said, gave him control over corporate dividend policy. By increasing, decreasing, or stopping dividends completely, it is argued that Byrum could "regulate the flow of income to the trust" and thereby shift or defer the beneficial enjoyment of trust income between the present beneficiaries and the remaindermen. The sum of this retained power is said to be tantamount to a grantor-trustee's power to accumulate income in the trust, which this Court has recognized constitutes the power to designate the persons who shall enjoy the income from transferred property.

At the outset we observe that this Court has never held that trust property must be included in a settlor's gross estate solely because the settlor retained the power to manage trust assets. On the contrary, since our decision in Reinecke v. Northern Trust Co., 278 U.S. 339 (1929), it has been recognized that a settlor's retention of broad powers of management does not necessarily subject an inter vivos trust to the federal estate tax. Although there was no statutory analogue to §2036(a)(2) when *Northern Trust* was decided, several lower court decisions decided after the enactment of the predecessor of §2036(a)(2) have upheld the settlor's right to exercise managerial powers without incurring estate-tax liability. In Estate of King v. Commissioner, 37 T.C. 973 (1962), a settlor reserved the power to direct the trustee in the management and investment of trust assets. The Government argued that the settlor was thereby empowered to cause investments to be made in such a manner as to control significantly the flow of income into the trust. The Tax Court rejected this argument, and held for the taxpayer. . . .

Essentially the power retained by Byrum is the same managerial power retained by the settlors in *Northern Trust* and in *King*. Although neither case controls this one . . . the existence of such precedents carries weight. The holding of *Northern Trust*, that the settlor of a trust may retain broad powers of management without adverse estate-tax consequences, may have been relied upon in the drafting of hundreds of inter vivos trusts. The modification of this principle now sought by the Government could have a seriously adverse impact, especially upon settlors (and their estates) who happen to have been "controlling" stockholders of a closely held corporation. Courts properly have been reluctant to depart from an interpretation of tax law which has been generally accepted when the departure could have potentially far-reaching consequences. When a principle of taxation requires reexamination, Congress is better equipped than a court to define precisely the type of conduct which results in tax consequences. When courts readily undertake such tasks, taxpayers may not rely with assurance on what appear to be established rules lest they be subsequently overturned. Legislative enactments, on the other hand, although not always free from ambiguity, at least afford the taxpayers advance warning. . . .

In our view, and for the purposes of this case, *O'Malley* adds nothing to the statute itself. The facts in that case were clearly within the ambit of what is now §2036(a). That section requires that the settlor must have "retained for his life . . . (2) the right . . . to designate the persons who shall possess or enjoy the property or the income therefrom." *O'Malley* was covered precisely by the statute for two reasons: (1) there the settlor had reserved a legal right, set forth in the trust instrument; and (2) this right expressly authorized the settlor, "in conjunction" with others, to accumulate income and thereby "to designate" the persons to enjoy it.

It must be conceded that Byrum reserved no such "right" in the trust instrument or otherwise. The term "right," certainly when used in a tax statute, must be given its normal and customary meaning. It connotes an ascertainable and legally enforceable power, such as that involved in *O'Malley*. Here, the right ascribed to Byrum was the power to use his majority position and influence over the corporate directors to "regulate the flow of dividends" to the trust. That "right" was neither ascertainable nor legally enforceable and hence was not a right in any normal sense of that term.

Byrum did retain the legal right to vote shares held by the trust and to veto investments and reinvestments. But the corporate trustee alone, not Byrum, had the right to pay out or withhold income and thereby to designate who among the beneficiaries enjoyed such income. Whatever power Byrum may have possessed with respect to the flow of income into the trust was derived not from an enforceable legal right specified in the trust instrument, but from the fact that he could elect a majority of the directors of the three corporations. The power to elect the directors conferred no legal right to command them to pay or not to pay dividends. A majority shareholder has a fiduciary duty not to misuse his power by promoting his personal interests at the expense of corporate interests. Moreover, the directors also have a fiduciary duty to promote the interests of the corporation. However great Byrum's influence may have been with the corporate directors, their responsibilities were to all stockholders and were enforceable according to legal standards entirely unrelated to the needs of the trust or to Byrum's desires with respect thereto.

The Government seeks to equate the de facto position of a controlling stockholder with the legally enforceable "right" specified by the statute. Retention of corporate control (through the right to vote the shares) is said to be "tantamount to the power to accumulate income" in the trust which resulted in estate-tax consequences in *O'Malley*. The Government goes on to assert that "(t)hrough exercise of that retained power, (Byrum) could increase or decrease corporate dividends . . . and thereby shift or defer the beneficial enjoyment of trust income." This approach seems to us not only to depart from the specific statutory language, but also to misconceive the realities of corporate life.

There is no reason to suppose that the three corporations controlled by Byrum were other than typical small businesses. The customary vicissitudes of such enterprises—bad years; product obsolescence; new competition; disastrous litigation; new, inhibiting Government regulations; even bankruptcy—prevent any certainty or predictability as to earnings or dividends. There is no assurance that a small corporation will have a flow of net earnings or that income earned will in fact be available for dividends. Thus, Byrum's alleged de facto "power to control the flow of dividends" to the trust was subject to business and economic variables over which he had little or no control.

Even where there are corporate earnings, the legal power to declare dividends is vested solely in the corporate board. In making decisions with respect to dividends, the board must consider a number of factors. It must balance the expectation of stockholders to reasonable dividends when earned against corporate needs for retention of earnings. The first responsibility of the board is to safeguard corporate financial viability for the long term. This means, among other things, the retention of sufficient earnings to assure adequate working capital as well as resources for retirement of debt, for replacement and modernization of plant and equipment, and for growth and expansion. The nature of a corporation's business, as well as the policies and long-range plans of management, are also relevant to dividend payment decisions. Directors of a closely held, small corporation must bear in mind the relatively limited access of such an enterprise to capital markets. This may require a more conservative policy with respect to dividends than would expected of an established corporation with securities listed on national exchanges. . . .

We conclude that Byrum did not have an unconstrained de facto power to regulate the flow of dividends to the trust, much less the "right" to designate who was to enjoy the income from trust property. His ability to affect, but not control, trust income, was a qualitatively different power from that of the settlor in *O'Malley*, who had a specific and enforceable right to control the income paid to the beneficiaries. Even had Byrum managed to flood the trust with income, he had no way of compelling the trustee to pay it out rather than accumulate it. Nor could he prevent the trustee from making payments from other trust assets, although admittedly there were few of these at the time of Byrum's death. We cannot assume, however, that no other assets would come into the trust from reinvestments or other gifts.

We find no merit to the Government's contention that Byrum's de facto "control," subject as it was to the economic and legal constraints set forth above, was tantamount to the right to designate the persons who shall enjoy trust income, specified by §2036(a)(2).

II

The Government asserts an alternative ground for including the shares transferred to the trust within Byrum's gross estate. It argues that by retaining control, Byrum guaranteed himself continued employment and remuneration, as well as the right to determine whether and when the corporations would be liquidated or merged. Byrum is thus said to have retained "the . . . enjoyment of . . . the property" making it includable within his gross estate under §2036(a)(1). The Government concedes that the retention of the voting rights of an "unimportant minority interest" would not require inclusion of the transferred shares under §2036(a)(1). It argues, however, "where the cumulative effect of the retained powers and the rights flowing from the shares not placed in trust leaves the grantor in control of a close corporation, and assures that control for his lifetime, he has retained the 'enjoyment' of the transferred stock.". . .

The Government points to the retention of two "benefits." The first of these, the power to liquidate or merge, is not a present benefit; rather, it is a speculative and contingent benefit which may or may not be realized. Nor is the probability of continued employment and compensation the substantial "enjoyment of . . . (the transferred) property" within the meaning of the statute. The dominant stockholder in a closely held corporation, if he is active and productive, is likely to hold a senior position and to enjoy the advantage of a significant voice in his own compensation. These are inevitable facts of the free-enterprise system, but the influence and capability of a controlling stockholder to favor himself are not without constraints. Where there are minority stockholders, as in this case, directors may be held accountable if their employment, compensation, and retention of officers violate their duty to act reasonably in the best interest of the corporation and all of its stockholders. Moreover, this duty is policed, albeit indirectly, by the Internal Revenue Service, which disallows the deduction of unreasonable compensation paid to a corporate executive as a business expense. We conclude that Byrum's retention of voting control was not the retention of the enjoyment of the transferred property within the meaning of the statute. . . .

Judgment affirmed.

Congress responded to the *Byrum* decision by enacting §2036(b), which provides that retention of the right to vote shares of a controlled corporation will be considered retention of the enjoyment of the transferred shares. A controlled corporation is defined as one where the decedent had the right to vote stock possession at least 20 percent of the total combined voting power of all classes of stock. In determining this right to vote, §318 applies to attribute stock owned by certain family members and entities to the decedent. While the scope of *Byrum* is thus limited by §2036(b), it continues to influence other cases involving §2036(a). The Tax Court invoked *Byrum*, emphasizing the fiduciary responsibility of corporate directors and majority shareholders, to reject the IRS claim that forgoing the right to corporate dividends creates a taxable gift. *See, e.g.,* Hutchens Non-Marital Trust v. Commissioner, 66 T.C.M. (CCH) 1599 (1993); Daniels v. Commissioner, 68 T.C.M. (CCH) 1310 (1994). In Estate of Strangi v. Commissioner, however, the Tax Court distinguished *Byrum* in applying §2036(a)(1) and (a)(2) to a family limited partnership. 85 T.C.M. (CCH) 1331 (2003), *infra* at page 292.

2. *Retention of Income from Business Assets*

The retention of income from a business occurs more frequently than the retention of voting rights. In the typical situation, Mom owns all the common stock of Family, Inc. She plans to retire and shift ownership of the company to her children, but she wants to retain a flow of income from the company. So she transfers the common stock back to Family, Inc. in exchange for new shares of common stock and new shares of preferred stock. She defines the preferred stock to have sufficient rights that it absorbs most of the current value of Family, Inc. and guarantees a flow of income through dividends. She then transfers the common stock to her children. The common stock has very little value, so the gift tax consequences are minimal or nonexistent. The common stock, however, carries with it the potential for future growth in the company. If this arrangement is successful, Mom is able to freeze the value of her estate and transfer the future appreciation in Family, Inc. to her children tax-free.

The IRS addressed this issue in Revenue Ruling 83-120, ruling that the common stock had significant value because of its potential for future appreciation. 1983-2 C.B. 170. This was not entirely satisfactory, and Congress then enacted §2036(c), which included in Mom's gross estate the date of death value of Family, Inc. if she had a substantial interest in the enterprise, transferred property with a disproportionately high share of potential future appreciation, and retained an income interest or other rights in the enterprise. The scope of §2036(c) extended well beyond the problem it was designed to address, and its complexities baffled even the most sophisticated. Congress quickly remedied its error by repealing §2036(c) and enacting Chapter 14. Section 2701 now governs the valuation of transfers of specified interests in corporations and partnerships, including the typical estate freezing technique described above. Section 2701 applies (1) to the transfer of an interest in a corporation or a partnership, (2) to a member of the transferor's family, (3) where the transferor or an applicable family member (4) retains "any applicable retained interest" except for interests for which market quotations are readily available. In other words, §2701 applies to the transfers of interests in closely held businesses from older generation family members to younger generation family members, but only if the older generation family member retains a distribution right (*i.e.*, the right to dividends) or a liquidation, put, call, or conversion right. Section 2701 specifies that the applicable retained interest will have a zero value unless it is the right to a qualified payment, which is a dividend payable on a periodic basis under cumulative preferred stock determined at a fixed rate. It also mandates that the junior equity interest have a minimum value of ten percent of the total value of all equity interests plus the total amount of indebtedness of the entity to the older generation family members. Sections 2703 and 2704 also affect valuation of business interests by disregarding certain rights and restrictions. As a result, the ability to transfer business interests at substantially reduced transfer tax costs has been significantly curtailed. Section 2701 also ensures that the owners of the preferred stock actually receive their dividends instead of allowing that money to remain in the corporation and, thus, increase the value of the common stock.

3. Family Limited Partnerships

The emergence of new forms of business entities has given rise to new estate planning techniques. The family limited partnership has come into vogue as a means to decrease the value of the decedent's property and thus minimize or eliminate transfer tax consequences. This device requires the decedent to transfer substantially all of his property to a limited partnership and then gives partnership interests to younger generation family members. Those gifts will have reduced values because they represent only minority interests in the partnership. Minority discounts will also apply to the value of the decedent's partnership interest at death.

If a decedent ignores the formalities of doing business as the partnership, however, the property is likely to be included in his gross estate by §2036(a)(1).

Estate of Schauerhamer v. Commissioner
73 T.C.M. (CCH) 2855 (1997)

FOLEY, Judge:
. . . In late November of 1990, decedent was diagnosed with colon cancer. In early December of that year, she retained an attorney, Travis Bowen, to set her business affairs in order. . . . On December 31, 1990, decedent, along with her

three children and their spouses, met with Mr. Bowen at his office. Mr. Bowen explained that three family limited partnerships would be formed and that David, Sandra, and Diane [and decedent] would each become a [limited partner and a] general partner in a partnership. He explained that after the limited partnerships were formed, decedent's business holdings would be transferred to the partnerships, with each partnership receiving an undivided one-third interest in the transferred assets. He further advised that, after the partnerships were formed and funded, decedent would transfer limited partnership interests to her children and their family members. On December 31, 1990, three substantially identical limited partnership agreements were executed. . . .

The partnership agreements set forth numerous terms and covenants with respect to the partnerships. . . . In addition, decedent was named the managing partner of each partnership. The partnership agreements provided that decedent, in her capacity as managing partner, had "full power to manage and conduct the Partnership's business operation in its usual course." From the time the partnerships were formed until shortly before decedent's death, she managed the partnership assets. . . . On December 31, 1990, and on November 5, 1991, decedent transferred some of her business assets, in undivided one-third shares, to the partnerships. The assets included real estate, partnership interests, and notes receivable. . . .

The partnership agreements each required that all income from the partnership be deposited into a partnership account. Shortly after the partnerships were formed, each partnership's initial capital was deposited into partnership bank accounts. Decedent deposited, into an account jointly held by her and David, all partnership income and income from other sources. She did not maintain any records to account separately for partnership and nonpartnership funds. Decedent utilized the account as her personal checking account, and from this account she paid personal and partnership expenses. . . .

In the notice of deficiency issued to petitioner, respondent determined a $947,049 deficiency . . . based on respondent's determination that the value of the assets contributed to the partnerships was includable in decedent's gross estate. . . . Respondent contends that the value of the assets transferred to the purported partnerships is includable in decedent's gross estate pursuant to section 2033, 2036(a)(1), or 2038. We conclude that the value of the assets is includable pursuant to section 2036(a)(1). As a result, we do not address sections 2033 and 2038.

Section 2036(a)(1) provides that a decedent's gross estate includes the value of all property interests transferred (other than for full and adequate consideration in money or money's worth) by a decedent during her life where she has retained for life the possession or enjoyment of the property, or the right to the income from the property. The term "enjoyment" refers to the economic benefits from the property. Estate of Gilman v. Commissioner, 65 T.C. 296, 307, 1975 WL 3005 (1975), *affd.* 547 F.2d 32 (2d Cir. 1976). Thus, "Enjoyment as used in the death tax statute is not a term of art, but is synonymous with substantial present economic benefit." McNichol's Estate v. Commissioner, 265 F.2d 667, 671 (3d Cir. 1959), *affg.* 29 T.C. 1179, 1958 WL 1158 (1958).

Retained enjoyment may exist where there is an express or implied understanding at the time of the transfer that the transferror will retain the economic benefits of the property. Guynn v. United States, 437 F.2d 1148, 1150 (4th Cir. 1971); Estate of Rapelje v. Commissioner, 73 T.C. 82, 86, 1979 WL 3799 (1979). The understanding need not be legally enforceable to trigger section 2036(a)(1). Estate of Rapelje v. Commissioner, *supra*. The retention of a property's income stream after the property has been transferred is "very clear evidence that the decedent did indeed retain 'possession or enjoyment.'" Estate of Hendry v. Commissioner, 62 T.C. 861, 873, 1974 WL 2655 (1974). Whether there was an implied agreement is a question of fact to be determined with reference to the facts and circumstances of the transfer and the subsequent use of the property. *Id.* at 872.

The facts of this case establish that an implied agreement existed among the partners. Decedent owned the assets subsequently transferred to the partnerships and collected the income these assets generated. On December 31, 1990, decedent formed the partnerships and contributed some of her business holdings. The partnership agreements required that each partnership maintain a bank account, and that all income from the partnerships be deposited into these accounts. After the formation of the partnerships, a partnership bank account was opened in the name of each partnership, and each partnership's $100 of initial capital was deposited into the account. As the partnerships earned income, however, decedent, in violation of the partnership agreements, did not deposit the income into the partnership accounts. Instead, she deposited the income into the account she utilized as her personal checking account, where it was commingled with income from other sources. Such deposits of income from transferred property into a personal account are highly indicative of "possession or enjoyment." *Id.*

David, Diane, and Sandra testified at trial that they were aware that decedent was depositing the funds into her personal, rather than a partnership, account. Moreover, they acknowledged that the formation of the partnerships was merely a way to enable decedent to assign interests in the partnership assets to members of her family. The assets and income would be managed by decedent exactly as they had been managed in the past. Where a decedent's relationship to transferred assets remains the same after as it was before the transfer, section 2036(a)(1) requires that the value of the assets be included in the decedent's gross estate. Guynn v. United States, *supra*; Estate of Hendry v. Commissioner, *supra* at 874.... As a result, the value of the partnership assets is includable in decedent's gross estate pursuant to section 2036(a)(1).

Even if the decedent observes the formalities, the assets of the limited partnership will be included in his gross estate under §2036(a)(1) if the decedent retains possession or enjoyment of the assets or the right to income from them. Courts will imply an agreement to retain income from the decedent's course of conduct. In the following case, the court also held that §2036(a)(2) applied because of terms in the limited partnership agreement.

Estate of Strangi v. Commissioner
85 T.C.M. (CCH) 1331 (2003)

COHEN, J.

This matter is before the Court on remand from the Court of Appeals for the Fifth Circuit for further consideration consistent with its opinion in Estate of Strangi v. Commissioner, 293 F.3d 279 (5th Cir. 2002) (*Strangi II*), *affg. in part and revg. and remanding in part* 115 T.C. 478 (2000) (*Strangi I*). The issue for decision on remand is whether the value of property transferred by Albert Strangi (decedent) to the Strangi Family Limited Partnership (SFLP) and Stranco, Inc. (Stranco), is includable in his gross estate pursuant to section 2036(a). . . .

[Decedent had four children: Jeanne, Rosalie, Albert T., and John. In 1985, Rosalie (Mrs. Gulig) married Michael J. Gulig, an attorney. On July 19, 1988, decedent executed a power of attorney naming Mr. Gulig as his attorney in fact and giving him broad and comprehensive powers. In 1993, after decedent was diagnosed with cancer and a brain disorder, Mr. Gulig took over decedent's affairs pursuant to this power of attorney. Mr. Gulig also developed a close personal relationship with decedent. On August 12, 1994, Mr. Gulig, acting as decedent's attorney in fact, formed SFLP, a Texas limited partnership, and Stranco, a Texas corporation, as its corporate general partner.]

By a series of transfer documents, Mr. Gulig assigned to SFLP property of decedent with a fair market value of $9,876,929, constituting approximately 98 percent of decedent's wealth, in exchange for a 99-percent limited partnership interest. The contributed property included decedent's interest in specified real estate (including the residence occupied by decedent), securities, accrued interest and dividends, insurance policies, an annuity, receivables, and partnership interests. About 75 percent of the contributed value was attributable to cash and securities. . . . Decedent purchased 47 percent of Stranco for $49,350, and Mrs. Gulig purchased the remaining 53 percent for $55,650 on behalf of herself and her three siblings. . . . Stranco's articles of incorporation named decedent and the Strangi children as the initial five directors. On August 17, 1994, the Strangi children and Mr. Gulig . . . authorized the corporate president to execute a management agreement employing Mr. Gulig. . . .

Decedent died of cancer on October 14, 1994, at the age of 81. . . . After its formation, various monetary outlays were made from SFLP. From September 1993 until his death, decedent required 24-hour home health care that was provided by Olsten Healthcare (Olsten) and supplemented by Ms. Stone.

During this time and while assisting decedent, Ms. Stone injured her back. The resultant back surgery was paid for by SFLP. SFLP also paid nearly $40,000 in 1994 for funeral expenses, estate administration expenses, and related debts of decedent, including a $19,810.28 check to Olsten for nursing services. SFLP then paid more than $65,000 in 1995 and 1996 for estate expenses and a specific bequest to decedent's sister. In July 1995, SFLP distributed $3,187,800 to decedent's estate for Federal estate and State inheritance taxes. When such disbursements were made to or for the benefit of decedent or his estate, Stranco received corresponding and proportionate sums either in cash or in the form of adjusting journal entries. For accounting purposes, certain amounts expended by SFLP were initially recorded on its books as advances to, and accounts receivable from, partners. SFLP also accrued rent on the residence occupied by decedent and reported the rental income on its 1994 income tax return. The accrued amount was paid in January 1997. . . .

On January 17, 1996, a Form 706, [was] . . . filed on behalf of decedent's estate. . . . The value reported on the Form 706 for the gross estate was $6,823,582, which included $6,560,730 for decedent's interest in SFLP and $24,551 for his stock in Stranco. The total value of the property held by SFLP as of the date of death was $11,100,922, to which discounts were applied in calculating the reported fair market value. The Form 706 also reflected other assets of $238,301 (including household and personal items, vehicles, securities, certain receivables, and bank account balances totaling $762) and claimed deductions of $43,280 for debts of decedent (including $5,161 for rents to SFLP) and $107,108 for expenses.

In a statutory notice dated December 1, 1998, respondent determined a deficiency in Federal estate tax of $2,545,826 and an alternative deficiency in Federal gift tax of $1,629,947. The estate tax deficiency resulted in large part from respondent's conclusion that decedent's interest in SFLP should be increased by $4,386,613 (to $10,947,343) and his interest in Stranco should be increased by $29,009 (to $53,560).

The proceedings in *Strangi I* were initiated in response to the foregoing notice of deficiency. Prior to trial, respondent attempted by motion to raise section 2036 as an issue. *Strangi I* at 486. That motion was denied as untimely. *Id.* With respect to the remaining issues, we held in *Strangi I* at 486-493: (1) The partnership was valid under State law and would be recognized for estate tax purposes; (2) section 2703 did not apply to the partnership agreement; (3) the transfer of assets to SFLP was not a taxable gift; and (4) decedent's interests in SFLP and Stranco should be valued using the discounts applied by respondent's expert. [On appeal, Court of Appeals for the Fifth Circuit reversed and remanded on the section 2036(a) issue. (*Strangi II.*)] . . . Over petitioner's objection, leave was granted for respondent's amendment to answer and a second amendment to answer raising section 2036. . . .

Hence, to summarize, the SFLP agreement named Stranco managing general partner with the sole discretion to determine distributions. The Stranco shareholders, including decedent (through Mr. Gulig), then acted together to delegate such authority to Mr. Gulig under the management agreement. Decedent's attorney in fact thereby stood in a position to make distribution decisions. Mrs. Gulig effectuated these decisions by signing checks to the recipients so designated.

I. Section 2036(a)(1)

Section 2036(a)(1) provides for inclusion of transferred property with respect to which the decedent retained, by express or implied agreement, possession, enjoyment, or the right to income. Enjoyment in this context is equated with present economic benefit.

A. Right to Income

As a threshold matter, we observe that our analysis above of the express documents suggests inclusion of the contributed property under section 2036(a)(1) based on the "right to the income" criterion, without need further to probe for an implied agreement regarding other benefits such as possession or enjoyment. The governing documents contain no restrictions that would preclude decedent himself, acting through Mr. Gulig, from being designated as a recipient of income from SFLP and Stranco. Such scenario is consistent with the reach of the right to income phrase as we described it in Estate of Pardee v. Commissioner, 49 T.C. 140, 148 (1967):

> section 2036(a)(1) refers not only to the possession or enjoyment of property but also to "right to the income" from property. The section does not require that the transferor pull the "string" or even intend to pull the string on the transferred property; it only requires that the string exist. *See* McNichol's Estate v. Commissioner, 265 F.2d 667, 671 (C.A.3, 1959), *affirming* 29 T.C. 1179 (1958). . . .

B. Possession or Enjoyment

The facts of this case [also] support the finding of an implied agreement for retained possession or enjoyment. We have previously considered implicit retention of these benefits under section 2036(a)(1) in situations involving family limited partnerships in Estate of Reichardt v. Commissioner, 114 T.C. 144 (2000); Estate of Thompson v. Commissioner, T.C. Memo.2002-246; Estate of Harper v. Commissioner, T.C. Memo.2002-121; and Estate of Schauerhamer v. Commissioner, T.C. Memo.1997-242. Although the instant case is based on limited post-transfer history, due in part to decedent's death only 2 months after creation of the partnership, we conclude that the reasoning underlying those opinions directs a like result here. Fundamentally, the preponderance of the evidence shows that decedent as a practical matter retained the same relationship to his assets that he had before formation of SFLP and Stranco.

Circumstances that have been found probative of an implicitly retained interest under section 2036(a)(1) include transfer of the majority of the decedent's assets, continued occupation of transferred property, commingling of personal and entity assets, disproportionate distributions, use of entity funds for personal expenses, and testamentary characteristics of the arrangement. Guynn v. United States, 437 F.2d at 1150; Estate of Reichardt v. Commissioner, *supra* at 152-154; Estate of Thompson v. Commissioner, *supra;* Estate of Harper v. Commissioner, *supra;* Estate of Trotter v. Commissioner, T.C. Memo. 2001-250; Estate of Schauerhamer v. Commissioner, *supra.*

At the outset, we acknowledge that, in contrast to certain of the prior cases, the participants involved in the SFLP/Stranco arrangement generally proceeded such that "the proverbial 'i's were dotted' and 't's were crossed.'" *Strangi I* at 486. Steps were taken to abide by the formal terms of the structure created. Such measures may give SFLP and Stranco sufficient substance to be recognized as legal entities in the context of valuation, which requires assumption of a hypothetical buyer and seller. They do not preclude implicit retention by decedent of economic benefit from the transferred property for purposes of section 2036(a)(1).

First, we cannot lose sight of the fact that decedent contributed approximately 98 percent of his wealth, including his residence, to the SFLP/Stranco arrangement. . . . [T]he relative dearth of liquefied (decedent's Form 706 showed two bank accounts with funds totaling $762), as opposed to "liquefiable," assets persuades us that decedent and his children and Mr. Gulig all expected that SFLP and Stranco would be a primary source of decedent's liquidity. It is unreasonable to expect that decedent would be forced to rely on sale of assets to meet his basic costs of living.

A second feature highly probative under section 2036(a)(1) is decedent's continued physical possession of his residence after its transfer to SFLP. The estate maintains that any otherwise negative implications of this circumstance are neutralized by the fact that SFLP "charged Mr. Strangi rent" on occupancy of the home and reported rental income on its 1994 tax return. Decedent likewise reported a rent obligation on his estate tax return. For accounting purposes, the accrued rent was recorded by SFLP on its books. Yet the accrued amount was not paid until January 1997. A residential lessor dealing at arm's length would hardly be content merely to accrue a rental obligation for eventual payment more than 2 years later. As we have remarked, accounting entries alone are of small moment in belying the existence of an agreement for retained possession and enjoyment. Estate of Reichardt v. Commissioner, 114 T.C. at 154-155; Estate of Harper v. Commissioner, T.C. Memo. 2002-121.

Concerning factors that relate to use of entity funds, the estate emphasizes that each disbursement for decedent or his estate was accompanied by a pro rata allotment to Stranco. Where, as here, the only interest in the partnership other than that held by the decedent is de minimis, a pro rata payment is hardly more than a token in nature. In these circumstances, pro rata disbursements are insufficient to negate the probability that the decedent retained economic enjoyment of his or her assets. After all, distributing 1 percent to Stranco would not in any substantial way operate to curb decedent's ability to benefit from SFLP property. Accordingly, we direct our attention to the purpose, as opposed to the mechanics, of partnership distributions and expenditures.

The record reveals several instances where SFLP expended funds in response to a need of decedent or his estate. SFLP paid for Ms. Stone's back surgery to alleviate an injury she sustained in caring for decedent prior to the formation of SFLP. In 1994, SFLP expended nearly $40,000 for funeral expenses, estate administration, and related debts, including a $19,810.28 check to Olsten to pay for nursing services rendered to decedent before his death. These sums were followed in 1995 and 1996 by further payment of over $65,000 for estate expenses and a specific bequest. SFLP also disbursed approximately $3 million directed toward decedent's estate and inheritance taxes. . . .

Regarding testamentary characteristics, the SFLP/Stranco arrangement also bears greater resemblance to one man's estate plan than to any sort of arm's-length, joint enterprise. As in Estate of Harper v. Commissioner, *supra,* "the largely unilateral nature of the formation, the extent and type of the assets contributed thereto, and decedent's personal situation are indicative." Mr. Gulig established the entities using [standardized] documents with little, if any, input from other family members. The contributed property included the majority of decedent's assets in general and his investments, a prime concern of estate planning, in particular. Decedent was advanced in age and suffering from serious health conditions. Furthermore, as discussed in *Strangi I* at 485-486, the purpose of the partnership arrangement was not to provide a joint investment vehicle for the management of decedent's assets, but was consistent with testamentary intent.

Moreover, the crucial characteristic is that virtually nothing beyond formal title changed in decedent's relationship to his assets. Mr. Gulig managed decedent's affairs both before and after the transfer. Decedent's children did not obtain a meaningful economic stake in the property during decedent's life. They raised no objections or concerns when large sums were advanced for expenditures of decedent or his estate, thus implying an understanding that decedent's access thereto would not be restricted. . . .

Hence, the preponderance of the evidence establishes that decedent retained possession of, enjoyment of, or the right to income from the property transferred within the meaning of section 2036(a)(1).

II. Section 2036(a)(2)

Although we have held *supra* that section 2036(a)(1) requires the estate to include the value of the transferred assets in the gross estate for Federal estate tax purposes, the parties have argued extensively over the issue of whether section 2036(a)(2) applies. Consequently, we address the applicability of section 2036(a)(2) to the instant case. As stated above, section 2036(a)(2) mandates inclusion in the gross estate of transferred property with respect to which the decedent retained the right to designate the persons who shall possess or enjoy the property or its income. This provision was interpreted by the Supreme Court in United States v. Byrum, 408 U.S. 125 (1972), and both parties devote a significant portion of their respective arguments to the implications of that decision. We address these arguments as an alternative to our conclusions concerning section 2036(a)(1) and with particular consideration of the facts of this case. . . .

A. Legally Enforceable Rights

On [the facts of this case], decedent can properly be described as retaining a right to designate who shall enjoy property and income from SFLP and Stranco within the meaning of section 2036(a)(2). In this regard, it is immaterial whether we characterize the pertinent documents and relationships as creating rights exercisable by decedent alone, in conjunction with other Stranco shareholders, or in conjunction with Stranco's president. *See* sec. 20.2036-1(b)(3), Estate Tax Regs.

With respect to SFLP income and as previously recounted in greater detail, the SFLP agreement named Stranco managing general partner and conferred on the managing general partner sole discretion to determine distributions. The Stranco shareholders, including decedent (through Mr. Gulig), then acted together to delegate this authority to Mr. Gulig through the management agreement. The effect of these actions placed decedent's attorney in fact in a position to make distribution decisions. Mrs. Gulig effectuated such decisions by executing checks to the recipients so designated.

In addition . . . decedent also retained the right, acting in conjunction with other Stranco shareholders, to designate who shall enjoy the transferred SFLP property itself. The Supreme Court indicated in United States v. Byrum, 408 U.S. at 143 n. 23 (citing Commissioner v. Estate of Holmes, 326 U.S. 480 (1946)), that a "power to terminate the trust and thereby designate the beneficiaries at a time selected by the settlor" would implicate section 2036(a)(2). Pursuant to the SFLP agreement, the partnership would be dissolved and terminated upon a unanimous vote of the limited partners and the unanimous consent of the general partner. The shareholders agreement likewise specifies that dissolution of SFLP requires the affirmative vote of all Stranco shareholders. Once dissolution and termination occur, liquidation is accomplished as set forth in the SFLP agreement. The managing general partner is named as the liquidator, which in turn disburses partnership assets first in payment of debts and then in repayment of partners' capital account balances. Authority is expressly granted for distributions in kind. Accordingly, decedent can act together with other Stranco shareholders essentially to revoke the SFLP arrangement and thereby to bring about or accelerate present enjoyment of partnership assets. Furthermore, it is noteworthy that such action would likely revest in decedent himself, as the 99-percent limited partner, the majority of the contributed property.

As regards property transferred to Stranco and income therefrom, decedent held the right, in conjunction with one or more other Stranco directors, to declare dividends. The corporation's bylaws authorize the board of directors to declare dividends from the entity. For the board to take such action, a majority vote of the directors at a meeting with a quorum present is sufficient. Under the bylaws, a majority of the directors then serving constitutes a quorum. Because Stranco had five directors, a quorum would consist of three, so two directors (e.g., decedent through Mr. Gulig and one other) could potentially act together to declare a dividend. The Stranco shareholders agreement further provided that each of the initial five directors would be reelected annually, thus effectively ensuring decedent's position on the board.

In response to various of the above concepts pertaining to joint action, particularly by stockowners, the estate suggests: "If the mere fact that a shareholder could band together with all of the other shareholders of a corporation and such banding together would be sufficient to cause inclusion under Section 2036, then it would have been impossible for the United States Supreme Court to reach the decision that it did in *Byrum.*" The estate's observation ignores the existence in United States v. Byrum, *supra,* of the independent trustee who alone had the ability to determine distributions from the disputed trust, notwithstanding any prior action by corporate owners or directors. It also ignores the identity of the shareholders in this case and the dual roles played by Mr. Gulig.

To summarize, review of the documentary evidence discussed above reveals that decedent here retained rights of a far different genre from those at issue in United States v. Byrum, *supra.* Rather than mere "control," management, or influence, there are traceable to decedent through the explicit provisions of the governing instruments ascertainable and legally enforceable rights to designate persons who shall enjoy the transferred property and its income. . . . The SFLP/Stranco arrangement placed decedent in a position to act, alone or in conjunction with others, through his attorney in fact, to cause distributions of property previously transferred to the entities or of income therefrom. Decedent's powers, absent sufficient limitation as discussed *infra,* therefore fall within the purview of section 2036(a)(2).

B. Constraints upon Rights to Designate

The Supreme Court in United States v. Byrum, *supra,* relied upon several impediments to the exercise of powers held by Mr. Byrum in concluding that such powers did not warrant inclusion under section 2036(a)(2). Here, the rights held by decedent are of a different nature and were not accompanied by comparable constraints. In our view, the constraints alleged by the estate are illusory. . . .

The fiduciary duties present in United States v. Byrum, 408 U .S. 125 (1972), ran to a significant number of unrelated parties and had their genesis in operating businesses that would lend meaning to the standard of acting in the best interests of the entity. As a result, there existed both a realistic possibility for enforcement and an objective business environment against which to judge potential dereliction. Given the emphasis that the Supreme Court laid on these factual realities, *Byrum* simply does not require blind application of its holding to scenarios where the purported fiduciary duties have no comparable substance. We therefore analyze the situation before us to determine whether the fiduciary duties relied upon by the estate would genuinely circumscribe use of powers to designate. . . .

Concerning Mr. Gulig, any fiduciary duties that Mr. Gulig might have had in his role as manager of Stranco (and thereby of SFLP) are entitled to comparatively little weight on these facts. Prior to his instigation of the SFLP/Stranco arrangement, Mr. Gulig stood in a confidential relationship, and owed fiduciary duties, to decedent personally as his attorney in fact. Thus, to the extent that Stranco or SFLP's interests might diverge from those of decedent, we do not believe that Mr. Gulig would disregard his preexisting obligation to decedent.

As regards fiduciary obligations of Stranco and its directors, these duties, too, have little significance in the present context. Although Stranco would owe a fiduciary duty to SFLP and to the limited partners, decedent owned the sole, 99-percent limited partnership interest. The rights to designate traceable to decedent through Stranco cannot be characterized as limited in any meaningful way by duties owed essentially to himself. Nor do the obligations of Stranco directors to the corporation itself warrant any different conclusion. Decedent held 47 percent of Stranco, and his own children held 52 of the remaining 53 percent. Intrafamily fiduciary duties within an investment vehicle simply are not equivalent in nature to the obligations created by the United States v. Byrum, *supra,* scenario.

With respect to the role of MCC Foundation, United States v. Byrum, *supra,* affords no basis for permitting outcomes under section 2036(a)(2) to turn on factors amounting to no more than window dressing. A charity given a gratuitous 1-percent interest would not realistically exercise any meaningful oversight. . . . We conclude that the value of assets transferred to SFLP and Stranco is includable in decedent's gross estate under section 2036(a)(2). . . .

Here, the record reveals that no part of the transferred property was exempt from the rights or enjoyment retained by decedent. The relevant documents make no distinction among the various assets contributed, nor does the evidence reflect that Mr. Gulig looked to particular assets in determining whether amounts should be distributed. The preponderance of the evidence therefore establishes that the full value of the transferred assets is includable under section 2036(a).

Pursuant to section 2036(a), 99 percent of the net asset value of SFLP and 47 percent of the value of assets held by Stranco should be included in decedent's gross estate.

PROBLEMS

1. Peter owns 25 percent of the stock of XYZ, Inc. Peter establishes an irrevocable trust for the benefit of Chester, his child.
   a. Peter appoints Thomas as Trustee. Peter then transfers the stock of XYZ, Inc. to the trust, but he retains the right to vote the stock. What are the estate tax consequences?
   b. Instead, Peter appoints himself as Trustee, and he is serving as Trustee when he dies. Peter does not explicitly retain the right to vote the stock. What are the estate tax consequences?
   c. Same as 1.a., except that Peter only owns ten percent of the stock.
   d. Same as 1.a., except that two years before his death, Peter relinquishes the right to vote the stock.

2. Which is the better rule—the holding in *Byrum* or §2036(b)? Why?

3. Pamela is the sole shareholder of MNO, Inc. MNO, Inc. has a fair market value of $1,000,000. Pamela owns 1,000 shares of common stock and 1,000 shares of nonvoting preferred stock. Pamela plans to transfer the 1,000 shares of common stock to Claire, her child.
   a. What are the gift tax consequences of the proposed transfer?
   b. Pamela dies five years after the transfer in 3.a. At the time of death Pamela owns the 1,000 shares of nonvoting preferred stock. Assume that MNO, Inc. has paid Pamela dividends regularly during the five years. What are the estate tax consequences?
   c. Same as b., only assume that MNO, Inc. has not paid any dividends during the five years.

4. Three years before his death, Patrick establishes Family Limited Partnership (FLP) and transfers his house, rental real estate, and his stock portfolio, with a total value of $5,500,000, to the partnership. Patrick's children, Claire and Carl, each transfer $25,000 cash to FLP. Patrick receives a limited partnership interest, and Claire and Carl receive limited and general partnership interests; these interests are proportionate to their contributions to FLP. In the year of formation and each subsequent year, Patrick transfers limited partnership interests, each valued at $11,000, to Claire, to Henry (Claire's husband), to Carl, to Wanda (Carl's wife), and to Patrick's five grandchildren. Patrick is the managing partner of FLP, and he continues to live in the house until his death.
   a. What are the gift tax consequences on formation of the partnership?
   b. What are the gift tax consequences on the subsequent transfers of limited partnership interests?
   c. What are the estate tax consequences if Patrick dies two years after FLP is formed? What if he dies five years later?
   d. If Patrick consulted you before creating FLP, what advice would you give him?

E. TRANSFERS AT DEATH
IRC §2037

As the title reflects, §2037 "Transfers Taking Effect at Death" is the direct descendant of the postponed possession and enjoyment clause of the original estate tax. Once the Supreme Court decided that all types of reversionary interests were to be included in the gross estate, there were very few questions of interpretation left.

The Supreme Court dealt with the gift tax issues and the relationship between the gift tax and this section in Smith v. Shaughnessy, 318 U.S. 176 (1943), where the decedent, age 72, created a trust to pay the income to his wife, age 44, for her life and at her death to return the property to the decedent if he was living, otherwise to those persons that his wife designated in her will. The issue before the Court was the taxability of the remainder. The donor argued that it was not a completed gift, because under Helvering v. Hallock, 309 U.S. 106 (1940), the value of the trust property less the value of the wife's outstanding life estate would be included in the decedent's gross estate. The Court rejected this argument as well as the claim that the contingent nature of the remainder rendered it valueless, stating:

> We cannot accept any suggestion that the complexity of a property interest created by a trust can serve to defeat a tax. For many years Congress has sought vigorously to close tax loopholes against ingenious trust instruments. Even though these concepts of property and value may be slippery and elusive they cannot escape taxation so long as they are used in the world of business. The language of the gift tax statute, "property . . . real or personal, tangible or intangible," is broad enough to include property, however conceptual or contingent.

Id. at 180.

Section 2037 applies if (1) the decedent has made a transfer in trust or otherwise, (2) the possession or enjoyment of the property can be obtained only by surviving the decedent, and (3) the decedent retains a reversionary interest and the value of that reversionary interest immediately before the decedent's death exceeds five percent of the value of the property. The transfer requirement of §2037 is the same as that of §§2036 and 2038. There is also an exception for bona fide sales for adequate and full consideration in money or money's worth.

The survivorship requirement is a more complex and elusive concept. The issue is: can possession or enjoyment of the property be obtained only by surviving decedent? If the answer is yes, and the other requirements of the statute are met, then the property is included in the gross estate. Assume that Decedent established an irrevocable trust to pay the income to A for life and the remainder to B. Neither A nor B has to survive Decedent to possess or enjoy the property. Once the trust is created, Decedent's death is irrelevant. The same is true if Decedent established a trust to accumulate the income for 30 years and then to distribute the accumulated income and trust property to B. B will obtain the trust property at the end of 30 years whether or not the Decedent is alive or dead. If Decedent is 60 or 70 years old when she established this trust, it may look, sound, and act like a testamentary transfer, *i.e.*, one that occurs at or after Decedent's death, but it has never been so considered, *see* Shukert v. Allen, 273 U.S. 545 (1929), and it is not one to which §2037 will apply.

Now suppose that Decedent creates a trust to pay the income to A for life and, at A's death, to distribute the trust property to B if living, otherwise to return the property to Decedent. Although B must survive A to obtain the property, B need not survive Decedent. As a result, §2037 does not apply to this transfer. Of course, even though Decedent predeceases B, there is a possibility that Decedent's heirs or beneficiaries might receive the trust property. This will happen if B predeceases A. Because of this, Decedent's reversion is in Decedent's gross estate under §2033. This reversion will pass from Decedent to her heirs or beneficiaries as a result of her death. Its value, of course, will depend on the probability that B will not survive A.

Section 2037 does apply where Decedent creates an irrevocable trust to pay the income to A for life and, at A's death, to distribute the trust property to Decedent if living, otherwise to distribute it to B. B will obtain possession of the trust property only if B survives Decedent. When A dies, either Decedent is alive and takes the property or Decedent is dead and B takes the property. Because B will only receive the property if Decedent is dead, B must survive Decedent to take.

The amount included in Decedent's gross estate in this case is the value of the trust property minus the value of A's life estate. A's life estate was a completed gift, and it is not governed by §2037. A's life estate is not dependent on A's surviving Decedent. Decedent's death vests the entire value of the remainder interest in B, and it is this value that is included in Decedent's gross estate by §2037.

The final requirement is that the decedent must retain a reversionary interest that exceeds five percent of the value of the property. The reversion may be one that is retained explicitly by the decedent, or it may be one that arises by operation of law because the decedent has not transferred the entire interest in the property. Reversions arising by operation of law are only included if the transfer occurred on or after October 8, 1949.

The value of the decedent's reversion is determined immediately before her death. If the reversion were to be valued at the moment of or immediately after death, it would be worthless because the decedent was dead and there would be no possibility that the decedent could obtain the property. The regulations and actuarial tables published by the IRS value the decedent's reversion based on the decedent's life expectancy. What happens if the decedent dies of a terminal illness? Will the value of the reversion be diminished because "immediately before death" the possibility of decedent's survival is almost nonexistent? Section 2037(b) provides that the reversionary interest will be valued "(without regard to the fact of the decedent's death) by usual methods of valuation, including the use of tables of mortality and actuarial principles, under regulations prescribed by the Secretary."

Estate of Roy v. Commissioner
54 T.C. 1317 (1970)

STERRETT, Judge:

. . . The facts involved are not complex and they are largely uncontested. On October 27, 1959, the decedent, who was then approximately 41 years old, and his brother transferred certain property in trust. Decedent's father, Benjamin, who was then approximately 69 years of age, was to have a life interest in the trust's net income. Upon Benjamin's death the trust corpus was to revert to the grantors, if living. If either grantor predeceased Benjamin his share of the trust corpus was to be administered for the benefit of his family.

Although the decedent was in relatively good health at the inception of the trust, in 1952 it was discovered that he was afflicted with glomerulonephritis. He, nonetheless, remained clinically well for approximately 11 years. In November of 1963 his condition began to steadily worsen until he succumbed to uremia on April 28, 1965. Benjamin did not die until approximately 4 years later, on April 6, 1969.

The controversy at issue arises because just prior to the decedent's death the state of his health indicated severely limited, actual life expectancy, while the respondent's mortality table indicate an expectancy for a man of 47, in normal health, of considerably longer duration. If we consider the decedent's actual health, in valuing his reversionary interest, that interest would have been less than 5 percent. If we are bound to consider only the average life expectancy of those in normal health as reflected in the mortality tables, his interest would have been approximately 70 percent as the respondent contends. The issue is thus narrowed to whether the decedent's personal life expectancy may be considered for purposes of valuing his reversionary interest under section 2037(a)(2).

Section 2037(b) prescribes the methods of evaluating reversionary interest as follows:

> The value of a reversionary interest immediately before the death of the decedent shall be determined (without regard to the fact of the decedent's death) by usual methods of valuation, including the use of tables of mortality and actuarial principles, under regulations prescribed by the Secretary or his delegate.

Since it is the method of evaluation that is at issue here, construction of the language quoted above will be determinative.

The predecessor of section 2037(a)(2) and (b) was enacted as section 811(c)(2) of the Internal Revenue Code of 1939 by section 8 of the Technical Changes Act of 1949. Prior to the enactment of this section, section 811(c)(1)(C) of the 1939 Code simply provided for the inclusion in the decedent's gross estate of interests that the decedent had transferred which were "intended to take effect in possession or enjoyment at or after his death."

Consequently, in Estate of Spiegel v. Commissioner, 335 U.S. 701 (1949), the Supreme Court required inclusion of a trust of approximately $1,140,000 due to the retention of a $70 reverter. . . . It was the congressional reaction to this decision which provided the impetus for the enactment of section 8 of the Technical Changes Act of 1949. S. Rept. No. 831, 81st Cong., 1st Sess., p. 8.

The circumstances surrounding this enactment indicate Congress' intention to reverse the holding in Estate of Spiegel v. Commissioner, *supra*, by the incorporation of a de minimis standard determinable with some mathematical precision. Certainty is of benefit to taxpayer and Internal Revenue Service alike.

As the statute obviously recognizes, no single method of valuation of a reversion can be prescribed in view of the large variety of reversionary interests. There must necessarily be some flexibility in the means used to make the appraisal. Thus, it is that mortality tables would be of little use in valuing an interest the receipt of which is contingent upon someone dying without issue. Yet there are, it is equally obvious, certain reversionary interests where the use of a mortality table is the fairest and most equitable method to be used.

In the case at bar petitioner would have us ignore the life expectancy as reflected in the mortality tables and use, in lieu thereof, the actual life expectancy of the decedent here involved. Admittedly such a position has appeal and ignites a sympathetic reaction under the facts here present. Further, the position is ably argued in the briefs.

Yet we feel its acceptance would emasculate section 2037 thereby vitiating the congressional intent to bring certainty to the law through the enactment of a de minimis provision. It would effectively write the words "including the use of tables of mortality" out of the statute. Surely Congress had certain reversionary interests in mind when it prescribed mortality tables as a means of evaluation. It is difficult to conceive of a "section 2037 revision" where the use of such tables would be more appropriate than the one before us. Thus, to deny the applicability of the "tables of mortality" language here would be to ignore what appears to be the specific mandate of Congress.

Should we accept the petitioner's arguments herein, section 2037 would not apply to comparable reversionary interests in any instance where the decedent was terminally ill prior the death. In cases of that sort of a drastically foreshortened actual life expectancy would bring any retained reversion below the 5-percent level. Section 2037 would then be applicable only in cases of sudden death; e.g., when a healthy individual is killed in an accident or when an ostensibly healthy individual dies as the result of a sudden coronary. We do not feel it reasonable to assume that Congress intended section 2037 to be limited to such narrow circumstances. Nor can we believe that Congress intended the mode of death, lingering or sudden, to be determinative of estate tax consequence.

Section 2037(b) states that the value of a retained reversionary interest "shall be determined (without regard to the fact of the decedent's death). . . ." If we were in the future to consider the manner of cause of a decedent's death we would, it seems to us, be in violation of this requirement.

PROBLEMS

1. Della establishes an irrevocable trust with Friendly National Bank as Trustee, to pay the income to Andrew for his life. At Andrew's death, the Trustee is to distribute the trust property to Bridget if she is living. If Bridget is not living, the Trustee is to distribute the trust property to Della. What are the gift and estate tax consequences?
2. Della establishes an irrevocable trust with Friendly National Bank as Trustee, to pay the income to Henry for his life. At Henry's death, the Trustee is to distribute the trust property to Della if she is alive. If Della predeceases Henry, the Trustee is to distribute the trust property to Isaac.
   a.   What are the gift tax consequences?
   b.   What are the estate tax consequences if Henry dies before Della?
   c.   What are the estate tax consequences if Della dies before Henry?
   d.   What are the estate tax consequences if Isaac dies before Della or Henry?
3. Della establishes an irrevocable trust with Friendly National Bank as Trustee, to pay the income to Ellen for her life and then to pay the income to Della for her life. After the death of both Ellen and Della, the Trustee is to distribute the trust property to Fred.
   a.   What are the gift tax consequences?
   b.   What are the estate tax consequences if Ellen dies before Della?
   c.   What are the estate tax consequences if Della dies before Ellen?

F.   TRANSFERS WITHIN THREE YEARS OF DEATH OR FOR CONSIDERATION
IRC §2035

Despite its colorful history, §2035 today plays a limited role in the estate tax. The general rule is that gratuitous transfers made within three years of death, even those made by the decedent on his deathbed, are not included in the gross estate. Once the gift and estate taxes were unified in 1976, there was no longer a need to do so because gifts are taxed at the same rate as transfers at death and there is one unified exemption amount.

The only remaining difference between the two taxes is that the gift tax is tax exclusive and the estate tax is tax inclusive. The gift tax is the primary responsibility of the donor and is paid from funds separate and distinct from the gift. This means that if the donor makes a taxable gift of $1,000,000, on which a gift tax of $350,000 is due, the recipient will actually receive $1,000,000, and the donor will have depleted his resources by a total of $1,350,000. Because the $350,000 gift tax is a debt owed to the government, there is no additional tax due on it. If, on the other hand, the donor has a taxable estate of $1,000,000 at death and the tax is $350,000, the beneficiary will only receive $650,000. The amount of the estate tax that is ultimately paid is included in the value of the taxable estate.

Because of this difference, there continues to be a significant advantage to making lifetime gifts. To eliminate this advantage and prevent decedents from giving away all of their property immediately before their death, Congress enacted §2035(b). This subsection requires that any gift tax paid on gifts made within three years of death be included in the decedent's gross estate. By doing so, Congress has eliminated the advantage of making lifetime gifts but only for gifts made within three years of death. To completely eliminate the difference, the rule of §2035(b) would need to apply to all lifetime transfers.

Section 2035 does include certain gifts in the gross estate. First, it includes gifts of life insurance made within three years of death. The reason for this should be obvious. The gift tax value of life insurance is the cost of the premium, in the case of term insurance, and the cost of the premium plus the investment component, in the case of cash value insurance. The estate tax includes the insurance proceeds received by the beneficiary rather than the value of the policy. §2042. The difference can be significant.

Section 2035 also includes gifts of retained interests made within three years of death.

Example 10-8

Douglas establishes a revocable trust in 1990. On May 1, 2002, Douglas releases the right to revoke the trust. He dies on September 15, 2004. Had Douglas not released the right to revoke, the trust would have been in his gross estate under §2038(a)(1). Because he released the right to revoke within the three-year period before his death, the full value of the trust will be in his gross estate under §2035(a).

Example 10-9

Daphne establishes an irrevocable trust in 1990 with Friendly National Bank as Trustee to pay her the income for life and at her death to distribute the trust property to her niece. On March 15, 2003, Daphne releases her right to receive trust income, transferring that right to her sister. She dies on April 10, 2004. Had she not released her right to income, the trust would have been in Daphne's gross estate under §2036(a)(1). Because she made a transfer of her retained life estate within three years of her death, the full value of the trust will be in her gross estate under §2035(a).

Example 10-10

Delores establishes an irrevocable trust in 1990 with Friendly National Bank as Trustee to pay the income to Ann for life. If Delores is living at Ann's death, the trust property will revert to her; otherwise, it will be distributed to Delores's children. On August 20, 2002, Delores releases her reversionary interest, thus ensuring that the property will pass to her children immediately upon Ann's death. Delores dies on January 9, 2004. Had Delores not released her reversion, the value of the trust property, less Ann's outstanding life estate, would have been in her gross estate under §2037. Because she transferred her reversion to her children within three years of her death, the same value will be in her gross estate under §2035(a).

Example 10-11

Dominic establishes an irrevocable trust in 1990 with Friendly National Bank as Trustee to pay the income to his children for their lives and, at the death of the last child, to distribute the trust property to his descendants. Dominic retains the right to add or delete beneficiaries with respect to both income and corpus. On October 31, 2003, Dominic releases his power to add or delete beneficiaries. He dies on November 10, 2004. Had Dominic retained this power, the trust would have been in his gross estate under either §2036(a)(2) or §2038(a)(1). Because he released the power within three years of his death, the value of the trust will be in his gross estate under §2035(a).

As these examples demonstrate, a decedent who retains an interest in the trust or a power over the trust that would have caused the trust to be included in her gross estate under §§2036, 2037, or 2038 and then releases that interest or power within three years of death must include the property in her gross estate. She cannot hold onto the interest or power until shortly before death and then avoid the estate tax.

Section 2035 makes sense for transfers of life insurance because of the difference in value between the gift tax and estate tax amounts. It does not make sense with respect to interests and powers subject to §§2036-2038. The release of the interest or power will be taxed as a gift, and the gift tax rates are the same as those of the estate tax. While there are some differences in value between the amount of the gift and the amount that would actually be in the decedent's gross estate, those differences are due to the passage of time or the time value of money. Despite this, it is unlikely that §2035(a) will be repealed with respect to these transfers.

A different issue arises if Decedent establishes a revocable trust and then directs the Trustee to make transfers to others. If Decedent has transferred most of her assets to the revocable trust, she may do this to take advantage of the gift tax annual exclusion and, thus, diminish the value of her gross estate. Had she made the gifts directly, there would be no claim that such gifts were included in her gross estate. When she makes gifts of trust property within three years of death, the IRS claimed that those transfers were relinquishments of the Decedent's power to revoke, bringing the amount of the gifted property into her gross under §2035. The IRS lost most of these cases. *See, e.g.*, Estate of Kisling v. Commissioner, 32 F.3d 1222 (8th Cir. 1994); McNeely v. United States, 16 F.3d 303 (8th Cir. 1994); Estate of Jalkut v. Commissioner, 96 T.C. 675 (1991), *acq.* 1991-2 C.B.1. Congress eventually clarified the law by enacting §2035(e), which treats such transfers as made directly by the Decedent as long as the Decedent is treated as the owner of the trust for income tax purposes. *See* §676.

Finally, there are a number of Code sections that confer special benefits depending on the inclusion of certain property in the gross estate and the proportionate value of that property to the total value of the gross estate: §303 (redemption of stock to pay death taxes), §2032A (special use valuation), §6166 (extension of time to pay estate tax), and subchapter C of Chapter 64 relating to liens. In all these situations, the decedent could manipulate his gross estate to qualify for the special treatment by making deathbed transfers. Section 2035(c) prevents this by including the value of all transfers made within three years of death in the gross estate for purposes of determining qualification for these sections. This rule is itself subject to an exception for gifts, other than life insurance, that do not require the filing of a gift tax return, *i.e.*, gifts that qualify for the gift tax annual exclusion or the marital deduction.

Rather than give property away within three years of death, the decedent may attempt to sell that property or a retained interest in property to avoid the estate tax. Sections 2035-2038 all contain an exception for bona fide sales for adequate and full consideration in money or money's worth. The exclusion for such sales applies whether the transfer occurred within three years of death or earlier. While there may be a question whether the sale was bona fide and at arm's length, *see, e.g.*, Estate of Maxwell v. Commissioner at page 247, the more troubling issue is whether the consideration is adequate and full.

United States v. Allen
293 F.2d 916 (10th Cir. 1961), *cert. denied* 368 U.S. 944 (1961)

MURRAH, Chief Judge.

. . . The pertinent facts are that the decedent, Maria McKean Allen, created an irrevocable trust in which she reserved ³/₅ths of the income for life, the remainder to pass to her two children, who are the beneficiaries of the other ²/₅ths interest in the income. When she was approximately seventy-eight years old, the trustor-decedent was advised that her retention of the life estate would result in her attributable share of the corpus being included in her gross estate, for estate tax purposes. With her sanction, counsel began searching for a competent means of divesture, and learned that decedent's son, Wharton Allen, would consider purchasing his mother's interest in the trust. At that time, the actuarial value of the retained life estate, based upon decedent's life expectancy, was approximately $135,000 and her attributable share of the corpus, i.e., ³/₅ths, was valued at some $900,000. Upon consultation with his business advisers, Allen agreed to pay $140,000 for the interest, believing that decedent's actual life span would be sufficient to return a profit to him on the investment. For all intents and purposes, he was a bona fide third party purchaser—not being in a position to benefit by any reduction in his mother's estate taxes. The sale was consummated and, upon paying the purchase price, Allen began receiving the income from the trust.

At the time of the transfer, decedent enjoyed relatively good health and was expected to live her normal life span. A short time thereafter, however, it was discovered that she had an incurable disease, which soon resulted in her untimely death. As a result of the death, Allen ceased receiving any trust income and suffered a considerable loss on his investment.

The Internal Revenue Commissioner determined that ³/₅ths of the corpus, less the $140,000 purchase money, should be included in decedent's gross estate because (1) the transfer was invalid because made in contemplation of death, and (2) the sale was not for an adequate and full consideration.

Plaintiff-executors paid the taxes in accord with the Commissioner's valuation of the estate, and brought this action for refund, alleging that the sale of the life interest was for an adequate consideration; and that, therefore, no part of the trust corpus was properly includible in the gross estate.

The trial court held for plaintiffs, finding that the transfer was in contemplation of death, but regardless of that fact, the consideration paid for the life estate was adequate and full, thereby serving to divest decedent of any interest in the trust, with the result that no part of the corpus is subject to estate taxes.

Our narrow question is thus whether the corpus of a reserved life estate is removed, for federal estate tax purposes, from a decedent's gross estate by a transfer at the value of such reserved life estate. In other words, must the consideration be paid for the interest transferred, or for the interest which would otherwise be included in the gross estate?

In one sense, the answer comes quite simply—decedent owned no more than a life estate, could not transfer any part of the corpus, and Allen received no more than the interest transferred. And, a taxpayer is, of course, entitled to use all proper means to reduce his tax liability. . . . It would thus seem to follow that the consideration was adequate, for it was in fact more than the value of the life estate. And, as a practical matter, it would have been virtually impossible to sell the life estate for an amount equal to her share in the corpus. . . .

It does not seem plausible, however, that Congress intended to allow such an easy avoidance of the taxable incidence befalling reserved life estates. This result would allow a taxpayer to reap the benefits of property for his lifetime and, in contemplation of death, sell only the interest entitling him to the income, thereby removing all of the property which he has enjoyed from his gross estate. Giving the statute a reasonable interpretation, we cannot believe this to be its intendment. It seems certain that in a situation like this, Congress meant the estate to include the corpus of the trust or, in its stead, an amount equal in value. . . .

The judgment of the trial court is therefore reversed and the case is remanded for further proceedings in conformity with the opinion filed herein.

BREITENSTEIN, Circuit Judge (concurring in result).

. . . As I read the statute the tax liability arises at the time of the inter vivos transfer under which there was a retention of the right to income for life. The disposition thereafter of that retained right does not eliminate the tax liability. The fact that full and adequate consideration was paid for the transfer of the retained life estate is immaterial. To remove the trust property from inclusion in decedent's estate there must be full and adequate consideration paid for the interest which would be taxed. That interest is not the right to income for life but the right to the property which was placed in the trust and from which the income is produced.

Estate of D'Ambrosio v. Commissioner
101 F.3d 309 (3d Cir. 1996), *cert. denied* 520 U.S. 1230 (1997)

NYGAARD, Circuit Judge.

Vita D'Ambrosio, executrix of the estate of Rose D'Ambrosio, appeals from a judgment of the United States Tax Court upholding a statutory notice of deficiency filed against the estate by the Commissioner of Internal Revenue. The tax court held that, even though the decedent had sold her remainder interest in closely held stock for its fair market value, 26 U.S.C. §2036(a)(1) brought its entire fee simple value back into her gross estate. We will reverse and remand with the direction that the tax court enter judgment in favor of appellant.

I

The facts in this case have been stipulated by the parties. Decedent owned, inter alia, one half of the preferred stock of Vaparo, Inc.; these 470 shares had a fair market value of $2,350,000. In 1987, at the age of 80, decedent transferred her remainder interest in her shares to Vaparo in exchange for an annuity which was to pay her $296,039 per year and retained her income interest in the shares. There is no evidence in the record to indicate that she made this transfer in contemplation of death or with testamentary motivation. According to the actuarial tables set forth in the Treasury Regulations, the annuity had a fair market value of $1,324,014. The parties stipulate that this was also the fair market value of the remainder interest.

Decedent died in 1990, after receiving only $592,078 in annuity payments and $23,500 in dividends. Her executrix did not include any interest in the Vaparo stock when she computed decedent's gross estate. The Commissioner disagreed, issuing a notice of deficiency in which she asserted that the gross estate included the full, fee simple value of the Vaparo shares at the date of death, still worth an estimated $2,350,000, less the amount of annuity payments decedent received during life.[1] The estate then petitioned the tax court for redetermination of the alleged tax deficiency.

The tax court, relying largely on Gradow v. United States, 11 Cl. Ct. 808 (1987), aff'd, 897 F.2d 516 (Fed. Cir. 1990), and Estate of Gregory v. Commissioner, 39 T.C. 1012, 1963 WL 1488 (1963), ruled in favor of the Commissioner. Eschewing any attempt to construe the language of either the Code or the applicable Treasury Regulations, the tax court reasoned that the transfer of the remainder interest in the Vaparo stock was an abusive tax avoidance scheme that should not be permitted:

> In the instant case, we conclude that Decedent's transfer of the remainder interest in her preferred stock does not fall within the bona fide sale exception of section 2036(a). Decedent's gross estate would be depleted if the value of the preferred stock, in which she had retained a life interest, was excluded therefrom. Decedent's transfer of the remainder interest was of a testamentary nature, made when she was 80 years old to a family-owned corporation in return for an annuity worth more than $1 million less than the stock itself. Given our conclusion that Decedent did not receive adequate and full consideration under section 2036(a) for her 470 shares of Vaparo preferred stock, we hold that her gross estate includes the date of death value of that stock, less the value of the annuity.

Estate of D'Ambrosio v. Commissioner, 105 T.C. 252, 260, 1995 WL 564078 (1995). The executrix now appeals; we have jurisdiction under 26 U.S.C. §7482. Both parties agree that our standard of review for this issue of law is plenary.

II

. . . There is no dispute that Rose D'Ambrosio retained a life interest in the Vaparo stock and sold the remainder back to the company. The issue is whether the sale of a remainder interest for its fair market value constitutes "adequate and full consideration" within the meaning of §2036(a). Appellant argues that it does. The Commissioner takes the position that only consideration equal to the fee simple value of the property is sufficient. Appellant has the better argument.

A

The tax court and the Commissioner rely principally on four cases, Gradow v. United States, 11 Cl. Ct. 808 (1987), aff'd for the reasons set forth by the Claims Court, 897 F.2d 516 (Fed. Cir. 1990); United States v. Past, 347 F.2d 7

---

1. The Commissioner now concedes that the estate must be credited for the fair market value of that annuity rather than the lifetime payments received under it.

(9th Cir. 1965); Estate of Gregory v. Commissioner, 39 T.C. 1012 (1963); United States v. Allen, 293 F.2d 916 (10th Cir. 1961). We find these cases either inapposite or unpersuasive; we will discuss them in chronological order.

In *Allen*, the decedent set up an irrevocable inter vivos trust in which she retained a partial life estate and gave the remainder (as well as the remaining portion of the income) to her children. Apparently realizing the tax liability she had created for her estate under the predecessor of §2036, she later attempted to sell her retained life interest to her son for an amount slightly in excess of its fair market value. After she died, the estate took the position that, because decedent had divested herself of her retained life interest for fair market value, none of the trust property was includable in her gross estate. The Court of Appeals disagreed, holding that consideration is only "adequate" if it equals or exceeds the value of the interest that would otherwise be included in the gross estate absent the transfer. *See* 293 F.2d at 917. . . .

Allen, however, is inapposite, as the Commissioner now concedes, because it involved the sale of a life estate after the remainder had already been disposed of by gift, a testamentary transaction with a palpable tax evasion motive. This case, in contrast, involves the sale of a remainder for its stipulated fair market value. Nevertheless, we agree with its rationale that consideration should be measured against the value that would have been drawn into the gross estate absent the transfer. As the Tax Court persuasively reasoned in a later case:

> [W]here the transferred property is replaced by other property of equal value received in exchange, there is no reason to impose an estate tax in respect of the transferred property, for it is reasonable to assume that the property acquired in exchange will find its way into the decedent's gross estate at his death unless consumed or otherwise disposed of in a nontestamentary transaction in much the same manner as would the transferred property itself had the transfer not taken place. . . . In short, unless replaced by property of equal value that could be exposed to inclusion in the decedent's gross estate, the property transferred in a testamentary transaction of the type described in the statute must be included in his gross estate.

Estate of Frothingham v. Commissioner, 60 T.C. 211, 215-16, (1973).

Gregory presents a closer factual analogy to D'Ambrosio's situation. *Gregory* was a "widow's election" case involving the testamentary disposition of community property. Typically in such cases, the husband wishes to pass the remainder interest in all of the marital property to his children, while providing for the lifetime needs of his surviving spouse. In a community property state, however, half of the marital property belongs to the wife as a matter of law, so he cannot pass it by his own will. To circumvent this problem, the will is drafted to give the widow a choice: take her one-half share in fee simple, according to law, or trust over her half of the community property in exchange for a life estate in the whole. Put another way, she trades the remainder interest in her half of the community property in exchange for a life estate in her husband's half.

In *Gregory*, the widow exchanged property worth approximately $66,000 for a life estate with an actuarial value of only around $12,000; by the time she died eight years later, the property she gave up had appreciated to approximately $102,000. The Tax Court compared the $102,000 outflow to the $12,000 consideration and concluded that the widow's election did not constitute a bona fide sale for an adequate and full consideration. 39 T.C. at 1015-16. It also stated that "the statute excepts only those bona fide sales where the consideration received was of a comparable value which would be includable in the transferor's gross estate." Id. at 1016.

We believe that the *Gregory* court erred in its analysis, although it reached the correct result on the particular facts of that case. There is no way to know ex ante what the value of an asset will be at the death of a testator; although the date of death can be estimated through the use of actuarial tables, the actual appreciation of the property is unknowable, as are the prevailing interest, inflation and tax rates. Consequently, there is no way to ever be certain in advance whether the consideration is adequate and thus no way to know what tax treatment a transfer will receive. This level of uncertainty all but destroys any economic incentive to ever sell a remainder interest; yet, Congress never said in §2036 that all transfers of such interests will be taxed at their fee simple value or that those transfers are illegal. Instead, it clearly contemplated situations in which a sale of a remainder would not cause the full value of the property to fall into the gross estate. Without some express indication from Congress, we will not presume it intended to eliminate wholesale the transfers of remainder interests. Therefore, rather than evaluate the adequacy of the consideration at the time the decedent dies, we will compare the value of the remainder transferred to the value of the consideration received, measured as of the date of the transfer. Here, we need not address that valuation issue, because it is stipulated that the fair market value of the stock was the same on the date of transfer as it was on the date of death.

In *Gregory*, however, the $12,000 the decedent received was grossly inadequate against the value of the property she transferred, regardless of the valuation date. The court was therefore correct that the transfer was not for adequate and full consideration. Because of that gross inadequacy, however, the holding of *Gregory* does not extend to the issue now before us: whether, when a remainder is sold for its stipulated fair market value, the consideration received is inadequate because it is less than the fee simple value of the property.

The *Past* case was factually somewhat different, in that it involved a divorce settlement, but the substance of the transaction was the same as in *Gregory*: the sale of a remainder in one-half of the marital property in exchange for a life estate in the whole. In that case, however, the court valued the property the divorcing spouse gave up at about $244,000 and the life estate she received at about $143,000; as a result, it held that the consideration was inadequate. 347 F.2d at 13-14. In making these valuations, however, the court took the fee simple value of the trust property and divided it in half. This was analytically incorrect, however, because the divorcing wife never gave up the life estate in her half of the marital property. She contributed only her remainder interest in that half, and that is the value that should have been used in the court's analysis. Alternatively, the *Past* court could have used the fee simple value of the wife's share, but it would then have needed to measure that against the value of the life estate in both halves of the property. Had the court employed this latter methodology, it would have seen that the $287,000 value of the life estate exceeded the $244,000 she contributed and would have found adequate consideration. Instead, it compared "apples and oranges" and, we believe, reached the wrong result.

B

The facts in *Gradow* were similar to those in *Gregory*; both are "widow's election" cases. That case is particularly significant, however, because the court focused on the statutory language of §2036. The court began its analysis, however, with a discussion of *Gregory*, *Past* and *Allen*. While acknowledging that it was not bound by those three cases, the *Gradow* court found them persuasive, for two reasons: 1) "the most natural reading of §2036(a) leads to the same result[;]" and 2) their holding is "most consistent with the purposes of §2036(a)." 11 Cl. Ct. at 813. We will discuss these rationales in turn.

1

We examine first the *Gradow* court's construction of the statute. It opined that

> there is no question that the term "property" in the phrase "The gross estate shall include . . . all property . . . of which the decedent has at any time made a transfer" means that part of the trust corpus attributable to plaintiff. If §2036(a) applies, all of Betty's former community property is brought into her gross estate. Fundamental principles of grammar dictate that the parenthetical exception which then follows—"(except in case of a bona fide sale . . .)"—refers to a transfer of that same property, i.e., the one-half of the community property she placed into the trust.

Id. (ellipses in original). We disagree; although the *Gradow* court's rationale appears plausible, we note that the court, in quoting the statute, left out significant portions of its language. Below is the text of §2036, with the omitted words emphasized:

> The *value of the* gross estate shall include *the value of* all property *to the extent of any interest therein* of which the decedent has at any time made a transfer (except in case of a bona fide sale for an adequate and full consideration in money or money's worth), by trust or otherwise, under which he has retained for his life . . . (1) the possession or enjoyment of, or the right to the income from, the property. . . .

After parsing this language, we cannot agree with the *Gradow* court's conclusions that "property" refers to the fee simple interest and that adequate consideration must be measured against that value. Rather, we believe that the clear import of the phrase "to the extent of any interest therein" is that the gross estate shall include the value of the remainder interest, unless it was sold for adequate and fair consideration. . . .

2

The *Gradow* court also believed that its construction of §2036 was "most consistent" with its purposes. 11 Cl. Ct. at 813. The tax court in this case, although recognizing that the issue has spawned considerable legal commentary and that scholars dispute its resolution, 105 T.C. at 254, was persuaded that decedent's sale of her remainder interest was testamentary in character and designed to avoid the payment of estate tax that otherwise would have been due. *Id.* at 260. It noted particularly that the transfer was made when decedent was eighty years old and that the value of the annuity she received was over $1 million less than the fee simple value of the stock she gave up. *Id.* Again, we disagree.

We too are cognizant that techniques for attempting to reduce estate taxes are limited only by the imagination of estate planners, and that new devices appear regularly. There is, to be sure, a role for the federal courts to play in properly limiting these techniques in accordance with the expressed intent of Congress. Under long-standing precedent, for example, we measure "consideration" in real economic terms, not as it might be evaluated under the common law of contract or property. *E.g.,* Commissioner v. Wemyss, 324 U.S. 303, 65 S. Ct. 652, 89 L. Ed. 958 (1945) (promise of marriage insufficient consideration, for gift tax purposes, for tax-free transfer of property); Merrill v. Fahs, 324 U.S. 308, 65 S. Ct. 655, 89 L. Ed. 963 (1945) (same). Likewise, when the transfer of the remainder interest is essentially gratuitous and testamentary in character, we focus on substance rather than form and require that the full value of trust property be included in the gross estate, unless "the settlor absolutely, unequivocally, irrevocably, and without possible reservations, parts with all of his title and all of his possession and all of his enjoyment of the transferred property." *See* Commissioner v. Estate of Church, 335 U.S. 632, 645, 69 S. Ct. 322, 329, 93 L. Ed. 288 (1949) (gratuitous transfer of remainder in trust for family members with possibility of reverter to estate); accord Helvering v. Hallock, 309 U.S. 106, 110, 60 S. Ct. 444, 447, 84 L. Ed. 604 (1940) (consolidation of three cases involving "dispositions of property by way of trust in which the settlement provides for return or reversion of the corpus to the donor upon a contingency terminable at his death").

On the other hand, it is not our role to police the techniques of estate planning by determining, based on our own policy views and perceptions, which transfers are abusive and which are not. That is properly the role of Congress, whose statutory enactments we are bound to interpret.[2] As stated *supra*, we think the statutory text better supports appellant's argument.

Even looking at this case in policy terms, however, it is difficult to fathom either the Tax Court's or the Commissioner's concerns about the "abusiveness" of this transaction. A hypothetical example will illustrate the point.

A fee simple interest is comprised of a life estate and a remainder. Returning to the widow's election cases, assume that the surviving spouse's share of the community property is valued at $2,000,000. Assuming that she decides not to accept the settlement and to keep that property, its whole value will be available for inclusion in the gross estate at death, but only as long as the widow lives entirely on the income from the property. If she invades principal and sells some of the property in order to meet living expenses or purchase luxury items, then at least some of that value will not be included in the gross estate. Tax law, of course (with the exception of the gift tax), imposes no burdens on how a person spends her money during life.

Next, assume that same widow decides to sell her remainder and keep a life estate. As long as she sells the remainder for its fair market value, it makes no difference whether she receives cash, other property, or an annuity. All can be discounted to their respective present values and quantified. If she continues to support herself from the income from her life estate, the consideration she received in exchange for the remainder, if properly invested, will still be available for inclusion in the gross estate when she dies, as *Frothingham* and *Gregory* require. On the other hand, if her life estate is insufficient to meet her living expenses, the widow will have to invade the consideration she received in exchange for her remainder, but to no different an extent than she would under the previous hypothetical in which she retained the fee simple interest. In sum, there is simply no change in the date-of-death value of the final estate, regardless of which option she selects, at any given standard of living.

On the other hand, if the full, fee simple value of the property at the time of death is pulled back into the gross estate under §2036(a), subject only to an offset for the consideration received, then the post-sale appreciation of the transferred asset will be taxed at death. Indeed, it will be double-taxed, because, all things being equal, the consideration she received will also have appreciated and will be subject to tax on its increased value. In addition, it would appear virtually impossible, under the tax court's reasoning, ever to sell a remainder interest; if the adequacy of the consideration must be measured against the fee simple value of the property at the time of the transfer, the transferor will have to find an arms-length buyer willing to pay a fee simple price for a future interest. Unless a buyer is willing to speculate that the future value of the asset will skyrocket, few if any such sales will take place.

Another potential concern, expressed by the *Gradow* court, is that, under appellant's theory, "[a] young person could sell a remainder interest for a fraction

---

2. Indeed, subsequent to the transfer at issue here, Congress did enact legislation dealing with abusive transfers of remainder interests. *See* 26 U.S.C. §§2036(c) (repealed), 2701.

of the property's [current, fee simple] worth, enjoy the property for life, and then pass it along without estate or gift tax consequences." 11 Cl. Ct. at 815. This reasoning is problematic, however, because it ignores the time value of money. Assume that a decedent sells his son a remainder interest in that much-debated and often-sold parcel of land called Blackacre, which is worth $1 million in fee simple, for its actuarial fair market value of $100,000 (an amount which implicitly includes the market value of Blackacre's expected appreciation). Decedent then invests the proceeds of the sale. If the rates of return for both assets are equal and decedent lives exactly as long as the actuarial tables predict, the consideration that decedent received for his remainder will equal the value of Blackacre on the date of his death. The equivalent value will, accordingly, still be included in the gross estate. Moreover, decedent's son will have only a $100,000 basis in Blackacre, because that is all he paid for it. He will then be subject to capital gains taxes on its appreciated value if he decides to ever sell the property. Had Blackacre been passed by decedent's will and included in the gross estate, the son would have received a stepped-up basis at the time of his father's death or the alternate valuation date. We therefore have great difficulty understanding how this transaction could be abusive. . . .

The Commissioner also asserts that the D'Ambrosio estate plan is "calculated to deplete decedent's estate in the event that she should not survive as long as her actuarially projected life expectancy." Commissioner's Brief at 34–35. We note first that the Commissioner does not argue that decedent transferred her remainder in contemplation of imminent death under such circumstances that the tables should not be applied. Leaving aside the untimely death of Rose D'Ambrosio, any given transferor of a remainder is equally likely to outlive the tables, in which case she would collect more from her annuity, the gross estate would be correspondingly larger and the Commissioner would collect more tax revenue than if the remainder had never been transferred.

PROBLEMS

1. Douglas gives Allison a gift each year equal to the amount of the gift tax annual exclusion. Douglas has not made any gifts in addition to this until this year when he gives Allison $3,000,000 cash.
   a. Calculate the gift tax due assuming that the top rate of tax is 45 percent and the applicable exemption amount is $2,000,000.
   b. Calculate the estate tax due if Douglas dies two years later. Assume that he owns other property worth $2,000,000 and has no estate tax deductions. Assume that the top rate is 45 percent and the applicable exemption amount is $2,000,000.
   c. Calculate the estate tax due in 1.b. assuming that Douglas dies four years after the gift.
2. In 2000, Douglas establishes a trust with Friendly National Bank as Trustee to pay the income to Allison for life, the remainder to Bruce,

and transfers $1,000,000 into the trust. Allison, Bruce, and Douglas are unrelated. (Do not calculate the tax due.)

a. The trust is irrevocable. The Trustee has total discretion to distribute or accumulate income and to add or delete beneficiaries. Douglas is not the Trustee, he cannot become the Trustee, and he has no power to appoint the Trustee. What are the gift tax consequences?

b. What are the estate tax consequences if Douglas dies in 2002? In 2004?

c. Instead, Douglas retains the right to revoke the trust. Each year the trust generates $50,000 of income, and that income is distributed to Allison. What are the gift tax consequences?

d. What are the gift tax consequences if Douglas also has the ability to withdraw principal for any reason or to direct the Trustee to make distributions of income or principal to others and he instructs the Trustee to distribute $10,000 each year to his three children?

e. What are the estate tax consequences if Douglas dies in 2002? In 2004?

f. Same facts as b., except that Douglas releases the right to revoke in 2002. What are the gift tax consequences?

g. What are the estate tax consequences if Douglas dies in 2004? In 2006?

3. Douglas establishes an irrevocable trust by transferring $500,000 to Friendly National Bank as Trustee to pay the income to Douglas for life and the remainder to Allison. Allison and Douglas are unrelated.

a. What are the gift tax consequences assuming Douglas was 50 at the time of the transfer, the value of the income interest was $356,220, and the value of the remainder interest was $143,780?

b. When Douglas is 75, he gives the life estate to Bruce. Douglas dies two years later. What are the gift and estate tax consequences?

c. Instead, when Douglas is 75, the corpus is still $500,000. Douglas sells the life interest to Bruce for $195,000. Douglas dies four years later. What are the gift and estate tax consequences to Douglas assuming the value of the income interest is $192,450 and the value of the remainder interest is $307,550?

4. Douglas owned Farmacre (FMV $300,000). On May 5, 2000, when Douglas is 60, he sells a remainder interest in Farmacre to his daughter, Martha, for $23,500. Assume that the actuarial value of the remainder interest is $121,872. Douglas dies on February 1, 2002.

a. What are the gift and estate tax consequences?

b. What are the gift and estate tax consequences if Martha had paid Douglas $125,000?

CHAPTER 11

Annuities and Employee Death Benefits

A. GENERAL PRINCIPLES
IRC §§2033, 2039

Section 2039 was enacted in 1954 to bring into the decedent's gross estate the value of annuities and similar payments receivable by a beneficiary who survives the decedent. An annuity is simply a contract to make payments for a specific period of time. Insurance companies sell many types of annuities, for example:

1. Fidelity Insurance Company agrees to pay Adam a specified amount each month for the remainder of his life.
2. Fidelity Insurance Company agrees to pay Adam a specified amount each month for a designated number of years.
3. Fidelity Insurance Company agrees to pay Adam a specified amount each month for the remainder of his life. If the sum of those payments does not equal a certain amount, Fidelity will pay the difference to Adam's estate.
4. Fidelity Insurance Company agrees to pay Adam a specified amount each month for the remainder of his life and then to pay Beth that sum for her life.
5. Fidelity Insurance Company agrees to pay Adam and Beth a specified amount each month for their joint lives.

Most retirement benefits are also paid as annuities.

Nothing will be in Adam's gross estate in the first example. All payments cease at his death, and no one is entitled to anything as a result of his death. If Adam lives longer than the term of the annuity in the second example, there is nothing in his gross estate. If he dies while receiving the annuity and the remaining payments are made to his estate, the value of the remaining payments will be in his gross estate under §2033. Section 2033 also applies to the third example if any amount is paid to Adam's estate. Section 2039 only applies to the fourth and fifth examples.

For §2039 to apply, (1) there must be a contract or agreement entered into after March 3, 1931, that is not life insurance, (2) there must be a beneficiary who will receive an annuity or other payment by reason of surviving the decedent, and (3) the decedent is either receiving annuity or other payments at the time of her death or she has an enforceable right to such payments. The payments to the decedent, or the decedent's right to the payments, must arise from the same contract or agreement as the beneficiary's payments, and they must continue for the decedent's life, for a period not ascertainable without reference to decedent's death, or for a period that did not in fact end before decedent's death.

The regulations interpret these requirements broadly. The term "annuity or other payment" refers to one or more payments extending over any period of time. The payments may be equal or unequal in amount; they may be conditional or unconditional; they may be periodic or sporadic. Reg. §20.2039-1(b)(1)(ii). A single payment to the beneficiary may be sufficient.

A "contract or agreement" includes any arrangement, understanding, or plan or any combination of arrangements, understandings, and plans. Reg. §20.2039-1(b)(1)(ii). A mere hope or even an expectancy that an employer will make payments is not sufficient. *See* Estate of Barr v. Commissioner, 40 T.C. 227 (1963), *acq.* 1964-2 C.B. 336, 1978-2 C.B. 1, discussed at page 336. A corporate resolution providing for payments made after decedent retires is usually not sufficient either. Courtney v. United States, 84-2 U.S.T.C. ¶13,580 at 86,140 (N.D. Ohio 1984). In Neely v. United States, 222 Ct. Cl. 250, 613 F.2d 802 (1980), however, the court held that a resolution of the board of directors was sufficient because the surviving wife, either personally or as personal representative of decedent's estate, owned 70 percent of the stock of the corporation, and her daughters and sons-in-law owned the remainder.

> Any possibility that the annuity payments to plaintiff would cease other than through a voluntary renunciation is extremely remote. We need not explore the outer boundaries regarding the extent to which section 2039(a) may apply to legally unenforceable arrangements, but to allow the annuity in this case to escape inclusion under section 2039(a) would seriously erode that section with regard to pensions and death benefits paid by a closely held corporation with any knowledgeable tax planning.

Id. at 808. In Courtney v. United States, the surviving spouse held only 15 percent of the stock of the corporation and was thus "not in a position to force the company to continue to make the payments at issue against the wishes of its management or the other stockholders." *Courtney* at 86,144.

The payments to the decedent and the beneficiary must arise from the same contract or agreement. In most annuities, whether purchased directly by the decedent or provided by an employer, the decedent and the beneficiary receive the same type of payments under one contract. Section 2039 may, however, reach beyond these traditional arrangements to include in decedent's gross

estate various payments from the decedent's employer to a beneficiary designated by the decedent. The primary issue is which employment benefits paid
to the decedent may be combined with the survivor's benefit for the purpose of
§2039. This issue is explored in section C of this chapter.

An annuity is payable to the decedent if she was in fact receiving it at the
time of her death even if she did not have an enforceable right to it. Moreover,
the decedent "possessed the right" to receive an annuity or other payment if she
had an enforceable right to receive payments in the future, even though the right
might be subject to conditions or forfeiture. Reg. §20.2039-1(b)(1)(ii). In Estate
of Wadewitz v. Commissioner, 339 F.2d 980 (7th Cir. 1964), the estate argued
that decedent did not have an enforceable right to any payments because they
were forfeitable if he engaged in competition with his employer after termination of his employment. The court rejected this claim, citing the regulation.

> It is, of course, true that under the statute a "right to possess" in the future
> must be nonforfeitable insofar as the obligator of the contracts is concerned; that
> is, the promise to make payments must be a continually enforceable one
> possessed by the obligatee. If [the employer] could have stopped payments at its
> discretion, Wadewitz would not have possessed a "right to receive," but a mere
> expectancy; thus, the statutory requirement would not have been satisfied. The
> promise of [the employer], however, to make payments if Wadewitz retired
> constituted a nonforfeitable right which the decedent possessed since [the
> employer] was unable to revoke its promise unless there was activity that could
> be initiated only by Wadewitz. Just as [the employer] had no discretion over the
> start of payments it had no discretion over their being stopped. Wadewitz's right
> to payments (if he retired and refrained from the proscribed acts listed in the
> contract) was entirely within his control. Hence, he possessed an enforceable
> nonforfeitable right to future payments.

Id. at 983. The court in Goodman v. Granger reached the same result under
§2033. 243 F.2d 264 (3d Cir. 1957), *cert. denied* 355 U.S. 835 (1957).

Example 11-1

Fidelity Insurance Company agrees to pay Dan an annuity of $2,000 per
month from age 70 until his death. Dan dies at age 72. Nothing is in his
gross estate because all payments cease at his death. The same result occurs
if Dan dies at age 64 before he begins receiving payments.

This may not be a good investment for Dan. If he wants to ensure the
return of his initial investment, Dan can contract with Fidelity to pay a lump
sum to his estate if he dies before receiving a certain number of payments.
Assume that the annuity requires Fidelity to pay Dan's estate $100,000 less
the sum of all payments received by Dan before his death. Dan dies after
receiving $60,000, and Fidelity pays his estate $40,000. Section 2039 does
not apply to the $40,000, because no "annuity or other payment" is received
by "any beneficiary by reason of surviving the decedent." Section 2033,
however, brings the $40,000 into Dan's gross estate because he had an interest

in that amount at the time of his death, and that amount passes from Dan to his beneficiaries or heirs either through his will or by intestacy.

Example 11-2

Fidelity Insurance Company agreed to pay Debra an annuity of $1,000 per month for her life and the same amount to her sister, Susan, for her life. When Debra dies, the value of the annuity to be paid to Susan will be in her gross estate under §2039. There is a contract between Debra and Fidelity Mutual Insurance Company; there are payments to a surviving beneficiary, Susan, under that contract, and there were payments to Debra, the decedent, under the same contract.

The amount included in the decedent's gross estate is the portion attributable to the decedent's contribution to the annuity. §2039(b). If the decedent paid the full purchase price, then the full value of the annuity payments will be in her gross estate. Amounts paid by the decedent's employer are considered as decedent's contribution if the payments are made by reason of employment.

Example 11-3

Debra and her sister, Susan, each contributed equally to the purchase of a joint and survivor annuity. Debra dies, survived by Susan. The value of the annuity at Debra's death is $50,000. Because Debra and Susan each contributed half of the purchase price, only $25,000 is in Debra's gross estate under §2039.

Section 2039 applies not only to annuities purchased directly by the decedent, but also to retirement annuities provided through employment. Retirement plans may be either qualified plans, *i.e.*, eligible for preferential income tax treatment, or nonqualified plans. When Congress enacted §2039 in 1954, it excluded qualified plan benefits. In 1982, Congress limited this exclusion and later repealed it entirely. Retirement annuities paid, or payable, to the decedent and then to a designated beneficiary are now included in the decedent's gross estate whether paid through a qualified or a nonqualified plan. Where the beneficiary is the decedent's spouse, the value of the annuity will usually qualify for the marital deduction. §2056(b)(7)(C).

Example 11-4

Dan retires and is collecting benefits from his §401(k) plan at the time of his death. His wife, Wanda, continues to receive benefits from the plan as his designated beneficiary. The present value of the benefits to Wanda will be included in Dan's gross estate under §2039, but they will qualify for the marital deduction under §2056 discussed in Chapter 16.

Example 11-5

Debra is collecting benefits from her IRA account at the time of her death. After her death, her sister, Susan, collects benefits as Debra's surviving beneficiary. The present value of the payments to Susan will be in Debra's gross estate under §2039.

PROBLEMS

1. David purchased an annuity from Fidelity Insurance Company.
   a. What are the estate tax consequences if David is to receive the greater of $1,500 per month for his life or $100,000, and David dies after receiving payments totaling $125,000? What if David has only received $75,000?
   b. What are the estate tax consequences if David is to receive $1,500 per month for his life and after his death his nephew, Ned, is to receive $1,500 per month for his life? David predeceases Ned.
2. Harold retired and received Social Security benefits of $1,000 per month. After his death, his spouse, Wendy, began receiving Social Security benefits of $1,000 because she was Harold's surviving spouse. Is the value of the Social Security benefits payable to Wendy in Harold's gross estate under §2039?
3. Diane was employed by XYZ Inc., which provided a retirement benefit plan. Under the plan, Diane was entitled to an annuity based on her salary and years of service at retirement or permanent disability. If Diane was married, the annuity would be paid to her surviving spouse after her death. If Diane was not married, she could also designate another beneficiary if she died before she began receiving payments. Assume the plan is a qualified retirement plan.
   a. What are the estate tax consequences if Diane dies while receiving benefits and her surviving spouse, Steve, continues to receive an annuity?
   b. What if Diane is not married and the annuity payments cease at her death?
   c. What if Diane dies before retirement and her daughter, Nancy, receives a lump sum payment?
   d. Would the result be different if this was a nonqualified plan?
4. Doris created an irrevocable trust with Friendly National Bank as Trustee to pay $50,000 to Doris for her life and to distribute the trust property to her son, Silas, at her death. If Doris's interest qualifies as a grantor retained annuity interest under §2702(b), what are the estate tax consequences when Doris dies?
5. Darren was severely injured in an accident at age ten. Settlement of the lawsuit included a payment of $45,000 per year. Payments were to continue for the greater of Darren's life or 25 years. Payments could not be accelerated, deferred, increased, or decreased. Darren dies at age 20. Is the value of the remaining settlement payments in his gross estate? Under what section?

6. Donna won the lottery and was entitled to receive 25 annual payments of $950,000. She could not sell, assign, or accelerate the lottery payments, but she could designate a beneficiary in the event of her death. Donna died after receiving five payments and had designated her brother, Ben, to receive the remaining payments. What are the estate tax consequences?

B. PRIVATE ANNUITIES AND SELF-CANCELING INSTALLMENT NOTES
IRC §§2033, 2036(a)(1), 2039, 7520

A private annuity is simply an annuity agreement between individuals rather than with a commercial enterprise such as an insurance company. Most private annuities arise from the sale of property by the decedent to a family member. The rules of §2039(a) apply to private annuities.

Example 11-6

Drew transfers Blackacre to his daughter, Lisa, in exchange for her promise to pay him $1,200 per month until his death. Drew dies seven years after the transfer. Nothing is in his gross estate because the payments cease at his death. If the value of the annuity is not equal to the fair market value of Blackacre on the date of transfer, the transaction will be characterized as a part-sale/part-gift.

Instead, Drew's agreement with his daughter requires her to pay the greater of $1,200 per month for his life or $250,000. Any amount not paid to Drew before death is to be paid to his estate. Drew dies after Lisa has made payments totaling $150,000. The $100,000 due on his death is in Drew's gross estate pursuant to §2033.

Instead, the agreement requires Lisa to pay Drew $1,200 per month until his death and then to pay that sum to Drew's spouse, Sarah. At Drew's death, the value of the annuity payments to Sarah will be in Drew's gross estate under §2039(a).

The estate tax consequences are the same for an installment sale where the sales agreement provides that all payments cease at the seller's death.

Estate of Moss v. Commissioner
74 T.C. 1239 (1980), *acq.* 1981-2 C.B. 1

IRWIN, Judge:
. . . John A. Moss (hereafter decedent) died on February 24, 1974. He was survived only by his wife, Dorothy. Prior to his death, decedent was president

of Moss Funeral Home, Inc. . . . As of September 11, 1972, decedent owned 231 shares of the 586 issued and outstanding shares of Moss Funeral Home. He also owned property (known as the North Fort Harrison property and parking areas) which was rented by Moss Funeral Home for use as one of its funeral homes.

All of the remaining stock of Moss Funeral Home was held by its employees who had either purchased the stock or been given shares as gifts from decedent over the years. All of the employee-shareholders were part of an agreement that upon their retirement or resignation from the corporation they would sell their shares of stock in Moss Funeral Home either to the corporation or pro rata to the remaining shareholders. . . .

On September 11, 1972, a special meeting of the stockholders and directors of Moss Funeral Home was held to consider decedent's offer to sell the corporation his 231 shares of Moss Funeral Home and the North Fort Harrison property and parking areas. The decedent offered to sell the stock for $184,800 and the North Fort Harrison property and parking area for $290,000, each to be paid by the issuance of a note by the corporation to the decedent. . . . The sale of the 231 shares of Moss Funeral Home, Inc., stock and the North Fort Harrison Chapel and parking areas was a bona fide sale for adequate and full consideration.

The notes issued for the purchase of the stock (hereafter Note B) and for the purchase of the North Fort Harrison property (hereafter Note C) provided for interest of 4 percent and equal monthly payments ($1,936.08 on Note B, and $3,053.92 on Note C) commencing October 1972, until paid in full, 9 years and 7 months from the first payment. The notes also contained the following clause: "Unless sooner paid, all sums, whether principal or interest, shall be deemed cancelled and extinguished as though paid upon death of J. A. Moss.". . .

On September 11, 1972, the physical and mental condition of decedent was average for a man of 72 years of age. There was nothing to indicate that his life expectancy would be shorter than the approximate 10 years of life expectancy which was indicated by generally accepted mortality tables. Decedent was admitted to the hospital on May 10, 1973, at which time it was discovered that he had cancer of the lymph nodes. Petitioner was told by his doctor at that time that his condition was probably terminal although treatment was prescribed. During the few days before his death on February 23, 1974, it was apparent that decedent was critically ill.

Decedent timely received each payment due under the notes from October 1972 until his death. At that time there remained unpaid balances of $257,396.08 on Note A-1, $161,575.50 on Note B, and $253,554.52 on Note C. No payments were made on Notes B and C subsequent to decedent's death. . . . We must first decide whether the promissory notes which were extinguished upon decedent's death are includable in his gross estate. . . .

In Estate of Buckwalter [v. Commissioner, 46 T.C. 805 (1966)], decedent's son was indebted to a bank on a 20-year note due in 1971 bearing 4½ percent interest. Decedent proposed that he and his son enter into an arrangement whereby decedent would pay off the unamortized principal of his son's note on December 31 1954. The son would pay him the identical monthly amounts which would have been due the bank, except that interest would be computed at 2½ percent so that the entire loan would be repaid in 1968 rather than in 1971. The son was instructed to keep the transaction secret, the payments were to be a "matter of honor" and the decedent stated that it was [his] intention not to show "in any way that (the son was) in any way indebted to me, otherwise (decedent) would be required to pay in [Pennsylvania] a personal property tax each year." Decedent recognized that he probably would not be alive at the end of the amortization period, and stated that his son was to be entirely free of any obligation to his estate. He added a long postscript to the letter setting forth a summary schedule of 30-day payments, showing components of interest and principal in each such payment in December of each year as well as "balance of amortized principal" until final payment in 1968. He also stated that his son might "cut away" the schedule and "destroy the rest of the letter after all details are consummated."

In a second letter to his son about a week later, after the proposal had been accepted, decedent stated that he was sending his son a schedule for payments and credits for the period January 1, 1955, to May 23, 1962, and that for the period thereafter he had "a schedule made up to show complete amortization of an honor loan," which he intended to seal and enclose in his lock box with a legend on the envelope in his son's handwriting reading "Personal Property of Abraham L. Buckwalter, Jr." In a single sentence, decedent informed his son that he could "consider the proposition on my part as a form of annuity at 2 and ½%."

We held that decedent had an interest in a debt owed to him by his son at the time of his death and that the unpaid principal was includable in his gross estate under section 2033. The taxpayer there argued that in substance, decedent merely had purchased an annuity from his son which terminated with his death, and therefore, nothing should be included in his gross estate. We disagreed with the contention that the substance of the transaction was an annuity and held that decedent had an interest in the loan at the time of his death. . . .

In *Buckwalter*, the decedent retained control of the entire debt until his death. The son was not relieved of the debt until he removed the evidence of the loan after the decedent's death. Therefore, at any time prior to his death, decedent could have revoked his decision to cancel the debt at his death and required the son to be obligated to his estate. The decedent sought to achieve the same result as a bequest in a will by keeping the details of the loan contained in a sealed envelope in his own lock box and permitting the son to cancel the debt at his death.

This is not the case here. The parties have stipulated that decedent's sale of stock for which the notes were issued was a bona fide sale for adequate and full consideration. The cancellation provision was part of the bargained for consideration provided by decedent for the purchase price of the stock. As such, it was an integral provision of the note. We do not have a situation, therefore, where the payee provided in his will or endorses or attaches a statement to a note stating that the payor is to be given a gift by the cancellation of his obligation on the payee's death.

We believe there are significant differences between the situation in which a note contains a cancellation provision as part of the terms agreed upon for its issue and where a debt is canceled in a will. The most significant difference for purposes of the estate tax is, as petitioner points out, that a person can unilaterally revoke a will during his lifetime, and, therefore, direct the transfer of his property, at his death. All interest that decedent had in the notes lapsed at his death. . . .

Even should we consider the payments to decedent as an "annuity" the value of the notes would still not be includable in his gross estate. In Estate of Bergan v. Commissioner, 1 T.C. 543 (1943), the decedent had made an inter vivos transfer to her sister of her interest in an estate in exchange for her sister's promise to care for and support the decedent for the remainder of the decedent's life. We held therein that the decedent did not retain a life interest in the income from the transferred property under the predecessor of section 2036 because no trust was created to secure the "annuity" nor did the decedent reserve to herself the right to the income from the transferred property. Estate of Bergan v. Commissioner, *supra* at 552. The decedent merely contracted with her sister for her support and her share of the estate was transferred as the consideration for such contract. Similarly, in the present case, decedent transferred his stock and the North Fort Harrison property as full consideration for Note B and Note C. While the notes were secured by a stock pledge agreement, this fact, alone, is insufficient to include the value of the notes in decedent's gross estate.

Although the estate tax consequences of annuities and installment sales with a cancellation provision are similar, the valuation for gift tax purposes may differ. The value of an annuity is the present value of the right to receive the projected stream of payments. Reg. §20.2031-7(d)(2)(iv). The annuity will be valued based on the seller's actuarial life expectancy except in unusual cases. §7520; Reg. §25.2512-8; Revenue Ruling 69-74, 1969-1 C.B. 43. The valuation of the self-canceling installment note, on the other hand, is more subjective. First, the facts and circumstances will be carefully scrutinized to determine whether or not there was a bona fide sale, at arm's length, with intent to enforce the promissory note. *See, e.g.,* Estate of Costanza v. Commissioner, 320 F.3d 595 (6th Cir. 2003). Second, there is no requirement that the actuarial tables be used so that the seller's health, the length of the promissory note, the interest rate, and any security may be evaluated to determine a fair market value for the note. *See* GCM 39503 (1985). Third, the interest rate is likely to be higher to reflect the risk of premature death. *See* Burgess J.W. Raby and William Raby, *Self-Canceling Installment Notes and Private Annuities,* 91 Tax Notes 2035

(2001). The income tax consequences of an annuity differ from those of an installment sale. *See* GCM 39503.

It is therefore critical to determine whether an agreement to transfer property in exchange for a promise to make periodic payments until a stated amount has been paid or until the transferor's death, whichever occurs first, is a private annuity or a self-canceling installment note. If the stated amount would be received by the transferor before the expiration of his actuarial life expectancy, determined as of the date of the transfer, the agreement will be treated as a self-canceling installment note. Otherwise, it will be treated as a private annuity. GCM 39503 (1985).

This does not, however, end the inquiry. It is possible that a private annuity will, in fact, be treated as a transfer with a retained life interest under §2036(a)(1). If this happens, the full date of death value of the transferred property will be in the decedent's gross estate. The substance of the transaction, not its form, will control.

Estate of Bergan v. Commissioner
1 T.C. 543 (1943)

BLACK, Judge:

. . . Margaret L. Goggin and the decedent, Sarah A. Bergan, were sisters. The decedent died in 1939. Kate A. Johnson, a third sister, died intestate December 6, 1932, leaving an estate of approximately $500,000, and her only distributees were her two above named sisters. Shortly after Mrs. Johnson's death, Miss Bergan, who was then 74 but in good health, approached Mrs. Goggin, who was five years younger, with the proposition that Mrs. Goggin was to take all of Mrs. Johnson's estate, except $50,000 in bonds which were to be transferred to Miss Bergan, and that there was to be an oral understanding between the two that Miss Bergan would live with Mrs. Goggin for the remainder of Miss Bergan's life and that Mrs. Goggin was to defray all of the living expenses. That proposition was agreed upon by both sisters and was fully executed. . . . Is this transfer of Miss Bergan's share of Mrs. Johnson's estate in excess of the $50,000 block of bonds includable in Miss Bergan's gross estate under [§2036(a)] of the Internal Revenue Code?. . .

The respondent strongly contends that in substance Miss Bergan retained for her life the right to the income from the property transferred, and that for this reason the property must be included in Miss Bergan's gross estate under [§2036(a)]. In this connection the respondent points out that the living expenses of Miss Bergan, Mrs. Goggin and her two adult sons, all of which were paid by Mrs. Goggin, were between $25,000 and $30,000 a year, and that, if it took $7,500 a year for Mrs. Goggin to support Miss Bergan, the income from the property transferred (1933 agreed value, $133,662.36) would hardly be sufficient. From this the respondent argues that the result of the agreement between the two sisters was in substance the same as if Miss Bergan had transferred the property in trust with instructions to pay her the income therefrom for life and upon her death to deliver the principal to Mrs. Goggin, citing Tips v. Bass [21 F.2d 460 (W.D. Texas 1927)] and Updike v. Commissioner [88 F.2d 807 (8th Cir. 1937), *cert. denied* 301 U.S. 708 (1937)].

We think these cases are distinguishable from the instant estate tax proceeding. In both these cases relied upon by the respondent actual trusts were created to secure the annuities, whereas no trust was created in the instant proceeding. Mrs. Goggin was free to use the property transferred to her in any way that she pleased. The title vested in Mrs. Goggin and not in any trustee. Miss Bergan did not reserve to herself the income from the property transferred. She had entered into a contract with her sister for support and transferred the property in question as consideration for the contract. . . . For reasons above stated, we hold that none of the $175,565.10 in question should be added to decedent's gross estate. On this issue we sustain petitioner.

We shall now consider the question whether any part of Miss Bergan's share of Mrs. Johnson's estate in excess of the $50,000 block of bonds is taxable as a gift made in 1933. . . . In deciding the estate tax question we held that Miss Bergan made a "transfer" during the year 1933 of her share of Mrs. Johnson's estate in excess of the $50,000 block of bonds in consideration for Mrs. Goggin's promise to support Miss Bergan for the remainder of Miss Bergan's life. The parties agree that in 1933 the value of the property thus transferred by Miss Bergan was the amount of $133,662.37. Petitioner contends that the transfer was for an adequate and full consideration in money or money's worth, and that there was, therefore, no gift. In the alternative, petitioner contends that if the transfer was for less than an adequate and full consideration, the minimum value of such consideration . . . would be $38,880.15, and that only the difference between $133,662.36 and $38,880.15 should be deemed a gift. . . . The respondent contends that the transfer was for less than an adequate and full consideration; that petitioner has failed to prove the value of the consideration, namely, Mrs. Goggin's promise to support Miss Bergan for the remainder of Miss Bergan's life; and that, therefore, the entire value of the property transferred ($133,662.37) should be deemed a gift under [§2512(b)]. . . .

In the instant gift tax proceeding there was a valid consideration for the transfer in question, namely, Mrs. Goggin's promise to support Miss Bergan for the remainder of Miss Bergan's life, but it was less than an adequate and full consideration for the property which was transferred. Is that consideration reducible to a money value? We think it is. Mrs. Goggin was to support Miss Bergan according to the standard then being enjoyed by the four adults which was at a cost of between $25,000 and $30,000 a year, or an average of between $6,250 and $7,500 for each adult. We adopt the lower figure in view of the insufficiency of the evidence to adequately establish a higher figure than that. We think such a consideration may be valued in the same way that an annuity of $6,250 for Miss Bergan's life would be valued. At the time of the transfer in 1933 Miss Bergan was 74 years of age. According to column 2 of table A mentioned in article 19(7) of Regulations 79, the present value of $1 due at the end of each year during the life of a person 74 years of age is $5.18402, or $32,400.13 for an annuity of $6,250. This is the same method of computation as petitioner used in arriving at the figures of $38,880.15 as being the value of Mrs. Goggin's agreement to support and maintain Miss Bergan during the remainder of her life. The difference in our figure and that arrived at by petitioner is that we use a figure of $6,250 as the cost of annual support and maintenance for Miss Bergan whereas petitioner used $7,500 as such annual figure. We find, therefore, that Miss Bergan transferred property of the value of $133,662.37 for an equivalent in money of $32,400.13, and . . . we hold that the excess of the value of the property transferred over the value of the consideration, or $101,262.24, shall be deemed a gift and shall be included in computing the amount of gifts made by Miss Bergan during the calendar year 1933.

Estate of Fabric v. Commissioner
83 T.C. 932 (1984)

STERRETT, Judge:

By notice of deficiency dated April 13, 1981, respondent determined a deficiency of $457,902 in the Federal estate tax of the Estate of Mollie P. Fabric. After concessions, the issues before us are: (1) Whether the decedent entered into a valid annuity or retained a life estate in the transferred properties, and (2) if a valid annuity existed, whether adequate and full consideration was given. . . .

Mollie P. Fabric (hereinafter referred to as decedent) was born on May 1, 1909, and died, testate, on February 21, 1977, a resident of Florida. She was survived by her four sons, Elliot, Robert, Bruce, and Stuart. . . . Decedent's family had a history of myocardial infarctions (heart attacks) and hypertension (elevated blood pressure). The decedent had had hypertension since at least 1962. On May 31, 1974, the decedent was hospitalized, suffering from multiple medical problems, including kidney problems, ulcerative colitis, and hypertension. Decedent was treated and released on July 3, 1974.

During the first 9 months of 1975, the decedent had severe chest pains, which were alleviated only with nitroglycerine. On September 5, 1975, the decedent's chest pains had increased in their intensity, resulting in an unexpected hospitalization. . . . [T]he decedent underwent coronary artery bypass surgery (open-heart surgery) on September 24, 1975. Prior to the surgery, the decedent's physicians predicted that she had a 60- to 75-percent chance of survival. Decedent survived the surgery, but it was not the end of her medical treatment. [Decedent was also hospitalized on October 8, 1975, in December 1975, on January 6, 1977, and in February 1977. In January 1976, her doctor expected her to live "several years, possibly even in excess of five years."]

The decedent was hospitalized for the last time on February 11, 1977, and died on February 21, 1977, from congestive heart failure. Decedent's death occurred approximately 1 year and 5 months after her September 24, 1975, operation.

On September 19, 1975, five days prior to her September 24, 1975, operation, the decedent executed numerous documents. These documents included her last will and testament, the creation of a foreign trust (hereinafter referred to as the Chai Trust), and a proposal to enter into an annuity agreement with the trustee of the Chai Trust. The proposal was accepted by the trustee on September 22 1975. . . .

In accordance with the annuity agreement, Cayman National Bank agreed to pay decedent the sum of $2,378.48 per week for the rest of her life. The annuity was a fixed obligation and was not dependent on the trust's income. Its amount was determined by use of the tables set forth in section 20.2031-10, Estate Tax Regs. In consideration for the bank's promise, decedent agreed to transfer assets to the trust totaling $1,150,000 in value. Under the laws of the Cayman Islands, the bank was liable to the full extent of its assets for paying the annuity in the event the Chai Trust assets had been exhausted.

Mr. Steinberg, a qualified expert actuary, testified that the purchase of a private annuity in 1975 under the same terms and conditions as the decedent's would have cost approximately $1,215,000. He was of the opinion that decedent had received adequate and full consideration for her transfer of assets in exchange for the annuity. . . .

We are faced with the question of how the above-described events should be characterized for estate tax purposes. Petitioner argues that the creation of the Chai Trust and the sale to, or exchange with, the trust for an annuity were two separate events. It is petitioner's contention that decedent entered into a valid and binding annuity agreement with the trust, for which adequate and full consideration was given. In support of the argument that adequate consideration was given, petitioner notes that the amounts of the annuity payments were determined from the actuarial tables set forth in section 20.2031-10, Estate Tax Regs. Thus, petitioner maintains that none of the assets that decedent transferred to the trust under the terms of the annuity agreement should be included in her estate.

Respondent maintains that the decedent did not purchase an annuity but instead retained a life estate in the transferred properties. Thus, under section 2036, respondent argues that the value of the transferred properties should be included in decedent's estate. Alternatively, respondent argues that if a valid annuity agreement existed, then adequate and full consideration was not given. This is premised upon the contention that decedent was not entitled to use the actuarial tables set forth in section 20.2031-10, Estate Tax Regs., in valuing the annuity. Respondent maintains that use of the tables was inappropriate because, at the time of the transfer, decedent's death was clearly imminent and her medical condition was incurable.

The critical issue is whether the disputed transaction is to be treated as an annuity, or a retained life estate in the transferred properties. This issue has been addressed in the income tax context by this Court in Lazarus v. Commissioner, 58 T.C. 854 (1972), *affd.* 513 F.2d 824 (9th Cir. 1975); in La Fargue v. Commissioner, 73 T.C. 40 (1979), *affd. in part and revd. in part* 689 F.2d 845

(9th Cir. 1982); and in Stern v. Commissioner, 77 T.C. 614 (1981), *revd. and remanded* 747 F.2d 555 (9th Cir. 1984). Since the annuity issue is separate and distinct from what income or estate tax consequences should attach to its resolution, the rationale of these cases is fully applicable to the case at bar.

In *Lazarus,* pursuant to a comprehensive plan, taxpayers established a foreign trust for the benefit of their family members. Taxpayers then entered into an annuity agreement with the trust whereby they transferred stock to the trust in exchange for the trust's promise to pay them $75,000 a year for life. As part of the prearranged plan, the trust sold the stock to a corporation for a nonnegotiable promissory note, which provided for annual interest payments of $75,000. We found that an annuity had not been purchased. Rather, the transaction was a transfer of the stock to the trust with a reservation of the right to have the annual income of $75,000 distributed to taxpayers.

In finding that a valid annuity was not created, the following factors were deemed important: (1) The alleged annuity payments exactly equaled the income generated by the trust. No distributions could have been made from the trust corpus because its sole asset was a nonnegotiable instrument. Thus, the corpus would remain intact for ultimate distribution to the remainderman. (2) The alleged annuity arrangement did not give taxpayers a downpayment, interest on the deferred purchase price, or security for its payment. (3) The only source of the payments to taxpayers was the income from the property they had transferred to the trust. (4) There was no relationship between the purported sales price and the value of the stock transferred.

In evaluating all of these factors, the Court concluded that the trust acted as a mere conduit for the distribution of trust income to petitioners.

In *La Fargue,* pursuant to an overall plan, taxpayer established a trust with an initial corpus of $100, naming her daughter as beneficiary. Taxpayer's sister, the son of friends, and her lawyer were the trustees. Two days later, taxpayer transferred various assets to the trust in return for equal annual payments for life from the trust. While there was not any precise tie-in between the income of the trust and the annuity payments, this Court did mention that the transferred property was the sole source of the annuity payments to taxpayer. There also was no relationship between the present value of the purported sales price and the fair market value of the transferred properties.

This Court ruled that the transfer of assets was not a sale or exchange for an annuity but rather a transfer in trust with a reserved interest. In so holding, the Court also mentioned that there were informalities in the trust's administration. The taxpayer had continued to receive dividends on the transferred stock; the taxpayer did not assert her contractual rights when her annuity payments were late; and the taxpayer expected to be kept informed on trust matters, even though she did not retain any control over the trust.

The Ninth Circuit reversed, holding that the "informalities" the Tax Court found did not justify looking through the formal terms of the annuity agreement. The Ninth Circuit also held that *Lazarus* did not apply because the annuity payments were not a conduit for the trust's income.

In *Stern* as an integral part of taxpayers' (Sidney and Vera Stern) financial and estate plan, two foreign trusts were created (the Hylton Trust and the Florcken Trust). The terms of the two trusts were essentially identical. The trustee of both trusts was an independent foreign bank, and taxpayers and their issue were the named beneficiaries of the respective trusts.

The trust instruments empowered the trustee to guarantee taxpayers' loans, to lend them money on an unsecured, interest-free basis, and to freely distribute corpus or income to them. In addition, the Hylton Trust gave Sidney, and the Florcken Trust gave Vera, a limited power of appointment over the trust properties and permitted them to replace the trustee without cause.

Shortly after the trusts were created, taxpayers transferred substantial blocks of stock to these trusts in exchange for lifetime annuities. The annual annuity payments were computed by dividing the fair market value of the stock by the appropriate annuity factor listed in the tables set forth in section 20.2031-10(b), Estate Tax Regs. Although the foreign bank trustee administered both trusts, taxpayers and their attorney played active roles in the trusts' affairs.

This Court found that the transactions did not constitute sales in exchange for annuities, but were transfers in trust with retained rights to annual payments. On appeal, the Ninth Circuit reversed, relying on their decision in *La Fargue*. They held that a valid annuity had been established, and emphasized that lack of tie-in between the amount of the annuity and the trust's income was essential to their analysis. In arriving at their decision, the court stated that the transfers of stock to a trust may not be recharacterized simply because the transfers were part of a prearranged plan designed to minimize tax liability or because the transferred property constituted the bulk of the trust assets. The court also mentioned that taxpayers did not possess the degree of control over the trusts to justify treating them as having retained an income interest in the transferred properties.

In the instant case, respondent insists that the decedent failed to purchase an annuity. He alleges that the following factors support his contention: (1) Many of the payments made to the decedent by the trustee were untimely; other payments due under the terms of the agreement were simply not made to the decedent. (2) Some interest payments on the transferred assets were made to the decedent rather than to the trustee. (3) Some of the assets were not transferred to the trustee until after September 1975. (4) The annuity agreement was not financially guaranteed by the trustee, and accordingly all payments were to be charged to the transferred property. (5) Decedent sent a letter to the trustee expressing her desire that he consult with her son and her attorney with respect to trust investment decisions.

This case is appealable to the Ninth Circuit, which reversed us in *La Fargue* and in *Stern*. We find that the facts here are substantially similar to those in *La Fargue* and in *Stern*. Further, the informalities in the trust and annuity administration were no more egregious than those we found in *La Fargue*. Therefore . . . we believe that we are compelled to hold that the decedent entered into a valid annuity agreement with the Chai Trust. . . .

The next issue presented is whether the decedent erred in using the actuarial tables set forth in section 20.2031-10 Estate Tax Regs., in valuing her annuity. Respondent maintains that the decedent's physical condition at the time she entered into the annuity agreement with the trust should have been considered. His position is that the annuity's value should have been determined from the decedent's actual life expectancy, not from her life expectancy as set forth in the actuarial tables.

The actuarial tables are provided as an administrative necessity and their general use has been readily approved by the courts. . . . This need for a simplified administration of the tax laws may result in occasional individual discrepancies from the use of the actuarial tables. . . . In exceptional circumstances, however, courts will permit departure from the actuarial tables. . . .

Prior opinions are distinguishable from the instant case. At the time of decedent's execution of the annuity agreement, it was not established that her maximum life expectancy was 1 year or less. In addition, while the decedent underwent open-heart surgery 5 days later, she survived the operation by 1 year and 5 months. Furthermore, the uncontroverted testimony of decedent's physician was that as of late 1975 decedent should live several more years, possibly even 5 more years. . . .

The evidence demonstrates that the decedent's death was not clearly imminent or predictable at the time she entered into the annuity agreement. Only where death is imminent or predictable will departure from the tables be justified. *See* Miami Beach First National Bank v. United States *supra,* at 120. Therefore, we rule that the decedent properly used the actuarial tables in valuing her annuity. The proper use of the tables, along with the testimony of Mr. Steinberg convinces us that adequate and full consideration was given for the annuity.

Section 7520 now prescribes valuation tables and principles to determine the value of annuities, life estates, terms of years, and remainders. Valuation of annuities depends on both an interest rate component, which is adjusted monthly, and a mortality component, which is adjusted after each census. Reg. §20.7520-1(b)(1), (2). The tables may not be used if the individual, who is the measuring life, is terminally ill on the valuation date, *i.e.,* there is at least a 50 percent probability that the individual will die within one year. Reg. §20.7520-3(b)(3)(i).

PROBLEMS

1. Doris owned Blackacre that had a fair market value of $350,000. When Doris was 70 years old, she transferred Blackacre to her daughter, Lauren. Lauren paid $35,000 on the date of transfer and agreed to pay the balance of $315,000, with interest, over 20 years. Doris's attorney prepared a

sales contract, a promissory note, and a mortgage. Assume Blackacre is investment real estate, earning approximately $18,000 per year.

   a. What are the estate tax consequences if Doris dies five years later and she forgives the debt in her will?

   b. What are the estate tax consequences if the contract and the promissory note provide that no payments will be due after Doris's death? Assume that Doris dies at age 75.

   c. What if Doris is 60 on the date of the transfer and dies at age 75? What if she is 85 at the time of the transfer and dies at age 88?

2. Derek owned a printing company and sold it to Peter, a longtime employee of the company.

   a. Peter agreed to pay Derek $3,000 per month until Derek died or until he had made payments totaling $1,200,000, whichever occurred first. What are the estate tax consequences if Derek dies after receiving payments totaling $350,000?

   b. Instead, Peter agreed to pay Derek 15 percent of the net profits of the printing business each year until Derek died or Peter had made payments totaling $1,200,000, whichever occurred first. If Peter sold the printing business before Derek died or before making payments of $1,200,000, he would owe Derek the difference between $1,200,000 and the amount of payments made. If 15 percent of the net profits were below a specified amount for three years in a row, the property would revert to Derek. Derek dies eight years later. What are the estate tax consequences?

3. Donna established an irrevocable trust for the benefit of her children and grandchildren with Friendly National Bank as Trustee. Six months after creating the trust, Donna transferred stock valued at $1,500,000 to the trust in exchange for a payment of $75,000 each year for 20 years. Donna died 12 years after creating the trust. What are the estate tax consequences?

C. EMPLOYEE DEATH BENEFITS
IRC §§2033, 2036(a)(2), 2038, 2039

Employers provide a variety of fringe benefits to their employees, including medical, life, and disability insurance as well as retirement benefits. Often employers also provide a survivor's benefit to an employee's spouse, domestic partner, dependent children, or other specified dependents if the employee dies during the term of employment. The amount paid is usually a percentage of the decedent's salary on the date of death. The percentage may depend on the length of decedent's employment. Benefits are paid for a number of years following the decedent's death or until the death of the designated beneficiary.

Whether anything is in decedent's gross estate depends on an analysis of §§2033, 2036, 2038, and 2039 and the terms and conditions of the benefit.

Estate of Barr v. Commissioner
40 T.C. 227 (1963), *acq.* 1964-2 C.B. 3, 1978-2 C.B. 1

PIERCE, Judge:

. . . In or about the year 1912, Eastman had inaugurated a practice of paying to its employees a year end "wage dividend," in recognition of their loyalty and services to the company. Each year in November, Eastman's board of directors held a meeting; and if at said meeting they declared a cash dividend payable to the holders of its common stock, the directors had been authorized and empowered by the stockholders to declare a "wage dividend" to be paid to eligible employees, if in the discretion of the directors, the cash position and the earnings and profits of the company would permit it. . . . The wage dividend was payable to those Eastman employees who were on the payroll of the company on the last day of its fiscal year; and it was actually paid to them in March of the year following its declaration.

Eastman paid a wage dividend to its employees in every year from 1912 through 1931, with the exception of 1934, when its directors determined that the company's earnings and profits were not sufficient, notwithstanding that a cash dividend was paid to its stockholders for said year. [A wage dividend could be paid to a deceased employee's surviving spouse, child or parent, the estate, or another beneficiary at the discretion of the company.]. . .

The second benefit amount involved in the instant case is the so-called salary death benefit. Decedent's death on March 30, 1957, occurred at the end of the first week of Eastman's fourth 4-week period in Kodak year 1957. Thereafter, on April 2, 1957, the company paid to the decedent's surviving spouse, Frances Barr, the sum of $1,742.31, which was equal to the amount that would have been paid to decedent as salary, if he had lived and continued to be employed by Eastman for the remaining 3 weeks of the pay period in which he died. The company charged the payment to an account on its books, designated "Death Benefit Expense."

Decedent's estate was paid in full by Eastman for the services which he had rendered to that company up to the date of his death.

As was the case with the wage dividend death benefit hereinabove described, a salary death benefit was not paid in the case of every employee who died. Such payments were made only after investigation by the company into the circumstances of the deceased employee's family. Also as has been found with respect to said wage dividend death benefit, the decedent made no contribution of his own funds for the salary death benefit; nor did the company insure against having to make such payment, or create any fund of its own from which to make such a payment. Moreover, no surviving spouse, or relative, executor, or administrator of any deceased employee has ever attempted to enforce a claim against Eastman for the payment of a salary death benefit; nor does the company consider that any such claim would be enforceable. . . .

The first issue relates to the so-called wage dividend death benefit which Eastman Kodak Co. paid to decedent's widow in March 1958 (approximately 1 year after decedent's death). And the question presented with respect to this, is whether the amount of such payment is includable in the gross estate of the decedent for Federal estate purposes, under either section 2033 or section 2039 of the 1954 Code. . . . It will be observed that [§2033] relates only to interests in property which the decedent had at the time of his death. And, as the Supreme Court pointed out in the leading case of Knowlton v. Moore 178 U.S. 41, the justification for the Government's power to subject such interests to the Federal estate tax rests on the principle that such interests pass from the decedent at death and that the estate tax is an excise tax on the privilege of transmitting property at death to the survivors of the decedent. . . .

It is our opinion that, in the present case, the decedent did not have at the time of his death any property interest, either in the "wage dividend" which Eastman's board of directors subsequently declared for the benefit of its living eligible employees (after it had declared a cash dividend for the benefit of its stockholders), or in the related death benefit which these directors then authorized to be paid to decedent's widow. Accordingly, there was no such interest which passed, or could have passed, from him to his widow; and hence no such interest upon which the excise tax on the privilege of transmitting property at death may be imposed under section 2033.

Both this Court and others have recognized that there is a distinction between rights of an employee to death benefits, and, on the other hand, mere hopes and expectancies on the part of an employee that death benefits may be paid. Thus, in the early case of Dimock v. Corwin, 19 F. Supp. 56 (E.D.N.Y.), *affirmed on other issues* 99 F.2d 799 (C.A. 2), *affd.* 306 U.S. 363, it was shown that the Standard Oil Co. had adopted an annuity and insurance plan, subject to withdrawal or modification by Standard at its discretion, under which death benefits roughly equal to a year's salary of an employee might be paid to the widow of a deceased employee. The District Court concluded that the decedent had "only the right to render it possible for (his surviving spouse) to receive a grant from the Standard Oil Co., and that this did not constitute property of his under the then applicable statute, section 302 of the Revenue Act of 1926, a statutory provision cognate to section 2033 of the 1954 Code. . . .

Authorities reaching differing results on the basis of the decedents having *enforceable vested* rights to have their employers pay death benefits to survivors, are typified by Estate of Charles B. Wolf, 29 T.C.441, 447, in which case we stated:

> At the date of decedent's death he had enforceable vested rights in the three trusts (one profit-sharing trust, and two pension trusts), procured by the rendition of services and by continuing in the employ of the respective corporations. He could be deprived of those rights only by deliberately terminating his employment or

being discharged for cause. He had unlimited power to designate or change beneficiaries, and payments to his named beneficiaries were obligatory. The rights thus created were valuable property rights, capable of valuation, and in fact valued by the parties. The decedent's death was the decisive event that resulted in the passage of those rights to the beneficiary. It seems clear to us that they are includible in his gross estate either under the sweeping provisions of section 811(a) or under the more specific provisions of section 811(f)(2) (dealing with powers of appointment). Cf. Estate of William L. Nevin, 11 T.C. 59.

We are convinced that in the instant case, decedent had no more than a hope or expectancy that his surviving spouse might receive a wage dividend death benefit. There were so many events that had to occur before such hope could be realized that we find it impossible to conclude that, at the date of death, he had any property right which he could pass to her. Eastman had to realize earnings and profits for the year 1957; the directors, in the exercise of their discretion, had to declare a dividend to its stockholders; the directors, in further exercise of their discretion, had to declare a wage dividend payment to those employees who were alive and employed by the company on the last day of the Kodak year; and the directors, in the still further exercise of their discretion, had to approve a wage dividend death benefit to the widow of the instant decedent who had theretofore died. Moreover, the company, in its Rules of Eligibility and Participation and in the pamphlet distributed to its employees, made it clear that whether it might approve a wage dividend death benefit to the estate or beneficiary of a deceased employee was solely within its "option"; and that such situation would be distinguishable from that of an employee who had continued to live until after the close of the Kodak year for which the wage dividend was declared, and who thereby had acquired a "right" to the same. . . .

On the basis of all the foregoing, we hold that the wage dividend death benefit here involved is not includable in the decedent's gross estate under either section 2033 or section 2039.

The second issue is whether the salary death benefit which was paid to the decedent's widow is includable in the decedent's gross estate, under either of the above-mentioned sections, 2033 or 2039.

It is our opinion that what we have stated with respect to each of these sections in our consideration of the wage dividend death benefit is equally applicable to this salary death benefit. Moreover, as regards section 2039, it is clear that the decedent himself could not reduce to possession, either immediately or in futuro at any time during his life, any death benefit payment. Hence there is here a failure to meet one of the essential requirements of section 2039, that the decedent must possess for his life or for any period not ascertainable without reference to his death or for any period which does not in fact end before his death, the right to receive an annuity or other payment, either alone or in conjunction with another person or persons. *See* Estate Tax Regs., sec. 20.2039-1(b)(ii).

In Goodman v. Granger, the decedent contracted with his employer, Gimbel Brothers, for the payment of $2,000 per year for 15 years after he terminated his employment. 243 F.2d 264 (3d Cir. 1957), *cert. denied* 355 U.S. 835 (1957). These payments were to be made only if decedent performed satisfactorily and did not engage in a competing business for a specified time after termination of employment. If he died before receiving all of the payments, they were to be made to his estate or the beneficiary named in his will. Decedent died while still employed by Gimbel Brothers, and payments were made to his estate. His estate argued that he did not have any property interest in the payments because they were to be valued at the moment before death and, at that time, the payments had no value because they were forfeitable upon certain conditions. The court rejected this argument, saying:

It is clear that the decedent's interest in the employment contracts was "property" includible in his gross estate under [§2033]. Determination of the time when that interest is to be valued is the crux of the dispute. . . . The taxpayer has ignored the very nature of the tax which it is urged is dispositive of this case. . . . Since death is the propelling force for the imposition of the tax, it is death which determines the interests to be includible in the gross estate. Interests which terminate on or before death are not a proper subject of the tax. Assets may be acquired or disposed of before death, possibilities of the loss of an asset may become actualities or may disappear. Upon the same principle underlying the inclusion of interests in a decedent's gross estate, valuation of an interest is neither logically made nor feasibly administered until death has occurred. The taxpayer's theory of valuing property before death disregards the fact that generally the estate tax is neither concerned with changes in property interests nor values prior to death. The tax is measured by the value of assets transferred by reason of death, the critical value being that which is determined as of the time of death. . . .

Here the employment contracts provided for additional "contingent" compensation of $6,000 per year for fifteen years to be paid to Blum or his estate after the termination of his employment by reason of death or otherwise. True, the right to these payments was forfeitable upon the occurrence of any of the specified contingencies. However, forfeiture as a result of the contingencies never occurred during Blum's lifetime, and any possibility of their occurrence was extinguished by his death. Gimbels has been making and the estate has been collecting the payments provided by the contracts. Valuation of the right to these payments must be determined as of the time of Blum's death when the limiting factor of the contingencies would no longer be considered. Death ripened the interest in the deferred payments into an absolute one, and death permitted the imposition of the tax measured by the value of that absolute interest in property.

Id. at 268-269.

Estate of Tully v. United States
528 F.2d 1401 (Ct. Cl. 1976)

KUNZIG, Judge.

The single issue presented in this estate tax case is the includability in decedent Edward A. Tully, Sr.'s gross estate of death benefits paid directly to Tully's widow by his employer. Plaintiffs (coexecutors) move for partial summary judgment claiming that no estate tax provision compels such treatment. Defendant's cross–motion counters that the death benefits must be added to the gross estate as required either by section 2038(a)(1) or section 2033 of the Internal Revenue Code of 1954. We agree with plaintiff's and hold the sum at issue not includable in Tully's gross estate.

The facts in this case are uncontested. Before his death, Tully was employed by Tully and DiNapoli, Inc. (T & D) a company owned 50% by decedent and 50% by Vincent P. DiNapoli. On July 1, [1959,] Tully, DiNapoli and T & D entered into a contract whereby T & D promised to pay death benefits to the Tully and DiNapoli widows. Later, in October 1963, the same parties amended the 1959 agreement to limit the maximum amount of death payments to $104,000. On March 7, 1964, Tully died. T & D paid his widow the $104,000 called for in the contract.

Because the death benefits were paid directly by T & D to the widow, plaintiffs did not include this sum in Tully's gross estate when they filed the estate tax return. On audit, the Internal Revenue Service (IRS) concluded that the $104,000 was part of Tully's gross estate and assessed an estate tax deficiency. Plaintiffs paid the deficiency, filed a refund claim and by timely petition filed in this court, brought the present action after the IRS disallowed their claim.

In essence, plaintiffs say section 2038(a)(1) is inapplicable because Tully never transferred an interest in the death benefits, either at the time of their creation or thereafter, and even if he had, he kept no power to "alter, amend, revoke or terminate" the interest. Further, plaintiffs assert, decedent had no "interest" in the death benefits at the time of his death, within the meaning of estate tax section 2033. Defendant takes an opposing viewpoint. It contends that Tully made a transfer of his interest in the benefits prior to his death, but kept a power to "alter, amend, revoke or terminate" such transfer until the time of his death. Defendant claims this power requires addition of the benefits to Tully's gross estate under section 2038(a)(1). Alternatively, the Government argues, Tully still had sufficient "interest" in the benefits at the time of his death to force the $104,000 into his gross estate under section 2033. . . .

I. Section 2038(a)(1)

Defendant argues that Tully transferred an interest in the death benefits at some point prior to his death and kept a section 2038(a)(1) power to "alter, amend, revoke or terminate" the enjoyment of the benefits after the transfer until his death. Plaintiffs counter that there was no "transfer" in the [1959] contract or thereafter because decedent never had any interest in the benefits which he could transfer. Even if a transfer is found, plaintiffs claim Tully did not keep a section 2038(a)(1) "power" after such transfer.

Contrary to plaintiffs' position, Tully did transfer an interest in the death benefits to his wife by executing the 1959 contract. In one of the three death benefit plans at issue in Estate of Bogeley v. United States, 514 F.2d 1027, 206 Ct. Cl. 695 (1975), the decedent (an employee, officer, director and 34% shareholder) entered into an enforceable contract with his employer. In consideration of decedent's past and future services, the employer promised to pay decedent's widow or the estate two years' salary after his death. We found that where decedent was married at the time of the execution of the contract he ". . . did make a transfer of his interest to his wife during his lifetime by making the contract with (the employer)." *Bogley, supra,* 514 F.2d at 1039, 206 Ct. Cl. at 715. In the instant case, the basic facts are nearly identical. The 1959 agreement looked to Tully's past and future services to T & D for consideration. The benefits here were also payable to the "widow" and decedent was married at the time of the 1959 contract. Tully in substance, if not in form, made a gift of a part of his future earnings to his wife.

However, within the meaning of section 2038(a)(1), Tully did not keep a power to "alter, amend, revoke or terminate" the death benefit transfer after the 1959 contract. There was no express reservation of such power in either in 1959 or 1963 contracts and no indication in the record of any other express agreements in which Tully obtained a section 2038(a)(1) power.

The Government implies that Tully's 50% stock ownership of T & D gave him unfettered power to change the death benefit plan to suit his own tastes. The facts do not bear this out. To the contrary, Tully's every movement could have been blocked by the other 50% shareholder. Tully did not have individual control of T & D and could not by himself, alter the terms of the death benefit, agreement. As stated by the court in Harris v. United States, 29 Am. Fed. Tax R.2d 1558 (C.D. Cal. 1972), section 2038(a)(1) powers must be demonstrable, real, apparent and evident, not speculative. . . . We agree with this test and find Tully did not have a section 2038(a)(1) power to "alter, amend, revoke or terminate" through his 50% stock ownership in T & D at the time of his death.

Moreover, the death benefits are not includable in Tully's gross estate despite the fact that Tully might have altered, amended, revoked or terminated them in conjunction with T & D and DiNapoli. A power to "alter, amend, revoke or terminate" expressly exercisable in conjunction with others falls within section 2038(a)(1), but "power" as used in this section does not extend to powers of persuasion. If section 2038(a)(1) reached the possibility that Tully might convince T & D and DiNapoli to change the death benefit plan, it would apply to speculative powers. Section 2038(a)(1) cannot be so construed. . . . In addition, if section 2038(a)(1) applies to situations where an employee might convince an employer to change a death benefit program, it would sweep all employee death benefit plans into the gross estates of employees. It would always be at least possible for an employee to convince the employer that it would be to their mutual benefit to modify the death benefit plan. In light of the numerous cases where employee death benefit plans similar to the instant plan were held not includable in the employee's gross estate, we find that Congress did not intend the "in conjunction" language of section 2038(a)(1) to extend to the mere possibility of bilateral contract modification. Therefore, merely because Tully might have changed the benefit plan "in conjunction" with T & D and DiNapoli, the death benefits are not forced into Tully's gross estate.

Tully also did not obtain a section 2038(a)(1) "power" from the remote possibility that he could have altered the amount of death benefits payable to his widow by changing his compensation scheme. The death benefits here were to be paid based on decedent's annual salary. From this, defendant reasons that up until the time of his death, Tully could have accepted lesser compensation or terminated his employment in order to alter or revoke the death benefits. In practical terms, we reject this possibility. This is not a factor which rises to the level of a section 2038(a)(1) "power." An employee might accept lesser compensation or terminate his employment for a myriad of reasons, but to conclude that a motive for such action would be the death benefit plan itself is not only speculative but ridiculous. And we have already made clear that a section 2038(a)(1) "power" cannot be speculative, but must be demonstrable, real, apparent and evident. . . . In addition, modification of Tully's employment contract would have required the cooperation of T & D or a breach by Tully. Neither of these two events constitutes a section 2038(a)(1) "power." Further, it is a common practice to "peg" employee death benefit plans to the employee's salary. To our knowledge, no court has ever held that such practice subjects death benefits to inclusion in the employee's gross estate. . . . [W]e hold that no section 2038(a)(1) power was created by the remote possibility that Tully might have changed the amount of death benefits prior to his death.

Finally, Tully did not retain a section 2038(a)(1) "power" to revoke or terminate the transfer to his wife by virtue of the possibility that he could have divorced her. The contract called for T & D to make the death benefit payments to Tully's widow. It might be argued that Tully could have divorced his wife to terminate her interest in the death benefits, but again such an argument ignores practicalities, reduces the term "power" to the speculative realm and is not in accord with prior cases. In reality, a man might divorce his wife, but to assume that he would fight through an entire divorce process merely to alter employee death benefits approaches the absurd. . . . Thus the use of "widow" in the death benefit contract did not give Tully a real power to revoke or terminate the death benefit transfer to his wife.

In short, in the 1959 contract Tully transferred certain interests to his wife by obtaining T & D's promise to pay death benefits. While it may be argued that Tully kept a certain de minimis association with the death benefit plan, such association never rose to the dignity of a power to "alter, amend, revoke, terminate" the transfer. . . . Therefore, section 2038(a)(1) does not operate to compel inclusion of the death benefits in decedent's gross estate.

II. Section 2033

Nor does section 2033 require addition of the benefits to Tully's gross estate. The Government argues that corporate control, "pegging" the benefits to Tully's salary, and naming "widow" as beneficiary constituted section 2033 "interests" kept by Tully until his death. We found above that these facts did not give rise to a section 2038(a)(1) "power." We also determine that they did not create a section 2033 "interest."

Having found that Tully transferred the death benefits to his wife and that he could not reach them for his own use, he could not have kept a section 2033 "interest." The de minimis associations Tully may have still had with the benefits are not strong enough to force a conclusion that decedent never transferred his interests in the benefits to his wife.

Defendant would use section 2033 as a "catch all." The simple answer to this is that section 2033 is not a "catch all" . . . but applies to situations where decedent kept so much control over an item of property that in substance he still owns the property. "Interest" as used in section 2033 connotes a stronger control than "power" as used in section 2038(a)(1). If controls over property cannot rise to the dignity of section 2038(a)(1) "powers" they equally cannot create section 2033 "interests." In the instant case, having failed to establish that corporate stock ownership, "pegging" the benefits to Tully's salary and naming the "widow" as beneficiary created section 2038(a)(1) "powers," defendant equally fails to demonstrate that the same facts create section 2033 "interests."

Not all courts agree that employment agreements including a death benefit constitute a transfer for purposes of §2038. *See, e.g.,* Harris v. United States, 72-1 U.S.T.C. ¶12,845 at 84,754 (C.D. Cal. 1972).

The IRS has been somewhat more successful including survivor's benefits in the gross estate under §2039. The primary issue under this section has been whether the decedent himself was receiving payments at the time of his death or had an enforceable right to payments pursuant to the same contract or agreement that provided the payment to the survivor. Although the regulations interpret this requirement broadly to include "any arrangement, understanding or plan or any combination of arrangements, understandings or plans arising by reason of the decedent's employment," reg. §20.2039-1(b)(1)(ii), not all benefits qualify. The receipt of pension or retirements benefits, or the right to receive these benefits, can be combined with a survivor's benefit or a death benefit to bring the latter within the reach of §2039. *See, e.g.,* All v. McCobb, 321 F.2d 633 (2d Cir. 1963); Estate of Wadewitz v. Commissioner, 339 F.2d 980 (7th Cir. 1964); Estate of Beal v. Commissioner, 47 T.C. 269 (1966), *acq.* 1967-2 C.B. 1; Gray v. United States, 410 F.2d 1094 (3d Cir. 1969). The receipt of salary or other compensation, on the other hand, is not sufficient.

See, e.g., Estate of Fusz v. Commissioner, 46 T.C. 214 (1966), *acq.* 1967-2 C.B. 1; Kramer v. United States, 186 Ct. Cl. 684, 406 F.2d 1363 (1969).

Estate of Siegel v. Commissioner
74 T.C. 613 (1980)

CHABOT, Judge:

Respondent determined a deficiency in Federal estate tax against petitioner in the amount of $382,815.89. . . . [T]he single issue now presented for decision is whether the commuted value of amounts payable to decedent's children under an employment contract between decedent and his employer is includable in decedent's gross estate either — (1) Under section 2039(a) because decedent might have been entitled to postemployment disability benefits under the employment contract or (2) Under section 2038(a)(1), because decedent retained a power to alter, amend, or revoke his children's rights under the employment contract. . . .

Decedent died of a coronary occlusion on September 21, 1971, at the age of 57. Immediately before his death decedent was employed by Vornado, Inc. . . . as its president and chief executive officer. He was also a member of Vornado's board of directors. Decedent served as president for the 6 years immediately before his death. Decedent was actively employed by Vornado until immediately before his death.

On September 30, 1965, decedent entered into a written employment agreement with Vornado, the relevant portions of which are as follows:. . .

FOURTH: The CORPORATION shall pay to SIEGEL, if living, or to others in the event of his death the following sums upon the terms and conditions and for the periods hereinafter set forth:

(a) In the event of death or disability of SIEGEL on or before the expiration date of this agreement while in the employ of the CORPORATION, the CORPORATION shall pay to him, if living, or others (as hereinafter provided) in the event of his death, monthly, the following sums which shall be in lieu of any and all payments provided for in Paragraph "THIRD" hereof:

(i) An amount equal to the balance of the monthly salary then payable to SIEGEL up to the end of the month in which death occurs or in which his employment is duly terminated because of disability.

(ii) An amount equal to his then monthly salary rate for all successive months up to the expiration date of this agreement.

(b) Payments of the monthly sums herein-above provided for shall begin at the end of the month set forth in subparagraph "(a)(i)" hereof. Such payments shall be made to SIEGEL if living, otherwise divided equally among SIEGEL'S children, living at the time of each scheduled payment. In the event there are no living children payment shall be made to the Estate of SIEGEL. . . .

It was the customary practice at Vornado that management employees, such as decedent, would continue to render services to the company during disability.

No management employee of Vornado had ever become disabled to such an extent that Vornado had terminated the employee's employment.

In the event of disability, decedent was obligated to render services to the best of his ability for the remaining term of the agreement and was under a continuing obligation during the term of the agreement to resume performing services as soon as he recovered sufficiently to do so.

Upon decedent's death, his children became entitled, under the agreement, to monthly payments from Vornado in the same amounts and for the same period of time as decedent would have been entitled to had he survived until November 30, 1979, and remained in Vornado's employ until that date. . . .

I. Section 2039

Respondent maintains that decedent had a right under the agreement to receive disability payments which are postemployment benefits, resulting in the value of the payments to decedent's children being includable in decedent's gross estate under section 2039(a). Petitioner asserts that the agreement provides only for salary or wage continuation payments, which are not includable under section 2039(a). We agree with petitioner. . . .

The parties agree that the following requirements for inclusion in decedent's gross estate under section 2039(a) have been met:

(1) The benefits are receivable pursuant to a form of contract or agreement (other than insurance on decedent's life) entered into after March 3 1931;
(2) The beneficiaries are entitled to receive the benefits by reason of surviving decedent; and
(3) Decedent had the right to receive payments under the contract or agreement for a period which did not in fact end before decedent's death.

The parties' dispute is as to whether decedent, at the time of his death, had the right to receive an "annuity or other payment," within the meaning of section 2039(a). If the agreement did not provide for an "annuity or other payment" to decedent, then section 2039(a) does not require the inclusion of the value of the payments in decedent's gross estate.

It is well established that the term "annuity or other payment" within the meaning of section 2039 does not include regular salary payments (Kramer v. United States, 186 Ct. Cl. 684, 406 F.2d 1363, 1366 (1969); Estate of Fusz v. Commissioner, 46 T.C. 214, 217-218 (1966)) or payments under wage continuation plans (*see* Estate of Schelberg v. Commissioner, 70 T.C. 690, 702 (1978), *revd.* 612 F.2d 25, 29 (2d Cir. 1979); *see also* materials cited in Rev. Rul. 77-183, 1977-1 C.B. 274, 275). The phrase "other payment" is qualitatively limited to postemployment benefits. Estate of Fusz v. Commissioner, 46 T.C. at 218. It is not necessary, however, that the decedent actually be receiving the postemployment benefits at the time of death. If at that time, even while yet employed and receiving only a salary, the decedent possessed the right to receive postemployment benefits at some time in the future, then the statutory requirement regarding the decedent's right to an "annuity or other payment" is met. It is immaterial that death prevents the decedent's receipt of the postemployment benefits. Gray v. United States, 410 F.2d 1094, 1110-1111 (3d Cir. 1969); Bahen's Estate v. United States, *supra*; Estate of Wadewitz v. Commissioner, 39 T.C. 925, 936–938 (1963), *affd.* 339 F.2d 980 (7th Cir. 1964). . . .

In the instant case, the following factors suggest that the agreement provided for postemployment benefits to decedent:

(1) The agreement stated as one of its purposes (third "Whereas"), the monetary provision for decedent in the event of his disability.
(2) The agreement provided for payments to decedent after "his employment is duly terminated because of disability." (Fourth (a)(i).)

The following factors suggest that the agreement did not provide for postemployment benefits to decedent:

(1) The agreement contemplated a continuing obligation on decedent's part to work for Vornado for the term of the agreement, over which term payments at the regular salary rate were to be made (Second).
(2) Decedent was to serve to the best of his ability on the same terms and conditions as were in effect before the agreement was signed (Third). It was the customary practice at Vornado that management employees, such as decedent, would continue to render services to the company during periods of disability.
(3) No employee of Vornado had ever become disabled to such an extent that Vornado had terminated the employee's employment.
(4) In the highly unlikely event that decedent's employment would have been terminated during the term of the agreement because of disability, with decedent still receiving payments, decedent would have had a continuing obligation to return to work when he became able to render services.

There is no reason in the record to conclude that the agreement contemplated that the services to be rendered in the event of disability would be nominal or pro forma. There is no reason in the record to conclude that the prescribed payments were really a retirement annuity; in fact, decedent would have been only 65 years old at the end of the term of the agreement. We conclude that if disability payments would have been made under the agreement then they would have constituted wages for services rendered or payments in lieu of wages during a period of absence from work because of sickness or other incapacity following which decedent would have been expected to return to work. We conclude that the agreement did not provide for postemployment benefits to decedent.

Contrary to respondent's analysis, this conclusion does not read the disability language out of the agreement. This conclusion merely means that disability would have excused decedent from performing services only to the extent of, and for the time of the disability. . . .

In Estate of Schelberg v. Commissioner, *supra,* Schelberg was entitled to participate in each of four separate plans of his employer. The life insurance plan provided for survivors' income benefits to eligible survivors; the value of Schelberg's survivors' income benefits under this plan was sought to be included in Schelberg's gross estate. Under the retirement plan, Schelberg would have been required to retire at age 65 and would have been entitled at that time to retirement benefits. Under the sickness and accident plan, Schelberg was entitled to receive full salary while absent from work on account of sickness or accident for up to 52 weeks in any 24-month period; benefits could be continued under this plan for more than 52 weeks at the employer's discretion in individual cases. Under the disability plan, Schelberg would be entitled to benefits if a special corporate panel determined he was totally and permanently disabled; the payments under this plan would begin on the expiration of the 52-week period of sickness and accident benefits (plus any period of individual consideration benefits under the sickness and accident plan) and continue until normal retirement date, at which time, Schelberg would become eligible for benefits under the retirement plan. Schelberg died while an active, full-time employee. This Court held that the potential benefits under the disability plan were postemployment benefits rather than wage continuation payments. We found strong considerations linking the disability plan to the retirement plan, and we thought it was critical that the disability plan assured a participating employee of income during a period of disablement notwithstanding that the employee was never expected to render any services. 70 T.C. at 701–702.

The Court of Appeals for the Second Circuit reversed, concluding that Schelberg's rights under the disability plan were too dissimilar in nature from an "annuity or other payment" and too contingent to meet the conditions of section 2039(a). 612 F.2d at 29. The Court of Appeals also viewed benefits under the disability plan as a partial continuation of wages when an employee's physical health deteriorated even further than that justifying benefits under the sickness and accident plan. 612 F.2d at 31. The Court of Appeals stated that we should not have presupposed a postretirement status from the disability benefits. 612 F.2d at 31.

Schelberg had a right to disability benefits only if he were determined to be totally and permanently disabled. If that determination were made, then Schelberg would have had no obligation to return to work if he became able. Schelberg would have had a right to disability payments with no continuing obligation to his employer once the corporate panel determined his total and permanent disability.

In contrast to *Schelberg,* as we interpret the agreement decedent had no right to disability benefits freed from an obligation to perform services "to the best of his ability."

In analyzing the agreement, we recognize that it is conceivable that decedent might become so disabled during the term of the agreement that he would be completely unable to render any services, and that Vornado might be so convinced of the permanence of the condition that it would never expect any future services from him. This situation may be what was contemplated by the reference in paragraph Fourth (a) to termination of employment. Also, the situation could theoretically arise in which Vornado would not only terminate decedent's employment as a result of a determination that he was totally and permanently disabled but would completely release decedent from any continuing obligation to return to work if he became capable of doing so. We do not believe that this was contemplated by the agreement, however. We see no reason why Vornado would gratuitously release the decedent from a continuing obligation to return to work. Certainly, the agreement does not clearly entitle decedent to such treatment in the event of his total and permanent disability. Considering all these factors, we conclude that the disability payments were intended to be salary or a wage continuation program in the event of sickness or disability. The agreement assured decedent of income during a period of disablement only if he rendered services which he was capable of, or resumed performing services if and when he recovered from a disability so serious as to preclude the rendering of services.

Since we find the nature of the payments in the instant case to be distinguishable from those in *Estate of Schelberg,* we do not need to reconsider, at this time, our holding in that case in light of the reversal by the Court of Appeals for the Second Circuit. . . .

II. Section 2038

Respondent asserts that decedent transferred property and retained a power to alter, amend, revoke, or terminate the enjoyment of the transferred property. This, respondent maintains, results in the value of the payments to decedent's children being includable in decedent's gross estate under section 2038(a)(1). Petitioner does not dispute that there was a transfer . . . but contends that the agreement's reference to modification "by the mutual consent" of decedent and Vornado adds nothing to the basic contract law rights of parties to renegotiate their contract. This, petitioner asserts, is not the sort of reserved power contemplated by the statute. Respondent answers that the cases upon which petitioner relies are irrelevant because the contracts there involved contained no express language as to rights to renegotiate, while the agreement authorized decedent, with Vornado's assent, to modify the rights or interests transferred to his children.

We agree with respondent.

Under section 2038(a)(1), the value of the payments to decedent's children are includable in decedent's gross estate if decedent retained a power to alter, amend, revoke, or terminate the right to these payments, either alone or in conjunction with any other person.

Paragraph Fifth of the agreement provides: "No right or interest is hereby granted to the children of Siegel except as set forth herein and such rights or interests are subject to any modification of this agreement by the mutual consent of Siegel and the Corporation." Thus, decedent reserved the power in conjunction with Vornado to modify the rights of the beneficiaries by a subsequent agreement. On its face, the agreement provides for the very power in decedent that results in inclusion under section 2038(a)(1).

Petitioner relies on Estate of Tully v. United States, *supra,* and Kramer v. United States, *supra,* for the proposition that "the ability of parties to a contract to agree to amend its terms is insufficient to satisfy the requirements of Code Section 2038." Petitioner acknowledges that Kramer did not reserve a right to renegotiate the amount of payments. In *Tully,* also, there was no express reservation of such a power. Petitioner maintains that *Tully* and *Kramer* are nevertheless on point because, "It is basic contract law that the parties to a contract may, at any time, renegotiate the terms of their contract. Vol. 6 Corbin on Contracts, § 1293 (1962). Thus the language contained in Article Fifth adds nothing to the rights that parties to contracts always possess." Petitioner draws comfort from an estate tax regulation . . . contending that the regulation recognizes that a power which exists under local law is not includable under section 2038(a)(1). Petitioner concludes that an identical power specified in the agreement also is not includable under section 2038(a)(1).

First, in fact no power was reserved by the agreements involved in *Tully* and *Kramer.* The issue in these cases was whether Tully's ownership of 50% of his employer's stock, or the "love and affection" for Kramer by the board of directors of Kramer's employer, caused Tully or Kramer to have a section 2038(a)(1) power. The Court of Claims held in each of these cases that that was not enough in the absence of a power reserved in an agreement. Estate of Tully v. United States, 528 F.2d at 1404; Kramer v. United States, 406 F.2d at 1369. It is precisely the element that the Court of Claims found to be missing in *Tully* and *Kramer* that the parties acknowledge is present in the instant case.

Secondly, as petitioner acknowledges, section 20.2038–1(a)(2), Estate Tax Regs., does not apply to the instant case, since the contingent beneficiaries were excluded by the agreement from any voice in revising their rights under the agreement. . . .

Thirdly, decedent and Vornado apparently did not trust the cited "basic contract law" to produce the results they desired and concluded that it was necessary or desirable to specify their power to vary the rights of decedent's children, and to exclude the children from the class of persons entitled to modify these rights. In contrast to the section 2039(a) dispute, *supra,* we have no evidence as to the meaning or purpose of paragraph Fifth of the agreement that might cast a different light on the matter.

Fourthly, neither side in the instant case has favored us with an analysis of New Jersey law bearing on the matter.

It is well-recognized that third-party beneficiaries, including third-party donee beneficiaries, have enforceable rights under New Jersey law in contracts made for their benefit. N.J. Stat. Ann. sec. 2A:15-2 (West 1952); Estate of Lingle, 72 N.J. 87, 367 A.2d 878, 882 (1976). . . . We are thus faced with the question of what power Vornado and decedent as promisor and promisee would have had to extinguish or modify the rights of the named beneficiaries in the absence of an express reserved power to modify the rights.

Under section 142 of the First Restatement of the Law of Contracts, the duty of the promisor to a donee beneficiary cannot be released by the promisee or affected by any agreement between the promisee and promisor unless the power to discharge or modify the contract is expressly reserved in specific terms. 4 A. Corbin, Contracts, secs. 813-814 pp. 244-255 (1951); 2 S. Williston, Contracts, sec. 396, pp. 1067-1070 (3d ed. 1959). Thus, the general rule is that a third-party donee beneficiary acquires a right immediately upon the making of a contract intended for his benefit, and that right becomes immediately indefeasible unless the contract reserves the right to change the beneficiary or modify the rights of the beneficiary.

Section 142 of the Second Restatement of Contracts (Tent. Draft No. 1-7 1973), pp. 307-313, provides a rule whereby a third-party beneficiary's rights are much more limited. Under the rule of the Second Restatement, a promisor and promisee may, by agreement, create a right in the third-party beneficiary which cannot be discharged or modified by a subsequent agreement between the promisor and promisee. In the absence of such a term, the promisor and promisee retain the power to discharge or modify the contract by subsequent amendment until the beneficiary materially changes his or her position in justifiable reliance on the promise, or brings suit on it, or manifests assent to it in a manner invited or required by the promisor or promisee. Petitioner has presented no authority indicating that New Jersey courts have adopted the rule described in the Second Restatement; nor have we found any. However, whichever rule is applied, we conclude that by expressly reserving the right to modify the rights of the beneficiaries, decedent and Vornado had greater rights than their rights under local law. Under the rule of the First Restatement, decedent and Vornado would not have been able to modify the rights of the beneficiaries without their consent in the absence of an expressly reserved power to do so. Under the rule of the Second Restatement, decedent's and Vornado's power to modify could have been terminated by specified actions by the beneficiaries in the absence of an expressly reserved power. Decedent, in the instant case, retained a power in conjunction with Vornado to modify the rights of the beneficiaries. This power could be exercised by decedent and Vornado without the consent of the beneficiaries; the language of the agreement having foreclosed the beneficiaries from taking steps (under the approach of the Second Restatement) to vest their rights as third-party beneficiaries. The power thus retained appears to be greater than the rights of the parties under local law.

In sum, by joining in the reservation of power set forth in paragraph Fifth of the agreement, decedent retained strings which appear to be greater than those arising from local contract law. The retention of such strings leads to inclusion under section 2038(a)(1).

The IRS has also argued, unsuccessfully, that survivor's benefits are to be taxed as a completed gift at the moment of death. *See* Estate of DiMarco v. Commissioner, 87 T.C. 653 (1986), *acq.* 1990-2 C.B. 1, discussed at page 164.

PROBLEMS

1. Donald is employed by J & K, Inc. on the date of his death. J & K, Inc. provides all employees with group term life insurance as well as medical and dental insurance. As a result of Donald's death, J & K, Inc. paid Emma, his surviving spouse, an amount equal to twice his annual salary.
    a. What are the estate tax consequences?
    b. What if J & K, Inc. also provided long- and short-term disability benefits to all employees?
    c. What if J & K, Inc. also provided a nonqualified retirement benefit?
    d. What if Donald is one of three equal owners of J & K, Inc.?
2. XYZ, Inc. consults you about the transfer tax consequences of establishing an employee death benefit plan in addition to its other fringe benefits. What advice would you give the company? Be specific.
3. Should survivor's death benefits be included in the decedent's gross estate? If so, what is the appropriate section?

CHAPTER 12

Powers of Appointment

A. GENERAL PRINCIPLES
IRC §§2041, 2514

A power of appointment is the right to designate who will enjoy property. No special words are needed to create a power of appointment; the right to appoint property, to demand property, to designate beneficiaries, to withdraw property, and to consume property are all powers of appointment. On the other hand, the power to invest or manage property that does not affect beneficial enjoyment is not a power of appointment.

The donor is the person who creates the power. The donee or power holder is the person who can exercise the power. The objects of the power are those individuals to whom the donee can appoint the property, and the takers in default are those individuals who will acquire the property in the absence of an exercise of the power. The donor must designate a donee and one or more objects of the power, but does not need to designate takers in default.

Example 12-1

Paul creates an irrevocable trust with Friendly National Bank as Trustee. The Trustee is to distribute income to Derrick during his lifetime. At Derrick's death, the trust property is to be distributed to those of Derrick's children that Derrick designates in his will. If Derrick does not appoint the trust property in his will, it is to be distributed to Derrick's heirs. Peter is the donor. Derrick is the donee or power holder. Derrick's children are the objects of the power. Derrick's heirs are the takers in default.

Section 2041 includes in the gross estate property over which the decedent has a general power of appointment at the time of death. A general power of appointment is the ability to appoint to oneself, one's creditors, one's estate, or the creditors of one's estate. In Example 12-1, nothing will be in Derrick's gross estate under §2041 because his power is limited, not general. He can only appoint to his children, not to himself, his creditors, his estate, or the creditors of his estate. Section 2041 also includes property over which the decedent has released or exercised a general power of appointment under conditions, which if the decedent had been the owner of the property, would have included that property in the decedent's gross estate pursuant to §§2035-2038.

Property subject to a general power of appointment was not initially included in the gross estate. The Revenue Act of 1916 included in the gross estate only property that was subject to claims and expenses in the decedent's estate and that was subject to distribution as part of his estate. In United States v. Field, 255 U.S. 257 (1921), the Supreme Court limited this provision to probate property and, thus, excluded from the decedent's gross estate property transferred pursuant to the exercise of his general power of appointment. In the Revenue Act of 1918, Congress added a provision to include property over which the decedent had a general power of appointment and the decedent exercised that power in his will, in contemplation of death, or in a transfer intended to take effect at his death. In light of this amendment, and considering its holding in United States v. Field, the Supreme Court refused to construe the predecessor of §2033 to include property subject to an unexercised general power of appointment. Helvering v. Safe Deposit & Trust Co., 316 U.S. 56 (1942).

Congress reacted once again in the Revenue Act of 1942. This time property over which the decedent had a general power of appointment was included in his gross estate if the decedent had the power of appointment at the time of his death or he had exercised or released the power in a transfer that would have brought the property into his gross estate under the predecessors to §§2035-2038 had the decedent been the owner of the property. Congress added the finishing touches in the Powers of Appointment Act of 1951 by simplifying the definition of a general power of appointment and by codifying the distinction between powers created on or before October 21, 1942, and those created after that date. Property subject to general powers created on or before October 21, 1942, is only included in the gross estate if the decedent exercised the power.

All this history, of course, begs the question whether property subject to a general power of appointment should be included in the decedent's gross estate or not. After all, the decedent does not, and never did, own the property over which he has the power. All the decedent has is the power to direct where that property goes.

Section 2041 taxes only general powers — those where the decedent can appoint the property to himself, his creditors, his estate, or the creditors of his estate. A general power of appointment is equivalent to property that the decedent owns outright but has deposited in a savings account or a certificate of deposit where the decedent has to ask for the property in a certain way or at a certain time. While the power to appoint to the decedent's estate is more limited, it still gives the decedent the ability to confer beneficial ownership of the property on anyone he wants. The only thing the decedent cannot do is acquire the property for his own benefit during his life. Given that the decedent in these situations has almost complete control over the property, it is appropriate to include such property in his gross estate. Failure to do so would allow significant opportunity for tax evasion.

Example 12-2

Dan creates an irrevocable trust with Friendly National Bank as Trustee to pay the income to Amy for her life and to distribute the trust property to Amy's children in equal shares at her death. The trust also gives Amy the right to withdraw trust property at any time for any purpose. Because Amy can withdraw trust property for her own benefit or to pay her creditors, Amy has a general power of appointment.

Example 12-3

Dan creates an irrevocable trust with Friendly National Bank as Trustee to accumulate trust income or to distribute it to Bruno as, and when, he requests it. At Bruno's death, the Trustee is to distribute the trust property to Bruno's children in equal shares. Because Bruno can withdraw trust income for his own benefit or to pay his creditors, he has a general power of appointment.

Example 12-4

Dan creates an irrevocable trust with Friendly National Bank as Trustee to pay the income to Celia for her life and to distribute the trust property to those of Celia's children as she designates in her will. Because Celia can only appoint the trust property among her children, she does not have a general power of appointment.

Assume that at Celia's death, the Trustee was to distribute the trust property to "such person or persons as Celia designates in her will." In most cases, this would be a general power of appointment because Celia could designate her estate. In Maryland, however, this language has been interpreted to preclude an appointment to the decedent, her creditors, her estate, or the creditors of her estate. As a result, in Maryland, such language does not create a general power of appointment. Maryland National Bank v. United States, 236 F. Supp 532 (D. Md. 1964). The right to appoint to anyone in a will coupled with a gift in default to the executor is, however, considered to be a general power of appointment under Maryland law. Martin v. United States, 780 F. 2d 1147 (4th Cir. 1986).

Courts have consistently held that state law creates the property rights and federal tax law determines how those rights will be taxed.

Keeter v. United States
461 F.2d 714 (5th Cir. 1972)

GOLDBERG, Circuit Judge:

. . . The decedent's husband, Daniel A. Shaw, died in 1930, the owner of an insurance policy on his own life in the amount of $100,000, which he had purchased in 1919. In 1926 Mr. Shaw (the "insured" or the "settlor") elected a settlement option which provided that the insurance proceeds should be held under four identical supplementary contracts, issued to the decedent, Mrs. Bessie Love Shaw, and their daughters in equal shares. By the terms of this settlement option decedent was to receive interest on her share of the proceeds for her life. . . . The settlement option also expressly provided that the principal and accrued interest from the proceeds were to be paid to "the executors or administrators" of the decedent at her death. Mrs. Shaw, domiciled in Florida, died in 1964, leaving a will, duly probated, that read in part:

> All the rest, residue and remainder of my property of every kind and description and wherever located, and any property over which I may hold the power of appointment or distribution, I give, devise, and bequeath in three equal portions for [her daughters].

Pursuant to the 1926 settlement election, the insurance company paid the $25,000 to the decedent's executor. The executor did not include that sum in the decedent's gross estate when he filed the estate tax return, and the Commissioner assessed a deficiency. The executor paid the deficiency and recovered a refund in the lower court. 323 F. Supp. 1093. The government has appealed that decision, and we reverse.

General powers of appointment created on or before October 21, 1942, are includable in the gross estate of a decedent only if they are "exercised," 26 U.S.C.A. §2041(a)(1). . . . The issue in this case is whether or not the settlor's election of annuities-cum-payments to the decedent's executor constitutes such a power of appointment for purposes of the estate tax. It is acknowledged by all parties that if the settlement option elected by the decedent's husband constituted a general power of appointment, the power was "created," for tax purposes, prior to 1942. . . . And it is also conceded by all that the power of appointment, if that is what it really was, was "exercised," for tax purposes, by a specific provision in the decedent's will that distributed any of her property held under power of appointment to her three daughters in equal shares.

We will look to applicable state law to determine whether the substance of the property interests created by the settlor fits within the federal tax law's definition of a power of appointment, but we emphasize that it is the substance of the state law that is relevant and not any labels that a state or the parties might attach to that substance. . . . The law in this case is as clear as the Internal Revenue Code and attendant regulations are ever wont to be. A general power of appointment is defined by the Code as "a power which is exercisable in favor of the decedent, *his estate,* his creditors, or the creditors of his estate," 26 U.S.C.A. §2041(b)(1) [emphasis added]. The Code definition is cast in the disjunctive, so that the donee is in possession of a general power of appointment if he or she is able to exercise that power in favor of *any one* of the four groups of beneficiaries specified in the statute. . . .

Mrs. Shaw's executor argues that the settlement option elected by Mrs. Shaw's husband was not a general power of appointment, resting his argument principally upon the assertion that Mrs. Shaw did not receive solely from that settlement option, and at the moment of the death of the insured, the unrestricted power to dispose of the insurance proceeds. Mrs. Shaw's power to distribute the funds came, the executor concludes, from the laws of Florida which empowered her to make a will and not from her husband's settlement option. In sum, the executor's argument is that because the proceeds would have to receive their direction under the will and not directly under the insurance clause, the option could not be called a power of appointment at the time of the insured's death. The executor's argument is unrealistic at best, conclusory at worst. We conclude that the making of a will was merely a conduit, not a rheostat, in the legal authority that ran between the decedent and the insurance option. . . .

We would add that a grant of distributory suzerainty over a fund is a general power of appointment within the habitat of the estate tax if the decedent holds the power to direct the funds freely and without restriction, regardless of the *source* of the fund. The principal or face amount of the insurance contracts formed the corpora of the power of appointment, but the manner of distribution came only upon the death and by the direction of the one who was designated by the settlor. Mr. Shaw, through his insurance policy, was not the director of the fund. It was the will of Mrs. Shaw that spread the largesse, and Mr. Shaw, by placing the proceeds in the hands of Mrs. Shaw's executors, simply named the decedent as the director of the fund. The settlor "created" a general power of appointment, for estate tax purposes, when he elected to place the residuum of the insurance proceeds into a position from which the decedent could appoint freely and without restriction. The fact that the position chosen by the donor was one formed by a previously-existing legal right of the decedent donee, in this case the statutory right to make a will, does not vitiate at all the practical and realistic consequences of the original grant from the settlor. . . .

Granting the residuum of the insurance proceeds to Mrs. Shaw's executors was tantamount to granting the residuum directly to Mrs. Shaw, subject only to the proviso that she appoint the fund by her will. Had the funds been expressly left for Mrs. Shaw's unfettered distribution by will, the fact that the grant was a power of appointment would be beyond doubt, even though her right to make a will arose only under a previously-existing state statute. . . . . Similarly, if the settlor had granted the insurance proceeds to a trust terminable at his wife's death over which his wife was sole trustee with sole power to distribute trust funds, we feel that the grant would clearly be a power of appointment and taxable as such, even though the trust itself might have been set up by a third party before Mr. Shaw ever purchased his insurance policy. It is the unrestricted power to direct the proceeds that is critical to the power of appointment, whether the director be called a testator, a trustee, or a donor. A director by any other name is still a director. . . .

In brief, Mrs. Shaw's husband directed the funds to Mrs. Shaw's executor, and Mrs. Shaw directed the executor. In practical terms, Mr. Shaw simply put the insurance proceeds into a receptacle from which his wife could appoint them, but it is Mrs. Shaw who substantively directed the funds to the ultimate recipients. And the fact that Mrs. Shaw spoke through her executor does not make her voice any less her own. For estate tax purposes, the critical question is whether the decedent directed her property after her death, not how that property got into the position from which she could direct it. In terms of the actual authority of direction over the insurance proceeds that was conferred and exercised, we see no substantive differences among an express grant of a general power of appointment, a grant utilizing a previously-existing trust with the donee as the sole trustee, an express grant of a general power of appointment exercisable only by will, and a grant employing a previously-existing law that allows the donee to distribute property freely by will. In each instance the power realistically conferred and exercised is the power to direct the fund as the donee sees fit at the point of her death, or in legalese the power to appoint. . . . Mrs. Shaw exercised her general power of appointment by specifically directing her executors in her will, and her estate is therefore taxable on the value of the exercise. The judgment of the district court is reversed.

Jenkins v. United States
428 F.2d 538 (5th Cir. 1970), *cert. denied* 400 U.S. 829 (1970)

GOLDBERG, Circuit Judge:
We consider here the application of federal estate tax provisions to an unexercised and evanescent power of appointment. The executors of the estate of Martha O. Jenkins seek approval of the decision below excluding from the decedent's estate the value of certain property subject to a power of appointment. Though equitable considerations invite us to affirm the ruling below in an effort to ameliorate the apparent harshness of the tax in this particular case, legal imperatives leave us no choice but to reverse and hold that the tax must be paid.

This case grew out of the lives — and deaths — of two sisters, Ada Lee Jenkins and Martha O. Jenkins. These sisters, both of whom were unmarried, lived together in Midland, Georgia, for many years prior to their deaths. Although they owned a substantial amount of property, they lived in a simple, frugal manner. On December 23, 1958, both sisters, who were then in their seventies, executed wills. These wills were very similar in wording and provisions, each sister leaving the other a life estate coupled with a power of invasion or consumption over the testatrix's property.

On September 24, 1962, Ada Lee Jenkins died. Shortly after her sister's death Martha O. Jenkins decided that she did not wish to serve as executrix under her sister's will, and on October 4, 1962, she executed a document renouncing her designation as executrix. She apparently took no other action with regard to the will of her sister. Although she had previously been in good health, on October 10, 1962, Martha suffered a heart attack, and on the following day she died. Because of the short period of time — only seventeen days — between the deaths of the two sisters, Ada's will had not been probated at the time of Martha's death. The wills of both sisters were filed and admitted for probate on October 25, 1962. Two nephews of the sisters, Alonzo Wimberly Jenkins, Jr., and McLendon Wash Jenkins, qualified as the executors of both estates.

The will of Ada Lee Jenkins contained several provisions leaving her surviving sister a life estate coupled with a power of invasion or consumption over certain real and personal property located in Muscogee County, Georgia. Each of the relevant provisions of the will included language substantially identical to the following:

> Should my sister, Martha O. Jenkins, survive me, then in that event, I give, bequeath and devise to Martha O. Jenkins all my right, title and interest in and to . . . (certain named property) . . . to have, hold, use and enjoy for and during her natural life, *with full and unlimited power and authority to dispose of the same in fee simple by gift or otherwise at any time during her life without accountability to anyone,* . . . and should my sister not dispose of my interest in said (property) during her lifetime, then on her death the same shall pass to and become the absolute property of (a certain named remainderman). . . .

These provisions of the will led to a disagreement between the Commissioner of Internal Revenue and the executors of the estate of Martha O. Jenkins as to the amount of estate taxes due. When the executors computed and filed an estate tax return for the estate of Martha O. Jenkins, they excluded from her gross estate the value of the property in which she received a life estate with powers of invasion by her sister's will. The Commissioner, however, ruled that the value of this property must be included because Martha's powers of invasion constituted a general power of appointment over such property. After paying the additional estate taxes required by the Commissioner's ruling, the executors filed a claim for a refund. . . . For the reasons hereinafter given, we are compelled to reject each of the plaintiffs' contentions, and we therefore reverse the judgment of the district court.

I

Plaintiffs' first contention is that decedent did not have a general power of appointment because her power could be exercised only inter vivos and not by will. We reject this contention because it involves a patent misconstruction of the relevant provisions of the Internal Revenue Code.

Section 2041 of the Code provides that the value of the decedent's gross estate shall include the value of property over which the decedent at the time of his death possessed a "general power of appointment." For estate tax purposes, therefore, property over which a decedent possessed such a power is treated as if the decedent actually "owned" the property in the conventional sense. Section 2041(b)(1) defines a "general power of appointment" as "a power which is exercisable in favor of the decedent, his estate, his creditors, or the creditors of his estate." The statutory definition is thus cast in the disjunctive. A power of appointment is a general power under 2041(b)(1) if the donee of the power can exercise it in favor of himself or his estate or his creditors or the creditors of his estate. . . .

In the case at bar the decedent received by virtue of her sister's will a life estate in the property involved with an unlimited power of disposition. Thus she had the power to make inter vivos dispositions of the property, but she could not dispose of the property by will. In statutory terminology, she had the power to appoint the property to herself or to her creditors, but she did not have the power to appoint the property to her estate or to the creditors of her estate. In view of the definition contained in 2041(b)(1), the fact that decedent could appoint to herself or to her creditors was sufficient to make her power of appointment a general power. Her inability to make appointments either to her estate or to the creditors of her estate was irrelevant. . . .

II

Plaintiffs next advance the contention that decedent's power of appointment was not a general power because it came within the "ascertainable standard" exception found in 2041(b)(1)(A). . . .

Plaintiffs make much of the fact that decedent had a substantial amount of property of her own and of the fact that she lived in an exceedingly frugal manner. Because of these facts, which are undisputed, plaintiffs contend that "there was no likelihood" that decedent would ever have exercised any of her powers of disposition over the property involved. Therefore, plaintiffs ask us to conclude, decedent's power of appointment was limited by an ascertainable standard within the meaning of the Code. We reject this contention, as did the court below. . . .

The district court was correct in holding that the relevant inquiry is not what the decedent may have planned to do with the property, but rather what she was empowered to do. An ascertainable standard must be a prescribed standard, not a post-prescriptive course of action. The acting out of the standard is irrelevant, for it is the script rather than the actor which controls a decision concerning the existence of an ascertainable standard. In determining what the decedent was empowered to do, courts must look to the express language of the instrument creating the power, or to the language of the instrument as modified by state law. . . .

In the instant case the instrument creating the power — the will of Ada Lee Jenkins — gave Martha O. Jenkins "full and unlimited power and authority to dispose of the (property) in fee simple by gift or otherwise at any time during her life without accountability to anyone." It is difficult to imagine a more unlimited, open-ended, freewheeling power than this. . . .

III

Plaintiffs' third contention is that decedent did not possess an exercisable general power of appointment at the time of her death because the will of Ada Lee Jenkins had not then been probated or filed or offered for probate. Plaintiffs prevailed on this issue in the district court. . . . Our examination of this contention, however, leads us to the conclusion that it must be rejected.

We note at the outset that there is no language in the will itself which evidences a desire on the part of Ada that Martha's possession of the power of appointment was to be postponed until some time after Ada's death. On the contrary, the relevant provisions of the will are couched in terms of the moment when Martha survived Ada, i.e., the moment of Ada's death: "Should my sister, Martha O. Jenkins, survive me, then in that event, I give, bequeath and devise of Martha O. Jenkins all my right, title and interest. . . ."

The district court, however, found significance in the language of Item Sixteen of the will, which provides in part:

> *Upon the probate and admission to record* of this my will, it is my desire that my executrix, executors or executor administer my estate with the control or supervision of any Court or other authority and to that end, reposing special confidence in them, I relieve them and each of them of accountability to any Court or other authority in the administration, management and final distribution of my estate. (Emphasis added.)

The district court placed special emphasis on the first seven of the quoted words. We cannot agree, however, with the court's apparent conclusion that these words expressed a desire on the part of the testatrix to postpone her surviving sister's possession of the power of appointment. On the contrary, when these words are read in the context of the entire sentence, it is clear that they have reference only to the procedure of probating the will, and not to the timing of the passage of the power of appointment to Martha O. Jenkins.

Moreover, we find nothing in Georgia law which leads us to conclude that Martha's possession of the power would have been postponed until probate or until any other point in time later than the death of Ada. In the absence of any contrary provision in the will itself, we think it is clear that Martha received an exercisable general power at the moment of Ada's death. . . .

We are compelled to reject plaintiffs' contention that Martha O. Jenkins could not have exercised her power of appointment prior to the probate of her sister's will. Under Georgia law she could have made conveyances of the property involved in this case at any time after her sister's death, subject only to subsequent perfection of the record title. The fact that she did not then possess a fully perfected record title is not controlling for federal estate tax purposes. The substantive powers she received at the time of her sister's death clearly came within the definition of a general power of appointment in 2041(b)(1) of the Internal Revenue Code, and these powers were clearly exercisable at the time of her death. . . .

IV

Plaintiffs finally contend that including the value of the property here involved in the gross estate of Martha O. Jenkins constitutes a deprivation of property without due process of law in violation of the Fifth Amendment. The district court did not reach this issue because of its findings favorable to the plaintiffs on two other issues. . . . We find it necessary to consider plaintiffs' constitutional argument, however, in view of the fact that on each of the preceding issues we have reached a decision adverse to the plaintiffs' position.

Plaintiffs base their constitutional argument on two premises. First, they contend that the property here involved passed directly from the estate of Ada Lee Jenkins to the remaindermen "without decedent at any time receiving the right to the use or benefit of those properties, or of the power or right to dispose of those properties." This argument is nothing more than a reiteration of plaintiffs' contention that Martha O. Jenkins received nothing by her sister's will at the time of her sister's death. In the light of our holding that Martha O. Jenkins did receive powers and rights at the time of her sister's death, this argument is untenable.

Secondly, plaintiffs contend that decedent was denied an opportunity to exercise her statutory right to disclaim or renounce the power of appointment. Section 2041(a)(2) grants to every donee of a post-1942 power the right to disclaim or renounce the power. If a decedent exercises this right, the value of the property as to which he has renounced the power will not be included in his gross estate. Moreover, the exercise of the right is not itself a taxable event.

Plaintiffs direct our attention to Treas. Reg. 20.2041-3(d)(6) . . . [contending] that every donee of a general power of appointment is entitled to a reasonable time to disclaim or renounce before he can be charged with possession of the power. Applying this principle to the facts of this case, plaintiffs argue that Martha O. Jenkins did not have a reasonable time in which to exercise her right to disclaim or renounce.

Even if we were to assume arguendo that the principle for which plaintiffs contend is correct, they still would fail in their attempt to apply such a "reasonable time" principle to the facts of this case. In the first place, if plaintiffs' contention in this regard is based on the theory that decedent had not yet received any power because her sister's will had not yet been probated, then the contention is untenable for the reasons previously given. In addition, plaintiffs' contention must be rejected even if it is not based on the time-of-probate argument. The sentence of the regulation upon which plaintiffs heavily rely provides that "in the absence of facts to the contrary, the failure to renounce or disclaim within a reasonable time after learning of its existence will be presumed to constitute an acceptance of the power." Treas. Reg. 20.2041-3(d)(6). Martha O. Jenkins was obviously aware of the existence of her power of appointment as soon as it came into her possession at the time of her sister's death. After all, she was not unfamiliar with the provisions of her sister's will. Moreover, after her sister's death she had sufficient time to execute a document renouncing her designation as executrix under her sister's will. Had she desired to disclaim or renounce her power of appointment, she could have done so at that time. We would ignore reality if we were to accept plaintiffs' argument that decedent was somehow robbed of her right to renounce.

Plaintiffs' constitutional argument, like their other contentions, is completely devoid of merit. The power of appointment possessed by Martha O. Jenkins had taxable existentiality at her death and was untainted by any constitutional disablement. The Commissioner's inclusion within her estate of the value of the properties embraced by the power is fully sanctioned by law.

The decedent is considered to have a power of appointment even if he has no knowledge of the power. Estate of Freeman v. Commissioner, 67 T.C. 202 (1976). In *Freeman* the decedent was receiving income from the trust and could have discovered the exact trust provisions simply by asking. If the decedent is unable to exercise the power because of incompetency, the property subject to the power is still in the decedent's gross estate. *See, e.g.*, Boeving v. United States, 650 F.2d 493 (8th Cir. 1981); Estate of Alperstein v. Commissioner, 613 F.2d 1213 (2d Cir. 1979), *cert. denied* 446 U.S. 918 (1980).

PROBLEMS

1. Peter establishes an irrevocable trust with Friendly National Bank as Trustee. The Trustee is to distribute income to Ann for her life and, at her death, to distribute the trust property to Ann's issue.
   a. Ann has the right to ask the Trustee to distribute corpus to her or to her issue at any time and for any purpose. Ann dies without exercising the power. What are the estate tax consequences?
   b. Instead, Ann can appoint the trust property in her will "to any person." What are the estate tax consequences?
   c. Instead, Ann can appoint the trust property in her will but only among her issue. What are the estate tax consequences?
   d. Same as c., except that Ann had borrowed money from her daughter, Ellen.
   e. Same as c., except that if Ann did not appoint the trust property, it passed to her executor. What are the estate tax consequences?
2. Penny establishes a testamentary trust by leaving money to Ben, her son, as Trustee, to pay the income to Ellen for life and at her death to distribute the trust property to Fred.
   a. As Trustee, Ben has the right to manage the trust property and to invest it. What are the estate tax consequences when Ben dies and he is still serving as Trustee?
   b. What are the estate tax consequences if Ben as Trustee has the right to accumulate income or to distribute it among Penny's children and grandchildren?
   c. Assume that the trust will terminate at Ben's death and that Ben has the right to designate which of Penny's descendants will share in the distribution of trust property at that time. What are the estate tax consequences?
3. Sally establishes an irrevocable trust with Tom as Trustee. The Trustee is to use the income and corpus of the trust for the benefit of Sally's

grandson, Larry, until he is 21. When Larry is 21, the Trustee is to distribute the trust property and accumulated income to Larry. If Larry dies before 21, the trust property is to be distributed to whomever Larry appoints in his will. In the absence of an appointment by Larry, the trust property is to be distributed to his surviving siblings.

    a.   What are the gift tax consequences to Sally on creation of this trust?

    b.   What are the estate tax consequences to Larry if he dies at age 17?

    c.   What are the estate tax consequences to Tom if he dies when Larry is 15? Assume that Tom is Larry's parent.

4.   Serena establishes an irrevocable trust with Friendly National Bank as Trustee. The Trustee is to distribute the income to Mary during her life. At Mary's death, the Trustee is to distribute as much of the trust property as is necessary to satisfy the claims against Mary's estate, the expenses of her funeral and administration of her estate, and any federal or state taxes due as a result of her death. Any property not so distributed is to be divided among Mary's descendants in equal shares. What are the estate tax consequences, if any, to Mary?

B. POWERS SUBJECT TO AN ASCERTAINABLE STANDARD
IRC §§2041(b), 2514(c)

A general power of appointment does not include a power that is limited by an ascertainable standard relating to health, education, support, or maintenance. §2041(b)(1)(A). The regulations explain:

> [T]he words "support" and "maintenance" are synonymous and their meaning is not limited to the bare necessities of life. A power to use property for the comfort, welfare, or happiness of the holder of the power is not limited by the requisite standard. . . . In determining whether a power is limited by an ascertainable standard, it is immaterial whether the beneficiary is required to exhaust his other income before the power can be exercised.

Reg. §20.2041-1(c)(2)

Estate of Vissering v. Commissioner
990 F.2d 578 (10th Cir. 1993)

LOGAN, Circuit Judge.

The estate of decedent Norman H. Vissering appeals from a judgment of the Tax Court determining that he held at his death a general power of appointment as defined by IRC §2041, and requiring that the assets of a trust of which he was cotrustee be included in his gross estate for federal estate tax purposes. The appeal turns on whether decedent held powers permitting him to invade the principal of the trust for his own benefit unrestrained by an ascertainable standard relating to health, education, support, or maintenance. . . .

Under IRC §2041 a decedent has a general power of appointment includable in his estate if he possesses at the time of his death a power over assets that permits him to benefit himself, his estate, his creditors, or creditors of his estate. A power vested in a trustee, even with a cotrustee who has no interest adverse to the exercise of the power, to invade principal of the trust for his own benefit is sufficient to find the decedent trustee to have a general power of appointment, unless the power to invade is limited by an ascertainable standard relating to health, education, support, or maintenance. Treas. Reg. §20.2041-1(c), -3(c)(2). . . .

The relevant provisions of the instant trust agreement are as follows:

> During the term of [this trust], the Trustees shall further be authorized to pay over or to use or expend for the direct or indirect benefit of any of the aforesaid beneficiaries, whatever amount or amounts of the principal of this Trust as may, in the discretion of the Trustees, be required for the continued comfort, support, maintenance, or education of said beneficiary.

Tax Ct. ex. 3-C at 5-6. The Internal Revenue Service (IRS) and the Tax Court focused on portions of the invasion provision providing that the trust principal could be expended for the "comfort" of decedent, declaring that this statement rendered the power of invasion incapable of limitation by the courts.

We look to state law (here Florida's) to determine the legal interests and rights created by a trust instrument, but federal law determines the tax consequences of those interests and rights. Morgan v. Commissioner, 309 U.S. 78, 80 (1940); Maytag v. United States, 493 F.2d 995, 998 (10th Cir. 1974). . . . Despite the decision in Barritt v. Tomlinson, 129 F. Supp. 642 (S.D. Fla. 1955), which involved a power of invasion broader than the one before us, we believe the Florida Supreme Court would hold that a trust document permitting invasion of principal for "comfort," without further qualifying language, creates a general power of appointment. Treas. Reg. §20.2041-1(c). See First Virginia Bank v. United States, 490 F.2d 532, 533 (4th Cir. 1974) (under Virginia law, right of invasion for beneficiary's "comfort and care as she may see fit" not limited by an ascertainable standard); Lehman v. United States, 448 F.2d 1318, 1320 (5th Cir. 1971) (under Texas law, power to invade corpus for "support, maintenance, comfort, and welfare" not limited by ascertainable standard); Miller v. United States, 387 F.2d 866, 869 (3d Cir. 1968) (under Pennsylvania law, power to make disbursements from principal in amounts "necessary or expedient for [beneficiary's] proper maintenance, support, medical care, hospitalization, or other expenses incidental to her comfort and well-being" not limited by ascertainable standard); Estate of Schlotterer v. United States, 421 F. Supp. 85, 91 (W.D. Pa. 1976) (power of consumption "to the extent deemed by [beneficiary] to be desirable not only for her support and maintenance but also for her comfort and pleasure" not limited by ascertainable standard); Doyle v. United States, 358 F. Supp. 300, 309-10 (E.D. Pa. 1973) (under Pennsylvania law, trustees' "uncontrolled discretion" to pay beneficiary "such part or parts of the principal of said trust fund as may be necessary for her comfort, maintenance and support" not limited by ascertainable standard); Stafford v. United States, 236 F. Supp. 132, 134 (E.D. Wash. 1964) (under Wisconsin law, trust permitting husband "for his use, benefit and enjoyment during his lifetime," unlimited power of disposition thereof "without permission of any court, and with the right to use and enjoy the principal, as well as the income, if he shall have need thereof for his care, comfort or enjoyment" not limited by ascertainable standard).

However, there is modifying language in the trust before us that we believe would lead the Florida courts to hold that "comfort," in context, does not permit an unlimited power of invasion. The instant language states that invasion of principal is permitted to the extent "*required* for the *continued* comfort" of the decedent, and is part of a clause referencing the support, maintenance and education of the beneficiary. Invasion of the corpus is not permitted to the extent "determined" or "desired" for the beneficiary's comfort but only to the extent that it is "required." Furthermore, the invasion must be for the beneficiary's "continued" comfort, implying, we believe, more than the minimum necessary for survival, but nevertheless reasonably necessary to maintain the beneficiary in his accustomed manner of living. These words in context state a standard essentially no different from the examples in the Treasury Regulation, in which phrases such as "support in reasonable comfort," "maintenance in health and reasonable comfort," and "support in his accustomed manner of living" are deemed to be limited by an ascertainable standard. Treas. Reg. §20.2041-1(c)(2). *See, e.g.*, United States v. Powell, 307 F.2d 821, 828 (10th Cir. 1962) (under Kansas law, invasion of the corpus if "it is necessary or advisable . . . for the maintenance, welfare, comfort or happiness" of beneficiaries, and only if the need justifies the reduction in principal, is subject to ascertainable standard); Hunter v. United States, 597 F. Supp. 1293, 1295 (W.D. Pa.1984) (power to invade for "comfortable support and maintenance" of beneficiaries is subject to ascertainable standard).

We believe that had decedent, during his life, sought to use the assets of the trust to increase significantly his standard of living beyond that which he had previously enjoyed, his cotrustee would have been obligated to refuse to consent, and the remainder beneficiaries of the trust could have successfully petitioned the court to disallow such expenditures as inconsistent with the intent of the trust instrument. The Tax Court erred in ruling that this power was a general power of appointment includable in decedent's estate.

Hyde v. United States
950 F. Supp. 418 (D.N.H. 1996)

McAuliffe, District Judge.

In this suit, the Estate of Dorothy Hyde seeks a refund of estate taxes it claims to have overpaid as a result of its having mistakenly included in the decedent's gross taxable estate the value of certain trust assets over which Hyde had a power of appointment. The Internal Revenue Service ("IRS") refused the refund claim on grounds that the decedent held a general power of appointment, effectively making the assets her own. Plaintiff appeals that decision on grounds that the power of appointment was not a general power for federal estate tax purposes because it was limited by "ascertainable standards" related to her health, education and support. . . .

Dorothy Hyde died testate on May 5, 1992. Her son, Richard C. Hyde, acting as executor, filed the estate's tax return and, among other assets, included in her estate the value of property left to Hyde in trust under the will of her mother, Amy F. Crowell, . . . which provided Hyde with a life estate interest in the trust's assets and empowered Hyde "to use the income and so much of the principal as in her *sole discretion* shall be *necessary and desirable.*" Crowell Will, Article Eighth. (Emphasis added).

A decedent's gross taxable estate, for federal estate tax purposes, includes "any property with respect to which the decedent has at the time of [her] death a general power of appointment created after October 21, 1942. . . ." 26 U.S.C.A. §2041(a)(2) (1986). A general power of appointment is one "which is exercisable in favor of the decedent, [her] estate, [her] creditors, or the creditors of [her] estate," subject to certain exceptions. 26 U.S.C.A. §2041(b)(1). The exception relied upon by the estate in this case provides that "[a] power to consume, invade, or appropriate property for the benefit of the decedent which is limited by an ascertainable standard relating to the health, education, support, or maintenance of the decedent shall not be deemed a general power of appointment." 26 U.S.C.A. §2041(b)(1)(A).

Applicable Treasury Regulations further define a power limited by an ascertainable standard. . . . Treas. Reg. §20.2041-1(c), -3(c)(2) (1995). So, for Hyde's power of appointment to qualify as a limited one under the exception it must meet two requirements: 1) it must be limited by an ascertainable standard; and 2) the limiting standard must relate to her own health, education, and/or support or maintenance. Crocker National Bank v. Commissioner, 87 T.C. 599, 600 (1986); Estate of Sowell v. Commissioner, 708 F.2d 1564 (10th Cir. 1983). Otherwise, the power is a general one, and the trust assets are taxable in Hyde's estate. Estate of Little, 87 T.C. at 600.

State law, here New Hampshire's, determines the scope of Hyde's right to invade and consume trust principal under the power, but federal law determines the tax consequences of Hyde's rights. . . . The parties have not cited, nor has the court found, any applicable New Hampshire authority that might operate to limit or define the terms "necessary" and "desirable" as meaning, in this context, that Hyde could only exercise her power to apply trust assets to meet her personal needs for education, support or maintenance, or to maintain her own health.

When state law does not limit or define the terms used, the instrument itself must supply the meaning. Estate of Little, 87 T.C. at 600. Therefore, applying the state's general rule of construction applicable to testamentary trusts, the court necessarily looks to the testator's (Crowell's) intent as conveyed by the language she used, . . . to determine whether the limitation asserted by Hyde's estate is sufficiently measurable and related to Hyde's health, education, and/or support or maintenance to qualify the power as a limited power of appointment for federal estate tax purposes. . . .

The inquiry then, is whether the terms "necessary and desirable" as used in the power were actually intended by Crowell to restrict her daughter's use of the trust principal by permitting Hyde to use those assets during Hyde's lifetime solely for her own education, her own support or maintenance, or her own health needs, and for no other purposes. The estate necessarily argues that that is precisely what Crowell intended, but its proffered construction seems far too harsh. Considering the terms used by Crowell in light of what she apparently wanted to accomplish, rather than from the vantage of hindsight illuminated by potential tax consequences, the only reasonable construction is that Crowell intended her daughter to have broad authority to use the trust's assets. Indeed, similarly worded powers have routinely been held to be general powers of appointment for federal tax purposes because the apparent limitations did not relate solely to the health, education, or support of the holders. *See* Lehman v. United States, 448 F.2d 1318 (5th Cir. 1971) (power to consume corpus of estate "for [decedent's] own use, benefit, comfort, support, and maintenance" was not limited by an ascertainable standard); Peoples Trust Co. v. United States, 412 F.2d 1156 (3d Cir. 1969) (power to invade principal as beneficiary "from time to time may require; she to be the sole judge as to the amounts and frequency of such principal payments" was not limited by an ascertainable standard); Miller v. United States, 387 F.2d 866 (3d Cir. 1968) (power to invade corpus as trustees "deem necessary or expedient for proper maintenance, support, medical care, hospitalization, or other expenses incidental to her comfort and well-being" was not limited by an ascertainable standard); Strite v. McGinnes, 330 F.2d 234 (3d. Cir.) (trustees power to invade principal "to provide for the reasonable needs and proper expenses for the benefit or comfort" of the decedent not limited by ascertainable standard), *cert. denied* 379 U.S. 836 (1964).

In this case, too, Crowell's will contains no express limitation upon the purposes for which trust principal could be used by Hyde. What might be "necessary and desirable" in Hyde's "sole discretion" is not, then, "reasonably measurable" in terms of the Regulations' qualifying limitations. As drafted, Hyde's power had no practical limitations, much less ones contemplated by the applicable exception.

Plaintiff understandably endeavors to limit the word "necessary" by reading into it the concept of "emergency," arguing that "necessary" as used by Crowell actually meant that which is "absolutely required" or "indispensable." . . . An express limitation requiring an "emergency" in order to invade principal has indeed been held, in context, to qualify a power of appointment as a limited one for federal tax purposes. *See, e.g.*, Estate of Sowell, 708 F.2d 1564 (10th Cir. 1983). But the term "necessary" standing alone is not apparently synonymous with "emergency," and the estate points to no precedent equating the two terms. "Emergency," as the term is generally used, includes in its meaning an unavoidable sense of exigency or immediacy not conveyed by the term "necessary." Estate of Sowell, 708 F.2d at 1567 (quoting Webster's Third International Dictionary). In *Estate of Sowell* the court expressly relied on the sense of immediacy conveyed by the term "emergency" to hold the power of appointment at issue there to be a limited one. *Id.*

The important question not specifically addressed in Crowell's will is, of course, "Necessary for *what?*" One can easily imagine a number of "necessary and desirable" expenditures from principal that Hyde could have made under her power unrelated to her own "health, or education, or support or maintenance." Paying for the education of her children (the remaindermen), paying for medical care for needy family members, traveling for purely recreational reasons, substantially improving her standard of living, or purchasing art to enhance her sense of happiness, are but a few of many possible examples of expenditures that Hyde could have deemed to be "necessary and desirable" in her sole discretion and that could not have reasonably been challenged as *ultra vires* under the power as written (and as undoubtedly intended by Hyde's mother), yet which would be well beyond the limitations necessary to avoid federal taxation. *See also* First Virginia Bank v. United States, 490 F.2d 532, 533 (4th Cir. 1974) (under Virginia law, right of invasion for beneficiaries' "comfort and care as she may see fit" not limited by an ascertainable standard). Crowell's use of the term "desirable" (again, desirable in Hyde's sole discretion) also confirms her intent to empower her daughter to apply the trust assets to whatever purposes Hyde might wish during her lifetime.

For estate tax purposes, then, Crowell's will provided Hyde with a general power of appointment, allowing her to basically treat the trust principal as her own and to use it for any purpose she in her sole discretion deemed necessary and desirable. Therefore, the trust's assets were properly included in Hyde's gross taxable estate when she died, because "the practical exercise of her powers of disposition and control for her own benefit was not confined within limitations at least as stringent as those prescribed by Federal law. . . ." *Lehman,* 448 F.2d at 1319-20 (citations omitted).

PROBLEMS

1. Gloria's will provided: "All the rest and residue of my property, of whatever kind and wherever situated, I leave to my son, Adam, for his life, to use in any manner that he deems proper. Any property remaining at the death of Adam is to be distributed to his surviving issue." Adam invested the property he acquired from Gloria and maintained it in an investment account separate from his other property. Is this property included in Adam's gross estate at his death?

2. George established an irrevocable trust with Friendly National Bank as Trustee.
    a. The trust provided that the Trustee was to distribute income or principal to Beth, George's daughter, as she requested for her support and maintenance. Is the trust in Beth's gross estate at her death?
    b. The trust provided that the Trustee was to distribute income and principal to Beth, if she deemed it necessary and desirable. Is the trust in Beth's gross estate at her death?
    c. The trust provided that Beth could withdraw trust principal if needed in an emergency. Is the trust in Beth's gross estate at her death?
3. Gretchen's will left her property to her nephew, Charles, as Trustee to distribute the income to himself for life and, at his death, to distribute the trust property to his surviving issue.
    a. The trust also provided that Charles could invade trust principal for his own comfort. Is the trust in Charles' gross estate at his death?
    b. What if the trust allowed Charles to invade principal for his own comfort and happiness?
    c. What if the trust allowed Charles to invade principal for his own care and comfort?
    d. What if the trust allowed Charles to invade principal for his support in reasonable comfort?
    e. What if the trust allowed Charles to invade trust principal to support himself in his accustomed standard of living?
    f. What if the trust allowed Charles to invade trust principal to continue his accustomed standard of living?
4. Why are powers that are limited by an ascertainable standard excluded from the definition of general powers? Should they be?

C. JOINT AND CONDITIONAL POWERS
IRC §§2041(b), 2514(c)

A power of appointment is not a general power, for purposes of §2041, if it can only be exercised by the decedent in conjunction with either the creator of the power or an individual having a substantial adverse interest in the property subject to the power. §2041(b)(1)(C). An individual has an adverse interest only if she has "a present or future chance to obtain a personal benefit from the property itself." Estate of Towle v. Commissioner, 54 T.C. 368, 372 (1970). An adverse interest is substantial "if its value in relation to the total value of the property subject to the power is not insignificant." Reg. §20.2041-3(c)(2).

A trustee does not have a substantial adverse interest in trust property unless she has a beneficial interest in the trust. Estate of Towle v. Commissioner, *supra.* A taker in default has an adverse interest, but a co-holder of the power does not have an adverse interest merely because he is a co-holder of the power or even if he is a permissible appointee. Reg. §20.2041-3(c)(2). In Revenue Ruling 75-145, 1975-1 C.B. 298, the IRS ruled that uncashed Social Security checks were not in the decedent's gross estate under §2041 because his wife was a joint payee and, as such, had a substantial adverse interest in the checks.

A general power of appointment exists on the date of decedent's death unless it is subject to a condition or event that has not occurred on or before that date. Reg. §20.2041-3(b). A requirement that the decedent give notice before exercising her power or that the exercise does not become effective for a specific period of time is not a condition sufficient to preclude inclusion of the trust property in the decedent's gross estate. *Id.* The condition must not be illusory and must have some significant nontax consequences independent of the decedent's ability to exercise the power. Estate of Kurz v. Commissioner, 101 T.C. 44 (1993), *aff'd* 68 F.3d 1027 (7th Cir. 1995). In *Kurz,* decedent's husband predeceased her, leaving his property in two trusts — a Marital Trust and a Family Trust.[1] Decedent received the income from both trusts. Decedent had the power to withdraw the entire principal of the Marital Trust upon written notification to the Trustee. She also had the right to withdraw five percent of the Family Trust, but only if the Marital Trust had been exhausted. Both trusts had substantial assets in them at decedent's death. The court held that five percent of the Family Trust was in her gross estate, because she could have depleted the Marital Trust by requesting distribution from the Trustee in writing, and rejected the argument that decedent did not have a general power of appointment, because her ability to withdraw the 5 percent was conditioned on the depletion of the Marital Trust, which had not occurred before her death.

PROBLEMS

1. Henry left his residuary estate to his wife, Wanda, and his son, Mark, as Trustees, to pay the income to Wanda for her life and, at her death, to distribute the trust property to Sam. During her life, Wanda had the power to invade corpus for her own benefit but only with the consent of Sam. At Wanda's death, is the trust property in her gross estate?

2. Mary created an irrevocable trust with Friendly National Bank as Trustee to pay the income to her daughter, Nancy, during her life. At Nancy's death, the trust property was to be distributed to Nancy's surviving issue. The trust also provided that Nancy could terminate the trust and receive the trust principal but only after she had graduated

---

1. The marital deduction is discussed in Chapter 16, and marital deduction trusts are discussed in section E of that chapter.

from law school and had been admitted to the bar. Nancy dies without having attended law school. Is the trust property in her gross estate?

3. Wendy left her residuary estate to Friendly National Bank as Trustee. The Trustee has absolute discretion to accumulate income or to distribute it to, or for the benefit of, Wendy's spouse, Hugh. At Hugh's death, the Trustee is to distribute the trust principal to Wendy's surviving issue. Hugh has the right to replace the Trustee at any time for any reason. Hugh dies without exercising his right to replace the Trustee. What are the estate tax consequences?

D. EXERCISE, RELEASE, AND LAPSE
IRC §§2041, 2514

Section 2041 also includes in the gross estate property over which the decedent had a general power of appointment but released or exercised that power in a transfer that, had the decedent owned the property outright, would have been included in her gross estate under §§2035-2038. In addition, §2514(b) treats the exercise or release of a general power as a transfer of property by the power holder (donee). As a result, the exercise or release of a general power of appointment will usually be taxed either as a gift or in the donee's gross estate.

Example 12-5

Robert leaves the residue of his estate to Friendly National Bank as Trustee, to pay the income to his daughter, Diane, for her life and, at her death, to distribute the trust principal to Diane's surviving issue. Robert gives Diane the power to invade trust corpus at any time for any purpose. If Diane instructs the Trustee to distribute $25,000 to her son, John, Diane will have made a gift of $25,000 to John. The exercise of her power is a transfer of property for gift tax purposes. The gift will qualify for the gift tax annual exclusion to the extent of $11,000. §§2503(b), 2514. If Diane instructs the Trustee to distribute the $25,000 to her, there is no gift because the transfer has been from Diane, the power holder, to herself.

Instead, assume that Diane releases her power to invade the trust corpus. Her release is a transfer to the trust of the full value of the trust corpus. It is as if Diane had withdrawn the entire trust corpus and created a new trust, income to herself (Diane) for life, remainder to her surviving issue. As a result, Diane has made a taxable gift of the remainder interest to her issue. Because this is a future interest, it does not qualify for the gift tax annual exclusion. When Diane dies, the full value of the trust will be in her gross estate under §2041 because of her income interest. Had she created the trust herself, it would have been in her gross estate under §2036(a)(1).

Example 12-6

Rebecca establishes an irrevocable trust with Friendly National Bank as Trustee, to pay the income to her son, Stephen, for life and, at Stephen's death, to distribute the trust property to Stephen's surviving issue. Rebecca also gives Stephen the power to terminate the trust at any time by requesting the Trustee to distribute the trust property to him or to another trust. After Rebecca's death, Stephen directs Friendly National Bank to distribute the trust property to a new trust that provides for the payment of income to his children in equal shares and the distribution of the trust property to his descendants at the death of his last child. Stephen reserves the right to alter this trust by adding or deleting beneficiaries. Stephen dies without altering or amending this trust.

Stephen's exercise of the power is a transfer under §2514. It is not a completed gift, however, because Stephen has retained the right to alter or amend the trust. If Stephen had been the original owner of the trust property, the second (revocable) trust would have been in his gross estate under §§2036(a)(2) and 2038 because of his right to alter or amend the trust. As a result, his exercise of the power brings the trust property into his gross estate under §2041.

Estate of Rolin v. Commissioner
588 F.2d 368 (2d Cir. 1978)

IRVING R. KAUFMAN, Chief Judge:

In this case, we must determine the effectiveness, for estate tax purposes, of an instrument by which the executors of the estate of Genevieve Rolin purported to renounce her interest in a trust created by her late husband, Daniel. The Tax Court held the renunciation effective. 68 T.C. 919 (1977). We affirm.

Daniel established the trust in 1958, retaining for life the income plus the power to amend or revoke the trust at any time. Upon his death, the corpus was to be divided into two parts: "Trust A" would receive an amount equal to the maximum marital deduction available to Daniel's estate under IRC §2056, and "Trust B" would receive the remainder. Genevieve would receive the income of both trusts for life. In addition she was granted the right to invade the corpus of Trust A at any time and in any amount during her life, and she also received a general testamentary power of appointment over its assets. If she failed to exercise the power, Trust A would be merged into Trust B at her death and the assets distributed to the Rolins' issue.

Daniel died on September 30, 1968. Genevieve, who was then 72 years old and suffering from a heart ailment, died four months later. Between Daniel's death and her own, Genevieve had not received the income from either trust, nor had she attempted to invoke the power of appointment over Trust A. As soon as Genevieve's executors qualified, they attempted to renounce her interest in the trust. Even without the Trust A assets, her estate was larger than Daniel's; consequently, the progressive rate structure of the federal estate tax would render inclusion of those assets in her estate disadvantageous to the Rolins' heirs. Thus, the tax saving to Daniel's estate created by the marital deduction of IRC §2056(b)(5) would be more than offset by the increased liability of Genevieve's estate under §2041, which taxes property over which the deceased held a general power of appointment at death. If the renunciation is held effective, Daniel's estate will pay about $35,000 more estate tax than otherwise, but Genevieve's will pay approximately $99,000 less.

We agree with the Tax Court that the renunciation was effective in this case. New York law permits executors, within a reasonable time, to disclaim legacies to which their testator was entitled. . . . Moreover, disclaimers "relate back" to the date of the gift (here, September 30, 1968, the date of Daniel's death) and prevent title from ever vesting. . . . The Commissioner does not dispute this, nor does he now contend that the Tax Court erred in holding that the power to disclaim is not limited to legatees, and extends to inter vivos gifts taking effect at death. . . . Rather, he argues that because a power of appointment is not a descendible property right but a personal privilege that expires at death, . . . there was nothing for the executors to disclaim. How, he asks, could they renounce a power they could not exercise?

We are of the view, however, that New York courts would permit executors to renounce powers and other interests held by their testator at death to the same extent they permit disclaimers of legacies. Outright ownership necessarily includes both a life estate and a general testamentary power of appointment. It is not any more anomalous to permit retroactive renunciation of those rights when they stand alone than it is when they are merely part of the bundle of rights constituting a fee simple. Furthermore, since the principle of retroactive renunciation is that a disclaimer of an interest may be treated as relating back in time, it seems irrelevant to the efficacy of that principle that the interest has expired. It is agreed on all sides that Hoenig and Dreyer correctly stated the law of New York with respect to legacies; accordingly, we conclude that a New York court would find the disclaimer in the instant case effective.

Nor does §2041 require a different result. That provision cannot be viewed in isolation from the rest of the Code. Section 2033 includes in the gross estate "the value of all property to the extent of the interest therein of the decedent," and the predecessor to §2041 was first enacted because Congress was doubtful whether the forerunner of §2033 would reach property as to which decedent did not hold fee simple title but merely a testamentary power of appointment. United States v. Field, 255 U.S. 257, 265 (1921). Moreover, the statute was amended in 1942 in response to Helvering v. Safe Deposit & Trust Co., 316 U.S. 56, 59-62 (1942), which held that only exercised powers were taxable. See, e.g., H.R.Rep.No. 2333, 77th Cong., 2d Sess. 160-61 (1942). . . . The clear congressional purpose in enacting §2041 was merely to ensure that, since the possessor of a general testamentary power of appointment may control the disposition of the property after his death as fully as the owner of a fee simple title, such powers are taxed in the same manner as outright ownership. Because, as Hoenig and Dreyer held, an executor's power to make a timely retroactive renunciation does not transgress the policy of §2033, neither is it inconsistent with §2041.

Indeed, this result comports well with more general considerations of estate tax policy. So long as assets do not escape taxation entirely and no specific provision of the Code is contravened, taxpayers are generally permitted to arrange their affairs to minimize estate tax liability. . . . Here, the trust agreement gave Genevieve the right to renounce her interest in the trust within 14 months of Daniel's death, and it specifically provided that her executors might exercise that right should she die before accepting the benefits of the trust. Since New York courts would uphold her executors' renunciation, and since the Trust A assets will be taxed as part of Daniel's estate, IRC §§2036, 2038, we see no reason to deny effect to this provision of the trust agreement. Accordingly, the judgment of the Tax Court is affirmed.

Lapse occurs when the donee has a limited amount of time to exercise a power of appointment and fails to do so.

Example 12-7

Richard creates an irrevocable trust with Friendly National Bank as Trustee. The Trustee has discretion to accumulate income or to distribute it to Richard's son, Simon. At Simon's death, the trust property is to be distributed to his issue. Simon has the right to demand $11,000 or the amount contributed to the trust, whichever is less, for 60 days after Richard makes a contribution to the trust. Richard transfers $11,000 to the trust on January 15. If Simon does not demand the money within the 60 days, the power lapses. He cannot exercise it. Simon's power in this situation is often referred to as a "*Crummey* power" and is used to qualify transfers to the trust for the gift tax annual exclusion. Crummey v. Commissioner and the gift tax annual exclusion are discussed at page 197.

The lapse of a power is considered to be a release of that power and, therefore, a transfer of property by the donee, but only to the extent that property that could have been appointed exceeds the greater of $5,000 or five percent of the trust assets out of which the exercise of the power could have been satisfied. §§2041(b)(2), 2514(e). Because Simon, in Example 12-7, did not exercise the power, it lapsed. He is, therefore, treated as making a transfer to the trust and a gift to his issue, the remaindermen. The amount of the gift depends on the value of the trust property out of which the demand could have been satisfied. Assume that the total trust assets are available to satisfy the demand.

If the trust corpus is $11,000, then Simon is deemed to have made a transfer of $6,000. This is the amount that exceeds $5,000.

If the trust corpus is $140,000, then Simon is deemed to have made a transfer of $4,000. Five percent of the trust corpus is $7,000, and this amount is deemed not to be a transfer by §2514(e).

If the trust corpus is $220,000, then Simon has not made a transfer because five percent of the trust corpus is $11,000, which is the amount of the property subject to the power that lapsed.

When the donee of a lapsed power dies, the value of the trust property attributable to the transfers that resulted from the lapse will be in the donee's gross estate. This happens only if the donee has an interest in the trust, such as the right to income, or a right, such as the right to terminate the trust. The interests and rights must be the type that would have brought the property into the donee's gross estate under §§2035 through 2038 had the donee been the original owner of the property.

Example 12-8

Rachel creates a trust with Friendly National Bank as Trustee, to pay the income to her daughter, Debra, for life. Debra has the right to withdraw $75,000 of trust income each year for her own use. This right is not cumulative. That is, Debra can only withdraw $75,000 in any year whether or not she has withdrawn money in a prior year. Debra dies 11 years after the trust is created without ever having exercised the right to withdraw. Assume that the trust corpus has remained at $1,000,000 for the entire term of the trust.

Debra's gross estate will include $325,000 of the trust property. First, $75,000 is in her gross estate because she has a general power of appointment over that amount at the time of her death. The right to withdraw for that year has not yet lapsed. Second, an additional $250,000 will be in her gross estate because there was a lapse in each of the prior ten years. Each lapse is treated as a transfer by Debra to the trust, but only to the extent that it exceeded the greater of $5,000 or five percent of the trust corpus. Since five percent of $1,000,000 is $50,000, each lapse is treated as a transfer of only $25,000, the amount in excess of five percent. In each year the transfer of $25,000 equals two and one-half percent of the trust assets. The percentage for each year is added together and the aggregate percentage, in this case 25 percent, of the trust assets is included in the decedent's gross estate. Reg. §§20.2041-3(d)(4), -3(d)(5).

A donee may convert a limited power of appointment into a taxable power if the donee can create "another power of appointment which under the applicable local law can be validly exercised so as to postpone the vesting of any estate or interest in such property, or suspend the absolute ownership or power of alienation of such property, for a person ascertainable without regard to the date of the creation of the first power." §§2041(a)(3), 2514(d). If the donee exercises a limited power of appointment by creating a new trust with a general power of appointment in another, that exercise will be taxable to the donee if the Rule Against Perpetuities period is measured from the donee's exercise rather than the creation of the donee's power. This provision, commonly referred to as the "Delaware Tax Trap," can cause unexpected estate tax consequences. It can also be an effective device to avoid the generation-skipping transfer tax.

Example 12-9

If Parent creates a testamentary trust to pay the income to Child for life and the remainder to Grandchild, there will be an estate tax on creation of the trust at Parent's death. The property is not in Child's gross estate because Child only has a life estate. As a result, Parent is considered the Transferor, and there will be a generation-skipping transfer tax at Child's death. §2612(a). If the trust property is included in Child's gross estate, *e.g.,* because Child has a general power of appointment, Child becomes the Transferor, and there will not be a generation-skipping transfer tax. Giving Child a limited power of appointment, with the ability to appoint further in trust with a power of appointment in another, allows Child to decide whether to exclude the property from his gross estate and pay a generation-skipping transfer tax or to exercise the power and thus escape that tax. This only works in jurisdictions where the period of the Rule Against Perpetuities is measured from the creation of the new power.

PROBLEMS

1. Peter establishes an irrevocable trust with Friendly National Bank as Trustee. The Trustee is to distribute income to Ann for her life and, at her death, to distribute the trust property to Ann's issue. Ann has the right to invade the trust principal at any time and for any purpose.
   a. What are the gift and estate tax consequences if Ann has the Trustee distribute $35,000 to her?
   b. What are the gift and estate tax consequences if Ann has the Trustee send $25,000 to Law School to pay her tuition? What if it is for her daughter's tuition?
   c. What are the gift and estate tax consequences if Ann has the Trustee distribute $11,000 to each of her three children and ten grandchildren?
2. Thomas creates a testamentary trust to pay the income to his son, Daniel, for life and to distribute the remainder to whomever Daniel appoints in his will, in default of appointment by Daniel to his issue per

stirpes. Thomas dies on March 13. Daniel has a heart attack and dies on April 15.

    a. Is the value of the trust in Daniel's gross estate? Why?

    b. Could Daniel avoid this result? How? Should Daniel do this?

    c. What if the remainder was to be paid to those of Daniel's issue as he appointed in his will?

    d. What if he appointed, in trust, income to his daughter, Carol, for her life and remainder to those of Carol's issue as she appoints in her will?

3. Gordon established an irrevocable trust by transferring $11,000 to Friendly National Bank as Trustee to pay the income to Archie for life and the remainder to Beatrice. Gordon gave Archie the right to withdraw annually the lesser of (1) $11,000, (2) the amount transferred to the trust, or (3) the greater of $5,000 or five percent of the trust corpus. Gordon transfers an additional $11,000 annually for the next five years, and Archie never exercises the right of withdrawal.

    a. What are the gift tax consequences to Gordon?

    b. What are the gift tax consequences to Archie?

    c. What are the estate tax consequences to Archie if Archie dies without ever exercising the power? Assume he dies in year 6 after transferring $11,000 to the trust each year.

    d. What are the gift and estate tax consequences if Archie has the right to withdraw $11,000 annually? Assume he dies in year 6 after transferring $11,000 to the trust each year.

CHAPTER 13

Life Insurance

A. GENERAL PRINCIPLES
IRC §§2042, 7702

Life insurance is a unique asset and a fundamental component of most estate plans. Families purchase life insurance to produce a flow of income in the event a wage earner dies prematurely, to create wealth to pass to the next generation, and to provide funds for death taxes and expenses. Businesses purchase life insurance to protect the company against the loss of a key employee or to fund buy-sell agreements. Employers frequently provide life insurance as a fringe benefit. The reason for owning life insurance will dictate what type of life insurance is purchased and, often, the transfer tax consequences.

The insured is the person whose life is covered by the policy. The insured may or may not be the purchaser or the owner of the policy. The owner is the person who has all the rights associated with that policy, including the right to name the beneficiary, determine the payment option, and the like. When the insured purchases a life insurance policy on her own life and transfers it to another, the insured must make sure that she transfers each and every right in that policy to the new owner. Many provisions of a life insurance policy refer to the rights of an insured rather than an owner. If all these rights are not transferred, the insured may still be considered to own the policy for purposes of the federal estate tax.

The insurer is the company issuing the policy. Although an insurer will not require the insured to be the purchaser or owner of the policy, it will not sell a policy to everyone who applies. The purchaser must have an insurable interest in the life of the insured. For example, you could not purchase life insurance on the life of your tax professor or the dean of your law school. If you are not a close family member, a business associate, or someone with a similar interest in the insured's life, the insurer will not sell you a policy. This is, after all, an insurance industry, not a gambling enterprise.

The beneficiary is the person, persons, or entity designated in the policy to receive the proceeds of the life insurance policy at the death of the insured. Many owners will designate both a primary beneficiary and a contingent beneficiary in the event the primary beneficiary predeceases the insured. Life insurance policies themselves frequently provide that the proceeds will be paid to the insured's estate or executor if all the named beneficiaries predecease the insured.

The premium is the cost of the life insurance policy. Premiums may be paid in one lump sum or at more frequent intervals such as annually, semiannually, or quarterly. Premiums may be paid by the insured, the owner, an employer, a business associate, or anyone. Premiums paid by someone who is not the owner of the policy will be considered gifts from the payor to the owner to the extent that the owner does not transfer adequate and full consideration in money or money's worth to the payor.

Insurance is simply a contract; the owner pays a specified amount (the premium), and the insurer agrees to pay a sum of money if a certain event happens. Insurance thus shifts the cost of the event from the owner, or the insured, through the insurer to the group insured by that company. There are two primary types of life insurance and many variations on these two basic forms.

The first type is term insurance, where the insurer agrees to pay a set amount if the insured dies. If the insured dies within the term, usually, but of course not always, a year, the insurer pays. If the insured survives the term, the insurer keeps the premium. At the end of the term, the insurer and the owner of the policy may, or may not, contract for another term. There are a number of variations. Renewable term allows the owner the option of renewing the policy, without proof of the insured's health. Decreasing term covers more than one year but decreases the amount of coverage over the term. Group term is simply term insurance purchased on a specified group of individuals, often employees of a company or members of an association.

The second type is cash value, whole life, or ordinary life. It is term insurance plus an investment, or savings, component. As a result, it has higher premiums than term insurance, and it will generate dividends and interest on the investment component of the policy. At some point in the insured's life, the total cost of the insurance may be paid, and no further premiums will be due. This type of insurance has a cash surrender value, *i.e.*, the amount the insurer will pay if the owner cancels the policy. Because of the investment component, the owner can also borrow from the insurer or use the policy as collateral for a loan.

Example 13-1

Husband buys a life insurance policy on his own life from Liberty Mutual Life Insurance Co., payable to his Wife and, if she predeceases him, to his Son and his Daughter in equal shares. Husband is the owner and the insured. Liberty Mutual Life Insurance Co. is the insurer. Wife is the primary beneficiary, and Son and Daughter are the contingent beneficiaries. If Husband assigns all his rights in the policy to his Wife, he is still the insured. Wife is now the owner as well as the primary beneficiary.

In Helvering v. LeGierse, 312 U.S. 531, 539 (1941), the Supreme Court defined life insurance as "a device to shift and distribute risk of loss from premature death." In that case, the decedent had purchased a single premium life insurance policy and an annuity policy from the same insurer when she was 80 years old. Considering the two policies as part of one agreement, the Court found no element of risk shifting because "[t]he fact remains that annuity and insurance are opposites; in this combination the one neutralizes the risk customarily inherent in the other." *Id.* at 541. The Court did include the amount received by the life insurance beneficiary in the decedent's gross estate as a transfer intended to take effect in possession or enjoyment at or after death [the statutory predecessor to §§2036-2038]. The Court's decision in *LeGierse* has been incorporated into the regulations. Reg. §20.2042-1(a)(2). The combination life insurance and annuity contract is now governed by §2039. *See, e.g.,* Estate of Montgomery v. Commissioner, 56 T.C. 489 (1971), *aff'd* 458 F.2d 616 (5th Cir. 1972), *cert. denied* 409 U.S. 849 (1972).

In Commissioner v. Estate of Noel, the Court held that accident flight insurance policies were life insurance policies even though such policies only insured against death from a specific event. 380 U.S. 678 (1965). The Court rejected the distinction between an *inevitable* loss (one that will necessarily occur) and an *evitable* loss (one that might or might not occur), saying that "[i]n each case the risk assumed by the insurer is the loss of the insured's life, and the payment of the insurance money is contingent upon the loss of life." *Id.* at 681. In Revenue Ruling 83-44, 1983-1 C.B. 228, the IRS included a death benefit payable under a required no-fault automobile insurance policy in the gross estate under §2042(1) because the contract shifted the risk of death to the insurer and the payment of the death benefit was not a substitute for a wrongful death action.

Section 7702 now defines "life insurance contract" for all purposes of the Internal Revenue Code. The contract must first be considered life insurance under the applicable law, usually state law. This restricts life insurance to the payment of death benefits and excludes annuity and investment arrangements that many companies market as life insurance. In addition, the contract must meet (1) the statutory cash value accumulation test or (2) the guideline premium requirements and fall within the cash value corridor, both defined in the statute. These statutory tests are quite technical, and perhaps the only way to determine if they are satisfied is to ask for verification from the insurance company.

B. PROCEEDS PAYABLE TO THE INSURED'S ESTATE
IRC §2042(1)

Section 2042(1) includes in the decedent's gross estate all proceeds of a life insurance policy that are receivable by the executor. The life insurance proceeds are received by the executor through an express designation by the decedent or through the terms of the life insurance policy itself. The proceeds are considered receivable by the executor even if the estate is not named as the beneficiary if the insurance proceeds are subject to a legally binding obligation to pay taxes, debts, or other expenses of, or claims against, the estate. Reg. §20.2042-1(b).

Example 13-2

Diane purchases a life insurance policy on her own life and transfers it to an irrevocable life insurance trust that allows, but does not require, the Trustee to use the proceeds to pay death taxes and expenses. In this situation only the amount of proceeds actually expended for death taxes and expenses will be included in Diane's gross estate. Assume the life insurance proceeds amounted to $250,000, death taxes were $100,000, and expenses were $50,000. Only $150,000 would be included by §2042(1) because this was the amount actually expended for obligations of the estate.

To avoid §2042(1), the decedent could give the trustee the power to loan the life insurance proceeds to the decedent's estate or the power to purchase assets of the estate. The loan or the sale provides liquidity for the decedent's estate, but it does not increase the assets available to the decedent's executor for payment of expenses and distribution to will beneficiaries. As a result, it will not subject the life insurance proceeds to the federal estate tax.

Section 2042(1) also encompasses life insurance payable to another that serves as collateral security for a debt. The insurance will be deemed payable to the estate to the extent of the loan outstanding on the date of death because it was the decedent's, and therefore his estate's, obligation to repay this debt. Reg. §20.2042-1(b)(1). Life insurance proceeds are also payable to the estate when the primary beneficiary dies before the insured and the insured has not designated any contingent beneficiaries. In this situation, the policy itself makes the proceeds payable to the decedent's executor or estate.

PROBLEMS

1. Doris purchased a cash value policy with a face amount of $250,000, naming her Executor as the beneficiary. Doris paid the annual premiums of $500 for five years.
   a. At Doris's death what, if anything, is included in her gross estate?
   b. Same facts except that Doris names Ann as the beneficiary of the life insurance policy and Ann predeceases Doris. Doris has not named a contingent beneficiary.
   c. Same as b., except that Doris and Ann die as the result of the same car accident, and the order of deaths cannot be determined.
2. Debra creates an irrevocable trust with Friendly National Bank as the Trustee. During Debra's life, the Trustee has discretion to accumulate

income or distribute it to Sam, Debra's spouse. After Debra's death, the Trustee must distribute all the income to Sam and has discretion to distribute corpus if it is necessary for Sam's support and maintenance. At Sam's death, the Trustee is to distribute the trust property to Debra's issue. Debra funds the trust with two life insurance policies, with a total face amount of $500,000, as well as cash and stocks.

   a. What are the estate tax consequences if the Trustee must transfer to the Executor of Debra's estate sufficient assets to pay the state and federal estate tax, the funeral expenses, the expenses of administration, debts, and claims before paying any income to Sam?

   b. What are the estate tax consequences if the Trustee has discretion, but is not required, to make the transfers specified in 2.a.? Assume that the Trustee exercises this discretion and transfers $450,000 to the Executor.

3. As a result of David's death, the following amounts were paid. What are the estate tax consequences, if any, of these payments?

   a. Marble State Bank, the mortgagee on David's house, received $75,000 from the mortgage insurance policy owned by David.

   b. David had purchased credit card insurance on his MasterCard account, and $8,200 was paid to City Bank under this policy to cover the charges outstanding on the date of David's death.

   c. David had obtained a $250,000 loan from Marble State Bank to operate his growing software business. David purchased a life insurance policy from Liberty Mutual Insurance Co. to cover the cost of this loan and pledged the policy to Marble State Bank as security for the loan. As a result of David's death, Liberty Mutual paid Marble State Bank $250,000.

C. INCIDENTS OF OWNERSHIP
IRC §2042(2)

1. General Principles

Section 2042(2) includes in the decedent's gross estate the amount received by a beneficiary other than the decedent's estate only if the decedent possessed an incident of ownership in the life insurance policy at the moment of her death. The term "incident of ownership" is defined broadly in the regulations to include any right of the insured or her estate to the economic benefits of the policy. The rights to name or alter the beneficiary, to cancel or surrender the policy for cash, to assign or transfer the policy, to pledge the policy as collateral for a loan, and to borrow against the policy are typical incidents of ownership.

Reg. §20.2042-1(c)(2). The incidents of ownership test is analogous to the retained interest provisions of §§2036-2038. Although the provisions are not identical, they serve the same purpose, *i.e.*, "to prevent the decedent from enjoying the effective ownership of property until death, and at the same time escape the tax on testamentary transfers by formally disposing of the property earlier." Estate of Rockwell v. Commissioner, 779 F.2d 931, 933 (3d Cir. 1985).

The decedent needs to retain only one incident of ownership to invoke §2042(2). The right to designate the beneficiary is, perhaps, the most important right to most owners of life insurance. This right, however, must be real, not illusory.

Example 13-3

Wife purchases a life insurance policy on Husband's life and owns all the incidents of ownership. To ensure a coordinated estate plan, Wife designates the Trustee of Husband's revocable trust as the beneficiary of the policy. Decedent can alter, amend, or revoke his trust at any time. By doing so, he can effectively change the beneficiary of the life insurance policy. Wife, however, still owns the life insurance policy, and she can change the beneficiary designation at any time and, thus, thwart Husband's attempt to direct the flow of the life insurance proceeds. The policy proceeds are not in Husband's gross estate, because Wife's power to change the beneficiary trumps the Husband's power to change the trust. *See* Estate of Margrave v. Commissioner, 618 F.2d 34 (8th Cir. 1980).

Instead, Wife makes an irrevocable assignment of the life insurance policy to the trust. Because she has given up the right to change the beneficiary, the insurance proceeds will be distributed to the trust. Now Husband does have the ability to control where those proceeds will go through his power to alter or revoke the trust. As a result, the insurance proceeds will be in his gross estate because his ability to amend the trust will be considered an incident of ownership. *See* Estate of Karagheusian v. Commissioner, 233 F.2d 197 (2d Cir. 1956).

The power to designate the beneficiary in conjunction with any other person is also an incident of ownership. What if the decedent has only the right to veto the owner's change of beneficiary? In Revenue Ruling 75-70 the IRS noted:

> For estate tax purposes, a power to consent to or veto the exercise of an incident of ownership by another is distinct from a power to initiate such exercise unilaterally, but there is little practical difference between the two. It is clear that by requiring that his written consent be obtained before the policy could be assigned or a change of beneficiary effected, the decedent had effectively retained substantial control over some of the incidents of ownership. The fact that his power could be exercised only after the wife had first taken action does not alter the basic nature of the decedent's veto right (by withholding his

consent) as a joint power exercisable by the decedent in conjunction with another person within the meaning of section 2042 of the Code.

1975-1 C.B. 301. The IRS determined that the policy proceeds were in the decedent's gross estate even though his right to veto was limited to those who did not have an insurable interest in his life.

In Estate of Rockwell v. Commissioner, however, the court excluded the life insurance from the decedent's gross estate where the decedent had transferred the policy to his wife, retaining the right to veto any designation of a person who did not have an insurable interest in his life. 779 F.2d 931 (3d Cir. 1985). In *Rockwell*, the decedent's wife had transferred the insurance policy to a trust, designating their children and issue as beneficiaries, and she died before the decedent. The court found that these facts rendered the decedent's veto power a nullity and effectively barred him from using it.

The right to borrow against the policy is also an important incident of ownership.

Example 13-4

Decedent purchases a cash value life insurance policy and transfers it to an irrevocable, funded life insurance trust. Friendly National Bank is the Trustee. Decedent retains the right to borrow against the policy up to the amount of the cash surrender value, but all other rights are held by the Trustee as owner of the policy. The retention of the ability to borrow against the policy right is sufficient to bring the policy proceeds into Decedent's gross estate as Decedent can receive the economic benefit of the policy merely by borrowing against it. Revenue Ruling 79-129, 1979-1 C.B. 306.

The term "incidents of ownership" also includes a reversionary interest in a life insurance policy, but only to the extent that the decedent's reversionary interest exceeds five percent of the value of the policy. Reg. §20.2042-1(c)(3). Consider what might happen if Decedent transfers a life insurance policy to his Wife. There is always the possibility that she might predecease him and the policy return to him through her will, by inheritance, or by exercise of his statutory rights. The regulations, however, specifically provide that these possibilities are neither reversionary interests nor incidents of ownership. *Id.* Despite this, it is still possible to create a reversionary interest in the decedent.

Example 13-5

Decedent and Spouse divorce. The divorce decree requires Decedent to maintain a life insurance policy on his own life payable to his Ex-Spouse. Under the terms of the divorce decree, the policy reverts to Decedent if his Ex-Spouse dies or remarries. When Decedent dies, his Ex-Spouse is alive and has not remarried. At the moment before his death, Decedent has a reversion in the life insurance policy. If that reversion exceeds five percent of the value of the life insurance policy, the proceeds will be in Decedent's gross estate even though they are payable to the Ex-Spouse. Revenue Ruling 76-113, 1976-1 C.B. 276. In that case, the IRS allowed a deduction for indebtedness under §2053(a)(4) for the proceeds actually paid to the Ex-Spouse.

Whether or not the decedent has an incident of ownership is determined at the time of death. Estate of Beauregard v. Commissioner, 74 T.C. 603 (1980), *acq.* 1981-2 C.B. 1. In *Beauregard*, the decedent was required by the divorce decree to maintain a life insurance policy on his own life for the benefit of his minor children. Although he had the ability to change the beneficiary designation once both children reached the age of 21, the decedent died when both his children were minors. The court held that since he could not change the beneficiary designation at the time of death, he did not possess an incident of ownership sufficient to bring the policy proceeds into his gross estate under §2042(2).

2. *Policy Facts Versus Intent Facts*

Courts will carefully scrutinize all the facts and circumstances to determine whether a decedent has an incident of ownership. While courts will focus primarily on the economic substance of the arrangement, they will not ignore the decedent's legal rights even if the decedent had no practical method of exercising those rights. In Commissioner v. Estate of Noel, 380 U.S. 678 (1965), decedent applied for two flight insurance policies at the airport. His wife paid for the policies, and the clerk gave her the policies. Decedent died three hours later when his plane crashed. The Supreme Court held that decedent possessed incidents of ownership in the policies because the policies themselves gave him, as the insured, the right to assign the policies or change the beneficiary. The wife's payment of the premiums did not give her these rights. The decedent's transfer of the policies to his wife was ineffective to convey these rights because he did not comply with the terms of the insurance contract. In response to the wife's claim that the decedent's power to assign the policy or change the beneficiary was illusory, the Court responded:

> Obviously, there was no practical opportunity for the decedent to assign the policies or change the beneficiary between the time he boarded the plane and the time he died. That time was too short and his wife had the policies in her possession at home. These circumstances disabled him for the moment from exercising those "incidents of ownership" over the policies which were undoubtedly his. Death intervened before this temporary disability was removed. But the same could be said about a man owning an ordinary life insurance policy who boarded the plane at the same time or for that matter about any man's exercise of ownership over his property while aboard an airplane in the three hours before a fatal crash. It would stretch the imagination to think that Congress intended to measure estate tax liability by an individual's fluctuating, day-by-day, hour-by-hour capacity to dispose of property which he owns. We hold that estate tax

liability for policies "with respect to which the decedent possessed at his death any of the incidents of ownership" depends on a general, legal power to exercise ownership, without regard to the owner's ability to exercise it at a particular moment. Nothing we have said is to be taken as meaning that a policyholder is without power to divest himself of all incidents of ownership over his insurance policies by a proper gift or assignment, so as to bar its inclusion in his gross estate under §2042(2). What we do hold is that no such transfer was made of the policies here involved.

Id. at 683-684.

United States v. Rhode Island Hospital Trust Company
355 F.2d 7 (1st Cir. 1966)

COFFIN, Circuit Judge.

This appeal presents the question whether the proceeds of a life insurance policy on decedent's life are properly includable in the gross estate of the decedent by reason of the alleged possession at his death of "any of the incidents of ownership, exercisable either alone or in conjunction with any other person," under Section 2042. . . . The Commissioner of Internal Revenue having included the proceeds of an insurance policy on the life of Holton W. Horton (decedent) in his gross estate . . . coexecutors under his will, made timely claim for refund. . . . The district court found for the plaintiffs . . . and the government appeals.

The facts, undisputed, are of two kinds: "intent facts" — those relating to the conduct and understanding of the insured and his father, who was the instigator, premium payer, and primary beneficiary of the policy; and the "policy facts" — those revealed by the insurance contract itself.

Decedent's father, Charles A. Horton, was a textile executive, a prominent businessman in his community, and, according to the testimony, "a man with strong convictions and vigorous action." Charles and his wife, Louise, had two sons, decedent and A. Trowbridge Horton. In 1924, when decedent was 18 and Trowbridge 19, their father purchased an insurance policy on the life of each boy from Massachusetts Mutual Life Insurance Company. The policies were identical, each having the face amount of $50,000, the proceeds being payable to Charles and Louise, equally, or to the survivor.

Charles Horton's purpose was to assure that funds would be available for his wife, should he and either son die. Charles kept the policies in his safe deposit box and paid all premiums throughout his life. Under the policies, however, the right to change beneficiaries had been reserved to the sons. In January, 1952, the boys' mother, Louise, died. In March, 1952, Charles told each of his sons to go to the insurance company's office and sign a change of beneficiary form. The amendment executed by decedent named his father as primary beneficiary, with decedent's wife, brother, and the executors or administrators of the last survivor being the successive beneficiaries. After this amendment, decedent continued to retain the right to make further changes, but none was made. Decedent died on April 1, 1958, survived by his wife and father. His father died on October 2, 1961.

The father, Charles, regarded the policies as belonging to him, saying at one point that it would be "out of the question" for the sons to claim them. Decedent's brother never discussed the policies with his father, never asked for a loan based on the policies, obediently signed the change of beneficiary form at his father's request, and considered the policy on his life as the property of his father. Decedent's widow recalled only that decedent had once told her that his father had a policy on himself and his brother but that "in no way did it mean anything to us or would it ever. It was completely his." She added that her husband, the decedent, had wanted more insurance of his own, but was not able to obtain it.

Coming to what we call "policy facts," a careful reading of the policy, captioned "Ordinary Life Policy — Convertible," reveals the following rights, privileges, or powers accorded to the decedent.

> — *Right to change beneficiary.* In the application, an unrestricted change of beneficiary provision was elected by striking out two alternative and more limited provisions. The policy itself indicated reservation of "the right successively to change the beneficiary" by the insertion of typewritten dashes where, otherwise, the word "not" would have been inserted.

> — *Assignment.* No assignment would be recognized until the original assignment, a duplicate, or a certified copy was filed with the company. The company did not assume responsibility for the validity of an assignment.

> — *Dividends.* The insured had the option to have dividends paid in cash, used to reduce premiums, used to purchase paid-up additions, or accumulate subject to withdrawal on demand.

> — *Loans.* On condition that the unlimited right to change the beneficiary was reserved, as in this case, the company would "loan on the signature of the insured alone."

> — *Survival.* Should no beneficiary survive the insured, the proceeds were payable to his executors and administrators.

> — *Alteration.* The policy could be altered only on the written request of the insured and of "other parties in interest." . . .

At the outset we are confronted with the issue of the nature of this review. It is undoubtedly true that the question of possession of incidents of ownership of a life insurance policy is one of fact, the plaintiff having the burden of proving non-possession of all. . . . But where all of the evidentiary facts appear, we are faced with a question of law not of fact. Were we to proceed otherwise, cases presenting identical or closely similar facts in this technical and complex field could be decided oppositely, to the disadvantage of equitable tax administration.

Taking the subsidiary facts as presented to the district court, we differ with its conclusion that "the decedent's father was actually the real owner of the various incidents of ownership in said policy." But in differing we recognize that early holdings and occasional dicta, early and late, have invited litigation. . . .

To begin, the statute which bears on this case has a reason for being, is part of a general rationale and tax law pattern, and is deliberately precise. Before the Revenue Act of 1942, the tax criterion governing cases in this area was "policies taken out" by the decedent on his own life . . . has led to difficult problems of interpretation, which the courts resolved by creating two criteria: "payment of premiums" and possession of "incidents of ownership." The Revenue Act of 1942 . . . eliminated the "policies taken out" language, and sanctified the judicial gloss, with Congress, in its committee reports, including an illustrative list of the kinds of rights included under "incidents of ownership." These included decedent's right to change beneficiaries, to borrow, to assign, to revoke an assignment, and to surrender or cancel. H.Rep.No.2333, 77th Cong., 2d Sess., p. 164, 1942-2 C.B. 372, 491.[3]

In acting this way, Congress was, we think, trying to introduce some certitude in a landscape of shifting sands. In the provision which was the predecessor of section 2042, it was not trying to tax the extent of the interest of the decedent. That it knew how to do this is evident, for example, from a reading of section 2033, which includes in the gross estate of the decedent "the value of all property . . . to the extent of the interest therein. . . ." What it was attempting to reach in section 2042 and some other sections was the power to dispose of property, the same power that the Supreme Court recognized as a basis for exercise of the tax instrument in Chase National Bank of City of New York v. United States, 1929, 278 U.S. 327. Power can be and is exercised by one possessed of less than complete legal and equitable title. The very phrase "incidents of ownership" connotes something partial, minor, or even fractional in its scope. It speaks more of possibility than of probability.

Plaintiffs seize on Section 20.2042-1(c)(2) of the Treasury Regulations on Estate Tax, which says ". . . the term 'incidents of ownership' is not limited in its meaning to ownership of the policy in the technical legal sense. Generally speaking, the term has reference to the right of the insured or his estate to the economic benefits of the policy." Plaintiffs urge that there must be "a real control over the economic benefits." To this there are two answers. First, it is clear that the reference to ownership in the "technical legal sense" is not

---

3. Subsequently, the Revenue Act of 1954 eliminated the premium payment test, leaving possession of "any incidents of ownership" as the sole criterion. 26 U.S.C. 2042. Sen.Rep. No. 1622, 83d Cong., 2d Sess., p. 472 et seq., U.S.Code Cong. & Admin.News 1954, p. 4629.

abandoned and supplanted by reference to "economic benefits." Second, the regulation goes on to list illustrative powers referred to by Congress in its reports. All of these are powers which may or may not enrich decedent's estate, but which can affect the transfer of the policy proceeds.

Viewed against this background, what power did decedent possess? This is the relevant question — not how did he feel or act. Did he have a capacity to do something to affect the disposition of the policy if he had wanted to? Without gaining possession of the policy itself, he could have borrowed on the policy. He could have changed the method of using dividends. He could have assigned the policy. He could have revoked the assignment. Should he have gained possession of the policy by trick (as by filing an affidavit that the policy was lost), force, or chance, he could have changed the beneficiary, and made the change of record irrevocable. . . . Other such possibilities might be imagined. We cite these only to evidence the existence of some power in decedent to affect the disposition of the policy proceeds. In addition, he always possessed a negative power. His signature was necessary to a change in beneficiary, to a surrender for cash value, to an alteration in the policy, to a change in dividend options. Even with this most limited power, he would be exercising an incident of ownership "in conjunction with" another person. . . .

The existence of such powers in the decedent is to be distinguished from such rights as may have existed in decedent's father or duties owed the father by decedent. It is, therefore, nó answer that decedent's father might have proceeded against him at law or in equity. The company made it clear in the contract that it bore no responsibility for the validity of an assignment, that it could pay a beneficiary without recourse, and that it was under no obligation to see to the carrying out of any trust. It even made clear that a beneficiary need only write to the home office to receive payment. Should a third party — for example, an innocent creditor who had given valuable consideration to decedent — receive the proceeds of the policy, the proceeds of a loan on the policy, or the cash value, it could not be said that the transaction between decedent and such third person would in all such cases be nugatory. For decedent had some powers — perhaps not rights, but powers — which could, if exercised alone or in conjunction with another, affect the disposition of some or all of the proceeds of the policy.

Nor is it a compelling argument that decedent lacked physical possession of the policy. . . . Moreover, as we have noted, some rights could be exercised without physical possession of the policy. . . .

While decisions against the estate of a passive but power-possessing decedent may often conflict with the honest intentions and understanding of premium-paying beneficiaries and insurers, the alternative of abandoning the insistence on the governing nature of the contract, in most cases, is less desirable. The drawing of a useful line would be impossible; there would be a much wider range of varying decisions on similar facts; and there would be an invitation to unprincipled estate manipulation. As government counsel has pointed out, there could always be a formally executed side agreement under which the insured clearly surrenders to the beneficiary all his rights to the policy, such agreement to be brought to light only in the event of the decedent's dying before the beneficiary.

In any event, the statute has been on the books since the Revenue Act of 1942. This is only one of a number of cases applying it in the face of considerable external evidence of intent. Charles Horton, who caused the policy to be taken out, saw fit to vest decedent with rights in the policy and to allow such rights to continue for thirty-four years. Charles was a successful businessman and with as much incentive, opportunity, and capacity to be aware of the laws of the land as most people. It is difficult to speculate what purpose he thought was being served by his son's retention of rights in the policy. Had he wished to deprive his son of all incidents of ownership in the policy, this result could easily have been accomplished. But the step was not taken. We find that the decedent died, possessing at least an incident of ownership in the policy on his life.

Morton v. United States
457 F.2d 750 (4th Cir. 1972)

CRAVEN, Circuit Judge:

. . . We think that the decedent did not possess any of the incidents of ownership of this insurance policy at the time of his death so as to require inclusion of the proceeds in the decedent's gross estate under Section 2042(2). . . . The facts are not disputed. . . . Briefly, the policy was taken out in 1932 by the decedent at the instigation of his father-in-law, who wanted to provide financial security for his daughter. The decedent paid none of the premiums on this insurance policy and it is clear that he never considered that he "owned" it. The premiums were paid by his father-in-law, then by a corporation owned by the decedent's wife and her sister, and finally by the decedent's wife until the decedent's death in 1963. The policy was kept in the office safe of another corporation owned by the decedent's wife and her sister. . . . In 1938 the decedent executed an endorsement of the policy effecting an irrevocable designation of beneficiaries and mode of settlement. It is the effect of this endorsement upon the other terms of the policy which is determinative of the issue raised. . . .

It is clear that before the execution of the irrevocable designation of beneficiaries and mode of settlement the policy conferred upon the decedent, as the insured, many, if not all of the powers which Congress had in mind as being incidents of ownership sufficient to cause the proceeds to be included in his gross estate. Ordinarily the possession by the insured of the power to cash the policy in, to elect the endowment option, to get a loan on the policy or to change the beneficiary is sufficient to cause the proceeds to be included in his gross estate. United States v. Rhode Island Hospital Trust Co., 355 F.2d 7 (1st Cir. 1966). However, we think that the irrevocable designation of beneficiaries and mode of settlement, coupled with payment of premiums by persons other than the insured, made it legally impossible for the decedent to exercise other powers purportedly given him as insured by the policy in such a way that any economic benefit would accrue to him or his estate or so that he could subsequently control the transfer of the proceeds of the policy.

The government concedes that the endorsement of April 7, 1938, divested the decedent of the right to change beneficiaries and to select another method of payment. However, it maintains that other provisions of the policy were left unaffected and there remained in the decedent some incidents of ownership.

It is well established that if the insured retains no right to change the beneficiary of a life insurance policy or, as here, gives up that right, the beneficiary stands in the position of a third party beneficiary to the insurance contract with indefeasibly vested rights in the proceeds. . . . Most authorities are also in agreement that the insured cannot deal with the policy in such a way as to defeat the irrevocably designated third party beneficiaries' interest in the proceeds, by, for example, surrendering the policy for its cash surrender value, without the consent of the beneficiaries, and we think the district court was clearly correct that this result would obtain in West Virginia. . . .

The inquiry is not ended here, however. The district court rejected the government's secondary contention that even if the insured had no independent power he nevertheless had the power to act "in conjunction with" the beneficiaries in exercising incidents of ownership and thus the proceeds of the policy would be includable in the decedent's gross estate under the express language of Section 2042(2) of the Code. We agree that the decisive factor is the existence of the power to exercise incidents of ownership either alone or in conjunction with any other person. Commissioner of Internal Revenue v. Noel's Estate, 380 U.S. 678, 684 (1965). If both the decedent and the beneficiaries were legally required to act in conjunction in order to affect any of the options of the policy which could be called incidents of ownership, and even if these options could only be exercised in the best financial interest of the beneficiaries and with the approval of a court, the decedent nevertheless possessed the power to exercise the incidents of ownership "in conjunction with any other person." That would suffice under Section 2042(2) to bring the proceeds of the policy within the gross estate. But we are convinced the beneficiaries could effectively act alone to exercise the incidents of ownership. Participation by the decedent "in conjunction with" the beneficiaries was not required, we think, on the facts of this case.

The law of West Virginia and other jurisdictions with regard to the right of irrevocably designated beneficiaries to exercise options of a life insurance policy without the consent of the insured is unclear at best. *See* 4 Couch on Insurance 2d §27:67. Other courts which have considered analogous insurance problems have done so in light of earlier revenue acts which did not make the proceeds taxable if any incident of ownership was exercisable in conjunction with another person, and hence did not fully consider whether the consent of the insured would be a prerequisite to the exercise of a particular power by an irrevocably designated beneficiary. We think that whether or not an irrevocably designated beneficiary would have the right to obtain a loan on the policy, cash it in, or elect the endowment option when the insured had paid the premiums is doubtful. The indefeasibly vested right to the proceeds by the beneficiary probably would not extend to the right to the use of the premiums which these options represent when the premiums were contributed by another. However, when the irrevocably designated beneficiary has also paid the premiums, we think that he has the legal power to exercise the options in the insurance contract which pertain to the use of these premiums without participation of the insured.

Full paid participating insurance, dividends, paid-up insurance, cash surrender value, premium loans and the endowment option all represent use of the premiums with the consent of the insurance company. We think that general principles of equity and contract law strongly suggest that exercise of such premium payment derived rights properly belong to the irrevocably designated beneficiary who has paid the premiums to the exclusion of the insured who contributed nothing. It is not necessary to ignore the policy facts in order to recognize that with respect to premium derived options it is clear that the decedent never considered the policy his, and had the question come up, that all parties would have doubtless agreed that the decedent's wife should be entitled to exercise these options.

The options for premium loans and reinstatement provide for methods of keeping the policy alive in the event of nonpayment of premiums, and the insured's participation would not be necessary where the beneficiary has a vested right to the proceeds. To hold otherwise would allow the insured to indirectly defeat this vested interest. We hold that where an insured has never paid a premium and has never for any purpose treated the policy as his own that his irrevocable designation of beneficiaries and mode of payment of proceeds is an effective assignment of all of his incidents of ownership in the policy.

3. *Incidents Held in a Fiduciary Capacity*

Suppose Decedent is the Trustee of a trust for the benefit of his children and that one of the trust assets is a life insurance policy on his own life. As Trustee, Decedent is the owner of the policy and can exercise all of the rights usually associated with ownership. He must, however, deal with the life insurance policy as a fiduciary, and thus he cannot sell, borrow, or assign the policy except for the benefit of the trust beneficiaries. Decedent dies while serving as Trustee. Are the life insurance proceeds brought into his gross estate by §2042(2)? In other words, are powers held in a fiduciary capacity treated as incidents of ownership?

The regulations specify that "a decedent is considered to have an 'incident of ownership' in an insurance policy on his life held in trust if, under the terms of the policy the decedent . . . has the power *(as trustee or otherwise)* to change the beneficial ownership in the policy or its proceeds . . . even though the decedent has no beneficial interest in the trust." Reg. §20.2042-1(c)(4). *Emphasis added.*

The Second Circuit interpreted this regulation to apply only to powers retained by the decedent. Estate of Skifter v. Commissioner, 468 F.2d 699 (2d Cir. 1972). The Fifth Circuit disagreed. Rose v. United States, 511 F.2d 259 (5th Cir. 1975). In *Rose*, decedent's brother created trusts for each of decedent's children and appointed decedent as trustee. The decedent, acting as the trustee, then applied for insurance on his own life, using trust property to pay the premiums. The court included the proceeds of the policies in his gross estate at his death because he could alter the time and manner of enjoyment of the policy proceeds through his ability to withdraw dividends, obtain loans, or cancel or convert the policies. In reaching this conclusion, the court distinguished §2042, which focuses on the possession of incidents of ownership at death, from §§2036-2038, which deal with interests retained by the decedent.

The IRS finally adopted the Second Circuit's position in Revenue Ruling 84-179, which provides:

> In accordance with the legislative history of section 2042(2), a decedent will not be deemed to have incidents of ownership over an insurance policy on decedent's life where decedent's powers are held in a fiduciary capacity, and are not exercisable for decedent's personal benefit, where the decedent did not transfer the policy or any of the consideration for purchasing or maintaining the policy to the trust from personal assets, and the devolution of the powers on decedent was not part of a prearranged plan involving the participation of decedent. This position is consistent with decisions by several courts of appeal. *See* Estate of Skifter; Estate of Fruehauf v. Commissioner, 427 F.2d 80 (6th Cir. 1970); Hunter v. United States, 624 F.2d 833 (8th Cir. 1980). *But see* Terriberry v. United States, 517 F.2d 286 (5th Cir. 1975), *cert. denied*, 424 U.S. 977 (1976); Rose v. United States, 511 F.2d 259 (5th Cir. 1975), which are to the contrary. Section 20.2042-1(c)(4) will be read in accordance with the position adopted herein.
>
> The decedent will be deemed to have incidents of ownership over an insurance policy on the decedent's life where decedent's powers are held in a fiduciary capacity and the decedent has transferred the policy or any of the consideration for purchasing and maintaining the policy to the trust. Also, where the decedent's powers could have been exercised for decedent's benefit, they will constitute incidents of ownership in the policy, without regard to how those powers were acquired and without consideration of whether the decedent transferred property to the trust. . . . Thus, if the decedent reacquires powers over insurance policies in an individual capacity, the powers will constitute incidents of ownership even though the decedent is a transferee.

1984-2 C.B. 195.

A decedent who wants to divest himself of all incidents of ownership need only comply with this Revenue Ruling to ensure that the policy be excluded from her gross estate. If, however, she directly transfers the policy to the trust or pays the premiums on the policy, she will be considered as owning an incident of ownership sufficient to bring the policy into her gross estate.

4. Employer-Provided Life Insurance

Many employers provide group term life insurance to their employees as a fringe benefit. If the employee designates her executor or estate as beneficiary, the proceeds are included in her gross estate by §2042(1). If she designates someone else, the proceeds are included in her gross estate by §2042(2) as long as she retains an incident of ownership. Most group term policies and the law of most jurisdictions allow employees to transfer such policies to others to avoid inclusion in their gross estates. The policies themselves, state law, or even employment agreements, however, might contain provisions that are deemed to be "incidents of ownership."

The right to cancel an insurance policy is an incident of ownership. Reg. §20.2042-1(c)(2). Does that mean that an employee has an incident of ownership in a group term policy that he has transferred to another because he can cancel the policy simply by terminating employment? Of course not. Only powers that directly affect the insurance policy will be considered incidents of ownership. Powers that affect it only collaterally are not. Revenue Ruling 72-307, 1972-1 C.B. 307. The decedent's ability to convert employer-purchased group term life insurance to some other form of life insurance upon termination of employment is also not considered to be an incident of ownership. The IRS will not distinguish between voluntary and involuntary termination of employment. *See* Revenue Ruling 84-130, 1984-2 C.B. 194.

The right to select a settlement option affects the time or manner of enjoyment. Is retention of such a right an incident of ownership? The cases that have discussed this arose in the context of employer-provided group term insurance, but they are applicable to all life insurance policies.

Estate of Lumpkin v. Commissioner
474 F.2d 1092 (5th Cir. 1973)

GEWIN, Circuit Judge:

This federal estate tax case squarely presents the question of whether an employee who under the provisions of a group term life insurance policy is given nothing more than the right to alter the time and manner of enjoyment of the proceeds possesses an "incident of ownership" with respect to that policy so that at his death the value of the proceeds must be included in his gross estate under §2042. . . . The Tax Court decided that §2042 does not require the value of the proceeds to be included in decedent's gross estate, and the Commissioner has appealed. We reverse.

At the time of his death Lumpkin was an employee of the Humble Oil & Refining Company (hereinafter Humble) and as such was covered by a non-contributory group term life insurance policy. . . . According to the terms of the policy, . . . two kinds of benefits were payable to survivors of covered employees who died while serving Humble, but of these only one is relevant to our inquiry, the "Contingent Survivors Group Life Insurance Coverage."

Benefits receivable under "Contingent Coverage" consisted of a lump sum payment of $200, to be paid immediately upon the employee's death, plus a series of monthly payments, each in the amount of half the employee's normal monthly compensation, to continue over a period the duration of which depended upon the number of full years of service the deceased employee had completed. The "Contingent Coverage" benefits were to be paid to one of the following classes of qualifying "preference relatives" in descending order of priority: (1) spouse, (2) children under 21 years of age or permanently incapable of self-support, and (3) parents. The order in which the employee's survivors succeeded to the right to receive the proceeds from the "Contingent Coverage" was irrevocably fixed; under no circumstances could the employee redetermine who the beneficiaries would be or the order of priority among them. . . . Payments were to cease as soon as there were no more survivors from the list of qualifying preference relatives; as a result it was never certain that all monthly installments earned by the employee would actually have to be disbursed.

We now come to the "Optional Modes of Settlement" provision exercisable in connection with the "Contingent Coverage" benefits, the provision said by the Commissioner to bring §2042 into play. One part of the optional settlement provision entitled the employee to elect, without the consent of any other person, to have any monthly installments becoming payable to his spouse in effect reduced by half. The insurer would then accumulate the unpaid balance of each monthly installment with interest into a fund, and, in the event all monthly installments earned by the employee were paid to the spouse, the fund would be used to continue reduced monthly payments to the spouse until it was exhausted. If the spouse were to die before the fund was consumed, the amount remaining in it would be paid to her estate in a lump sum. But in no event would her estate receive more than what was in the accumulated fund. If the spouse were to die before all monthly installments earned had become due, the remaining installments would still be paid to surviving members of the next priority of preference relatives as previously outlined. Thus this part of the optional settlement provision enabled the insured employee to extend the period of time over which monthly payments would be made to his spouse and consequently to reduce them in amount. It did not empower him to divest her of any portion of the proceeds to which she (or her estate) was entitled under the terms of the preference relative provisions.

In addition to offering the employee this specific optional mode of settlement, the optional settlement provision entitled him, upon obtaining the
approval of his employer and the insurer, to establish any other scheme he
might devise for the disbursement of the proceeds once they became payable
to a particular relative. The exercise of this more general part of the optional
settlement provision was also limited in that under it the employee still could
not rearrange the order in which his preference relatives succeeded to the right
to receive monthly installments and hence could not divest any preference relative of the share of the proceeds to which he was entitled. The optional settlement provision concluded with the stipulation that under it the employee had
no right to designate beneficiaries either by request or by assignment but that
he could assign all rights given to him by the policy.

Before proceeding any further we should delineate the exact nature of the
power that was conferred upon Lumpkin by the provision entitling him to elect
optional modes of settlement, the only provision in the entire policy which
gave him any control over the proceeds. By exercising his rights under this
provision Lumpkin could not benefit himself or his estate, nor could he designate who the beneficiary of the proceeds would be. What the optional settlement provision did give him the right to do was to vary the time and manner in
which the proceeds would be paid to the policy-designated beneficiaries after
his death. . . . In short the right to elect optional modes of settlement gave
Lumpkin a degree of control over the time when the proceeds of the policy
would be enjoyed and nothing more.

[Section] 2042 is the statute in the federal estate tax scheme under which
the value of life insurance proceeds is taxed to the estate of the insured.
With respect to proceeds receivable by beneficiaries other than the insured,
it is triggered only if at death the insured possessed any "incidents of
ownership" in the insurance. When the "incidents of ownership" term first
appeared as part of an amendment to §2042's predecessor, no definition
accompanied it; however, Congress, in its committee reports, did include an
illustrative list of the kinds of rights comprehended by the phrase. Among
these were the right of the insured to the economic benefits of the insurance, the right to change beneficiaries, the right to surrender or cancel the
policy, the right to assign the policy, the right to pledge the policy for a loan,
and others.

From this list it can be inferred that by using the "incidents of ownership"
term Congress was attempting to tax the value of life insurance proceeds over
which the insured at death still possessed a substantial degree of control. This
inference is strengthened if we recognize that by enacting §2042 Congress
intended to give life insurance policies estate tax treatment roughly equivalent
to that accorded other types of property under related sections of the Code.
Under §§2036 (transfers with retained life estate), 2037 (transfers taking effect
at death), 2038 (revocable transfers), and 2041 (powers of appointment)
substantial control is often the touchstone by which the determination is made
that inclusion is necessary. . . .

The question before this court is whether the right to alter the time and manner of enjoyment, a fractional right to be sure, affords its holder the kind of control over the proceeds that will make it an "incident of ownership" within the meaning of §2042(2). The Tax Court thought not. In reaching this decision it relied on an earlier Board of Tax Appeals case which to our knowledge is the only one in which the question has been considered. In Billings v. Commissioner, B.T.A. 1147 (1937), *acq.* 1937-2 C.B. 3, the decedent had a right to elect optional modes of settlement similar to that conferred upon Lumpkin by the group term policy in this case; the Tax Court's predecessor held that the right to determine when the proceeds should be paid to the beneficiary was too limited and insignificant to amount to control over the proceeds.

To offset the impact of this 1937 decision, the Commissioner relies upon two relatively more recent Supreme Court decisions. In Lober v. United States, 346 U.S. 335 (1953), the decedent had created three separate irrevocable trusts, one for the benefit of each of his three minor children. Although the trust instruments gave each child a "vested interest" under state law so that if one of them had died after creation of the trusts respective interest would still have passed to his estate, the decedent as trustee had retained the right to turn all or any part of the principal trusts over to the beneficiaries at any time he saw fit. Thus Lober had forsaken the right to determine who the beneficiaries of the trust would be but had retained the right to determine when the trust property would be enjoyed. The court held that retention of this right rendered the value of the trust property includible in Lober's gross estate under the forerunner to §2038; that section, as does §2038, required the inclusion of the value of all property that the decedent had previously transferred in trust but over the enjoyment of which he had retained the power to "alter, amend, revoke or terminate." In reference to Lober's right to alter the time of enjoyment, the court said: " '[A] donor who keeps so strong a hold over the actual and immediate enjoyment of what he puts beyond his own power to retake has not divested himself of that degree of control which §811(d)(2) requires in order to avoid the tax." ' *Id.* at 337.

In essence United States v. O'Malley, 383 U.S. 627 (1966), the second case relied upon by the Commissioner, is not substantially different from *Lober*. The decedent Fabrice created several irrevocable trusts for the benefit of different members of his family. As one of the trustees he was empowered to pay the trust income to the beneficiaries or to accumulate it and add it to the principal, in which event the beneficiaries would be denied the privilege of immediate enjoyment and their eventual enjoyment would be conditioned upon their surviving the termination of the trusts. Thus Fabrice also had the right to alter the time and manner of enjoyment; however, the control afforded him by this right was somewhat less than Lober had possessed because it extended to the trust income only and not the principal which was inalterably committed to pass to the beneficiary (or his estate) when the trust terminated. Nevertheless the Supreme Court held that O'Malley's power over the time and manner of enjoyment was significant and of sufficient substance to activate the predecessor to §2036 which required inclusion whenever the transferor of property in trust had retained the right to "designate" who was to enjoy it.

Quite clearly the lesson to be drawn from *Lober* and *O'Malley* is that the right to alter the time and manner of enjoyment does give its holder a substantial degree of control, at least insofar as §§2036 and 2038 are concerned. In view of the Congressional intention to make the estate tax treatment of life insurance roughly analogous to that bestowed upon other types of property, somewhat of an anomaly would be created if power over the time and manner of enjoyment was said to impart enough control to activate §§2036 and 2038 yet not enough to make it an "incident of ownership" within the context of §2042.

The only significant distinction between §§2036 and 2038 on the one hand and §2042 on the other is that under the former there must be an incomplete transfer by the decedent whereas under the latter a transfer is unnecessary. Thus under §§2036 and 2038 the decedent must have retained some control over property he initially transferred while under §2042 it is enough if at death the decedent merely possessed an incident of ownership, the means by which he came into possession being irrelevant. This distinction does not, however, suggest that there is a further difference among these sections of the estate tax as to the degree of power a decedent must hold over the property in question — whether it be life insurance or some other form of wealth — in order to render its value includible in his gross estate.

These sections are all part of a Congressional scheme to tax the value of property transferred at death, whether the decedent accomplishes the transfer by will, by intestacy, or by allowing his substantial control over the property to remain unexercised until death so that the shifting of its economic benefits to the beneficiary only then becomes complete. It is the lapse of substantial control at death that triggers their application. *Lober* and *O'Malley* teach that one endowed with power over the time of enjoyment has the kind of substantial control Congress intended to reach by enacting these sections. Because the control it affords is substantial, we conclude that a right to alter the time of enjoyment such as that conferred upon Lumpkin by the optional modes of settlement provision in this case is an "incident of ownership" under §2042(2). Lumpkin could easily have assigned the right to elect optional settlements, thereby completely divesting himself of control over the insurance proceeds and avoiding inclusion of their value within his gross estate. Since he did not, his estate must suffer the consequences.

_____

The Third Circuit Court of Appeals rejected this approach in Estate of Connelly v. United States, 551 F.2d 545 (3d Cir. 1977), saying:

> The *Lumpkin* court strongly relied on what it viewed as the intent of Congress to tax life insurance and other types of property equivalently. However, *Lumpkin's* construction of §2042 would make it the only section in the Code that could reach

property in which the decedent had no beneficial interest and over which he had no power exercisable for his own. It is clear that Congress does not consider life insurance to be inherently testamentary. Thus if *Lumpkin* is correct in concluding that Congress meant to have the tax consequences of life insurance conform to other types of property, it would certainly seem more logical that Congress intended to equate incidents of ownership with the right to economic benefits of the policy. Indeed, there is a long line of cases which explicitly makes that equation. *See, e.g.*, Estate of Skifter v. Commissioner, 468 F.2d 699 (2d Cir. 1972); Estate of Fruehauf v. Commissioner, 427 F.2d 80 (6th Cir. 1970); Chase Nat'l Bank v. United States, 278 U.S. 327, 49 S. Ct. 126, 73 L. Ed. 405 (1929); Prichard v. United States, 397 F.2d 60 (5th Cir. 1960); Commissioner v. Chase Manhattan Bank, 259 F.2d 231 (5th Cir. 1958).

Furthermore, Treasury Regulation section 2042-1(c)(2) specifically provides that "incidents of ownership" refers "to the right of the insured or his estate to the economic benefits of the policy." Mr. Connelly had no rights whatsoever to the economic benefits of the policy.

Lumpkin's reliance upon *Lober* and *O'Malley* in defining section 2042 is misplaced. The facts of *Lober* and *O'Malley* were specifically covered by other sections of the Code. Moreover, the powers involved in *Lober* and *O'Malley* are directly parallel to explicit provisions of the regulations for life insurance, Reg. 20-2042-1(c). If the same powers which were involved in *Lober* and *O'Malley* were translated to the parallel provisions for life insurance, the explicit language of the regulations would require inclusion. Both decisions are controlled by explicit regulations. Such is not the case here. *Lumpkin* erroneously extended *Lober* and *O'Malley* to a fact situation foreign to both and controlled by different statutory provisions.

Id. at 551-552. The IRS will only follow *Connelly* in the Third Circuit. Revenue Ruling 81-128, 1981-1 C.B. 469. The Fifth Circuit relied heavily on its decision in *Lumpkin* when it decided Rose v. United States, but its position in *Rose* was ultimately rejected by the IRS in Revenue Ruling 84-179, 1984-2 C.B. 195. The IRS, however, has not yet rejected the rationale of the Fifth Circuit in *Lumpkin*.

5. *Policies Owned by a Corporation Controlled by the Insured*

Regulation §20.2042-1(c)(6) provides that incidents of ownership held by a corporation will not be attributable to a controlling, or even the sole, shareholder when the insurance proceeds are payable directly to the corporation. The rationale for this regulation is that insurance proceeds paid to, or for the benefit of, the corporation will increase the value of the corporation. As a result, the value of the decedent's stock will also increase. *See* Reg. §20.2031-2(f); Estate of Huntsman v. Commissioner, 66 T.C. 861 (1976), *acq.* 1977-2 C.B.1. The net effect on the decedent's estate will be the same. Any proceeds payable to a third party for a valid business reason are also not attributed to the shareholder. If the insurance proceeds are payable to another beneficiary, such as the decedent's spouse or child, however, any incidents of ownership held by the corporation *will* be attributed to the shareholder if the decedent is the sole or controlling shareholder. Reg. §20.2042-1(c)(6). The regulation defines a "controlling" shareholder as one with 50 percent or more of the voting power.

In Revenue Ruling 82-85, 1982-1 C.B. 137, the IRS considered the appropriate tax treatment when the corporate-owned life insurance proceeds were used to purchase decedent's stock from his estate. Relying on Estate of Huntsman v. Commissioner, the IRS held that the proceeds, although realistically flowing through the corporation to the decedent's estate, would not be included in the decedent's gross estate by §2042 but instead would be reflected in the value of decedent's stock in the corporation and thus included in the gross estate by §2033.

Estate of Levy v. Commissioner
70 T.C. 873 (1978)

GOFFE, Judge:

. . . At the time of his death decedent owned 80.4 percent of the issued and outstanding voting stock and 100 percent of the issued and outstanding nonvoting stock of Levy Bros. of Elizabeth, New Jersey, Inc. (Levy Bros.). He was never the sole stockholder of the corporation. Levy Bros. owned the . . . two life insurance policies on the life of decedent. . . . The life insurance policies were characterized as "split-dollar" policies whereby Levy Bros. owned the policies and were entitled to the net interpolated cash value as set forth above ($1,726.06). In addition, Levy Bros. held the right to change the beneficiary of the cash value, the right of assignment, the right of borrowing against the policies, and the right to modify the policies. The decedent, apart from his stock ownership of Levy Bros., had no incidents of ownership in either life insurance policy at the time of his death. Mrs. Levy, decedent's widow, as beneficiary, was entitled to and was paid proceeds from the policies in the amount of $206,701 as set forth above. The beneficiary of the death benefits under the policies could not be changed without the approval of Mrs. Levy.

The proceeds of the policies paid to Mrs. Levy were not included in the estate tax return of decedent's estate. The Commissioner, in his statutory notice of deficiency, determined that the proceeds of the policies paid to Mrs. Levy were includable in decedent's estate pursuant to section 2042. . . .

Therefore, the ultimate question for our decision on this final issue is whether a controlling stockholder (80.4 percent of all voting stock in the instant case) is to be treated in the same manner as a sole stockholder for purposes of attribution. We see no distinction between a sole or controlling stockholder with regard to the application of the provisions of section 2042. In either situation the stockholder possesses the power over the activities of the corporation so as to affect the disposition of the insurance proceeds. Clearly,

Congress did not intend to attribute corporate incidents of ownership to a sole stockholder while excluding a stockholder owning 99 percent of the voting stock of a corporation, or 80.4 percent in the instant case. Petitioner relies upon Casale v. Commissioner, 247 F.2d 440 (2d Cir. 1957), *revg.* 26 T.C. 1020 (1956), for the proposition that the application of the "sole stockholder example" to a controlling stockholder is inconsistent with the separate entity approach to corporations. However, the holding in *Casale* is inapposite to the facts in the instant case because our focus is limited to the application of section 2042(2). In *Casale*, a corporation purchased a combined life and annuity contract insuring a taxpayer who was the president and majority stockholder (98 percent) of the corporation. Under the provisions of the insurance policy, the corporation was the designated owner of the policy and held the rights to assign the policy, to change its beneficiary, to receive dividends as declared by the insurer, and to borrow on the policy in an amount not exceeding its loan value. The president and majority stockholder had the right under a compensation agreement to designate a beneficiary in the event he died only after he became entitled to annual annuity payments. We held that the premium payments (made by the corporation) were equivalent to a dividend distribution to taxpayer. On appeal, the Second Circuit Court of Appeals reversed and held that the taxpayer received no immediate benefit from the premium payments and that any rights possessed by the taxpayer were subject to termination prior to his receiving annuity payments in the future. In addition, the court, taking the position that the corporation was not a sham operating as a conduit on behalf of the taxpayer merely because the taxpayer was a controlling stockholder, stated: "We have been cited to no case or legislative proposition which supports the proposition that the entity of a corporation which is actually engaged in a commercial enterprise may be disregarded for tax purposes merely because it is wholly owned or controlled by a single person."

Levy Bros. possessed the right to change the beneficiary of the cash value, the right of assignment, the right to borrow against the policies, and the right to modify the policies. Although the parties did not stipulate the specific terms of the policies, it is apparent that the corporation, by the exercise of its rights in the policies, had the power to realize all or at least the greater portion of the proceeds of the policies prior to decedent's death and thus prevent decedent's widow from receiving much of the insurance proceeds. By his stock ownership, decedent had the power to elect the board of directors who, in turn, had the power to elect corporate officers who would be amenable to decedent's wishes as to the exercise of the incidents of ownership held by the corporation. United States v. Rhode Island Hospital Trust Co., 355 F.2d 7 (1st Cir. 1966). Decedent could indirectly exercise such power with ownership of less than all of the voting stock.

Petitioner further argues that any incidents of ownership held by a corporation controlled by the decedent are restricted by a fiduciary capacity, citing Estate of Fruehauf v. Commissioner, 427 F.2d 80 (6th Cir. 1970), *affg.* 50 T.C. 915 (1968). In that case, the decedent held the incidents of ownership as cotrustee of a testamentary trust created in his wife's will. We held that merely because decedent could exercise the incidents of ownership in a fiduciary capacity, nevertheless such capacity was no bar to inclusion by reason of possession of incidents of ownership. The Court of Appeals affirmed but rejected the broad rule we adopted and held that under the special facts of the case the incidents of ownership were attributable to decedent. In the instant case, decedent did not possess the incidents of ownership as a fiduciary. The record is silent as to whether petitioner was an officer or director of Levy Bros., in either event of which he would be in a fiduciary capacity. But it is not contended by either party that the incidents of ownership are attributable to decedent in such a capacity but, instead, by reason of his controlling stock ownership. Even if decedent, as a shareholder, were considered in a fiduciary capacity, it is difficult to see how the corporation or minority shareholders could be injured by exercising the incidents of ownership to defeat the widow. Numerous situations are apparent where it would be in the best interests of the corporation to exercise its incidents of ownership and deprive decedent's widow of the proceeds, i.e., e.g., borrowing against the insurance policies at a lower rate of interest than borrowing from other sources, especially if the loan could be deducted from the proceeds and repayment by the corporation never be required.

Includability of the proceeds under section 2042(2) is based upon stock ownership as demonstrated in its legislative history and not upon retention of control or enjoyment as in section 2036(a)(1). . . . Accordingly, we hold that proceeds of the two life insurance policies on the life of decedent payable to his widow are includable in decedent's gross estate.

PROBLEMS

1. Dwight purchases a life insurance policy from Metropolitan Life Insurance Co., naming his spouse, Sarah, as primary beneficiary and his children as contingent beneficiaries.
    a. What are the estate tax consequences when Dwight dies and Sarah receives $500,000 from Metropolitan Life Insurance Co.?
    b. What are the estate tax consequences if Dwight purchases the policy and then transfers it to Sarah? Assume that Dwight paid all of the premiums even after the transfer and that Sarah's will leaves all of her property outright to Dwight. Dwight dies five years after the transfer to Sarah.
    c. Same as 1.b., except that Dwight reserved the right to borrow against the policy. He assigned all other rights to Sarah.
    d. Same as 1.b., except that Dwight must consent to any change of beneficiary.
2. What are "policy facts"? How do they differ from "intent facts"? Of what relevance are "policy facts" and "intent facts" to §2042(2)? Who

has the burden of proof with respect to incidents of ownership and what is that burden?

3.   Is it possible to avoid the result in *Estate of Noel* and *United States v. Rhode Island Hospital Trust Company*? If so, how?

4.   Can you distinguish *Morton* from *Rhode Island Hospital Trust Company*? How?

5.   Delwin purchases a $400,000 life insurance policy on his own life and transfers it to his spouse, Sally. Sally dies five years later. Her will leaves all of her property, including the life insurance policy, to Delwin. Two years later Delwin dies.

    a.   Is anything in Delwin's gross estate? Why?

    b.   Would it make any difference if Sally had been the original purchaser of the policy and if Delwin never owned any incidents of ownership until Sally's death?

6.   Diane purchases a $400,000 life insurance policy on her own life. She then creates an irrevocable insurance trust, transferring the policy and other investments to the trust. The Trustee is to accumulate income during Diane's life and, at her death, pay the income to Diane's spouse for his life, with the remainder going to Diane's issue. Assume that trust income is used to pay the insurance premiums.

    a.   What are the estate tax consequences if Diane appoints herself Trustee and is serving as Trustee at the time of her death?

    b.   What if Diane has appointed Thomas as the original Trustee, but Thomas resigned and Diane became the successor Trustee? Assume Diane was serving as Trustee at the time of her death.

    c.   Instead, Diane's spouse purchased the policy, and he set up the trust. He appointed Diane as Trustee, and Diane was serving as Trustee at her death. What are the estate tax consequences when Diane dies? Would the result be different if the transfers were part of one coordinated estate plan?

    d.   Same as 6.c., except that Diane pays the premiums.

7.   Dawn's employer, ABC, Inc., purchases a group term life insurance policy on all employees. Each employee is insured for twice her annual salary and may designate the beneficiary of the policy.

    a.   Dawn transfers all her rights in the policy to Harold, her spouse. Is anything in her gross estate assuming that neither state law nor the employment agreement creates any rights in Dawn?

    b.   Same as 7.a., except that Dawn retains the right to cancel the policy.

    c.   Same as 7.a., except that Dawn has no right to cancel the policy other than by terminating employment with ABC, Inc.

    d.   What are the estate tax consequences in 7.a. if state law gives Dawn the right to convert the group term life insurance policy to an individual policy upon termination of employment?

    e.   Same as 7.a., except that Dawn retains the right to alter the settlement option but not the beneficiary designation?

8. Dale is one of three equal co-owners of X, Inc. The by-laws of X, Inc. require that all shareholder actions be agreed upon by 75 percent of the shareholders, in effect giving each shareholder veto power. X, Inc. purchases a $1 million life insurance policy on each of the three shareholders and pays the premiums.

   a. What are the estate tax consequences to Dale when he dies?

   b. How does the life insurance affect the valuation of X, Inc.?

   c. Assume that Davie is the sole shareholder. What is the result if X, Inc. uses the insurance proceeds to redeem Dale's stock from his estate?

   d. Assume that Davie is the sole shareholder. What is the result if the insurance policy is a "split-dollar policy" paying X, Inc. the cash surrender value of the policy and paying Helen, Dale's spouse, the rest?

D. LIFE INSURANCE ON THE LIFE OF ANOTHER
IRC §§2033, 2036(a)(1)

Life insurance may be included in the decedent's gross estate by a section other than §2042 if the owner is not the insured.

Example 13-6

Husband purchases a life insurance policy on his own life and irrevocably assigns all the rights in the policy to Wife. Five years later, Wife dies. The insurance policy is property that she owned at death, and its value will be in her gross estate under §2033. The amount that is included in her gross estate is the value of the life insurance policy, not the face amount or the proceeds that would have been received on that date if Husband had died.

Sections other than 2033 might also apply.

Example 13-7

Wife purchases a life insurance policy on her Husband's life and owns all the incidents of ownership in the policy. She selects the settlement option that leaves the insurance proceeds with the insurance company and pays her only interest and dividends for her life. At her death, the policy proceeds will be paid to her children. This settlement option becomes irrevocable at Husband's death. Husband dies, and Wife begins receiving interest and dividends on the insurance policy. Five years later, Wife dies. The life insurance proceeds are brought into Wife's gross estate by §2036(a)(1), because she made a lifetime transfer and retained the right to income. *See* In re Estate of Pyle v. Commissioner, 313 F.2d 328 (3d Cir. 1963).

E. GIFTS OF LIFE INSURANCE
IRC §§2035(a), 2503(b), 2512

A life insurance policy is an asset that can be transferred to another. The insured frequently gives life insurance policies to other family members or to a trust to avoid inclusion of the policy proceeds in her gross estate under §2042. When making a gift of life insurance, the insured must transfer all incidents of ownership to the new owner. As Commissioner v. Estate of Noel and United States v. Rhode Island Hospital Trust Co. demonstrate, the insured must clearly assign all rights in the policy to avoid §2042.

The value of the life insurance policy depends on the type of policy. The value of a single-premium whole life policy is the cost, not the cash surrender value. Guggenheim v. Rasquin, 312 U.S. 254 (1941); Reg. §25.2512-6(a) (Ex. 3). The value of term insurance is also the cost. If the insured makes the gift at the very beginning of the term, the value of the gift is the premium paid. If the insured makes the gift in the middle of the term, the value is simply the prorated premium for the remainder of the term.

Valuation of cash value policies is more complicated because there are both insurance and investment elements. In this situation, the value of the insurance element is once again the prorated premium for the remainder of the term. The value of the investment element is the interpolated terminal reserve, an amount calculated by the insurance company that is approximately the same as the cash surrender value. Example 4 of regulation §25.2512-6 demonstrates how to value such a gift. An easier, and more common, method is simply to contact the insurance company and request the value for the date of the gift.

An outright gift of a life insurance policy qualifies for the gift tax annual exclusion because the new owner has the right to immediate use, possession, or enjoyment of the policy. It is irrelevant that the insured is still alive and, thus, enjoyment of the policy proceeds is delayed. Reg. §25.2503-3(a). A gift of life insurance to a trust will not qualify as a present interest unless the trust beneficiaries have the right to demand payment, for example, through a *Crummey* power. Reg. §25.2503-3 (Ex. 2).

Life insurance is a unique asset. For a very modest payment, the insured can create instant wealth.

Example 13-8

Insured purchases $500,000 of term life insurance by paying the premium due of $500 and names his Spouse as the beneficiary. Two weeks later, Insured dies in an automobile accident. The value of the insurance policy immediately before Insured's death was the $500 premium paid. Spouse, however, receives $500,000. Section 2042 recognizes this discrepancy between value and amount received and includes in the gross estate the amount receivable, not the value.

As a result of this difference in value, an insured who makes a lifetime gift of his insurance policies may be able to achieve significant transfer tax savings. If, however, the insured wants to retain control of the policies until shortly before death, he may not be able to accomplish this goal. Section 2035 still includes gifts of life insurance made within three years of death in the gross estate. Given the difference between the value of the policy for gift tax purposes and the amount included in the gross estate, the failure to provide a rule such as §2035 would create a very large loophole in the transfer tax system.

An insured who owns cash value life insurance may not be able to achieve significant transfer tax savings by retaining such a policy until shortly before death. With cash value insurance, the increase in the investment portion of the policy will raise the value of the policy for gift tax purposes to, or even exceeding, the face amount. As a result, owners of cash value insurance should give those policies away as early in life as possible.

Another way to avoid §2035 is for the insured never to own the policy in the first place. A spouse, child, or trustee can purchase the policy directly from the life insurance company. In this case, neither §2042 nor §2035 would apply because the decedent/insured never had any incidents of ownership in the policy and never made a transfer of that policy. When someone other than the insured purchases a life insurance policy, however, they must make sure that all of the rights given to the insured in the policy are transferred to the owner/purchases. If they do not do this, the policy will be in the insured's gross estate at death. *See, e.g.*, Commissioner v. Estate of Noel, *supra*. Despite the repeal of the premiums paid test in 1954, the Commissioner has argued that payments of premiums within three years of death will bring a life insurance policy into the gross estate of the decedent. The Commissioner has lost this argument. *See, e.g.,* Estate of Headrick v. Commissioner, 918 F.2d 1263 (6th Cir. 1990); Estate of Leder v. Commissioner, 893 F.2d 237 (10th Cir. 1989).

PROBLEMS

1. Daniel purchases a cash value life insurance policy with a face amount of $250,000. He gives that policy to his spouse, Wendy, assigning all his rights in the policy to her. Daniel continues to pay the premiums.
    a. What are the gift tax consequences? What if the policy were a term policy rather than cash value?
    b. Wendy dies five years after the policy is transferred to her. What are the estate tax consequences?
    c. Instead of b., Daniel dies. What are the estate tax consequences if he dies two years after transferring the policy? What if it is four years later?
2. Same as problem 1, except that Daniel transfers the policy to an irrevocable life insurance trust and appoints Friendly National Bank as Trustee. What are the gift tax consequences?

3. Same as problem 1, except that Wendy now establishes an irrevocable
    trust with Friendly National Bank as Trustee, to pay the income to
    herself for life, then to pay the income to Daniel if he is living, and to
    distribute the trust property to her children in equal shares. Wendy trans-
    fers the life insurance policy to the trust.
    a. What are the estate tax consequences when Daniel dies?
    b. What are the estate tax consequences when Wendy dies?

PART IV

Deductions and Credits

CHAPTER 14

Expenses, Claims, Debts, Taxes, and Losses

A. GENERAL PRINCIPLES
IRC §§642(g), 2053

The federal estate tax is imposed on property that passes from the decedent to others as a result of death. In defining the taxable estate, the IRC allows two types of deductions: (1) those that represent amounts that do not pass gratuitously from the decedent to others and (2) those that promote specific policies. The deductions allowed by §§2053, 2054, and 2058 fall into the first category. These are expenses of administering the decedent's estate and claims that are legal obligations of the decedent and her estate. Because this property does not pass to the decedent's heirs or beneficiaries, it should not be taxed. These deductions are discussed in this chapter.

The second category of deductions is designed to foster specific policies and include: the deduction for charitable gifts, §2055, the deduction for transfers to the surviving spouse, §2056, and the deduction for family-owned business interests, §2057. The property represented by these deductions does pass from the decedent to her heirs and beneficiaries but, for policy reasons, passes free of transfer tax. Sections 2055 and 2056 are analyzed in subsequent chapters.[1]

A deduction reduces the size of the taxable estate and thus the amount of tax. The amount of tax saved depends on the marginal tax bracket of the estate. A deduction of $100,000 saves $50,000 of taxes at the 50 percent marginal tax rate and $40,000 at the 40 percent marginal tax rate. A credit, on the other hand, reduces taxes dollar for dollar. A $100,000 credit saves $100,000 of taxes. As a result, a credit affects all estates the same, while a deduction provides a greater benefit to estates in a higher marginal tax bracket. Both deductions and credits may be limited to specific percentages or dollar amounts.

---

1. Section 2057 was repealed by the 2001 Tax Act.

The administrator of the decedent's estate files three different tax returns: the decedent's final income tax return (Form 1040), the estate's income tax return (Form 1041), and the estate tax return (Form 706). Individuals are cash basis taxpayers, reporting income when it is received and deductions when they are paid. As a result, only expenses paid before death may be deducted on the decedent's final income tax return. Section 213(c) provides an exception for medical expenses paid by the estate during the year after decedent's death. These expenses are claims against decedent's estate and, as such, may alternatively be deducted on the estate tax return.

The estate is a taxable entity, collecting income and incurring expenses. Many of the expenses may be deducted on either the estate's income tax return or the estate tax return; they cannot be deducted on both. §642(g). If the decedent has a taxable estate, most deductions are claimed on the estate tax return because the rate of tax is higher, and thus the benefit is greater. Moreover, income tax deductions may have percentage or other limitations that are usually absent from the estate tax. In deciding where to claim a particular expense, however, the administrator must also consider who benefits from the deduction. Some heirs may benefit more if items are claimed as income tax deductions rather than as estate tax deductions.

Section 2053 allows a deduction for funeral and administration expenses, claims against the estate including certain taxes, and debts. These items are deductible only to the extent they are allowable by state law. This does not mean that deductibility is governed exclusively by state law. Rather, it creates a two-part test. First, the expense must be one of those listed in §2053. Federal law dictates what is, or is not, a funeral expense or an administration expense or a claim against the estate. Second, the expense must be allowable under the law of the jurisdiction administering the estate in terms of both character and amount.

Example 14-1

State has a nonclaim statute that requires all claims against Decedent's estate to be presented for payment within nine months of Decedent's death. Decedent owes Debtor $25,000 but fails to present the claim within nine months. The claim is unenforceable as a result. Decedent's estate cannot deduct the $25,000, even if it pays Debtor, because the claim was not allowable under state law.

The determination of the probate court will ordinarily establish the validity and amount of the claim or expense as long as that court has decided the issue on its merits. Reg. §20.2053-1(b)(2). *See* Commissioner v. Estate of Bosch, 387 U.S. 456 (1967), discussed at page 32.

Section 2053 distinguishes between amounts that are payable out of property subject to claims (first category) and amounts incurred in administering nonprobate property that is included in the gross estate (second category). Section 2053(c)(2) limits the deduction for the first category to the value of the property subject to claims plus any amount paid within the time for filing the estate tax return.

Example 14-2

David's gross estate includes bank accounts of $50,000, life insurance of $500,000 payable to his daughter, and jointly owned property worth $1,000,000. Funeral expenses were $5,000, administration expenses were $10,000, and claims were $75,000. Only the bank account is probate property. David's daughter contributes $40,000 of the life insurance proceeds toward the payment of the claims, and David's executor uses the $50,000 bank account to pay the remainder of the claims and expenses. If all the claims and expenses were paid within the time specified for filing the estate tax return, *i.e.*, nine months, then the full $90,000 will be allowed as a §2053 deduction.

Assume that $30,000 of the claims was not paid until six months after the date for filing the estate tax return. In that case, only $60,000 would be allowed as a §2053 deduction.

Expenses for nonprobate property are deductible as long as they are paid before the expiration of the period of limitation for assessment of the estate tax, *i.e.*, usually three years. Reg. §20.2053-1(a)(2), -8.

B. EXPENSES
IRC §2053

Section 2053 permits the deduction of reasonable funeral expenses that are actually expended, Reg. §20.2053-2, and expenses that are actually and necessarily incurred in the administration of the estate, Reg. §20.2053-3. This includes executors' commissions, attorneys' fees, appraisers' fees, court costs, and the like. *Id.*

Hibernia Bank v. United States
581 F.2d 741 (9th Cir. 1978)

WALLACE, Circuit Judge:

. . . In May 1965, Celia Tobin Clark died testate leaving an estate worth several million dollars. Mrs. Clark's will provided for several specific bequests of personal property. The will also directed that the residue, which included the bulk of the estate, be divided among four testamentary trusts. The income of each trust was to be paid to one of Mrs. Clark's children with the remainder to be divided equally among Mrs. Clark's grandchildren. The residue of Mrs. Clark's estate included two principal components: a mansion situated on 240 acres in Hillsborough, California, and approximately 10,000 common shares of Hibernia Bank stock.

Mrs. Clark's will named Hibernia as trustee for the four testamentary trusts. . . .

On June 2, 1965, Mrs. Clark's will was admitted to probate. By December 1967, all of the specific bequests and virtually all claims against the estate had been paid. Apparently, at this time, Hibernia, acting as the administrator, could have sought permission to distribute the remaining assets, including the mansion and the Hibernia stock, to the testamentary trusts and to close the estate. Rather than do so, however, Hibernia elected first to liquidate the Hillsborough mansion.

Hibernia encountered substantial difficulty in disposing of the mansion, and it was not finally sold until the spring of 1972. During this period, the administrator was required to spend some $60,000 per year in order to maintain the residence. Thus, Hibernia believed that it was necessary either to sell the estate's share of Hibernia stock or, alternatively, to borrow the funds required to maintain the mansion. Hibernia elected to borrow.

In each of the years from 1966 through 1969, Hibernia executed a substantial loan from a commercial bank. The net proceeds from these loans equaled $775,000. Hibernia itself acted as lender for two of the four loans, the proceeds of which totaled $625,000. The interest payments for the four loans totaled $196,210.[1]

In June 1971, Hibernia filed with the Commissioner a claim for a refund of part of the estate taxes paid on the Clark estate. As part of this claim, Hibernia asserted that it was entitled to deduct from the gross estate as expenses of administration the amount it had paid in interest on the four bank loans. The Commissioner disallowed the claimed deduction for the interest and denied the corresponding refund.

In March 1974, Hibernia brought suit in the district court asserting that it was entitled to deduct the loan interest and claiming a corresponding refund. . . . [T]he essence of Hibernia's argument is that the deductibility of administration expenses is exclusively a question of state law. Since in this case the California

---

1. Although the ethical quality of Hibernia's conduct as the estate's administrator does not bear on our disposition of this case, we do observe that Hibernia allowed itself to be placed in positions fraught with potential for abuse. First, Hibernia's decision to borrow funds and thereby subject the estate to substantial interest payments rather than sell the Hibernia stock carries at least the outward appearance of an attempt by Hibernia to avoid placing a large block of its own stock on the market at the expense of the Clark estate. Second is Hibernia's decision to borrow from itself. This act placed Hibernia in a position where its interest sharply conflicted with that of the estate. As long as the loans remained unpaid, Hibernia received substantial interest payments at the expense and diminution of the estate. Of the $196,210 paid in total interest for the four loans, $133,241 was paid to Hibernia.

probate court expressly approved the $196,210 interest payments as administration expenses, Hibernia contends that the Commissioner was required to permit a corresponding deduction.

Hibernia's contention is supported by Estate of Park v. Commissioner of Internal Revenue, 475 F.2d 673 (6th Cir. 1973), in which the Sixth Circuit expressly rejected the cases to the contrary and held "that the deductibility of an expense under 2053(a) (or its predecessor) is governed by state law alone." *Id.* at 676.

The district judge rejected Hibernia's argument and expressly declined to follow *Estate of Park.* The district judge ruled that in addition to showing that the claimed expense is allowable under state law, "the taxpayer must show that the claimed administrative expense was a reasonable, necessary administrative expense within the meaning of federal law."

There is no dispute in this case as to whether the interest rate was reasonable or as to the total amount of interest payments. Thus, the dispute centers around whether or not the interest payments were expenses of administration within the meaning of federal estate tax law. In order to resolve this issue, the district judge focused on Treas.Reg. §20.2053-3(a), which provides in part:

> The amounts deductible from a decedent's gross estate as "administration expenses" . . . are limited to such expenses as are actually and necessarily incurred in the administration of the decedent's estate; that is, in the collection of assets, payment of debts, and distribution of property to the persons entitled to it. The expenses contemplated in the law are such only as attend the settlement of an estate and the transfer of the property of the estate to individual beneficiaries or to a trustee. . . . Expenditures not essential to the proper settlement of the estate, but incurred for the individual benefit of the heirs, legatees, or devisees, may not be taken as deductions.

Viewing the issue in this light, the district judge found that the estate had been kept open much longer than necessary, thereby rendering the loans and interest payments made during the excess period also unnecessary. Specifically, the judge found as a matter of fact that "(w)ithin fifteen months of the testator's death (Hibernia), in its capacity as administrator of the estate, had sold all the assets of the estate except the mansion with its surrounding acreage and the Hibernia Bank stock." In addition, the district judge concluded that Hibernia had failed "factually (to) demonstrate an existing necessity to keep the Clark estate open for seven years." The district judge reasoned that since it was wholly unnecessary to keep the estate open during the period of the loans, the loans and interest payments were therefore also unnecessary to the administration of the estate. The implication is that the estate was left open in order to sell the mansion not because the sale was necessary for the administration of the estate, but rather because the heirs preferred to have cash distributed to the trusts rather than an undivided interest in the mansion. Thus, the expenses were not deductible.

We agree with the district judge that allowability under state law is not the sole criterion for determining the deductibility of a particular expenditure under section 2053(a)(2).

> In Pitner v. United States, 388 F.2d 651 (5th Cir. 1967), the Fifth Circuit held that (i)n the determination of deductibility under section 2053(a)(2), it is not enough that the deduction be allowable under state law. It is necessary as well that the deduction be for an "administration expense" within the meaning of that term as it is used in the statute, and that the amount sought to be deducted be reasonable under the circumstances. These are both questions of federal law and establish the outside limits for what may be considered allowable deductions under section 2053(a)(2).

Id. at 659.[4] . . .

We agree with the Fifth Circuit. We cannot read section 2053(a)(2) as permitting the deduction of expenditures which simply are not expenses of administration within the meaning afforded that term by federal estate tax law. Our holding is firmly supported by prior decisions as well as sound principles of policy.

United States v. Stapf, 375 U.S. 118, 84 S. Ct. 248, 11 L.Ed.2d 195 (1963), involved the will of a Texas decedent which directed that if the surviving spouse elected to take under the will rather than retain her one-half interest in the community, then the executors were to pay "all and not merely one-half" of the community debts and administration expenses. . . . On certiorari, the Supreme Court instructed that "(t)he first question to consider is whether the claim is of the type intended to be deductible." 375 U.S. at 130, 84 S. Ct. at 256. Applying this analysis, the Court observed that the decedent's assumption of debts and expenses which ordinarily would have attached to the property of his wife was "in effect . . . a testamentary gift to his wife." Id. at 133, 84 S. Ct. at 258. The Court held that such a gift or "gratuitous assumption of debts," Id. at 131, 84 S. Ct. 248, even though permissible under state law was not a claim against the estate within the meaning of the statute. The Court applied the same analysis in denying the deductibility of administration expenses which, absent the will provision, would have been chargeable to the estate of the surviving spouse. Id. at 133-34, 84 S. Ct. 248.

We believe Stapf firmly undergirds our conclusion that even though an expenditure of estate funds is permitted by state law, it must in fact be an "administration expense( )" as contemplated by section 2053(a)(2) to be deductible as such. . . .

---

4. In *Pitner*, the court did observe, and we agree, that in most instances "the state law may be relied upon as a guide to what deductions may reasonably be permitted for federal estate tax purposes." 388 F.2d at 659. As the court explained, however, deference to state law as a guide cannot justify the deduction of expenses which simply are not "administration expenses" within the meaning of federal estate tax law.

Policy considerations also militate in favor of our holding. The federal estate tax is not a tax on the decedent's property, but rather a tax on the transfer of that property. . . . The mechanics of the estate tax give meaning to this distinction by permitting deductions from the decedent's gross estate for debts, administration expenses, and certain other liabilities. The resulting "taxable estate" on which the estate tax is calculated is the amount actually transferred to the heirs. Although fairness dictates that the taxable estate not include assets which will not be available for transfer to the heirs, fairness does not require the deduction of amounts which are not true liabilities of the estate. Thus, "(e)xpenditures not essential to the proper settlement of the estate, but incurred for the individual benefit of the heirs, legatees, or devisees" are not expenses of administration within the meaning of section 2053. 26 C.F.R. §20.2053-3(a).

The district judge's conclusion that the Clark estate was left open much too long is amply supported by the record. Fed.R.Civ.P. 52(a). Since it was unnecessary to leave the estate open during the period of the loans, it is clear that the loans were not necessary to the administration of the estate. Accordingly, the district judge was correct in disallowing an administration expense deduction for the amount of the interest payments.

The Sixth Circuit overruled *Estate of Park* in Estate of Millikin v. Commissioner, 125 F.3d 339 (6th Cir. 1997). At issue in *Millikin* was the $750,000 expense of maintaining and selling the decedent's residence. Decedent's gross estate was valued at $22,851,356.30 and included a 150-acre estate. Decedent authorized her executor to sell any asset without obtaining court approval. She gave the Cleveland Museum of Art the right to select any art objects it desired. Decedent died on June 18, 1989, the Cleveland Museum of Art had finished its selection process by March 16, 1990, and the house was finally sold on April 20, 1994. On remand from the Sixth Circuit, the Tax Court held that the estate could only deduct the cost of maintaining the residence through March 16, 1990, when the museum had finished its selection of art objects. After that, the expenses of maintaining and selling the residence were not deductible because the principal reason for the sale was to accommodate the beneficiaries, not to benefit the estate. Estate of Millikin v. Commissioner, 76 T.C.M. (CCH) 1076 (1998).

C. CLAIMS AND DEBTS
IRC §2053

Section 2053 also provides a deduction for claims against the decedent's estate as well as the decedent's debts. Claims that are founded on a promise or agreement must be bona fide and contracted for adequate consideration in money or money's worth. Only debts that are the personal obligation of the decedent may be deducted. If the decedent is the guarantor of a debt, no deduction will be allowed unless the debtor is unable to pay. Debts need not have matured; in fact, state law usually imposes a limited amount of time for debtors to file claims against the estate.

Estate of Flandreau v. Commissioner
994 F.2d 91 (2d Cir. 1993)

LOKEN, Circuit Judge:

The Estate of Lulu K. Flandreau appeals a decision of the United States Tax Court, Clapp, J., denying the Estate an estate tax deduction under IRC §2053 for the unpaid balance of promissory notes executed by decedent payable to her sons and daughters-in-law. Estate of Flandreau v. Commissioner, T.C. Memo 1992-173, 63 T.C.M. (CCH) ¶2512 (1992). We affirm.

IRC §2053(a)(3) provides an estate tax deduction "for claims against the estate." A deduction "founded on a promise or agreement," however, is "limited to the extent that [the claims] were contracted bona fide and for an adequate and full consideration in money or money's worth." IRC §2053(c)(1). In this case, the Estate claims a $102,000 deduction for the face amounts of fourteen non-interest bearing, unsecured promissory notes executed by decedent in December 1970, January 1971, and January 1972 payable to her two sons and their wives.

Each note was preceded by a gift of the same amount from decedent to the purported lender. Decedent reported each of these transfers on a gift tax return but paid only $126 in federal gift taxes as all but two of the transfers were within the then-applicable gift tax exclusion. The recipients then transferred the gifted amounts back to decedent and received the notes in question. The notes were payable in 1995, when decedent would be 95 years old, or upon her death.

Mrs. Flandreau died on February 20, 1986, without having repaid any portion of the notes. The Estate claimed a deduction of $102,000 for the full amount due. The Commissioner issued a Notice of Deficiency denying the deduction on the ground that, "The debts were not bona fide debts contracted for adequate and full consideration under Section 2053 of the Internal Revenue Code." The tax court denied the Estate's petition for redetermination. The court concluded that "these were merely circular transfers of money from decedent to her children and back to decedent." As such, the notes did not represent debts, but were rather "unenforceable gratuitous promises to make a gift, based upon neither money nor money's worth," and therefore did not qualify as deductible claims under §2053. The Estate appeals.

We have consistently rejected taxpayer attempts to use gifts to family members followed by loans back to the taxpayer to avoid federal taxes that would otherwise be imposed. In Johnson v. Commissioner, 86 F.2d 710 (2d Cir. 1936), taxpayer gave $400,000 to his wife. The wife established two trusts, assigning insurance policies on taxpayer's life, with the wife as beneficiary, to an "insurance" trust, and depositing the $400,000 in a "funded" trust. The funded trust then loaned taxpayer the $400,000. Mr. Johnson claimed a deduction for his interest payments to the funded trust. Of course, the trustee used the interest payments to pay the premiums on the life insurance policies. We affirmed the disallowance of this "ingenious attempt to reduce taxes," concluding that this was all part of a single transaction and that taxpayer never lost control of his gift. "The payment to Johnson of money which he himself supplied to the trustee for the very purpose [of making the loan] cannot be a loan to him or furnish consideration for his note." 86 F.2d at 712.

In Guaranty Trust Co. of New York v. Commissioner, 98 F.2d 62 (2d Cir. 1938), decedent gave his wife $1,048,000 over a five year period. She put the moneys in trust, and the trusts loaned decedent the same amounts in exchange for ten-year interest bearing notes. We affirmed the denial of an estate tax deduction for the $1,048,000 owing on the notes at his death. Relying upon Johnson v. Commissioner, we reasoned that, because the gifts were conditioned upon the subsequent loans, the trusts had only "loaned" decedent his own money.

In Muserlian v. Commissioner, 932 F.2d 109 (2d Cir. 1991), the taxpayer made forty loans of about $5,000 each to his adult children who immediately loaned the same amounts back to him. Again, we affirmed the denial of a deduction for interest payments on these loans, concluding that this was not bona fide indebtedness. "By making 'gifts' and then receiving 'loans' from his donees, the taxpayer was actually borrowing his own money to create [an] interest expense." 932 F.2d at 113.

The tax court's findings and conclusions in this case are entirely consistent with the above precedents. The gifts, loans, and notes were exchanged contemporaneously, and the amounts of the gifts were identical to the amounts subsequently loaned. The Estate argues that the tax court improperly considered the source of the funds that decedent's sons and daughters-in-law "loaned" to her in exchange for the notes. However, *Guaranty Trust* confirms that it is appropriate to look beyond the form of the transactions and to determine, as the tax court did here, that the gifts and loans back to decedent were "component parts of single transactions." 98 F.2d at 66.

As the Supreme Court has observed, "the family relationship often makes it possible for one to shift tax incidence by surface changes of ownership without disturbing in the least his dominion and control over the subject of the gift or the purposes for which the income from the property is used." Commissioner v. Culbertson, 337 U.S. 733, 746 (1949). For this reason, courts examine such intrafamily transactions with heightened scrutiny; when the bona fides of promissory notes is at issue, the taxpayer must demonstrate affirmatively that "there existed at the time of the transaction a real expectation of repayment and an intent to enforce the collection of the indebtedness." Estate of Van Anda

v. Commissioner, 12 T.C. 1158, 1162, 1949 WL 301 (1949), *aff'd per curiam,* 192 F.2d 391 (2d Cir.1951). *See also* Estate of Labombarde v. Commissioner, 58 T.C. 745, 754-55, 1972 WL 2474 (1972), *aff'd,* 73-2 U.S. Tax Cas. (CCH) ¶12953 (1st Cir. 1973). Here, the tax court expressly found that the sons and daughters-in-law never expected that the money they transferred to decedent would be repaid.

Having carefully considered the entire transaction, we agree with the tax court that the Estate failed to carry its burden of showing the notes were "contracted bona fide and for an adequate and full consideration in money or money's worth." . . . The judgment of the tax court is affirmed.

Leopold v. United States
510 F.2d 617 (9th Cir. 1975)

ALFRED T. GOODWIN, Circuit Judge:

. . . The second issue on this appeal involves the deductibility for estate-tax purposes of a $264,000 payment by the executors of decedent's estate to Constance Trevor de Schulthess, as guardian for her daughter Beatrice Tina.

The decedent and his second wife, Constance, were married on February 2, 1958. On August 13, 1958, their daughter, Beatrice Tina, was born. One year later Constance filed an action for divorce. Following extensive negotiations, the decedent and Constance entered into a property-settlement agreement, [which required decedent to make a will leaving Beatrice Tina $250,000 plus an amount determined by reference to certain trusts.]. . . This property-settlement agreement was approved and incorporated into an interlocutory judgment of divorce entered on January 17, 1961.

Although the decedent did make a bequest to Beatrice Tina, the amount was uncertain. Constance filed a creditor's claim for $273,900 based on the quoted clause of the property-settlement agreement. The executors rejected the claim in part, but after Constance had filed suit in state court, the matter was settled, and $264,000 was paid to Constance in satisfaction of the claim filed on behalf of Beatrice Tina.

In their claim for refund, the taxpayers contended that this payment was a deductible claim against the estate under section 2053(a)(3) of the Internal Revenue Code, 26 U.S.C. §2053(a)(3). The government replied that although Beatrice Tina had an enforceable claim under local law, the claim was not supported by adequate and full consideration in money or money's worth, as required by section 2053(c)(1)(A). . . . The district court agreed with the taxpayers, finding that the $264,000 payment was based upon a promise by the decedent contracted bona fide and for an adequate and full consideration, and concluding that the payment was deductible.

Section 2053(a)(3) does authorize deductions from the gross estate for amounts paid to satisfy "claims against the estate." However, subsection (c)(1)(A) further provides that deductions "shall, when founded on a promise or agreement, be limited to the extent that they were contracted bona fide and for an adequate and full consideration in money or money's worth. . . ." One purpose of this limitation is to prevent testators from depleting their estates by transforming bequests to the natural objects of their bounty into deductible claims. . . .

We begin our analysis by looking to two decisions of this court construing an analogous provision of the Internal Revenue Code. In United States v. Past, 347 F.2d 7 (9th Cir. 1965), we scrutinized a property-settlement agreement made in anticipation of divorce. There the husband and wife jointly transferred certain community property into a trust, with the income payable to the wife for her life and the remainder payable to the couple's children. When the wife died, the Commissioner included the entire corpus of the trust in her gross estate. The district court held instead that none of the property was includible because the decedent had received adequate and full consideration from her husband for making the transfer. We reversed, holding that the fact that the transfer was part of a property-settlement agreement incident to a divorce was insufficient in itself to make the transfer one for an adequate and full consideration. The value of what the decedent received must be measured against the value of what she transferred. Since in *Past* the decedent received less than she transferred, we held that the trust property was not excludible from federal estate tax upon her death.

In Estate of Haskins v. United States, 357 F.2d 492 (9th Cir. 1966), we again were faced with a property-settlement agreement incident to a divorce. There, as part of the agreement, the husband placed money in a trust in which he reserved a life estate with the remainder to his children. We affirmed a district court decision holding that the corpus of this trust was includible in the decedent's gross estate. We noted that both parents were devoted to their children and keenly mindful of parental obligation. Testamentary provisions for the care of children, even though required by a property-settlement agreement, were not necessarily made for monetary consideration but could be viewed as a form of estate planning by the couple.

The government contends that *Haskins* requires us to reverse the judgment of the district court holding that the payment to Constance was a deductible claim against the estate. However, in *Haskins* the district court specifically found that there was no consideration for the transfer; here, the district court found that there was. Moreover, *Haskins* did not establish a per-se rule that a testamentary provision for one's own children could never be made for monetary consideration.

In Hartshorne v. Commissioner, 402 F.2d 592, 594 n. 2 (2d Cir. 1968), the government did take the position that a bequest to one's own children can never be a "claim against the estate" within the meaning of section 2053 because such a bequest is simply an agreement to make a testamentary disposition to persons who are the natural objects of one's bounty. The Court of Appeals for the Second Circuit rejected this absolute position, and so do we.

The Second Circuit noted, in language which conforms to the test laid down in
Past and *Haskins*:

> . . . Under exceptional circumstances . . . it may be that a claim by someone who
> might otherwise inherit from the decedent should be deductible under section
> 2053. If the claim is not simply a subterfuge for a nondeductible legacy, if the
> claim is supported by "adequate and full consideration," and if the consideration
> is a non-zero sum which augmented the decedent's estate, then it would seem
> that the deduction should be allowed. Whether or not a particular claim is
> deductible, then, will depend on the facts in each case. 402 F.2d at 594-595 n.2.

Constance's claim on behalf of Beatrice Tina meets this standard. The case
presents the "exceptional circumstances" to which the Second Circuit alluded.

The testimony before the district court was sharply conflicting on the question whether the decedent's agreement to make the bequest to Beatrice Tina
was bargained for or merely gratuitous . . . Decedent's will suggests that
Beatrice Tina might not necessarily have been a natural object of the decedent's bounty. His will established his first wife and her daughters as the residuary beneficiaries of his estate; by contrast, nothing was left to Constance and
no more to Beatrice Tina than was required by the property-settlement agreement. His attorney testified that the decedent knew that his first two daughters'
share of the residuary estate would be worth considerably more than the
amount promised to Beatrice Tina. Moreover, these two daughters already had
the inter vivos trusts which are the subject of the first issue on this appeal.

The record strongly suggests that the decedent and Constance were not
equally concerned with the financial walfare of their daughter, and that
Constance felt she had to wrench from her husband — or at least from her
husband's lawyers — the promise to leave a bequest to Beatrice Tina. She
feared that because of the circumstances concerning the marriage and the birth
of their daughter, her child might not be treated equally with the children of
the first marriage. The decedent's attorney testified that the decedent did give a
preference in financial matters to his first two daughters, in part because he felt
that Constance was more self-assertive than his first wife and would always
manage to provide for her child.

Constance's initial demands for support payments for herself were within
the range of California court awards in similar cases. Nonetheless, she
accepted a substantially smaller sum, partly in consideration for her husband's
promise to bequeath more than $250,000 to their daughter. Constance appar-
ently felt that she could spend her support payments more freely and would
not have to set aside part for her estate if she knew that her child would be
taken care of in the event of her ex-husband's death. Thus, by accepting
reduced alimony, Constance paid for her husband's promise to leave money to
their daughter; in effect, she diverted to her daughter that consideration which
otherwise would have flowed to herself. Although the property-settlement
agreement might have spelled out more precisely what Constance relinquished
in exchange for her husband's promise to leave their daughter a bequest, the

record supports the finding that the promise was contracted for in good faith for value which augmented the decedent's estate.

Estate of Smith v. Commissioner
198 F.3d 515 (5th Cir. 1999)

WIENER, Circuit Judge:

In this complex federal tax case, involving both estate and income tax issues, Petitioner-Appellant Estate of Algerine Allen Smith (the "Estate") appeals an adverse decision of the Tax Court. At the time of her death, Algerine Allen Smith (the "Decedent") was one of many defendants in a lawsuit brought by Exxon Corporation that arose out of royalty provisions in numerous oil and gas leases. Exxon had overpaid royalty owners, including the Decedent, and was suing to recoup the overpayments.

Four questions are presented in this appeal: (1) As of what date is a claim against the Decedent that is deductible from gross estate under §2053(a)(3) to be valued? (2) How and to what extent, if any, does an estate's inchoate right to an *income* tax deduction (or refund) under §1341(a) — a right that ripens only when and if an estate makes a payment on a claim deducted under §2053(a)(3) — affect the §2053(a)(3) *estate* tax deduction allowed to the estate for such claim?. . .

In answer to the first two questions, we hold that the claim generating the estate tax deduction under §2053(a)(3) — as well as the §1341(a) income tax relief that will necessarily attend any payment by an estate on that claim — must be valued as of the date of the death of the decedent and thus must [be] appraised on information known or available up to (but not after) that date. We therefore vacate and remand with instructions to the Tax Court that it admit and consider evidence of pre-death facts and occurrences that are relevant to the date-of-death value of Exxon's claim, without admitting or considering post-death facts and occurrences such as the Estate's settlement with Exxon, which occurred some fifteen months after Decedent's death. . . .

I. Facts and Proceedings

In 1970, Decedent . . . leased tracts of land located in Wood County, Texas, [designated as the Hawkins Field Unit "HFU")] to Exxon's predecessor, Humble Oil & Refining Company ("Humble Oil"). The lessors were to receive royalty payments calculated as a fraction of the price received by the lessee for any oil and gas produced from the leased tracts. The lease agreements provided that if the price of the minerals produced under the lease were ever regulated by the government, royalties would be adjusted accordingly. . . .

[The federal government sued Exxon for violating federal price regulations. (The D.O.E. litigation) A group of royalty owners including Decedent then sued Exxon for the full amount of the royalties designated in the contract. In the first suit, the court] held that Exxon had violated the federal price-control regulations. The court determined that Exxon was liable, in restitution, for over $895 million. In February of 1986 — following affirmance of the [court's] judgment and shortly after the Supreme Court denied certiorari — Exxon paid the judgment, which, including both pre and post-judgment interest, totaled approximately $2.1 billion.

In 1988, Exxon sued the HFU royalty owners, seeking to recoup a portion of the $2.1 billion judgment. . . . In August 1989, fifteen months before Decedent's death, the district court that was adjudicating the [royalty owner's suit] ruled that Exxon had "an implied cause of action [against the HFU royalty owners, including the Decedent] under federal common law for reimbursement." . . . In January 1990, the royalty owners, including Decedent, moved for summary judgment. . . .

Decedent died on November 16, 1990. At the time of her death, the royalty owners' Motion for Summary Judgment was still pending. Exxon subsequently filed its own motion for summary judgment, and in February 1991 — after Decedent's death but before the filing of her estate tax return (Form 706) — the district court granted summary judgment in favor of Exxon. The court held that (1) the royalty owners were liable to Exxon; (2) Exxon's damages would equal the difference between the regulated price of oil and the higher price Exxon had charged its customers; and (3) Exxon could recover interest on its damages for the period beginning on the date that Exxon had paid the judgment in the DOE litigation (February 27, 1986) and ending on the date that the interest owners paid Exxon. The court expressly *did not* allow Exxon to collect interest accruing before it paid the judgment in the DOE litigation, reasoning that to do so would be "unjust and inequitable" because Exxon could have avoided this portion of the judgment by paying the DOE earlier. The court then referred the calculation of damages to a special master. Exxon claimed that it was owed a total of $2.48 million by the Estate.

Decedent's Form 706 was filed in July, 1991, approximately eight months after her death and five months after the summary judgment favorable to Exxon but while the Special Master was calculating the quantum of Exxon's claims. Pursuant to §2053(a)(3), Decedent's Form 706 included a $2.48 million deduction for Exxon's claim against the Estate. In March 1992, fifteen months *after* Decedent's death and nine months after the filing of her Form 706, the Estate paid Exxon $681,840 to settle the case, a sum equal to 27.5 percent of the §2053(a)(3) deduction claimed by the Estate.

The Commissioner determined that, as Exxon's claim was disputed on the date of Decedent's death, the Estate was entitled to deduct only the amount paid in settlement ($681,840), even though that was not done until fifteen months after Decedent's death. Accordingly, the Commissioner issued a notice of deficiency for $663,785 in *estate* taxes, based in part on the reduced deduction. . . .

On the merits, the Tax Court ultimately held that because (1) Exxon's claim was neither certain nor enforceable as of the decedent's death, the estate was entitled to deduct only the post-death settlement payment of $681,840; and (2) the income tax benefit the estate derived under §1341(a) for paying Exxon $681,840 in settlement constituted property of the Estate, as of Decedent's death. . . .

II. Analysis

. . . A tax is imposed on the transfer of the "taxable estate" of every decedent who is a citizen or resident of the United States. The "taxable estate" is the "gross estate" less those deductions allowable under §§2051 through 2056. The first issue in this case is whether post-death facts and occurrences can be considered in valuing the deduction authorized by §2053(a)(3) for "claims against the estate . . . as are allowable by the laws of the jurisdiction . . . under which the estate is being administered". . .

Although we are persuaded that, on these facts, the Commissioner is not permitted to consider — much less rely exclusively on — the amount of the post-death settlement of the Exxon claim when valuing Decedent's allowable estate tax deduction, we are also persuaded that the estate is not entitled to deduct the full amount that was being claimed by Exxon at Decedent's death. Rather, for the reasons that follow, we conclude that the correct analysis requires appraising the value of Exxon's claim based on the facts as they existed as of death.

Section 2053(a)(3) is silent regarding the "as of" date for valuing claims against an estate. The Commissioner cites Treasury Regulation ("Reg.") §20.2053-1(b)(3), which allows a deduction for a claim "though its exact amount is not then known, provided it is ascertainable with reasonable certainty, and will be paid." The Commissioner urges that because the "reasonable certainty" and "will be paid" requirements were not met as of the date of death, post-death events can and should be considered in establishing the value of the claim. The Estate, on the other hand, emphasizes that Reg. §20.2053-4 allows a deduction for those "personal obligations of the decedent *existing at the time of his death.*" According to the Estate, this temporal reference establishes the precise date as of which claims are to be valued. Thus, insists the Estate, because the district court had held that Exxon had a cause of action, and because Exxon was asserting a debt of $2.48 million as of Decedent's death, this is the proper amount of the deduction.

The most that can be discerned from these Regulations is that the situation we now face is not expressly contemplated, and that there is, arguably, language that supports the opposite contentions of the parties. Finding no definitive answer in the statute or regulations, we turn to the case law.

Ithaca Trust Co. v. United States is the Supreme Court's clearest statement of the general rule that "[t]he estate so far as may be is settled as of the date of the testator's death." [279 U.S. 151, 155 (1929).] *Ithaca Trust* involved the value of a charitable remainder subject to a life estate. The question before the Court was whether the charitable remainder became more valuable (as a deduction from the gross estate) because the life tenant, who survived the testator, died before reaching her actuarial life expectancy. The Court, per Justice Holmes, held that the estate tax is a levy on the transfer of property, a discrete act, and that

> the value of the thing to be taxed must be *estimated* as of the time when the act is done. But the value of property at a given time depends upon the relative intensity of the social desire for it at that time, expressed in the money that it would bring in the market. Like all values, as the word is used by the law, it

depends largely on more or less certain prophecies of the future; and *the value is no less real at that time if later the prophecy turns out false than when it comes out true.* Tempting as it is to correct uncertain probabilities by the now certain fact, we are of opinion that it cannot be done, but that the value of the wife's life interest must be estimated by the mortality tables. Our opinion is not changed by the necessary exceptions to the general rule specifically made by the Act. [*Ithaca Trust Co.,* 279 U.S. at 155 (citations omitted)(emphasis added).]

As many courts have noted, decisions following *Ithaca Trust Co.* are irreconcilable. In the context of the §2053(a)(3) "claims against the estate" deduction, some courts have strictly adhered to the Supreme Court's directive to value deductions based on the "more or less certain prophecies of the future" [*Ithaca Trust Co.,* 279 U.S. at 155] existing on the date of death[18]; others have not.[19]

Propstra v. United States from the Ninth Circuit is a leading case that strictly applies the date-of-death valuation principle to a claim against the estate. [680 F.2d 1248 (9th Cir. 1982).] As of his death, the decedent in *Propstra* owned property encumbered with liens exceeding $400,000. More than two years later, his estate paid the lien holder approximately $135,000 in full satisfaction of its claims. The Commissioner argued, as he does here, that the estate was permitted to deduct only the amount actually paid. The court disagreed: "We rule that, as a matter of law, when claims are for sums certain and are legally enforceable as of the date of death, post-death events are not relevant in computing the permissible deduction."[21]

The *Propstra* court cited three reasons for its conclusion. First, it found significant a change in the wording of the relevant Code section when Congress enacted the Internal Revenue Code of 1954. Prior to 1954, the predecessor to §2053(a) had authorized deduction for claims "as are *allowed* by the

---

18. In the following cases interpreting §2053(a)(3) or its predecessors, the courts refused to consider post-death events: *Estate of Van Horne,* 720 F.2d 1114 (9th Cir. 1983); Propstra v. United States, 680 F.2d 1248 (9th Cir. 1982); Greene v. United States, 447 F. Supp. 885 (N.D.Ill. 1978); Estate of Lester v. Commissioner, 57 T.C. 503, 1972 WL 2478 (1972); Russell v. United States, 260 F. Supp. 493 (1966); Winer v. United States, 153 F. Supp. 941 (1957).

19. In the following cases the courts did consider post-death events: Estate of Sachs v. Commissioner, 856 F.2d 1158 (1988); Jacobs v. Commissioner, 34 F.2d 233 (1929); Estate of Kyle v. Commissioner, 94 T.C. 829, 1990 WL 77198 (1990); Estate of Hagmann v. Commissioner, 60 T.C. 465, 1973 WL 2507 (1973), *aff'd per curium,* 492 F.2d 796 (5th Cir. 1974); Estate of Cafaro v. Commissioner, T.C. Memo. 1989-348, 1989 WL 79310; Estate of Quintard v. Commissioner, 62 T.C. 317, 1974 WL 2633 (1974).

21. *Propstra,* 680 F.2d at 1254. We acknowledge that the *Propstra* court drew a distinction between "disputed or contingent" claims on one hand, and "certain and enforceable" claims on the other. *Id.* at 1253. It stated, in *dicta,* that post-death events are relevant in computing the allowable deduction in the case of "disputed or contingent" claims, but the court gave no indication of the meaning that it assigned to these imprecise terms.

laws of the jurisdiction . . . under which the estate is being administered." [*Id.*] Courts were divided regarding whether the use of "allowed" meant that the estate actually had to pay the claim for it to be deductible. [*Id.* at 1254-55.] In the 1954 re-enactment of the Code, "allowed" was replaced with "allowable." The *Propstra* court found this change indicative of Congress's preference for the line of cases that measured a claim's viability and value as of the date of death without imposing the additional element of actual post-mortem payment by the estate. [*Id.* at 1254-55.]

Second, the *Propstra* court reasoned that its holding was supported by Treasury Regulation §20.2053-4, which allows an estate to deduct "personal obligations of the decedent existing at *the time of [the decedent's] death.*" [Emphasis added.] Finally, the court reasoned that its holding comported with the teaching of *Ithaca Trust.*

The Ninth Circuit again applied the date-of-death valuation principal to a claim against an estate in Estate of Van Horne v. Commissioner. [720 F.2d 1114, 1117 (9th Cir. 1983).] The decedent in *Van Horne* was obligated, pursuant to a valid judgment, to make support payments to her ex-husband for the duration of his life, notwithstanding either his remarriage or her death. The judgment provided that if the decedent predeceased her ex-husband, the support obligation would be payable by her estate. She predeceased him, and shortly after her death — but far short of his actuarial life expectancy — her ex-husband died. Consequently, the estate's ultimate liability on the claim was only a small fraction of the actuarial prediction as of her death. Consistent with *Ithaca Trust* and *Propstra,* the *Van Horne* court held that "legally enforceable claims valued by reference to an actuarial table meet the test of certainty for estate tax purposes. Because decedent's spousal support obligation meets that test, it is subject to the *Propstra* rule." [720 F.2d 1114, 1117 (9th Cir. 1983).] . . .

We are persuaded that the Ninth Circuit's decisions in *Propstra* and *Estate of Van Horne* correctly apply the *Ithaca Trust* date-of-death valuation principle to enforceable claims against the estate. As we interpret *Ithaca Trust,* when the Supreme Court announced the date-of-death valuation principle, it was making a judgment about the nature of the federal estate tax — specifically, that it is a tax imposed on the act of transferring property by will or intestacy and, because the act on which the tax is levied occurs at a discrete time, i.e., the instant of death, the net value of the property transferred should be ascertained, as nearly as possible, as of that time. This analysis supports broad application of the date-of-death valuation rule. . . .

That there are, as the *Ithaca Trust* Court recognized, statutory exceptions to this rule[36] does not command or even permit further judge-made exceptions.

---

36. Current exceptions to date-of-death valuation include §§2053(a)(1) (funeral expenses), 2053(a)(2) (estate administration expenses), and 2054 (casualty losses).

To the contrary, it suggests that when Congress wants to derogate from the date-of-death valuation principle it knows how to do so. We note in passing that since *Ithaca Trust,* Congress has thrice reenacted the entire Internal Revenue Code and has made countless other modifications to the statute, but has never seen fit to overrule *Ithaca Trust* legislatively. We decline the Commissioner's invitation to rewrite the law ourselves.

Other courts (including the Tax Court in this case) that have delved into this confused jurisprudence have perceived a distinction between (1) cases concerning the *valuation* of claims that are certain and enforceable as of death, and (2) cases concerning disputed or contingent claims, the *enforceability* of which is unknown as of death. Claims falling into the first category are — according to the courts that have accepted this distinction — deductible at their date-of-death value. Claims falling into the second category, by contrast, are deductible in the amount of their ultimate resolution. In the instant case, the Tax Court classified Exxon's claim as one of uncertain validity and enforceability on the date of death and, accordingly, relied on post-death facts, specifically, the settlement.

Although this dichotomy, which distinguishes between enforceability on the one hand and valuation on the other, has superficial appeal, closer examination reveals that it is not a sound basis for distinguishing claims in this context. There is only a semantic difference between a claim that may prove to be invalid and a valid claim that may prove to have a value of zero. For example, if given the choice between being the obligor of (1) a claim known to be worth $1 million with a 50 percent chance of being adjudged unenforceable, or (2) a claim known to be enforceable with a value equally likely to be $1 million or zero, a rational person would discern no difference in choosing between the claims, as both have an expected value $500,000. Nevertheless, it could be argued that in some cases, the date-of-death claim against the estate is so specious that its value should be ignored because for practical purposes it is worthless. This is not such a case.

Here, the district court adjudicating the [royalty owner's] litigation had held, prior to Decedent's death, that Exxon had a cause of action against the royalty owners. Thus, the Estate was not claiming a deduction for a potential claim without an existing claimant — or, conversely, an identifiable claimant without a cognizable claim. The actual value of Exxon's claim prior to either settlement or entry of a judgment is inherently imprecise, yet "even a disputed claim may have a value, to which lawyers who settle cases every day may well testify, fully as measurable as the possible future amounts that may eventually accrue on an uncontested claim.". . .

In light of the foregoing analysis, we hold that the Tax Court erred reversibly when it determined that the amount that the Estate ultimately paid Exxon ($681,840) in a settlement achieved fifteen months after Decedent's death set the value of the Estate's §2053(a)(3) deduction. On remand, the Tax Court is instructed neither to admit nor consider evidence of post-death occurrences when determining the date-of-death value of Exxon's claim. . . .

[The court then held that the income tax relief provided by §1341 was one factor to be taken into account in valuing the date-of-death value of the Exxon claim and that it was not a separate asset of the estate.]

On remand, the IRS presented expert testimony that the claim against Smith's estate was in fact worth less on the date of her death than the amount ultimately received in settlement because of the uncertainty of Exxon's claim against the royalty owners. Estate of Smith v. Commissioner, 82 T.C.M. (CCH) 909 (2001). The estate presented no new evidence, arguing instead that because the parties had stipulated to the fact that "[w]ith interest, Exxon in the [litigation by the royalty owners] claimed $2,482,719.00 from the decedent," this amount was the established value of the claim. *Id.* at 914. The estate also ignored the instructions in the Fifth Circuit's opinion that "it is incumbent on each party to supply the Tax Court with relevant evidence of pre-death facts and occurrences supporting the value of the Exxon claim advocated by that party." Estate of Smith v. Commissioner, 198 F.3d 515, 526 (5th Cir. 1999). The Tax Court found that the value of the claim was $450,948.30 based on the evidence of the IRS expert and held that "[a]lthough this amount is less than the amount previously allowed in the notice of deficiency, respondent does not seek to reduce the estate's section 2053(a)(3) deduction below the amount allowed in the notice of deficiency. We find that the net fair market value of Exxon's claim at the time of decedent's death was not more than $681,840." Estate of Smith v. Commissioner, 82 T.C.M. (CCH) at 918. The Fifth Circuit affirmed in an unpublished opinion. Estate of Smith v. Commissioner, 54 Fed. Appx. 413 (5th Cir. 2002).

The Tenth and Eleventh Circuits have agreed with the Fifth Circuit. In Estate of McMorris v. Commissioner, 243 F.3d 1254 (10th Cir. 2001), the estate deducted federal and state income taxes resulting from the redemption of stock decedent had received from her husband. When the value of the stock was finally established after an estate tax audit and settlement in her husband's estate, decedent's basis in the stock was adjusted, creating a loss on the redemption and, thus, decreasing her income tax liability. In Estate of O'Neal v. Commissioner, 258 F.3d 1265 (11th Cir. 2001), the decedent and her husband made gifts of closely held stock to their children and grandchildren who agreed to contribute toward any transferee gift tax liability. Decedent agreed to reimburse her children and grandchildren for any increase in this transferee liability if the stock was revalued. The government audited the gift tax returns, increasing the value of the stock significantly. Decedent died, and her estate claimed a deduction for reimbursing the donees based on the government's stock valuation. Subsequently, the donees settled with the government for far less than the government asserted. The estate filed an amended return, deducting only the amount actually paid to the donees but claimed a refund. In both cases, the courts held that the claims must be valued on the date of death and all events occurring after that date must be disregarded.

D. TAXES
IRC §§2011, 2053, 2058

Taxes are allowed as a deduction under §2053 only as claims against the estate. Property taxes that have actually accrued before death and that are enforceable obligations at the time of death may be deducted. Reg. §20.2053-6(b). Taxes due on gifts made before death are also deductible if not in fact paid before death. Reg. §20.2053-6(d). Income taxes for amounts received before death are also deductible. Reg. §20.2053-6(f).

Death taxes paid to a state or other jurisdiction are not deductible under §2053. Prior to 2001, the estate received a credit under §2011 for state death taxes. Section 2011 is discussed at page 508. The 2001 Tax Act phases out §2011 during 2002-2004 and repeals it for decedents dying after December 31, 2004. Beginning in 2005, there will be a deduction under §2058 for state death taxes. The 2001 Act, however, includes a sunset provision that repeals all its amendments effective January 1, 2011. If Congress takes no further action, §2011 will be resurrected at that time and §2058 will disappear.

E. LOSSES
IRC §2054

Section 2054 allows a deduction for losses, but only those arising from "fires, storms, shipwrecks, or other casualties, or from theft" and only to the extent that the "losses are not compensated for by insurance or otherwise." The loss must occur during the settlement of the estate. If it occurs before decedent's death, the loss must be taken as a deduction, if at all, on the decedent's final income tax return. If the loss occurs after distribution of the asset, the loss must be claimed by the beneficiary receiving the asset.

The types of losses allowed by §2054 are the same as those allowed by §165(c)(3). Because the estate is a taxable entity filing its own tax return, the executor must decide whether to claim the loss on the estate tax return or the estate's income tax return. Because casualty losses are limited by §165(h), it is usually more advantageous to claim the loss on the estate tax return. The estate cannot claim a deduction on both returns. §642(g).

PROBLEMS

1. Dennis died on December 31, 2003, owning a house worth $200,000, a car worth $20,000, stocks worth $2,500,000, bank accounts containing $50,000, and household furnishings and personal effects valued at

$30,000. Dennis also owned a life insurance policy that paid $500,000 to Cathy. Dennis also owned a summer home with his sister, Sally, as joint tenants with the right of survivorship. The house had a fair market value of $200,000, and Dennis had paid the entire purchase price. Dennis had established a revocable trust in 1995 with the Friendly National Bank as Trustee to pay the income to Dennis during his life and the principal to Cathy at his death. The value of the trust principal at the date of Dennis's death was $3,000,000.

Dennis had been married twice. Wanda, his first wife, is deceased. There were two children from that marriage, Alice and Bert; both are adults. Dennis divorced his second wife, Flora; Cathy is the child of that marriage.

Dennis's will specifically provided that his executor, his brother Ezra, was to pay the expenses of his last illness, his just debts, and funeral expenses. Dennis's will left his property to Cathy. Dennis did not mention Alice, Bert, or Flora at all in his will.

Ezra incurred the following expenses for Dennis's burial: $15,000 to the Blake Brothers, Inc. Funeral Chapel that included the cost of the casket, the hearse, a limousine for the children, and the funeral director; $25,000 for a marble tombstone and statue as directed by Dennis in his will. Dennis's will directed that $10,000 be paid to the Park Lawn Cemetery Association for the perpetual care of his plot.

Ezra paid the medical bills for Dennis's last illness that were not covered by insurance totaling $85,000. At the time of his death, Dennis still owed $13,000 on his car. He also had outstanding a personal note for $20,000, and miscellaneous bills totaling $25,000. The $20,000 personal note was not presented to the executor until six months after the time to file claims with the estate. In addition, $5,000 of the miscellaneous bills was unenforceable due to the statute of limitations.

There was a mortgage on the home of $100,000. Cathy did not want the home and directed Ezra to sell it. Pending sale the house was rented at $1,500 per month. During the period of administration, Ezra expended $3,000 on the house in the rental process. Ezra incurred expenses of $15,000 in selling the house.

Ezra paid court costs of $2,000, accountant's fees of $18,000, and appraisers' fees of $5,000. Executor's fees are estimated to be $20,000. Attorneys' fees to probate the estate are estimated to be $25,000. Alice and Bert filed a will contest claiming undue influence and lack of testamentary capacity. The will contest settled, and the estate agreed to pay Alice and Bert each $500,000. Ezra also paid $35,000 attorneys' fees to defend the will contest begun by Alice and Bert. Alice and Bert also paid $25,000 attorneys' fees for the will contest.

Flora submitted a claim of $250,000 against the estate, claiming that Dennis had agreed to leave her that amount in his will in exchange for her agreement to accept limited alimony during his life.

Dennis made gifts to Cathy of $11,000 each year in the five years preceding his death. Immediately after making each gift, Dennis borrowed $11,000 from Cathy. Each loan was evidenced by a promissory note, payable on demand, and bearing interest at the applicable federal rate. Cathy presented these notes to Ezra for payment as claims against the estate. Ezra also incurred $7,500 attorneys' fees and trustees' fees on the revocable trust. He spent $1,500 to clear title to the summer home.

Dennis had made taxable gifts in 2002, and Ezra paid the gift tax due of $150,000 after Dennis's death. He also paid the federal and state income tax of $85,000 due on Dennis's 2002 income. Ezra, as executor, also paid the state estate taxes due totaling $450,000.

Property taxes on Dennis's residence are $5,000 per year, due in a single installment on October 1 of each year. Property taxes on the house owned in joint tenancy are $4,000 per year, due in a single installment on November 1 of each year.

The state probate court approved the executor's final accounts, including all the above mentioned expenses. What is Dennis's gross estate? What is his taxable estate? Assume that nonprobate property is not subject to the claims of the estate.

2. Eighteen months before her death, Debra was sued by Janice for patent infringement. Janice claimed damages of $1,500,000. Discovery was completed two months before Debra's death, and both Debra and Janice had moved for summary judgement. Six months after Debra's death, the trial court denied both motions for summary judgment. One year after Debra's death, Debra's estate and Janice settled the case for $150,000.

Debra died as a result of a car accident, and her estate sued the other driver for wrongful death, claiming damages of $750,000. Two years later the case came to trial, and the estate recovered $500,000.

Debra purchased Greenacre five years before her death for $650,000. When her estate put Greenacre up for sale, it discovered that there were old fuel tanks buried on the property that had leaked. After spending $100,000 to clean up the property, the estate sold Greenacre for $425,000.

Six months before her death, Debra had sued Luke for breach of contract. The claim arose out of Debra's business that she operated as a sole proprietor. Debra claimed damages of $250,000, and Luke denied all liability. Six months after her death, Debra's estate recovered $150,000 from Luke.

Debra borrowed $150,000 from her sister, Sally, and was making annual payments of principal and interest. At the time of her death, Debra owed Sally $100,000. Sally did not present a claim against Debra's estate until the estate filed its final accounting in probate court, three years after Debra's death.

What are the estate tax consequences to Debra's estate of these events?

3. David's estate included a summer home valued at $350,000. Two months after David's death, the summer home burned. What are the tax consequences if the insurance company paid David's estate $300,000?

4. In problem 6 on page 217, is Dominic's estate entitled to any deduction for the seizure of the drugs or the forfeiture of the house and car? Should it be?

5. Fiona had a close relationship with her brother, Doug. When Doug started up a business, Fiona agreed to help him. Doug promised that he would pay Fiona "when the business became established." For three years, Fiona worked approximately 20 hours a week. At one point, Fiona asked Doug about payment, and he again promised to pay her. Doug died without ever paying Fiona. His will left all his property to her and appointed her as executor. Including the business, Doug owned approximately $5,000,000 at the time of his death. The reasonable value of Fiona's services to Doug's business was $75,000. The executor's fee would be $50,000. Fiona consults you to determine whether she should file a claim against the estate for the value of her services and whether she should waive the executor's fee. What advice would you give her?

CHAPTER 15

Transfers to Charity

A. GENERAL PRINCIPLES
IRC §§170, 2055, 2522

Section 2055 allows the decedent's estate to deduct the value of certain transfers to charity. This deduction arises from a policy decision rather than from an attempt to accurately reflect the net value of the decedent's gratuitous transfers. Transfers to charity promote the general welfare and relieve government of the need to provide certain services.

The rules governing both charitable donations and tax exempt organizations are detailed and complex. There are many commonalities among the income tax, gift tax, estate tax, and tax-exempt organization provisions, but there are also significant differences. For example, a nonprofit cemetery association is exempt from income tax, §501(c)(13), and a donation to it is deductible for purposes of income taxation, §170(c)(5), but not for purposes of estate taxation, *see, e.g.*, Mellon Bank v. United States, 762 F.2d 283 (3d Cir. 1985), First National Bank of Omaha v. United States, 681 F.2d 534 (8th Cir. 1982), *cert. denied* 459 U.S. 1104 (1983), unless the cemetery is owned and operated by a governmental unit such as a city or state, Revenue Ruling 79-159, 1979-1 C.B. 308. Unlike the income tax, §170(b), there are no monetary or percentage limits on the estate tax or the gift tax charitable deduction except that the deduction cannot exceed the value of the transferred property. §2055(d). The same restrictions on gifts of partial interests apply to the income, gift, and estate tax deductions. §§170(f), 2055(e), 2522(c).

For an estate to obtain a charitable deduction, the decedent must designate a qualifying organization. Only donations to the organizations enumerated in §§2055(a) and 2522(a) will qualify and then only if the donation is for the purposes specified in the statute. Bequests to the United States, any State, or a political subdivision are deductible as long as the property must be used exclusively for public purposes. §2055(a)(1). Property that escheats to the state when the decedent dies intestate does not qualify because the decedent did not transfer the property to the state; it passed by operation of law. Senft v. United States, 319 F.2d 642 (3d Cir. 1963). A bequest to a foreign government is not deductible under subsection (a)(1), but it may be deductible under subsection

435

(a)(2) or (a)(3) if the property must be used only for charitable purposes. Revenue Ruling 74-523, 1974-2 C.B. 304.

Bequests to corporations that are organized and operated exclusively for religious, scientific, literary, educational, or charitable purposes or to trusts or fraternal associations if the gift is to be used exclusively for religious, scientific, literary, educational, or charitable purposes are also deductible. §2055(a)(2), (a)(3). The organization cannot be disqualified from tax exempt status because of lobbying or participating in political campaigns. The concept of "charity" is much the same as in the income tax, although, for example, as noted above, gifts to cemetery associations are not considered charitable. A deduction is also allowed for certain transfers to veterans organizations, §2055(a)(4), and employee stock ownership plans, §2055(a)(5).

Revenue Ruling 77-232
1977-2 C.B. 71

The Internal Revenue Service has reconsidered its position announced in Rev. Rul. 59-152, 1959-1 C.B. 54, that contributions by members and other donors to or for the use of an integrated State Bar are deductible in computing taxable income in the manner and to the extent provided by section 170 of the Internal Revenue Code of 1954 and are deductible for Federal estate tax and gift tax purposes under the provisions of sections 2055(a)(1) and 2522(a)(1), respectively.

Rev. Rul. 59-152 states that the integrated State Bar of a certain state was created by statute as a public corporation. This State Bar works with the Supreme Court of the state in implementing certain statutory rules regarding the practice of law in the state with respect to the admission, suspension, disbarment, and reprimanding of attorneys. In addition, the State Bar promotes the professional interests of members. . . .

In this case the integrated State Bar has certain public purposes principally in the areas of admission, suspension, disbarment, and reprimand of attorneys licensed to practice in the state. However, it also has certain private purposes such as the encouragement of stimulating discussion among attorneys and the protection of the professional interests of members of the State Bar. Thus, the State Bar is a dual purpose organization.

The State Bar is not an arm of the state because it is a separate entity and has private as well as public purposes. It is not a political subdivision because it has no meaningful sovereign powers. . . . Therefore, contributions to the State Bar are not "to" a state or a political subdivision thereof.

Contributions to the State Bar are also not for the use of a state or a political subdivision thereof since there are no restrictions imposed by the donor or by the bar itself that require that the state or a political subdivision thereof will benefit from the contributions. Such contributions can be used for the private purposes of the State Bar and its members.

In addition to the above, when an organization has both public and private purposes, unrestricted contributions to that organization cannot be said to be made for exclusively public purposes. In such situations there is nothing to insure that contributions will be used in furtherance of whatever public functions the organization might perform. . . .

Accordingly, the contributions made to the State Bar by members and other donors are not deductible as charitable contributions as defined in section 170(c)(1) of the Code. Similarly, such contributions are not deductible for Federal estate tax and gift tax purposes under the provisions of sections 2055(a)(1) and 2522(a)(1).

Compare Revenue Ruling 77-232 with Dulles v. Johnson, where the court held that bequests to city, county, and state bar associations were deductible under the predecessor of §2055(a)(2), finding that the activities of these associations were charitable, scientific, and educational. 273 F.2d 362 (2d Cir. 1959), *cert. denied* 364 U.S. 834 (1960). The court held that the associations' activities in regulating the unauthorized practice of law, disciplining attorneys, improving court procedures, endorsing judicial candidates, and influencing legislation were designed to protect the public and improve the law. Other activities, such as maintaining libraries, sponsoring lectures, providing free legal service, and operating a legal referral system, were also considered charitable, scientific, and educational.

Cemetery associations do not qualify under either §2055(a)(2) or (a)(3), because they are not operated exclusively for charitable purposes. Even if the cemetery permits burial of indigents or sells lots at a reduced rate, it will not be considered charitable because the primary purpose of the association is to sell lots at full value to the public. Revenue Ruling 67-170, 1967-1 C.B. 272. In Child v. United States, the court rejected the argument that relief of the public fisc was sufficient, by itself, to consider an activity charitable. 540 F.2d 579 (2d Cir. 1976), *cert. denied* 429 U.S. 1092 (1977). The court distinguished Dulles v. Johnson, saying:

> In *Dulles*, however, it is clear that substantial "charitable" and "educational" activities of a more traditional sort were continuously being performed by the beneficiary associations: "maintaining libraries for legal research, sponsoring lectures and forums on the law, providing free legal service through participation in legal aid, and providing low cost legal service through participation in a legal referral system." 273 F.2d at 367-68. In our view, *Dulles* should be read for the proposition that public dedication of services by an organization may be colored by a history of that organization's performance of more traditional charitable activities to such an extent that the entire enterprise, or the "total operations" of the association, *id.* at 368, assume the aspect of charitable service to the community. The activities which are not charitable or educational, *e.g.*, social or economic, must be merely "auxiliary" or "incidental in nature." *Id.* . . .

Relief of general tax burdens alone, in a society with some progressivity in its tax structure, cannot be deemed a single, inalienable mark of charity.

Our view is that relief for the public fisc is more symptomatic than evidentiary regarding whether an activity is charitable: charity often results in an absorption of a burden otherwise falling upon the state, particularly where the social welfare is a principal purpose of the state. But this does not mean that activities lessening public expense in any of a myriad of areas of public interest are perforce charitable.

Id. at 583.

The court was also influenced by the fact that Congress had made specific provision for cemetery associations in §170 and in §501 but not in §2055 or §2522. *Accord,* Mellon Bank v. United States, *supra*; First National Bank of Omaha v. United States, *supra*.

Except for donations of qualified conservation easements, which are discussed in section C, the decedent herself must specifically provide for the charitable contribution in her will. Neither the executor nor the beneficiaries can create a charitable deduction in the absence of a clear indication from the decedent.

Estate of Pickard v. Commissioner
60 T.C. 618 (1973)

TANENWALD, Judge:

. . . On June 24, 1954, decedent, Claire Fern Pickard, established a revocable trust (hereinafter referred to as the Pickard Trust) with the Ohio National Bank of Columbus and Herbert S. Peterson (decedent's stepfather) as trustees. The trust instrument provided for payment of income and principal to decedent upon request during her life. After decedent's death, an annuity of $3,000 was to be paid to decedent's mother, Etta Mae Peterson, during her life and, upon the mother's death (or upon decedent's death, if her mother predeceased her), "the Trustees shall transfer, assign and convey the entire Trust Estate then remaining in its hands absolutely and in fee simple to Herbert S. Peterson to be his absolute property."

The decedent died testate on December 3, 1967. . . . The decedent was survived by her mother, Etta Mae Peterson. . . . Decedent's stepfather, Herbert S. Peterson (hereinafter referred to as Peterson), died testate on October 14, 1967, 7 weeks prior to the date of decedent's death. His will, duly admitted to probate, bequeathed and devised the residue of his estate to a revocable trust (sometimes hereinafter referred to as the Peterson Trust). . . . The Peterson Trust named Peterson's wife (decedent's mother) as life beneficiary after Peterson's death and provided that, upon the death of Peterson, his said wife, and decedent, $10,000 of the trust assets should be distributed to two named individuals if living, and the balance as follows:

One-half of the remaining assets to the First English Lutheran Church of Columbus, Ohio, or its successors.

One-half of the remaining assets to the Columbus Foundation, Columbus, Ohio.

On June 26, 1968, the Ohio National Bank of Columbus, as executor of the Estate of Claire Fern Pickard, deceased, commenced an action in the Probate Court of Franklin County, Ohio, naming as defendants the First English Lutheran Church of Columbus, Ohio, the Pickard Trust, the Estate of Herbert S. Peterson, the Peterson Trust, the Columbus Foundation, and Etta Mae Peterson. The action had as its purpose the obtaining of a court determination as to how the probate assets of decedent's estate and the assets of the Pickard Trust should be distributed. . . . [The Probate Court decreed that Herbert S. Peterson's interest in the Pickard Trust became absolute at the death of Claire Fern Pickard and that his estate or the Peterson Trust was the residuary beneficiary of the Pickard Trust. As a result, the Trustee of the Pickard Trust was ordered to pay $3,000 annually to Etta Mae Peterson during her life and at her death to pay the residue either to the Herbert S. Peterson Estate or, if the estate had been closed, to the Herbert S. Peterson Trust.]

Section 2055 provides, among other things, that "the value of the taxable estate shall be determined by deducting from the value of the gross estate the amount of all bequests, legacies, devises, or transfers . . . to or for the use of any corporation organized and operated exclusively for religious, charitable, scientific, literary, or educational purposes."

The parties herein are in agreement as to the exempt character of the two organizations involved and as to the amount of the deduction, if found to be allowable. Additionally, no question has been raised whether the provisions of any of the instruments involved or the possibility of claims against either the Pickard or Peterson estates or trusts might operate in such a way as to make the interests of those organizations unascertainable or subject to the so-remote-as-to-be-negligible possibility that the transfers would not become effective. *See* sec. 20.2055-2, Estate Tax Regs.

The sole question to be decided herein is whether the provisions of decedent's will and the Pickard Trust are operative within the framework of the above-quoted statutory language. Petitioner asserts that there are three elements contained in section 2055, all of which are satisfied in this case, namely, (1) decedent made a transfer, (2) of property includable in her gross estate, and (3), by virtue of her stepfather's death and the provisions of his will and the Peterson Trust, to or for the use of a qualified entity. Such assertion is premised upon the assumption that each of three elements is independent of each other and that section 2055 can therefore be fragmented in order to determine whether a deduction is allowable. Under petitioner's reasoning, the route of devolution is immaterial; it is enough if there is a transfer of includable property which must, because of the surrounding circumstances, inevitably find its way into the coffers of an exempt organization.

In our opinion, such separation of the three elements is improper. We believe that the first and third elements are mutually interdependent and that the "transfer . . . to or for the use of" such organization must be manifest from the provisions of the decedent's testamentary instrument. The impact of the route of devolution has been considered in a variety of contexts. Thus, in Senft v. United States, 319 F.2d 642 (C.A. 3, 1963), property of the decedent, who died intestate, escheated to the Commonwealth of Pennsylvania. In denying the decedent a deduction under section 2055, the Court of Appeals emphasized decedent's failure to make the transfer, as opposed to the property passing to the qualified recipient by another force, *i.e.*, by operation of law.

In Cox v. Commissioner, 297 F.2d 36 (C.A. 2, 1961), affirming a Memorandum Opinion of this Court, a deduction under the predecessor of section 2055 was denied where the testatrix, with full knowledge of all relevant facts and her express approval of the ultimate recipient of the bequest, bequeathed part of her estate to her son, a priest, who had, prior to her death but subsequent to the making of the testatrix's will, taken solemn vows of poverty and renounced all his interests in property (including donations and legacies) in favor of the Society of Jesus, a qualified entity under the statute. . . .

In each of the foregoing cases, the fact that the designated portion of the decedent's estate inevitably inured to the benefit of the charity did not save the day. To be sure, they can be distinguished on their facts, but the common element which forms the foundation for decision is that the transfer to or for the use of the charity was not effectuated by a testamentary transfer on decedent's part but rather by the operation of an external force. The same is true herein, where it was the testamentary disposition of decedent's stepfather via the Peterson Trust which accomplished the transfer.

Concededly, the charities herein would not have received decedent's property if the decedent had not made the testamentary disposition to her stepfather. The lesson from the decided cases, however, is that a simple "but for" test is not, as petitioner would have us hold, sufficient. There must be something more, namely, the testamentary facts as gleaned from the decedent's own disposition must manifest the transfer to the charity. . . . In so stating, we do not imply that the decedent must specify the charitable recipient in so many words. But, at the very least, the instrument of testamentary disposition must sufficiently articulate, either directly or through appropriate incorporation by reference of another instrument, the manifestation of decedent's charitable bounty. . . . Such a situation simply does not obtain herein and, accordingly, the claimed deduction is not allowable.

Buder v. United States
7 F.3d 1382 (8th Cir. 1993)

BOWMAN, Circuit Judge.

. . . Buder, a St. Louis business and tax attorney, died in 1984, leaving a will he personally drafted and a substantial estate. . . . The pivotal issue in this case concerns Article V of the will, which states that "twenty-five percent (25 %) of my remaining net estate . . . shall be divided among and paid to the following charitable, benevolent or educational organizations or entities, or their respective successors[,] in the following proportions." Article V then lists thirteen charitable organizations that were to receive bequests. Pursuant to 26 U.S.C. §2055(a)(3) (1988), the estate deducted these bequests in determining its federal estate tax liability. The only deduction challenged by the Government is that of the bequest of Paragraph D (the "Paragraph D Trust"), which provides that

> D. Ten per cent (10%) [of the assets disposed of by this Article shall be given to five listed persons], IN TRUST, however, to be used solely and exclusively in fostering and promoting the cause of patriotism, loyalty and fundamental constitutional government in the United States of America, and in combating subversive activities, socialism and communism, including, if deemed advisable, assistance in the teaching of the principles of conservatism in public affairs among college and high school students. The said Trustees and their successors in office are authorized and empowered to use the principal and income of such fund as they may agree to be most advisable and effective for the accomplishment of the objectives mentioned in this paragraph; and may, in their discretion, make contributions to other organizations or specific programs constituted and operated to achieve the purposes herein mentioned. . . .

The District Court concluded that the Paragraph D Trust qualified as a charitable deduction. . . . The Government appeals, and we affirm.

We turn first to the issue of whether the estate properly deducted from its return Buder's bequest to the Paragraph D Trust. The Government, renewing the argument it made to the District Court, contends that the bequest does not qualify for a charitable deduction because the trustees have the discretion to dispense funds to organizations that engage in such noncharitable activities as lobbying and campaigning. Hence, the Government concludes, the Paragraph D Trust does not comply with the requirements established by the Internal Revenue Code, and the estate's deduction of the bequest was erroneous.

An estate may deduct bequests in trust that are to be used "exclusively for religious, charitable, scientific, literary, or educational purposes, or for the prevention of cruelty to children or animals"; the deduction is improper, however, if the trust "would . . . be disqualified for tax exemption under section 501(c)(3) by reason of attempting to influence legislation" or if the trustees "participate in, or intervene in (including the publishing or distributing of statements), any political campaign on behalf of (or in opposition to) any candidate for public office." 26 U.S.C. §2055(a)(3) (1988).

Wills are construed in accordance with state law. Teller v. Kaufman, 426 F.2d 128, 131 (8th Cir. 1970). Under Missouri law, the settlor's intent controls the interpretation of the bequest, and we must ascertain this intent "from the whole will and not from single words, passages or sentences." Mercantile Trust Co. v. Mercantile Trust Co., 677 S.W.2d 343, 346 (Mo.Ct. App. 1984).

Because Missouri courts use the same rules for construing both trusts and wills . . . we construe Buder's Paragraph D Trust by examining the will in its entirety. Buder organized his will into several sections. After providing for his debts and the natural objects of his bounty, Buder turned in Article V to his charitable interests. At the beginning of the Article, he provided that his assets were to be distributed "to the following charitable, benevolent or educational organizations or entities." Buder then listed thirteen different charitable organizations, twelve of which were already established, the other being the Paragraph D Trust he created in the Article. The language Buder used at the beginning of the Article is consistent with that of the donations he made throughout the Article, and Buder clearly intended that the instructions he included at the beginning of Article V were to govern all bequests made by that Article. We find persuasive here the reasoning of St. Louis Union Trust Co. v. Burnet, 59 F.2d 922, 928-29 (8th Cir. 1932):

> It was undoubtedly the intention of the testator that this bequest should be devoted to charitable uses. It occurs in that section of his will dealing exclusively with gifts of the same general nature. It was devised to trustees with authority to select the beneficiaries from the general class described.

We find support for our reading of the Paragraph D Trust's language from the facts that the trustees have read the language in the same manner, made their donations to charitable organizations, and executed an ancillary Indenture of Trust that binds them to this reading of the Trust's terms. Indeed, the IRS has determined that the G.A. Buder, Jr. Charitable Trust is a tax-exempt organization.

The Government's argument that the trustees have discretion to make noncharitable donations would have force if the Trust were created independently of the charitable restrictions of Article V. However, because we construe the Paragraph D Trust as one of a series of bequests in a self-contained article of the will, and thus construe its provisions in light of Buder's instructions at the beginning of Article V, the Government's argument loses its force. Indeed, Buder's listing of his purposes serves to limit the trustees' discretion, rather than give them too much, because to comply with Buder's directions, the trustees must make donations that are to "charitable, benevolent or educational organizations or entities" *and that* "foster[ ] and promot[e] the cause of patriotism, loyalty and fundamental constitutional government in the United States of America, and . . . combat [ ] subversive activities, socialism and communism."

If we apply the Government's argument, the estate would have been able to deduct Buder's charitable bequest only if Buder had included directions, in addition to those at the beginning of Article V, that his trustees not attempt to influence legislation or participate or intervene in any political campaigns. The Government's cramped interpretation of Buder's charitable language is unavailing. Although it is certainly true that the words "charitable, benevolent or educational" do not by definition mean "all charitable, benevolent or educational activities except those proscribed by the Code provisions on charitable bequests," which is the sort of restrictive language the Government's argument would require, this Court has never held philanthropic testators to the exacting standard that the Government proposes. *See, e.g., Burnet,* 59 F.2d at 926 (holding that, although "benevolent" may have a broader meaning than does "charitable," a bequest was charitable within the meaning of the Code even though the will provided only that the trustees were to use the funds for "benevolent" purposes). We decline to set a standard that is so rigorous that the average testator who is attempting to make a charitable donation will fail to meet it.

The Government cites several cases holding that particular bequests were not charitable. None of these cases is relevant to this case, however, because Buder's intentions, as evidenced by the language of Article V, plainly were charitable and the terms of his will impose on his trustees the obligation to make charitable donations. Accordingly, we affirm the judgment of the District Court that the estate was entitled to a charitable deduction for the amount of the bequest made to the Paragraph D Trust.

To be deductible, state law must (1) uphold the validity of the charitable donation and (2) restrict the distribution of property to organizations that are charitable within the meaning of §2055. In Revenue Ruling 69-285, the decedent, a Massachusetts resident, left the residue of his estate to his executor "to be distributed to whatever charities she may deem worthy." The IRS determined that under Massachusetts law the definition of "charitable" was at least as restrictive as the definition under §2055 and that the executor had a fiduciary obligation to distribute the residue only for purposes that were exclusively charitable. As a result, it allowed a charitable deduction. 1969-1 C.B. 222. In Revenue Ruling 71-441, however, the IRS denied a charitable deduction for a gift in trust to "such charitable organization to be selected by the trustee in his sole discretion" because Alabama law would not uphold the validity of this disposition as a charitable trust. The cy pres doctrine would not save the bequest because the decedent had not indicated a specific charitable purpose, only a general charitable intent. 1971-2 C.B. 335.

Postmortem events can affect the deductibility of a charitable bequest. If a beneficiary makes a qualified disclaimer under §2518, that beneficiary is treated as predeceasing the decedent. This may qualify a bequest that would otherwise fail to meet the requirements of §2055.

Example 15-1

David bequeathed $50,000 to his sister, Sarah, if she survived him, otherwise to University Law School. Sarah survived David, but she disclaimed her interest in the $50,000 in a manner that met the requirements of §2518. As a result, the executor distributed the $50,000 to University Law School. David will be treated as the transferor, and his estate will be entitled to a charitable deduction.

The complete termination of a power to consume, invade, or appropriate property made before the date of filing the estate tax return is deemed to be a qualified disclaimer. §2055(a); Reg. §20.2055-2(c)(1). Death of the life tenant within this prescribed period, however, does not qualify as a disclaimer of that interest in order to increase the amount of a charitable contribution. *See* Merchants National Bank v. United States, 583 F.2d 19 (1st Cir. 1978); Revenue Ruling 76-546, 1976-2 C.B. 290. Death will only be considered as the renunciation of a power to consume principal that would otherwise disqualify a trust under §2055(e)(2), not as a disclaimer that meets the requirements of §2518.

The estate will be entitled to a charitable deduction for payments to a charitable organization in settlement of will contest, but only if it is a bona fide contest and not a collusive suit to reform a bequest that does not otherwise qualify under §2055(e)(2). The IRS will scrutinize settlements to ensure they are the result of actual controversies. Revenue Ruling 89-31, 1989-1 C.B. 277. Only the amount actually paid to the charity will qualify for the deduction.

Section 2055(e)(3) provides detailed rules for reforming charitable bequests to comply with the split interest provisions of subsection (e)(2). Modifications or reformations based on nontax considerations will be given effect even though they do not satisfy the requirements of subsection (e)(3), but not otherwise. *See, e.g.,* Estate of La Meres v. Commissioner, 98 T.C. 294 (1992); Estate of Burdick v. Commissioner, 96 T.C. 168 (1991), *aff'd* 979 F.2d 1369 (9th Cir. 1992).

A deduction will be allowed for a conditional bequest, but only if the possibility that the charitable transfer will not become effective is so remote as to be negligible. Reg. §20.2055-2(b)(1). If the probability that the condition will defeat the charitable interest does not exceed five percent, then it will be considered so remote as to be negligible. Revenue Ruling 70-452, 1970-2 C.B. 199.

Example 15-2

Debra's will provides "if my spouse, Sam, does not survive me by 90 days, I leave $250,000 to his brother, Carl, but if Sam does survive me, this sum will become part of my residuary estate." The residue of Debra's estate was left to a trust that qualified under §2055(e)(2), giving Sam an interest for life and the remainder to College. At Debra's death, Sam was 75 years old, and he did in fact survive her by 90 days. If the likelihood that a 75-year-old male would die within 90 days, measured on the day of Debra's death, is less than five percent (based on the mortality tables), Debra's estate will receive a charitable deduction for the transfer to the trust. Revenue Ruling 78-255, 1978-1 C.B. 294.

PROBLEMS

1. Duane bequeathed $100,000 to each of his three children, Mary, Nancy, and Oscar. At the time that Duane drafted his will, Nancy belonged to an order of Catholic nuns and had taken a vow of poverty. Pursuant to

that vow, any property that Nancy acquired became the property of the Catholic Church. Duane's executor distributed the property as directed in his will, and Nancy paid over her $100,000 to the Catholic Church. What are the estate tax consequences to Duane's estate?

2. Diane's will leaves the residue of her property in trust to provide scholarships for individuals attending college or professional school. What are the estate tax consequences in the following situations?

   a. The Trustees are to provide scholarships first to the lineal descendants of Diane's grandparents and then to other needy persons.

   b. The Trustees are to provide scholarships to individuals who have the same last name as Diane.

   c. The Trustees are to provide scholarships to individuals who are living in a designated county in a particular state at the time they apply to college if that individual or one of the individual's parents has lived in that county for at least two years prior to the individual's matriculation in college.

3. What are the estate tax consequences in the following situations?

   a. Dierdre sends a $100,000 check to Law School on December 26. She dies on January 2 before Law School deposits the check. Law School deposits the check on January 3 unaware of her death. Dierdre's bank pays the check in the normal course of business.

   b. Dierdre had agreed to give $100,000 to Law School's capital campaign, payable over four years. She died after making the first payment. Her estate pays the remaining $75,000.

   c. Dierdre was interested in endowing a tax professorship at Law School. Although she had extensive discussions with her family and the Dean of Law School, she had made no provisions for a contribution before her death. Her will leaves her property to her son, Silas, who is also her executor. Silas decides to honor Dierdre's wishes and he sends $2,000,000 from the estate to Law School to endow a tax professorship.

4. Douglas leaves the residue of his estate in trust to pay the income to Alex for life and, at Alex's death, to distribute the trust property to whomever Alex designates in his will. In default of appointment by Alex, the property is to be distributed to Church.

   a. What are the estate tax consequences to Douglas?

   b. What are the estate tax consequences to Alex if he does not appoint the trust property, and it goes to Church?

   c. What are the estate tax consequences to Douglas if Douglas's will had left the residue of his estate to "whatever charitable organization my son, Alex, designates," and Alex designates the local homeless shelter, which is a §501(c)(3) organization?

   d. Assume that Douglas's will had left the residue of his estate in trust to pay the income to Alex for his life, and at Alex's death, the trust property was to be distributed to "whatever charitable organization my son, Alex, designates in his will." Alex designates a child care center that is a §501(c)(3) organization. What are the estate tax consequences to Douglas? To Alex?

5. Diane leaves the residue of her estate to City to build and maintain a swimming pool for the use of residents of City. What are the estate tax consequences?

B.   TRANSFERS IN TRUST
IRC §§170, 642(c), 664, 2055(e), 2522(c)

In 1969, Congress adopted stringent rules for gifts of split interests in property, *i.e.*, where the decedent gives interests in the same property to both a charitable and a noncharitable beneficiary. These rules are designed to ensure that the amount of the charitable deduction matches the value of what the charity actually receives.

Senate Report 91-552, 91st Cong., 1st Sess. 1969
reprinted in **1969 U.S.C.C.A.N. 2027, 2116**

General reasons for change. — The rules of present law for determining the amount of a charitable contribution deduction in the case of gifts of remainder interests in trust do not necessarily have any relation to the value of the benefit which the charity receives. This is because the trust assets may be invested in a manner so as to maximize the income interest with the result that there is little relation between the interest assumptions used in calculating present values and the amount received by the charity. For example, the trust corpus can be invested in high-income, high-risk assets. This enhances the value of the income interest but decreases the value of the charity's remainder interest.

The committee agrees with the House that a taxpayer should not be allowed to obtain a charitable contribution deduction for a gift of a remainder interest in trust to a charity which is substantially in excess of the amount the charity may ultimately receive. To provide a closer correlation between the charitable contributions deduction and the ultimate benefit to charity, the House bill generally provided that a deduction would not be allowed for a gift of a remainder interest in trust to charity unless the gift took a specified form: namely, an annuity trust (under which the income beneficiary is to receive a stated dollar amount annually) or a unitrust (under which the income beneficiary is to receive an annual payment based on a fixed percentage of the trust's assets). Another provision of the bill . . . denied a deduction for an outright gift of a remainder interest to charity except to the extent a deduction would have been allowed if the gift had been in trust. This had the effect of denying a charitable contributions deduction in the case of a non-trust gift or a remainder interest to charity.

Although . . . . the committee is in general agreement with the House regarding the need for a closer correlation between the charitable contributions deduction allowed for a gift of a remainder interest to charity and the benefit ultimately received by the charity, the committee believes that the House provision is unduly restrictive. The requirement that a deduction is to be allowed only if the remainder interest given to charity is in the form of an annuity trust or unitrust could have a significant adverse effect on established forms of charitable giving, such as pooled income fund arrangements, and outright gifts of real property, such as a residence, where the donor reserves a life estate in the property. Since these types of charitable giving cannot be framed in the form of an annuity trust or unitrust, the House provision would deny a deduction for the charitable gift. The committee believes that it is possible to continue to allow a charitable deduction in these types of cases with appropriate limitations, however, to prevent the overstating of the charitable contribution deduction. . . .

Explanation of provision. — For the reasons discussed above, the committee amendments provide limitations (for income tax, gift tax, and estate tax purposes) on the allowance of a charitable contribution deduction for a charitable gift of a remainder interest. As under the House bill, a deduction is to be allowed for a charitable gift of a remainder interest in trust, where there is a noncharitable income beneficiary, if the trust is either a charitable remainder annuity trust or a charitable remainder unitrust. The committee agrees with the House that this requirement will provide a better means of assuring that the amount received by the charity will accord with the charitable deduction allowed to the donor on creation of the trust. This is because the requirement will remove the present incentive to favor the income beneficiary over the remainder beneficiary by means of manipulating the trust's investments. The amount received each year by the income beneficiary, generally, will have to be either a stated dollar amount or a fixed percentage of the value of the trust property.

In addition, under the committee amendment a deduction is to be allowed for a gift of a charitable remainder interest in trust which takes the form of a transfer of property to a pooled income fund. . . . In order to prevent manipulation to overstate the appropriate charitable contribution deduction in the case of this type of gift, it is further provided that the amount of the charitable contribution deduction allowed the donor upon the transfer of property to the pooled income fund is to be determined by valuing the income interest on the basis of the highest rate of return earned by the particular pooled income fund in any of the three taxable years preceding the taxable year of the fund in which the transfer occurs. Where a fund has not been in existence for this period of time, the rate of return is to be assumed to be six percent, unless a different rate is prescribed by the Secretary of the Treasury or his delegate.

Another additional situation in which the committee amendments allow a charitable contribution deduction for the gift of a remainder interest to charity is in the case of a nontrust gift of a remainder interest in real property to charity. Thus, for example, a charitable contribution deduction is to be allowed where an individual makes a gift of his residence to charity and retains the right to live in the residence for his life. The committee does not believe that this type of situation generally presents the kind of abuse which both the House and the committee believe it appropriate to curtail. . . .

The committee has modified the House provision to make it clear an annuity trust or a unitrust may have more than one noncharitable income beneficiary, if the interest of each such beneficiary either is for a term of years which does not exceed 20 years or is for the life of the beneficiary. An individual who is not living at the time of creation of the trust, however, may not be an income beneficiary of a charitable remainder trust.

Under the regulations existing in 1969, life estates and remainders were valued assuming an interest rate of three and one-half percent. Because the interest rate was static, taxpayers were able to manipulate the valuation when market conditions changed. They were also able, as the Senate report indicates, to affect the amount flowing to the income beneficiaries by the nature of the investments. When interest rates began to change dramatically, the IRS amended the regulations to provide first for a six percent rate and later for a nine percent rate. These amendments were not entirely satisfactory, and Congress ultimately adopted §7520, which requires the Treasury Secretary to issue monthly interest rates for valuing life estates, remainders, and similar interests. Section 7520 applies not only to charitable remainder trusts, but to all such interests whether given to a charity or an individual.

As a result of the 1969 amendments, §2055(e)(2) now allows an estate tax deduction for split interest gifts only if the interest given to charity is one of the following: (1) a charitable remainder annuity trust, (2) a charitable remainder unitrust, (3) a pooled income fund, (4) a guaranteed annuity or unitrust interest, (5) a remainder interest in a personal residence or farm, (6) an undivided portion of the taxpayer's entire interest in the property, or (7) a qualified conservation contribution. These restrictions also apply to the income tax and gift tax charitable deductions.

A charitable remainder annuity trust (CRAT) is an irrevocable trust where an income interest is paid to one or more beneficiaries, at least one of whom is not a charitable organization. The income interest may be paid for one life, for two or more lives, or for a term of years that does not exceed 20 years. If an income interest is to be paid to an individual, that individual must be living on the date the CRAT is created. The income interest must be a specified sum that is at least five percent of the initial fair market value of the property placed in trust and not more than 50 percent of that value. The sum certain can be expressed as a dollar amount or as a fraction or percentage amount of the initial fair market value of the property placed in trust. The income interest must be distributed at least annually, and the value of the remainder interest, as determined under §7520, must be at least ten percent of the initial fair market value of all the property placed in trust. §664(d)(1); Reg. §§1.664-1, 1.664-2.

Example 15-3

Duncan transfers $750,000 to Friendly National Bank as Trustee to pay $25,000 each year to his mother, Martha, for her life and, at her death, to distribute the trust property to College. If the remainder interest has a value of at least $75,000, this trust meets the requirements of §664(d)(1), and Duncan will be allowed a gift tax deduction for the value of the remainder interest.

Example 15-4

Donna bequeaths $900,000 to Friendly National Bank as Trustee to pay her son, Sam, an amount equal to 7 percent of the fair market value of the trust, determined as of the date her estate tax return is due, each year for 15 years. After 15 years, the trust property is to be distributed to Church. If the remainder interest has a value of at least $90,000, this trust meets the requirements of §664(d)(1), and Donna will be allowed an estate tax deduction for the value of the remainder interest.

A charitable remainder unitrust (CRUT) must meet the same requirements as a CRAT, except that the income interest must be a fixed percentage of the net fair market value of the trust assets, valued annually. That percentage must be not less than five percent or more than 50 percent of the net fair market value determined annually. §664(d)(2); Reg. §§1.664-1, 1.664-3. While the income interest in a CRAT can be stated as a specified sum, the income interest in a CRUT must be stated as a fixed percentage. The amount of income distributed from a CRUT will change each year as the value of the trust assets increases or decreases. In contrast, the amount of income from a CRAT will remain the same despite changes in the value of the trust property. As a result, the income beneficiary of a CRAT is protected from a decrease in value in trust assets, but does not benefit from an increase in value. Because the income payment from a CRAT is a fixed amount, the income beneficiary will receive less value in periods of significant inflation.

Example 15-5

Daniel bequeaths $800,000 to Friendly National Bank as Trustee to pay his spouse, Sarah, 6 percent of the net fair market value of the trust assets, valued annually, in quarterly installments. At Sarah's death, the Trustee is to transfer the trust property to the American Red Cross. If the remainder interest has a value of at least $80,000, this trust meets the requirements of §664(d)(2), and Daniel will be allowed an estate tax deduction for the value of the remainder interest.

The IRS has published sample forms of trusts that meet the requirements of §664(d)(1) and (2) for charitable remainder annuity trusts and unitrusts. Revenue Procedure 90-30, 1990-1 C.B. 534; Revenue Procedure 90-31, 1990-1 C.B. 539; Revenue Procedure 90-32, 1990-1 C.B. 546.

A donor or decedent will also receive a charitable deduction for the value of a remainder interest donated to a pooled income fund for a public charity, as defined in §170(b)(1)(A), other than charities in clauses (vii) and (viii). The pooled income fund must be a trust maintained by the charity that is the remainder beneficiary. The income interest must be paid to one or more beneficiaries who are living at the time of the transfer to the fund for their lives. The income interest is determined by the rate of return on the fund. The property donated will be commingled with that of others making similar transfers, and only amounts that qualify under §642(c)(5) can be in the fund. No investments can be made in tax-exempt securities, and no donor or income beneficiary can be a trustee of the charitable organization. The value of the charitable contribution will be based on the highest rate of return earned by the fund for any of the three tax years preceding the year of the transfer. §642(c)(5); Reg. §1.642(c)-5.

A decedent's estate may also receive a charitable deduction for transfers where the charity receives an income interest rather than a remainder interest. The charitable organization must receive either a guaranteed annuity or a fixed percentage of the fair market value of the trust assets determined annually, *i.e.*, a unitrust interest. §2055(e)(2)(B).

Finally, a decedent's estate may also receive a deduction under §2055(e)(2) for contributions specified in §170(f)(3)(B), *i.e.*, an undivided portion of the decedent's entire interest in property, a remainder interest in a personal residence or a farm, or a qualified conservation contribution.

PROBLEMS

1. Daphne dies and devises Blackacre, which is investment real estate and is valued at $1,500,000, to her niece, Nancy, and to College as tenants in common. Daphne devises Farmacre, valued at $500,000, to her nephew, Peter, for his life with the remainder to University. She bequeaths the residue of her estate, $2,000,000, to Friendly National Bank as Trustee, to pay the income to her husband, Henry, for his life, and at his death to distribute the trust property to Church. Will Daphne's estate be entitled to a deduction under §2055 for any of these bequests? Explain.

2. Dennis bequeaths the residue of his estate, $5,000,000, to Friendly National Bank as Trustee to pay the income to Charity for 15 years and then to distribute the trust property in equal shares to his surviving issue.
   a. Will Dennis's estate be entitled to a deduction under §2055 for this bequest?
   b. What if the Trustee is to pay Charity $300,000 per year for 15 years?

     c.   What if the Trustee is to pay Charity 6 percent of the value of the trust each year?

  3. Doris bequeaths $10,000,000 to Friendly National Bank as Trustee to pay the income to her child, Chris, for life and at his death to distribute the trust property to Charity.

     a.   Will Doris's estate be entitled to a deduction under §2055 for this bequest?

     b.   What if the Trustee is to pay Chris $35,000 each year?

     c.   What if the Trustee is to pay Chris $60,000 each year for 25 years and at the end of the 25 years distribute the trust property to Charity?

C.   CONSERVATION EASEMENTS
IRC §§170(h), 2031(c), 2055(f), 2522(d)

Section 2031(c) excludes from the decedent's gross estate a portion of the value of land subject to a qualified conservation easement in addition to any income, gift, or estate tax deduction under §§170(h), 2055(f), and 2522(d). The §2031(c) exclusion is available for postmortem contributions by the decedent's executor or trustee or a member of the decedent's family even if the decedent did not provide for such a contribution in her will. Both the gift tax and the estate tax incorporate the income tax definitions and restrictions contained in §170(h) but with some exceptions. §§2031(c)(8)(B), 2055(f), 2522(d). Section 170(h) defines a qualified conservation contribution as a contribution of a qualified real property interest, to a qualified organization, exclusively for conservation purposes.

A qualified real property interest may be (1) the donor's entire interest other than a qualified mineral interest, (2) a remainder interest, or (3) a restriction on the use of the property granted in perpetuity. §170(h)(2). For purposes of the gift and estate taxes, however, only the third interest, *i.e.*, a conservation easement, will qualify for a deduction or the §2031(c) exclusion. Section 2031(c) also requires a prohibition on more than a de minimis use for commercial recreational activity. §2031(c)(8)(B).

Qualified organizations are a governmental entity, a public charity, or a private foundation if it meets the requirements in §509(a)(2) or meets the requirements in §509(a)(3) and is controlled by a governmental entity, a public charity, or a §509(a)(2) private foundation. §170(h)(3).

Conservation purposes include: (1) the preservation of land for outdoor recreation by, or the education of, the general public; (2) the protection of a relatively natural habitat of fish, wildlife, or plants, or similar ecosystem; (3) the preservation of open space, including farmland and forests, for the scenic enjoyment of the general public or pursuant to a clearly delineated governmental policy; and (4) the preservation of a historically important land area or a certified historic structure. §170(h)(4)(A). The contribution must be exclusively for one of these purposes, and the purpose must be protected in perpetuity. The estate tax exclusion in §2031(c) is not available for historic preservation. §2031(c)(8)(B). On the other hand, the gift and estate tax charitable deductions are available without regard to §170(h)(4)(A). §§2055(f), 2522(d). This means that the donor or decedent only needs to contribute a conservation easement to a qualified organization to obtain the deduction. Of course, if she wants to exclude part of the value of the land subject to that easement under §2031(c), the easement must be limited to one of the first three conservation purposes listed in §170(h)(4)(A).

The amount of the charitable deduction is the fair market value of the conservation easement. In Revenue Ruling 73-339, the IRS provided that:

> Open space easements in perpetuity may be valued separately and distinctly. However, more often than not open space easements in perpetuity are granted by deed of gift so there is usually no substantial record of market place sales to use as a meaningful or valid comparison. As a consequence, the valuation of an open space easement in perpetuity is generally made on the basis of the "before and after" approach. Thus, the difference between the fair market value of the total property before the granting of the easement and the fair market value of the property after the grant is the fair market value of the easement given up.

1973-2 C.B. 68, clarified by Revenue Ruling 76-376, 1976-2 C.B. 53.

Section 170(b) limits the amount of all charitable contributions, including qualified conservation contributions, that may be deducted for income tax purposes. The gift and estate tax deductions are unlimited in amount. §§2055(a), 2522(a). Section 2031(c) imposes both a monetary limit and a percentage restriction on the amount excluded from the decedent's estate. It also further restricts the type of property interests qualifying for the exclusion.

Section 2031(c) was added to the estate tax as part of the Revenue Reconciliation Act of 1997, P.L. 105-304, §508(a), because "a reduction in estate taxes for land subject to a qualified conservation easement will ease existing pressures to develop or sell off open spaces in order to raise funds to pay estate tax, and will thereby help to preserve environmentally significant land." S. Rep. 105-33, 105th Cong., 1st Sess. 1997, 46. The exclusion is restricted to land located in the United States or one of its possessions that was owned by the decedent or a member of her family at all times during the three-year period ending on the date of decedent's death and that meets the definition of a qualified conservation easement, as described above. §2031(c)(8). For decedents dying before January 1, 2001, the land must have been located in, or within 25 miles of, a metropolitan area, a national park, or a wilderness area, or within 10 miles of an Urban National Forest. This limitation was removed by the 2001 Tax Act, but will be reimposed in 2011 as a result of the sunset provision of the 2001 Tax Act if no further action is taken to make this amendment permanent.

The executor must elect the §2031(c) exclusion on the estate tax return and no later than the due date (including extensions) for filing that return. §2031(c)(6). The decedent need not have donated the easement before her death or in her will. This section allows the executor, the trustee of a trust that includes the land to be subject to the qualified conservation easement, or a member of the decedent's family to make the donation. If this happens, the decedent's estate is also allowed a charitable deduction under §2055(f) but only if no person is allowed an income tax deduction for the donation. §2031(c)(8)(A)(iii), (c)(9).

Section 2031(c) excludes the lesser of (1) $500,000 (for decedents dying after 2001) or (2) the applicable percentage of the value of land subject to a qualified conservation easement reduced by the amount of any §2055(f) deduction with respect to such land. The applicable percentage is 40 percent if the value of the qualified conservation easement is at least 30 percent of the value of the land, determined without regard to the easement. If the value of the easement is less than 30 percent of the value of the land, then the applicable percentage (40 percent) is reduced by two percentage points for each percentage point that the value of the easement is less than 30 percent of the value of the land.

Example 15-6

Diane owns Greenacre, which has a fair market value of $300,000, and other property worth $2,000,000. In her will, Diane donates a qualified conservation easement on Greenacre to Local Land Trust, a §501(c)(3) public charity. The value of the easement is $100,000. Her estate will be allowed a charitable deduction under §2055(f) of $100,000. The §2031(c) exclusion will be 40 percent of the value of the land without the easement ($300,000) minus the value of the §2055(f) deduction ($100,000) or $80,000.

Diane's gross estate will be $2,220,000, *i.e.*, the value of the other property plus the value of Greenacres less the §2031(c) exclusion. Her taxable estate will be $2,120,000 because of the §2055(f) deduction.

The section §2031(c) exclusion also applies to conservation easements donated during life.

Example 15-7

Assume that Diane had made the donation of the easement on Greenacre during her life. She received an income tax deduction of $100,000 under §170(f), and the transfer of the easement qualified for the gift tax charitable deduction under §2522(d). Her gross estate includes the value of the other property, *i.e.*, $2,000,000, the value of Greenacre $200,000 less the §2031(c) exclusion of $80,000 or $120,000. Her gross estate will therefore be $2,120,000. Her taxable estate will be the same amount because she is not entitled to a §2055 deduction. Instead, she received a gift tax and an income tax deduction.

The amount of the qualified conservation easement will not be included in the tax base under §2001 because it is not an adjusted taxable gift. Because it qualified for the gift tax charitable deduction, it was not a taxable gift.

The §2031(c) exclusion is also available if the decedent's executor, trustee, or family member makes the donation and the appropriate election. If Diane had not donated the easement on Greenacre during her life and had neglected to do so in her will, her estate can still receive the benefit of both the §2031(c) exclusion and a §2055(f) deduction if the executor makes the donation and the election. The result would be the same as in Example 15-6. The estate would not be entitled to an income tax deduction for this donation.

PROBLEMS

1. Dexter owns Greenacre, which has a fair market value of $200,000. He donates a conservation easement on the property to Land Trust, a §501(c)(3) organization. The easement has a fair market value of $75,000. Dexter dies five years later owning Greenacre and other property valued at $3,000,000. What are the gift and estate tax consequences?

2. Della owns Whiteacre, which has a fair market value of $1,000,000. In her will, she donates a conservation easement on Whiteacre to Land Trust, a §501(c)(3) organization. The value of the easement is $200,000.
   a. What are the estate tax consequences?
   b. What if Whiteacre has a value of $3,000,000 and the easement is worth $1,000,000?
   c. Same as 2.b., except that Della's will did not include a donation to Land Trust. Her executor donates the easement.

CHAPTER 16

Transfers to the Surviving Spouse

A. GENERAL PRINCIPLES

While marriage is currently considered to be a partnership and the family a single economic unit for tax purposes, it was not always this way. When the estate and gift taxes were first enacted, they included no special provisions for transfers between spouses. Each taxpayer was taxed separately on his or her own transfers, even to each other. This applied only in common law property jurisdictions, where each individual was treated as the sole owner of the property except, of course, for property owned as joint tenants with the right of survivorship or as tenants by the entirety. In community property jurisdictions, each spouse was considered to own one-half of the property regardless of how title was held. At death, the propertied spouse had the right to dispose of only one-half of the community property. As a result, any tax was assessed against only that half of the property. The following example demonstrates the difference in tax treatment between these two systems of property in a transfer tax system that did not contain any special provision for transfers between spouses.

Example 16-1

A and B are married and live in a common law property jurisdiction, while C and D are married and live in a community property jurisdiction. A and C each owns $3,000,000 of property. A dies in 2004, leaving all his property to B. C also dies in 2004, leaving all his property to D. A's estate will pay a tax of $705,000. C's estate will pay no tax because C is deemed to own only one-half of the community property, $1,500,000, which is entirely sheltered from tax by the applicable exemption amount.

Assume further that B and D do not own any other property of their own other than what they have inherited; they do not consume any of the property left to them by A and C; and there is no appreciation or depreciation in the value of that property. Assuming the tax rate remains at the 2004 level, when B dies, her estate will owe tax of $366,600 (on the $2,295,000 she received from A). When D dies, her estate will owe tax of $705,000 (on the $3,000,000 she received from C). Not only did A and B pay more estate tax than C and D — $1,071,600 compared to $705,000 — but B had less property than D after the death of their spouses.

In 1942, Congress attempted to remedy this inequity by treating community property the same as common law property. The amendment required that the gross estate include all property owned by the decedent regardless of the survivor's community property interest. As a result, C, in the example above, would have had a gross estate of $3,000,000. If the surviving spouse could establish that some of this property was in fact her separate property or resulted from compensation for her personal services, that amount was deducted. This was essentially the same rule that applied to joint tenancy property. *See* §2040(a). If the spouse who did not own the property died first, however, her estate continued to include 50 percent of the community property because she had the right to dispose of that property. The 1942 amendment merely shifted the inequity from common law jurisdictions to community property jurisdictions, and it created additional problems. If the spouse owning the property died first, the estate tax was based on the entire value of the property, despite the surviving spouse's interest in it, and the tax in some situations could exceed the value of the property over which the decedent had the power of disposition.

Problematic as this was, a far greater problem was produced by the income tax. In a common law property jurisdiction, the wage earner was taxed on all of his or her earnings. In a community property jurisdiction, however, half of the income was attributed to each spouse. Given the progressive rate structure of the income tax, this produced a significant advantage for couples in community property jurisdictions because twice as much income was taxed at the lowest rates. As income tax rates increased during the 1940s, the disparity became more obvious, and common law property jurisdictions began to adopt community property laws.

This movement stopped in 1948 when Congress enacted provisions: (1) allowing couples to file a joint income tax return and thus essentially split their income; (2) allowing couples to consider gifts as made one-half by each (the split gift provision codified in §2513); and (3) creating a deduction in both the gift and estate taxes for transfers from one spouse to the other. The theory of these provisions was to treat owners of common law property the same as owners of community property. A decedent in a common law property jurisdiction could leave one-half of his property to his surviving spouse without paying any estate tax. If property was left to the surviving spouse in trust, she had to have the right to the income from the trust property and the ability to dispose of that property during her life or at death, the same rights that she would have had in a community property jurisdiction. These provisions did not apply to community property.

This policy of treating common law property like community property was assailed almost from the beginning. In 1954, proposals for an unlimited marital deduction were submitted to Congress, but no action was taken. In 1976, proponents of the unlimited deduction achieved a modest success when

Congress amended the marital deduction provisions to allow $100,000 of lifetime gifts to pass tax-free between spouses and the greater of $250,000 or 50 percent of the adjusted gross estate to pass tax-free to the surviving spouse at death. This opened the door to removing all monetary limitations on the deduction, which Congress finally did in 1981. At the same time, Congress enacted a new exception to the terminable interest rule, allowing a decedent to leave property in trust for his surviving spouse, without requiring the decedent to give the survivor the right to dispose of the property during her life or at her death. These amendments reflected a significant shift in policy, recognizing that spouses were one economic unit regardless of who earned the income or held title to the property.

Property given to a spouse that qualifies for the marital deduction will be subject to the estate tax when the survivor spouse dies unless she consumed it or gave it away during her life. This reflects the policy adopted by Congress in 1976 that property should be taxed once each generation as spouses are considered to be in the same generation, regardless of age.

Example 16-2

H and W are married. H owns property valued at $2,500,000. H bequeaths his entire estate to W. H's gross estate is $2,500,000, the value of property he owned at the time of his death. §2033. His taxable estate, however, will be $0 because he transferred all of his property to W. §2056(a). When W dies in 2004, her gross estate will be $2,500,000 (assuming she owned no other property, she did not consume or give away the property she inherited from H, and that H's property neither appreciated nor depreciated in value) because she has fee simple title to this property. §2033. Assuming no other deductions, W's estate will pay a tax of $465,000. With appropriate planning (*see* subsection F), H and W could eliminate this tax burden entirely.

B. THE STATUTORY REQUIREMENTS
§§2056, 2523

The basic requirements of the marital deduction are the same for both the estate tax and the gift tax even though the following discussion focuses on the estate tax provisions. First, the marital deduction is available to any decedent who is subject to the federal estate tax even if he is not a citizen or resident of the United States. The marital deduction is only available to a noncitizen, nonresident if the property is included in his gross estate (property located in the United States) and the other requirements of §2056 are met. *See* §2106(a)(3).

Second, the property must be given to a spouse. Marital status is determined by state law. Only a final divorce decree terminating marriage is sufficient to change marital status; legal separation or initiation of divorce proceedings is insufficient. If there is a question about the validity of a divorce or marriage, the decision of a court with primary jurisdiction over the administration of the decedent's estate will determine the decedent's marital status. Before no-fault divorce became common, divorces obtained in jurisdictions such as Mexico and Nevada were not always recognized. *See, e.g.,* Estate of Steffke v. Commissioner, 538 F.2d 730 (7th Cir. 1976), *cert. denied* 429 U.S. 1022 (1976); Estate of Spalding v. Commissioner, 537 F.2d 666 (2d Cir. 1976); Estate of Goldwater v. Commissioner, 539 F.2d 878 (2d Cir. 1976), *cert. denied* 429 U.S. 1023 (1976). If common law marriage is recognized by the jurisdiction, the survivor must establish that all requirements of state law have been satisfied to obtain the benefits of the marital deduction.

The spouse need not be a citizen or even a resident of the United States. If the spouse is not a citizen, the property must be left to a qualified domestic trust as defined in §2056A, which is discussed in subsection C.

The donor and donee must be married at the time of the transfer to qualify for the gift tax marital deduction. For purposes of the estate tax marital deduction, however, the decedent need not have been married to the recipient at the time of the transfer as long as (1) the decedent and recipient are married at the time of death and (2) the property is included in the decedent's gross estate. The converse is also true; if the decedent and recipient are married at the time of the transfer but subsequently divorced, the property will not qualify for the marital deduction even if it is in the decedent's gross estate at death. Revenue Ruling 79-354, 1979-2 C.B. 334.

Third, the spouse must survive the decedent. As long as the order of deaths can be established, survivorship, even for a matter of seconds, is sufficient. If the order cannot be determined, state law will create a presumption that each spouse survived with respect to his or her own property. There are special rules for jointly owned property, life insurance, and trusts. These presumptions can interfere with a couple's estate plan if that plan depends on one spouse's estate obtaining the benefit of the marital deduction. In such situations, both spouses' estate plans should include survivorship provisions that override the statutory presumptions.

Two issues arise in drafting these survivorship provisions. The first occurs if the survivorship provision only applies if the deaths result from a common disaster. For federal transfer tax purposes, such a provision would be ineffective if the order of deaths, even resulting from a common disaster, could be established. Moreover, in some rare cases both spouses will die in circumstances where the order of death cannot be established but there was no common disaster. This problem can be easily avoided by drafting the provision to apply "whenever the order of death cannot be determined."

The second arises when identical language is used in both wills. A provision in both wills that says "if my spouse and I die in circumstances where the order of deaths cannot be determined, my spouse is deemed to survive me" will create exactly the same result as the state law presumptions of survivorship and undermine the estate plan. Instead, the survivorship clauses should specify that one person, *e.g.*, the wife, be deemed the survivor.

Example 16-3

A and B are married, and their estate plan depends on A's estate qualifying for the marital deduction. A's will should include a provision that states, "if my spouse (B) and I die in circumstances where the order of deaths cannot be determined, my spouse (B) is deemed to survive me." B's will should include a provision that states, "if my spouse (A) and I die in circumstances where the order of deaths cannot be determined, I am deemed to survive my spouse (A)." As a result, A's property will pass to B and qualify for the marital deduction.

Fourth, the property must be in the decedent's gross estate as determined by §§2033 to 2044. If the property is not in the decedent's gross estate, allowing a marital deduction would create a double benefit.

Example 16-4

H and W are married. W owns property valued at $2,000,000. She also has the right to appoint the corpus of a trust, created by her father, to her spouse or her surviving children. The value of the trust property is $1,000,000 at the time of her death. Her gross estate includes only the $2,000,000 of property because her interest in the trust is not a general power of appointment. §2041(b). If she leaves the $2,000,000 to her children and appoints the trust property to her spouse, her estate will not be entitled to the marital deduction. She will therefore pay a tax on the $2,000,000 less the applicable credit amount. To allow her estate a deduction for the property passing to her spouse would mean that her estate paid no estate tax — $2,000,000 gross estate minus the $1,000,000 deduction for the trust property, leaving only $1,000,000, all of which would be sheltered by the applicable credit amount. This ignores the fact that her taxable estate, which was $2,000,000, passed to her children.

W could avoid paying any tax. If she wants to give her children $2,000,000 and her spouse $1,000,000, she should appoint the trust property to her children, give her spouse half of the remaining property, and give the residue of her property to her children. Again, her gross estate would be $2,000,000. This time her estate would be entitled to the marital deduction, reducing her taxable estate to $1,000,000, all of which would be sheltered by the applicable credit amount.

Fifth, the property must "pass" from the decedent to the surviving spouse. If the property is in the decedent's gross estate and if the survivor acquires the property as a result of the decedent's death, this requirement will be met. Section 2056(c) provides that bequests and devises, inheritances, dower or curtsey interests or the statutory share, joint tenancy property, life insurance, property subject to a power of appointment, and property subject to §§2035 through 2038 are considered as passing if the decedent transferred them to the surviving spouse. A surviving spouse's interest in pension plans, employer death benefits, and similar arrangements are also considered to "pass." Reg. §20.2056(c)-1(a)(6).

If the surviving spouse disclaims an interest in property left by the decedent, that property will not be considered as passing to him. On the other hand, if the decedent left property to a third person, such as a child, and that third person disclaimed so that the property went to the surviving spouse, the property will be considered as passing from the decedent to the surviving spouse. Reg. §20.2056(d)-2(b). This is simply an application of §2518, which treats the person disclaiming as if he had predeceased the decedent. As a result, the decedent, not the disclaimant, is treated as the transferor.

If the surviving spouse elects against the will, the statutory share is considered as passing from the decedent. A similar rule applies if the survivor challenges the will and wins. Even will contest settlements qualify as long as they represent "a bona fide recognition of enforceable rights." Reg. §20.2056(c)-2(d)(2). The IRS will scrutinize all family arrangements and even court approved settlements to determine that this standard has been met.

The passing requirement limits the amount of the marital deduction to the net value of the property received by the surviving spouse. §2056(b)(4). The net value limitation applies if the decedent leaves the survivor property that is subject to debt.

Example 16-5

H and W are married. W owns an apartment building that has a fair market value of $350,000 and a mortgage of $200,000. W devises this property to H. Her gross estate includes the $350,000 value. §2033. Her estate is entitled to a marital deduction of only $150,000, the net value of the property passing to H. Reg. §20.2056(b)-4(b). Her estate will, however, be entitled to a §2053 deduction for the $200,000 mortgage. As a result, the amount in her taxable estate will be zero.

The net value limitation also applies when the bequest to the surviving spouse bears the burden of the federal estate tax, the state death tax, or expenses of administration. Once again, the amount of the marital deduction must be reduced by these taxes or expenses. The deduction cannot exceed the amount actually distributed to the surviving spouse.

The same principle applies when the decedent leaves the surviving spouse a conditional bequest.

United States v. Stapf
375 U.S. 118 (1963)

Mr. Justice GOLDBERG delivered the opinion of the Court.

Respondents brought this suit . . . for a refund of estate taxes . . . the Court of Appeals for the Fifth Circuit held that respondents were entitled to certain marital deductions under §812(e) [now §2056(b)(4)(B)] of the Internal Revenue Code of 1939. . . .

Lowell H. Stapf died testate on July 29, 1953, a resident and domiciliary of Texas, a community property jurisdiction. At the time of his death he owned, in addition to his separate estate, a substantial amount of property in community with his wife. His will required that his widow elect either to retain her one-half interest in the community or to take under the will and allow its terms to govern the disposition of her community interest. If Mrs. Stapf were to elect to take under the will, she would be given, after specific bequests to others, one-third of the community property and one-third of her husband's separate estate. By accepting this bequest she would allow her one-half interest in the community to pass, in accordance with the will, into a trust for the benefit of the children. . . .

The relevant facts and computations are not in dispute. The decedent's separate property was valued at $65,100 and the community property at $258,105. . . . If Mrs. Stapf had not elected to take under the will, she would have retained her fully vested one-half interest in the community property ($129,052) which would have been charged with one-half of the community debts ($16,184) and 35 percent of the administration expenses ($1,426). Thus, as the parties agree, she would have received a net of $111,443.

In fact Mrs. Stapf elected to take under the will. She received, after specific bequests to others, one-third of the combined separate and community property, a devise valued at $106,268, which was $5,175 less than she would have received had she retained her community property and refused to take under the will.

In computing the net taxable estate, the executors claimed a marital deduction under §812(e)(1) of the Internal Revenue Code of 1939 for the full value of the one-third of decedent's separate estate ($22,367) which passed to his wife under the will. . . . The District Court allowed the full marital deduction but disallowed the disputed claims and expenses. 189 F. Supp. 830. On cross-appeals the Court of Appeals, with one judge dissenting on all issues, held that each of the claimed deductions was allowable in full. 309 F.2d 592. For reasons stated below, we hold that the Commissioner was correct and that none of the disputed deductions is allowable.

By electing to take under the will, Mrs. Stapf, in effect, agreed to accept the property devised to her and, in turn, to surrender property of greater value to the trust for the benefit of the children. This raises the question of whether a decedent's estate is allowed a marital deduction under §812(e)(1)(E)(ii) of the 1939 Code where the bequest to the surviving spouse is on the condition that she convey property of equivalent or greater value to her children. The Government contends that, for purposes of a marital deduction, "the value of the interest passing to the wife is the value of the property given her less the value of the property she is required to give another as a condition to receiving it." On this view, since the widow had no net benefit from the exercise of her election, the estate would be entitled to no marital deduction. Respondents reject this net benefit approach and argue that the plain meaning of the statute makes detriment to the surviving spouse immaterial.

Section 812(e)(1)(A) provides that "in general" the marital deduction is for "the value of any interest in property which passes . . . from the decedent to his surviving spouse." Subparagraph (E) then deals specifically with the question of valuation:

(E) Valuation of interest passing to surviving spouse. In determining for the purposes of subparagraph (A) the value of any interest in property passing to the surviving spouse for which a deduction is allowed by this subsection —

(ii) where such interest or property is incumbered in any manner, or where the surviving spouse incurs any obligation imposed by the decedent with respect to the passing of such interest, such incumbrance or obligation shall be taken into account in the same manner as if the amount of a gift to such spouse of such interest were being determined.

The disputed deduction turns upon the interpretation of (1) the introductory phrase "any obligation imposed by the decedent with respect to the passing of such interest," and (2) the concluding provision that "such . . . obligation shall be taken into account in the same manner as if the amount of a gift to such spouse of such interest were being determined."

The Court of Appeals, in allowing the claimed marital deduction, reasoned that since the valuation is to be "as if" a gift were being taxed, the legal analysis should be the same as if a husband had made an inter vivos gift to his wife on the condition that she give something to the children. In such a case, it was stated, the husband is taxable in the full amount for his gift. The detriment incurred by the wife would not ordinarily reduce the amount of the gift taxable to the husband, the original donor. The court concluded:

Within gift tax confines the community property of the widow passing under the will of the husband to others may not be "netted" against the devise to the widow, and thus testator, were the transfer inter vivos, would be liable for gift taxes on the full value of the devise. 309 F.2d 592, 598.

This conclusion, based on the alleged plain meaning of the final gift-amount clause of §812(e)(1)(E)(ii), is not supported by a reading of the entire statutory provision. First, §812(e) allows a marital deduction only for the decedent's gifts or bequests which pass "to his surviving spouse." In the present case the effect of the devise was not to distribute wealth to the surviving spouse, but instead to transmit, through the widow, a gift to the couple's children. The gift-to-the-surviving-spouse terminology reflects concern with the status of the actual recipient or donee of the gift. What the statute provides is a "marital deduction" — a deduction for gifts to the surviving spouse — not a deduction for gifts to the children or a deduction for gifts to privately selected beneficiaries. The appropriate reference, therefore, is not to the value of the gift moving from the deceased spouse but to the net value of the gift received by the surviving spouse.

Second, the introductory phrases of §812(e)(1)(E)(ii) provide that the gift-amount determination is to be made "where such interest or property is incumbered in any manner, or where the surviving spouse incurs any obligation imposed by the decedent with respect to the passing of such interest. . . ." The Government, drawing upon the broad import of this language, argues: "An undertaking by the wife to convey property to a third person, upon which her receipt of property under the decedent's will is conditioned, is plainly an 'obligation imposed by the decedent with respect to the passing of such interest.'" Respondents contend that "incumbrance or obligation" refers only to "a payment to be made out of property passing to the surviving spouse." Respondents' narrow construction certainly is not compelled by a literal interpretation of the statutory language. Their construction would embrace only, for example, an obligation on the property passing whereas the statute speaks of an obligation "with respect to the passing" gift. Finally, to arrive at the real value of the gift "such . . . obligation shall be taken into account. . . ." In context we think this relates the gift-amount determination to the net economic interest received by the surviving spouse.

This interpretation is supported by authoritative declarations of congressional intent. The Senate Committee on Finance, in explaining the operation of the marital deduction, stated its understanding as follows:

> If the decedent bequeaths certain property to his surviving spouse *subject*, however, *to her agreement*, or a charge on the property, for payment of $1,000 to X, the value of the bequest (and, accordingly, the value of the interest passing to the surviving spouse) is the value, reduced by $1,000, of such property. S.Rep. No. 1013, 80th Cong., 2d Sess., Pt. 2, p. 6; U.S.Code Cong.Service 1948, p. 1228. (Emphasis added.)

The relevant Treasury Regulation is directly based upon, if not literally taken from, such expressions of legislative intent. Treas.Reg. 105, §81.47c(b) (1949). The Regulation specifically includes an example of the kind of testamentary disposition involved in this case:

> A decedent bequeathed certain securities to his wife in lieu of her interest in property held by them as community property under the law of the State of their residence. The wife elected to relinquish her community property interest and to take the bequest. For the purpose of the marital deduction, the value of the bequest is to be reduced by the value of the community property interest relinquished by the wife.

We conclude, therefore, that the governing principle, approved by Congress and embodied in the Treasury Regulation, must be that a marital deduction is allowable only to the extent that the property bequeathed to the surviving spouse exceeds in value the property such spouse is required to relinquish.

Our conclusion concerning the congressionally intended result under §812(e) (1) accords with the general purpose of Congress in creating the marital deduction. The 1948 tax amendments were intended to equalize the effect of the estate taxes in community property and common-law jurisdictions. Under a community property system, such as that in Texas, the spouse receives outright ownership of one-half of the community property and only the other one-half is included in the decedent's estate. To equalize the incidence of progressively scaled estate taxes and to adhere to the patterns of state law, the marital deduction permits a deceased spouse, subject to certain requirements, to transfer free of taxes one-half of the non-community property to the surviving spouse. Although applicable to separately held property in a community property state, the primary thrust of this is to extend to taxpayers in common-law States the advantages of "estate splitting" otherwise available only in community property States. The purpose, however, is only to permit a married couple's property to be taxed in two stages and not to allow a tax-exempt transfer of wealth into succeeding generations. Thus the marital deduction is generally restricted to the transfer of property interests that will be includible in the surviving spouse's gross estate. Respondents' construction of §812(e)(1) would, nevertheless, permit one-half of a spouse's wealth to pass from one generation to another without being subject either to gift or estate taxes. We do not believe that this result, squarely contrary to the concept of the marital deduction, can be justified by the language of §812(e)(1). Furthermore, since in a community property jurisdiction one-half of the community normally vests in the wife, approval of the claimed deduction would create an opportunity for tax reduction that, as a practical matter, would be more readily available to couples in community property jurisdictions than to couples in common-law jurisdictions. Such a result, again, would be unnecessarily inconsistent with a basic purpose of the statute.

Since in our opinion the plain meaning of §812(e)(1) does not require the interpretation advanced by respondents, the statute must be construed to accord with the clearly expressed congressional purposes and the relevant Treasury Regulation. We conclude that, for estate tax purposes, the value of a conditional bequest to a widow should be the value of the property given to her less the value of the property she is required to give to another. In this case the value of the property transferred to Mrs. Stapf ($106,268) must be reduced by the value of the community property she was required to relinquish ($111,443). Since she received no net benefit, the estate is entitled to no marital deduction.

The final statutory requirement is that the interest not be a nondeductible terminable interest. This terminable interest rule is discussed in section D, and the exceptions to it are discussed in section E.

PROBLEMS

1. Harold and Wanda are married. They own a home (valued at $500,000) as joint tenants with the right of survivorship. Harold also owns a life insurance policy (face amount $700,000) payable to Wanda and investments (valued at $800,000). In addition, Harold's mother had established a testamentary trust to pay the income to Harold for life and remainder to whomever he appoints by will, and in default of appointment by Harold to his children in equal shares. At the time of Harold's death, the trust corpus is worth $2,000,000.

    a. Harold's will leaves all his property to Wanda, his spouse. In addition, Harold exercises his power of appointment in favor of Wanda. What is the value of Harold's gross estate? What is the value of his taxable estate? Why?

    b. Harold had consulted an attorney about estate planning, indicating that he wanted to leave everything to Wanda. Harold, however, dies before he can execute his will or exercise his power of appointment. Wanda inherits one-half the investment property under the intestacy laws. Chris, Harold's son, inherits the other half. The trust property passes under the default clause to Chris.

        (1) What is the value of Harold's taxable estate? Why?

        (2) Chris disclaims his interest in the investments, and his interest passes to Wanda pursuant to state law. Assume that Chris's disclaimer meets the requirements of §2518. What is the value of Harold's taxable estate? Why?

        (3) Instead of (2), Chris and Wanda engage in lengthy discussions and negotiations. They finally agree that Chris will transfer the investments and half of the value of the trust property to Wanda. This agreement does not meet state property law requirements as a disclaimer, nor does it meet the requirements of §2518. What is the value of Harold's taxable estate? Why?

    c. Instead, Harold made the insurance proceeds payable to Chris, left all his other property to Chris, and appointed the trust property to Chris. (The house is still in joint tenancy with Wanda.)

        (1) If Wanda elects against the will, will the amount she receives qualify for the marital deduction? Why?

        (2) What if, instead, she challenged the will on grounds of mental capacity and undue influence and won? Assume that there was a prior will leaving everything to Wanda and exercising the power of appointment in favor of her. The court decree upholds the prior will.

        (3) Same as (2), except that Wanda and Chris settle before trial. Will the amount that Wanda receives under the settlement qualify for the marital deduction? Why?

    d. Assume that the trust gave Harold only a special power of appointment to appoint to Wanda or his lineal descendants. What are the estate tax consequences if Harold leaves his investments to Chris and appoints the trust property to Wanda? (Assume the insurance proceeds are still payable to Wanda.)

    e. What are the estate tax consequences in problem 1.a. if the house is subject to $300,000 mortgage?

2. Leslie and Robin have lived together for 25 years and have always identified themselves as a couple. Leslie's will provides: "I leave all of my property to my partner, Robin." Leslie owned property valued at $2,500,000. What is the value of Leslie's taxable estate? Why?

3. Alan and Brenda are married and have two adult children, Ethan and Faith. Alan owns investments of $1,500,000; Brenda owns investments of $600,000. Alan's will leaves all his property to Brenda, and if she does not survive him to their children. Brenda's will leaves all her property to Alex, and if he does not survive her to their children. Alex shoots Brenda and then himself. State law provides that a killer is considered to have predeceased his victim.

    a. What is the value of Alex's gross estate? His taxable estate?

    b. What is the value of Brenda's gross estate? Her taxable estate?

4. George and Martha are married and have one child, Sam. George leaves Martha Farmacre valued at $3,500,000 on condition that she allow Sam to live on the property. What are the estate tax consequences?

C. QUALIFIED DOMESTIC TRUSTS
IRC §§2056(d), 2056A, 2523(i)

The marital deduction rules differ when the recipient spouse is not a citizen of the United States. First, the gift tax marital deduction is not available at all. §2523(i). Instead, the annual exclusion is increased to $100,000 (and adjusted for inflation) for transfers to such spouses. §2523(i)(2). Second, the §2040(b) rule for spousal joint tenancies does not apply. §2056(d)(1)(B). Third, the estate tax marital deduction is only available if the property is left to a qualified domestic trust (QDOT) as defined in §2056A.

A QDOT must have a trustee who is either a citizen of the United States or a domestic corporation. The trustee must have the right to withhold the estate tax imposed by §2056A(b) on any distribution, other than a distribution of income. Moreover, the trust must meet the requirements of §2056(b)(5), a power of appointment trust, §2056(b)(7), a QTIP trust, §2056(b)(8), a charitable remainder trust with the spouse as the only noncharitable beneficiary, or an estate trust as defined by Reg. §20.2056(c)-2(b)(1). Finally, the executor must make the appropriate election, and the trust must comply with all the requirements designed to ensure collection of the tax.

The rationale is that a noncitizen recipient spouse might not be a resident of the United States at death and therefore not subject to the federal estate tax. To prevent tax avoidance, §2056A imposes an estate tax on any lifetime transfer from the QDOT, other than a distribution of income, as well as on the value of the trust property remaining in the trust at the recipient spouse's death. §2056A(b)(1). The estate tax imposed by §2056A(b) is not a tax on the spouse's property. Rather, it is an estate tax on the original decedent's transfer of property that is simply deferred until the death of the recipient spouse or any lifetime distribution from the QDOT.

D. NONDEDUCTIBLE TERMINABLE INTERESTS
IRC §§2056(b), 2523(b)

Property left to a surviving spouse will qualify for the marital deduction only if the spouse's interest is not a "nondeductible terminable interest." Transfers of partial interests in property and transfers in trust must be carefully analyzed to determine if they violate this rule.

The first step is to understand what is, or is not, a terminable interest. A terminable interest is simply an interest in property that will terminate or fail on the lapse of time or the occurrence or nonoccurrence of an event or contingency. The classic terminable interest is a life estate because the life tenant's interest will terminate at his death. The second step is to determine whether or not the terminable interest is deductible. If the decedent transferred an additional interest in the property to someone other than the surviving spouse and that person will enjoy the property after the surviving spouse, the interest is nondeductible.

Example 16-6

Decedent leaves property in trust to pay the income to Spouse for life and the remainder to her Children. The gift to Spouse is a nondeductible terminable interest. Decedent transferred an interest to the surviving Spouse that will terminate at his death. Decedent also transferred an interest to her Children, who will enjoy the property after the spouse's death. No marital deduction is allowed for the transfer to the Spouse because it is a nondeductible terminable interest.

Example 16-7

Decedent leaves a patent to Spouse. The patent will expire in ten years. The property interest is a terminable interest because of the limited protection granted by statute, but Decedent has not transferred an interest in the patent to anyone other than Spouse. As a result, the value of the patent qualifies for the marital deduction.

There are, of course, exceptions to this rule. The primary exceptions are discussed in the next section. There are two other situations where terminable interests will qualify for the marital deduction. The first occurs when the third person pays the decedent adequate and full consideration in money or money's worth for his interest. The second occurs when the decedent creates a trust to pay the income to the surviving spouse for life and the remainder to the surviving spouse's estate. In both situations the decedent's estate will be entitled to the marital deduction. These exceptions are consistent with the policy underlying the marital deduction, *i.e.*, that spouses are considered one economic unit and their property should be taxed once and only once. As a result, if the property will be taxed, either when the decedent dies or when the spouse dies, the property should qualify for the marital deduction.

In the first situation, the children pay adequate and full consideration for their remainder interest. Because this payment is made directly to the decedent, it will be in her gross estate pursuant to §2033. There is, of course, debate as to what qualifies as adequate and full consideration. Is it simply the value of the remainder interest? Or is it the value of the entire property? In United States v. Allen, the court held that a decedent selling a life estate needed to receive the full value of the property, not just the value of the life estate, to meet the adequate and full consideration test of §2036(a)(1). 293 F.2d 916 (10th Cir. 1961), *cert. denied* 368 U.S. 944 (1961). In Estate of D'Ambrosio v. Commissioner, however, the court held that §2036(a)(1) required only that the decedent receive the value of the remainder interest, not the full value of the property, to avoid inclusion in the gross estate. 101 F.3d 309 (3d Cir. 1996), *cert. denied* 520 U.S. 1230 (1997.) (These cases are discussed at pages 308 and 310.) The appropriate amount should be the value that would have been in the decedent's estate had the decedent retained the property.

In the second situation, the property will pass from the decedent to the survivor's estate. Because the survivor can then transfer that property to anyone by his will, it will be included in his gross estate pursuant to §2033. The estate trust is very similar to a power of appointment trust, §2056(b)(5), where the surviving spouse is given a testamentary power of appointment. The primary difference is that the surviving spouse need not be given an income interest in an estate trust. If the decedent has nonincome producing assets or wants the trustee to have discretion to accumulate or distribute income to the surviving spouse, an estate trust would be the appropriate disposition.

The following case demonstrates the interplay of a statutory widow's allowance and the terminable interest rule.

Jackson v. United States
376 U.S. 503 (1964)

Mr. Justice WHITE delivered the opinion of the Court.

Since 1948 §2056(a) of the Internal Revenue Code of 1939 has allowed a "marital deduction" from a decedent's gross taxable estate for the value of interests in property passing from the decedent to his surviving spouse. Subsection (b) adds the qualification, however, that interests defined therein as "terminable" shall not qualify as an interest in property to which the marital deduction applies. The question raised by this case is whether the allowance provided by California law for the support of a widow during the settlement of her husband's estate is a terminable interest.

Petitioners are the widow-executrix and testamentary trustee under the will of George Richards who died a resident of California on May 27, 1951. Acting under the Probate Code of California, the state court, on June 30, 1952, allowed Mrs. Richards the sum of $3,000 per month from the corpus of the estate for her support and maintenance, beginning as of May 27, 1951, and continuing for a period of 24 months from that date. Under the terms of the order, an allowance of $42,000 had accrued during the 14 months since her husband's death. This amount, plus an additional $3,000 per month for the remainder of the two-year period, making a total of $72,000, was in fact paid to Mrs. Richards as [a] widow's allowance.

On the federal estate tax return filed on behalf of the estate, the full $72,000 was claimed as a marital deduction. . . . The deduction was disallowed, as was a claim for refund after payment of the deficiency, and the present suit for refund was then brought in the District Court. The District Court granted summary judgment for the United States, holding . . . that the allowance to the widow was a terminable interest and not deductible under the marital provision of the Internal Revenue Code. The Court of Appeals affirmed. . . . For the reasons given below, we affirm the decision of the Court of Appeals.

In enacting the Revenue Act of 1948, . . . with its provision for the marital deduction, Congress left undisturbed §812(b)(5) of the 1939 Code, which allowed an estate tax deduction, as an expense of administration, for amounts "reasonably required and actually expended for the support during the settlement of the estate of those dependent upon the decedent." . . . As the legislative history shows, support payments under §812(b)(5) were not to be treated as part of the marital deduction allowed by §812(e)(1). The Revenue Act of 1950, 64 Stat. 906, however, repealed §812(b)(5) because, among other reasons, Congress believed the section resulted in discriminations in favor of States having liberal family allowances. Thereafter allowances paid for the support of a widow during the settlement of an estate "heretofore deductible under section 812(b) will be allowable as a marital deduction subject to the conditions and limitations of section 812(e)." S.Rep. No. 2375, 81st Cong., 2d Sess., p. 130, U.S. Congressional Service, 1950, p. 3191.

The "conditions and limitations" of the marital deduction under [§2056] are several but we need concern ourselves with only one aspect of [§2056(b)(1)], which disallows the deduction of "terminable" interests passing to the surviving spouse. It was conceded in the Court of Appeals that the right to the widow's allowance here involved is an interest in property passing from the decedent within the meaning of [§2056(c)], that it is an interest to which the terminable interest rule of [§2056(b)(1)(B)] is applicable, and that the conditions set forth in (i) and (ii) of [§2056(b)(1)] were satisfied under the decedent's will and codicils thereto. The issue, therefore, is whether the interest in property passing to Mrs. Richards as widow's allowance would "terminate or fail" upon the "lapse of time, upon the occurrence of an event or contingency, or upon the failure of an event or contingency to occur."

We accept the Court of Appeals' description of the nature and characteristics of the widow's allowance under California law. In that State, the right to a widow's allowance is not a vested right and nothing accrues before the order granting it. The right to an allowance is lost when the one for whom it is asked has lost the status upon which the right depends. If a widow dies or remarries prior to securing an order for a widow's allowance, the right does not survive such death or remarriage. The amount of the widow's allowance which has accrued and is unpaid at the date of death of the widow is payable to her estate but the right to future payments abates upon her death. The remarriage of a widow subsequent to an order for an allowance likewise abates her right to future payments. 317 F.2d 821, 825.

In light of these characteristics of the California widow's allowance, Mrs. Richards did not have an indefeasible interest in property at the moment of her husband's death since either her death or remarriage would defeat it. If the order for support allowance had been entered on the day of her husband's death, her death or remarriage at any time within two years thereafter would terminate that portion of the interest allocable to the remainder of the two-year period. As of the date of Mr. Richards' death, therefore, the allowance was subject to failure or termination "upon the occurrence of an event or contingency." That the support order was entered in this case 14 months later does not, in our opinion, change the defeasible nature of the interest.

Petitioners ask us to judge the terminability of the widow's interest in property represented by her allowance as of the date of the Probate Court's order rather than as of the date of her husband's death. The court's order, they argue, unconditionally entitled the widow to $42,000 in accrued allowance of which she could not be deprived by either her death or remarriage. It is true that some courts have followed this path, but it is difficult to accept an approach which would allow a deduction of $42,000 on the facts of this case, a deduction of $72,000 if the order had been entered at the end of two years from Mr. Richards' death and none at all if the order had been entered immediately upon his death. Moreover, judging deductibility as of the date of the Probate Court's order ignores the Senate Committee's admonition that in considering terminability of an interest for purposes of a marital deduction "the situation is viewed as at the date of the decedent's death." S.Rep.No. 1013, Part 2, 80th Cong., 2d Sess., p. 10. We prefer the course followed by both the Court of Appeals for the Ninth Circuit in *Cunha's Estate, supra,* and by the Court of Appeals for the Eighth Circuit in United States v. Quivey, 292 F.2d 252. Both courts have held the date of death of the testator to be the correct point of time from which to judge the nature of a widow's allowance for the purpose of deciding terminability and deductibility under [§2056]. This is in accord with the rule uniformly followed with regard to interests other than the widow's allowance, that qualification for the marital deduction must be determined as of the time of death.

Our conclusion is confirmed by [§2056(b)(3)] which saves from the operation of the terminable interest rule interests which by their terms may (but do not in fact) terminate only upon failure of the widow to survive her husband for a period not in excess of six months. The premise of this provision is that an interest passing to a widow is normally to be judged as of the time of the testator's death rather than at a later time when the condition imposed may be satisfied; hence the necessity to provide an exception to the rule in the case of a six months' survivorship contingency in a will. A gift conditioned upon eight months' survivorship, rather than six, is a nondeductible terminable interest for reasons which also disqualify the statutory widow's allowance in California where the widow must survive and remain unmarried at least to the date of an allowance order to become indefeasibly entitled to any widow's allowance at all.

Petitioners contend, however, that the sole purpose of the terminable-interest provisions of the Code is to assure that interests deducted from the estate of the deceased spouse will not also escape taxation in the estate of the survivor. This argument leads to the conclusion that since it is now clear that unless consumed or given away during Mrs. Richards' life, the entire $72,000 will be taxed to her estate, it should not be included in her husband's. But as we have already seen, there is no provision in the Code for deducting all terminable interests which become nonterminable at a later date and therefore taxable in the estate of the surviving spouse if not consumed or transferred. The examples cited in the legislative history make it clear that the determinative factor is not taxability to the surviving spouse but terminability as defined by the statute. Under the view advanced by petitioners all cash allowances actually paid would fall outside [§2056(b)(1)]; on two different occasions the Senate has refused to give its approval to House-passed amendments to the 1954 Code which would have made the terminable-interest rule inapplicable to all widow's allowances actually paid within specified periods of time.

We are mindful that the general goal of the marital deduction provisions was to achieve uniformity of federal estate tax impact between those States with community property laws and those without them. But the device of the marital deduction which Congress chose to achieve uniformity was knowingly hedged with limitations, including the terminable-interest rule. These provisions may be imperfect devices to achieve the desired end, but they are the means which Congress chose. To the extent it was thought desirable to modify the rigors of the terminable-interest rule, exceptions to the rule were written into the Code. Courts should hesitate to provide still another exception by straying so far from the statutory language as to allow a marital deduction for the widow's allowance provided by the California statute. The achievement of the purposes of the marital deduction is dependent to a great degree upon the careful drafting of wills; we have no fear that our decision today will prevent either the full utilization of the marital deduction or the proper support of widows during the pendency of an estate proceeding.

Affirmed.

PROBLEMS

1. John and Nancy are married, and Nancy dies. Her will leaves all her property ($2,500,000) in trust, income to John for life, remainder to their children. (Assume the executor does not make the election under §2056(b)(7).)

   a. What are the estate tax consequences to Nancy?

   b. What are the estate tax consequences if John and the children (who are adults) agree that John will receive $1,500,000 outright, which is the actuarial value of his life estate, and that the children will receive the remainder?

   c. What are the estate tax consequences if the trust paid the income to John only until his remarriage? What if it paid the income to him only for ten years?

   d. What are the estate tax consequences if the trust had provided, income to Nancy's mother for life, remainder to John?

2. David and Sally are married, and David dies. David sold an apartment building and, as part of the sale proceeds, he receives 30 percent of the net rents for 15 years. David dies after ten years. At the time of death David also owns a portfolio of stocks and bonds, a house in joint tenancy with Sally, property in Maine as tenants in common with Carol and Evan, a patent that will expire in ten years, a condominium in Boston, and a life insurance policy payable to Sally. David's other heirs are Carol and Evan, who are David's children from a prior marriage.

   a. David's will leaves all his property outright to Sally. What are the estate tax consequences?

   b. Same as a., only David's will leaves the condominium in Boston to Sally and Carol as joint tenants with the right of survivorship. What are the estate tax consequences?

   c. The probate court allows Sally as surviving spouse an allowance of $1,500 per month until the estate is settled. What are the estate tax consequences?

3. Karen and Lance are married, and Karen dies. Karen and Lance own a house as joint tenants valued at $350,000. Karen purchased a joint and

survivor annuity with Lance that has a value at her death of $250,000. Karen created a revocable trust to pay the income to herself during her life, then the income to Lance during his life, and at his death, to distribute the trust property to Lance's estate. At her death, the trust property had a value of $800,000.

a.   What is the value of Karen's gross estate? What is the value of her taxable estate?

b.   What if the annuity included a provision that would pay Karen's daughter, Gail, the difference between the purchase price and the amount distributed to Karen and Lance if they both died before receiving payments totaling the purchase price?

c.   Assume that Karen had not purchased the annuity during life. Instead, she instructed her executor to purchase an annuity for Lance. The cost of the annuity was $250,000.

E.   EXCEPTIONS TO THE TERMINABLE INTEREST RULE
IRC §§2041, 2044, 2056(b), 2523(b)–(f)

1. *Survivorship Conditions: §2056(b)(3)*

To avoid the cost of two probate proceedings within a short time, the decedent may require that the spouse survive for a specified period of time. Such a clause also ensures that the property passes to the decedent's designated beneficiaries, rather than to the spouse's beneficiaries. These survivorship clauses should be distinguished from the provisions discussed above, which designated who survived in situations where the order of deaths could not be determined. The survivorship clauses at issue here are provisions that specifically require the beneficiary to survive by a stated number of hours or days. For example, the decedent might leave property to his surviving spouse only if she survives him by 30 days or six months or one year. State law might also impose a condition of survivorship. The Uniform Probate Code §2-702(a), for example, provides that an individual who does not survive the decedent by 120 hours is deemed to have predeceased the decedent.

This type of survivorship clause will not necessarily deprive the decedent's estate of the marital deduction. Section 2056(b)(3) provides that a bequest to a spouse conditioned upon survival will qualify for the marital deduction as long as (1) the survivorship condition is limited to a period not exceeding six months after the decedent's death or to death from a common disaster and (2) the spouse in fact survives. If the spouse does not, in fact, survive, the property passes to another and will not qualify for the marital deduction.

Example 16-8

H and W are married. W leaves all of her property to H but only if he survives her by 180 days. W dies on March 1. H dies on December 15 of the same year. H has survived W by more than 180 days. He will receive her property, and her estate will be entitled to the marital deduction.

Now assume that W dies on March 1 and that H dies on May 1. Because H did not survive for the period required by the will, he will not receive the property from W, and her estate will not be entitled to the marital deduction.

Why six months? The answer is simple. There has to be some limitation, and six months is just as good as five months or seven months. Additionally, and perhaps more importantly, the decedent's estate tax return must be filed within nine months of his death. §6075(a). At that time, the executor must be able to determine whether or not the decedent's estate is entitled to the marital deduction.

Survivorship clauses are usually drafted in terms of days rather than months. This avoids argument about how many days are in the month of the decedent's death and whether the spouse did in fact survive for the required time period. *See* Revenue Ruling 70-400, 1970-2 C.B. 196, which provides the survivorship period of §2056(b)(3) expires on the same day of the sixth month following decedent's death. Moreover, survivorship clauses should not refer to surviving specific events. It does not matter if the event actually occurs within the six-month period. The marital deduction will be denied if there was the possibility that the event could have occurred beyond that six-month period.

Example 16-9

H and W are married. H leaves his property outright to W "provided that if she dies before my will is probated, I leave all of my property to my son, A." H's will is probated within four months of his death. W survives and receives the property. H's estate will not be entitled to the marital deduction because it was possible, viewed at the moment of his death, that probate might not occur within the six months required by §2056(b)(3). Because it was not absolutely certain on the date of his death, his estate will not be able to claim the marital deduction. Reg. §20.2056(b)-3(d)(Ex. 4).

2.   *Life Estate with Power of Appointment: §2056(b)(5)*

Prior to 1981, the primary exception to the terminable interest rule was the power of appointment trust, which reflected the initial purpose of the marital deduction, *i.e.*, to provide equality between common law and community property jurisdictions. In community property jurisdictions, the non-propertied spouse shares in the income from the community property and has the right to dispose of one-half of the community property. Requiring the surviving spouse to receive all income annually and to have a power of appointment over the trust property provides equivalent treatment. The requirement that the surviving spouse have the power to appoint the trust property to herself or her estate also ensures that the property will be included in her gross estate by §2041.

Section 2056(b)(5) provides that the decedent's estate will be entitled to a marital deduction for property left to a surviving spouse in trust if the spouse is entitled to all of the income (or a specific portion of it) for life, the income is paid annually or at more frequent intervals, the spouse has the power to appoint the entire interest (or a specific portion of it) to herself or to her estate, and no person has the power to appoint to anyone other than the surviving spouse.

a. Right to Income

The first requirement is that the surviving spouse be entitled to the income for her life, payable annually or at more frequent intervals. The regulations require that the spouse be given "substantially that degree of beneficial enjoyment . . . which the principles of the law of trusts accord to a person who is . . . the beneficiary of a trust." Reg. §20.2056(b)-5(f)(1). This means, first and foremost, that the trustee cannot be given discretion to accumulate income; payments of income must be mandatory. It also means that the trust property must either produce income or be personal use property, such as a residence. If the trust property is unproductive, the trustee must have the ability to convert it to income-producing property. Reg. §20.2056(b)-5(f)(5), -5(f)(7).

The trustee may be given administrative powers to allocate receipts and expenditures between income and corpus without jeopardizing the marital deduction. The issue is whether the spouse will substantially enjoy the benefits of the property during her life. Consideration will be given to the terms of the trust, local law, and the nature of the trust assets. Reg. §20.2056(b)-5(f)(3), -5(f)(4). Revenue Ruling 69-56, 1969-1 C.B. 224, specifically provides that the following administrative powers will not disqualify the trust: to allocate interest income and expenses, rental income and expenses, real estate taxes; to treat ordinary cash dividends as income; to treat extraordinary cash dividends, stock dividends, and capital gains as principal; to charge fees and expenses to income or principal; or to maintain reasonable reserves for depreciation, depletion, or amortization. Any combination of administrative powers will be allowed as long as the surviving spouse is not deprived of beneficial enjoyment of the trust property, the remainder beneficiaries are not preferred over the surviving spouse, or the primary thrust of the administrative powers is to preserve trust property rather than make it productive.

Finally, all the trust income must be paid to the surviving spouse. Income is usually distributed on some periodic basis, such as monthly or quarterly. So what happens to the income that is earned between the time of the latest distribution and the date of the surviving spouse's death? This is commonly referred to as the "stub income," and the regulations provide that this income must either be paid to the surviving spouse's estate or be subject to a general testamentary power of appointment in the surviving spouse. Reg. §20.2056(b)-5(f)(8).

b. Power of Appointment

The surviving spouse must also have the power to appoint the trust property to herself or to her estate, alone and in all events. Reg. §20.2056(b)-5(g)(1). The spouse must be treated as the unqualified owner of the trust property, and there must be no substantial limitations on her right to appoint the property. Reg. §20.2056(b)-5(g)(2). This means that the surviving spouse cannot contract with the decedent only to exercise the power in favor of their children or someone else. On the other hand, it does not prevent the decedent from naming takers in default in case the surviving spouse does not exercise her power. *Id.*

The surviving spouse must have the ability to exercise her power without the consent of anyone else, including the trustee. She must also have the ability to exercise the power "in all events." This means that the power cannot be limited in terms of time, *e.g.*, only after the decedent's will is probated, or in terms of contingencies, *e.g.*, only in an emergency or to provide for illness or education. Reg. §20.2056(b)-5(g)(3). This does not mean, however, that the spouse must be able to exercise her power both during life and in her will. One or other power is sufficient. *Id.*

Example 16-10

H and W are married. W dies, leaving her property in trust with Friendly National Bank as Trustee to pay H all of the income from the trust every quarter. H has the right to demand trust corpus during his life at any time for any purpose. This trust will qualify for the marital deduction under §2056(b)(5) even though H is not able to appoint trust property in his will.

Same facts, except that H does not have the ability to obtain trust corpus during his life. Instead, the trust property is to be distributed as H designates in his will. Because H can appoint the property to his estate, the trust will qualify for the marital deduction under §2056(b)(5) even though H has no ability to obtain trust property during his life.

The surviving spouse may have additional powers as long as she has the power to appoint to herself or her estate. Reg. §20.2056(b)-5(g)(5).

Example 16-11

H and W are married. W dies, leaving her property in trust with Friendly National Bank as Trustee to pay H all of the income from the trust every quarter. H has the right to demand trust corpus during his life at any time for any purpose. He also has the power to appoint the trust corpus among W's children at his death. This trust will qualify for the marital deduction even though H's power to appoint in his will is limited to W's children because he also has the power to appoint to himself during life at any time for any reason. Reg. §20.2056(b)-5(g)(5).

Instead, H has the right to demand trust corpus during his life but only for his own support and maintenance. He also has the power to appoint the trust corpus by will to anyone. Because H can appoint the property to his estate, the trust will qualify for the marital deduction even though H's ability to obtain trust property during his life is limited by the ascertainable standard of support and maintenance. If H had only the power to demand trust corpus during his life for his own support and maintenance, the trust would not qualify for the marital deduction because he did not have the right to appoint trust property "in all events." Reg. §20.2056(b)-5(g)(1).

Someone other than the surviving spouse may also have a power to appoint the trust property as long as this power is not in opposition to that of the surviving spouse. Reg. §20.2056(b)-5(j). Thus, a trustee can be given the power to appoint trust corpus to the surviving spouse. This power can be limited or unlimited. By itself, this power in the trustee will be insufficient to qualify the trust for the marital deduction under §2056(b)(5). The surviving spouse must also have the power to appoint to herself or her estate. A power in the trustee to appoint to the surviving spouse can be very useful if the surviving spouse becomes incapacitated or otherwise unable to exercise her own power of appointment.

The power of the surviving spouse to appoint to herself or her estate is a general power of appointment and will bring the property into her gross estate at her death under §2041. Not every general power of appointment, however, qualifies for the marital deduction under §2056(b)(5). The definition of a general power of appointment in §2041 includes the power to appoint to one's creditors or the creditors of one's estate. These powers are sufficient to bring the property into the gross estate but they do not satisfy the requirements of §2056(b)(5). Likewise, a power in the surviving spouse to appoint to herself with the consent of the trustee is a general power of appointment under §2041, but it will not qualify for the marital deduction under §2056(b)(5).

c.   Specific Portion

Section 2056(b)(5) allows a marital deduction if the spouse's right to income or power of appointment is limited to a specific portion of the trust. This provision allows the decedent to create one trust, a portion of which will qualify for the marital deduction and a portion of which will not. A specific portion is limited to a fractional or percentage share of the trust. §2056(b)(10). This means that a provision giving the surviving spouse one-half of the income or 30 percent of the income will qualify as a specific portion. A provision giving the spouse $5,000 of income per month or $50,000 income per year will not qualify. Although the Supreme Court in Northeastern Pennsylvania National Bank and Trust Co. v. United States, 387, U.S. 213 (1967), held that one could determine actuarially that amount of trust property needed to generate a specific sum of money and that this satisfied the language of §2056(b)(5), Congress overturned this result when it added subsection (10) to §2056(b).

The surviving spouse's right to income or her power to appoint or both can be limited to a specific portion. The marital deduction will be allowed, however, only for the smaller portion. Reg. §20.2056(b)-5(b). Thus, if the surviving spouse is given the right to one-half the income from the trust and the power to appoint the entire trust corpus in her will, the marital deduction will be limited to one-half the value of the trust. Likewise, if the spouse is given the right to all of the income during her life, but has the power to appoint only 40 percent of the trust corpus during her life or at death, the marital deduction will be limited to 40 percent of the value of the trust property.

3. Life Insurance Settlement Options: §2056(b)(6)

Section 2056(b)(6) includes similar requirements for proceeds of a life insurance, endowment, or annuity contract if the proceeds are payable in installments or only interest is to be paid to surviving spouse. The installments or interest payments must be made annually or at more frequent intervals, commencing no later than 13 months after the decedent's death. In addition, the surviving spouse must have the power to appoint the proceeds to herself or her estate, alone and in all events, and no person can have the power to appoint to someone other than the surviving spouse. An insurance settlement option will still qualify for the marital deduction even though the surviving spouse must comply with certain formalities, such as furnishing proof of death. Reg. §20.2056(b)-6(d).

4. Qualified Terminable Interest Property: §2056(b)(7)

In 1981, Congress uncoupled the marital deduction from the concept of community property, lifted all restrictions on the amount of the deduction, and adopted a new exception to the terminable interest rule — qualified terminable interest property (QTIP). §2056(b)(7). The QTIP exception furthers the fundamental policy of treating a married couple as one economic unit. Any QTIP property given away during life by the surviving spouse will be subject to gift tax by §2519, and any QTIP property remaining at death will be included in the surviving spouse's gross estate under §2044. Section 2056(b)(7), however, extends far beyond this and allows a decedent to control the ultimate disposition of the property without depriving him of the benefits of the marital deduction, thus recognizing the issues arising in second (or subsequent) marriages or other non-nuclear family arrangements.

To qualify under §2056(b)(7), (1) the surviving spouse must be entitled to all of the income (or a specific portion of it) from the property payable annually or at more frequent intervals; (2) no person may have the power to appoint trust property to anyone other than the surviving spouse during that spouse's life; and (3) the executor must elect QTIP treatment. Thus, a decedent can now leave his property in trust to pay the income to his surviving spouse for her life and at her death to distribute trust property to his children and receive the benefit of the marital deduction without giving his spouse the ability to dispose of the trust property either during life or at death.

a. Right to Income

The income and specific portion requirements of §2056(b)(7) are the same as those of §2056(b)(5) with one exception: income earned by the trust between the last distribution date and the date of the surviving spouse's death, *i.e.*, the stub income, need not be distributed to the surviving spouse nor need it be subject to a power of appointment in the surviving spouse. Reg. §20.2056(b)-7(d)(4). The rationale for this distinction is that the undistributed stub income will be taxed in the survivor's gross estate by §2044. Reg. §20.2044-1(d)(2). Although this regulation appears to work to the advantage of taxpayers, some taxpayers have challenged it.

Estate of Shelfer v. Commissioner
86 F.3d 1045 (11th Cir. 1996)

KRAVITCH, Circuit Judge:

The Commissioner of the Internal Revenue Service ("Commissioner") appeals the Tax Court's decision in favor of the estate of Lucille Shelfer. The court held that Lucille's estate was not liable for a tax deficiency assessed on the value of a trust from which she had received income during her lifetime. The estate of Lucille Shelfer's husband, Elbert, previously had taken a marital deduction for these trust assets, claiming that the trust met the definition of a qualified terminable interest property trust ("QTIP") pursuant to 26 U.S.C. §2056(b)(7).

This case presents an issue of first impression for this circuit: whether a QTIP trust is established when, under the terms of the trust, the surviving spouse is neither entitled to, nor given the power of appointment over, the trust income accumulating between the date of the last distribution and her death, otherwise known as the "stub income." The Commissioner interprets the QTIP statutory provisions to allow such trusts to qualify for the marital deduction in the decedent's estate; accordingly, the value of the trust assets must be included in the surviving spouse's estate. We agree with the Commissioner and REVERSE the Tax Court.

I

Elbert Shelfer died on September 13, 1986 and was survived by his wife, Lucille. Elbert's will provided that his estate was to be divided into two shares, that were to be held in separate trusts. The income from each trust was to be paid to Lucille in quarterly installments during her lifetime. The first trust was a standard marital deduction trust consisting of one-third of the estate. It is not at issue in this case. The second trust, comprising the remaining two-thirds of the estate, terminated upon Lucille's death. The principal and all undistributed income was payable to Elbert's niece, Betty Ann Shelfer.

Elbert's will designated Quincy State Bank as the personal representative for his estate, and on June 16, 1987, the bank filed a tax return on behalf of the estate. The bank elected to claim a deduction for approximately half of the assets of the second trust under the QTIP trust provisions of 26 U.S.C. §2056(b)(7). The IRS examined the return, allowed the QTIP deduction, and issued Quincy Bank a closing letter on May 10, 1989. The statute of limitations for an assessment of deficiency with respect to Elbert's return expired on June 16, 1990.

On January 18, 1989, Lucille died; Quincy State Bank served as personal representative for her estate. The bank filed an estate tax return on October 18, 1989 and did not include the value of the assets in the trust, even though the assets previously had been deducted on her husband's estate tax return. The IRS audited the return and assessed a tax deficiency for the trust assets on the ground that the trust was a QTIP trust subject to taxation. Quincy State Bank commenced a proceeding in tax court on behalf of Lucille's estate, claiming that the trust did not meet the definition of a QTIP trust because Lucille did not control the stub income; therefore, the Bank argued, the estate was not liable for tax on the trust assets under 26 U.S.C. §2044. The Tax Court agreed. The Commissioner appeals this decision.

II

The proper construction of a statutory provision is a purely legal issue; thus, we apply a de novo standard of review to the Tax Court's decision. Kirchman v. Commissioner, 862 F.2d 1486, 1490 (11th Cir. 1989). As in any case involving the meaning of a statute, we begin our analysis with the language at issue. . . .

Lucille's estate contends, and the Tax Court held, that the phrase "all of the income" includes income that has accrued between the last distribution and the date of the spouse's death, or the stub income. They argue that "all" refers to every type of income. Stub income is a kind of income, and thus the surviving spouse must be entitled to stub income in order for the trust to qualify as a QTIP trust. They conclude that because Elbert's will did not grant Lucille control over the stub income, the QTIP election fails.

In contrast, the Commissioner and amicus argue that the statute is satisfied if the surviving spouse controls "all of the income" that has been distributed. They contend that the requirement that income be "payable annually or at more frequent intervals" limits "all of the income" to distributed income, namely those payments that have been made to the surviving spouse during her life. . . .

The estate replies that the phrase "payable annually or at more frequent intervals" is separated from the preceding clause by commas, and thus is a parenthetical clause. Because parenthetical clauses are non-restrictive, it contends that the clause is merely a description of the distribution process and does not in any way limit the preceding requirement that the spouse must be entitled to "all of the income."

Both parties insist that their reading of the statute is "plain." We do not agree. Although the use of commas around the clause "payable annually or at more frequent intervals" does indicate a parenthetical clause, we refuse to place inordinate weight on punctuation and ignore the remainder of the sentence. It is equally plausible that the next clause is designed to provide a context from which to define "all of the income." . . . Nothing in this statutory provision on its face allows us to choose between these interpretations. Accordingly, we must look to other sources for guidance.

The Commissioner contends that the second part of the statute, subclause (ii)(II), mandates her reading of the statute. This clause states that no one can have the power to appoint any of the property to someone other than the surviving spouse. This prohibition is modified by the language beneath this clause, known as the "flush language," which states that subclause II expressly does not apply to a power exercisable only at or after the death of the surviving spouse. . . . The flush language allows the decedent to appoint the trust property to another beneficiary after the death of the surviving spouse. The Commissioner argues that the language also refers to disposition of the stub income after the spouse's death.

Although the flush language limiting subclause (ii)(II) is consistent with the Commissioner's argument, it does not directly apply to the independent requirement in subclause (ii)(I) that the spouse be entitled to "all of the income," which remains ambiguous. Thus, the statutory language alone does not resolve the issue before this court. . . .

Accordingly, we must look beyond the "plain language" of the statute for guidance. When faced with a similarly ambiguous tax code provision, the Supreme Court thoroughly examined the history and purpose of the tax provision at issue, past practices, and the practical implications of its ruling. . . . We follow suit, beginning with the history and purpose of the marital deduction.

III

The marital deduction for estate taxes first appeared in §812(e) of the Internal Revenue Code of 1939, which was enacted by the Revenue Code of 1948. The marital deduction provisions served the dual purposes of equalizing the tax treatment between persons in common-law and community property states and "codify[ing] the long-standing notion that marital property belongs to the unitary estate of both spouses. . . ."

An essential goal of the marital deduction statutory scheme "from its very beginning, however, was that any property of the first spouse to die that passed untaxed to the surviving spouse should be taxed in the estate of the surviving spouse." Estate of Clayton v. Commissioner, 976 F.2d 1486, 1491 (5th. Cir. 1992). In accordance with this intent, the statute proscribed deductions for terminable property interests. Terminable property interests are those interests that will terminate upon the occurrence of an event, the failure of an event to take place, or after a certain time period. Because these interests could terminate prior to the death of the surviving spouse, they posed a risk that the assets would escape taxation in the spouse's estate tax return.

The original statute allowed three exceptions to the terminable property rule for interests that would not escape taxation in the spouse's estate. . . . To take advantage of these exceptions, however, the decedent had to relinquish all control over the marital property to the surviving spouse.

As divorce and remarriage rates rose, Congress became increasingly concerned with the difficult choice facing those in second marriages, who could either provide for their spouse to the possible detriment of the children of a prior marriage or risk under-endowing their spouse to provide directly for the children. In the Economic Recovery Act of 1981, Congress addressed this problem by creating the QTIP exception to the terminable property interest rule. . . . Thus, the purpose of the QTIP trust provisions was to liberalize the marital deduction to cover trust instruments that provide ongoing income support for the surviving spouse while retaining the corpus for the children or other beneficiaries.

In addition to creating the QTIP trust provisions, the 1981 Act also substantially changed the marital deduction by lifting the limitations on the amount of the deduction. The Senate Report for the 1981 Act states the reason for the change: "The committee believes that a husband and wife should be treated as one economic unit for purposes of estate and gift taxes, as they generally are for income tax purposes. Accordingly, no tax should be imposed on transfers between a husband and wife." S.Rep. No. 144, 97th Cong., 1st Sess. 127 (1981), reprinted in 1981 U.S.C.C.A.N. 105, 228.

Although the legislative history of the 1981 Act sets forth Congress's reasons for enacting the statute, it does not directly address the stub income issue. . . . Accordingly, we must decide which interpretation of the statute best comports with the two general goals discussed above: expanding the marital deduction to provide for the spouse while granting the decedent more control over the ultimate disposition of the property, and treating a husband and wife as one economic entity for the purposes of estate taxation.

Under the Commissioner's interpretation of the statute, the decedent would gain the tax benefit, retain control of the trust corpus, and provide the spouse with all of the periodic payments for her personal support. The stub income, which accrues after her death and is thus not used for her maintenance, could be appointed to someone else. This result is consistent with the statutory goals of expanding the deduction while providing for the spouse's support. In contrast, the Tax Court's reading of the statute would condition the tax benefit for the entire trust corpus on ceding control over a much smaller amount that is not needed for the spouse's support.

The statute's second goal, treating a married couple as one economic entity, was effected in a comprehensive statutory scheme. In addition to the QTIP provisions of §2056(b)(7), Congress added §2044, which requires the estate of the surviving spouse to include all property for which a marital deduction was previously allowed, and §2056(b)(7)(B)(v), which states that a QTIP "election, once made, shall be irrevocable." Taken together, these sections of the code provide that assets can pass between spouses without being subject to taxation. Upon the death of the surviving spouse, the spouse's estate will be required to pay tax on all of the previously deducted marital assets. The Commissioner's position comports with the statutory scheme because it compels the surviving spouse to abide by the irrevocable election of a QTIP trust and to pay taxes on property that had previously been subject to a deduction. . . .

[E]ven if we accept the Tax Court's construction of the Senate report for §2056(b)(5), we do not reach the same conclusion with respect to §2056(b)(7). Although this court presumes that the same words in different parts of the statute have the same meaning, such a presumption is rebuttable. Doctors Hosp., Inc. of Plantation v. Bowen, 811 F.2d 1448, 1452-53 (11th Cir. 1987). In the instant case, the Commissioner has presented sufficient evidence to overcome the presumption.

First, the two sections were enacted in entirely different statutes, separated by a significant time period. The Senate report for the power of appointment trusts in §2056(b)(5) was written over thirty years prior to the 1981 enactment of the QTIP provisions at issue here. Thus, we give more weight to the objectives stated in the more recent legislative history of the QTIP provisions. . . .

Second, the QTIP provisions were a substantial break with the past. The whole purpose of §2056(b)(7) was to eliminate the requirement that the surviving spouse retain control of all of the property, as was previously required under §2056(b)(5). In furtherance of this goal, Congress added flush language to the QTIP statute providing that the power to appoint property to someone other than the surviving spouse is exercisable after the spouse's death.

Importantly, the Tax Court did not rely solely on the similar wording of the two statutes in reaching its conclusion. The court held that although the Shelfer trust did not qualify for a marital deduction, a trust could qualify for the deduction if the surviving spouse had a power of appointment over the stub income. . . . Neither of the statutes, however, specifically equates "entitled to all of the income" with "the power of appointment." The Senate Report cited above also does not mention "power of appointment." Thus, the Tax Court had to go beyond the statutory language and the legislative history to find a realistic meaning for the critical statutory terms.

The Tax Court relied primarily upon the regulations accompanying §2056(b)(5) for its determination that the spouse's power of appointment over the stub income would satisfy the statute. Estate Tax Regulations §20.2056(b)-5(f). These regulations are particularly pertinent because they are referenced in the legislative history of the QTIP provisions of §2056(b)(7). . . . The Tax Court quoted from subsection 5(f)(8) of the regulations:

> [A]s respects the income for the period between the last distribution date and the date of the spouse's death, it is sufficient if that income is subject to the spouse's power to appoint. Thus, if the trust instrument provides that income accrued or undistributed on the date of the spouse's death is to be disposed of as if it had been received after her death, and if the spouse has a power of appointment over the trust corpus, the power necessarily extends to the undistributed income.

The court read this regulation as requiring that the stub income "must be disposed of as the spouse directs." *Howard*, 91 T.C. at 333.

We disagree. The regulations must be interpreted in light of the statutory provisions of §2056(b)(5), for which it was written. As previously discussed, §2056(b)(5) creates an exception to the terminable property rule for property over which the surviving spouse has a power of appointment. The property is subject to taxation upon the spouse's death because the tax code requires an estate to pay taxes on all property over which the decedent had the power of appointment. To complete the statutory scheme and to ensure taxation, the regulations require that the stub income be subject to the spouse's power of appointment or treated as part of the corpus over which the spouse had [the] power of appointment.

Following the logic of the regulations, the person with the power to appoint the property in the trust corpus should be permitted to have the power to appoint the stub income; the stub income will then be subject to taxation along with the corpus property. Under the QTIP provisions, that person is the decedent. The trust corpus and the stub income would be taxable pursuant to §2044, which requires the spouse to include all previously deducted property in which she has a qualifying interest for life. This comprehensive scheme, like that of the power of appointment trust, allows an initial deduction and later taxation of the property. . . .

IV

Our construction of the statute has several practical advantages over the Tax Court's position. First, it would assure certainty in estate planning. . . . The status of trust instruments that were set up in accordance with the Commissioner's advice will not be in question and the validity of the Commissioner's final regulation on this matter will be affirmed.

Second, our result comports with standard trust practices. Under the Tax Court's approach, a trust fund that made daily payments to the surviving spouse would qualify for the deduction because there would be no undistributed income; in contrast, one that made quarterly payments would be ineligible. . . . Our reading of the statute gives meaning to the statutory terms requiring annual or more frequent distribution, not daily disbursements. . . .

Finally, a broad reading of the marital deduction provisions benefits the federal Treasury and furthers Congressional intent to ensure taxation of all previously deducted property. In the instant case, for example, the corpus of $2,829,610 would be subject to taxation, for a gain of over $1,000,000 in tax deficiencies. The Tax Court's opinion would grant similar estates a substantial windfall, encouraging other executors of wills to disclaim the previously taken deduction.

For all of these reasons, we conclude that our interpretation of the statute will better serve the practical realities of trust administration and estate taxation. . . . Accordingly, we REVERSE the Tax Court.

This decision is consistent with that of the Ninth Circuit Court of Appeals in Estate of Howard v. Commissioner, 910 F.2d 633 (9th Cir. 1990), and was followed by the Court of Federal Claims in Talman v. United States, 37 Fed. Cl. 741, 97-1 U.S.T.C. ¶60,270 at 88,393 (1997). Now that the regulations specifically provide that stub income need not be distributed to the surviving spouse's estate, Reg. §20.2056(b)-7(d)(4), and that the stub income will be included in the spouse's gross estate, Reg. §20.2044-1(d)(2), it is less likely that taxpayers will claim that failure to distribute the stub income to the surviving spouse prevents taxation under §2044.

Because the stakes can be significant, the validity of these regulations may be challenged. In *Shelfer* and in *Talman* the will of the first spouse to die created what appeared to be a QTIP trust. The executor claimed the marital deduction. These estates were then closed, and the statute of limitations on the federal estate tax had run before the issue of taxation in the survivors' estates was litigated. If the estates of the surviving spouses had prevailed in *Shelfer* and in *Talman*, then the trust property would have escaped taxation altogether. As Estate of Letts v. Commissioner, *infra*, demonstrates, the surviving spouse's estate might be required to include the value of the trust property in her gross estate even if it did not satisfy all the requirements of §2044.

b. No Power to Appoint to Other than the Surviving Spouse

To qualify for §2056(b)(7), no person can have the power to appoint any part of the QTIP property to anyone other than the surviving spouse during her life. §2056(b)(7)(ii)(II). Of course, the trustee, the spouse, or anyone else can have the power to appoint to the surviving spouse during her life. Reg. §20.2056(b)-7(d)(6). How the surviving spouse subsequently disposes of the property is irrelevant unless the surviving spouse is legally obligated to transfer it to another gratuitously. *Id.* If the decedent wants to provide access to trust property to the surviving spouse, it is generally advisable to give that power to the trustee who is not the surviving spouse. If the surviving spouse has the ability to withdraw trust property for her own benefit, she will have a general power of appointment. This power may convert the trust from a QTIP trust to a power of appointment trust. As a result, the decedent will lose not only benefit of controlling the ultimate disposition of the trust property, but also the ability to make the reverse QTIP election to qualify the trust for the generation-skipping transfer tax exemption. *See* Chapter 18, section D.

The trustee, the surviving spouse, or anyone else can have the power to appoint the trust property at, or after, the surviving spouse's death.

Example 16-12

Decedent's will leaves $3,000,000 in trust with Friendly National Bank as Trustee, to pay the income quarterly to Spouse. At Spouse's death, the Trustee is to distribute the trust property to those of Decedent's children as Spouse appoints in his will and, in default of appointment, to Decedent's children equally. If the executor elects, the trust will qualify under §2056(b)(7) even though Spouse has a limited power to appoint among Decedent's children because that power does not arise until Spouse's death, and thus he cannot avoid inclusion of the trust property in his gross estate under §2044.

Example 16-13

Decedent's will leaves $3,000,000 in trust with Friendly National Bank as Trustee, to pay the income quarterly to Spouse. After Spouse's death, the Trustee is to distribute income to Decedent's children equally and has discretion to distribute trust property to Decedent's children for their health, education, support, or in an emergency. If the executor elects, the trust will qualify under §2056(b)(7) because the Trustee's power does not arise until after Spouse's death and the trust property will be in Spouse's gross estate under §2044.

Although no one can appoint trust property to anyone other than the surviving spouse during her lifetime, the surviving spouse can give away or sell her income interest. If she does so, §2519 treats the transaction as a transfer of the underlying trust assets minus her income interest.

Example 16-14

Decedent's will leaves $1,000,000 in trust with Friendly National Bank as Trustee, to pay the income quarterly to Spouse, and at her death, to distribute the trust property to Decedent's children equally. When Spouse's income interest has a value of $400,000, she gives that interest to her Daughter. Section 2519 treats this as a gift of $600,000, the value of the trust property minus the value of Spouse's income interest. Section 2511 treats the transfer of the $400,000 income interest as a gift. As a result, S has made gifts totaling $1,000,000. Reg. §25.2519-1(g)(Ex. 1, Ex. 3).

If Spouse sold her income interest to Daughter for its actuarial value of $400,000, she would still have made a gift of $600,000, the value of the remainder interest. Reg. §25.2519-1(g)(Ex. 2).

Section 2519 thus prevents the surviving spouse from avoiding §2044 through a lifetime transfer.

c. Election

To qualify for §2056(b)(7), the executor must make the appropriate election on the decedent's estate tax return. Although the statute states clearly that the executor must make an affirmative election to qualify trust property as QTIP, many executors fail to do so. As a result, the IRS now presumes that an executor is making the QTIP election if the estate tax is calculated as if the marital deduction is in fact claimed or unless the executor affirmatively indicates that he or she is not making the QTIP election. While this presumption may be necessary to accord with the realities of estate tax returns, it is contrary to the statute and leaves the door open for executors to later challenge the designation of the trust property as QTIP and its inclusion in the survivor's gross estate under §2044.

Estate of Letts v. Commissioner
109 T.C. 290 (1997)

COLVIN, Judge:

Respondent determined that petitioner is liable for a $461,601 deficiency in Federal estate tax. The issue for decision is whether, because of the duty of consistency, decedent's estate includes the value of property that decedent's husband left to her. We hold that it does. . . .

Decedent was Mildred Geraldine Letts. Her husband was James P. Letts, Jr. . . . James P. Letts, Jr., signed his will in 1983 and amended it by codicil in 1984. . . . In Item II of his will, he devised the residue of his estate, after payment of funeral expenses, debts, and expenses of administration, to decedent and their two children in trust (Item II trust). . . . The Item II trust authorized decedent to receive all of the income from the trust for life at least quarterly, authorized decedent to withdraw up to $40,000 per year, and authorized the trustees to distribute the corpus to decedent for her comfort, maintenance, and support. The corpus of the Item II trust consisted of terminable interest property in which decedent had an income interest for life. The Item II trust authorized the executors of the Estate of James Letts, Jr., to elect to treat the trust as "qualified terminable interest property" (QTIP) for purposes of the Federal estate tax marital deduction. . . . Item III of the will of James Letts, Jr., created a trust (Item III trust) for the benefit of decedent and the living descendants of James Letts, Jr. When decedent died, the undistributed income from the Item II trust was to be paid to decedent's estate and the corpus was to be paid to the Item III trust. . . .

The Estate of James Letts, Jr., claimed a $1,317,969 marital deduction. Of that amount, $317,705 was attributable to assets passing to decedent as joint tenant with the right of survivorship. The remaining $1,000,264 was for the Item II trust, which was described on Schedule M as a "qualified marital trust." The Estate of James Letts, Jr., did not state on its return whether or not the Item II trust property was terminable interest property. The Estate of James Letts, Jr., passed $1,317,969 to decedent and paid no estate taxes.

On page 2 of the return filed by the Estate of James Letts, Jr., under "Elections by the Executor," the following question appears on line 4: "Do you elect to claim a marital deduction for qualified terminable interest property (QTIP) under section 2056(b)(7)?" The executor of the Estate of James Letts, Jr., placed an "x" in the box for "No." The instructions for line 4 say that if the gross estate exceeds $500,000, the property for which the election is being made must be listed on Schedule M and clearly marked as "qualified terminable interest property." The executor listed no property on Schedule M as QTIP. . . .

James P. Letts III signed the Federal estate tax return for the Estate of James Letts, Jr. It was filed on September 8, 1986. Respondent did not examine or make any adjustments to that return. The time to assess tax against the Estate of James Letts, Jr., expired on September 8, 1989, before decedent died. . . . Decedent died on April 20, 1991, in Atlanta, Georgia, and was survived by her son, James P. Letts III, and her daughter, JoAnne L. Magbee. The Item II trust had not been funded before decedent died. . . . Decedent's Federal estate tax return noted that the executors of James Letts, Jr.'s estate had not elected QTIP treatment for the Item II trust. Decedent's estate did not include the value of the Item II trust in decedent's gross estate. Petitioner attached the following statement to its estate tax return:

> Item Two of the Will of James P. Letts, Jr., the late husband of Mildred G. Letts, created a trust for her benefit. Pursuant to the terms of that trust, Mildred G. Letts was to receive all of the income from the trust for life. She also was given the power to withdraw up to $40,000 from the trust each year (see Schedule H), but had no other general power of appointment. On the Form 706 filed on behalf of the estate of James P. Letts, Jr., a copy of which is attached hereto, the executor did not elect to treat the Item Two trust as qualified terminable interest property. Consequently, the assets held in the item two trust are not includible in the gross estate of Mildred G. Letts under section 2044.

. . . Respondent determined that the value of the Item II trust is includable in decedent's gross estate. Petitioner concedes that $40,000 of the trust property is includable in decedent's gross estate because it was subject to decedent's power of withdrawal or appointment at her death.

Petitioner points out, and respondent does not dispute, that assessment of tax against the Estate of James Letts, Jr., is barred by the statute of limitations. Petitioner also points out that section 2044 does not include in the gross estate of a surviving spouse the value of property for which no QTIP election was made. Thus, petitioner contends that the value of the Item II trust is not includable in decedent's gross estate.

Respondent contends that petitioner must include the value of the Item II trust in decedent's gross estate under the duty of consistency. For reasons discussed next, we agree with respondent.

A tax is imposed on the transfer of the taxable estate of every decedent who is a citizen or resident of the United States. Sec.2001(a). In computing the value of the taxable estate, an estate may deduct the value of certain interests which pass from the decedent to the decedent's spouse (marital deduction). Sec.2056(a). . . . It is a basic policy of the marital deduction that property that passes untaxed from a predeceasing spouse to a surviving spouse is included in the estate of the surviving spouse. Estate of Shelfer v. Commissioner, 86 F.3d 1045, 1048 (11th Cir. 1996), *revg.* 103 T.C. 10 (1994); Estate of Cavenaugh v. Commissioner, 100 T.C. 407, 416 (1993), *affd. in part and revd. in part on other grounds* 51 F.3d 597 (5th Cir. 1995).

The marital deduction provides special rules for gifts of terminable interest property (e.g., life interests). Sec.2056(b). A terminable interest is an interest passing to a surviving spouse that will end on the lapse of time, on the occurrence of an event or contingency, or on the failure of an event or contingency to occur. Sec.2056(b)(1). The marital deduction is not available for terminable interest property given to the surviving spouse unless the estate of the predeceasing spouse elects to treat the property as QTIP. Sec.2056(b)(1), (7). The estate of the predeceasing spouse is denied a marital deduction for terminable interest property if that estate does not make the QTIP election. These rules permit the predeceasing spouse's estate to choose QTIP treatment and thus defer taxation of a terminable interest, at the price of having it included in the gross estate of the surviving spouse under section 2044.

The duty of consistency prevents a taxpayer from benefitting in a later year from an error or omission in an earlier year which cannot be corrected because the time to assess tax for the earlier year has expired. Herrington v. Commissioner, 854 F.2d 755, 757 (5th Cir. 1988), *affg.* Glass v. Commissioner, 87 T.C. 1087 (1986); Southern Pac. Transp. Co. v. Commissioner, 75 T.C. 497, 838-839 (1980). The duty of consistency prevents a taxpayer who has benefitted from a past representation from adopting a position inconsistent with that taken in a year barred by the statute of limitations; the doctrine thus prevents a taxpayer from claiming that he or she should have paid more tax before and so avoiding the present tax. Eagan v. United States, 80 F.3d 13, 16 (1st Cir. 1996); Lewis v. Commissioner, 18 F.3d 20, 26 (1st Cir. 1994). . . . Courts have applied the duty of consistency to prevent taxpayers from permanently excluding income that is taxable in some year, *e.g.*, Grayson v. United States, 437 F. Supp. 58, 60 (N.D.Ala. 1977), or from deducting the same expense in 2 or more taxable years, *e.g.*, Robinson v. Commissioner, 181 F.2d 17, 18 (5th Cir. 1950), *affg.* 12 T.C. 246 (1949). The roots of the taxpayer's duty of consistency are found in R.H. Stearns Co. v. United States, 291 U.S. 54 (1934), in which the

Supreme Court applied the duty based on the principle that no one may base a claim on an inequity of his or her own making. *Id.* at 61-62. . . .

The taxpayer's duty of consistency applies if:

(a) The taxpayer made a representation of fact or reported an item for tax purposes in one tax year;

(b) the Commissioner acquiesced in or relied on that fact for that year; and

(c) the taxpayer desires to change the representation previously made in a later tax year after the earlier year has been closed by the statute of limitations.

. . . When these requirements are met, the Commissioner may act as if the previous representation is true, even if it is not, and the taxpayer may not assert the contrary. . . .

The three elements of the duty of consistency refer to conflicting representations that are made by a taxpayer. However, as discussed next, the duty of consistency can also be applied to bind one person to a representation made by another where the two are deemed to be in privity. We will first decide whether the duty of consistency applies between the Estates of James Letts, Jr., and of decedent; we will then decide whether the three elements of the duty of consistency are present in this case. . . .

The duty of consistency can bind a beneficiary of an estate to a representation made on an estate tax return if the beneficiary was a fiduciary of the estate . . . husband and wife can have interests so closely aligned that one may be estopped under the duty of consistency by a prior representation of the other. . . . The same can be true of the estates of a husband and a wife. Whether there is sufficient identity of interests between the parties to apply the duty of consistency depends on the facts and circumstances of each case. . . .

There is a sufficient identity of interests between the Estates of James Letts, Jr., and of decedent to trigger the duty of consistency. Decedent and James Letts, Jr., were married. Their estates were a single economic unit. Decedent's husband left his estate to decedent, James P. Letts III, and JoAnne Magbee; and decedent left her estate to James P. Letts III and JoAnne Magbee. Decedent was an executrix of her husband's estate. James P. Letts III signed both estate tax returns. JoAnne Magbee is also a coexecutor of, and signed the estate tax return for, decedent's estate. . . . We conclude that decedent's estate and the Estate of James Letts, Jr., are sufficiently related to be treated as one taxpayer for purposes of the duty of consistency.

We next decide whether respondent has shown that the three elements of the duty of consistency are present here.

The Estate of James Letts, Jr., included the value of the Item II trust in the marital deduction. That estate was entitled to claim the marital deduction for the property only (1) if it was not terminable interest property, or (2) if it was terminable interest property for which a QTIP election was made.

The Estate of James Letts, Jr., clearly indicated that the property was not QTIP. James P. Letts III, as executor for the Estate of James Letts, Jr., answered

"No" to the question on line 4 of the return, "Do you elect to claim a marital deduction for qualified terminable interest property (QTIP) under section 2056(b)(7)?" Consistent with that answer, he did not separately list any terminable interest property in Schedule M. Thus, the estate eliminated one of the two grounds stated above for deducting the value of the Item II trust property as a marital deduction. The only other ground for including the value of the Item II trust property in the marital deduction would be if the Item II trust property was not terminable interest property. Thus, the Estate of James Letts, Jr., represented that the Item II trust property was not terminable interest property.

For purposes of the duty of consistency, a taxpayer's treatment of an item on a return can be a representation that facts exist which are consistent with how the taxpayer reports the item on the return. . . . We conclude that the first element for the duty of consistency is satisfied.

The Commissioner acquiesces in or relies on a fact if a taxpayer files a return that contains an inadequately disclosed item of which the Commissioner was not otherwise aware, the Commissioner accepts that return, and the time to assess tax expires without an audit of that return. . . . The Estate of James Letts, Jr., did not provide any facts to respondent that would show that the Item II trust property was terminable interest property. For example, the estate tax return of the Estate of James Letts, Jr., did not include a copy of his will. The Commissioner may rely on a presumption of correctness of a return or report that is given to the Commissioner under penalties of perjury. . . . The time to assess tax against the Estate of James Letts, Jr., expired. Thus, the second element has been satisfied. . . .

Petitioner represented on its estate tax return that the Item II trust property was terminable interest property. That representation is inconsistent with the representation made on the return of the Estate of James Letts, Jr., that the Item II trust property was not terminable interest property. Decedent died after the time to assess tax against the Estate of James Letts, Jr., had passed. Thus, the third element for the duty of consistency is satisfied.

Petitioner points out that both it and the Estate of James Letts, Jr., represented that the Estate of James Letts, Jr., did not elect to treat the Item II trust property as QTIP. However, the fact that both estates made a consistent representation about the QTIP election does not erase the fact that the estates made inconsistent representations about whether the Item II trust property was terminable interest property.

We conclude that all three elements for the duty of consistency are satisfied.

Revenue Procedure 2001-38, 2001-1 C.B. 1335, provides relief for some estates that erroneously elect QTIP treatment. With the increase in the unified credit exemption amount, fewer estates need to shelter property from the estate tax using the marital deduction. Revenue Procedure 2001-38 allows the surviving spouse to establish that a QTIP election was erroneous "where the election was not necessary to reduce the estate tax liability to zero." It does not apply (1) to a partial QTIP election where the executor elected QTIP treatment for more property than was necessary to reduce estate tax liability to zero, (2) to elections stated in terms of a formula designed to reduce estate tax liability to zero, and (3) to protective QTIP elections. Revenue Procedure 2001-38 would not have provided relief for Mildred Letts, because her husband's estate was greater than the applicable unified credit exemption amount.

Initially, the IRS argued that the ability of the executor to elect QTIP treatment for only a portion of the trust prevented the trust from qualifying for the marital deduction under §2056(b)(7), because the executor's ability to elect was tantamount to a power of appointment for the benefit of persons other than the surviving spouse. Although the Tax Court agreed with this analysis, Estate of Clayton v. Commissioner, 97 T.C. 327 (1991), the Fifth Circuit Court of Appeals reversed, 976 F.2d 1486 (5th Cir. 1992). Other circuits followed the Fifth Circuit. Estate of Robertson v. Commissioner, 15 F.3d 779 (8th Cir. 1994); Estate of Spencer v. Commissioner, 43 F.3d 226 (6th Cir. 1995). The Tax Court finally conceded defeat in Estate of Clack v. Commissioner, but noted that these cases had been decided prior to the effective date of the regulation that stated the IRS position. 106 T.C. 131 (1996), *acq.* 1996-2 C.B. 1. Rather than continue to litigate this issue, the Treasury revised the regulation to provide that the ability to elect QTIP treatment is not considered to be a prohibited power of appointment. Reg. §20.2056(b)-7(d)(3), -7(h)(Ex. 6).

PROBLEMS

1. Alice and Bruce are married, and Alice dies. The residuary clause of her will provides: "all the rest and residue of my property I leave to my spouse, Bruce, if he survives me by ninety days; if he does not survive me, I leave this property to my children equally, share and share alike."
   a. What are the estate tax consequences if Bruce survives Alice by five years?
   b. What are the estate tax consequences if he dies 30 days after her?
   c. Instead, what if the residuary clause required Bruce to survive by nine months and he did, in fact, survive?

2. Oliver and Carol are married, and Carol dies. One asset of Carol's estate was a $1,000,000 life insurance policy naming Oliver as beneficiary. Carol had provided that the insurance company was only to pay Oliver the interest on this policy during his life. Will this property interest qualify for the marital deduction? Why?

3. Donna and Simon are married, and Donna dies. Donna leaves her estate to Friendly National Bank as Trustee, income to Simon for life, remainder to such persons as Simon shall appoint by will; in default of appointment by Simon, remainder to Donna's children in equal shares. Analyze this trust under §2056(b)(5).

    a. Does this trust qualify if Friendly National Bank must distribute income quarterly to Simon?

    b. What if Friendly National Bank is to distribute "all the income" to Simon, but the trust does not specify how often?

    c. What if Friendly National Bank has complete discretion to accumulate or expend income for Simon?

    d. What if Simon has the right, exercisable annually, to demand distribution of all income earned that year with any income that he does not demand being added to the trust principal?

    e. What if Friendly National Bank has discretion to distribute income for Simon's welfare, comfort, and happiness?

    f. Assume no discretion to accumulate. What if Simon has only the right to one-half the income? To 25 percent?

    g. What if Simon has the right to $2,000 per month of the income until the children are 25; then he has the right to $1,000 per month of the income until his death?

4. Hugh and Wendy are married, and Hugh dies. Hugh leaves his property to Friendly National Bank, income to Wendy for life, remainder to their children in equal shares. Analyze this trust first under §2056(b)(5) and then under §2056(b)(7).

    a. Does this trust qualify for the marital deduction? Why?

    b. What if Wendy has the power to appoint the corpus in her will among Hugh's children?

    c. What if Wendy has the power to appoint the corpus during her life or in her will, but only to Hugh's children and her creditors?

    d. What if Wendy has the power to appoint the corpus to herself during her life?

    e. What if Wendy is the Trustee and has the power to invade the corpus for any purpose?

    f. What if the power in e. is limited by an ascertainable standard of Wendy's health, education, or welfare?

    g. The Trustee who is not Wendy has the power to invade corpus for the benefit of Wendy.

    h. The Trustee who is not Wendy has the power to invade corpus for the health, education, or welfare of Wendy.

5. Tom and Ellen are married. Tom dies and leaves his residuary estate of $5,000,000 to Friendly National Bank as Trustee to pay the income to Ellen for life, and the remainder to his surviving children. Tom names Friendly National Bank as executor and gives the bank discretion to elect QTIP treatment with respect to some or all of the residue. Property for which Friendly National Bank does not elect QTIP treatment passes into a separate trust.

    a. Does this qualify for the marital deduction under §2056(b)(7)?

    b. What if the income earned after the last distribution to Ellen and before her death passes to Tom's children?

      c. Assume that Friendly National Bank does not specifically elect QTIP treatment on Tom's estate tax return, but it does calculate the estate tax on the basis that $4,000,000 of Tom's estate qualified for the marital deduction. Ellen dies five years later, and Friendly National Bank is the executor of her will. Friendly National Bank claims that the $4,000,000 trust is not includible in Ellen's gross estate under §2044 because it was not QTIP property. Will Friendly National Bank prevail? Why?

    6. Compare §2056(b)(5) with §2056(b)(7). What are the advantages and disadvantages of each subsection? Under what circumstances should a decedent use §2056(b)(5) and under what circumstances should she use §2056(b)(7)?

F. PLANNING

1. *The Annual Exclusion and the Unified Credit*
    IRC §§2010, 2503(b), 2505, 2513

Married couples seeking to diminish or eliminate transfer taxes utilize a combination of the gift tax annual exclusion, the unified credit, and the marital deduction to accomplish their goal. The gift tax annual exclusion allows each person to transfer $11,000 per year per donee without paying any gift tax, and thus, a married couple can transfer $22,000 per year to each of their children. If one person (A) owns all, or most, of the property, the spouse (B) cannot take full advantage of this estate planning technique. There are two possible solutions to this dilemma. First, A can transfer property to B, who can then make gifts that qualify for the annual exclusion. This will work in most situations. There may, however, be significant transaction costs to the transfer, for example, when the property is real estate. Moreover, A cannot require that B give the property to others. If A does so, A will be treated as making the gift, not B. *See, e.g.,* Heyen v. United States, 731 F. Supp. 1488 (D. Kan. 1990), *aff'd,* 945 F.2d 359 (10th Cir. 1991).

Second, A can transfer $22,000 to each child if B consents to split the gift under §2513. This section does not increase the amount of the tax-free transfers that the couple can make because the spouse cannot make additional gifts to the same recipient that qualify for the annual exclusion. Section 2513 is discussed in Chapter 7, section B.

Example 16-15

H and W are married. W has two children, E and F, from a prior marriage. W has significant wealth and wants to take full advantage of the gift tax annual exclusion to diminish her estate. If she transfers $22,000 each year to H, who then transfers $11,000 each year to A and $11,000 each year to B, there is a significant possibility that the IRS will challenge this arrangement as indirect gifts from W to A and B. Instead, if H agrees, W can transfer $22,000 each year to A and $22,000 each year to B. As long as H and W file a gift tax return and both consent, these gifts will be considered as made one-half by H and one-half by W and will be entirely tax-free. Of course, H and W must agree to split all gifts they make in that year, not just the gifts to E and F.

A second component of a married couple's estate plan is to fully utilize the unified credit in the estates of both spouses. Failure to do so can have significant estate tax consequences and would be considered malpractice.

Example 16-16

H and W are married. H owns $3,000,000 of property and W owns nothing. H dies in 2004 and leaves all of his property outright to W. H's estate will pay no tax because the $3,000,000 will qualify for the marital deduction. If W dies in 2005, her estate will pay a tax of $695,000. If H had left half of his property in a credit shelter trust for the benefit of W, she would have paid no estate tax on her death because the taxable estate of each would be only $1,500,000 — the amount that is sheltered by the unified credit.

The purpose of a credit shelter trust, also called a bypass trust or a family trust, is to take advantage of the unified credit in the estate of the first spouse to die. This trust should not qualify for the marital deduction, *i.e.*, the surviving spouse cannot be given a general power of appointment over the trust assets and that the executor should not elect QTIP treatment for this trust. The surviving spouse can, of course, have the right to income from this trust. She might even have the power to withdraw trust corpus for her own health, education, support, and maintenance since such a power is not a general power of appointment and thus would not bring the corpus of this trust into her gross estate. An independent trustee could be given even broader powers to distribute trust corpus to the surviving spouse as long as the surviving spouse cannot become the trustee and thus acquire what would be considered a general power of appointment. This trust will be in the decedent's taxable estate because it does not qualify for the marital deduction. If the trust is limited to the applicable exemption amount, the decedent's estate will pay no tax because of the unified credit in §2010.

The typical estate plan will usually include two trusts: the credit shelter trust and the marital deduction trust. To maximize the estate tax benefits, the trustee of the credit shelter trust should not be required to distribute trust income or corpus to the surviving spouse. The property in this trust will not be in the survivor's gross estate, so the greater the accumulation in that trust, the more estate tax will be saved. Instead, assets in the marital deduction trust should be distributed first to meet the needs of the surviving spouse. Depleting this trust will decrease the amount taxable on the death of the surviving spouse.

Example 16-16 raises another problem. What if W dies before H? She owns no property in her own name, and thus her estate cannot take advantage of the unified credit. When H dies, the full $3,000,000 will be in his gross estate. The only way to avoid this problem is for H to transfer property to W during life so that if W dies first, her estate can take advantage of the unified credit. The simplest way to achieve this is for H to give W either half the property or an amount equal to the applicable exemption amount, whichever is less. W can then leave this property in a credit shelter trust for the benefit of H if she dies before him. Of course, many people in H's situation are reluctant to transfer significant wealth outright, even to their spouse, during life. H might prefer to transfer the property in trust for the benefit of W during life. H, of course, can do so using a power of appointment trust or a QTIP trust. If H does so, and reserves a secondary life estate for his own benefit in case he should survive W, the trust will end up in his gross estate because of §2036(a)(1), and the plan to take advantage of the unified credit of both spouses will be thwarted.

2. Deferral versus Equalization
IRC §§2001(c), 2010

The two-trust estate plan is not necessary for the couple that owns relatively little property, *i.e.*, not more than the equivalent of the applicable exemption amount. For these couples, there is little need for tax planning. Their combined assets will be sheltered by the unified credit in the estate of the survivor.

On the other hand, the married couple that owns more than twice the applicable exemption amount must decide whether to equalize their estates or defer all tax until the death of the survivor. The benefit of equalization is that the combined estates will pay less estate tax. The benefit of deferral is that the survivor will have the use of the money that would otherwise be paid to the government as estate tax at the death of the first spouse. Example 16-17 demonstrates the difference between equalization and deferral, using the estate tax rates in effect before the 2001 Tax Act and assuming an applicable exemption amount of $1,000,000.

Example 16-17

H and W are married and own $6,000,000 of property. They equalize their estates through lifetime gifts, and each owns $3,000,000. H dies first, leaving his $3,000,000 in a credit shelter trust for the benefit of W and their children. This trust does not qualify for the marital deduction. The tax due on H's death will be $945,000. Assuming no change in the value of the property, the applicable exemption amount, or the tax rates, the tax due on W's death will also be $945,000. The combined estate tax paid by H and W will be, therefore, $1,890,000.

Instead, H leaves only $1,000,000 in the credit shelter trust and the rest of his property in a trust for the benefit of W that qualifies for the marital deduction. H will pay no estate tax because the $1,000,000 will be sheltered by the applicable credit, and the property bequeathed to W will be sheltered by the marital deduction. W's estate will pay an estate tax of $2,045,000, which is $155,000 more than the estate tax paid when H and W equalized their estates.

If H and W choose to equalize their estates, W, in this example, will also lose the benefit of the $945,000 paid to the government as estate tax. This property will not be in the credit shelter or marital deduction trust earning income for the benefit of W or available for her needs.

The conventional wisdom has been to defer estate taxes and allow W the benefit of these additional resources. The economics, however, do not support deferral. *See* Jeffrey N. Pennell and R. Mark Williamson, *The Economics of Prepaying Wealth Transfer Tax*, 136 Trusts & Estates 49 (June 1997); Jeffrey N. Pennell, *Estate Tax Marital Deduction*, 843 BNA Tax Mgt. Portfolio A-16 (1996). Moreover, if W dies within two years of H, her estate will be entitled to a §2013 credit for any estate tax paid with respect to the property received from H. If W dies more than two but less than ten years after H, her estate will be entitled to a §2013 credit equal to a percentage of the estate tax paid with respect to the property received from H. (Section 2013 is discussed at page 506.) If the spouses had deferred all estate tax, no §2013 credit would be available. *See* Anna C. Fowler and Sally M. Jones, *The Trade-Off Between the Marital Deduction and the 2013 Credit*, 44 Tax Notes 207 (1989).

The changes in the tax brackets and the applicable exemption amount in the 2001 Tax Act have mooted this dilemma, at least temporarily.

Example 16-18

H and W are married and own $6,000,000 of property. Assume they equalize their estates and each owns $3,000,000. H dies first, in 2007, when the applicable exemption amount is $2,000,000, and the maximum tax rate is 45 percent. He leaves his $3,000,000 in a credit shelter trust for the benefit of W and their children. This trust does not qualify for the marital deduction. The tax due on H's death will be $450,000. W dies in 2008, when the applicable exemption amount and tax rates are exactly the same. Assuming no change in the value of the property, the tax due on W's death will also be $450,000. The combined estate tax paid by H's and W's estates will be $900,000.

Instead, H leaves only $1,000,000 in the credit shelter trust and the rest of his property outright to W. H's estate will pay no estate tax because the $1,000,000 will be sheltered by §2010 and the remainder by the marital deduction. W's estate will pay an estate tax of $900,000, exactly the same amount as the combined estate tax paid by H's and W's estates in the prior paragraph. This occurs because all of the property in both estates is taxed at the 45 percent rate, which is the rate imposed on amount exceeding the applicable exemption amount.

The benefit of equalization increases as the tax rates become more progressive. As Example 16-18 demonstrates, there is no benefit to equalization when the tax rate is exactly the same in both estates. There is a modest tax savings when the tax rates are moderately graduated and more property is taxed at a lower rate. In Example 16-17, the tax rates applicable to W's (the survivor's) taxable estate were 39, 41, 43, 45, 49, and 50 percent. The tax savings would increase significantly if the tax rates had, for example, extended from 18 percent to 55 percent.[1]

There are many factors beyond the amount of the estate tax that will influence a couple's decision whether to incur estate tax at the death of the first to die or to defer all taxes until the death of the survivor. The most important factor is usually the ability of the survivor to spend the funds that would otherwise have been paid to the government as tax on the estate of the first to die or to give that money away or to invest it and use the income generated from it. Other factors include the total value of the spouse's estates, the nature of the assets, the desire (or reluctance) to transfer property to the next generation at the first death, uncertainty regarding the survivor's financial needs, uncertainty regarding the future of the estate tax, and the need for liquidity in either estate to pay taxes, claims, and other expenses.

3. Disclaimers, Savings Clauses, and Trust Reformation

If H and W fail to plan appropriately in terms of either the amount of the marital deduction or its form, all is not necessarily lost. In Example 16-16, H owned $3,000,000 and left it all to W, thereby losing the benefit of the unified credit. If W is willing to disclaim part of her interest in H's property, H's estate will be able to utilize the unified credit. Pursuant to state law, any property interest that W disclaims will pass as if she predeceased H. Under §2518 H, not W, will be considered as the transferor. Thus, any property that W disclaims could be sheltered from tax by the unified credit, up to the exemption amount. The obvious disadvantage of such post-mortem planning is that W will lose the benefit of that property. She will not receive any income that it generates, and it will not be available in case of an emergency or financial loss. Disclaimers are used primarily when the surviving spouse has a short life expectancy or significant wealth of her own.

Another option is a savings clause, which typically will provide as follows:

> It is my intent that [Trust A] will qualify for the federal estate tax marital deduction. The executor [trustee] shall allocate to [Trust A] only property that will

---

1. These are the tax rates in §2001(c). The lowest brackets no longer apply because of the applicable credit amount in §2010. As the applicable exemption amount increases, it eliminates the effect of the lower tax rates.

qualify for the marital deduction. Furthermore, all powers and discretions in the administration of this trust shall be interpreted and exercised in a manner consistent with the marital deduction.

Whether or not such a clause will be given effect will depend on the settlor's intent as expressed in all the trust provisions as well as the nature of the defect.

In Estate of Ellingson v. Commissioner, 964 F.2d 959 (9th Cir. 1992), a husband and wife created three inter vivos trusts, including one designated as the "Marital Deduction Trust." After the husband's death, the trustee of the Marital Deduction Trust was to distribute the entire net income of that trust at least annually to the wife, but the trustee also had discretion to accumulate income if the trust income exceeded the amount necessary for the wife's "needs, best interests, and welfare." The Commissioner claimed that this accumulation provision prevented the trust from qualifying for the marital deduction, and the Tax Court agreed. The Ninth Circuit, however, reversed, holding that "[t]he Commissioner's reading of the Trust Agreement causes the agreement to self-destruct in defiance of the settlor's obvious intent." *Id.* at 963. In reaching this conclusion, the court gave effect to the saving clause included in the trust, but agreed with the Commissioner that the savings clause alone was insufficient to qualify the trust for the marital deduction. Instead, the court interpreted the "best interests" language of the accumulation provision to mean that the trustees were to pay the entire net income of the trust to the wife.

> The Accumulation Proviso states that the trustee may accumulate income which is in excess of the amount necessary for Lavedna's "needs, best interests and welfare." The agreement does not define "best interests." As the Estate notes, it would not be in Lavedna's best interests for the trustee to be forced to sell the family farm so that the Estate could pay in excess of $8 million in estate taxes out of the Marital Deduction Trust property. Accordingly, they argue, the trustee of the Marital Deduction Trust actually possessed no discretion to accumulate income. To effectuate the settlors' intent, the trustee would have to pay all of the income of the trust to Lavedna during her life. In other words, paying Lavedna such amount of the income necessary for her "best interests" means paying Lavedna *all* of the income.

Id. at 964.

A savings clause in Estate of Walsh v. Commissioner, 110 T.C. 393 (1998), however, was not sufficient to qualify the trust for the marital deduction. In that trust, if the surviving spouse became incompetent, the trust terminated and the trust property was to be distributed according to the spouse's general power of appointment. Because the trust terminated if the surviving spouse became incompetent, the court held that it was a terminable interest.

> We also disagree with the estate's alternative argument. The estate has set forth no good reason why we should disregard the validity of the Trust, and we decline to do so. Although the estate states correctly that we must (and do) interpret the language of the Agreement in accordance with the settlors' intent, . . . the

mere fact that the settlors meant for Trust A to qualify for the marital deduction does not mean that it does so qualify. . . . In order for the estate to avail itself of the marital deduction, the Trust must fall within the statutory and regulatory requirements for that deduction. . . . As discussed above, it does not.

We note that the Trust serves more than just the settlors' stated intent to avail themselves of the marital deduction. The Agreement indicates that a principal purpose for the Trust was to provide subsistence for the surviving spouse during his or her competency and, thereafter, to allow the spouse to qualify for medical assistance at minimal family expense. The Agreement states that the Trust's assets shall be distributed to the settlors' children upon the surviving spouse's incompetency, or, in other words, when the surviving spouse may potentially incur increased medical expenses for physician care and/or the need for a nursing home. Because the Trust's assets would be outside the Trust, they would not be counted as an asset of the surviving spouse for purposes of ascertaining the amount that he or she would have to pay for these expenses. Thus, more of the settlors' assets would pass to the settlors' children.

Id. at 401-402.

In the absence of a savings clause, the executor or the surviving spouse might petition the probate court to reform the decedent's will to conform with the requirements of §2056. The Commissioner, of course, is not bound by the probate court's determination even if that decision has become final and is, therefore, unappealable. *See, e.g.*, Estate of Rapp v. Commissioner, 140 F.3d 1211 (9th Cir. 1998). Under Commissioner v. Estate of Bosch, 387 U.S. 456 (1967), only the decision of the state's highest court will be considered as controlling the state property law issue. In the absence of such a ruling, the "federal authorities must apply what they find to be the state law after giving the 'proper regard' to relevant rulings of other courts of the State." *Id.* at 465.

4. Allocation of Taxes and Expenses

Taxes and administrative expenses that are allocated to property that qualifies for the marital deduction will reduce the amount of that deduction. §2056(b)(4); Reg. §20.2056(b)-4(c), (d). Whether such amounts are charged against the marital deduction property will depend on the terms of the decedent's will. In the absence of specification by decedent, state law will determine the allocation.

Example 16-19

D and S are married and D dies, owning property valued at $6,000,000. D's will leaves half of the property to D's children and half of the property to S. Assume that federal estate taxes, state death taxes, and administrative expenses total $800,000. If these amounts are allocated to the property passing to S, they will reduce the amount of the marital deduction and thus increase the amount of tax due. This will leave even less property for S.

Decedent's will should specify how to allocate these items. Administrative expenses usually reduce the residuary estate. Taxes may reduce the residuary estate or be allocated proportionately to bequests that are subject to tax. If the marital deduction bequest is the residuary clause, it will be charged with taxes and expenses unless the decedent's will provides otherwise.

An additional problem arises when decedent's estate is composed of non-probate assets that are subject to tax. Sections 2205 to 2207B provide decedent's estate with a right of recovery from beneficiaries who receive such assets.

PROBLEMS

1. Henry and Whitney are married and have two adult children. They own a house valued at $200,000 as joint tenants. They also own cars, household goods, and personal effects valued at $50,000. Their joint bank accounts are $25,000. They each own $100,000 of life insurance, with their spouse as primary beneficiary and their children as secondary beneficiaries. Henry has $200,000 in his retirement fund, and Whitney has $100,000 in her retirement fund. They want each other to have the benefit of the maximum amount of property, but they don't want to pay any more estate tax than necessary. How would you structure their estates? Why?

2. Debra and Simon are married and have four adult children. They own a house valued at $250,000 as joint tenants. They also own cars, household goods, and personal effects valued at $50,000. Their joint bank accounts are $100,000. Debra has investments valued at $4,500,000.
   a. How should they structure their estate plans if they want to provide the maximum economic benefit for the survivor and ultimately for the property to pass to their children?
   b. How would your answer change, if at all, if Debra owned $3,000,000 of the investments and Simon owned $2,000,000 of the investments?
   c. Same as 2.a., except that Debra and Simon have no children together, Debra has two children from a prior marriage, and Simon has three children from a prior marriage.

3. Chris and Terry are married and own $10,000,000 of real estate as joint tenants. Both have wills that leave all their property to the survivor. Assume that Chris dies in 2004 and Terry dies in 2007.
   a. What is the estate tax due on Chris's death? What is the estate tax due on Terry's death?
   b. How, if at all, should they restructure their estate plans to minimize transfer taxes?

CHAPTER 17

Credits

A. UNIFIED CREDIT
IRC §§2010, 2505

Prior to 1976, the gift tax and the estate tax had separate exemptions amounts; the gift tax had a $30,000 exemption, while the estate tax had a $60,000 exemption. An exemption, like a deduction, benefits taxpayers in a higher marginal tax bracket more than those in a lower bracket. For example, an estate in the 10 percent bracket saved only $6,000 in estate taxes because of the estate tax exemption, while an estate in the 70 percent bracket saved $42,000 because of the exemption. Moreover, wealthy taxpayers were able to take advantage of the separate gift tax exemption by making taxable gifts, but poorer taxpayers, who could not afford to do so, lost the benefit of this exemption.

To remedy these disparities, Congress replaced the separate gift tax and estate tax exemptions with a single credit of $47,000 when it unified the two taxes in 1976. In doing so, Congress increased the amount of property sheltered from tax to approximately $175,500. By shifting from an exemption to a credit, Congress also remedied the disparity between taxpayers. A credit, unlike an exemption or a deduction, provides the same benefit to each taxpayer because it is subtracted after the tentative tax is calculated, not before.

In 1981, with the $47,000 unified credit barely phased in, Congress increased it to $192,800 (the equivalent of $600,000 of property), phasing the increase in over a number of years. Again in 1997, Congress increased the applicable credit amount to the equivalent of $1,000,000, phasing this increase in between 1998 and 2006. Before that amendment was fully effective, Congress in 2001 once again increased the credit equivalent amount to $1,000,000 for 2002 and 2003, to $1,500,000 for 2004 and 2005, to $2,000,000 for 2006 to 2008, and to $3,500,000 for 2009.

During this same period, Congress modified the tax brackets. Prior to 1976, the estate tax rates ranged from 3 percent to 77 percent. In 1976, Congress amended the rates to range from 18 percent to 70 percent. In 1981, Congress lowered the top marginal rate to 55 percent. Because of the unified credit, the lowest effective tax rate was 24 percent. When the unified credit of $192,800 was fully phased in, the lowest rate of tax became 37 percent. The 2001 Tax Act again amended both the unified credit and the tax rates. As a result, in 2002, the lowest estate tax rate became 37 percent and the highest rate became 50 percent; in 2004, the lowest rate is 45 percent, and the highest rate is 48 percent; in 2006, there will be a flat rate of tax of 46 percent; and in 2007, there will be a flat rate of tax of 45 percent. The gift tax applicable exemption amount, however, will remain at $1,000,000, so that gifts will be taxable beginning at 41 percent. With an essentially flat rate of tax of 45 percent, a deduction benefits a very wealthy taxpayer the same as one with moderate wealth, but a deduction of $100,000 will only reduce taxes by $45,000, while a credit of $100,000 will reduce taxes by $100,000.

Although the unified credit appears in both §2010 and §2505, a taxpayer does not receive a double benefit.

Example 17-1

Debra has made no prior taxable gifts and makes a taxable gift in 2002 of $1,000,000. She dies in 2003 with a taxable estate of $1,000,000. The gift and estate taxes are calculated as follows:

Gift Tax

Taxable gift	$1,000,000	
Tentative tax on taxable gift		$345,800
§2505 applicable credit amount		$345,800
Gift tax due		$ 0

Estate Tax

Taxable estate	$1,000,000	
Adjusted taxable gifts	$1,000,000	
Tax base	$2,000,000	
Tentative tax on tax base		$780,800
Less gift tax paid		$ 0
Less §2010 applicable credit amount		$345,800
Estate tax due		$435,000

Debra pays an estate tax of $435,000 because she had already transferred $1,000,000 tax-free and thus used up her applicable credit amount. Compare her with Denise, who did not make any taxable gifts and had a taxable estate of $2,000,000 when she died in 2003. Denise's estate tax is calculated as follows:

Taxable estate	$2,000,000	
Adjusted taxable gifts	$ 0	
Total tax base	$2,000,000	
Tentative tax on total tax base		$780,800
Less gift tax paid		$ 0
Less §2010 applicable credit amount		$345,800
Estate tax due		$435,000

Denise's estate tax bill is the same as Debra's even though she used her applicable credit amount to transfer property tax-free at death instead of during life.

Because §2001 includes adjusted taxable gifts, *i.e.*, those taxable gifts that are not in the gross estate, in the calculation of the tax, it does not matter when the transfer occurred. Because those adjusted taxable gifts are included in the calculation, the §2010 credit is the same in both situations.

This principle — that a taxpayer cannot increase the amount of property passing tax-free by making lifetime taxable gifts — remains the same even when the §2505 exemption amount for gifts remains at $1,000,000 and the §2010 exemption amount for estates increases to $1,500,000, $2,000,000, or $3,500,000.

Example 17-2

Delwin has made no prior taxable gifts and makes a taxable gift in 2004 of $1,000,000. Delwin dies in 2006 with a taxable estate of $1,000,000. The gift and estate taxes are calculated as follows:

Taxable gift	$1,000,000
Tentative tax on taxable gift	$345,800
§2505 applicable credit amount	$345,800
Gift tax due	$ 0
Taxable estate	$1,000,000
Adjusted taxable gifts	$1,000,000
Total tax base	$2,000,000
Tentative tax on total tax base	$780,800
Less gift tax paid	$ 0
Less §2010 applicable credit amount	$780,800
Estate tax due	$ 0

Had Delwin not made the taxable gift, his taxable estate would have been $2,000,000 and his estate tax calculated as follows:

Taxable estate	$2,000,000
Adjusted taxable gifts	$ 0
Total tax base	$2,000,000
Tentative tax on total tax base	$780,800
Less gift tax paid	$ 0
Less §2010 applicable credit amount	$780,800
Estate tax due	$ 0

Delwin pays no tax because the estate tax applicable exemption amount is $2,000,000.

For most taxpayers, the applicable credit amount will shelter their estates from any estate tax. For wealthy taxpayers, it is important to ensure that the benefit of this credit is not lost. This can happen if a married couple leaves all of the property of the first person to die to the surviving spouse.

Example 17-3

Henry and Wanda are married. Henry owns $5,000,000 worth of property, and Wanda owns no property. If Henry leaves all of his property to Wanda outright or to a qualified trust for her benefit, his estate will pay no tax because of the unlimited marital deduction. While deferring all tax until Wanda's death, this estate plan eliminates the benefit of the unified credit in Henry's estate.

If Henry dies in 2003, when the applicable exemption amount is $1,000,000, and Wanda dies in 2005, when the applicable exemption amount is $1,500,000, her estate will pay an additional estate tax of $470,000 because Henry failed to use the unified credit. If Henry dies in 2006, and Wanda in 2008 when the credit amount is $2,000,000, her estate will pay an additional estate tax of $900,000.

Henry could have avoided this by creating a "credit-shelter" or "bypass" trust equal to the applicable exemption amount. Wanda could be the income beneficiary and could even be given a limited power of appointment to withdraw trust property for her health, education, support, or maintenance. As long as she has only a life estate and a special power of appointment and no QTIP election is made, the trust property will not be in her gross estate at death. Failure to adopt such a plan to utilize the §2010 credit in a decedent's estate will be considered legal malpractice.

B. CREDIT FOR PRIOR TRANSFERS
IRC §2013

Section 2013 provides a credit for the federal estate tax that was paid when the decedent acquired property from an individual (the "transferor") who died within ten years before or two years after the decedent. This provision, like the unified credit, began as a deduction rather than a credit. When Congress recodified the Internal Revenue Code in 1954, it changed this deduction to a credit and eliminated the requirement that the decedent actually own the property acquired from the transferor at death.

The purpose of §2013 is simple: to relieve the estate tax burden in successive estates when individuals die within a relatively short time period of each other.

Example 17-4

Tom bequeaths all his property to his brother, Doug, and Doug dies six months after Tom, bequeathing all his property to his son, Sam. Assume a flat 50 percent rate of tax, no unified credit, and no credit for prior transfers. Tom has $1,000,000 of property. After taxes, Doug receives $500,000. Doug has an additional $1,000,000 of his own property. Because of the two estate taxes imposed, one on Tom's estate and one on Doug's estate, Sam receives only $750,000.

Now assume a credit for prior transfers. The tax on Doug's estate will only be $250,000 compared to $750,000 without such a credit. As a result, Sam will receive $1,250,000 of property not $750,000.

Although the purpose of §2013 is simple, the application is rather complicated. The regulations provide detailed examples of how to calculate the credit. Reg. §20.2013-6.

There are two limitations on the §2013 credit. First, the credit cannot exceed the federal estate tax attributable to inclusion of the property in the transferor's estate.[1] §2013(b); Reg. §20.2013-2. Second, the credit cannot exceed the federal estate tax attributable to including the property received from the transferor in the decedent's estate. §2013(c); Reg. §20.2013-3. Furthermore, the credit is reduced to 80 percent if the decedent died more than two but less than four years after the transferor, to 60 percent if the decedent died more than four but less than six years after the transferor, to 40 percent if the decedent died more than six but less than eight years after the transferor, and to 20 percent if the decedent died more than eight but less than ten years after the transferor. Finally, for purposes of calculating the §2013 credit, the value of the property transferred to the decedent is deemed to be the value of the property used in calculating the transferor's estate tax adjusted for federal estate and state death taxes, encumbrances on the property, and any marital deduction attributable to the property.

Example 17-5

Tracy died on January 5, 2002, with a taxable estate of $2,000,000. She bequeathed all her property to Diane. Diane died on January 3, 2003. The federal estate tax due on Tracy's estate was $435,000, and there was no state death tax. Diane had a taxable estate of $1,000,000, other than the property she acquired from Tracy. Diane's federal estate tax is calculated as follows:

Diane's taxable estate:

Diane's own property	$ 1,000,000	
Property from Tracy	$ 1,565,000	
	$ 2,565,000	

Tentative tax on $2,565,000

$$\$780,800 + \begin{array}{r} \$\ 2,565,000 \\ -\ 2,000,000 \\ \hline \$\ \ \ 565,000 \\ \times\ \ \ \ \ .49 \\ \hline \$\ \ \ 276,850 \end{array} = \$1,057,650$$

Less §2010 applicable credit amount	$ 345,800
Less §2013 credit	$ 435,000
Estate tax due	$ 276,850

---

1. The "transferor" is usually the first to die. The §2013 credit is calculated for the estate of the "decedent," *i.e.*, the person who received the property from the transferor.

Calculation of the §2013 credit:

First limitation, §2013(b)

transferor's federal estate tax $\times$ <u>value of property transferred to decedent</u>
transferor's taxable estate less death taxes

$435,000 $\times$ <u>$1,565,000</u>   = $435,000
                    $1,565,000

Because Tracy transferred all of her property to Diane, the full amount of the estate tax is attributable to the property transferred to her.

Second limitation, §2013(c)

Estate tax on Diane's estate ($2,565,000) without regard to §2013

Tentative tax	$1,057,650
Applicable credit amount	$ 345,800
	$ 711,850

Less

Estate tax on Diane's estate without the property received from Tracy ($1,000,000)

Tentative tax on $1,000,000	$ 345,800
Applicable credit amount	$ 345,800
	$ 0

Second limitation $ 711,850

Thus, the §2013 credit is $435,000, the lesser of the §2013(b) amount or the §2013(c) amount.

Diane's estate pays an estate tax of $276,850 even though her property without the addition of Tracy's would have been fully sheltered by the applicable credit amount in §2010, and her estate received a credit equal to the amount of federal estate tax paid by Tracy's estate. This occurs for two reasons. First, the amount sheltered from tax in Tracy's estate, the applicable exemption amount, is now subject to tax in Diane's estate. Second, the amount taxed in Tracy's estate was taxed at 41 percent, 43 percent, and 45 percent, but because of the progressive nature of the estate tax and the addition of the property that Diane owned, some of the property ($565,000) in Diane's estate is taxed at 49 percent. Had Diane died three years after Tracy (and assuming that the tax brackets and unified credit amounts did not change), the §2013 credit would have been 80 percent of $435,000 or $348,000.

C.   CREDIT FOR TAXES
IRC §§2011, 2012, 2014

There are three sections allowing an offset against the federal estate tax for other transfer taxes: §2011 allows a credit for state death taxes; §2012 allows a credit for certain gift taxes; and §2014 allows a credit for certain foreign death taxes.

Section 2011 provides a credit for all types of death taxes — estate, inheritance, legacy, or succession — paid to a state or the District of Columbia. Unlike the unified credit or the credit for prior transfers, the credit for state death taxes was originally enacted in 1924 as a credit, not as a deduction or an exemption. Death taxes were considered to be the province of the states, so Congress enacted a credit equal to 25 percent of the tax paid to the states. In response to pressure from the states, who wanted to protect a major source of revenue, Congress increased the credit to 80 percent in 1926. In 1932, Congress raised the estate tax rates significantly and limited the state death tax credit by creating a basic estate tax using the 1926 rates against which the 80 percent credit was allowed and an additional tax with new rates against which no credit was allowed. Although Congress simplified this provision in 1954, the credit for state death taxes still reflects the 80 percent limitation based on the 1926 estate tax rates and the $60,000 estate tax exemption.

There are a number of limitations on the §2011 credit. First, the credit cannot exceed the amount of state death taxes actually paid. Second, the credit is allowed only for taxes paid within four years of filing the federal estate tax return unless the estate files a petition in Tax Court, receives an extension to pay estate taxes under §6166, or files a claim for a refund. Third, the credit is limited to the amount specified in §2011(b). Fourth, the credit cannot exceed the amount of the federal estate tax reduced by the applicable credit amount in §2010. Finally, the §2011 credit is phased out for decedents dying after December 31, 2001, and replaced by the §2058 deduction for state death taxes for decedents dying after December 31, 2004.

Example 17-6

Dale dies in 2003 with a taxable estate of $3,600,000. Assume his state imposes an estate tax of $250,000 on his estate. His federal estate tax is calculated as follows:

Tentative tax on $3,600,000:

	$780,800 +	$ 3,600,000	
		− 2,000,000	
		$ 1,600,000	
		× .49	
		$ 784,000 =	$1,564,800
Less §2010 credit			$ 345,800
Less §2011 credit			$ 119,400
Estate tax due			$1,099,600

Calculation of the §2011 credit:

Taxable estate	$3,600,000
Less $60,000	$ 60,000
Adjusted taxable estate	$3,540,000

§2011(b)(1) amount	$ 238,800
Applicable percentage, §2011(b)(2)	× .50
§2011(b) amount	$ 119,400

Because the §2011(b) amount is less than the amount of tax paid, the credit is equal to the §2011(b) amount.

Had Dale died in 2001, his estate would have been entitled to a §2011 credit of $238,800; had he died in 2005, his estate would have received a deduction equal to the amount of state death taxes paid, *i.e.*, $250,000. Because the highest marginal tax rate in 2005 is 47 percent, this deduction will save his estate only $117,500 in federal estate taxes.

All the amendments to the estate tax made by the 2001 Tax Act will be repealed for decedents dying after December 31, 2010, unless Congress takes further action. If Congress does not act, the §2011 credit will reappear without the percentage reduction of §2011(b)(2), and the §2058 deduction will disappear on January 1, 2011.

Section 2012 allows a credit for federal gift taxes paid on gifts made prior to 1977 if the value of the property is included in the decedent's gross estate. For example, assume that Dennis purchased property in 1972 taking title as joint tenants with the right of survivorship with his son, Ed. Dennis paid the entire purchase price of the property. As a result, when Dennis dies in 2004, the value of the property will be in his gross estate under §2040(a) even though he had paid a gift tax on the value of half the property at the time of the purchase. Section 2012 will allow his estate a credit for the gift tax paid. The §2012 credit is not necessary for gifts made after January 1, 1977, because the gift tax paid is subtracted from the tentative tax under §2001(b).

Section 2014 allows a credit for death taxes paid to a foreign country if property located in that country is also subject to the federal estate tax. Because the federal estate tax is imposed on all property of citizens and residents regardless of its location, property located outside the United States will frequently be subject to double taxation. Section 2014 avoids the harshness of double taxation. Relief may also be provided by a tax treaty with the foreign country. The decedent's estate will be allowed either relief under the treaty or the §2014 credit, but not both.

PROBLEMS

1. Which of the following should be a credit, and which should be a deduction?
   a. Expenses of administration of the decedent's estate
   b. State death taxes
   c. Property transferred to charity
   d. Property transferred to a surviving spouse

e. The amount of property allowed to be transferred free of transfer taxes

2. What amount of property should a taxpayer be allowed to transfer before paying any transfer tax?

3. Should the transfer tax be a flat rate of tax or progressive rates? If a flat rate of tax, what should the tax rate be? If progressive, what should the highest rate be? The lowest rate? How many different rates should there be?

4. Amanda and Belinda are sisters. Amanda dies on September 24, 2003, leaving all her property in trust to pay the income to Belinda for life and giving Belinda the power to invade the corpus for her own benefit. Amanda's taxable estate is $3,000,000. Belinda dies on October 10, 2003, before Amanda's estate is probated. Belinda has a taxable estate of her own of $3,000,000.

    a. Calculate the estate tax due on Amanda's death and on Belinda's death. Assume there is no state death tax.

    b. Is there any way to avoid the additional estate tax in Belinda's estate?

5. Dawn dies in 2004 with a taxable estate of $5,100,000.

    a. What is the amount of the §2011 credit if her jurisdiction imposes an estate tax of $350,000?

    b. What if, instead, the state imposes an inheritance tax of $85,000?

6. You are a member of your State House of Representatives. Your state had an estate tax equal to the §2011 state death tax credit. Because Congress has replaced that credit with a deduction, your State is considering a proposal to adopt an accessions tax, *i.e.*, a cumulative tax on the receipt of gifts and inheritances. Be prepared to discuss and vote on this bill.

PART V

The Taxation of Generation-Skipping Transfers

CHAPTER 18

The Generation-Skipping Transfer Tax

A. GENERAL PRINCIPLES

The generation-skipping transfer tax is based on the policy that the transfer of property should be taxed at least once at each generation. The following scenarios demonstrate the inconsistency and lack of fairness in a transfer tax system without such a tax. These scenarios are greatly simplified and assume a flat rate of gift and estate tax of 50 percent.

The Smith Family transfers wealth by omitting alternate generations. The Smith Family has $40 million and splits that wealth between generation one and generation two, incurring a gift tax of $10 million on the transfer. Generation one retains $20 million and generation two has acquired $10 million. The Smith Family than transfers that wealth to alternate generations. Generation one passes its wealth to generation three, who passes it to generation five, who passes it to generation seven. At a 50 percent tax rate, the wealth diminishes from $20 million (generation one) to $10 million (generation three) to $5 million (generation five) to $2.5 million (generation seven). In the meantime, generation two passes its wealth to generation four, who passes it to generation six, who passes it to generation eight. Given a 50 percent tax rate, generation eight receives $1.25 million. The total wealth in the Smith Family after these transfers is $3.25 million. All of this, of course, assumes no appreciation in the value of the assets, no inflation, no depreciation, and no consumption.

In contrast to the Smiths, the Jones Family also has $40 million but transfers that wealth to each succeeding generation, paying a 50 percent tax rate on each transfer. At generation eight, the Jones Family will have only $312,500, approximately one-tenth the wealth of the Smith Family. With appropriate advice, the Jones Family will adopt the same plan as the Smith Family. The difficulty is that only families with significant wealth can structure their assets and transfers in this way. Those of moderate or little wealth cannot afford to do so and, thus, incur transfer taxes at every generation often paying more tax than those of greater wealth.

Now consider the Nelson Family, who, on advice of counsel, transfers $40 million to a trust to pay the income to their children for life, then the income to their grandchildren for life, and so on. Assume that the Nelson Family lives in a jurisdiction that has eliminated the Rule Against Perpetuities. There will be a transfer tax on the creation of the trust, leaving $20 million in the trust. There will be no further transfer taxes because the income interest will not be in the estate of any beneficiary. The eighth generation will still enjoy the income from the $20 million in trust, far more than either the Smith Family ($3.25 million) or the Jones Family ($312,500).

If the Nelsons wanted to give each generation access to trust principal without subjecting the property to transfer taxation, they could do this by giving an independent trustee power to make discretionary distributions of principal or by giving the younger generations special or limited powers of appointment. Because a power to invade for health, education, support, or maintenance is not a general power of appointment, the younger generation Nelsons could enjoy substantial access to the trust property without ever paying a transfer tax.

These scenarios demonstrate a lack of fundamental fairness. In the tax world, fairness is measured both horizontally and vertically. Horizontal fairness requires that similar tax consequences be imposed on taxpayers who are similarly situated. Vertical fairness depends on progressivity, that is, that taxpayers with greater resources pay a greater share in taxes. A transfer tax system without a generation-skipping tax violates both these principles. Taxpayers who are similarly situated may pay different amounts of tax depending only on the method in which they choose to transfer their wealth. Both scenarios described above demonstrate this problem. Vertical fairness is also absent because only the very wealthy can afford to transfer wealth in the manner of the Smiths and the Nelsons. Those of moderate or low wealth must resort to the transfer techniques used by the Joneses, techniques that impose a greater tax burden than those used by the Smiths and the Nelsons. This also violates another basic premise of tax policy — neutrality. The more that a tax system dictates the form of transactions, the less neutral it is. Transactions should be structured for their economic, social, or familial effects and should be influenced as little as possible by tax considerations.

These disparities led Congress to enact a tax on generation-skipping transfers in 1976. That tax attempted to approximate the estate tax that would have been due if the property had been subject to tax in the estate of the parent of the recipient. This created extreme complexity and confusion, particularly for transfers to those who were not lineal descendants of the transferor. Moreover, the 1976 generation-skipping transfer tax did not address the transfer that actually skipped a generation, taxing only the transfers like those of the Nelson Family, where each generation had an interest in or power over the trust property. In 1986, Congress repealed the 1976 generation-skipping transfer tax retroactively and substituted the current provisions of Chapter 13.

The 1986 generation-skipping transfer tax ensures that tax is paid on the transfer of property to each generation as well as on transfers that skip generations. It includes an exemption amount of $1,000,000, which will increase to $3,500,000 in 2009, and the rate of tax is equal to the maximum estate tax rate. While simpler than the 1976 version, the current generation-skipping transfer tax provisions remain complicated and still allow some transfers to avoid taxation at every generation.

Example 18-1

Peter dies and leaves a bequest of $5 million to his great-granddaughter. There will be an estate tax on his death (*i.e.*, a tax on the transfer to the first generation). Because this transfer is a direct skip, there will also be a generation-skipping tax (*i.e.*, a tax on the transfer to the second generation). There will not be a second imposition of the generation-skipping transfer tax, so the transfer to the third generation in this example avoids transfer taxation altogether.

The number of instances where donors and decedents make transfers that actually skip two generations will be rare. To remedy this omission would require significantly more complexity in an already complicated statute, and it simply does not appear to be worth the price.

B. TERMINOLOGY AND GENERATION ASSIGNMENTS
IRC §§2612, 2613, 2651, 2652

The generation-skipping transfer tax is imposed on direct skips, taxable terminations, and taxable distributions. Generation-skipping transfers include not only outright transfers, such as gifts and bequests, but also distributions from trusts or termination of interests in trusts. Whether or not a particular transfer qualifies as one of these taxable events depends on the identity of the transferor, the generation assignment of the recipients, whether the recipients have an interest in the trust, and whether the recipients are skip persons.

Section 2652(a) defines a transferor as the donor, if the property is subject to the gift tax, or the decedent, if the property is subject to the estate tax. The donor or the decedent is the transferor even if no gift or estate tax is actually paid because of applicable exclusions, exemptions, deductions, or credits. Reg. §26.2652-1(a)(3).

Example 18-2

Pam gives her granddaughter, Gail, $100,000 but does not pay any gift tax because of the applicable credit amount in §2505. Pam is considered the donor for purposes of the gift tax and is, therefore, the transferor for purposes of the generation-skipping transfer tax.

If Pam left the property to her granddaughter, Gail, in her will, the result would be the same. Pam is the decedent for purposes of the estate tax even if no estate tax is due because of the applicable credit amount in §2010. She is still the transferor for purposes of the generation-skipping transfer tax.

Both these transfers are direct skips because Gail is two generations below Pam. Whether Pam, or her estate, pays any generation-skipping transfer tax will depend on the allocation of her GST exemption.

If an individual and her spouse elect to split gifts under §2513, then each is treated as the transferor with respect to one-half of the gift. If Pam in Example 18-2 is married and her spouse agrees to split the gift, each will be considered the transferor of $50,000 to Gail. §2652(a)(2).

The identity of the transferor may shift even if there is not a subsequent transfer. The holder of a power of appointment may or may not be a transferor for purposes of the generation-skipping transfer tax.

Example 18-3

David leaves his residuary estate in trust to pay the income to his son, Peter, for his life. After Peter's death, the Trustee is to distribute the trust property to whomever Peter appoints in his will. Because Peter can appoint to anyone, including his creditors, the creditors of his estate, or his estate, the power is a general power of appointment, and the trust property will be in Peter's gross estate under §2041. As a result, Peter will be considered the transferor of the trust property after his death whether or not he actually exercises the power and appoints the property. There may, or may not, be a generation-skipping transfer depending on to whom Peter appoints the trust property.

Instead, assume that Peter could only appoint the trust property among his children and, if he does not appoint, the trust property will be distributed equally to those children. Because this is not a general power of appointment, the property will not be in Peter's gross estate. As a result, David remains the transferor and there will be a generation-skipping transfer when Peter dies because the property goes from David to *his* grandchildren.

If the power holder has a lapsing power, such as a *Crummey* power, the power holder will be considered the transferor if the power lapses, but only to the extent that the lapse exceeds the greater of $5,000 or five percent of the trust property.

Example 18-4

Dori establishes an irrevocable trust with Friendly National Bank as Trustee to pay the income to her daughter, Paula, during her life and at her death to distribute the property to Paula's issue. Dori also gives her daughter,

Paula, the right to withdraw the lesser of $10,000 or the amount contributed to the trust in that year. Paula must exercise her right to withdraw within 90 days of any contribution to the trust or the power lapses. Dori is originally considered the transferor because she has made a taxable gift. It is irrelevant that the gift will be sheltered from gift tax by §2503(b). If this is the first contribution to the trust, there is only a lapse with respect to $5,000. As a result, Paula will be considered as the transferor with respect to only $5,000. Reg. §26.2652-1(a)(5)(Ex. 5).

Assume that there is $200,000 in the trust when Dori makes a subsequent transfer. Dori is still the original transferor. Now, Paula will not be considered a transferor because the lapse does not exceed five percent of the value of the trust corpus. *Id.*

The identity of the transferor may also shift in a marital deduction trust.

Example 18-5

Decedent dies leaving a testamentary trust to pay the income at least annually to Spouse and, at Spouse's death, to distribute the trust property to their surviving issue. Executor elects qualified terminable interest property (QTIP) treatment under §2056(b)(7), and the trust qualifies for the marital deduction in Decedent's estate. Decedent is the transferor for purposes of the generation-skipping transfer tax. Then Spouse dies. The trust property is in Spouse's gross estate pursuant to §2044. Because Spouse is now the decedent and the property is in Spouse's gross estate, Spouse becomes the transferor for purposes of the generation-skipping transfer tax. §2652(a)(1).

This can present a problem for Decedent if he wants to allocate his GST exemption to this trust. Because Spouse is now the transferor, Decedent's exemption will be lost. To allow both spouses in this situation to use their GST exemption amounts, Congress enacted §2652(a)(3), which allows the Decedent's estate to elect "reverse QTIP treatment." This means that the QTIP election is ignored but only for purposes of the generation-skipping transfer tax. The trust will still qualify for the marital deduction at Decedent's death, but Decedent will continue to be treated as the transferor even though the property will be in Spouse's gross estate pursuant to §2044.

Example 18-6

Assume that Decedent dies in 2004 when the estate tax applicable exemption amount is $1,500,000 and the GST exemption amount is $1,500,000. Decedent's will left $1,500,000 outright to his children and created two trusts (Trust A and Trust B) with identical provisions to pay the income to Spouse for her life, then to pay the income to their children for their lives, and at the death of the last child to distribute the trust property to Decedent's surviving descendants. Decedent's executor elected QTIP treatment for both Trust A and Trust B. The executor also made the election allowed by

§2652(a)(3) to treat Trust B as if no QTIP election had been made. Both Trust A and Trust B were funded with $1,500,000.

As a result of this arrangement, Decedent is initially considered the transferor with respect to both Trust A and Trust B. There will, however, be no generation-skipping transfer tax consequences because there will be no distributions to anyone other than Spouse during her life. After Spouse's death, Decedent will continue to be the transferor with respect to Trust B because of the §2652(a)(3) election. If Decedent allocates his GST exemption amount to this trust, no generation-skipping transfer tax will be paid. After Spouse's death, she will become the transferor with respect to Trust A. If she allocates her GST exemption amount to this trust, no generation-skipping transfer tax will be paid. Both Trust A and Trust B will be in Spouse's gross estate at her death pursuant to §2044. Reg. §26.2652-1(a)(5)(Ex. 6). *See also* Revenue Ruling 92-26, 1992-1 C.B. 314.

The generation-skipping transfer tax will only be imposed if there is an outright transfer to a skip person or if there is a taxable event transferring property to a recipient who has an interest as defined by §2652(c) and who is a skip person. Section 2652(c) provides that a person has an interest in property held in trust if that person either has the present right to receive income or corpus or is a permissible current recipient of income or corpus and is not a charity. A future right to income or corpus is not an interest for purposes of §2652(c) even if it is a vested interest.

Example 18-7

Dwight establishes an irrevocable trust to pay the income to Ann for her life and at her death to distribute the trust property to Ann's daughter, Beth. Ann has an interest in the trust because she has the present right to receive income. Beth does not have an interest in the trust for purposes of the generation-skipping transfer tax because her vested remainder is a future interest.

Example 18-8

Dwight establishes an irrevocable trust with Friendly National Bank as Trustee. The Trustee has discretion to distribute income to any of Dwight's three children, Ann, Adam, and Agnes. The Trustee also has discretion to distribute corpus to any of Dwight's grandchildren, Beth, Bob, Barbara, and Ben. All three children and all four grandchildren have interests because they are current permissible recipients of income or corpus.

Interests designed to postpone or avoid the generation-skipping transfer tax will be disregarded. §2652(c)(2). The fact that income or corpus from a trust may be used to satisfy a legal obligation of support will also be disregarded in determining whether a person has an interest in a trust as long as the use of trust funds is either discretionary or pursuant to state law such as the Uniform Transfers to Minors Act. §2652(c)(3).

Generation-skipping transfers are also defined in terms of transfers to skip persons. A skip person is a natural person assigned to a generation that is two or more generations below that of the transferor. A trust can be a skip person if either all the interests in the trust are held by skip persons or no person holds an interest in the trust and there cannot be a distribution to a non-skip person. §2613(a). A "nonskip" person is a person who is not a skip person. §2613(b). The transferor's grandchild and great-grandchild are skip persons. So are her grandnieces and grandnephews. Her children, her nieces, and her nephews are nonskip persons.

Example 18-9

Diane establishes an irrevocable trust with Friendly National Bank as Trustee. The Trustee has discretion to distribute income among Diane's grandchildren during their lives. At the death of her last grandchild, the trust property is to be distributed to the grandchildren's issue. Diane's grandchildren all have interests in this trust because the Trustee may distribute income to them. They are all skip persons because they are two generations below Diane, the transferor. As a result, the trust is a skip person, and the creation of the trust will be considered a direct skip and a taxable gift.

Assume that, instead, Diane provides that the Trustee is to accumulate income until her youngest grandchild reaches the age of 21. At that time, the Trustee has discretion to distribute income among the grandchildren in whatever proportion the Trustee determines. At the death of the last grandchild, the trust property is to be distributed to the grandchildren's issue. Immediately after the trust is created, no person has an interest in the trust as defined by §2652(c) and no distribution may be made to a nonskip person. As a result, the trust is a skip person, and the creation of the trust will be considered a direct skip as well as a taxable gift.

Generation assignment depends on the recipient's relationship to the transferor. Most transfers are from one family member to another, and most generation assignments are based on family relationships. For purposes of the generation-skipping transfer tax, generation assignments based on family relationships extend to all lineal descendants of a grandparent of the transferor. §2651(b)(1). As a result, lineal descendants of the transferor, lineal descendants of the transferor's siblings, and lineal descendants of the transferor's first cousins will be assigned to generations by comparing the number of generations between the grandparent and the individual with the number of generations between the grandparent and the transferor. In these cases it does not matter how old the relative is. The transferor's children, nieces and nephews, and first cousins once removed are all in the first generation below the transferor. Her grandchildren, grandnieces and grandnephews, and first cousins twice removed are in the second generation below her. And so on. The same rules apply to lineal descendants of a grandparent of a spouse or a former spouse. §2651(b)(2).

The transferor's spouse is assigned to the transferor's generation regardless of age. §2651(c)(1). The generation assignment does not change upon death or divorce. The spouse of any lineal descendant of either the transferor's grandparent or the transferor's spouse's grandparent is also assigned to the same generation as that lineal descendant.

Anyone who is not assigned to a generation based on family relationship is assigned based on age. A person born no more than 12.5 years after the transferor is assigned to the same generation. A person born more than 12.5 and less than 37.5 years is assigned to the next generation. Each subsequent generation is 25 years. §2651(d). As a result, persons born more than 37.5 years after the transferor will be skip persons. Anyone born before then will be a nonskip person.

Section 2651(e) provides an exception if the parent of a lineal descendant is dead at the time of a generation-skipping transfer. In this case the child moves up one generation.

Example 18-10

Theresa has two children, Mary and Nancy. Mary dies, survived by her son, Simon. Theresa dies and her will leaves half her property to Nancy and half to Simon. Because Simon's mother was dead at the time of the transfer from Theresa, §2651(e) will apply and Simon will move up to his parent's generation. As a result, he will not be a skip person, and the bequest to him will not be a generation-skipping transfer.

Originally this exception applied only to direct skips, *i.e.*, outright gifts and bequests. In 1997, Congress expanded this exception to apply to all generation-skipping transfers but only if the parent is dead at the time of the initial transfer that subjected the transferor to the gift or the estate tax. In the case of taxable terminations and taxable distributions, the parent must have died before the transferor created the trust.

Section 2651(f)(1) provides that if an individual would be assigned to more than one generation, that person will be assigned to the youngest generation. Section 2651(f)(2) provides that if an entity has an interest, each individual with a beneficial interest in the entity is considered to have an interest and is assigned to generations based on the family relationship or age rules. Section 2651(f)(3) provides that a charitable organization or governmental entity will be assigned to the transferor's generation.

Section 2651(b)(3) provides that a person who is legally adopted will be treated as a blood relative. If the transferor or a lineal descendant adopts an unrelated person, the adopted person is, thus, assigned to the appropriate generation. For example, if the transferor's child adopts an unrelated child, the adopted child will be the transferor's grandchild and assigned to that generation.

The result is not as clear if the individual adopted already had a generation assignment based on the family relationship with the transferor. For example, Transferor's Niece has one child, Ned. Under the generation assignment rules in §2651(b), Ned would be assigned to a generation that is two generations below Transferor. Niece dies and her mother, Transferor's Sister, adopts Ned. If Ned is treated as having two generation assignments, then the rule of §2651(f)(1) applies and Ned remains assigned to the generation that is two generations below Transferor. If, on the other hand, the adoption eliminates the original generation assignment and replaces it with a new generation assignment, the door is opened for transferors or their relatives to adopt younger generation relatives for tax avoidance purposes. This will not usually be a problem in the example of Niece and Ned because the deceased parent exception would apply to raise Ned one generation even without the adoption. If Ned is an adult, however, and Niece is still alive, the tax avoidance issue is quite real.

Another issue arises when a grandchild or similar relative is adopted after the death of a parent.

Example 18-11

Transferor has two children, A and B. B dies leaving one child, C. A adopts C. Transferor plans to leave a bequest to C. If the adoption eliminates the first generation assignment and ignores the relationship between C and B, the deceased parent exception will not apply. The bequest to B would be a direct skip and would be a generation-skipping taxable event. The IRS has ruled that adoption does not alter the relationship between the deceased parent and the adopted child and, thus, the deceased parent exception will continue to apply. PLR 199907015; PLR 9310005.

C. TAXABLE EVENTS
IRC §§2611, 2612, 2651(e), 2653

There are three events that trigger the generation-skipping transfer tax: a direct skip, a taxable termination, and a taxable distribution. §2611(a). Two additional rules affect these taxable events: the deceased parent exception of §2651(e) and the multiple skip rule of §2653.

A direct skip is a transfer that is subject to the gift tax or the estate tax and that is made to a skip person. §2612(c). A gift to a grandchild, a great-grandchild, a grandniece, or a great-grandnephew is a direct skip. A bequest to any of them is also a direct skip.

The creation of a trust may also be a direct skip if either all interests in the trust are held by skip persons or no person holds an interest in the trust and there may never be a distribution to a non-skip person.

Example 18-12

Theo establishes an irrevocable trust to pay the income to his grandchildren for their lives and, at the death of the last grandchild, to distribute the trust property to their surviving descendants. All of the grandchildren's parents are alive at the time Theo establishes the trust. The creation of the trust is a taxable gift. It is also a direct skip because the only persons with interests in the trust are the grandchildren and they are all skip persons.

Example 18-13

Tess establishes an irrevocable trust and directs the Trustee to accumulate income until the death of her last child. After the death of the last surviving child, the Trustee is to distribute the accumulated income and principal to Tess's surviving issue. At the time that Tess creates the trust no one has an interest in it because no one either has a present right to income or principal or is a permissible current recipient of income or principal. Distribution of the trust property may only be made to skip persons. As a result, the trust is a skip person. The creation of the trust is a taxable gift, and it is also a direct skip because it is a transfer to a skip person, *i.e.*, the trust.

A taxable termination is the termination, by death, lapse of time, release of a power, or similar event, of an interest in property held in trust unless immediately after the termination a nonskip person has an interest in the trust or at no time after the termination may a distribution be made to a skip person. §2612(a).

Example 18-14

Sam's will establishes a trust to pay the income to his child for life and, at his child's death, to distribute the trust property to his grandchildren in equal shares. The trust property is in Sam's gross estate at his death. The creation of the trust is not a direct skip because Sam's child, who is a nonskip person, has an interest in the trust. The death of Sam's child, however, is a taxable termination because immediately after his death, the only persons with interests in the trust are Sam's grandchildren, who are all skip persons.

Example 18-15

Tom's will leaves his property in trust to pay the income to his Spouse for her life. After Spouse's death, the Trustee is to distribute income to Tom's two children, Mark and Luke, for their lives. After the death of both Mark and Luke, the Trustee is to distribute the trust property in equal shares to Tom's surviving descendants. The property will be in Tom's gross estate; it is irrelevant that it might qualify for the marital deduction. Spouse's death is not a taxable termination because after her death both Mark and Luke have interests in the trust and they are nonskip persons.

Assume that Mark dies before Luke. His death is not a taxable termination because Luke continues to have an interest in the trust. If, however, the trust were to be divided into two separate shares at Mark's death and if Mark's share were then distributed to his surviving descendants, his death would be a taxable termination. §2612(a)(2).

Assume that Tom's will provides that at the death of the first child, the trust is split into separate shares. Tom gives each child a power to appoint his share of the trust property to whomever he designates in his will; in default of appointment, the property will be distributed to the son's surviving issue. There is no taxable termination at Mark's death. He has a general power of appointment, and, as a result, his share of the trust property will be in his gross estate pursuant to §2041. Reg. §26.2612-1(b)(1). There is no need for a generation-skipping transfer tax on this transfer because the property will be subjected to the transfer tax as part of Mark's gross estate.

If Mark had a power to appoint only among his surviving descendants, however, the power would not be a general power and the trust property would not be in Mark's gross estate. In this case, Mark's death would be a taxable termination.

A taxable distribution is a distribution from a trust to a skip person as long as that distribution is not a taxable termination or a direct skip. §2612(b). The distribution of trust property to Sam's grandchildren in Example 18-14 is not a taxable distribution because it is a taxable termination. The same is true in Example 18-15 when trust property is distributed to Mark's issue at his death.

Example 18-16

Sarah's will creates a trust, giving the Trustee discretion to distribute income in whatever proportion deemed advisable to any of Sarah's children or grandchildren. The Trustee also has discretion to distribute corpus to any of Sarah's children or grandchildren for their health, education, or in an emergency. A distribution of either income or corpus to a child will not be taxable distribution because the children are not skip persons. A distribution of income or corpus to a grandchild will be a taxable distribution because the grandchildren are skip persons.

Section 2653 establishes a rule for multiple skips and prevents them from being taxed twice as generation-skipping transfers. The rule is based on the principle that the transfer of property should be taxed once, but only once, at each generation.

Example 18-17

Parent establishes an irrevocable trust to pay the income to Child for her life, then to pay the income to Grandchild for his life, and then to distribute the trust property to Great-Grandchild. The creation of the trust is a taxable gift. It is not a direct skip because Child is a nonskip person. Distributions of income to Child are not taxable distributions because Child is a nonskip person. Child's death is a taxable termination. It is necessary to impose a generation-skipping transfer tax at this time because the trust property is not in Child's gross estate.

Because of the rule of multiple skips, distributions of income to Grandchild after Child's death are not taxable distributions. Section 2653 achieves this result by moving Parent down to the generation immediately above that of Grandchild. Since Grandchild is now only one generation removed from Transferor, Grandchild is no longer a skip person and distributions to Grandchild will no longer be taxable distributions because they are now being made to a nonskip person.

Assume that Parent's State has abolished the Rule Against Perpetuities and Parent's trust provided for income first to Child, then to Grandchild, then to Great-Grandchild, and then to Great-Great-Grandchild. The trust property is to be distributed to Great-Great-Great-Grandchild after the death of Great-Great-Grandchild. In this situation, Child's death is a taxable termination. Distribution of income to Grandchild is not a taxable distribution because of the multiple skip rule, which moves Parent down to the generation level immediately above that of Grandchild.

Grandchild's death will also be a taxable termination. The rule of multiple skips will apply again and move Parent down to the generation immediately above Great-Grandchild. As a result, distributions to Great-Grandchild will not be taxable distributions because Great-Grandchild is now considered a nonskip person.

Likewise, Great-Grandchild's death will be a taxable termination and the rule of multiple skips will move parent down to the generation immediately above Great-Great-Grandchild. Once again, distributions to Great-Great-Grandchild will not be taxable distributions.

The rule of multiple skips also applies when the creation of the trust was a direct skip.

Example 18-18

Gretta established an irrevocable trust to pay the income to Abigail, her granddaughter, until she is 35. The trust property is to be distributed to Abigail at age 35. If Abigail dies before age 35, the trust property will be distributed to her descendants. Assuming that Abigail's parent (who is Gretta's child) is alive at the time the trust is created, the creation of the trust is both a taxable gift and a direct skip. Distributions of trust income to Abigail will not be taxable distributions. Because the creation of the trust was a direct skip and thus subject to the generation-skipping transfer tax, Gretta will be moved down to the generation immediately above Abigail. As a result, Abigail will no longer be considered a skip person and distributions to her will not be subject to the generation-skipping transfer tax.

The predeceased parent exception of §2651(e) prevents unnecessarily harsh tax treatment if the parent of a recipient predeceases a transferor-ancestor. The rule applies to an individual who is the descendant of a parent of the transferor. This means it applies to the transferor's lineal descendants

— her children, grandchildren, etc. — and to the transferor's siblings and their descendant's — the transferor's siblings, nieces and nephews, grandnieces and grandnephews, and the like. If this individual is the parent of the recipient and is dead at the time of the transfer, the recipient is moved up a generation. This rule only applies to the transferor's collateral heirs, *i.e.*, her siblings and their descendants, if the transferor has no living lineal descendants. §2651(e)(2).

Example 18-19

Greg has two children, Max and Nina. Max dies and is survived by a daughter, Chloe. Nina has one child, Ellen. Greg gives each of his grandchildren $250,000. The gift to Chloe is not a direct skip because her father, Max, is a descendant of Greg's parent and is dead at the time of the gift. As a result, Chloe moves up to the generation that is one generation below Greg and is no longer a skip person. The gift to Ellen is a direct skip, because the death of Max is irrelevant to the gift to Ellen.

Example 18-20

Joan's will leaves her property in trust to pay the income to Lauren, her grandchild, for life and then to distribute the trust property to Mark, her great-grandchild. Lauren's father, David, who was Joan's child, predeceased Joan. The deceased parent exception applies to move Lauren up one generation to that of David, her deceased parent. As a result, the creation of the trust is not a direct skip, and distributions to Lauren are not taxable distributions. There will be a taxable termination on Lauren's death and a generation-skipping tax imposed at that time.

Instead, assume that David is alive but that Lauren predeceased Joan. The trust is to pay the income to David for his life and then to distribute the trust property to Mark. The creation of the trust is not a taxable event because David is a nonskip person. His death will be a taxable termination, despite the deceased parent exception. Mark is moved up only to his parent's generation, *i.e.*, that of Joan's grandchild. Since he is still two generations removed from Joan, David's death will be a taxable termination.

Adoption does not necessarily preclude the deceased parent exception from applying. In PLR 9310005, the transferor, A, had a daughter, B. The daughter had one child, C. The daughter died and her husband, H, remarried. His wife, W, adopted C. A intended to make a gift to C. If C were given a new generation assignment because of the adoption, C would be two generations below A and the gift would be a direct skip. The IRS ruled that C retained her relationship with B and A, and thus the deceased parent exception applied. As a result, C was moved up to B's generation, and the gift was not a direct skip. *See also* PLR 9709015.

D. EXCLUSIONS, EXEMPTIONS, AND CALCULATION OF THE TAX
IRC §§2503(b), 2602, 2611, 2631, 2641, 2642

Few transferors actually pay the generation-skipping transfer tax due to its exemptions and exclusions. Because the tax rate is equal to the maximum estate tax rate, the generation-skipping transfer tax is usually a tax to be avoided.

The primary exclusion is the GST exemption in §2631. Originally set at $1,000,000, the GST exemption is indexed for inflation after 1998. The 2001 Tax Act amended the GST exemption amount to equal the applicable exemption amount for estate tax purposes beginning in 2004. Thus, the GST exemption becomes $1,500,000 in 2004, $2,000,000 in 2006, and $3,500,000 in 2009. The 2001 Act also repealed the generation-skipping transfer tax for transfers made in 2010. If nothing changes, the generation-skipping transfer tax will be reinstated on January 1, 2011, with an exemption amount of $1,000,000 as adjusted for inflation. It is impossible to predict at this time whether the repeal will become permanent, the repeal will itself be repealed, or other reforms and adjustments will be enacted, such as an increase in the exemption amount or a decrease in rates.

The transferor or her executor must decide how to allocate the GST exemption. Unlike the applicable credit amount in §§2010 and 2505, which is applied automatically to the first taxable transfers made by a donor or decedent, the GST exemption amount can be allocated in any way the transferor chooses. Section 2632 provides detailed rules for allocating the GST exemption.

Allocation is critical because, once made, the allocation is irrevocable. If a transferor establishes a trust and that trust later becomes subject to another gift or estate tax, the new donor or decedent becomes the transferor. Any GST exemption allocated by the original transferor disappears with respect to that transfer.

Example 18-21

Harvey and Wendy are married. Harvey's will creates a trust to pay the income to Wendy for her life, then the income to Carl, their son, for his life, and then to distribute the trust property to Carl's descendants. The trust is funded with $2,000,000. Harvey is the transferor for purposes of the generation-skipping transfer tax. Harvey's executor elects QTIP treatment for this trust, and he allocates Harvey's GST exemption to this trust.

When Wendy dies, the trust property will be in her gross estate pursuant to §2044 and she, therefore, becomes the transferor of the trust for purposes of the generation-skipping transfer tax. If she does not allocate any of her GST exemption to this trust, the taxable termination that occurs at Carl's death will be taxed at the maximum rate. Harvey's allocation of his exemption amount to this trust is irrelevant because Harvey is not the transferor of this trust at the time the generation-skipping transfer tax is imposed.

If Harvey wants to remain the transferor of this trust, he or his executor must make the reverse QTIP election in §2652(a)(3).

Couples such as Harvey and Wendy often establish two separate trusts to ensure maximum use of both individual's GST exemptions. If one owns most of the wealth, the wealthy individual must decide whether or not to transfer sufficient assets to the poorer individual so that the poorer individual can establish his or her own trust that qualifies for the GST exemption. If the wealthy spouse does not want to do this, he or she will end up establishing two trusts, both of which will qualify for QTIP treatment, in order to remain the transferor of one of the trusts.

The generation-skipping transfer tax is calculated by multiplying the taxable amount by the applicable rate. §2602. The applicable rate is the maximum federal estate tax rate multiplied by the inclusion ratio. §2641(a). The inclusion ratio is one minus the applicable fraction. §2642(a)(1). And the applicable fraction is the GST exemption amount applied to the transfer divided by the value of the property minus death taxes and any charitable deduction.[1] The formula is:

tax = taxable amount × applicable rate
   = taxable amount × [maximum estate tax rate × inclusion ratio]
   = taxable amount × [maximum estate tax rate
     × (1 − GST exemption allocated to transfer)]
                        Value of property   )]

As a result, the allocation of the GST exemption affects the taxation of all generation-skipping transfers associated with that trust.

Example 18-22

In 2006, Tom establishes an irrevocable trust for the benefit of his children and grandchildren. The Trustee has discretion to distribute income or corpus to any child or grandchild. Distributions to the grandchildren during the life of the children will be taxable distributions. Tom transfers $2,000,000 to the trust and allocates his entire GST exemption to the trust. (In 2006, the GST exemption is $2,000,000.) The applicable fraction is $2,000,000 / $2,000,000 or 1. The inclusion ratio is 1 − 1 or 0. The rate of tax is thus 0. As a result, any distributions to the grandchildren would have a rate of tax of 0.

If Tom had not allocated any of his GST exemption to this trust, the applicable fraction would have been $0 / $2,000,000 or $0. The inclusion ratio

---

1. For the sake of simplicity, the calculations and examples will assume no federal estate tax or state death tax and no charitable deduction.

would have been $1 - 0$ or 1. And the rate of tax would have been the maximum federal estate tax rate, which is 46 percent in 2006. As a result, every distribution to a grandchild in 2006 would be taxed at 46 percent. The rate of tax for subsequent years would change only if the maximum federal estate tax rate changed.

If Tom had allocated $1,000,000 of his GST exemption to the trust, the applicable fraction would have been $1,000,000 / $2,000,000 or 0.5. The inclusion ratio would have been $1 - 0.5$ or 0.5. And the rate of tax would have been the maximum federal estate tax rate, which is 46 percent in 2006, times 0.5 or 23 percent. As a result, every distribution to a grandchild in 2006 would be taxed at 23 percent. The rate of tax for subsequent years would change if the maximum federal estate tax rate changed.

A new applicable fraction is computed if there is a new transferor because the trust becomes subject to gift or estate tax at a later date, for example, when a surviving spouse dies and the property is in that spouse's gross estate or when an individual dies possessing a general power of appointment. A new applicable fraction is also computed if there are subsequent transfers to the trust as the amount of the donated property will increase the denominator of the fraction. In this situation, the applicable fraction will decrease, and the rate of tax will increase. A new applicable fraction must also be computed if the transferor allocates additional GST exemption to the trust. In this situation, the numerator will increase, the applicable fraction will increase, and the rate of tax will decrease. Finally, the inclusion ratio is adjusted for the generation-skipping transfer tax in cases of multiple skips. §2653(b).

There are additional exclusions, beyond the GST exemption, that shelter transfers from the generation-skipping transfer tax. The predeceased parent rule is not really an exclusion or exemption as the recipient is simply moved up to a higher generation assignment when her parent dies before the transferor makes the generation-skipping transfer. In many cases the recipient is no longer a skip person, and there is thus no generation-skipping transfer. In some cases, however, the reassignment to a higher generation does not prevent the imposition of a generation-skipping transfer.

Example 18-23

Thelma has a daughter, Cathy, who has a son, Greg. Greg has a daughter, Mary. Greg dies. Thelma establishes an irrevocable trust with Friendly National Bank as Trustee to pay the income to Mary until she is 40 and then to distribute the property to her. The creation of the trust is a direct skip. Although Greg is dead at the time of the transfer, Mary is only moved up to his generation. She is still two generations below that of the transferor, Thelma, so the creation of the trust is a generation-skipping transfer.

Section 2611(b)(1) excludes transfers for medical expenses and tuition paid directly to the provider, which are also excluded from the gift tax by §2503(e).

Section 2611(b)(1) shelters not only transfers made directly by the transferor to the medical or educational institution but also distributions from trusts for the benefit of skip persons.

Example 18-24

Gordon pays the $25,000 law school tuition bill for his granddaughter, Lily. This transfer is not a taxable gift because of §2503(e), and it is excluded from the generation-skipping transfer tax by §2611(b)(1). It does not use up Gordon's gift tax annual exclusion, applicable credit amount, or GST exemption.

Instead, Gordon establishes an irrevocable trust with Friendly National Bank as Trustee. The Trustee has discretion to distribute income to Gordon's children during their lives. The Trustee may also distribute income or corpus for the health, education, or in an emergency for any of Gordon's grandchildren or great-grandchildren. The creation of the trust will be a taxable gift that does not qualify for the annual exclusion, but it may be sheltered by the applicable credit amount in §2505. The creation of the trust is not a direct skip because Gordon's children are permissible recipients of income. Distributions from the trust directly to educational institutions for tuition or to medical providers on behalf of Gordon's grandchildren or great-grandchildren will not be taxable distributions because those transfers would have qualified under §2503(e) had Gordon made them directly during his life. *See* PLR 9109032.

Section 2642(c) also excludes direct skips that qualify for the gift tax annual exclusion by defining the inclusion ratio for these gifts as zero. This exclusion does not apply to gifts in trust unless (1) the trust is for the benefit of one individual, (2) during that individual's life no portion of the income or corpus may be distributed to anyone other than that individual, and (3) the trust assets will be in that individual's gross estate if the trust does not terminate before the individual dies. §2642(c)(2).

Example 18-25

Greg sends his grandson, Ed, a check for $11,000. This gift qualifies for the gift tax annual exclusion. This transfer meets the definition of a direct skip — a transfer to an individual who is two or more generations below the transferor. Because this is a direct skip that qualifies for the gift tax annual exclusion and it is not a gift in trust, §2642(c) defines the inclusion ratio as zero. Because the inclusion ratio is zero, the generation-skipping tax rate will also be zero, and Greg will not need to allocate any of his GST exemption to this transfer to avoid the tax.

Example 18-26

Gail creates an irrevocable trust with Friendly National Bank as Trustee for the benefit of her granddaughter, Ellen. The Trustee may distribute income or corpus to or for the benefit of Ellen until she is 21 years old. When Ellen is 21, the trust property and any accumulated income will be distributed to her. If she dies before age 21, the trust property will be distributed to whomever she appoints in her will.

This trust qualifies for the gift tax annual exclusion pursuant to §2503(c). It also qualifies under §2642(c). The creation of the trust is a direct skip because Ellen is the only beneficiary, and she is two generations below Gail. In addition, only Ellen may receive income or corpus during her life, and if she dies before the trust terminates, the property will be in her gross estate because she has a general power of appointment.

Example 18-27

Gail decides that she does not want Ellen to receive the trust property at age 21, so instead she provides the Trustee with discretion to distribute income or corpus to Ellen until she is 35. When Ellen is 35, the trust property and any accumulated income will be distributed to her. If she dies before age 35, the trust property will be distributed to whomever she appoints in her will. Gail also gives Ellen the right to withdraw the lesser of the amount contributed to the trust in any year or $11,000 within 60 days of a contribution to the trust. Gail contributes $11,000 to the trust each year.

Gail's contributions will qualify for the gift tax annual exclusion because she has given Ellen a *Crummey* withdrawal right. Those contributions would be considered direct skips because Ellen is two generations below Gail. Because only Ellen can receive income or corpus and because the trust will be in her gross estate, the inclusion ratio is zero under §2642(c), and this trust will avoid the generation-skipping transfer tax.

The exclusion of §2642(c) is limited to gifts that qualify for the gift tax annual exclusion or to gifts that qualify for §2503(e). If there are more than one beneficiary of the trust, it will not qualify under §2642(c).

PROBLEMS

1. Teresa establishes an irrevocable trust by transferring $5,000,000 to Friendly National Bank as Trustee to pay the income to Paul (Teresa's child) for life, then the income to Carol (Teresa's grandchild) for life, with the remainder to Edward (Teresa's great-grandchild). The Trustee has absolute discretion to pay any amount of income or corpus to either Paul or Carol during Paul's life. What are the generation-skipping transfer tax consequences of the following situations?
    a. The Trustee distributes income to Paul.
    b. The Trustee distributes income to Carol during Paul's life.
    c. The Trustee distributes corpus to Paul.

    d. The Trustee distributes corpus to Carol during Paul's life.

    e. Paul dies.

    f. The Trustee distributes income to Carol after Paul dies.

    g. Carol dies.

2. Tracy has 4 children and 12 grandchildren. On December 1, Tracy sends each of them a check for $11,000.

    a. What are the gift and generation-skipping transfer tax consequences?

    b. What if Tracy is married to Frank, and she sends each child and each grandchild a check for $22,000?

    c. Same as 2.b., except that each check is for $200,000.

3. Todd establishes an irrevocable trust with Friendly National Bank as Trustee, to pay the income to his three grandchildren, Arthur, Brent, and Cindy, for their lives and, at the death of the last surviving grandchild, to distribute the trust property to their descendants. Todd gives each grandchild the power to withdraw the lesser of $11,000 or their pro rata share of the amount contributed to the trust for 60 days after any contribution is made.

    a. Todd transfers $33,000 to the trust. What are the gift and generation-skipping transfer tax consequences?

    b. What are the generation-skipping transfer tax consequences when Arthur dies?

4. Tanya has two children — Mary and Nancy. Mary has one child, Amanda, and Nancy has two children, Ellen and Faith. Faith was adopted by Nancy and her husband when she was an infant. Tanya's will leaves the residue of her estate to her children in equal shares; if a child dies before Tanya, that child's share goes to that child's issue. Nancy dies before Tanya.

    a. What are the generation-skipping transfer tax consequences when Tanya dies?

    b. Both Nancy and her husband die before Tanya, and Mary adopts Ellen and Faith. What are the generation-skipping transfers tax consequences if Tanya's will leaves the residue of her estate to her grandchildren equally?

5. Tom establishes an irrevocable trust with Friendly National Bank as Trustee, to distribute income or corpus for the education of Tom's grandchildren. When the last grandchild has graduated from college or when the youngest grandchild has reached the age of 30, the trust is to terminate and the trust property and any accumulated income is to be distributed to the grandchildren in equal shares.

    a. What are the gift and generation-skipping transfer tax consequences on the creation of the trust?

    b. What are the gift and generation-skipping transfer tax consequences when Friendly National Bank pays University $15,000 for tuition for Gretchen, Tom's granddaughter?

    c. What are the gift and generation-skipping transfer tax consequences when Friendly National Bank distributes $20,000 to Gary, Tom's grandson, to reimburse him for payment of tuition to College?

    d. What are the generation-skipping transfer tax consequences when the trust terminates?

6. Tyler's will leaves the residue of his estate ($5 million) to Chris, his son, as Trustee, to provide care for those of Tyler's dogs that survive him. When the last dog dies or 20 years after Tyler's death, whichever occurs first, the trust will terminate and the trust property will be distributed to Tyler's surviving grandchildren. What are the generation-skipping transfer tax consequences?

7. Tara is married to Sam. They have two children, Jake and Krista. Jake is married to Isabel and they have one child, Mark. Krista is married to Larry, and they have one child, Faith. Isabel dies; then Krista dies; then Tara dies. Tara's will leaves the residue of her estate to Mark and Faith. What are the generation-skipping transfer tax consequences?

8. Tristan is married to Wanda. Wanda had three children, Alex, Barbara, and Claude, from her prior marriage. At the time of his death, Tristan is 70, Wanda is 60, Alex is 35, Barbara is 30, and Claude is 25. Tristan leaves the residue of his estate ($10 million) in trust to pay the income to Wanda for her life and, at her death, to distribute the trust property to her surviving issue. Assume that Tristan's executor elected QTIP treatment for this trust.

    a. What are the estate and generation-skipping transfer tax consequences when Tristan dies?

    b. What are the estate and generation-skipping transfer tax consequences when Wanda dies?

    c. What are the generation-skipping transfer tax consequences on Wanda's death if Tristan's executor elects "reverse QTIP" treatment for this trust?

9. Every year in January, Tiffany gives her grandchild, Carol, $11,000. In May 2006, Tiffany gives Carol $5,000,000. Assume that Tiffany has already made gifts of $2,000,000 to her children.

    a. Calculate the gift and generation-skipping transfer tax due on the May gift to Carol. Assume that Tiffany allocates her generation-skipping exemption to this transfer. Note: §2515 treats any generation-skipping tax paid by Tiffany as a gift to Carol.

    b. What is the result if Tiffany does not allocate her generation-skipping exemption to this transfer?

TABLE OF CASES

535

TABLE OF REVENUE RULINGS

TABLE OF TREASURY DECISIONS

INDEX